Weaving
A Handbook
of the Fiber Arts

Cover photograph by David Vine
Materials from the studio of Judith Rosenberg
Cover design by Karen Salsgiver

Weaving

second edition

A Handbook of the Fiber Arts

Shirley E. Held

Iowa State University

Holt, Rinehart and Winston

*New York   Chicago   San Francisco   Atlanta   Dallas
Montreal   Toronto   London   Sydney*

Editor   Rita Gilbert
Picture Editor   Joan Curtis
Production Assistants   Susan Adams, Barbara Curialle, Polly Myhrum
Production Supervisor   Robert de Villeneuve
Illustrators   Ronald Gilbert, Jim Bolles
Designer   Marlene Rothkin Vine
Associate Designer   Karen Salsgiver

Library of Congress Cataloging in Publication Data

Held, Shirley E.
  Weaving.
    Bibliography: p. 373
    Includes index.
    1. Hand weaving.   I. Title
TT848.H43   1978   746.1′4   77-24219

ISBN 0-03-022691-0 College Softcover Edition
ISBN 0-03-042821-1 General Book Hardcover Edition

Composition and camera work by York Graphic Services, Inc., Pennsylvania
Color separations and printing by Lehigh Press Lithographers, New Jersey
Printing and binding by Capital City Press, Vermont
      0 1 2 138 9 8 7 6 5 4 3 2

Preface

Weaving is a basic introduction to the fiber arts. It is intended for those who have no experience in fiber and wish to explore this fascinating medium to a developed level of expression. Many of the people who use this book will have the advantage of working with an instructor. This can be an invaluable aid, since it often takes four times as long to explain something in words as it does to show it. Nevertheless, the text and illustrations have been prepared in such a way that the weaver working independently should have no difficulty understanding the processes. Too, an instructor with limited class time usually must concentrate on certain aspects of a field, whereas a book has more leisure to explore variations.

Part I of *Weaving* presents an illustrated history of the art from earliest times through the 20th-century craft revival. It is my hope that this section will stimulate and inspire the reader with the beauty of the works shown and the engrossing story of their creation. It should also discourage any hesitation about trying ambitious projects because one does not have an expensive loom. Some of the most glorious, intricate fabrics shown in Part I were made on equipment that we would consider very crude.

Part II covers the various materials that can be used by the weaver and the variety of equipment available. It continues with a detailed introduction to loom weaving, including the mechanics of dressing the loom, then explores the extremely helpful system of draft notation, or graphic representation of a weave and its mechanics. The body of the text gives only enough information about drafting to make the remainder of the book easy to follow. Readers who are especially interested in drafting will find more concentration in the Appendix. The next chapter deals with "loom-controlled" weaves—those made through the pre-set interlacement of warp and weft; and the following chapter treats "weaver-controlled" weaves, or those that entail some hand work. Here will be found a full discussion of tapestry techniques, lace weaves, pattern double weaves, and brocade. The all-important step of finishing a woven object forms the subject of the final chapter in this Part.

Part III deals with specialized methods, such as pile weaves. A chapter on simple looms gives complete instructions for building backstrap, frame, and inkle looms with basic carpentry skills. The off-loom techniques of macramé, sprang, netting, plaiting, braiding, spool knitting, and card weaving are explained as well, with many illustrations.

Like most creative artists, people who work in fiber often experiment with various aspects of the medium. For this reason, Part IV of *Weaving* introduces the handspinning of yarns, yarn dyeing with natural or synthetic dyes, and the patterning of yarns or fabrics by means of ikat, tie-dye, silkscreen, and batik processes.

A concluding Part analyzes the elements and principles of design as they apply to fiber art and considers the factors involved in designing for the loom, with many sample diagrams and drafts. The fiber art of the 20th century—so vital as a craft and sculpture medium—is the subject of the last chapter.

Given the limitations of a book's size, it is not possible to delve into any subject in great detail, with the possible exception of basic loom-weaving mechanics. My purpose has been to enrich the repertoire of the weaver, to open areas of exploration, and to show the endless possibilities for work in fiber. Readers who wish to investigate a particular subject in greater depth will find direction from the sources listed in the Bibliography.

Those familiar with the first edition of *Weaving* will find a number of changes in this volume. First, the most prominent weavers in the United States and abroad have been generous in permitting the reproduction of their works; photographs of their art illuminate the text and do more than any words could to show the dynamism of fiber art today. Another general change is in the presentation of directions for various techniques. Each "how-to" section is isolated in a boxed, bullet list, rather than in running prose, so that it is easy to find and to follow. For the first time, too, metric equivalents have been given in the text. Those in the picture captions have been rounded off, since they are meant only to show the scale of an object; metric quantities in yarn measure or formula, however, are as precise as I and my editors could make them.

One particular caution should be mentioned. Throughout the book I have given very specific directions for the various processes and provided illustrations of them. However, as is noted frequently, never should any list of directions be considered the *one* acceptable way of working. Indeed, every weaver has shortcuts and tricks and individual styles. The only criterion for acceptability is success. The techniques given *will* yield the results promised, and they have been tested by hundreds of weavers and students. Once these steps have been mastered, the reasons for various operations will become clear. Each individual can then go on to find the methods he or she finds most comfortable.

It is, in fact, this personal approach that I have stressed all through *Weaving*. The author of a book can teach only ways and means. It remains for the individual to supply that indefinable quality we call creativeness.

Acknowledgments

Many people must be thanked for their contributions toward making this second edition of *Weaving* the book it is. Above all, I am grateful to my students, who have served as exacting critics when they interpreted the directions and illustrations during their early attempts at weaving. To the many readers of the first edition who have written praise or offered suggestions, I express my deep appreciation.

No art book could be considered a success without illustrations of the best work being done by talented, creative people around the world. I have been extremely fortunate in the generosity of weavers who have sent parcels full of beautiful photographs to be included in this edition. Thanks are due also to the museums and private collectors who were gracious enough to permit reproduction of works they own.

My friend James D. Okey had the patience to read through a draft of the manuscript and the astuteness to provide a searching commentary on its content and organization. I am grateful to Carolyn Saul Logan for several valuable illustrations of Peruvian textiles. Dr. Margaret Warning and Dr. Agatha Huepenbecker made it possible for me to exploit the riches to be found in the historical textile collection maintained at Iowa State University. Professor Donald Cyr of Southern Connecticut State College and Ms. Kate Edgerton of Edgerton's Handcrafts prepared the excellent photographs now illustrating the chapters on dyeing and spinning.

I must express my special gratitude to Judith Rosenberg—weaver and editor emeritus—who has read every line of the text and brought to this task the quest for perfection of one who sits before the loom each day. Her willingness to test procedures, her broad knowledge of the literature of weaving, and above all her reluctance to settle for less than the ideal have been a great asset to this edition. Ms. Rosenberg also supplied the materials for the wonderful photograph on the book's cover.

I am indebted to the staff at Holt, Rinehart and Winston who produced this second edition. My editor, Rita Gilbert, deserves my heartfelt thanks for her special perception, combined with unique skills and knowledge needed to bring this book to its final form. Joan Curtis, picture editor for the art books at Holt, has almost sole responsibility for the excellence of the illustrations, for it was she who undertook the diligent search for the best work by the best weavers. The fresh, new design of this edition is the creation of Marlene Rothkin Vine, and she, together with Karen Salsgiver, have prepared a visually exciting and functional layout. Again I must praise the splendid line illustrations made by Ronald Gilbert, who translated the barest sketches supplied him into clear, elegant drawings. For this edition, his work was supplemented by that of Jim Bolles. Barbara Curialle, Polly Myhrum, and Susan Adams had the often thankless task of controlling all the myriad editorial details that are part of any complex book. And Robert de Villeneuve brought his own special enthusiasm and expertise to the actual production.

Finally, my gratitude goes, as always, to my family and friends who have sustained me through the ordeal that is known as writing a book.

Ames, Iowa   S. E. H.
January 1978

Contents

I
The History
of Fiber Arts

Weaving is one of the oldest crafts—and arts—to be developed. In the very early stages of civilization weaving satisfied two essential needs: those of clothing and shelter. Moreover, the creation of fabric is inextricably bound with the quest for the third basic need—food, for when primitive peoples made the transition from a food-gathering to a food-producing way of life, they learned to use the hair from the animals they domesticated and the fruits of the crops they cultivated to construct garments and dwellings.

The Need for Fabric

Shelter

Second only to the requirement for bodily sustenance is the need for shelter—from the elements and from predators, both animal and human. Even before prehistoric people emerged from the caves they learned to devise ways of making those

1
The Origins of Fabric

crude abodes more comfortable and secure. They discovered that by laying an animal skin on the floor they could diminish the dampness, thus making the cave somewhat warmer. By hanging a pelt in the entryway they could inhibit the passage of inclement weather and wild animals.

When early peoples began to wander in search of more plentiful food supplies, they developed the technique of creating simple shelters, first by covering branches with animal skins and subsequently by plaiting, twining, knotting, or interweaving branches or grasses to erect freestanding structures. Such crude "houses," although temporary, had to be assembled quickly and securely. A method was devised whereby rigid poles made of tree branches were set in the ground, and flexible materials were twined around them at right angles. In warmer regions, a somewhat more permanent abode could be fashioned from baked mud, with a door of woven branches or rushes (Fig. 1). Animal skins were still put to use as door coverings and as "rugs" to insulate the earthen floor. They were slit into strips to make cords or binders. Where skins were not abundant or desirable, the same methods used for constructing a shelter were adapted to other useful items. A rough fabric could be attached by its ends to the walls of the dwelling for a suspended sleeping bag—a hammock. At first these hammocks served mainly as cradles for the young, but later they were built with sufficient strength to support the weight of a full-grown man or woman, thus providing a far more satisfactory arrangement than sleeping on the damp ground. Once the technique of fabric construction had been mastered, it could be applied to an endless variety of products—carriers for food and equipment, blankets, and, of course, body coverings.

Clothing

Authorities have long debated the initial impetus that led humans to clothe their bodies. As the species *Homo sapiens* evolved, the thick mat of hair that had covered the body gradually disappeared, and the denuded creatures were impelled to don artificial coverings. Was it a quest for protection from the elements, a desire for power and prestige, or simple modesty that made them take this step? Most writers agree that, although virtually every culture we know has employed some sort of clothing (if only a tiny loincloth), modesty was a later development. Not until the wearing of clothes had become commonplace did people acquire vanity and the feeling that nudity was shameful. Furthermore, since the earliest civilizations were established in the warm regions of the earth, clothing was not essential for comfort or for protection from the elements. It seems likely, then, that clothing first developed in a display of power,

1. Mud hut with basketry door, Africa.

to frighten the enemy or to demonstrate the skill of the hunter, who adorned himself with furs as a testament to success in the hunt. Later, rudimentary textiles were substituted for the pelts, and clothing became a means of gaining social approval (Fig. 2). The increasing popularity of clothing led to a heightened demand for textiles, which in turn stimulated weaving. As variety in fabric patterns emerged, tribes began to engage in an exchange of designs.

The Aesthetic Impulse

It is believed that variety in design and the desire for enhancement of the created object followed closely upon the invention of fabric. Supporting this idea are examples from primitive cultures of mats, fishing nets, and baskets in which several materials, such as grasses, rushes, sinews, or strips of skin, have been combined, indicating a basic interest in color and design. Weavers selected grasses with different natural colors and combined them to create patterns (Fig. 3). Later, they added colors by dyeing or painting the fibers or strips of skin with berries, nuts, or other natural materials. It seems that even when the business of survival occupied all waking hours and life was precarious at best, people still found time to supersede mere functionalism and create objects that were beautiful in and of themselves.

above: 2. *Ebikil,* superintendent of the Ishtar temple at Mari. Sumerian, 3rd millennium B.C. Louvre, Paris.

right: 3. Sweenie Willis, a Choctaw from Mississippi. Mat. 1965. River cane (natural and walnut-dyed), plaited; 4′11″ × 3′11″ (1.5 × 1.2 m). U. S. Department of the Interior, Indian Arts and Crafts Board.

4. Oriole's nest—the work of a natural fiber artist.

The Inspiration for
Fabric Construction

Humans always have been observant of and influenced by nature's lesser creatures—their forms and behavior as well as their products. Thus, we can assume that birds, animals, and insects have helped to provide ideas that could be adapted for fashioning coverings for the body, tools for capturing food, and carriers for goods or for the young. For example, scientists have devoted considerable attention to the spider's method of spinning its web and the way in which birds build their nests (Fig. 4). A sturdy, intricate nest such as that of the oriole may well have inspired early peoples to construct their shelters in a similar manner. A beaver's dam could have suggested barricades for capturing fish and small game. And it is not too farfetched to imagine that the opossum and other animals with pouches for transporting their young might have sparked the idea for the papoose carrier of the American Indian. Many skills that the animals possess by virtue of their instinct we must learn by imitation.

Early Construction Techniques

Wattling or twining is probably the oldest of the preweaving construction techniques. The process was employed for linking rushes along the banks of streams in order to snare fish, as well as for creating the framework of shelters. This was followed by thatching, braiding or looping, knotting, and netting—all procedures that could be applied to readily available materials in their natural state, with no special pretreatment.

Matted and felted fabrics, both of which are produced by pounding rather than interlacing, undoubtedly preceded weaving. Matting developed in tropical areas. The bark of a tree is cut into thin layers, soaked, and then beaten until it takes the form of a mat. The resultant fabric is called *tapa cloth* (Fig. 5).

Historians theorize that the idea for felting developed from observation of the natural matting that occurs when a sheep's wool is left unsheared for a long period of time. The same tendency toward matting appeared in fur pelts worn for clothing. These skins were worn fur side in for comfort, and the combination of body heat and perspiration, plus the friction that was created by rubbing against the body, caused the wool to become permanently matted, forming a tough, resilient fabric. Later, artificial means of applying heat, moisture, and pressure were used to create quite serviceable cloth (Fig. 6).

Both plaiting techniques and basketry are believed to have been employed earlier than weaving. One authority considers plaiting to have been the precursor of the primitive harness loom of the American Indian. Basketry is actually a limited form of weaving. It was an essential development during the prehistoric wandering period, since people required carriers for food and equipment. When a waterproof container was needed, the basket was lined with clay, much as some birds add mud to their nests to hold the sticks together. It is generally agreed that pottery was invented when such a clay-lined basket accidentally fell into the fire.

Once the technique of basketry had been mastered, the underlying principle of weaving was at hand. At first weaving was accomplished by simple means. Perhaps the rushes or reeds were laid out on the ground and the more limber vegetable fibers were interlaced over and under the rushes. Only when weavers began to choose more flexible materials for the warp—the lengthwise strips—did they require some device to hold the warp ends rigid during the weaving process. The first loom most likely consisted of two stakes between which one set of fibers was stretched. The earliest woven textiles were used to cover tent poles and were placed on the ground inside the shelter to serve as a floor covering.

Primitive Materials

Although it is difficult to determine just which fibers were used in prehistoric times, it seems evident that weavers employed all the obvious materials in their environment: hemp, raffia, leaf fibers, hair, wool, strips of fur, and sinew (Fig. 7). Human hair, deer hair, and the hair from dogs, cattle, and apes all were used to spin weaving yarns. One culture of prehistoric Denmark epitomized the maxim "waste not, want not" by making total use of the cow. The animal supplied both

left: 5. Patchwork skirt, detail,
from Kuba, Republic of Zaire.
Tapa cloth, 24 × 11″ (67.5 × 28.8 cm) overall.
Minnesota Museum of Art, St. Paul.

below: 6. Hood, Naxca culture, Peru.
Felted human hair, width 13½″ (33.8 cm).
Museum of the American Indian,
Heye Foundation, New York.

The introduction of the loom was followed quickly by the need for spinning. Spinning made possible the use of a greater variety of fibers, many of which were too short in their natural state to be woven. Although some materials could be extended by knotting their ends together, spinning was a much more satisfactory method and greatly enlarged the repertoire of the weaver. Spindle whorls unearthed in archaeological digs indicate that spinning was done during the Paleolithic Age in Europe—about 20,000 years ago.

7. Detail of Figure 8,
hair strainer.

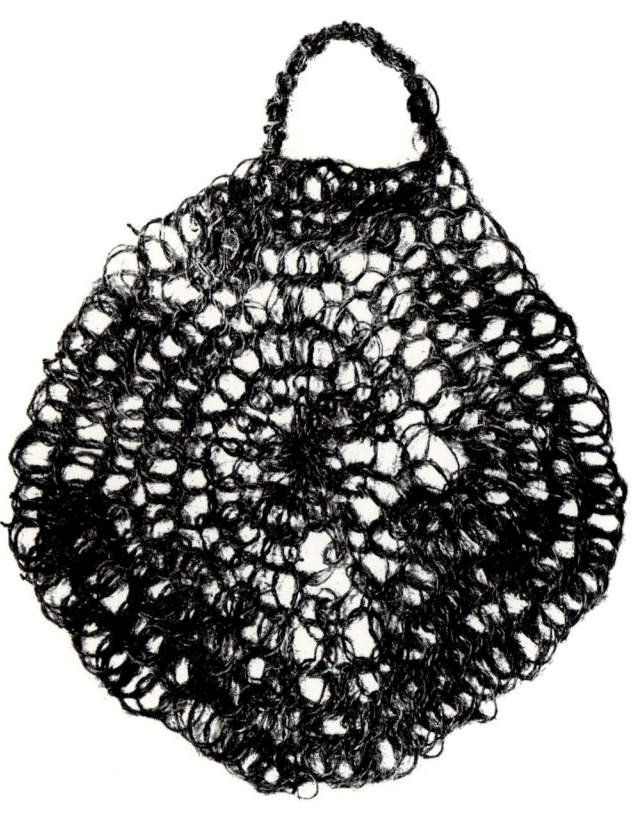

left: 8. Strainer, North Helgeland, Norway. Hair, 15¾ × 12⅞" (39.3 × 32 cm). Norsk Folkemuseum, Oslo.

below: 9. Man's garment, Trindhøj, Jutland. Early Bronze Age (1500–1100 B.C.). National Museum of Copenhagen.

food and drink, the horn served as a drinking vessel as well as a musical instrument, the skin and sinews could yield material for garments, and the bones were made into sewing needles. Finally, the cow's tail was cut before winter and used as a strainer for milk (Fig. 8). By spring the tail had regrown, long enough for chasing flies. Tail hair was also spun into a coarse yarn and made into a mesh. Even today cow's hair is a weaving staple in this area, commonly spun to make weft for the backing of rya rugs.

Cotton fibers and wool became usable with the invention of spinning. It is believed that spinning was developed first among peoples who employed vegetable fibers for fabric construction, because evidence indicates that cotton and flax were spun earlier than wool. Cotton yarns were produced in India as early as 3500 B.C., and spun linen was available by 2000 B.C., although the fiber had been used in Egypt before that time by twining the strands. Wool became accessible with the domestication of sheep, a feat that was accomplished in Afghanistan and Iran by Neolithic times.

Evidences of Prehistoric Weaving

It is challenging, to say the least, to obtain accurate information about a craft whose origins date back perhaps 35,000 years. Much of our understanding of very early fabric making is based on conjecture. Nevertheless, scientists have been quite successful in piecing together scraps of evidence from a variety of sources, including archaeological findings, written and painted records, patterns on clay vessels, and modern-day societies that operate on a primitive level. The first of these sources is, of course, the most reliable.

Archaeological Findings

The archaeologist seeking the remains of a long history of fabric construction has an unusually difficult task because of the impermanence of the material. Dampness, mildew, moths, fire, and chemicals in the soil all destroy animal and vegetable fibers, so that very few remnants of early woven goods survive. Fortunately, certain areas in the world have climatic conditions more favorable to the preservation of textiles. Among these are the extremely cold northern part of Siberia, the boglands of Scandinavia, the hot, arid Sahara region, and the Andes and coastal plains of Peru.

Remnants of woven fabric dating possibly from 5000 B.C. have been found in the tombs of Egypt, sealed under conditions ideal to preservation. One of the richest lodes of archaeological evidence for prehistoric weaving has been uncovered in the region of the Swiss Lake Dwellers, a culture dating to about 2500 B.C. Here scientists have discovered textile scraps, spinning whorls, and other artifacts that indicate an advanced capability for spinning and weaving during the Stone Age. The robe illustrated in Figure 9 was unearthed in Trindhøj, Jutland. It is one of seven complete garments found in oak coffin graves in the Danish boglands and is believed to date from the beginning of the Early Bronze Age (1500–1100 B.C.), before the custom changed to cremation.

Until 1949 it had been believed that the oldest existing rugs dated from the 3rd century of the Christian era. However, in that year a Soviet expedition uncovered an ice-bound grave in Pazyryk in the Altai and made an amazing discovery. The grave contained a wool rug, approximately 6 feet square and almost perfectly preserved (Fig. 10). The rug, which is dated to the 4th or 5th century B.C., was created by Scythian nomads, who were highly skilled craftsmen. It is less that ¹⁄₁₀ inch

10. Pile rug, Scythian, from Tomb No. 5 at Pazyryk, Siberia. 5th–4th century B.C. c. 6′ (1.8 m) square. The Hermitage, Leningrad.

thick and has 230 knots per square inch. The design consists of central squares with rosettes and a five-band border containing rows of winged griffins, grazing elk, and horsemen. Since the carpet exhibits such advanced technical prowess, it can be safely assumed that the method was in use from at least the 1st millenium B.C.

Clues from Other Art Forms

Where fabric remains are not available, historians must rely on evidence from other sources. They can examine the pictures made by ancient peoples to get an idea of the tools used (Fig. 11). Wall paintings in tombs at Beni Hassan show weavers and spinners at work, and a model room recovered by archaeologists provides a three-dimensional illustration of a weaving shop in ancient Egypt (Fig. 12). Such pictures also convey the artist's version of garments worn by the people.

After about the 5th century B.C. the archaeologist has additional help from written records—accounts kept by weavers' guilds and tradesmen, as well as the writings of contemporary historians. Both Herodotus and Pliny have left us good descriptions of weaving in the ancient world.

In their excavations archaeologists often come upon bits of early pottery showing textile imprints (Fig. 13). Long after the fabric itself has disintegrated, the fired clay endures to preserve a record of the weaves employed.

above: 11. Black-figure lekythos, Greece, with image of vertical warp-weighted loom. c. 560 B.C. Terra cotta, height 6¾″ (16.9 cm). Metropolitan Museum of Art, New York (Fletcher Fund, 1931).

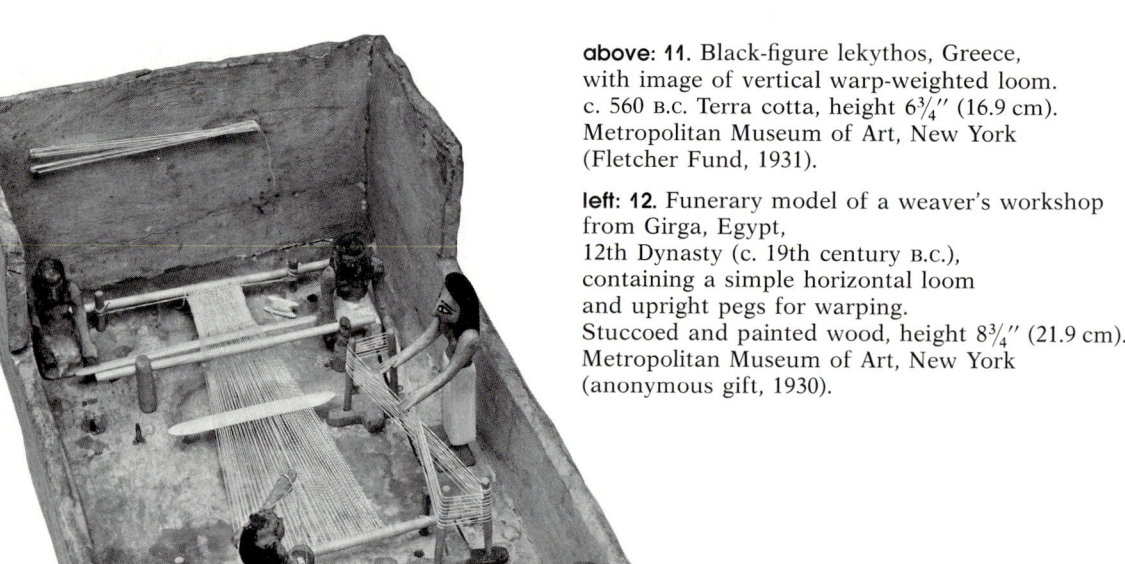

left: 12. Funerary model of a weaver's workshop from Girga, Egypt, 12th Dynasty (c. 19th century B.C.), containing a simple horizontal loom and upright pegs for warping. Stuccoed and painted wood, height 8¾″ (21.9 cm). Metropolitan Museum of Art, New York (anonymous gift, 1930).

above: **13.** Neolithic pottery with weave imprint, found in the Thames near Mortlake. Terra cotta, height 5¼″ (13.1 cm). British Museum, London.

below: **14.** Shirt, Minahase, Celebes. Collected before 1887. Bamboo fiber, knotted to increase length; height 3′11″ (1.2 m). Tropical Museum, Amsterdam.

Primitive Societies Today

In a world that sends astronauts traveling to the Moon it is hard to believe that Stone Age societies still exist in remote parts of the globe, but this is indeed the case. There are groups of people living in isolated areas who still practice the most primitive manipulations of materials, using the crudest forms of equipment. This is true of some tribes in Central and South America, as well as in Africa and Southeast Asia. By studying such societies it is possible to project their pattern of development in textiles onto their ancient counterparts.

In Southeast Asia bamboo fibers serve to make cloth for sacks, sails, and decorated garments (Fig. 14). Young stems of bamboo are harvested, slit lengthwise, and soaked for the bast fibers. Chewing provides further preparation, as it does for the bast fibers of banana trees. Once knotted together, the relatively short fibers thus obtained can be employed as yarns and subsequently woven on primitive looms (Fig. 15).

Since before the advent of recorded history textiles have served in a multitude of ways. They not only protect from extremes of temperature but they also are identified with people's ideas about themselves. For thousands of years fabrics have symbolized power, authority, humanity, social position, success on the battlefield, spiritual attitudes, economic position, and the adoration of the body.

15. Detail of the shirt reproduced in Figure 14.

The Evolution of Nonloom Processes

With two exceptions the techniques described in this chapter predated the invention of the loom. Long before people discovered the advantages of weaving flexible materials through a set of stretched warps they had devised various methods for interlocking fibers or strands to create usable fabric. The oldest of these processes were in use during the Stone Age; the last to be considered—lacemaking—is new relative to the long history of fabric construction, having achieved its fullest development only in the 16th century. All, however, are practiced to some extent today.

Matting

Fabric made from pounded bark is usually associated with Hawaii and the South Sea Islands, but much tapa cloth was also produced in Africa, Southeast Asia, and Central and South America (Pl. 1, p. 37). It is almost exclusively a product of the tropical regions. One rarely finds examples of the technique outside the equatorial zone bounded by the 25th parallels.

The preferred material for tapa cloth is the bark of the paper mulberry tree, colored light tan in its natural state. Although lightweight, soft, pliable, and attractive, the best tapa does not have great durability. Worn or damaged tapa fabric can be repaired by pounding in new bark, but the result is never satisfactory.

Tapa was most frequently used for clothing, both utilitarian and ceremonial. The Rio Negro Indians of Brazil made splendid dance masks that covered the entire body, and masks fashioned of tapa have appeared in many other cultures. The people of the Admiralty Islands produced lavish dance skirts decorated with seeds, shells, and feathers. Bedding was another common end-product. Immense sheets, often more decorative than serviceable, were made in Hawaii by felting strips of tapa cloth together. The fabric also served for funeral wrappings and for architectural adornment.

Despite the attractiveness of the natural tan color of bark cloth, the fabric was often dyed, usually in earth tones of red, brown, and black. The practice of stamping or pressing dye-soaked leaves or flowers into the cloth was widespread. Tahitian tapa became famous for its imprinted leaf patterns in crimson on yellow cloth. In some regions natural colors were rubbed directly into the fabric. Another common method of decorating bark cloth involved sewing strips of the fabric together in predetermined patterns. The Bushongo of Africa stitched alternating triangles of white and gray tapa into an allover geometric design.

Because of its poor strength, little utilitarian tapa cloth is made today. Almost always bark cloth disappears once weaving has been introduced into a society. However, the manufacture of tapa cloth is still practiced as an art form in Polynesia, mainly for the tourist trade.

Felting

Felting involves the interlocking of loose fibers by a process that combines heat, moisture, and pressure. In the colder regions of the world felting took the place of matting as an early method of fabric construction (Fig. 16). The best raw material for felt is sheep's wool, but the hair from many other animals—and even human hair—can be successfully felted.

It is possible to study primitive methods for making felt, because these same techniques are still in use today in Central Asia (Fig. 17). The wool

above: 16. *Eagle-Griffin Attacking an Ibex,* from the Pazyryk tombs, Siberia. 5th–4th century B.C. Appliquéd dyed felt. The Hermitage, Leningrad.

left: 17. Wetting and rolling wool fibers to make felt, Mongolia.

13

is first laid in layers on a large mat, the top layer having the highest quality of wool. When the desired thickness has been reached, the "sandwich" can be bound with grease or with a mixture of oil and water. The entire mat is then rolled tightly like a jelly roll, unrolled, and rerolled from the opposite end. This process continues for four or five hours. Finally, the matted wool is washed and dried, then dampened and stretched on the mat to dry in the sun.

Today these same steps are accomplished at high speed by sophisticated felting machines, and manufacturers have found ways to include a certain percentage of nonfelting materials—such as rayon—into the finished product. Despite the prevalence of woven fabrics, felt remains much sought after because of its unique characteristics. Since there is no grain line, felt will not ravel or tear. An excellent insulator against cold, shock, and sound, it can also be shaped easily.

Historians believe that the earliest felt garments were caps and hoods, probably because felt could be molded readily to the shape of the head (Fig. 6). By the time of the Romans felt had more varied applications. One of Caesar's armies was equipped with felt breastplates, tunics, boots, and socks. Even Roman slaves wore felt, in the form of skullcaps to cover their shaved heads. Shops un-earthed at Pompeii appear to have specialized in the production of felt hats and gloves.

The use of felt was not limited to Western civilizations. The nomads of Siberia worked delicate appliqués in dyed felts (Fig. 16). Chinese historical records indicate that their warriors went to battle with felt shields, clothing, and hats. The popularity of felt for warfare is not surprising when one considers its nontearing qualities, which would have somewhat impeded penetration of missiles.

Perhaps the most ingenious use of felt was and still is made by the nomadic Mongols of Central Asia, who construct huge tents known as *yourtas* or *yurts* from felted goat hair. For this purpose goat hair has proved more practical than wool, owing to its superior ability to contract when wet and expand when dry. Thus, the yurt is watertight in rain yet breathes in dry weather.

Modern uses for felt extend from the cradle to the grave, from diapers to shrouds. Felt is widely used in curtains, handkerchiefs, bandages, napkins, place mats, and numerous other products. The contemporary fiber artist has also explored this versatile medium (Fig. 18).

Netting

Netting is a looping and knotting technique done on a single continuous strand. It is also a rudimentary form of lacemaking. Netting produces an openwork fabric suitable for carrying or for fishing and trapping wild game. Prehistoric people used nets for just these purposes, and the descendants of primitive nets can be seen today on the fishing boats that set out each morning from coastal towns.

The ancient Egyptians used nets for garments, often in the form of an openwork tunic worn over a solid fabric. A related technique—though not really a netting process at all—was Egyptian leatherwork netting. A piece of leather was slit in rows to form an open pattern. The result was a fabric that could be lifted as a unit but at the same time could be stretched sideways to cover a larger area than the original piece of leather.

Netting served a variety of utilitarian purposes in the New World. The Indians of Peru made slings for carrying their babies, as well as caplike head coverings (Fig. 19). A waterproof cape could be constructed from a net foundation, with straw or tied leaves interlaced with the net.

18. Gayle Luchessa. *Untitled #5.* 1976.
White felt with lint, 24 × 24 × 2″ (50 × 50 × 5 cm).
Copyright © Gayle Luchessa.

In medieval Europe nets of exquisite beauty were made, often for purely decorative purposes. The Cid reportedly presented the Sultan of Persia with a tunic of netting. Five centuries later, when Charles V of Spain (1500–58) led his armies on an expedition against Tunis, his horses were equipped with trappings of gold and scarlet silk net over crimson. At the same time, the popularity of nets for hunting and other utilitarian purposes continued. In the late 18th century a fashionable Spanish lady's wardrobe included an upper skirt made of

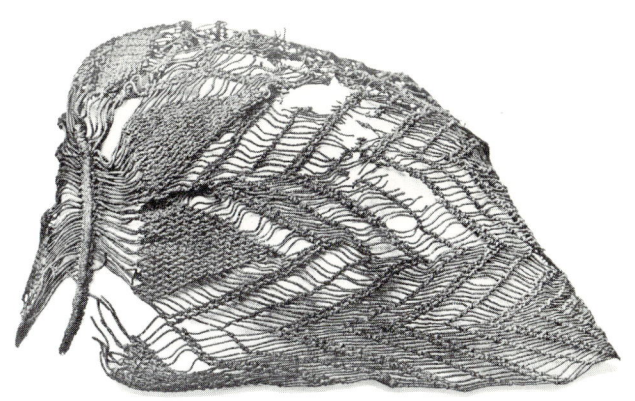

above: 19. Cap, central coast, Peru. Netted cotton worked in a symmetrical pattern of knots. Collection Fritz Iklé, St. Gall, Switzerland.

left: 20. Dance costume, from Liberia. Collected 1926. Knotted netting with cut-pile edging, length 17″ (42.5 cm). Milwaukee Public Museum.

below: 21. Gayle Luchessa. *Netted Paper Tapestry.* 1975. Dyed, unwrapped, and netted paper rush; 6 × 9′ (1.8 × 2.7 m). Copyright © Gayle Luchessa.

knotted net finished at the bottom with tassels. Nets are still popular for decorative and ceremonial garments (Fig. 20).

Today modern industry produces nets of great strength, often using space-age fibers. So common are netted materials that they are taken for granted: fish nets, hair nets, tennis nets, net curtains—an endless variety of functional objects. However, the aesthetic possibilities of netting have not been ignored, for a number of fiber artists have experimented with the technique (Fig. 21).

Basketry

Basketry is the process of making objects from various semirigid vegetable materials, such as grasses, rushes, reeds, and sticks. Known throughout the world, the technique has been practiced in one region or another for at least eleven thousand years. So versatile is the basket construction that it has been applied to containers and carrying vessels of every kind, cooking utensils, hats, sandals, mats, fish traps, armor, furniture, and even boats.

There are three principal methods of basketry. In *coiled basketry* a foundation or core of grasses or other materials is coiled upon itself, and then the coils are fastened together with a wrapping element. Coiled baskets usually have round or oval shapes. For *woven* or *plaited basketry* two sets of strips—a warp and a crosswise *weft*—are interlaced, usually at right angles to one another. It was

22. Cherokee woman making a basket.
Shown at Oconaluftee Indian Village.
Cherokee Historical Association, Cherokee, N.C.

the latter technique that led to the development of weaving, for when the use of more flexible materials became desirable, a crude loom had to be devised to hold the warp ends rigid. The third method, *twining*, combines traits common to both plaiting and true weaving. Here again two contrasting elements are joined to develop the mat or basket. The stiff rushes or bundles of flax stems were laid side by side, and a pair of flexible strands were worked in and out of them, intersecting and twisting after each reed or bundle. Twined baskets were made in ancient Egypt and Palestine to serve as sieves for flour and grain. Many of the Indians of the area now comprising the western United States twined baskets, including the Nez Percé, the Pomo, the Aleuts, and the Tlingit.

Several kinds of decoration have been applied to baskets. The most obvious combines different colored grasses or reeds, often one color for the warp and a contrasting color for the weft. In highly developed basketry, richly patterned weaves can be created (Fig. 22). Some cultures have incorporated shells, beads, or feathers into their basketwork, either woven in during the construction or attached to the outside of the completed basket.

Baskets found in the western region of the United States have been dated between 9000 and 7000 B.C., and the level of technical mastery in these examples indicates that the method had been practiced for a considerable time before that period. Evidence suggests that basketry developed in Eurasia even earlier.

The ancient Egyptians employed basketry to construct a wide variety of objects, including canoelike fishing boats bound together with papyrus. Numerous Biblical references attest to the widespread use of basketry throughout the ancient Middle East, and the Greeks and Romans continued this reliance on baskets for containers and carriers.

By far the highest development in the art of basketry was attained by the so-called primitive cultures, notably the Indians of the western regions of North America. The Pomo, Pima, and Tulare tribes have been especially renowned for the beauty of their coiled baskets, in which the colorful geometric designs reflect the shape of the object (Fig. 23).

During the Middle Ages in Europe the basket makers were organized into guilds, whose rules prevailed until the end of the 18th century. Basketry objects and furniture were popular throughout the 18th and 19th centuries, and several designers have adapted this technique to strikingly modern forms in our era (Pl. 2, p. 37; Fig. 24).

Twining

Twining developed from the twined basketry process. One or both of the sets of strands may be flexible, and consequently the product is more pliable, though not so soft as a woven fabric. A frame or *warp-weighted loom* (Fig. 26) is often used; that is, the warp threads are suspended from a rod of some kind and weighted at the bottom to hold them in position. In twining, each weft is a double strand. One strand passes in front of the warp and the other strand behind it; then the two strands are twisted together before continuing to the next warp thread or set of threads. In many cases the warp is completely covered by the weft. Twining served as the link between basketry and true weaving. Textile artisans had learned to weave with the aid of a simple frame, but they had not yet produced a soft, drapable fabric from flexible materials.

The oldest known twined fabrics were discovered in Asia Minor and date from about 6500 B.C. These remnants show a fairly basic grasp of the principles of twining and indicate that the skill had been only recently acquired. Far more developed was the twining practiced by the Indians of ancient America. Fabrics dating from approximately 2500 B.C. have been found on the northern coast of Peru. It is apparent that twining coexisted for a time with weaving, but after their weaving became sufficiently expert, the Peruvian Indians abandoned twining as a construction method.

25. Maori cloak (detail)
with taaniko border,
New Zealand.
Field Museum
of Natural History, Chicago.

26. Chilkat warp-weighted loom
with partly woven legging, Alaska.
c. 1880. Width of loom 18″ (45 cm).
Museum of the American Indian,
Heye Foundation, New York.

Unlike most other groups, the Maori of New Zealand used no frame for their twining, but simply held the strands in the lap and manipulated them with the hands. The women wore shaped garments made entirely of twined fabric. Taaniko weaving (Fig. 25), a highly sophisticated variation of pattern twining, was in common use when James Cook first visited New Zealand in the latter part of the 18th century.

The Indians of North America were especially ingenious in adapting local materials to the requirements of twining. The cliff dwellers of the Southwest, for example, employed yucca for twining their carrier bands. The bags and pouches of the Plains Indians were twined from cornhusks, stems of rushes, the bast fibers of trees, or buffalo yarn. In each area of the world the natives learned to utilize raw materials indigenous to that region.

Most striking of all twined fabrics were the famous Chilkat blankets (Pl. 3, p. 37), actually large ceremonial robes made by the Tlingit Indians of Alaska. The blankets typically combined a stylized animal form flanked by symmetrical abstract shapes and human heads, all of which formed the family crest of a particular clan. The Chilkat tribe used a warp-weighted loom (Fig. 26) for their intricate three-strand twining. The warp threads, which were completely covered by the twining, consisted of mountain goat hair spun around strands of bark from the yellow cedar tree. The pattern-carrying weft was made only of goat hair dyed in shades of black, white, green, and yellow. Elaborately designed and meticulously executed, Chilkat blankets often required a whole year's work for a single garment to be produced. Very few of the blankets still exist, for the Tlingit customarily cremated them with their dead chiefs.

Sprang

Sprang involves a set of stretched parallel yarns twisted upon one another. There is no weft, or crosswise thread. The warp ends are twisted to form a lacelike pattern and then secured at the center, so that the two ends of the meshwork become absolutely symmetrical. Sprang is extremely elastic in all directions. In order for the design to be visible, the yarns should be held taut.

Sprang is sometimes called *meshwork, interlacing,* or *Egyptian plaitwork.* Remnants of such meshwork have been found in the Danish boglands, in the Swiss Lake region, and in Peru. Of these, the oldest examples come from the Bronze Age burial grounds in Denmark. The prehistoric Danes used sprang for a variety of utilitarian objects, such as stockings, cloaks, head coverings, mittens, strainers (Fig. 8), and dish cloths. Often, spun pig bristles or horsehair served as the yarn. Sprang was also known to the ancient Egyptians and to the Copts (Fig. 27). Many primitive cultures, including the Eskimos and the Australian aborigines, used sprang to make carrying bags and hammocks for sleeping.

In most parts of the world, sprang is no longer a familiar fabric process. However, the Indians of Mexico still use the technique to make hammocks and market bags (often for international export), and at least one commune in the United States has supported itself by the manufacture of sprang hammocks.

In recent years a number of fiber artists have experimented with sprang for decorative pieces. Foremost among them is Peter Collingwood, the noted English weaver, who has created some exceptionally effective wall hangings (Fig. 28). In an age of multiple media, it is to be expected that sprang will be incorporated with other techniques to broaden the range of handcrafts.

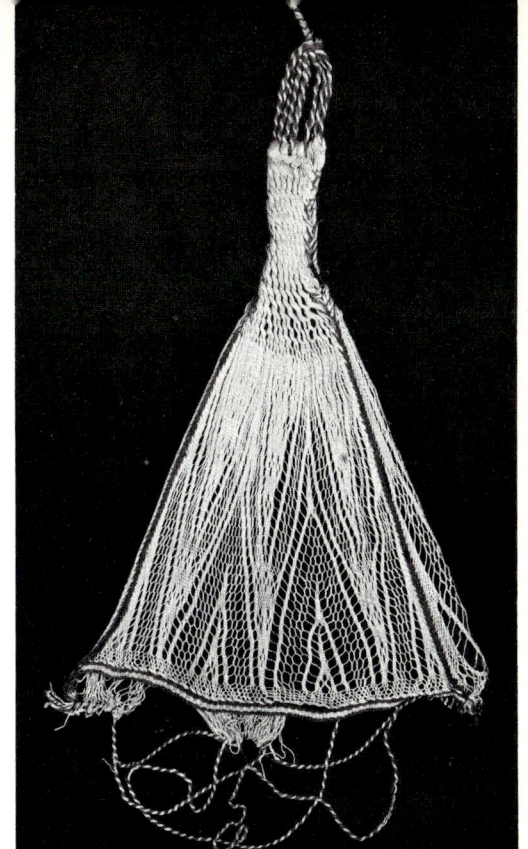

above right: 27. Coptic sprangwork cap or bag.
A.D. 4th–5th century.
Linen, 15¼ × 9¼″ (58 × 24 cm).
Textile Museum Collection, Washington, D.C.

right: 28. Peter Collingwood.
Screen of double-twist sprang. 1966.
Horsehair and monofilament nylon
in a copper frame, 6′ × 1′3″ (1.8 × .4 m).
Victoria & Albert Museum, London.

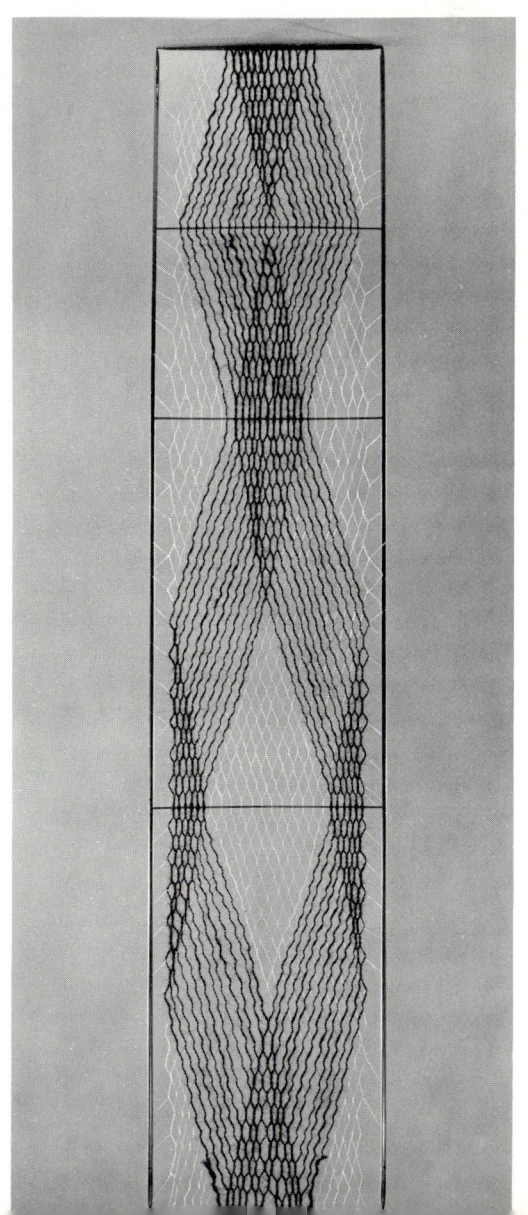

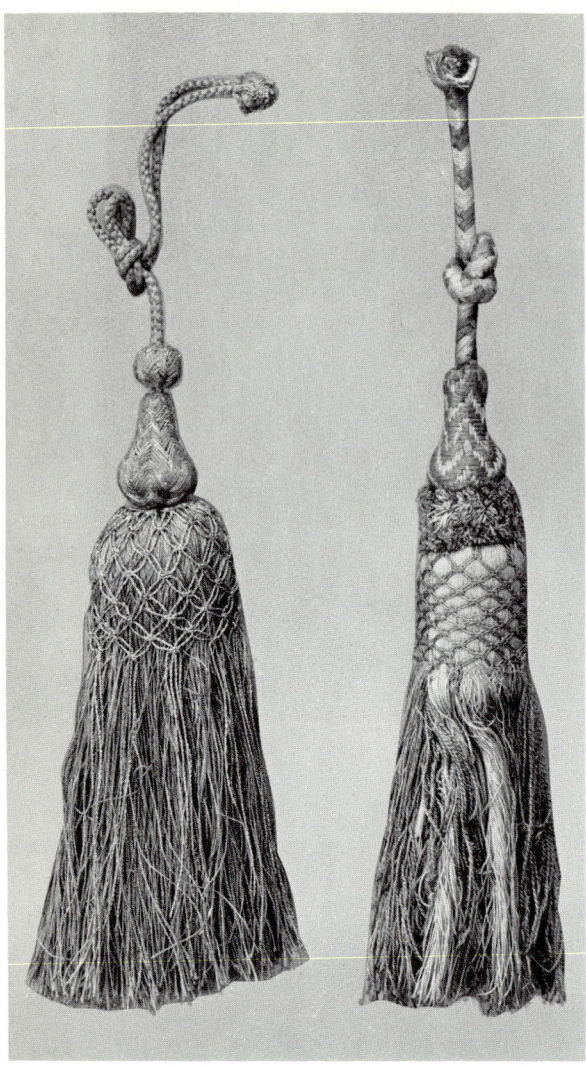

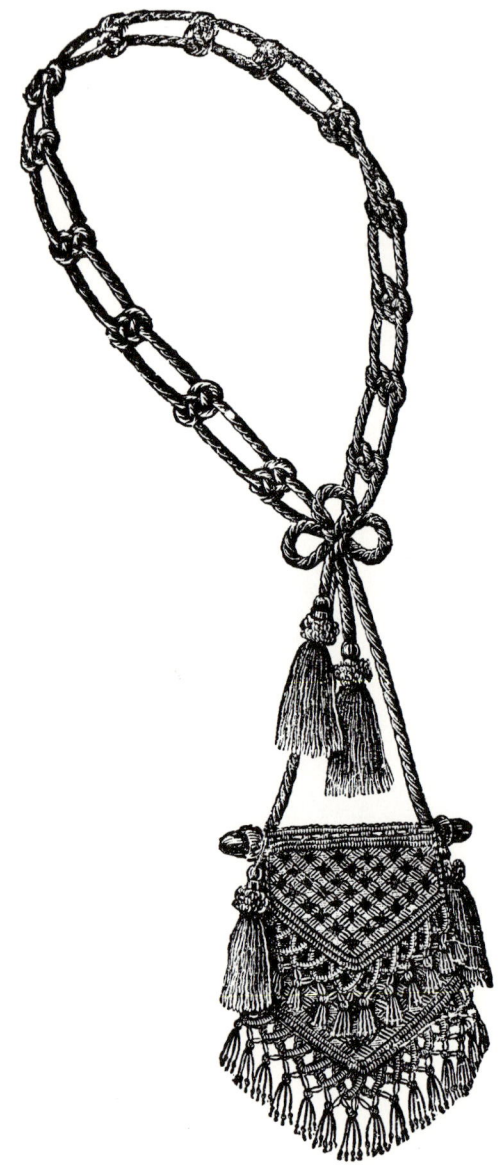

Macramé

The idea of knotting is so elementary that it hardly seems to qualify as a technique. However, for a prehistoric civilization the idea that one could tie two short strands of fiber together to make a longer strand was a giant step. The oldest known examples of knotted fabrics are nets originally made for catching wild game.

Macramé is a specialized form of knotting perfected by the Arabs perhaps as early as the 7th century. Like sprang, it involves only one set of strands, a vertical warp. However, in the case of macramé, the strands can move either vertically or horizontally, so that the effect of a weft is created. Only two simple knots form the basis of macramé, but they can be combined in endless variations to achieve different effects.

The word *macramé* comes from the Arabic *migramah*, meaning fringe, and the technique was apparently first used for a decorative fringe on towels. In the 8th century the conquering Moors carried the knowledge of macramé into Spain, whence it spread to France and Italy. In medieval Europe macramé was used widely in decorative fringes or tassels for ecclesiastical vestments (Fig. 29). The banners carried in procession on holy days were often embellished with macramé, as were special altar cloths. Instead of merely hemming the edges of the cloth, weavers would knot the warp ends into elaborate patterns.

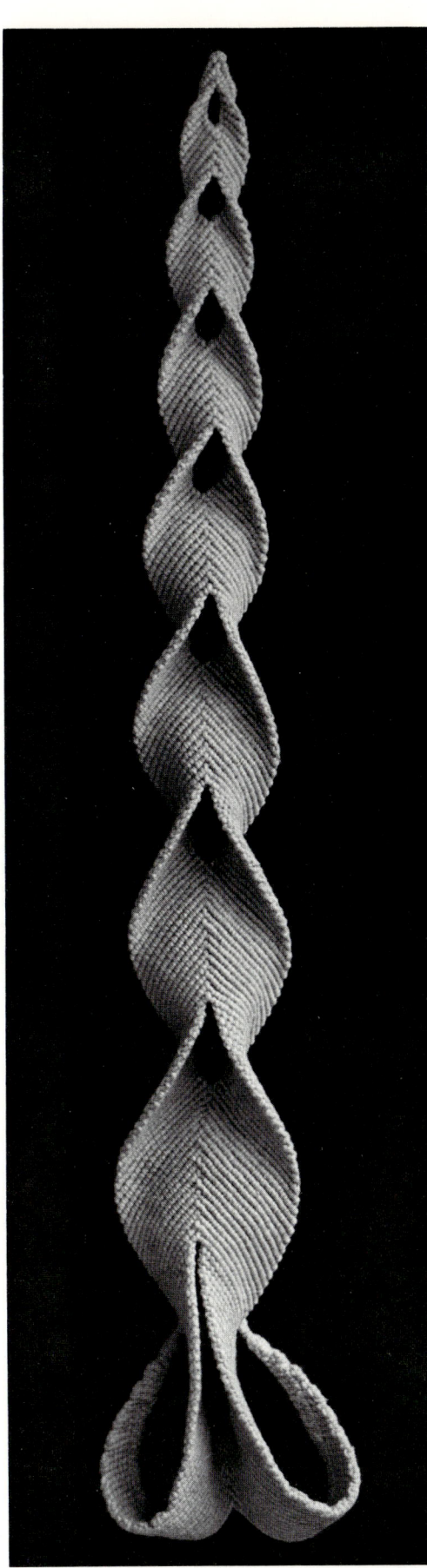

31. Joan Michaels Paque.
Moebius Extension. 1977.
Knotted and woven synthetic fiber,
length c. 8′ (2.4 m).
Collection Dr. and Mrs. Robert Monk, Waukesha, Wis.

The work was extremely fine and came to be known as *macramé lace.* Gold and silver threads were often included for special enrichment. The costume of the knight and the trappings of his horse provided another opportunity for decoration. Bed curtains, face towels, purses, veils, headdresses, pillows, and gloves were all considered appropriate subjects for macramé fringes.

The art of macramé declined after the 17th century, only to be revived in the mid-19th century under several different circumstances. Victorian England worked macramé fringes on table coverings, lampshades, umbrellas, baby carriages, clerical vestments, and accessories (Fig. 30). The craft became a staple of Latin America and to this day is taught to school children in several South American countries. However, it was among sailors, away at sea for months at a time, that macramé reached a pinnacle of popularity. Knotting came naturally to these seamen, for it was a part of their everyday work on the ship's rigging. In their leisure hours they demonstrated remarkable ingenuity in finding surfaces to embellish with macramé, or as they called it, *square knotting.* Unfortunately, few of these knotted articles have survived, for the sailors typically sold them or gave them away as soon as they reached port. But it was in this way that the knowledge of macramé spread.

Toward the end of the 19th century macramé again declined and virtually disappeared. Then, in the mid-1960s the craft enjoyed another renaissance. Craftsmen interested in structural design in fabrics have explored the possibilities of knotting in both two- and three-dimensional forms and have even experimented with large sculptural constructions (Fig. 31).

Lacemaking

Lace is an intricate twisting of fine threads done in such a way as to form a pattern. It is a descendant of netting, knotting, and plaitwork, as well as of *cutwork embroidery,* in which the cloth backing of an embroidered piece is cut away to leave only the stitched areas. An entire piece of fabric may be composed of lace, or the lacework may serve as an edging for a woven cloth. There are essentially three types of lace: needle or point lace, bobbin lace, and decorated nets.

above: **32**. Border of needle lace (*punto in aria*), Spain.
Late 16th–early 17th century. Height 9¼″ (23 cm).
Cooper-Hewitt Museum of Decorative Arts and Design, Smithsonian Institution, New York
(gift of Richard Cranch Greenleaf in memory of his mother Adeline Emma Greenleaf).

below: **33**. Border of straight bobbin lace,
from Genoa. Early 17th century.
Cooper-Hewitt Museum of Decorative Arts and Design, Smithsonian Institution, New York
(bequest of Richard Cranch Greenleaf in memory of his mother Adeline Emma Greenleaf).

Needle lace (Fig. 32) is probably the oldest variety and was inspired by cutwork embroidery. It is composed of stitches and knots made with a single yarn in a needle. Most needle lace construction derives from the buttonhole stitch. The pattern to be worked is drawn on a small piece of parchment or paper, and the latter is attached to cloth for support. After the pattern has been outlined in a foundation thread *couched* (that is, tacked down

with thread) to the backing, the design is worked inside the foundation. Cutting the couching threads removes the finished lace from the parchment and cloth.

Bobbin lace is worked with several individual yarns each wrapped around a bobbin—a short stick with a spool at the end. It is sometimes called *bone lace*, because many bobbins were made of bone, or *pillow lace*, because a pillow serves as a

34. Ed Rossbach.
White and Yellow Lace.
Bobbin lace of vinyl tape,
4′4″ × 3′6″ (1.3 × 1 m).
Courtesy the artist.

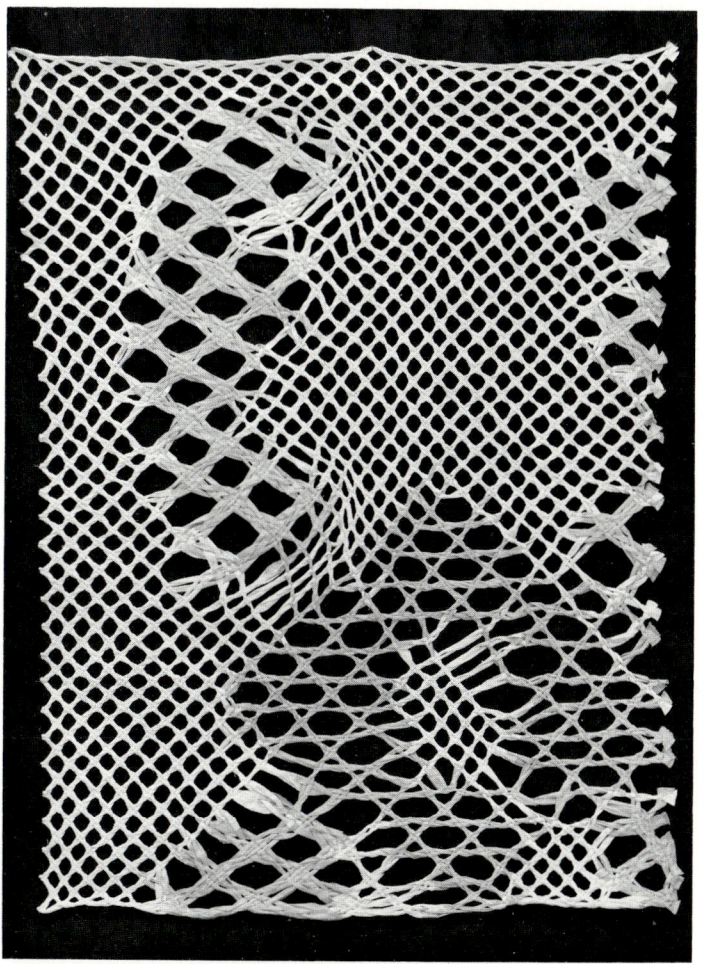

support in constructing the lace. The introduction of the bobbin made it possible for quantities of yarn to be worked simultaneously without the problem of tangling. A paper or parchment pattern is first laid over the pillow, and marking needles are inserted at strategic points in the design. With a bobbin held in each hand, the threads are twisted, crossed, or plaited and cast around the marking needles to build a firm network of lace. Bobbin lace can be further subdivided into two types, straight lace and free lace. *Straight lace* (Fig. 33), as the name implies, is a strip of lace such as might be used for a border or inset. It sometimes requires a vast number of bobbins: as many as three or four hundred might be used to produce a complex pattern only 3 or 4 inches wide. All the threads are attached at the top of the pillow and allowed to hang down over the pattern. The yarns are worked down to the bottom of the pattern and then reestablished at the top to begin the repeat. *Free lace* (Fig. 34) can take any form the lacemaker wishes. It is often worked over a round pillow so that the pillow can be turned to follow the pattern. Far fewer bobbins are required for free lace—seldom more than twenty or thirty.

The third category of lace, *decorated net*, consists of patterns darned or embroidered with the chain stitch on a net structure ranging from coarse to extremely fine (Fig. 35). It is less common than needle lace and bobbin lace.

35. Panel of embroidered net, Russia.
18th century. Height 29″ (72 cm).
Brooklyn Museum (gift of Mrs. Edward S. Harkness).

The Evolution of Nonloom Processes　　**23**

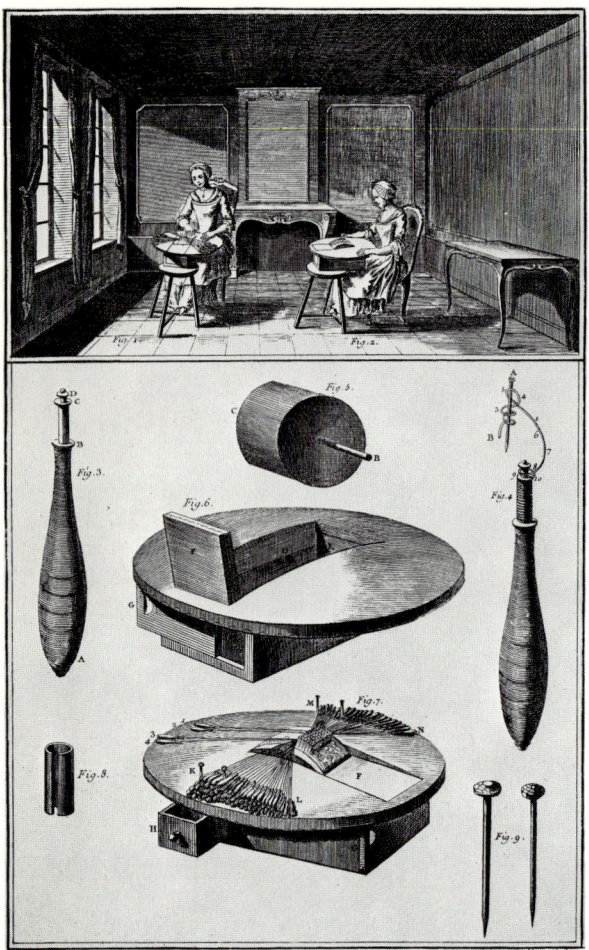

above: 36. Lacemaking in 18th-century France,
from Diderot's *Encyclopédie*, 1753.
Fig. 1: the lacemaker; *Fig. 2:* another worker
pricks the lace, which is placed on a bit
of green awning material stretched on the cushion;
Fig. 3: an empty spindle; *Fig. 4:* a full spindle
and the pin to which one attaches it by means
of a loop of thread; *Fig. 5:* a so-called "cushion,"
actually a cylindrical piece of wood;
Fig. 6: frame for holding the cushion;
Fig. 7: frame with the cushion in place;
Fig. 8: a half-case of horn or reed;
Fig. 9: coarse pins with heads
of diamond or Spanish wax.

To the extent that lacemaking traces its ancestry to plaitwork and netting, the technique has been known for a very long time. Rods that may have served as bobbins have been found in Etruscan graves in Italy, thus dating them well before the Christian era. However, true lace can be said to have been invented in 16th-century Venice, when the *punto in aria*—the stitch drawn freely in the air—broke free of older embroidery methods. The first lace patterns were based on embroidery designs, but as early as 1530 a book of patterns intended specifically for lace was published in Italy. By 1557 a collection of bobbin lace patterns had appeared in print. Gold and silver threads were often used for the construction of 16th-century bobbin laces. Unfortunately, few specimens of these sumptuous laces still exist, for they were later melted down and sold for the precious metal.

Lacemaking was introduced into France in the 17th century, when the French government, under the leadership of Colbert, imported workers from Italy and Flanders. A lace center was established at Alençon, where needle laces, primarily, were made. Chantilly and Cluny, among other cities, produced bobbin lace. Closely supervised by the state, the French lace industry worked by such high standards that France dominated Europe in lacemaking through the 19th century (Fig. 36).

During the Industrial Revolution machines were introduced that could duplicate very closely the fine handmade laces. In fact, as early as 1769 Robert Frost of Nottingham invented a machine on which he made plain lacy webbing. To date no machine can fabricate the buttonhole stitch, which is the basis of needle laces, but bobbin lace can be copied quite faithfully. With these developments it seemed, for a time, that the traditional lace industry was doomed. However, a small market for handmade lace remained, and the art of lacemaking has endured in most of the well-known centers into the 20th century. Today one can still find lacemakers in Spain, Italy, Ireland, England, Finland, Belgium, and Czechoslovakia. Marian Powys, who studied in Brussels, was considered by many to be the foremost lacemaker ever to have worked in the United States (Fig. 37).

Some of the more inspired contemporary lacework is currently being done in Czechoslovakia. Marie Vaňková of Prague constructs in bobbin lace works that are both delicate in structure and massive in scale (Fig. 38). Free-form laceworks

37. Marian Powys. *Fawns.* c. 1930.
Devon pillow lace.
Collection Peter P. Grey, Blauvelt, N.Y.

left: 38. Marie Vaňková. *Space Lace Form*, detail. 1970. Pillow lace of flax and silver threads; height 13′ (3.9 m), diameter 1′7½″ (.475 m). International Biennial of Tapestries, Lausanne, 1971.

below: 39. Kaethe Kliot. *Maiblumen*. 1974. Bobbin lace. Courtesy the artist.

now have taken on an architectural presence, as in the creations of Kaethe Kliot (Fig. 39).

It should be clear from the foregoing discussion that the sum of knowledge in the textile arts need not overshadow its individual parts. Although we have developed highly sophisticated machines and techniques for the production of fabric, the old methods are still open to restatement. Skilled, imaginative fiber artists throughout the world are proving this today.

Handweaving of the Past: The First Six Millennia

Weaving is the process by which two sets of threads of any substance are interlaced at right angles to form a continuous web. Although simple weaving can be done with the fingers alone, nearly every culture with a tradition of weaving has devised some kind of frame to simplify the interlacing of the yarns. This chapter, therefore, traces the history of techniques that are usually associated with the loom, primarily weaving and tapestry.

The process of weaving is treated fully in Part II. However, in order to understand better the discussion that follows, the reader should be familiar with certain terms. The *web* referred to above is the product of the loom—the fabric or other material that the weaver creates. As noted in Chapter 1, the *warp* threads or *ends* are the lengthwise yarns, which are set up first on the loom. The *weft* yarns—also called *pick*, *woof*, or *fill*—are the crosswise intersecting yarns. The finished edge at either side of the web is referred to as the *selvedge* (or *selvage*). A *tapestry* can be defined as a woven cloth in which the pattern-carrying weft yarns, for the most part, are visible on the surface, for they are closely packed on a less-concentrated warp.

This definition will assume more meaning in the context of Chapter 11, in which the tapestry technique is explained in detail.

Many of the most splendid and complicated weaves had their origins in antiquity, so it is useful for the weaver to have some background knowledge of a craft almost as old as civilization.

The Ancient Middle East

Egypt

Like most accounts of the development of art and civilization, our history of weaving starts along the banks of the Nile, where the highly sophisticated culture we call ancient Egypt began to take form more than five thousand years ago. Weaving undoubtedly was practiced in many parts of the ancient world at a very early date, but in Egypt, with its hot, dry climate, evidence of this accomplishment has been preserved (Fig. 40). Remnants of fabrics found in the areas of Fayum and Badari in the Nile Valley have been dated as early as 5000 B.C. These fabrics are of a plain weave—a simple one-up-one-down weave (Figs. 233, 234)—as were all textiles woven in the Middle East until roughly 2500 B.C. They are made of linen, and this preference for the product of the flax plant prevailed throughout the era of Egyptian civilization.

Although the Egyptians knew and certainly wore wool, they did not regard it highly. Sheep and goat herders belonged to the lowest caste of Egyptian society, and, similarly, the wool from the animals they tended was considered profane. Garments of wool are rarely found in Egyptian tombs. The Egyptian legal code contained sumptuary laws that restricted the use of wool. Members of the priesthood were forbidden to wear wool clothing next to their skin and were required to remove all woolen garments before entering a temple.

Cotton was cultivated widely in Egypt, and many excellent examples of cotton textiles have been unearthed in tombs. However, the finest linen was reserved for royal garments (Fig. 41) and

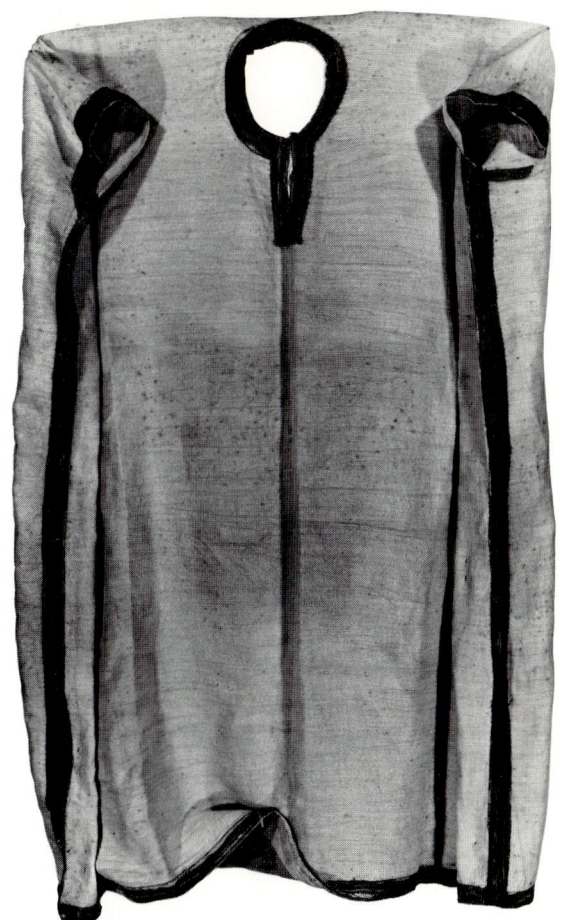

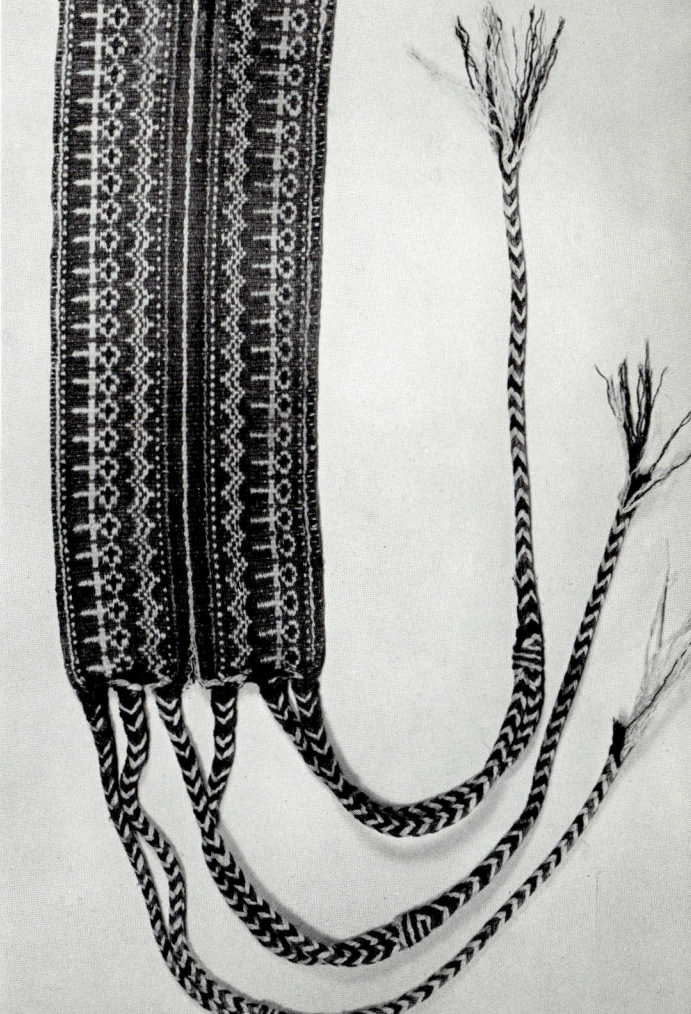

above right: 40. Tunic edged with colored braid, Amenophis III–IV, Tomb of Kha, Thebes. 18th Dynasty, 1405–1352 B.C. Turin Museum.

right: 41. Girdle of Ramses III, Egypt. c. 1200 B.C. Linen, overall length 17′ (5.1 m). Merseyside County Museums, Liverpool (Mayer Collection).

42. Mummy cloth fragments, Egypt.
Plain-weave linen.
Textile and Clothing
Department Collection,
Iowa State University, Ames.
The fragment at lower right
is coated with paint
on an earthlike material,
and is probably an outer wrapping.

for mummy wrappings (Fig. 42). During the First Dynasty (c. 3000 B.C.) mummy cloths with as many as 160 warps and 120 wefts per inch were made. (By comparison, fine modern cambric has 70 warps and 70 wefts per inch.) Silk was not introduced until the Christian era.

Tablet weaving (also known as *card weaving*, Figs. 453, 454) preceded conventional loom weaving. Later the Egyptians developed a warp-weighted loom similar to that used throughout the ancient world (Fig. 11). Pictorial representations of yarn spinning and weaving during the period of the Middle Kingdom (2133–1991 B.C.) have been found in the tombs at Beni Hassan (Fig. 43). The horizontal frame loom that was finally adopted by the Egyptians is almost identical to the common floor loom in use today.

The Egyptians were skilled dyers and are known to have employed acids and salts. Threads were often dyed before weaving, so that elaborate, patterned effects could be achieved on the loom (Fig. 44). The art of embroidery was also practiced to a high degree of perfection, and the earliest known embroidered fabrics have been found in

43. *Women Weaving and Spinning*, tempera copy after an Egyptian wall painting from the reign of Se'n Wosret II, 12th Dynasty (c. 19th century B.C.). Metropolitan Museum of Art, New York.

44. Tapestry-woven rug with lotus pattern, from the tomb of Kha, Thebes. 18th Dynasty (c. 14th century B.C.). Linen, 25⅝" × 19¾" (63.8 × 49.4 cm). Museo Egizio, Turin.

B.C. Archaeologists have uncovered clay tablets, some dated as early as 2200 B.C., which served as account books for the weavers. The robes favored by the kings and priests of Sumeria consisted of many overlapping layers of fringe, apparently in imitation of the fur pelts worn by their Stone Age ancestors (Fig. 2). The women's garments, also tiers of fringe, were cut and sewn to form a round neckline and a cape effect.

The Babylonian culture, which replaced the Sumerian about 1800 B.C., also laid great emphasis on weaving. Not only were the weavers highly skilled, but they specialized as well, with each of the craftsmen responsible for a particular kind of cloth. The Babylonian weavers' guild embraced the canvas weaver, the cloth weaver, the wool weaver, and the weaver who employed a variety of yarns. Even more important to the Babylonians was the art of embroidery. From Mesopotamia and from Phrygia to the west, the knowledge of embroidery spread to the entire Mediterranean world. According to Pliny, Babylonian embroideries enjoyed such great esteem that the technique was generally called "Babylonian."

The invading Assyrians adopted much of the culture of Babylon, including the art of embroidery. The Assyrians were equally energetic in propagating the weaving industry, and Queen Semiramis, who conquered Egypt, was responsible for establishing many cotton manufactures along the Nile River.

The Hebrews

Despite the lack of surviving examples, we know more about the weaving practiced by the Hebrew peoples than about that of any other ancient race, thanks to detailed accounts in the Old Testament.

Fragments of wool and linen fabrics dating from as early as 3000 B.C. have been found in Palestine. Cotton was available by the time of Solomon (968–937 B.C.), having been imported from Egypt, but wool was the most common fiber. Considered choice, white wool was reserved for the finest weaving. The inferior, coarse wool, or mixtures of black wool and camel hair, was used for making tents and nets. However, garments of mixed fibers were absolutely proscribed. The book of Deuteronomy (22:11) instructs that: "Thou shalt

Egypt. However, both polychrome textiles and embroidery were considered by the Egyptians to be alien to their taste; they were reserved for specific deities, such as the cat goddess Bast. Appliqué with leather and beads was known, and tapestry was common.

This high level of expertise in all facets of textile art continued until the decline of Egypt toward the end of the second millennium B.C., only to be revived again several centuries later by the Copts (see pp. 34–35).

Mesopotamia

At the same time that the Egyptian civilization was developing along the banks of the Nile, another culture, equally remarkable, flourished between the Tigris and the Euphrates in the land known as Mesopotamia. This area, dominated in turn by the Sumerians, the Babylonians, and the Assyrians, was renowned in the ancient world for the quality of the textiles produced.

Evidence indicates that the Sumerians had developed a weaving industry by the 3rd millennium

left: 45. *Cock,* Sassanian. c. 600.
Silk twill, diameter
of medallion 10¼″ (25.6 cm).
Museo Cristiano, Vatican.

below: 46. *Penelope at the Loom,*
detail of an Attic red-figure
skyphos, Greece. 5th century B.C.
Terra cotta. Chiusi Museum, Italy.

not wear a garment of divers sorts, as of woolen and linen together." In fact, such fabrics had to be transported to market on sticks to prevent their touching the bodies of the carriers. Only garments of pure linen could be worn by the high priest entering the holy of holies.

The Old Testament mentions three types of weavers: the weavers of plain weaves, the weavers of multicolor materials, and the "art-weavers," who embroidered figures on fabrics for clothing and curtains. Joseph's coat of many colors is believed to have been woven in narrow strips that were later sewn together, but garments generally were woven in a single piece. The ends of the warps often served to connect the new web with cloth already woven.

In Palestine spinning was the work of women and even considered by law to be the woman's property. In the event of a divorce, all yarns that had been made by the wife on her spindle remained in her possession. Hebrew law declared that: "Married women should not spin in the street nor in the open, certainly not at night by the light of the moon." If a woman were to spin outdoors, it would necessitate revealing her arms, and this might be cause for divorce.

It is known that the ancient Hebrews were capable of producing very complex yarns. Jewish law tells of yarns of as many as 28 ply—that is, 28 single strands twisted together. According to tradition, the curtain of the last Temple was woven from 24- and 72-ply yarns. The Hebrews used both gold and silver threads in their weaving, and as is evident from the Biblical descriptions, they had a knowledge of dyeing techniques.

The Persian Empire

In the 6th century B.C. the Persians, under the leadership of Darius I and Xerxes, built an empire far larger than any of its predecessors in the ancient world. At its height the Persian Empire extended from Greece and Egypt in the west to the borders of India in the east.

The textile arts were valued highly in ancient Persia, and testament to this can still be seen in the architectural sculpture of the great cities of Persepolis and Susa. Tapestry weaving was particularly important and became even more so in the 6th century of the Christian era, when silk culture was introduced from China (see p. 36). Exquisite silk tapestries that have seldom been equaled in richness of color and pattern were made during the period of the Sassanian dynasty (A.D. 226–637). These tapestries (Fig. 45) were widely exported to both the Byzantine and the Roman worlds. They were later to have a profound effect on European, Byzantine, Islamic, and even Chinese art. The Persians are also credited with production of the first velvets, which were similarly exported to all parts of the ancient world.

As commerce increased, Persia became the crossroads for trade routes between Europe and the Far East. European merchants brought home not only the spices and silks of the Orient but design concepts acquired in Persia along the way. This influence lasted until the middle of the 7th century, when Persia was swept up in the all-encompassing tide of Islam.

The Classical World

Greece

That the ancient Greeks were accomplished weavers we know primarily from written and pictorial records, for no examples of their craft survive. The most famous episode involving weaving in Classical Greece is in the legend of Penelope, wife of Odysseus and universal symbol of constancy (Fig. 46). Although Odysseus had been away on his voyage for many years and was presumed lost,

Penelope continued to refuse the many suitors who pressed for her hand in marriage. As her excuse she explained that, before she could re-marry, she must complete a winding sheet for her father-in-law. By day she would sit at her loom and weave, and at night she would unravel all the work she had done. Eventually, the suitors began to realize that her progress was unusually slow, and she was forced to finish the shroud and urged to choose a new husband. However, Odysseus returned in the nick of time, routed the suitors singlehandedly from his home, and reclaimed his devoted wife.

Representations of Penelope show her at work on a warp-weighted loom (Fig. 11), and this is apparently the type that was used throughout the ancient world. For her fiber she might have chosen wool or linen, for both were common in Greece. Later, wool exclusively was used for men's garments throughout Greece, while *byssus*, a very fine linen, was the material for women's dresses. Silk was also available, for it had been introduced from China perhaps as early as 1000 B.C. Cotton, grown abundantly in India during this period, would have been known to the Greeks from the writings of Herodotus.

The Greeks were accomplished in embroidery and tapestry weaving—in fact, in all the decorative textile arts then known. Their mastery in the fields of architecture, sculpture, painting, and pottery making tends to overshadow their other skills. However, were it not for the absence of surviving examples, they might be equally renowned for their work in fabric.

Rome

The mighty empire of the Romans absorbed most of the cultures previously discussed. Thus, the accumulated expertise in weaving techniques acquired by various groups was at the disposal of Rome.

The free Roman citizenry did very little weaving, considering it to be beneath them. Fabrics were imported from Greece, or else Greek and other slaves were employed in the weaving of cloth and making of garments.

It was the custom in aristocratic Roman households to own slaves for the exclusive purpose of spinning, weaving, and making garments for the members of the family. Those who could not afford the luxury of a personal weaver relied on the groups of free tradesmen who sold their wares in shops. The weavers of Pompeii apparently lived in a particular district of the town. Frescoes on the entrance pillars of one building

47. Sign from the shop of Vecilius Verecundus, cloth merchant of Pompeii. Before A.D. 79.

depict the interior of the factory (Fig. 47), showing four felters at the table, three weavers at their looms, and the proprietor displaying finished wares. In Rome itself the weavers, spinners, and dyers were organized into a guild, which had its headquarters in the Temple of Minerva Medica. So highly organized was its membership that it reminds one of a modern trade union. There were dues, guild regulations, individual and group privileges, and even a widows' fund.

Each weaving center produced a distinctive type of fabric. For example, the Po Valley and parts of Gaul supplied the city of Rome with the woolen fabric used for togas and tunics. Padua specialized in expensive carpets and elaborate textiles, while the rougher fabrics that clothed the workmen and slaves came from Gaul. Until the beginning of the Christian era the principal fibers were linen and wool, with linen used primarily in underclothing. For a particularly lavish effect, wealthy Romans might don a garment into which gold threads had been woven. Agrippina, the wife of Emperor Claudius (A.D. 41–57) reportedly owned a robe made entirely of gold.

Toward the end of the 1st century B.C. silk came into vogue, first in mixtures with linen or cotton and later in the form of pure silk fabrics. It is said that the Emperor Heliogabalus (A.D. 218–222) was the first to wear garments all of silk. In order to weave with silk the Romans imported fabrics from China, then painstakingly unraveled and rewove them. This factor partially explains the very high cost of silk in Rome: in A.D. 16 a pound of silk was sold for 12 ounces of gold. Later, the supply of silk became more plentiful and the price declined.

However, the tedious process of unraveling the fabric was still necessary, for the secrets of *sericulture*—the cultivation of the silkworm and production of silk—were locked in China.

Early Weaving in the Far East: Pre-Buddhist China

It is customary to think of the "cradles of civilization" in terms of the Nile River Valley in Egypt and the plains between the Tigris and the Euphrates in Mesopotamia. However, by the 3rd millennium B.C. two other great cultures were flourishing in the valleys of the Indus of India and the Yellow River of China. Many written records attest to the knowledge of weaving in ancient India, but no concrete evidence of this skill prior to the 7th century A.D. has survived. Much more is known about the evolution of the textile arts in China.

The history of weaving in China centers almost exclusively around the one commodity deemed most precious in the West: silk. A number of legends are told about the discovery of silk, but the most famous concerns the empress Hsi-Ling-shi.

Emperor Huang-Ti, who reigned sometime during the 27th century B.C., had become increasingly worried about a blight that was gradually destroying the royal mulberry grove, and so he asked his empress to study the problem. Hsi-Ling-shi noticed that the mulberry leaves were being consumed by hundreds of tiny white worms, which would then crawl from the leaves to the stem and spin pale, glossy cocoons. She took several of the cocoons into her apartments for further investigation, and accidentally dropped one into a basin of hot water. In water, the cocoon separated into a delicate network of fibers, and the empress discovered that she could draw a thin, continuous filament into the air. The more she drew out the

above left: 48. Kitagawa Utamaro, Japan. *Reeling of Silk.* 18th century. Woodcut. Textile Museum Collection, Washington, D.C.

above right: 49. Kitagawa Utamaro, Japan. *Weaving of Silk.* 18th century. Woodcut. Textile Museum Collection, Washington, D.C.

right: 50. Woven mitts, found at Ch'ang-sha, Hunan Province, China. c. 3rd century B.C. Silk with warp pattern and plain weave, length 8¼″ (20.6 cm). Cooper-Hewitt Museum of Decorative Arts and Design, Smithsonian Institution, New York (purchase, AuPanier Fleuri Fund).

filament, the smaller the cocoon became. Thus, Hsi-Ling-shi stumbled upon a technique that would be jealously sought after by the rest of the world—and just as jealously guarded by the Chinese—for almost three thousand years. Not until about A.D. 300 did Japan learn the secret, and it reached the West only in the 6th century.

With the introduction of silk, the Chinese had no need for spinning; a filament from a single cocoon frequently measures more than 1000 yards. The weavers would merely soften the cocoon and unravel the filament, after which it would be ready for the loom (Figs. 48, 49).

The earliest surviving silk textiles date from the end of the Eastern Chou Dynasty (771–256 B.C.). They are extremely fine, indicating a long period of development in the textile arts. The pair of silk mitts in Figure 50 suggest mastery of the ikat technique of dyeing (see Chap. 18). Highly complex figurative weaves were produced during the Han Dynasty (206 B.C.–A.D. 220), some with stylized nat-

Handweaving of the Past: The First Six Millennia **33**

top: 51. *Mountains and Birds,* from Noin-ula, China.
Han Dynasty (206 B.C.–A.D. 220).
Silk damask, height 12″ (30 cm).
The Hermitage, Leningrad.

above: 52. Gauze fragment with a pattern
of triple lozenges on a ground of small lozenges,
from Noin-ula, China. Han Dynasty (206 B.C.–A.D. 220).
Cream-colored silk, 3⅛ × 2″ (7.75 × 5 cm).
Philadelphia Museum of Art.

ural motifs and others with an overall lozenge
pattern (Figs. 51, 52).

According to tradition, Buddhism was introduced into China in A.D. 68. By the 3rd century
Buddhist elements had begun to appear in Chinese art, just as, in the West, the Christian influence had started to manifest itself.

The Christian World:
Alexandria and Byzantium

The Copts

During the first three centuries of the Christian
era, when the new religion was beginning to take
hold throughout the disintegrating Roman Empire, numerous converts were made in Egypt, then
still under the domination of Imperial Rome.
Among the first to embrace the Christian faith
were members of a peasant class known as the
Copts, who traced their ancestry back directly to
the ancient Egyptians. Records tell of Coptic mar-
tyrs to Christianity in the middle of the 3rd century, when the religion was still forbidden
throughout the Empire. A Coptic version of the
Bible was prepared during the same period. By the
5th century Christianity had become dominant in
Egypt; it remained so until the Arab conquest.

Coptic art is particularly distinguished for its
splendid textiles. Early Coptic fabrics show the
influence of the flowing naturalism and refined
taste of later Greek art, but from the 3rd century
until the 6th—when Coptic art achieved its highest
development—the tendency was increasingly toward abstract, highly stylized forms. Since the
Copts were primarily a peasant class, they rejected
the cosmopolitan styles of the cities in favor of a
more provincial, "Oriental" mode. Stylized animals, the tree of life, the acanthus leaf, palmettes,
and floral designs were all characteristic motifs. In
the 5th century Christian elements began to appear, and a rich iconography, or "story" content,
emerged (Pl. 4, p. 38).

The Copts were especially skilled at tapestry
weaving. They formed their tapestries in the manner of a mosaic, combining many small pieces of
simple weaving in different colors. The best known
of their forms is the so-called *medallion,* a woolen
insert, usually circular but sometimes square,
woven into the linen garments as they were being

above: **53.** Coptic tunic, probably from Tuna (Ashmunein). 6th–7th century. Undyed wool with clavi and orbiculi tapestry woven in colors, 5'5⁄8'' × 3'5'' (1.5 × 1 m). Metropolitan Museum of Art, New York (gift of Maurice Nahman, 1912).

right: **54.** Panel of a curtain with a large central medallion, Coptic. 4th–5th century. Black wool border on undyed loop-weave linen ground, 25½ × 20'' (64 × 50 cm). Cooper-Hewitt Museum of Decorative Arts and Design, Smithsonian Institution, New York (gift of J. P. Morgan).

below: **55.** Coptic *Head*. Loop weave in wool, height 6'' (15 cm). Collection Norman Ives, New Haven, Conn.

made (Fig. 53). The medallions were often applied to clothing at the shoulders, knees, and other points of wear. Medallions also appeared in curtains and church hangings (Fig. 54). Tapestry weaves with *pile* (that is, with protruding strands of wool) were invented in Coptic Egypt (Fig. 55).

With the assistance of the Copts, the Arabs conquered Egypt in 627, and this event marked the beginning of a decline in Coptic art. The Coptic weavers were pressed into the service of the Moslem caliphs, with the result that Islamic motifs intermingled with Coptic forms. Under the Arabs the Copts performed remarkable feats of weaving. One woven tent is described as having been so large that it required a train of seventy camels to haul the tent and its furnishings.

Despite their domination by the forces of Mohammed, the Copts never intermarried with their conquerors, so they retained the characteristics of their race—traceable to ancient Egypt—into the modern era. The prevalence of Coptic forms in Egyptian woolens endured until the 12th century.

Handweaving of the Past: The First Six Millennia **35**

above: 56. Monks presenting Chinese silkworm eggs to the Byzantine Emperor Justinian I.
Etching by Philippe Galle
after a painting by Johannes Stradanus (1536–1605).

right: 57. *Samson and the Lion,*
Byzantine, from Alexandria.
6th–7th century. Silk compound twill,
$37\frac{3}{8} \times 15\frac{7}{8}$" (94 × 40 cm).
Dumbarton Oaks Collection, Washington, D.C.

The Byzantine Empire

In A.D. 323 the Roman Emperor Constantine decided to move the capital of the Empire to the city of Byzantium, renaming it Constantinople. With the western portions of the Empire weakening and subject to periodic barbarian invasions, the power of the eastern capital gradually increased, so that by the 5th century it is possible to speak of a "Byzantine" Empire, distinct in culture, tastes, and particularly in art, from the Roman west.

The weaving of Byzantium, like that of China, focuses primarily on silk. In A.D. 522 the Emperor Justinian succeeded in penetrating the wall of secrecy that had protected the Chinese monopoly of sericulture for three thousand years. Two Nestorian monks concealed silkworm eggs in a hollow walking cane and smuggled them out of China. The monks brought the eggs to Constantinople and gave them to Justinian (Fig. 56), along with some mulberry leaves—also smuggled out—to feed the silk larvae when they hatched. Justinian appointed a special caretaker for the precious eggs and at the same time began to import silks from abroad, presumably to serve as models for his own weavers. Subsequently Constantinople became a major center for the manufacture of silk textiles.

State workshops, in which most of the weavers were women, supported a thriving commerce in silks and silk products.

Lavish figure weaves characterize the finest Byzantine textiles. Among the most famous silks made in the workshops of Constantinople are: that from the 7th century showing Samson struggling with a lion (Fig. 57); the splendid 10th-century elephant weave from the tomb of Charlemagne, placed there about two hundred years after the

Plate 1. Mask associated with the Snake Dance, from Baining, New Britain, Papua New Guinea. Collected 1910. Tapa cloth. American Museum of Natural History, New York.

left: Plate 2. Gary Trentham. Basket. 1977. Brown paper twine. Courtesy Hadler Galleries, New York.

below left: Plate 3. Chilkat blanket, Northwest Coast Indians. Collected 1880. Warp of cedar bark and mountain goat hair, weft of mountain goat hair. American Museum of National History, New York.

above: Plate 4.
Sacrifice of Isaac, Coptic.
7th century. Tapestry,
$4\frac{5}{8} \times 10\frac{1}{8}''$ (11 × 25 cm).
Musée Historique des Tissus,
Lyons.

left: Plate 5. Gunta Stölzl.
Slit Gobelin wall hanging. 1927–28.
Linen warp, cotton weft;
$4'7'' \times 3'7''$ (1.4 × 1.1 m).
Bauhaus-Archiv, West Berlin
(on permanent loan from
the Carpet Association
of Wuppertal).

Emperor's death (Fig. 58); and a dalmatic said to have belonged to Charlemagne (Fig. 59).

Unlike Coptic Egypt, Byzantium withstood the onslaughts of Islam. Constantinople remained preeminent in textiles well into the 14th century.

The Moslem Conquest

When the Prophet Mohammed died at Medina in 632, the religion he had preached—Islam—was known only in the Arabian peninsula. Within one hundred years his followers had conquered all the land as far east as the Indus River, the entire northern coast of Africa, all of Spain, and even parts of southern France. They carried with them not only the word of Allah but a political system, a language, and a culture that amalgamated the Oriental elements of its origins with the most refined tastes and skills of the conquered nations. We can thus speak of *Islamic* weaving as that practiced by Arab craftsmen as well as by native artisans in all the lands under the domination of the Caliphate.

Islamic decoration in the arts tended to be highly abstract and geometric, partially because of the Koranic ban on representations of the human form. When animal forms did appear, they were usually stylized and purely decorative in character

above: 58. Byzantine textile with elephant pattern, from the tomb of Charlemagne. c. 1000. Silk, 5'3¾" × 4'4" (1.6 × 1.3 m). Cathedral Museum, Aachen.

right: 59. Dalmatic alleged to have belonged to Charlemagne. c. 9th century. Vatican Basilica Treasury, Rome.

(Fig. 60). Another prohibition concerned the use of silk, which in the early Islamic period was considered too luxurious for clothing. Wool, cotton, and linen were the preferred materials, but these were often enriched with silk borders or bands (Fig. 61). Gradually, the silk bands became wider and wider, and laws were passed regarding the amount of silk that could be added to a garment. In time the ban was forgotten, and the weaving of silk textiles became a profitable industry throughout the Islamic world.

Persia fell to the Arabs in the first decade after Mohammed's death, and the invaders thus became heir to the rich heritage of Sassanian weaving (Fig. 45). Recognizing, perhaps, the artistry of Sassanian tapestries—or perhaps their commercial importance—the caliphs never enforced the injunction against silk weaving in Persia. Therefore, the Sassanian silk industry continued without interruption after the conquest (Fig. 62). There was, however, a gradual change in style, as the more abstract Moslem forms, including the Kufic script, began to dominate.

With the conquest of Egypt the Arabs inherited a second great cultural tradition—from the Copts. The transition to the Islamic decorative styles cannot have been too difficult for the Copts, so abstract were their own artistic forms. Many textiles produced in Egypt under Moslem domination showed elaborate Arabic calligraphy (Fig. 63).

above: 62. Iranian textile fragment showing
a pair of fantastic birds grasping ibexes.
Buyid Period, 10th century.
Silk diasper weave,
28 × 37⅛″ (70 × 92 cm).
Cleveland Museum of Art
(purchase from the J. H. Wade Fund).

right: 63. Fatimid sash, from Egypt.
12th century.
Linen and silk, width, 11″ (27.5 cm).
Museum of Islamic Art, Cairo.

When Islam reached Spain in the early part of the 8th century, it subjugated a people who had been under the influence of the Byzantine Empire and thus of Byzantine culture. Nevertheless, so thoroughly was the Moorish aesthetic absorbed into Spanish art that it remained a visible presence until the 15th century. Spanish textiles of the Islamic period include the Kufic script and other Arab motifs, and Spanish silks were reputed to be as fine as those woven in Persia.

The expulsion of the Arabs from Spain began in the 10th century, but many Arab craftsmen stayed in Spain and continued to work in their accustomed modes. This period of Spanish art—from the Christian reconquest to the final expulsion of all Moors in 1492—is referred to as *Hispano-Moresque*. The most characteristic textiles from this era are in the "Alhambra" style (Fig. 64)—geometric plait-band patterns based on designs found in the stucco and tile of that remarkable palace at Granada.

The decline in power of the Islamic empire corresponded in time to the emergence of the European kingdoms. From this point, with a few digressions, the history of weaving can be traced in Christian Europe.

64. Textile, Hispano-Moresque.
15th century.
Silk, height 39¼″ (98 cm).
Metropolitan Museum of Art, New York
(Fletcher Fund, 1929).

Until medieval times families supplied all their textile needs from fabrics made in the home (Fig. 65). When they produced more than they required, the extra cloth would be paid to their feudal lords as part of their taxes. The lord would then mark each piece of fabric with his personal brand and sell it in the local market. The brand might be a symbolic representation of the baron's name or castle or, in the case of a monastery, the patron saint. Since the brands readily identified the source of the fabric, they became a guarantee of quality, a kind of trademark.

Certain fabrics became so important to barter and payment that they served as a currency in themselves. This was true particularly of *wadmal* (Fig. 66), a woolen fabric woven in Scandinavia and in England. Wadmal was commonly made into clothing, sails, and bedding, but in standardized measure—2 by 20 ells (an ell equals 45 inches)—lengths of wadmal took the place of legal tender for commerce.

The nobles could afford more variety and luxury in their textiles. Trade with the Middle East had long been in effect, and in the 13th century Marco Polo opened the lucrative trade routes to China and India.

Handweaving of the Past: Europe, the Far East, and the New World

left: 65. Women carding, spinning, and
weaving wool. From a 15th-century
illuminated manuscript.
British Museum, London.

below: 66. Hood, Herjolfsnes, Greenland.
14th century.
Wadmal in brown four-shaft twill,
height c. 24″ (60 cm).
National Museum, Copenhagen.

below: 67. *Harold Swearing Oath,*
detail of *Bayeux Tapestry.* c. 1073–88.
Wool embroidery on linen;
height 20″ (50 cm),
overall length 231′ (69.3 m).
Town Hall, Bayeux.

The Middle Ages in Europe

Before the development of towns, monasteries and convents often provided space for the weavers and spinners to work. As the manufacture of cloth gradually moved out of the home and into the workshop, weaving became more and more standardized, and guilds were established. Weavers on the Continent had formed guilds even before the Norman Conquest in 1066. By the 12th century the Weavers' Guild, the oldest of the English guilds, had been organized. The manufacture of woolen cloth introduced England to industry and commerce. It also created a number of new occupations, not only weaver and spinner but cloth merchant as well. The manufacture of cloth required that a considerable amount of money be tied up for quite a long time. Consequently, the cloth merchants were among the wealthiest citizens of the town.

The guilds served a twofold purpose: They helped the artisans by eliminating unfair competition and by enabling them to buy raw materials at wholesale prices; on the other hand, the standards set by the guilds protected the consumer. Until this time quality of workmanship had been a variable factor. The guild standards assured the purchaser of high quality at a fair price. King Henry I of England (1100–35) is credited with establishing a standard yard measurement—the length of his own arm. Such universal measures were essential to weavers who were merchandising their cloth.

Many of the controls introduced by cloth inspectors were intended as a gauge for assessing fines, so they benefited the consumer only indirectly. These regulations governed the length and width of fabric, the number of warp yarns, and the evenness of dyeing. In France a law of 1258 prohibited the weaving of tapestry by artificial light, which might cause poor workmanship.

One of the most common fabrics used by the peasant class during this period was *fustian*, a cloth originally woven in Fustat (present-day Cairo). In many ways similar to wadmal, fustian had a linen warp and a coarse cotton weft. It was woven in a twill (Figs. 238–242), with a low pile formed by protruding loops of weft yarn on one side.

At the opposite end of the social spectrum, *cloth of gold*, a rich brocade ornamented with gold yarns, was much sought by European royalty throughout the medieval and Renaissance periods. It was woven in the Middle East, probably in Persia, from yarns produced by winding the solid metal leaf around a core of silk or cotton. Cloth of gold was in particular demand for ceremonial occasions, such as coronations. Everything imaginable would be draped extravagantly with this exquisite fabric—horses, banners, canopies, the stage, the throne, the banquet hall, and, of course, the king himself.

The art of tapestry weaving was practiced in many parts of Europe by the 11th century. Tapestries of the 12th and 13th centuries in Western Europe owe their existence to the patronage of the abbeys and the great churches. Later, the kings, dukes, and bourgeoisie, particularly in France, helped the craft to flourish. Until the Renaissance, however, the production of fine silks and brocades achieved commercial importance only in Italy.

France

The most famous tapestry dating from the Middle Ages—perhaps the most famous textile of all time—is not really a tapestry at all. A remarkable work of embroidery measuring 231 feet in length, the *Bayeux Tapestry* (Fig. 67) was made to cover the masonry frieze of Bayeux Cathedral. Its 79 panels, worked in wool on a coarse linen cloth,

68. Nicolas Bataille, after a design by Jean de Bandol (Hennequin de Bruges). *The Apocalypse,* detail. c. 1381. Tapestry, height of detail 6'6" (1.95 m). Musée des Tapisseries, Angers.

depict the conquest of Saxon England by William of Normandy, culminating in the Battle of Hastings in 1066.

The tapestry is much like an enormous book, for its scenes are read, for the most part, from left to right, following the sequence of events. The episode illustrated, *Harold Swearing Oath,* is from the first segment of the narrative, in which Earl Harold of Wessex apparently pledged himself to support William's claim to the English throne. No effort is spared to make the tapestry's message abundantly clear, from the Latin inscriptions that accompany each episode, to the presence of symbolic beasts along the top border. In this case, the inclusion of the fox and crow, the wolf and stork, and the ewe, goat, and cow with a lion all signify Harold's potential treachery.

Conventional tapestries, in which the figures were woven into the cloth rather than applied to it, served a functional as well as a decorative purpose during the Middle Ages. They were often made as large wall coverings for the cold, dismal "great halls" of castles and churches. In addition to cutting drafts, the tapestries created a feeling of warmth. Only in the earliest times did tapestries hang directly on the walls. Later, they provided a corridor, used by the servants, between the hanging and the wall.

Tapestry weaving was flourishing in Paris in the 13th century, but it did not reach its pinnacle until the latter part of the 14th. In the Middle Ages, for

the first time, it is possible to ascribe certain textiles to the hand of a known artisan. Three French master-weavers dominated the field: Jacques Dourdin, Pierre de Beaumetz, and Nicolas Bataille. Bataille's masterpiece was the *Apocalypse* (Fig. 68), a series of seven hangings commissioned by Louis d'Anjou. Records indicate that the tapestry, which was paid for (and presumably underway) in 1377, was inspired by an illuminated manuscript lent by Louis' brother, King Charles V. Each of the seven panels was 80 feet long by 20 feet high, and, when hung in series, the backgrounds alternated between red and turquoise. The figures are drawn in a rather coarse weave with approximately twenty colors. In spite of these limited technical means, the subjects are portrayed with great sensitivity.

Another monumental tapestry series of the period depicts the *Nine Heroes* (Fig. 69), a theme that was very popular in the 14th century, largely because of the mystical connotations of three and three times three. The roster includes three pagan heroes (Hector, Alexander, and Julius Caesar), three Hebrew heroes (David, Joshua, and Judas Maccabeus), and three Christian heroes (Arthur, Charlemagne, and Godfrey of Bouillon). Several of the tapestries bear the arms of that formidable patron of the arts Jean, Duc de Berry, also brother of Charles V, although it is not certain that they actually belonged to him. A number of similarities between the *Heroes* and the *Apocalypse* suggest that Bataille's workshop was responsible for both, but this, too, cannot be proved. Because the composition of the *Nine Heroes* is much more complex, the series is dated a bit later than the *Apocalypse*, about 1390.

It is often assumed that all the splendid medieval tapestries were designed to be hung on the wall, where they could be admired in all their beauty. This is far from the case. The very large pieces, such as the *Nine Heroes* and the *Apocalypse*, could scarcely be put anywhere else, but many smaller tapestries served as table covers, window curtains, bench covers, or even nonspecific textiles that could be put to use wherever the need arose. On commission from Philip the Bold, duke of Burgundy (yet another brother of King Charles), Nicolas Bataille wove tapestry mule blankets and a garment for the nobleman's favorite leopard.

The Hundred Years' War had a devastating effect on the French tapestry industry. With much of France, including Paris, lost to the English, the weaving workshops were disbanded.

Flanders

In the Early Middle Ages the city of Arras established itself as a major textile center, and it held that position for several hundred years. By the 14th century both the weaving and the tapestry workshops had attained so large a scale that they could almost be called factories. These workshops flourished under the patronage of such discriminating clients as the French court and the dukes of Burgundy. The tapestry industry had close connections with its counterpart in Paris. Jacques Dourdin, one of the French master-weavers and merchants, was a citizen of Arras.

Most of our knowledge of early Flemish tapestry weaving comes from contemporary documents, for little has been preserved. These records describe extravagant representations of themes then popular in France: religious and heroic subjects, battle scenes, and legends of love. Among the few remaining examples of medieval Flemish tapestry are the *Saga of Jourdain de Blaye* (Fig. 70),

above right: 69. Nicolas Bataille (?).
King Arthur, from *Nine Heroes*. Late 14th century.
Wool tapestry, 11'6½" × 10' (3.5 × 3 m) overall.
Metropolitan Museum of Art, New York
(Munsey Fund, 1932).

right: 70. *Saga of Jourdain de Blaye*,
detail, from Arras. c. 1400.
Wool tapestry,
10'9" × 12'6" (3.25 × 3.75 m).
Museo Civico, Padua.

made in Arras about 1400, and *The Story of Saint Piat and Saint Eleuthère* (Fig. 71), a work also attributed to the weavers of Arras and dated to the turn of the 15th century.

Norway

The Norwegians have been skilled at figural weaving since Viking times. Among the items uncovered at the 9th-century Oseberg ship-burial site are figure weaves of great richness and imagination (Fig. 72). However, the most important surviving example of early tapestry weaving in Norway dates from four centuries later. The *Baldishol Tapestry* (Fig. 73) is a fragment of a bench cover depicting the months of April ("Prilis," a bearded and robed figure) and May ("Ivis," a knight in armor). It is woven in six colors, with geometric and other decorative motifs covering the entire surface. In many respects—the flatness of the fig-

left: 71. *The Story of Saint Piat and Saint Eleuthère,* detail, from Arras. 1402. Tapestry, 8'10¼″ × 6'3″ (2.66 × 1.88 m). Notre Dame de Tournai.

below: 72. Textile from the Oseberg Burial Ship, Norway. A.D. 830. Tapestry. Copyright University Museum of National Antiquities, Oslo.

above: 73. *Baldishol Tapestry*, found in the Church of Baldishol at Nes, Hedmark. Early 13th century (?). Wool and linen, 3'10" × 6'6" (1.15 × 1.95 m). Oslo Museum of Applied Art.

below: 74. Coronation cloak of Roger II, from Palermo. 1133. Gold and bead embroidery on purple cloth. Kunsthistorisches Museum, Viena.

ures and space, the presence of heraldic beasts—it is similar to the *Bayeux Tapestry* (Fig. 67) of two centuries earlier.

Italy

When the great Islamic Empire fell into decline, its position of importance in the production of fine textiles, particularly silks, was ceded to Italy. The revival of the textile arts came earliest in Sicily, which had been under Moslem domination in the 10th century. Before the Moslem conquest Sicily had been first Roman and then Byzantine; afterward it was successively Norman, Swabian, and Spanish. This curious mixture of influences was naturally reflected in the textiles (Fig. 74). A specialty of the Sicilian workshops was the weaving of borders made from gold thread. These ornamental borders were exported to all parts of Europe for use in decorative fabrics.

It would be impossible to discuss the history of weaving in Europe without mention of Lucca, the most important textile center of the Middle Ages. By the 14th century there were about three thousand looms operating in Lucca alone, and commercial offices had been established in many European and Middle Eastern cities. In addition to the domestic production, fine textiles were imported from Persia, Syria, Egypt and eastern Asia. Silk weaving remained an important industry in Lucca until the 18th century.

The city of Venice was second only to Lucca in both weaving and commerce. Venetian merchants had close contact with textile centers in Byzantium and the Middle East, with the result that Byzantine and Islamic motifs were adopted by local craftsmen. In 1269 Marco Polo, with his father and uncle, set out from Venice on an overland route to the Far East, arriving in the Chinese capital of Pekin two years later. Marco remained in the service of Kublai Khan for seventeen years. When he finally returned to Venice, he related tales of unimaginable wealth to be found in the East, and, as a result of his journey, direct importation of silk from China was begun. Some of the Oriental silk that reached medieval Europe took the form of fine cloth woven on Chinese looms; the remainder was raw silk that the Italians themselves processed into fabric, frequently combining the silk with a certain amount of linen fiber in order to produce a more durable textile.

The travels of the Polo family, and the memoirs published by Marco upon his return to Venice, awakened Europeans to the riches that existed beyond their own world. It was this quest for exotic treasure that led them, ultimately, to the shores of the Americas.

Pre-Columbian America

Archaeologists and art historians have long debated whether the textile arts flowered spontaneously among the tribes that inhabited Central and South America before the arrival of the *conquistadores*, or whether some previously unsuspected contact existed between these groups and the ancient peoples of the Middle East, by which weaving knowledge was transmitted. The voyages of Thor Heyerdahl opened the *possibility* that Egyptian or other Mediterranean sailors, in their fragile papyrus boats, managed to cross the Atlantic and land in Latin America. Furthermore, a number of authorities have pointed to the striking similarity between the textiles of ancient Peru and those of Egypt. In any event, we can say that a very high level of expertise in all the textile arts was achieved by the tribes who inhabited the Americas from the pre-Christian era to the 16th century.

The Pueblo Indians of what is now the southwestern United States had developed the art of weaving cotton to a fairly advanced degree by A.D. 700. They also used fibers from the yucca plant, and, for cold-weather protection, the chiefs wore wraps made from strips of rabbit skins interlaced with the yucca warps. For their bedding the Pueblos made thick cotton sheets and blankets woven from feathers. Over the centuries the art of weaving declined among the Pueblos and eventually disappeared altogether. Fortunately, their techniques and decorative styles were passed along to a neighboring tribe, the Navajo, who later applied the same methods to wool after the Spaniards introduced sheep in the 17th century.

From surviving pottery, sculpture, and painting, archaeologists have deduced that the Indians of Mexico and Central America were also adept at weaving, but of their craft nothing remains. However, thanks to the special preserving qualities of

75. Head ornament, Nazca Valley, Peru. c. 2500 B.C. Cotton or agave and feathers, 11 × 8″ (27.5 × 20 cm). Collection the author.

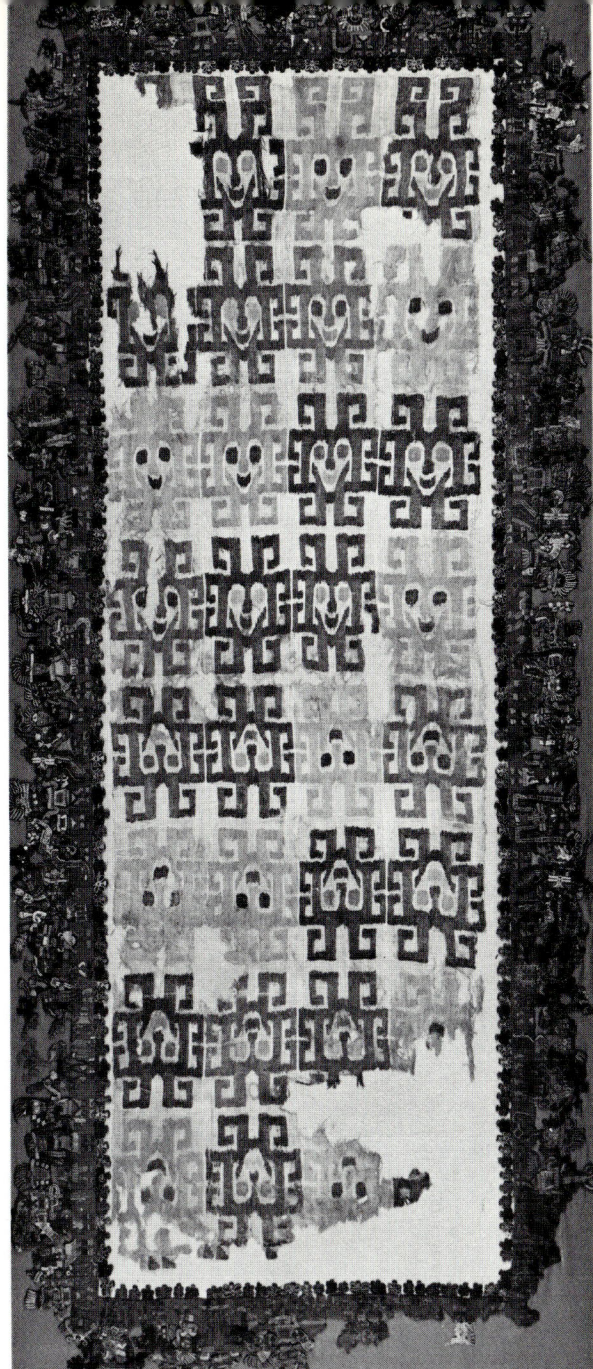

left: **76.** *Paracas Textile*, Cabeza Larga,
south coast of Peru.
Late 1st century B.C.–A.D. early 1st century.
Woven cotton with loop stitch border of wool,
5′5″ × 1′8″ (1.63 × .50 m).
Brooklyn Museum, New York
(John T. Underwood Memorial Fund).

below: 77. Detail of Figure 76, *Paracas Textile*.

the climate, a fabulous wealth of woven textiles has been unearthed in the coastal plains of Peru.

Most of the textiles found in Peru have come from tombs, for it was the custom among the Indians to wrap the bodies of their dead and to provide them with an array of new clothing for use in the afterlife. Agave fiber, cotton, and wool from the llama, the alpaca, and the vicuña were their principal materials; silk and linen were never available. Often, fibers were combined. The warps were of cotton, and wool, which readily accepted the natural dyes, served as the pattern-carrying weft. Reds were obtained from cochineal, yellow from ocherous earth, brown from vegetable juices, and blue and green from indigo. By simple means they achieved a wide range of hues.

The oldest Peruvian fabrics known date from the preceramic period, that is, before 1200 B.C. The example in Figure 75 has a braided fringe ending in tiny feathers. By the Experimenter Period (400 B.C.–A.D. 400) the range of the Peruvian fabric maker had grown impressive indeed, despite the fact that a loom consisted of little more than two sticks. Stripes, abstract designs, and even figures were woven into cloth through the use of colored wefts. Figure 76 illustrates a mantle so fabulous that for many years after its discovery it was called simply *The Paracas Textile*. The central portion, patterned with stylized faces, is of loosely woven wool on cotton, while the elaborate border (Fig. 77) consists of a procession of figures—warriors, serpents, mythological beasts—worked in a loop

stitch that resembles knitting. The embroiderer's repertoire was astonishing, as evidenced by the sampler reproduced in Figure 78. Human forms, birds, animals, fish, monsters, and abstract patterns of various kinds were all handled skillfully.

The most striking textiles from this period are the Paracas funerary mantles (Fig. 79). These were wrapped around mummies before burial, and interspersed between the layers of the mantle were ponchos, headbands, and ceremonial gear that the deceased might require. (When archaeologists excavated the tombs, it often took them weeks to unwrap these burial bundles.) Measuring about 3 yards by 1 yard, the mantles are of plain cloth

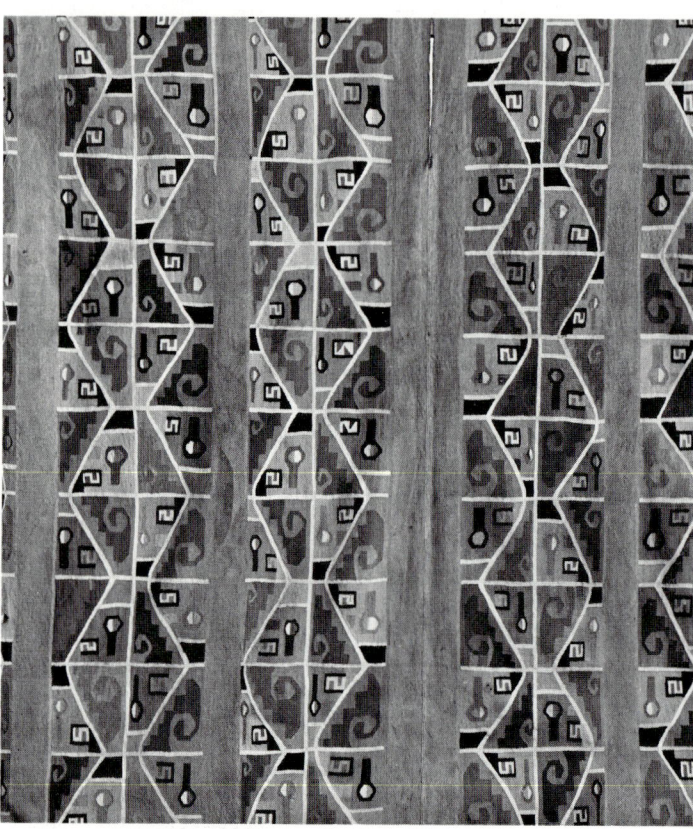

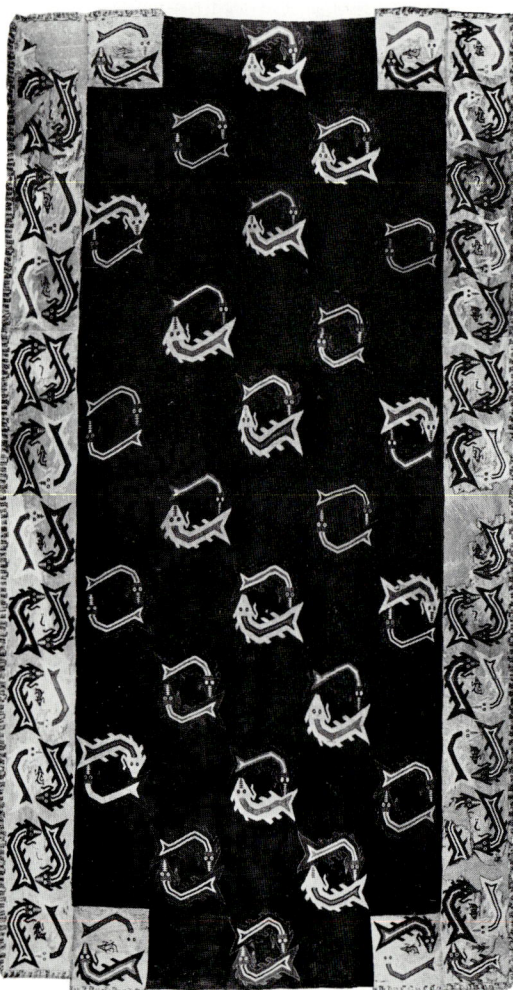

top left: **78.** Sampler, Nazca, south coast of Peru, detail.
100 B.C.–A.D. 200.
Wool and cotton, 42 × 28½″ (1.05 × .71 m).
Metropolitan Museum of Art, New York
(Michael C. Rockefeller Memorial Collection of Primitive Art).

left: **79.** *Paracas Funerary Mantle*, south coast of Peru.
Late 1st century B.C.–A.D. early 1st century.
Wool with embroidered border,
5′3″ × 10′ (1.6 × 3 m).
Brooklyn Museum, New York (Alfred W. Jenkins Fund).

above: **80.** Poncho-shirt, detail, Tiahuanaco,
south coast of Peru. A.D. 800–1100.
Interlocking tapestry weave in cotton and wool,
3′6″ × 7′4″ (1.05 × 2.2 m).
Art Institute of Chicago (purchase, Buckingham Fund).

right: **81.** Hanging, Chancay, central coast of Peru. 1000–1450. Wool and cotton, 6'4" × 8'5" (1.9 × 2.53 m). Metropolitan Museum of Art, New York (Michael C. Rockefeller Memorial Collection of Primitive Art).

below: **82.** Shirt, Ica, south coast of Peru. 1000–1450. Wool and cotton. Metropolitan Museum of Art, New York (Michael C. Rockefeller Memorial Collection of Primitive Art).

embroidered with free-floating human or animal forms—cat demons, fish, butterfly gods, birds, or combinations of various elements.

The following period—A.D. 400 to 1000—is aptly termed the "Age of the Mastercraftsmen." Not only in textiles, but in pottery, metalwork, and other crafts the Peruvian artist reached a pinnacle of achievement. Paracas burial mantles were still made, and they were often accompanied by matched sets of shirts, ponchos, and shawls with the same overall polychrome embroidery. During this period the cultural center shifted from the Paracas peninsula on the coast to Tiahuanaco on the shores of Lake Titicaca in modern Bolivia. The Tiahuanaco style emphasized tapestry weaves characterized by straight, rectilinear, strongly outlined forms, as in the sleeveless shirt reproduced in Figure 80.

The period between 1000 and 1438 brought a decline in the pan-Peruvian Tiahuanaco style and the emergence of regional styles—Chancay, Chimu, and Ica (Figs. 81, 82). The three styles have in common a more lighthearted, even humorous approach and a preference for stylized animal forms.

Handweaving of the Past: Europe, the Far East, and the New World **53**

below: 84. Sleeveless checkerboard shirt,
Inca, Peru. 1438–1532.
Tapestry weave in alpaca wool,
34 × 31″ (85 × 77.5 cm).
Museum of Fine Arts, Boston
(William Francis Warden Fund).

above: 83. Mantle, Chancay,
north coast of Peru. 1000–1300.
Feathers and fiber, 45 × 44½″ (113 × 111 cm).
Nelson Gallery–Atkins Museum,
Kansas City (Nelson Fund).

A number of fabric innovations were perfected
during this era, including the complicated feather
textiles (Fig. 83). After weaving a fine cloth, the
artisan sewed in tiny bird's feathers, selected for
their color.

The mighty empire of the Incas (1438–1532)
marks the last great period in the art of pre-
Columbian Peru. Most of the surviving textiles
from this culture are articles of clothing, particularly the shirt or *cuzma*. They are characterized by
bright, contrasting colors and geometric forms—
crosses, lozenges, spirals, meanders, and checker-
boards (Fig. 84). Inca weaving was, in a sense, a
refinement of all that had gone before—a purifica-
tion of form combined with a mastery of fiber
technique.

In 1527 a small band of Spaniards led by Francisco Pizarro landed in Peru. The Incas welcomed
their European visitors, and for five years the two
groups coexisted peacefully. Then, in 1532 Pizarro
seized the ruling Inca and established Spanish
colonial government. The art of the Indians, so
different from that of Europe, was either ignored
or destroyed.

The Meeting of East and West: China and Japan

China

Unlike Pizarro, Marco Polo knew full well the
value of the textiles and other works of art he
encountered in the Chinese court. Almost immediately fine silks from China began to appear in the
churches and royal houses of Europe. Among the
first of these was a gold brocaded silk vestment
used as a burial garment for Pope Benedict, who
died in 1304 (Fig. 85). Apart from stylistic differences, Chinese gold textiles can be distinguished
from those made in the Middle East and in Europe
because the precious metal was applied to thin
strips of leather.

Silk tapestries had been popular in China since
the Sung Dynasty (960–1279), when they were
fashioned after contemporary painting styles. By
the Ming Dynasty (1368–1644) tapestry weaving
had become an art in its own right. The *K'o-ssu*
silks of that period (Fig. 86) were often copies of
lost paintings, but they were never direct imita-

left: 85. Dalmatic, Chinese,
said to be from the tomb
of Pope Benedict XI (d. 1304).
Silk and gold brocade with embroidery.
San Domenico, Perugia.

right: 86. Fragment of a panel, China. Ming Dynasty (1368–1644).
K'o-ssu (silk tapestry) with gold thread, 6′6″ × 2′2″ (1.95 × .65 m).
Cleveland Museum of Art (gift of Mr. and Mrs. J. H. Wade).

below: 87. *Emperor's Dragon Medallion*, China. Ming Dynasty (1368–1644).
Silk with embroidery and couched gold, diameter 12″ (30 cm).
Metropolitan Museum of Art, New York (anonymous gift, 1946).

tions. Instead, the original design was reinterpreted in the tapestry technique, with soft colors and flattened forms. Tapestries also served for court robes, furnishing fabrics, and accessories.

The borrowing of designs from one art form to another was quite common under the Ming Dynasty. It has been established that many patterns on the famous Ming porcelains were adapted from silk embroidery and brocades. Typical forms included phoenixes, lions, peacocks, storks, flying fish, and dragons (Fig. 87).

the Nara Period (645–794) the government had become so stratified that elaborate rules of dress were instituted. Each official rank was assigned a particular color and pattern of clothing, and this, of course, greatly stimulated the weaving and dyeing industries. Brocades, called *nishiki*, were especially ornate, with patterns woven in either the warp or the weft. Silk textiles were most highly prized, but cotton and hemp were also used. The textile industries continued to flourish during the Heian Period (794–1185). Rich and diversified colors were important, and silk was the main fiber.

During the Kamakura and Muromachi periods weaving declined, and the most elegant fabrics were imported from China—the textiles referred to as *meibutsu-gire,* "famous materials." The Momoyama Period (1573–1615) revived the textile arts most splendidly in the costumes of the *Noh* theater. The more extravagant costumes were painted or embroidered, but a few simple and lovely gold brocades survive. Everyday clothing among members of the samurai class reflected the tendency toward greater luxury. Both sexes wore a one-piece kimono called a *kosode* decorated with bright, large-scale designs.

The tastes of the Edo Period (1615–1868) were, if possible, even more lavish. The *kosode* (Fig. 90) was adopted by all levels of society, and longer sleeves and wider *obi* (sashes) were fashionable in

above: 88. Pile rug, China. 18th century. Wool and cotton, 8′8″ × 5′3″ (2.6 × 1.58 m). Textile Museum, Washington, D.C.

right: 89. *Ban* (Buddhist ritual pendant), detail, Japan. Asuka Period (552–645). Silk ikat. Tokyo National Museum.

The Chinese were exceptionally proficient in the manufacture of velvets. In the 17th century the most sumptuous velvets had alternately cut and uncut pile, which enhanced the quality of reflected light. Pile carpets (Fig. 88), often featuring Buddhist and Taoist images, also date from this period. The most unusual were the "pillar" carpets, meant to be hung around a column.

Japan

The origins of Japanese art are most often traced to the Asuka period, beginning with the introduction of Buddhism from China in A.D. 552. From written records it is known that the Japanese were already skilled in the production of fine silks, damasks, brocades, and embroideries (Fig. 89). By

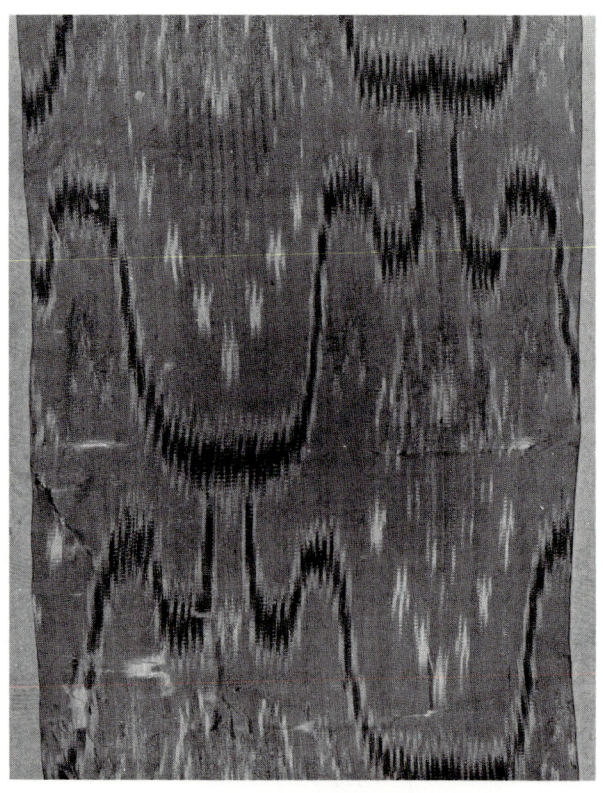

90. Kosode, Japan. 18th century. Kara-ori brocade, silk; height 5′ (1.5 m). Metropolitan Museum of Art, New York (bequest of Edward C. Moore, 1891).

women's dress. Printing and dyeing rather eclipsed woven patterns, because the former were capable of stronger effects. During this period Kyoto was the center of the textile industry, but many other cities and towns became famous for their individual styles. Some of these local manufactures are in operation to this day.

Both the Portuguese and the Spanish Jesuits reached Japan in 1542, with the result that a few Japanese textiles were introduced to Europe. However, it was the Dutch, arriving half a century later, who instigated active trade between Europe and Japan.

Europe In Renaissance

The fantastic rebirth of arts and sciences that engulfed Europe in the centuries following what we call the "Middle Ages" did not occur simultaneously on all parts of the Continent. It came first to Italy and Flanders, then spread later to Spain, France, England, and Germany. However, for purposes of discussion it is convenient to label as "Renaissance" the period between 1400 and

1600—an era made fabulous by the Medici in Florence, the art patron popes in Rome, Ferdinand and Isabella of Spain, Francis I of France, and Henry VIII of England.

Weaving shared in the enormous popularity enjoyed by all the arts. In both quantity and quality, the product of the Reniassance looms rivals that of any other age, with the possible exception of our own. To satisfy the tastes of wealthy clients, a number of opulent fabrics were developed. Velvets—plain, cut, embroidered, appliquéd, brocaded—were much sought for garments and clerical vestments. Silk brocades, enriched with gold and silver threads, served as clothing, upholstery fabrics, wall coverings, and draperies. Furthermore, the nobility no longer held a monopoly on elegant fabrics, for a newly prosperous bourgeoisie competed in the demand for iridescent taffetas, fine silks, and damasks.

Tapestry weaving, in particular, reached the height of its form; indeed, the Renaissance and early Baroque periods have been termed "the golden age of tapestry." Among those who could afford it, the fashion of the day called for rooms hung entirely with intricate, highly decorated tapestries. We can get some idea of the expense involved in keeping up this fashion from the fact that *The Story of Alexander the Great* reproduced in Figure 92 was acquired by Philip the Good, Duke of Burgundy, for the extraordinary sum of five thousand gold pieces.

During the Renaissance nearly every region of Europe had its tapestry weavers, but in the production of large-scale epic tapestries the supremacy of Flanders was unchallenged.

Flanders

For the first half of the 15th century Arras maintained its prominent position in the field of tapestry weaving. Its closest rival was the neighboring city of Tournai, and after about 1450 the balance gradually shifted in favor of the latter, which had captured that most enviable prize—the patronage of the dukes of Burgundy. Throughout

the period the two cities had very close artistic and commercial ties, so it is often difficult to attribute a particular work to one or another. But most authorities agree that the splendid *Offering of the Heart* in Figure 91 was woven in Arras.

The Story of Alexander the Great (Fig. 92) was created in the workshop of Pasquier Grenier (d. 1493), the most famous merchant-weaver of Tournai. The manufactures had, by this time, been organized on an industrial level; their products attained monumentality in both scale and concept. One has only to list the titles of major tapestry series to understand their epic nature: *The History of the Sacrament, The History of St. Peter, The History of Julius Caesar.*

After a hundred years of leadership, Tournai declined as a tapestry capital. In the latter half of the 15th century wealthy patrons had begun to turn to Brussels, where the style of weaving was more closely oriented toward painting. A characteristic of many Brussels tapestries is the segmenting of narrative episodes in an architectural setting reminiscent of wooden altarpieces. The extravagant use of gold threads in these works inspired the name *tapis d'or* ("cloth of gold"). Such tapestries were considered precious works of art and intended purely for decoration.

Among the more prominent merchant-weavers in early 16th-century Brussels were Pieter Pannemaker and Pieter van Aelst. Van Aelst was responsible for executing *The Acts of the Apostles* (Fig. 93), for which Raphael prepared the cartoons (Fig. 94). The tapestry was woven for the Sistine Chapel and completed in 1519, seven years after Michelangelo had finished the ceiling frescoes. In style it is more like Italian painting than northern textile art, for Raphael emphasized a sense of mass and three-dimensional space, both of which had previously been minimal in tapestry decoration.

Flemish tapestries of the Renaissance are so magnificent that they tend to overshadow the other textile arts. However, simple weaving was also a highly profitable industry during that period, and in the 15th century Flanders became the European center for wool weaving. Exquisite damasks, often with complicated figural designs (Fig. 95), also came from Flemish looms.

left: **93. Pieter van Aelst,**
after a design by Raphael.
The Miraculous Draught of Fishes,
from *The Acts of the Apostles.* 1516–19.
Tapestry weave in wool, silk,
and gold threads;
15'11" × 16'7" (4.78 × 4.97 m).
Vatican Museum, Rome.

above: **94. Raphael.**
Cartoon for *The Miraculous Draught of Fishes.*
1515–16. Watercolor,
10'5½" × 13'1" (3.14 × 3.93 m).
Victoria & Albert Museum, London
(on loan from Her Majesty the Queen).

right: **95.** *Annunciation,* Flanders. c. 1500.
Linen damask, 3'11½" × 2'6¾" (1.19 × .77 m).
Victoria & Albert Museum, London.

England

Many of the Protestant weavers who emigrated from France during the Counter-Reformation settled in England, where they became part of a thriving enterprise. Queen Elizabeth I made the weaving industry the basis for England's trade and the establishment of her merchant marine. Ships laden with English fabrics reached ports throughout the Mediterranean, and their captains were charged with selling the entire cargo in a lot. If this proved impossible, foreign merchants were encouraged to buy at least one item for their own use. The most desirable customer was Spain, which would pay in the gold she was draining from her recently conquered territories in the New World. In time English woolens for bed covers, cushions, draperies, and hangings became stylish in Europe, replacing the much more expensive silk, which had prevailed earlier.

In 1510, under the direction of William Sheldon of Weston House, a series of county maps were woven in tapestry. The example in Figure 96 shows a portion of the tapestry map of Worcestershire—a charming mixture of geographical representation and decorative design.

top: 96. Sheldon tapestry map of Worcestershire, detail. 1588. Wool, 12'3" × 16' (3.68 × 4.8 m) overall. Collection Bodleian Library, Oxford, presently at the Victoria & Albert Museum, London.

right: 97. *The Capture of the Unicorn,* from *The Hunt of the Unicorn,* Franco-Flemish. c. 1500. Tapestry weave, 12'1" × 12'5" (3.6 × 3.75 m). Metropolitan Museum of Art, New York (gift of John D. Rockefeller, Jr., 1937).

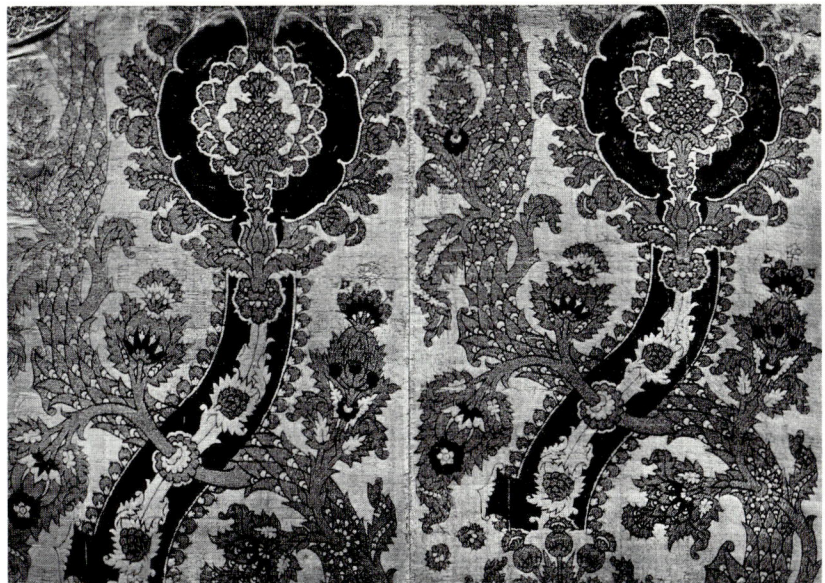

left: 98. Altar frontal, detail
with pomegranate motif, Florence.
Late 15th century.
Voided velvet with brocade.
Museo Poldi Pezzoli, Milan.

below: 99. Ecclesiastical cape,
Spain. c. 1438.
Velvet with ferronnerie design
embroidered in couched gold thread
and embroidered orphreys,
height 4′8½″ (1.41 m).
Metropolitan Museum of Art,
New York
(Cloisters Collection,
Purchase, 1953).

France

No single tapestry center comparable to Arras or Tournai existed in France during the Renaissance. Some writers have suggested that most French tapestry weaving of the period was accomplished by itinerant artisans who moved from town to town, setting up their looms whenever they found a patron. Consequently, it is almost impossible to determine where a particular tapestry was woven.

The Hunt of the Unicorn (Fig. 97), a series of seven tapestries depicting a favorite Renaissance theme, is among the works whose exact origins are unknown. Five of the tapestries were almost certainly woven to celebrate the marriage of Anne of Brittany to Louis XII of France in 1499, and the other two may have been added to the series a decade and a half later in honor of the wedding of Anne's daughter. The *Unicorn* tapestries have much in common with contemporary production in Tournai, so they may actually have been woven in that city, or at least by a weaver familiar with the Flemish style.

Italy and Spain

Most of the sumptuous velvets used in clothing and ecclesiastical vestments were woven in Italy and Spain. Venice and Florence in particular specialized in the production of rich cut velvets, in which the height of the pile was varied to create a "carved" effect. Several Italian painters, including Pisanello and Jacopo Bellini, designed patterns for cut velvet. A favorite motif in Italy was the pomegranate (Fig. 98), while in Spain, still influenced by the Hispano-Moresque tradition, the pomegranate

often appeared side by side with the Turkish tulip and arabesque. All the refined techniques for fabric ornamentation were brought to bear in the design of clerical vestments. The more elaborate garments consisted of cut and voided velvet, heavily appliquéd in silk and metallic threads (Fig. 99).

Until the 16th century the great patrons of Italy commissioned their tapestries in the North, for the art of tapestry weaving was not well established. In 1546 Cosimo I de' Medici contracted with Nicolaus Carcher, a Flemish weaver, to organize a tapestry works in Florence. A number of Florentine painters—notably Pontormo and Agnolo Bronzino—contributed cartoons. Carcher had also set up a workshop in Ferrara, but its production was short-lived. On the whole, tapestry weaving was never a significant industry in either Italy or Spain, for the textile manufacture of both countries was dominated by the cut velvets and, especially in Italy, the fine silks.

The Baroque Period in Europe

In its original usage the word "baroque" meant something bizarre, grotesque, and distorted. However, as applied to the arts, especially music and the visual arts, *baroque* has come to designate the dynamic, opulent, curvilinear style prevalent in Europe between 1600 and 1750.

Flanders

Just as Raphael had left his mark on the tapestry style of 16th-century Brussels, another great master of painting—Peter Paul Rubens—exercised enormous influence on 17th-century production in that city. In the very early part of the century the most popular subjects had been small hunting scenes; Rubens set out to restore the monumental character of tapestry weaving. To this end he designed a number of tapestry series all with epic themes and powerful figures. *The History of Constantine* (Fig. 100), commissioned by Louis XIII, illustrates Rubens' preference for heroic figures in the foreground, with a minimum of background interest. The implied analogy between Louis and Constantine obviously served to glorify the king. Many sets of these tapestries exist, for it was common in the 17th century for several different workshops throughout Europe to copy the same design, with minor alterations. Rubens continued to prepare sketches for the tapestry ateliers of Brussels and France until his death in 1640.

France

During the 17th century France assumed the position long held by Italy in the production of fine silks. The silk manufactures at Lyons had been established in the mid-15th century, but for about two hundred years their output consisted mainly of copies from Italian imports. Then, under the sponsorship of Henry IV (1589–1610) and Louis XIV (1643–1715) the French weaving industry got the stimulus needed to dominate Europe.

As part of his program for revitalizing the French economy, Henry IV introduced silk cultivation to France (Fig. 101). The Edict of Nantes in

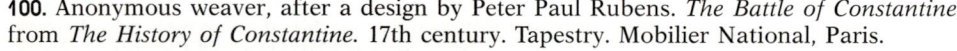

100. Anonymous weaver, after a design by Peter Paul Rubens. *The Battle of Constantine,* from *The History of Constantine.* 17th century. Tapestry. Mobilier National, Paris.

above: **101.** *Culture of Silkworms in France.* 1602. Engraving. Bibliothèque Nationale, Paris.

right: **102.** Wall panel with scenes of silk manufacture, from France. Second half of 18th century. Silk brocade *chinoiserie*, 4'11" × 2'6¼" (1.48 × .76 m). Musée Historique de Tissus, Lyons.

1598, which granted religious freedom to the Huguenots, enabled many Protestant weavers to return to France. However, most crucial to the success of the weaving industry was the founding in Paris, in 1667, of the Manufacture Royale des Meubles de la Couronne, a state-subsidized workshop planned by Louis XIV and expedited by his minister Colbert. Originally, the Manufacture Royale included cabinetmakers, goldsmiths, and engravers, and it incorporated the famous Gobelins tapestry works. Although a government superintendent controlled the workshop's operation, artistic activity was under the direction of the painter Charles Lebrun.

The silk ateliers were prolific in their output of clothing, wall hangings, and upholstery. Improved looms enabled the weavers to use an immense number of colors—as many as 1800, all derived from natural dyestuffs, were available by the 18th century—and to achieve unusual effects. After the establishment of the royal manufactury, only domestic silks were obtainable throughout France. The radiant example set by the French court greatly stimulated exportation, as did the representation of French silks in paintings by such masters as Watteau.

A special category of silk textiles were the *chinoiseries* (Fig. 102), westernized adaptations of the Chinese silks that circulated throughout Europe during the latter part of the 17th century. It is said that Madame de Pompadour personally directed the design of *chinoiseries* in Lyons.

Over a period of three years the most important tapestry centers of France were granted royal recognition. In 1664 the title Manufacture Royale de Tapisserie was conferred upon the workshops at Beauvais, and the same honor was bestowed upon the Aubusson factory the following year. In both towns production consisted mainly of *verdures*, small tapestries featuring trees and foliage. The Gobelins workshops of Paris, organized under the royal manufactury in 1667, held the monopoly on crown commissions, with the inevitable result that much of their output was designed to glorify the Sun King, Louis XIV. Typical examples were

103. Charles Lebrun design, executed at Gobelins.
Marriage of Louis XIV of France and the Infanta Marie-Thérèse of Spain, from *The Life of the King.*
1665–80. Tapestry of wool, silk, and gold thread; 16′3″ × 31′5″ (4.88 × 9.43 m). Palace at Versailles.

Royal Palaces and *The Life of the King* (Fig. 103), both completed under the direction of Lebrun in about 1680.

The textile and tapestry workshops were severely affected by the French Revolution of 1789. Silk production was brought to a virtual standstill, and only tapestries featuring patriotic themes were permitted. However, a different kind of revolution—that caused by the invention of mechanical weaving devices—would have much more spectacular implications for the entire weaving industry in the century to come.

The American Settlers

In the 17th century weaving was still a common household chore in rural parts of Europe. Consequently, the settlers who traveled to the American colonies brought with them a tradition of home weaving. They also brought their looms and their patterns, for contact with the mother country was uncertain at best, and the colonists had to be entirely self-sufficient. At first each family satisfied all its own textile needs, from clothing to blankets to bed and table linens. Later, traveling weavers or *journeymen*—the term "journey" meaning a day's work—supplied the scattered colonists with goods they could not produce themselves.

Raw materials were a constant problem to the colonists. The most abundant fiber was linen, for the early settlers had brought flax seeds with them, and their crops achieved success in most parts of the colonies. Cotton was scarce, because it could not be cultivated in the northern regions, and the cotton industry in the South did not become significant until the 1830s. Columbus had carried sheep to the New World on his second voyage in 1493, but this was of little use to the settlers in the thirteen colonies. The Revolution halted the flow of wool from England, but small quantities were purchased from Spain. However, not until the 19th century, with the importation of Merino sheep, did wool become plentiful.

As the settlements grew increasingly permanent and ships called more frequently at colonial ports, some fabrics from Europe began to filter in, but only the wealthiest families could afford them. By 1638 the first textile factory in America had been established in the Massachusetts Bay Colony by one Ezekiel Rogers. Later, William Penn himself introduced the textile industry to Pennsylvania, when he rented a house to be used for the manufacture of cloth. In time, most colonies had a small factory, and there were professional weavers in every community who produced wool blankets, linen and flannel sheets, fustian (called "thick-

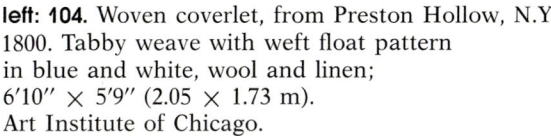

left: **104.** Woven coverlet, from Preston Hollow, N.Y. 1800. Tabby weave with weft float pattern in blue and white, wool and linen; 6'10'' × 5'9'' (2.05 × 1.73 m). Art Institute of Chicago.

below left: **105. Abram William van Doren.** Coverlet, from Oakland County, Mich. 1845. Wool and cotton in red and white double weave, 6'4'' × 7'4'' (1.9 × 2.2 m). Art Institute of Chicago (Dr. F. Gunsaulus Collection).

below: **106.** Double cloth coverlet, Indiana. Early 19th century. Linen, 8' × 8'8'' (2.4 × 2.6 m). Private collection.

sett," see p. 45), and striped linsey-woolsey for everyday clothing.

Notwithstanding the growing number of professional weavers, a large percentage of the textiles were still produced in the home. In 1810 more than ten thousand looms existed in the Ohio country alone. Virtually all yarn, even that provided to journeyman weavers, was homespun. In affluent families the slaves did the weaving, but the spinning and winding of yarn were still considered the task of the housewife.

Of the early textiles that have been preserved, the most common item is the coverlet (Figs. 104, 105). Woven on simple looms, usually with a natural linen warp and a colored wool weft, these beautiful fabrics display an amazing intricacy and a very high level of craftsmanship. The coverlet in Figure 106 is a form of double cloth (see Figs. 254–261), with two warp threads and two weft threads woven together at points where the design areas meet. The pattern is called "Nine Snowballs with Pine Tree Border."

107. *Love Conquered Fear,* engraving showing women and children laborers in a textile mill, from a London publication of April 20, 1839. British Museum, London.

The Industrial Revolution reached America very shortly after it had taken hold in England. With the coming of the machines, a factory system developed, and home weaving virtually ceased.

The Industrial Revolution

Insofar as the textile industry was concerned, the Industrial Revolution began in 1764, with the historic introduction of James Hargreaves' spinning jenny. This rather crude invention was replaced within fifteen years by Samuel Crompton's spinning mule, which, tended by one worker, could match the output of two hundred hand spinners. On a hand-operated loom a single weaver could produce about 8 yards of fabric a day, and eight hand spinners were kept busy supplying the yarn consumed. The spinning mule and the new power looms that came into use at the end of the century dramatically accelerated the rate of production. Incensed at the loss of their jobs, many hand-weavers and spinners rebelled. Machines were smashed, and at one point a factory containing four hundred power looms was burned. But the new system was so profitable that the workers could not possibly reverse the trend. With the rebels hanged or deported, the machines relentlessly clanked on.

An immediate result of this mechanical revolution was the emergence of a factory system. Workers were taken out of their homes or shops and herded together in huge plants. The weaver who had once taken pride in the work, had seen a project through from beginning to end, was now reduced to an automaton, occasionally pushing a lever or tying a broken thread. It was soon discovered that women and children would work more cheaply than men, and these unfortunate creatures were forced to spend mercilessly long hours—often as many as eighteen hours a day—under ghastly conditions (Fig. 107).

Despite the vast quantity of textiles produced, a price was paid in the marked deterioration of quality. The machines could operate best when conditions were standardized, so that thousands of yards of identical material were manufactured. The resultant fabric might be technically perfect, but the human touch of the weaver disappeared forever. Furthermore, the increasing complexity of the looms tempted entrepreneurs, like children with new toys, to experiment with more and more highly decorated fabrics.

The Industrial Revolution proceeded most rapidly in England, where the product of the weaving mills stimulated trade and fed an expanding economy. By 1864, just a century after the invention of the spinning jenny, handweaving in England was almost a forgotten craft.

By the end of the 19th century public interest in the handcrafts had all but vanished from the industrialized nations of the world. The machine was king: its products were bigger, better, more uniform; they could be manufactured faster and much more cheaply than old-fashioned handmade goods. Artists, writers, and musicians competed to outdo one another in praising the age of technology. Half a century later the crafts were once again flourishing. Weaving, ceramics, jewelry making, needlecraft—in fact, all the hand processes, including a few that had been out of vogue for hundreds of years—were more popular than ever before.

Many writers have attempted to explain this fantastic resurrection. The most common theory suggests an aesthetic reaction to an overstandardized environment, a world in which one's house, furniture, car, clothing, and personal effects look much like everyone else's. Combined with this is a growing dismay at shoddy workmanship. A machine cannot take pride in its job; it cannot be held accountable if its product falls apart the first

20th-Century Handweaving

time it is used. In increasing numbers people are seeking the handcrafted object—the slight irregularities, the meticulous care of execution, the burst of inspiration that give evidence of humanity.

William Morris

The roots of this 20th-century craft revival must be sought in the latter part of the 19th, when a few individuals began to speak out against the machine. William Morris (1834–96) was trained as a

108. **William Morris** design,
executed at Merton Abbey by Morris & Company.
The Woodpecker. 1885.
Wool tapestry, 9′7″ × 5′ (2.88 × 1.51 m).
William Morris Gallery, London.

painter and architect. In 1857 he set out to furnish his first studio in London. To Morris' shock he found that, even by assembling the best of the industrial products then available, he could not possibly construct an environment suitable for painting magnificent pictures. Morris theorized that artists, surrounded by poorly built and grossly overdecorated objects, would ultimately see their own ideals corrupted. Consequently, in 1861 Morris took the initiative in organizing the firm of Morris, Marshall & Faulkner, Fine Art Workmen in Painting, Carving, Furniture, and the Metals. The company designed and manufactured chairs "such as Barbarossa might have sat in," strong, functional tables, carpeting, stained glass, and metal objects—all in the highest possible standards of taste and craftsmanship. Morris also designed fabrics, wallpaper, and tapestries, a splendid example of which is the *Woodpecker* (Fig. 108), woven at Merton Abbey in 1885.

For the rest of his life Morris wrote and lectured extensively in an attempt to popularize his ideas. Moreover, Morris, who was a Socialist, did not merely seek an elitist concept of excellence. He believed that well-designed and well-crafted objects should be within the reach of even the poorest individual, that the public could be educated to good taste as well as bad.

A direct outgrowth of Morris' preaching was the Arts and Crafts Movement in England. As part of their campaign to restore the handcrafts, followers of the movement sought out native artisans in areas of continental Europe where the Industrial Revolution had not completely taken over. The peasant class of Sweden, Norway, and Denmark were still producing handwoven articles for their daily needs on their own looms, and these skilled weavers taught their methods to the students from England. To this day the Scandinavian countries have an enormous influence on the design of handcrafted—and to some extent mass-produced—items throughout the world.

The Bauhaus

Not all the proponents of excellence in design and construction wished to abolish the machine. Many people believed, instead, that the machine could be harnessed, that sound workmanship and good taste were not incompatible with mass production. The most ambitious statement of this ideal was developed in the Bauhaus.

The Bauhaus was founded as a school of design in 1919 in Weimar, Germany. Its stated aim was to "create a new guild of craftsmen, without the class distinctions which raise an arrogant bar-

109. Anni Albers. Bauhaus tapestry. 1926.
Silk, 6 × 4′ (1.8 × 1.2 m).
Busch-Reisinger Museum,
Harvard University, Cambridge, Mass.
(purchase, Germanic Museum Association).

rier between craftsman and artist." To this end, studies were organized on a workshop basis, and the medieval guild roles of "master," "journeyman," and "apprentice" substituted for those of teacher and student. The original director of the Bauhaus was the architect Walter Gropius, whose belief that "form follows function" became gospel for his adherents.

The weaving workshop was the first to be fairly well organized. Its co-masters were Hélène Börner and George Muche, but many resident painters supplied ideas and designs for the weavers.

Increasing pressure from the government, which accused the school of subversion and even Bolshevism, forced the Bauhaus, in 1924, to move to Dessau. There, under the direction of Gunta Stölzl (Pl. 5, p. 38), the weaving workshop achieved its first commercial success. Systematic training in weaving and dyeing techniques was undertaken, and the course of study was aimed ultimately at design for industry. Many of the weavers, including Otti Berger and Anni Albers (Fig. 109), did, in fact, have their textile designs mass-produced by German manufacturers.

On April 11, 1933, the Gestapo occupied the Bauhaus. Attempts to reconcile the ideals of the school with those of the new regime were doomed to failure, and in July of 1933 the Bauhaus was closed. To the incalculable good fortune of the American crafts movement, the great majority of the faculty and students ultimately emigrated to the United States.

Art Deco

A style that paralleled the Bauhaus in time and—to some extent—in ideals was Art Deco, which grew out of the Exposition Internationale des Arts Decoratifs held in Paris in 1925. Like the Bauhaus style, Art Deco emphasized machine production. However, in contrast to the plain, unadorned, often austere Bauhaus designs, Art Deco gloried in a profusion of decorative elements. The favored materials were bright and shiny, symbolic of the machine age. Pattern was laid upon contrasting pattern, and the most common motifs were geometric shapes, including triangles, zig-zags, thunderbolts, and semicircles. A woven fabric from this

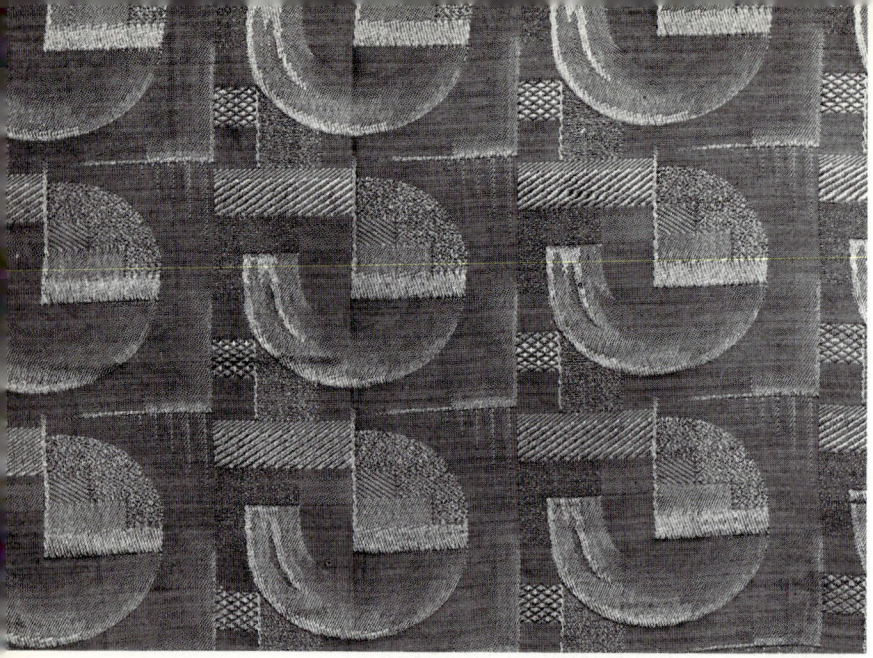

period (Fig. 110) shows a typical pattern of dynamic forms set against one another.

As a movement, Art Deco did not last very long, disappearing in the late 1930s. However, interest in the style was revived during the 1970s, and many objects from that period are treasured for themselves and for their inspiration.

The Revival of Handweaving in the United States

The Arts and Crafts Movement in England had its equivalent in the United States with the Craftsman Style, which flourished around the turn of the 20th century. Like its British counterpart, the Craftsman Style emphasized sound workmanship, honest use of materials, and simple, forthright design. A rug from this period (Fig. 111) illustrates all these principles and seems to have been influenced by American Indian designs, which were beginning to attract popularity.

American interest in handweaving began to reassert itself seriously in the later part of the 1920s. One of the pioneers in this movement was Mary Atwater (1878–1956), who as a bride arrived in a remote Montana mining town shortly after the turn of the century. Recreational opportunities for women were limited in that isolated community, so as a diversion Atwater taught herself to weave. She had been shown an heirloom coverlet belonging to one of the townspeople, and this inspired

111. Gustav Stickley (?), Eastwood, N.Y.
Rug. Early 20th century.
Plain weave in cotton, wool,
and soft wood paper fibers;
6'10¾" × 3'10⅞" (2.07 × 1.18 m).
Art Institute of Chicago
(gift of Mr. and Mrs. John J. Evans, Jr., 1971).

above left: Plate 6. Joan Michaels Paque. *Reversals,* from the series *Double Entendre.* 1973.
Macramé in nylon fiber, 18½ × 10″ (46 × 25 cm). Collection Mr. and Mrs. Russel Martin, Asheville, N.C.

above right: Plate 7. Judith Rosenberg. *Beach Scene,* detail. 1976.
Mixed fibers, 6′ (1.8 m) square overall. Collection Susan Rayfield, New York. (See also Fig. 556.)

below: Plate 8. Thelma Becherer. *Jingle Shells.* 1970. Plain weave in Velon monofilament,
hand-spun silk, wool, mohair, and jingle shells; 34 × 24″ (85 × 60 cm).
Collection Thomas B. Williams, Brookhaven, N.Y.

above: **Plate 9. Jean Stamsta.**
Progression of Ten. 1974.
Tubular weave in wool and synthetics,
3′6″ × 12′6″ (1.05 × 3.75 m).
Courtesy Hadler Galleries, New York.

left: **Plate 10. Karen White Boyd.**
Homage to Betsy Ross. 1972.
Triple weave and tapestry
in cow hair and polyester,
12′ × 4′6″ × 5″ (3.6 × 1.35 × .15 m).
Courtesy the artist.

her to try her own designs (Fig. 112). Soon she began to share her newly acquired knowledge with other women in the town. Her interest in pre-Columbian textiles was awakened when she accompanied her husband on a series of business trips to Central and South America. There she had an opportunity to examine the ancient fabrics and record their patterns.

During World War I Atwater served as an occupational therapist for injured servicemen. This experience encouraged her to write a book about the possibilities of weaving in rehabilitation. Later, she organized the first weavers' guild in the United States. As a service to her members she developed *Shuttlecraft Bulletin*, at the time the only magazine written expressly for handweavers. Her research in Early American fabrics made it possible for modern weavers to understand and copy the traditional patterns for their own adaptation.

Until the 1940s pattern weaving, based on old coverlets and other Colonial designs, was the prevalent style in the United States. Women collected weaving patterns like cooking recipes, and sometimes guarded them just as jealously. How-

ever, during and after World War II the trend shifted to an interest in texture created with the simplest weaves. To some extent the new fashion was stimulated by the Bauhaus expatriates.

Anni Albers, with her husband Josef, the noted painter and colorist, came to the United States in the thirties. Like many of her compatriots, she taught for a time at Black Mountain College in North Carolina. Later, her influence was exercised through extensive lecturing and through her books on design and weaving.

Although Albers' early training emphasized design for industry, she was very much a master of the hand loom. For her, the two were never incompatible. Essentially an analytical weaver, Albers concentrated on the elements—linear, coloristic, textural—that are combined in creating a textile (Pl. 11, p. 171).

Another German-trained weaver, Lili Blumenau, had a comparable influence on the spread of handweaving in the United States. Until the early 1950s the main product of the handloom was yardage. Blumenau's interest was the titled wall hanging—the woven object as a work of art ex-

112. Mary Meigs Atwater.
Crackle Weave, detail.
Six-strand floss on three-ply cotton warp,
10 × 12″ (25 × 30 cm).
Southern California Handweavers' Guild,
Los Angeles (Mary Meigs Atwater Memorial Collection).

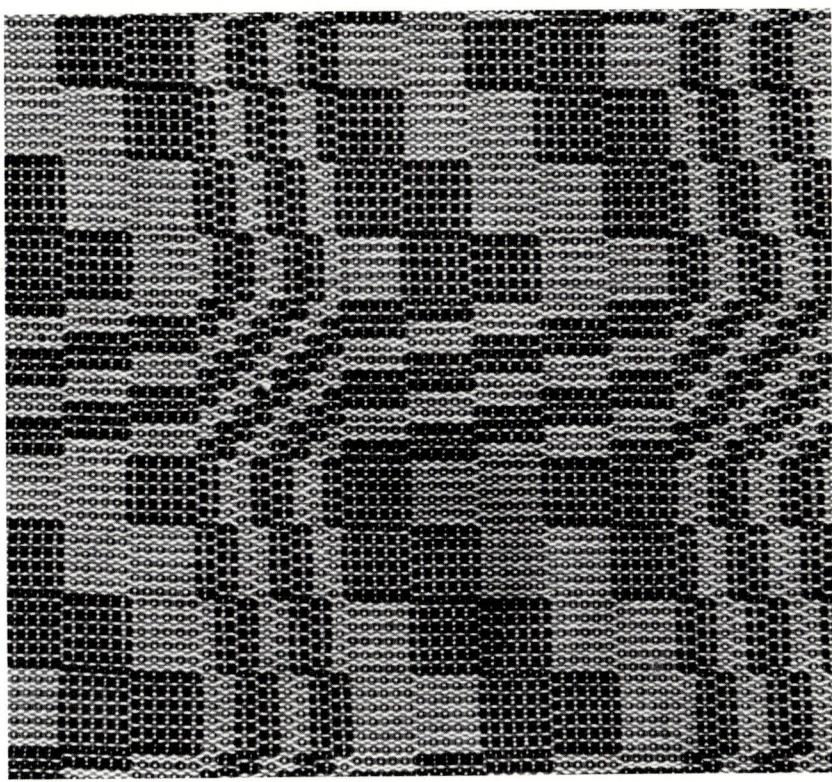

113. Lili Blumenau. *Transparent and Opaque.* 1958. Braided ribbon and fine rayon, 7′ × 2′9″ (2.1 × .83 m). From *Objects: USA*, Johnson Wax Collection of Contemporary Crafts, Racine, Wis.

pressing her thoughts and ideas (Fig. 113). She was active in nearly every phase of the crafts movement, as teacher, author, museum curator, lecturer, and industrial designer.

Much of the current interest in vivid colors and unusual materials can be traced to the work of Dorothy Liebes, a California-born weaver-designer who was often referred to as "America's first lady of the loom." Trained as a painter, Liebes turned to weaving when she realized that the standard of excellence she sought could best be attained in fiber. Her early inspiration was drawn from the vibrant Oriental colors and patterns she found in San Francisco's Chinatown (Fig. 114), and bright lacquer red became a mainstay of her repertoire. Incredible as it seems, she was among the first of her generation to combine blue and green in a textile—a daring color scheme that seemed to many a violation of color theory.

In her search for exciting textures, Liebes experimented with leather strips, ticker tape, tape measures, and especially metallic yarns, including pure gold. Her best-known textiles exhibit a striking glitter effect derived also from the early Chinese influence. Perhaps her most important contribution was in raising the quality of design in mass-produced, moderately priced fabrics.

Craft Organizations

As more and more individuals were attracted to the crafts, the number of organizations and publications specifically dedicated to their needs began to grow. The American Crafts Council (originally named the American Craftsmen's Council) was founded in 1943, chiefly through the efforts of Aileen O. Webb. The council's stated aim from the outset was to "stimulate interest in the work of handcraftsmen." To this end the ACC has been instrumental in reteaching the techniques of age-old crafts, as well as newer ones, and in helping crafts people to market their goods. Membership is open to any interested person.

The council also operates the Museum of Contemporary Crafts in New York, which develops a year-round program of craft and craft-related exhibitions. In recent years the members in nearly every state have formed their own branch organizations. These groups conduct exhibitions, fairs, seminars, competitions, and many other activities on a local level. The World Crafts Council, launched in 1964 and now affiliated with the UNESCO branch of the United Nations, helps to unite crafts people from all parts of the world.

The American Crafts Council publishes *Craft Horizons*, a bi-monthly magazine that reports cur-

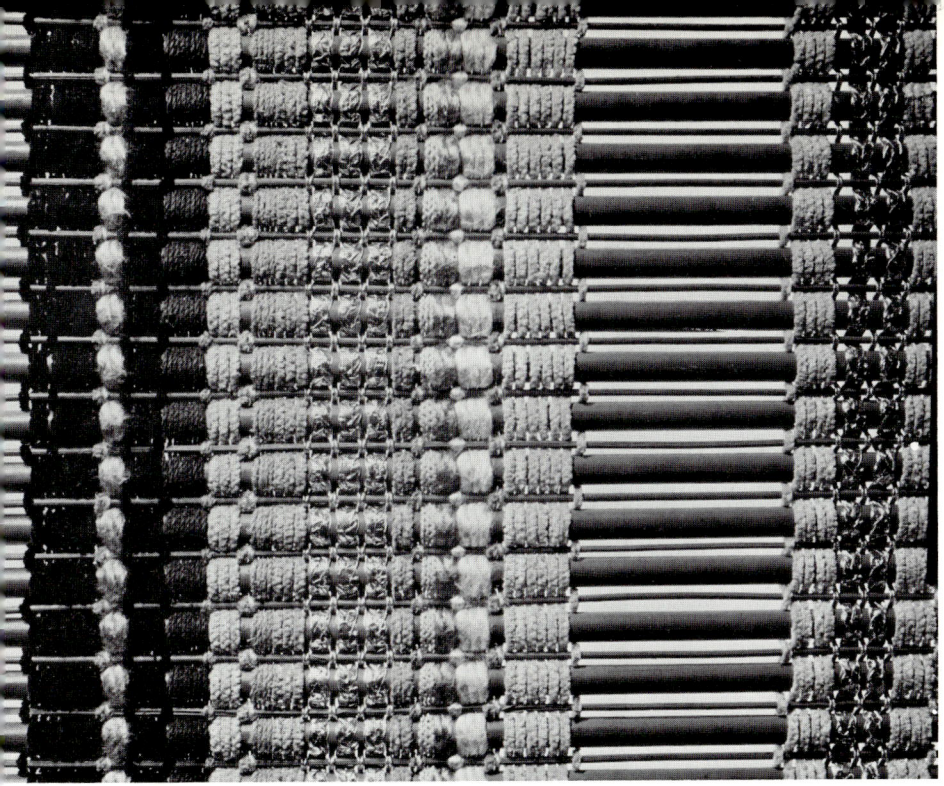

114. Dorothy Liebes.
Handwoven blinds, detail. 1952.
Rayon, cotton, and braided
metallic yarns, with Oriental reeds
and painted wood dowels.
Courtesy Museum of
Contemporary Crafts, New York.

rent happenings in all craft areas, both nationally and internationally.

The Handweavers' Guild of America was organized in the summer of 1969 and became the first national organization concerned totally with the fiber crafts. In December of that same year the Guild's publication, *Shuttle, Spindle and Dye-Pot*, was initiated. It has since become the outstanding magazine serving all those interested in weaving and related areas, as well as providing an effective organ for the association. The HGA holds its national meeting, "Convergence," biennially in different parts of the United States.

The Craft Revival in the Southern Highlands

It is easy to forget that not all parts of the world have been touched equally by the Industrial Revolution. There are sections of the United States, the most heavily industrialized nation on earth, where the machine age has gone virtually unnoticed. The mountain regions of the Virginias, the Carolinas, Maryland, Kentucky, Tennessee, Georgia, and Alabama—known collectively as the Southern Highlands—are such a special area. There, daily life has changed little over the last three hundred years. Long isolated in their remote mountain homes, inaccessible to any railroad, jet plane, or superhighway, the Appalachian peoples have learned to be almost totally self-sufficient. The folk handcrafts passed down from generation to generation satisfy their daily needs for woven fabrics, baskets, pottery utensils, and wooden ob-

jects (Fig. 115). They also provide a form of recreation. According to the Works Progress Administration *Guide to North Carolina* (1939), "Colonial handicrafts have survived in North Carolina despite the flood of machine-made products from

115. Coverlet, from the Southern Appalachian Mountains. c. 1920. Wool. Southern Highland Handicraft Guild, Asheville, N.C. (Frances Goodrich Collection).

the factories. The influence of tradition, poverty, isolation, and some steady local markets have served to keep alive these native skills."

The Southern Highland Handicraft Guild was first organized in 1930 to aid local artisans in establishing a broader market for their goods. In recent years interested outsiders have encouraged the mountain women to turn their household crafts into cottage industries. Woven fabrics, patchwork, and other fiber products have begun to appear in fashionable shops in the large cities, where their meticulous craftsmanship and exquisite designs fetch handsome prices from a sophisticated clientele.

Since the 1940s the output of the handloom has changed considerably. New materials—nylon, rayon, plastics, metallics—have broadened the resources of the weaver immeasurably. The production of yardage, accomplished much more efficiently by power looms, has declined, and there is a new emphasis on wall hangings, garments, rugs, and sculptural constructions. The tapestry technique was revived in the late fifties, at first as a medium for copying paintings. Artists commissioned to prepare the designs executed their cartoons in terms of paint on canvas. Later, tapestry weaving earned respect as a serious art form in its own right.

The example of the Southern Highlands is symptomatic of a trend evident in all the crafts. Folk handcrafts from all parts of the world are being explored by contemporary artists who seek a fresh outlook in their own work. This fact explains the current interest in macramé, sprang, twining, patchwork (in essence a form of collage), and many other techniques. To a very real extent, the future of the handcrafts lies in the past.

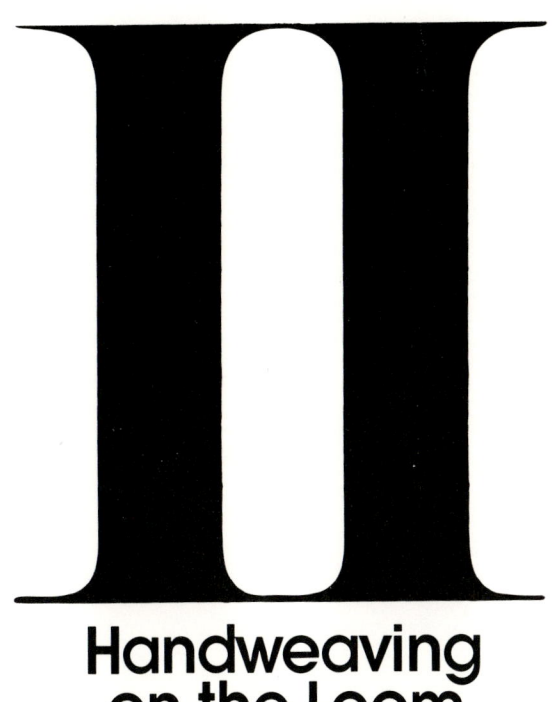

II

Handweaving on the Loom

Yarn is to the weaver what clay is to the potter, metal to the jeweler, and wood to the cabinet-maker: the raw material needed to make the finished product. In the case of weaving, the character of a textile depends to a large extent on the properties of the yarns chosen for a specific project (Fig. 116).

All yarns are composed of *fibers*, either the natural fibers derived from living and growing things or the manufactured fibers extruded from the spinnerette. Until the 20th century most weaving was confined to the four major natural fibers—cotton, linen, wool, and silk (Figs. 117–120). However, since the 1930s fiber manufacturers have introduced a vast number of synthetic materials, many of which are suitable for handweaving. Furthermore, in their search for new modes of expression, contemporary weavers have begun to show an interest in less common fibers (such as jute, sisal, and hemp), materials used by primitive peoples (such as feathers, grasses, and rushes),

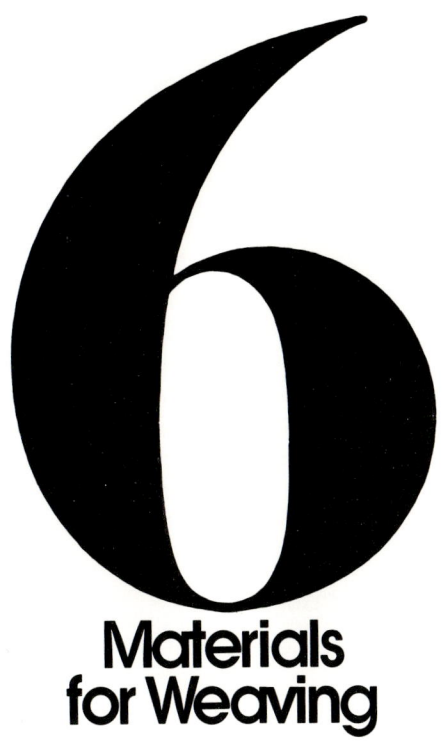

6

**Materials
for Weaving**

116. Maria Chojnacka.
Mobile Spatial Composition—Chains, detail. 1973.
Sisal, overall height 16′6″ (5 m).
Courtesy the artist.

117–120. *Photomicrographs of the four principal fibers, in longitudinal view.*

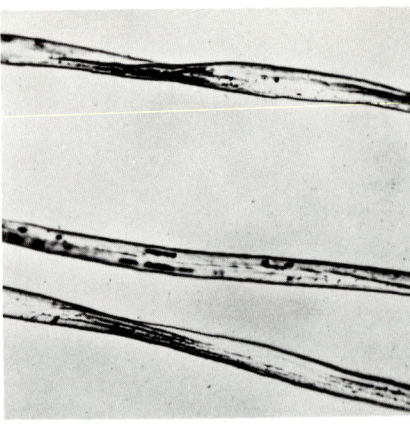

117. Cotton.

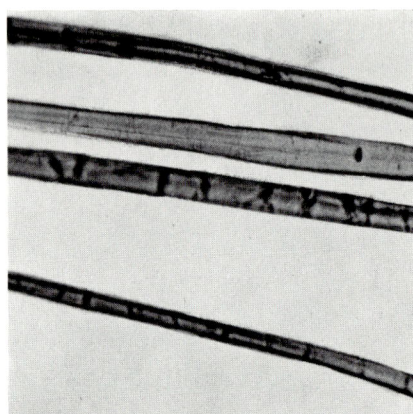

118. Linen.

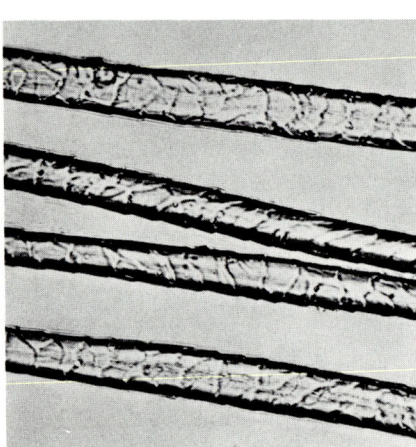

119. Wool.

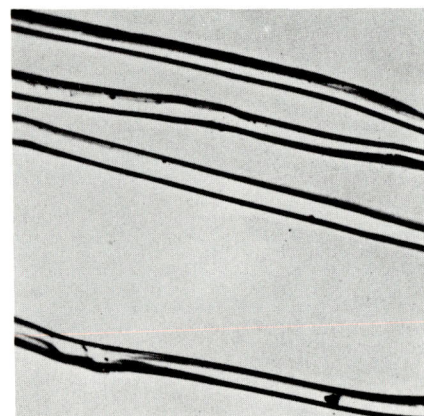

120. Silk.

and totally nonfibrous materials (such as wire and plastic, Fig. 121). The suitability of a material for weaving is limited only by its appropriateness to the project for which it is intended. The weaver should have at hand a wide range of yarns and other materials—providing a variety of color, size, texture, and fiber—from which to select.

Fiber Classification

Considering the numberless fibers on today's market, it is essential, in order to avoid confusion, that some means of classification be established. Many

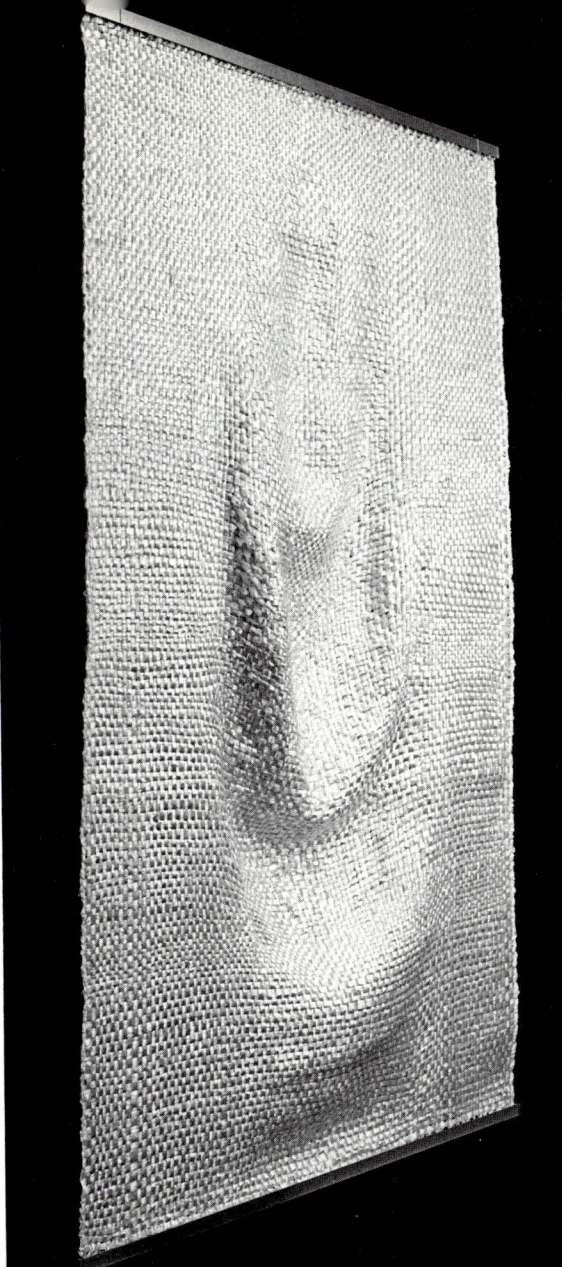

121. Loes van der Horst.
Who Has Been Sleeping in My Bed? 1974.
White polyethylene, 6'1½" × 4'6" (1.75 × 1.3 m).
Stedelijk Museum, Amsterdam.

Natural Fibers

Vegetable (cellulosic) fibers
seed hairs
  cotton
  kapok
  milkweed
  cattail
bast (stem) fibers
  flax
  hemp
  jute
  ramie
  bamboo
leaf fibers
  sisal
  yucca
  abaca (Manila hemp)
  raffia (palm leaf)
  piña (pineapple)
  reed
  grass
fruit fibers
  coir (coconut)
bark and root
  broom
  cedar

Animal (protein) fibers
hair fibers
  wool
  cashmere (Tibetan goat)
  mohair (Angora goat)
  llama
  alpaca
  vicuña
  camel hair
  cow hair
  horsehair
  dog hair
  rabbit hair
  bristle hair
  buffalo hair
  beard hair
  reindeer hair
  qiviut (musk ox)
internal animal parts
  sinews
  intestines
animal secretions
  silk

different systems have been proposed, but the most common is based on the source of each individual fiber. The simplest breakdown separates the natural from the synthetic fibers; under each of these broad categories one can isolate several important subdivisions. In the outline that follows, the synthetic fibers are identified by their *generic* or family names, plus a few of the more common *trade* names used by individual manufacturers (the trade names distinguished by an initial capital letter).

Until recent years it was common to differentiate between *synthetic* fibers—those created in the laboratory but composed partly of vegetable materials—and *manufactured* fibers, which contain no natural ingredients. In this text the terms are used synonymously to embrace all nonnatural fibers, regardless of their composition.

Materials for Weaving **81**

Mineral fibers
asbestos
metal
 aluminum
 gold
 silver

Manufactured Fibers

Cellulosic fibers
 rayon
 high-wet-modulus rayon

Modified cellulosic fibers
acetate
 secondary acetate (Celanese, Chromspun, etc.)
 triacetate (Arnel)

Protein fibers
azlon

Synthesized fibers
condensation polymer fibers
 nylon
 polyester (Dacron, etc.)
additional polymer fibers
 anidex
 acrylic (Acrilan, Orlon, etc.)
 modacrylic (Dynel, Verel, etc.)
 nytril

olefin
saran
vinal
vinyon
elastomers
 spandex
 rubber

Mineral fibers
 glass

Fiber Characteristics

It is often necessary for a weaver to know in advance how a particular fiber will behave both on and off the loom—how much it will stretch or sag, whether it is flammable, how readily it will accept dyes, and so forth. If a heavy wall hanging is woven from relatively elastic fibers, the entire composition may stretch out of shape merely from its own weight. Such foreknowledge is especially important for industrial designers and for those handweavers involved in executing large-scale commissions. For example, a theater curtain made of flammable materials would probably be rejected on the basis of local fire laws. The table below lists several of the more common fibers used for handweaving and the qualities associated with each *in its natural state.* Various finishes can be applied to the fibers or the yarns made from them, markedly altering their properties.

Fiber Characteristics

Fiber	Strength	Elasticity	Receptiveness to dyes	Flammability
cotton	medium	low	good	high
linen	high	low	good	high
hemp	high	low	difficult to bleach, but will accept bright or dark dyes	high
jute	medium; rots when exposed to moisture	low	difficult to bleach, but will accept bright or dark dyes	high
wool	low	medium to high	excellent	medium
silk	medium to high	medium	good	medium
rayon	varies with type	medium	good	high
nylon	high	high	poor	medium

Weaving Yarns

The properties of a yarn are affected by several factors, including the origin, size, and texture of the fiber, the type of yarn construction, the time and method of coloring, and the presence or absence of a finish. A cotton yarn, for example, may be composed of short or long fibers; it can be given high or low twist, or constructed to achieve certain novelty effects; it can be dyed by the manufacturer or by the user, in the latter case before or after weaving; it can be mercerized (treated with caustic soda) or left in its natural state. All these variables will influence the behavior of a yarn on the loom and its appearance in the finished project.

Yarn Construction

Yarns can be composed of either filament or staple fibers. *Filament* fibers are those that are measured in yards or even miles, primarily the synthetic fibers, which can be extruded in an infinite unbroken length from the machines. Among the natural fibers, only silk is classified as a filament fiber, since the unraveled cocoon sometimes measures up to 3000 yards. Yarns made from filament fibers are either *monofilament*—consisting of a single continuous strand; or *multifilament*—composed of two or more filaments twisted together. Some fibers, such as nylon, lend themselves to monofilament weaving (Pl. 6, p. 71).

Staple fibers are measured in inches or fractions of inches and must be spun to produce a thread. All natural fibers except silk are staple length, and occasionally short ends of silk from broken cocoons are spun to create a staple yarn. In addition, most synthetic fibers can be cut apart and spun in the usual manner. *Long-staple* yarns are considered top quality. They are sturdier, more lustrous, and capable of being spun tighter, thus making them fine and smooth.

Cotton is divided into three staple lengths: long staple (roughly, greater than an inch), short staple, and waste or *linters* (fibers picked directly from the seeds). Linters are used primarily in the manufacture of rayon. Hair staple fibers vary from 1 to 15 inches in length. Coarse wools and Angora goat hair are the longest, while fine wools, such as Merino, are usually about 5 to 6 inches long. The most luxurious hairs, including cashmere and vicuña, are shorter. Woolen yarns are spun from short, uncombed fibers; worsted yarns are composed of longer wool fibers that have been *combed*, or straightened (pp. 264–265). Flax fibers for linen are classified as either *line* (greater than

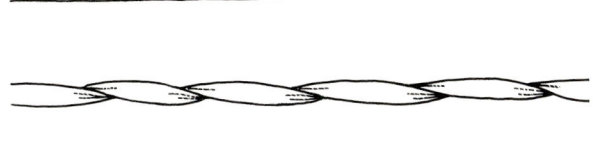

above: **122.** Yarns are subjected to varying degrees of twist, depending on the nature of the fiber involved and the use to which the yarn will be put. *Top to bottom:* roving or untwisted yarn, low-twist yarn, crepe or high-twist yarn.

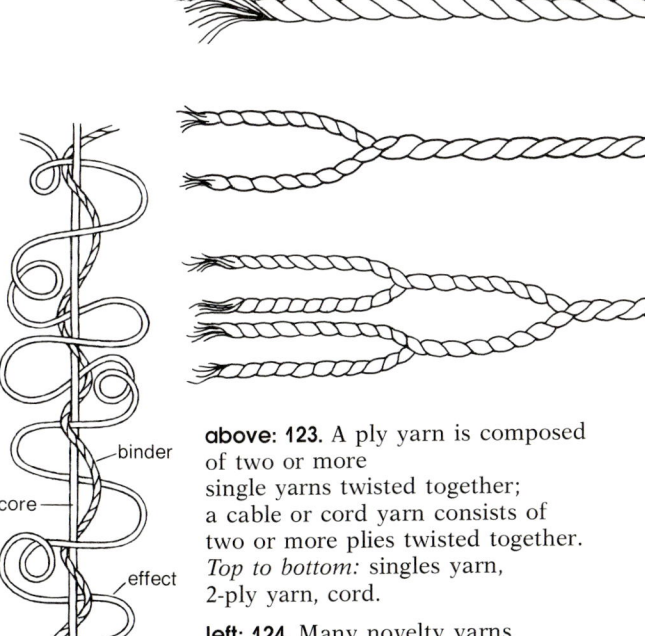

above: **123.** A ply yarn is composed of two or more single yarns twisted together; a cable or cord yarn consists of two or more plies twisted together. *Top to bottom:* singles yarn, 2-ply yarn, cord.

left: **124.** Many novelty yarns are composed of three parts: a core yarn, an effect yarn, and a binder that holds the effect yarn in place.

12 inches) or *tow* (less than 12 inches). Sometimes an intermediate grade—*demi-line*—is recognized.

Most yarns, both filament and staple, are given a certain amount of twist in order to hold the fibers together. The degree of twist required depends upon the particular fiber (Fig. 122); it varies from no twist at all (*roving*) to high twist (*crepe*). When two or more yarns are twisted together, the result is known as a *ply* (Fig. 123). A 2-ply yarn, for example, is composed of two single yarns plied together. A *cable* or *cord* yarn is even more complicated: it results from two or more *plies* twisted together. Many *novelty yarns* are ply yarns consisting of a *core*, a *decorative* or *effect yarn*, and a *binder* (Fig. 124). They are characterized by spaced

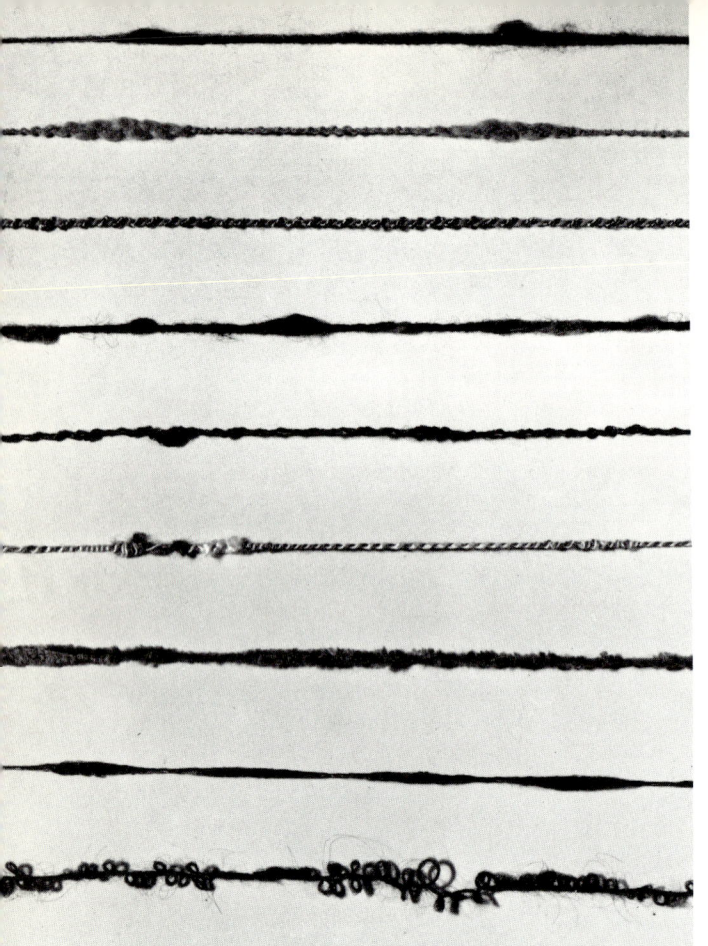

125. Novelty yarns are characterized by spaced irregularities of size, twist, or effect. *Top to bottom:* slub, ratiné, bouclé, nub, seed, corkscrew, chenille, flake, loop.

irregularities of size, twist, or effect (Fig. 125). Among the more common novelty yarns are:

Slub yarns, which are left untwisted at different intervals to produce bulky areas (Pl. 7, p. 71);

Ratiné and *guimpe yarns,* in which a bulky yarn is looped around a core yarn, with the two held in place by a binder;

Bouclé yarns, similar to ratiné and guimpe, but with wider spacing between the loops;

Nub or *knob yarns,* in which the decorative yarn is wrapped repeatedly around the core yarn at a given point to form an enlarged segment;

Seed yarns, which have smaller nubs;

Corkscrew yarns, created by twisting together yarns of different diameters, sizes, or fiber content, or by varying the speed or direction in which the yarns are twisted;

Chenille yarns, narrow strips cut from a special fabric;

Flake yarns, to which small tufts of fiber have been added at irregular intervals;

Loop yarns, in which a curling effect yarn is held in place around a core by a binder yarn.

In addition to these standard designations, yarns are often subjectively described as smooth (carpet warp), nubby (bouclé), velvety (chenille), shiny (monofilament rayon), or dull (spun silk).

Metallics, such as gold and silver, are produced in sheets, then cut into fine, flat strips.

Dyes and Finishes

The fiber composition of a yarn has a marked effect on the degree to which it will accept a dye. As indicated in the table, most natural fibers are dye receptive; however, animal and vegetable fibers will often absorb dyes at different rates. Therefore, if fibers of varying composition, such as silk (protein) and linen (cellulose) are spun or twisted together, the resulting yarn will not dye evenly. Some manufactured fibers cannot be dyed at all, and so color must be introduced into the chemical solution before the fibers are extruded. A complete discussion of yarn dyeing appears in Chapter 17.

In recent decades scientists have developed a great many chemical finishes to enhance fiber properties. While most of these are intended for use on completed fabrics, a few can be applied to yarns. *Mercerization,* a manufacturer's process, improves the luster, dyeability, and strength of cotton. (*Perle* cotton is a ply yarn twisted from two single mercerized yarns.) Wool yarns can be treated with mothproofing compounds or with finishes designed to retard shrinkage. Other finishes introduce luster, stretch, or resistance to fire. Directions for *sizing* yarns appear in Chapter 8 (p. 109). Before purchasing a yarn, the weaver should be aware of the finishes employed.

Yarn Properties

Despite the wide variety of "miracle" fibers available, most handweavers still rely heavily on the basic four: wool, linen, cotton, and silk (Fig. 126). However, few can resist the temptation to experiment with other materials.

Wool Wool yarns may bear special labels that indicate the previous life of the fiber. *Virgin wool* is new wool that has never before been made into yarn. Included in this category is *lamb's wool,* which has been clipped from sheep less than eight months old. *Reprocessed wool* has been reclaimed from fabric scraps that were never used, perhaps from remnants of material cut for sewing. The fabric is shredded and respun into yarn. *Reused wool* or *shoddy* is wool reclaimed from used fabric, such as rags or second-hand clothing. Both reused wool and reprocessed wool are lower in quality—notably in strength—than virgin wool. In most cases they are not worth the time and energy expended in a handwoven project.

Wool is rarely used for a warp, because its stretchiness prevents it from maintaining proper tension on the loom. It is probably the most common weft material, however, because of its strength, durability, and high acceptance of dyes. For a weft-face fabric, in which the warp is to be partially or completely covered, wool has the packing ability to give this result.

Linen Linen yarns are preferred for a warp. They are highly stable and maintain warp tension well. But linen can be very difficult for a beginner to work with. You may find it less frustrating to learn the mechanics of weaving with cotton yarns, and to experiment with linen only after you achieve a degree of confidence.

Cotton Cotton yarns are perhaps the most versatile of the natural fibers. They serve for both the warp and the weft, accept dyes readily, are stable and durable. The range is almost infinite.

Jute and Sisal In recent years many weavers have been attracted to jute, sisal, and other bast fibers because of their "natural" qualities. These yarns are attractive and often seem particularly appropriate for a handwoven project. However, you should be aware that bast fibers, and especially jute, are *highly* susceptible to deterioration. If exposed to moisture, jute will rot very quickly, and even under dry conditions it will gradually disintegrate. No major project that is to be permanent should ever be woven in jute, unless the fiber is finished in some way to protect it, such as spraying with silicone. Even with finishing, jute should not be used outdoors or for such items as planters, which will be subjected to water.

Silk Like wool, silk yarns fall into different categories. *Tussah* silk, also called *wild silk*, is obtained from the cocoons of uncultivated silkworms found in India and Assam. The fiber has a pale brown tint. *Raw silk* has not been degummed, so it still contains the sericin secreted by the insect. Raw silk yarns produce a fabric that is rather stiff and has a tendency to waterspot. A *thrown silk* yarn is a ply yarn into which twist has been inserted. It is not as lustrous as the original silk filament.

Asbestos For centuries people have been intrigued with the idea of incorporating fireproof asbestos into textiles. According to one legend, Charlemagne took great delight in astonishing his guests by throwing a tablecloth woven from asbestos into the fire and then removing it unharmed. The functional fireplace illustrated in

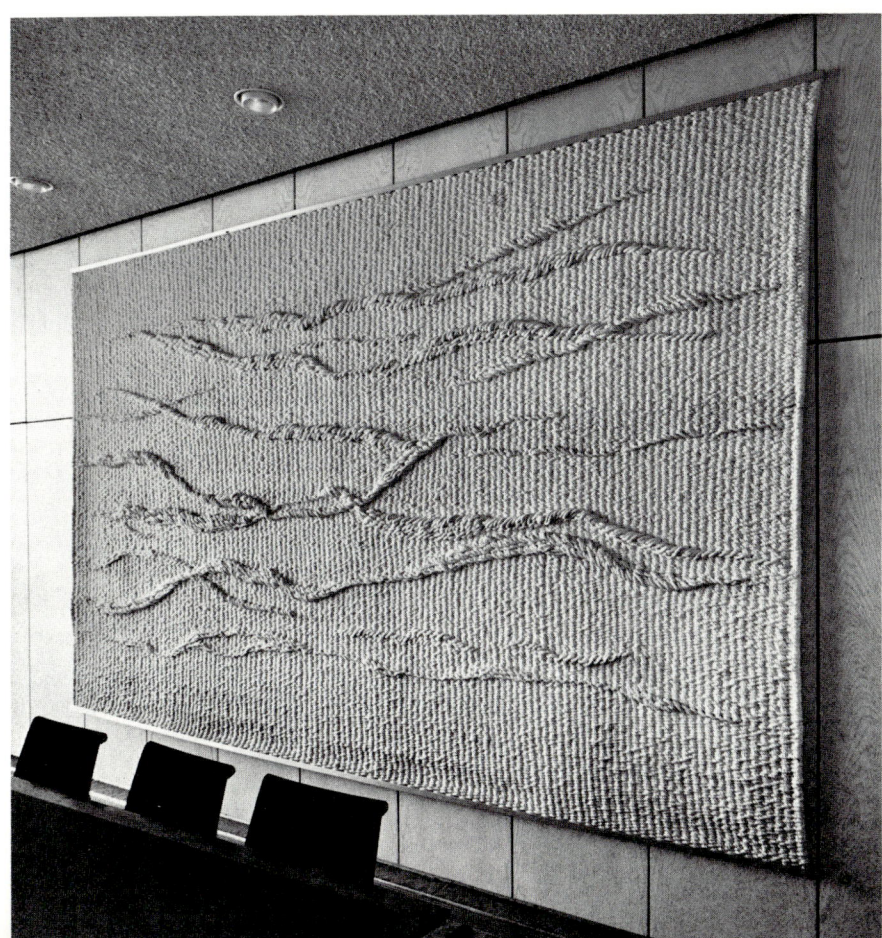

126. Wil Fruytier.
Airwaves. 1973. White cotton,
8′8″ × 26′3″ (2.75 × 7.5 m).
Collection KLM Royal Dutch
Airlines, Amstelveen.

127. Bonnie MacGilchrist. *Soft Fireplace.* 1970.
Handwoven bands of asbestos fiber, 12 × 3′ (3.6 × .9 m).
Courtesy California Design XI, Pasadena, Calif.

reassess their potential. As a result, the usefulness of natural fibers has been greatly extended, chiefly through the development of new finishes.

Yarn Sizes

At present there is no widely accepted uniform system for measuring yarn size or *count;* different standards are applied to the various fibers.

Filament yarns—that is, silk and the manufactured fibers—are measured in *deniers* (Fig. 128), a denier being equivalent to the weight in grams of 9000 meters of yarn. A 30-denier yarn is three times as large as a 10 denier. Thus, in dealing with filament yarns, the greater the number, the *coarser* the yarn.

Staple fiber yarns reverse this process: the greater the number, the *finer* the yarn (Fig. 129). Such yarns are measured according to the number of *hanks* required to make 1 pound of yarn. A hank of *cotton* equals 840 yards. Therefore, the coarsest cotton singles yarn is labeled 1s, since one

Figure 127 shows one possible, if slightly eccentric, application of the fiber by handweavers.

Synthetic Fibers   The earliest synthetic fibers were developed in an attempt to imitate the natural fibers. In fact, when rayon was introduced in the latter half of the 19th century, it was called "artificial silk" and was not given a proper name of its own until 1924. Serious research in manufactured fibers was undertaken during the 1930s, but it was not until World War II, when the supply of silk was cut off and the demand for fibers in military applications was enormous, that experimentation became reality. After the war, the new fibers were made available to the general public, and acceptance was immediate. Instead of trying to simulate the natural fibers, manufacturers stressed the *superior* qualities of their product. For example, nylon, which is nonabsorbent, has practical applications for rainwear and other items in which water resistance is important. Its mothproof quality has fostered the development of coarse, heavy yarns for carpeting. Nylon possesses far greater elasticity than silk or wool, so it is often used in stretch yarns. Weavers choose it for its strength and luster (Pl. 6, p. 71).

Serious competition from synthetic fibers has prompted the manufacturers of natural yarns to

above: 128. Filament-fiber yarns, including silk and most synthetics, are measured in deniers; the greater the number, the coarser the yarn. *Top to bottom:* 1-denier yarn, 3-denier yarn.

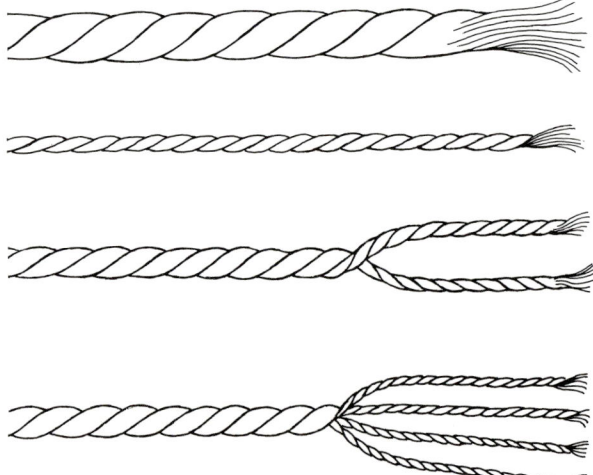

129. For staple-fiber yarns, the greater the number the finer the yarn. The numerator in the fraction indicates the singles yarn size, the denominator the ply number. *Top to bottom:* 1/1 yarn, 4/1 yarn, 4/2 yarn, 8/4 yarn.

left: 130. Aurelia Munoz. *Cathedral.* 1974. Sisal with mica, 8'3" × 3' (2.35 × .9 m). Courtesy the artist.

right: 131. Maria Chojnacka. *At the Sea Shore,* detail. 1973. Fishing thread and seashells, 4'4" × 3' (1.3 × .9 m). Courtesy the artist.

hank alone will weigh a pound. A 3s yarn would be one-third as coarse, and so on. Ply yarns are designated by two numbers separated by a slash. A yarn marked 5/3, for instance is a *size* 5, *3-ply* yarn.

The same system applies to other spun yarns, except that the unit of measure varies. A hank of *worsted* yarn equals 560 yards; a hank of *woolen* yarn equals 300 yards when indicated in cuts, 1600 yards when indicated in runs; a hank of *spun silk* equals 840 yards. For *linen* yarns the unit of measure is a *lea*, equivalent to 300 yards.

Nonyarn Materials

The contemporary handweaver is by no means restricted to the use of classic yarns. You can experiment with many different kinds of nonfibrous materials, both natural and synthetic, in order to achieve the expression you seek. Corn husks, cattails, seed pods, horsehair, seaweed, river cane, feathers, grasses, pine needles, and shells are only a few of the possibilities among the natural materials (Pl. 8, p. 71; Figs. 130–132).

132. Peter Jacobi and Ritzi Jacobi. *Transylvania II.* 1973. Horsehair and goat hair, 10'6" × 21' × 3'6" (3 × 6 × 1 m). Kunsthalle, Mannheim, Germany.

Native materials vary according to the geographical region and the season of the year in which they are collected (Fig. 133). Some of these, such as common milkweed, are best harvested in late summer or fall, while others can be gathered at any time. Native materials must be dried thoroughly before they can be used in order to shrink them and to prevent mold. Drying away from light will help to preserve the color. Before weaving, the materials should be remoistened to make them pliable. Cattails, grasses, and similar plants can be treated with glycerin to maintain their suppleness. A coating of clear plastic will retard insect damage. A few suggestions for gathering and handling native materials are listed below.

Corn husks can be gathered in any season, but if they are collected at the normal harvesting time, they are already dried. They can be used in their natural state or dyed. The inner husks are most desirable. To restore their pliability, place the

133. Many native materials
can be incorporated in a weaving.

dried husks for several hours in a sealed plastic bag to which some moisture has been added. During the weaving process the cloth beam of the loom must be protected from dampness with newspapers or plastic. The woven fabric cannot be left too long on the loom, for the corn husks will mildew.

Cattails must be gathered as soon as possible after they have reached the desired size. Small heads will be found in late June or early July.

Rushes should be harvested during the summer months, before they grow brown and brittle.

Sedges are recognized by their triangular stems. For weaving purposes they are best collected in summer.

Grasses suitable for weaving include wheat, rye, oats, timothy, tall reed grass, sweet vernal grass, and bromegrass. Most will accept dyes. The grains should be collected when they are ripe (in July), before they are combined or broken by baling. Grasses can be bleached and used without the addition of color. The most effective process for bleaching is to boil the materials with or without the addition of a small amount of fabric bleach to hasten the process. After the green color has gone from the grass, the bundled grass can be hung to dry in the sun to complete the removal of all color. It is best to cut off the blades, leaving only the stems. Boiling does not seem to destroy the grass. It is wise to straighten the stems and hold them together loosely with a cord during the heating process to prevent the mass from becoming tangled. You can remove the cords after drying.

Milkweed is usable in either the swamp or the common form.

Dogbane provides a fiber from its inner bark. It is best gathered in summer.

Willow shoots can be harvested either in spring or in fall. If white shoots are desired, they should be gathered in the spring, after the sap begins to flow and the buds swell. Shoots harvested in the fall will be tan.

Blue stem grass (original Illinois prairie grass) is best collected in the fall.

Feathers of many sorts, including white chicken or turkey feathers, will accept dyes. Pheasant feathers have an interesting variety of colors in their natural state. Often feathers make a natural termination for a fiber piece (Fig. 134).

Pine needles can be gathered at any time of the year. It is best to remove them directly from the tree, but the brown needles on the ground are satisfactory. The long-leaved needles of the southeastern United States have more character and are easier to work with than the shorter needles found in the midwestern states.

right: 134.
Chris Yarborough.
Necklace.
Feathers and glass,
12 × 4½″
(30 × 11.25 cm).
Courtesy the artist.

far right: 135.
Mary Walker Phillips.
Bell Frilling Knitting,
detail. 1976.
Red armature wire
with white and red glass
beads and gold bells.
Courtesy the artist.
(See also Fig. 584.)

In order to fulfill the requirements of a special project, the handweaver may have recourse to an endless variety of synthetic materials. Among these are wire, nails, strips of Plexiglas or acetate, plastic, newspaper, beads, chain, and ceramic pieces (Figs. 135–138). No material, regardless of its size, shape, composition, color, or degree of rigidity, can be conclusively eliminated as a possibility for weaving.

136. **Evelyn Anselevicius.**
Bead Face. 1970.
Opaque and transparent
plastic beads
with plastic ribbon
on steel hoop with
chicken-tail feathers,
diameter 9′ (2.7 m).
Courtesy the artist.

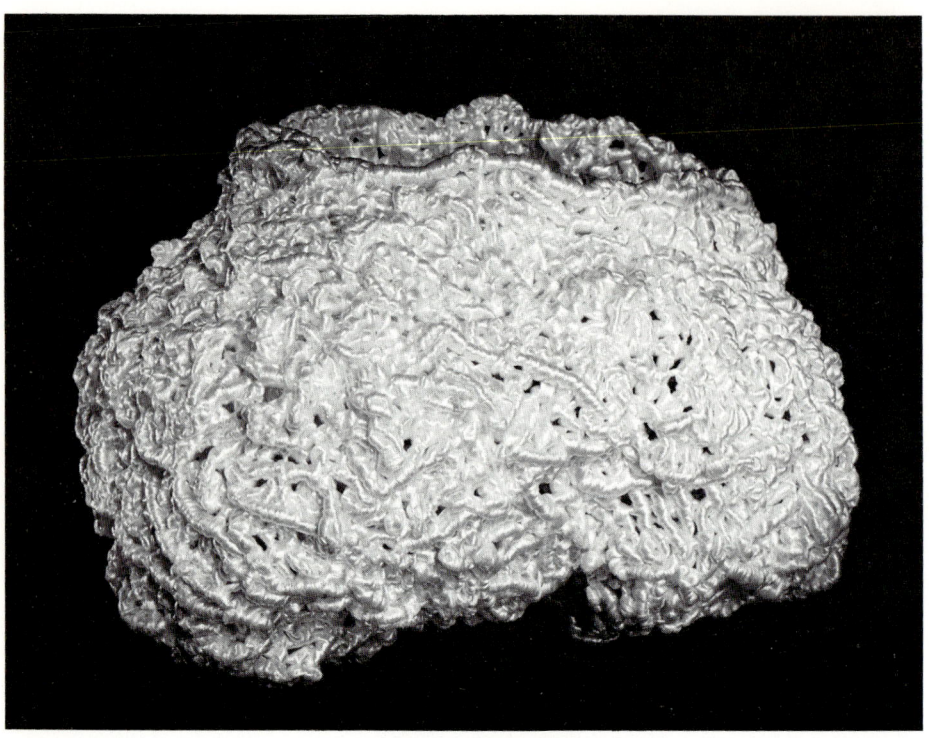

above: **137. Gary Trentham.** *Glad Wrap Basket.* 1974.
Knotted clear polyethylene, 14 × 30″ (35 × 75 cm).
Collection Virginia Seitz Mahone, Marietta, Ohio.

below: **138. Ed Rossbach.** *Newspaper Basket.* Twined newspapers,
4 × 4 × 3′ (1.2 × 1.2 × .9 m). Courtesy the artist.

Weaving can be done without any tools at all. Primitive peoples learned to weave long before they had invented the loom. However, nonloom weaving is a tedious business, and the outcome may not be very satisfactory. The contemporary handweaver has access to a wide variety of precision looms and other equipment to aid the weaving process and encourage professional results.

The Loom

In its most basic form the loom consists of a framework to hold the warp yarns rigid while the weft is interlaced. Despite the complexity of modern looms, only two refinements, essentially, have been added to this simple structure: a *shedding* device, to raise or lower certain warp threads so that the weft can be inserted; and a *beating* device, to push the weft into position. A loom is a sensitive machine, and you must learn to use it. Only when you understand its full potential can you match its performance to your creative ideas. Few looms come equipped with operating instructions, and

**Tools
and Equipment**

91

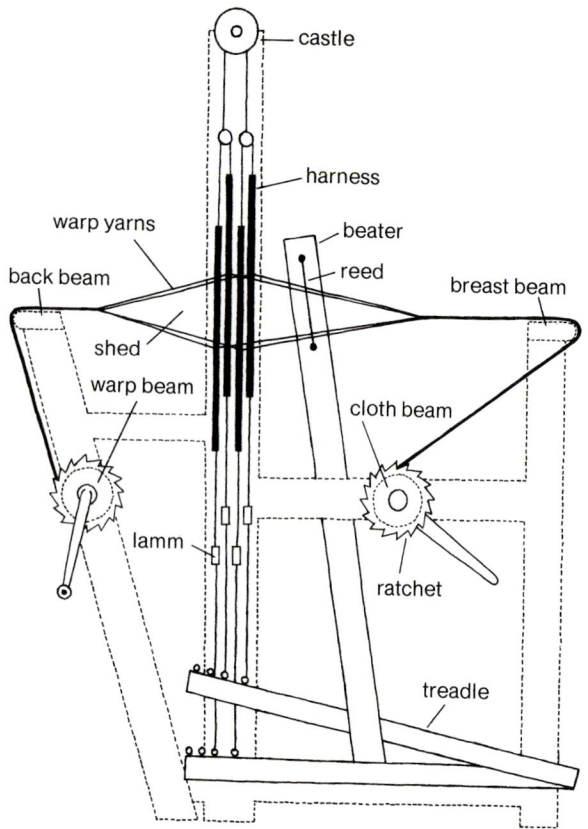

139. Diagram of a counterbalance loom,
illustrating the basic parts
common to all modern floor looms.

1. The *warp beam*, which stores the warp until it is needed. The warp beam is equipped with a *ratchet* to hold it stationary, thus regulating the tension of the warp yarns. When additional warp is needed, the weaver releases the ratchet and rolls the warp beam forward. Many looms have a lever at the front that restores tension to the warp.
2. The *back beam*, a rigid beam that supports the warp and maintains its horizontal position in a line to the breast beam.
3. The *breast beam*, an equivalent support at the front of the loom.
4. The *cloth beam*, which stores the web after it has been woven. The cloth beam also has a ratchet, which maintains warp tension when a section of completed web is to be taken up onto the cloth beam.
5. The *castle*, the uppermost part of the loom, which supports the harnesses.

The Shedding Mechanism The shedding mechanism incorporates all the parts necessary to create a *shed*, the space between spread warps through which the weft is thrown. The shedding mechanism includes:

1. The *heddles* (Fig. 140), vertical cords or strips of metal. Each has an *eye* in the center, and an individual warp yarn is threaded through each eye. Occasionally, two or more yarns are passed through a single heddle. In aluminum or steel heddles the length of the eye varies from $\frac{1}{4}$ to $\frac{1}{2}$ inch; if linen cord is used to make heddles, the opening can be as large as the weaver needs.

It sometimes happens that an extra heddle is required in the middle of a harness, perhaps because the weaver has made an error in threading. In this case, a *corrective heddle* (Fig. 140) can be snapped into place, or a string heddle can be added. String heddles often are used on tapestry looms and on various kinds of simple frame looms.

often they lack directions for assembly. Therefore, even the beginning weaver must be thoroughly familiar with the parts of a loom and their functions. Once mastered, the individual elements should be easy to recognize on any loom.

Parts of the Basic Loom

Figure 139 is a diagram of the basic loom with each of its parts indicated.

The Frame The frame is the overall structure of the loom. It holds the warp yarns in tension and supports the moving parts of the loom. It includes:

140. Top to bottom: metal heddle; corrective heddle, which can be snapped in place in the center of a harness without disturbing the adjacent heddles; string heddle.

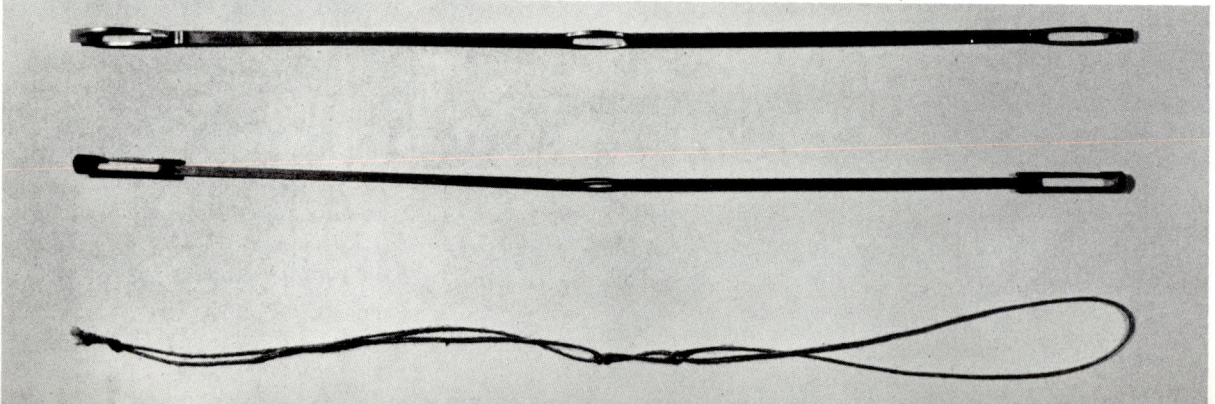

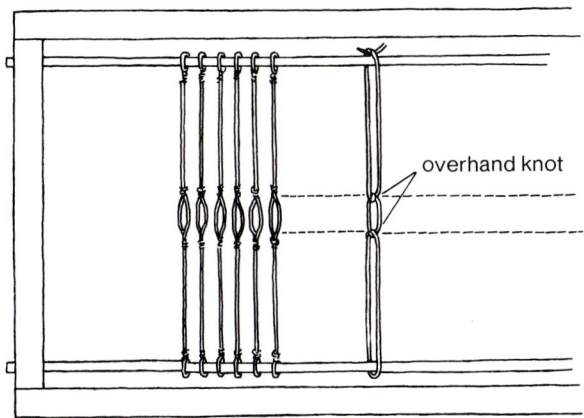

above: 141. A string heddle is made
from linen carpet warp looped over
the bottom of the harness, tied in an overhand knot
at the bottom and top of the eye,
and knotted securely over the top of the harness.

below: 142. The beater of the loom,
with a reed in position.

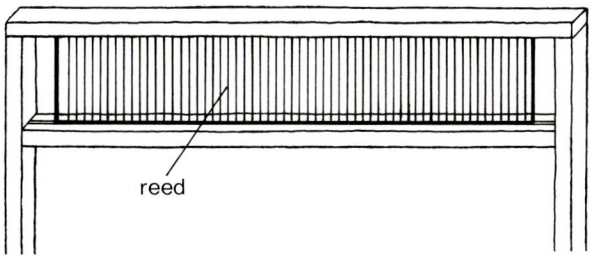

reed

Making a String Heddle

□ Take a piece of cotton string or linen carpet warp 3 or 4 inches longer than twice the height of the heddle frame.
□ Loop the cord over the bottom of the frame (Fig. 141).
□ Tie the cord in an overhand knot at the bottom and top of the eye.
□ Knot the cord securely on the top of the frame.
□ The string should be fairly taut, so that the eye will remain in line with those of the other heddles.
□ Trim off the extra length of cord.

2. The *harnesses* or *heddle frames*, which support the heddles. The number of harnesses on a given loom controls the complexity of weaves it can produce. Two harnesses are enough for plain weave, tapestry, and other simple weaves, but an elaborate pattern weave may require twenty or more.
3. The *treadles*, foot levers that raise and lower the harnesses.
4. The *lamms*, bars that connect the harnesses to the treadles.

The Beating Mechanism   The beating mechanism (Fig. 142) orders the warp yarns, controls their density, and packs the weft yarns into position. It has two parts:

1. The *reed*, a comblike device, parallel to the harnesses, through which the warp yarns are threaded after they leave the heddles. Its function is to keep the warp yarns perfectly aligned. The spaces in the reed are called *dents*. They vary in size from 4 per inch to 40 or more.
2. The *beater*, a framework that holds the reed. It is attached to either the top or the bottom of the loom by a pair of uprights, which allow it to swing freely. After each new shot of weft yarn has been passed through the shed, the beater is pulled against the web so that the reed places the new weft against the previous one.

Evolution of the Loom

When weaving was done entirely by hand, rushes were laid lengthwise on the ground and lifted alternately to allow the weft to be threaded across. The first improvement on this system was a method of holding the warp yarns taut. Primitive weavers undoubtedly drove two stakes into the ground and stretched their warps between them. Such a "loom" was portable—or even disposable—a serious consideration for the nomadic peoples of the Stone Age. A variation on this simple device was the Solomon Islands hand loom (Fig. 143), a slit piece of wood held apart by two vertical

143. The Solomon Islands hand loom,
a very simple loom with no heddles or harnesses.

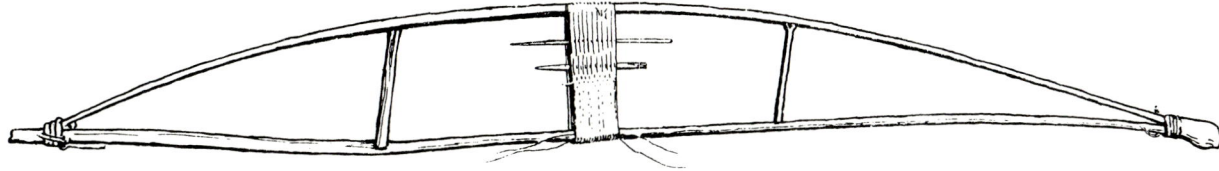

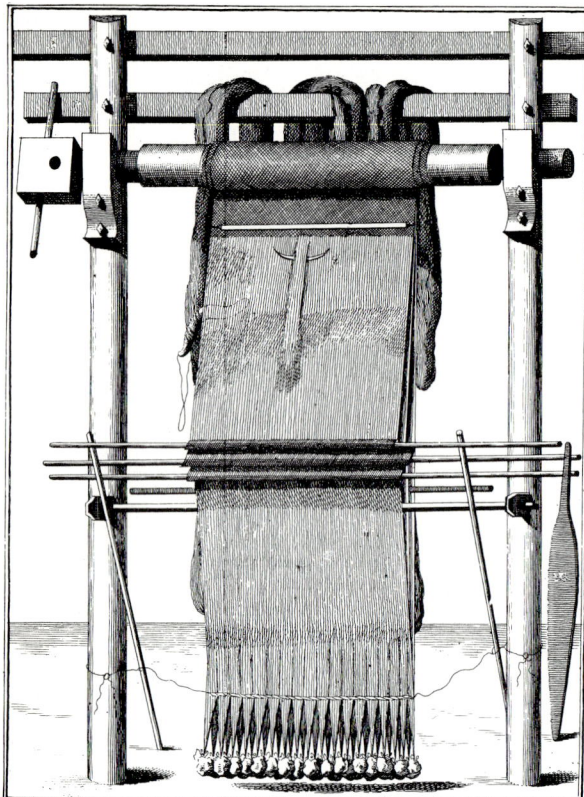

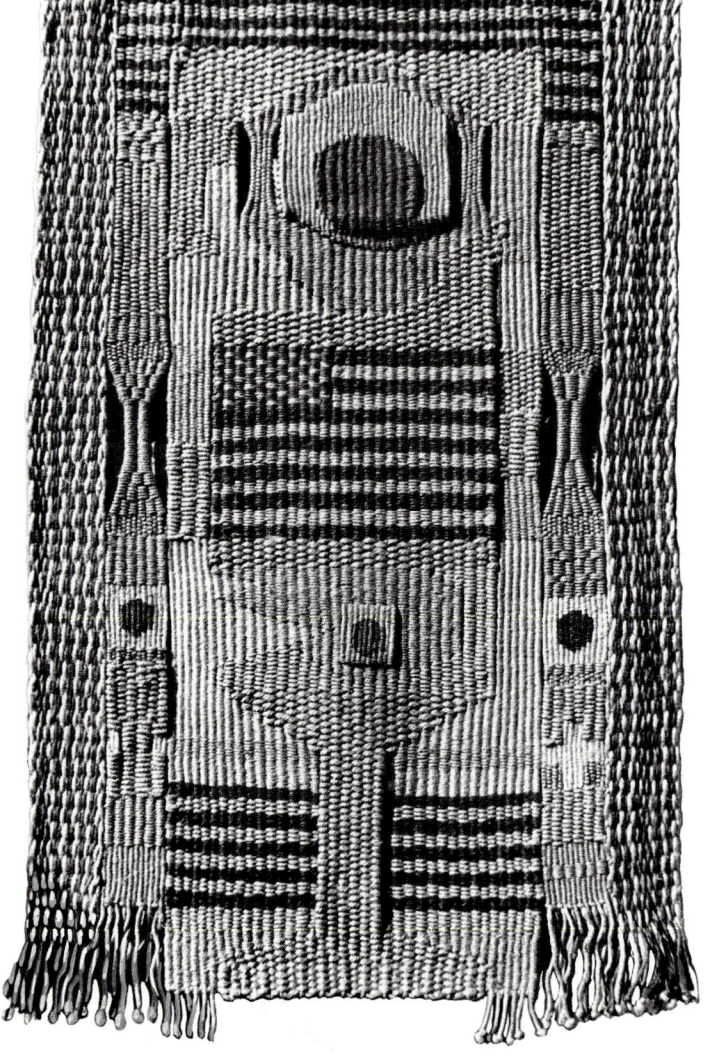

left: 144. Vertical warp-weighted loom used in 18th-century Iceland. From Olaus Olavius, *Oeconomisk Reise igiennem de nordvestlige, nordlige, og nordostlige Kanter af Island,* Dresden and Leipzig, 1780.

below: 145. Momo Nagano. *Three Cheers for the White, Blue, and Red.* 1975. Woven jute tapestry made on vertical warp-weighted loom, 5′6″ × 4′ (1.65 × 1.2 m).

below: 146. A Laha woman weaving on a backstrap loom in the hills of northern Thailand.

wooden props and tied at the ends to prevent further separation. The warp was a continuous bast fiber wound around the center section of the loom. A crude needle assisted the weaver's fingers in inserting the weft threads.

The Warp-Weighted Loom   The vertical warp-weighted loom was an outgrowth of the twining process (pp. 196–197). It appeared first in Egypt during the second millennium B.C. and was eventually adopted by the Swiss Lake Dwellers, the Greeks, the Romans, the Scandinavians, and the Indians of North and South America (Figs. 11, 26, 43, 46). The loom consisted of a horizontal beam—supported at either end by a vertical post—around which the warp threads were tied. As a rule, each warp yarn or group of yarns was weighted at the bottom with a stone or a piece of metal. A shed rod and a heddle rod helped to change the shed. In the Greek version of the loom (Fig. 46) weaving moved from the top downward, and the warp beam revolved, so that as sections of web were completed, they could be rolled up over the beam. Both the Romans and the New Kingdom Egyptians (Fig. 43) used a type of loom in which the warp yarns were weighted by another horizontal beam at the bottom. Weaving moved upwards, and the weft was beat into place by a comb that was the ancestor of our modern-day reed.

The Icelandic loom illustrated in Figure 144 is an 18th-century version of the Greek warp-weighted loom. It is equipped with three heddle rods and two shed rods. When the shed was to be changed, a heddle rod was lifted to raise selected warp yarns, and the movable shed rod was inserted, followed by a bobbin containing the weft yarn. Such a loom was quite practical for the nomadic Lapps. When they moved, they carried only the warp beam and heddle rods. Uprights were constructed from available timber at the new location. Warp-weighted looms are probably still used in isolated parts of Lapland and in other remote areas; they have attracted some interest among handweavers in the United States (Fig. 145).

The Backstrap Loom   Among the simplest of horizontal looms is the backstrap loom (Fig. 385), in which the warp yarns are held taut between a tree or other fixed object and the body of the weaver (see pp. 212–215). A strap or band attached to the loom is passed around the weaver's waist, so that tension in the warp yarns can be controlled by a simple shift of weight. Originally, weaving was done with the fingers alone, but more advanced backstrap looms use heddle rods and separators to create the shed, as well as a beater stick to pack the weft yarns into position. The backstrap loom was common among the Indians of Peru during the pre-Inca period. It is still used by native peoples of Southeast Asia and the Americas, including the Navajo of Arizona and New Mexico and the Indians of Mexico (Fig. 146). Full instructions for the assembly and use of a backstrap loom are given in Chapter 14.

147. The pit loom, as used in India, one form of horizontal ground loom.

Horizontal Ground Looms   It is not known precisely when the horizontal ground loom was developed. This loom provides for a fixed support at *both* ends of the warp, thus freeing the weaver physically from the loom. One version was the *pit loom* (Fig. 147), so called because it was designed to be placed over a pit dug in the ground. The weaver sat on the ground at a level with the loom. The weaver's feet, in the pit, operated the treadles. Each warp yarn had its own heddle. The heddles were divided into two groups and suspended from two shafts, which could be raised or lowered alternately to change the shed. A reed controlled the horizontal spacing of the warp yarns. Pit looms were used in India for weaving cotton.

Another type of horizontal ground loom is the *tripod loom* (Fig. 148), still used by the natives of

148. The tripod loom, used in various parts of Africa for making narrow bands of cloth.

The Draw Loom   The draw loom was invented in China about the time of the birth of Christ. As the Japanese print in Figure 151 shows, it was designed for two operators: the master weaver manipulated the heddle frames and threw the shuttle, while the assistant, stationed at the top of the loom, controlled individual warp yarns, independent of the heddle frames. This system permitted amazing intricacy of pattern. Each warp yarn was attached to a cord run through a comber board to the top of the loom. On command from the weaver, the assistant, in marionettelike fashion, could raise any warp or group of warps, thus providing infinite variety in the shed.

Along with the knowledge of sericulture, the draw loom migrated westward. All the elaborate pattern weaves of the Renaissance and Baroque periods were created on a European version of the draw loom. Until 1733 the maximum fabric width was about 22 inches, but in that year John and Robert Kay introduced the fly shuttle, which made it possible to weave fabrics in greater widths. The Kays' invention also speeded the weaving process considerably. The draw loom was used in Europe until the end of the 18th century, when it was replaced by the Jacquard loom.

Liberia for weaving their narrow bands of country cloth. This loom provides a more efficient method for separating the warps. It is equipped with string heddles and a reed beater. The tripod supports the heddle frames, while tension in the warp is maintained by a stake driven into the ground at either end. When sticks, performing as treadles, are attached to the heddle frames, the tripod loom functions much like a more complex counterbalance loom.

Horizontal Frame Looms   The horizontal frame loom was known in ancient Egypt, but it may have been invented in China much earlier. Although many refinements have been added over the centuries, in operating principle it was identical to the common floor loom used today. A complex version of the horizontal frame loom—with treadle-operated harnesses, a reed beater, and a movable warp beam—appeared in Europe by the 13th century, but its mechanisms must have been perfected long before. Hans Holbein's conception of *Penelope at the Loom* (Fig. 149) suggests the type of instrument employed by Renaissance weavers. Even after the Industrial Revolution much cloth was woven on the horizontal frame loom in non-industrialized parts of Europe and in rural areas (Fig. 150).

150. Ludwig Vogel. *Two Women Weaving in the "Schachental," Canton of Uri, Switzerland.* 19th century. Pencil drawing, $8\frac{7}{8} \times 8\frac{3}{8}$" (22 × 20.6 cm). Swiss National Museum, Zurich.

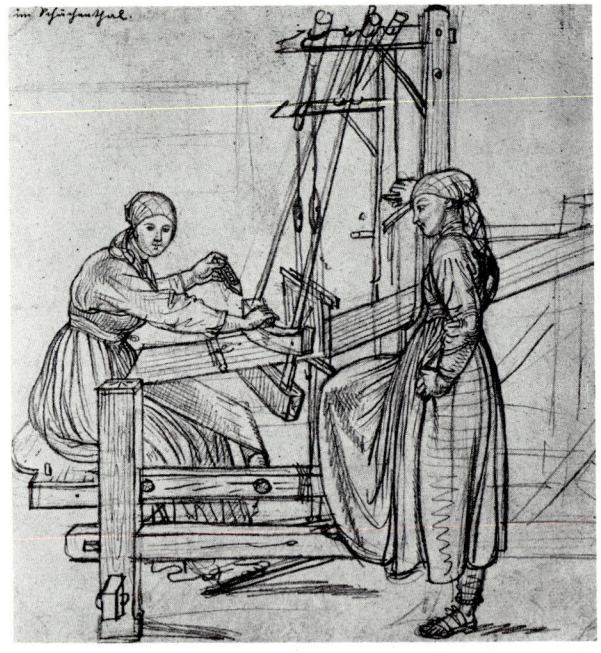

151. Tachibana Minko, Japan. Chinese draw loom, from the artisan series *Saiga Shokunin Burui.* 1770s. Woodcut.

The Jacquard Loom   When a new device has been introduced, it is not unusual for one individual's name to become associated with it, even though many people may have contributed their ingenuity. Such was the case with the Jacquard loom, the first pattern loom to operate successfully on a mechanized basis. As far back as 1725 Basile Bonchon had experimented with perforated paper as a means of selecting the cords to be raised on a draw loom. In 1745, Jacques de Vaucanson improved the mechanism by adding a *griffe*, a metal bar that could be cranked up or down, carrying with it those wires selected by Bonchon's perforations. Vaucanson is also credited with placing the entire apparatus on the top of the loom, a position it still occupies today.

Joseph Marie Jacquard was born in 1752 at Lyons, France. His first textile innovation seems to have been a machine for weaving net, which captured the prize in a London competition. Jacquard thought little of his invention and forgot about it, until he was suddenly arrested on orders from Napoleon. He was taken to Paris and charged with, in effect, technological blasphemy, for having pretended "to do that which God Almighty cannot do, tie a knot in a stretched string." To clear himself of the charge, Jacquard built a model of his machine. This so impressed his interrogators

that he was asked to examine a loom—probably one built on Vaucanson's principle—that had failed to weave satisfactorily certain rich fabrics intended for the Emperor's personal use. Jacquard succeeded in correcting the flaws, and in 1806 the French government accepted what came to be known as the Jacquard loom (Fig. 152).

152. The original Jacquard loom, constructed in 1804 for the French government by Joseph Marie Jacquard.

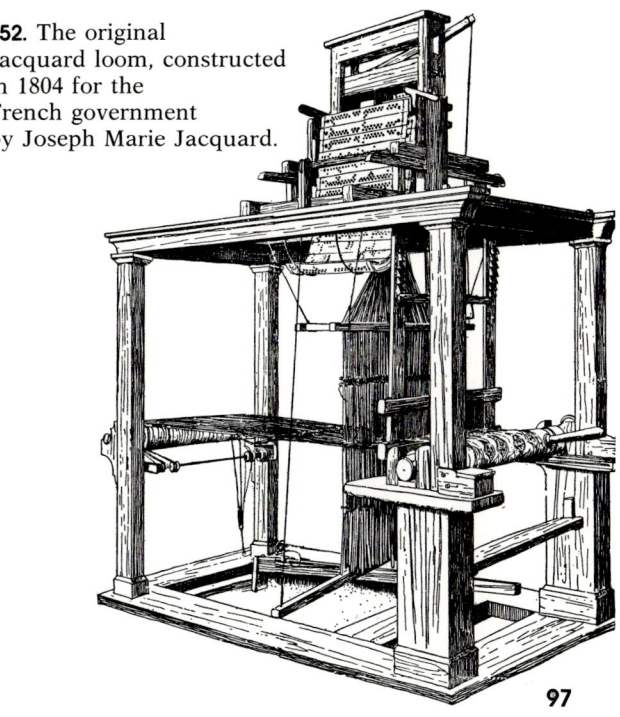

153. Annette Kaplan. *Geometric Resolutions.* 1976.
Wool tapestry, Jacquard woven; 4'9" × 7'6" (1.42 × 2.25 m).
Courtesy Modern Master Tapestries, Inc., New York.

on, and a new card takes its place for the next shed. When all the cards are used, the series begins again and the pattern is repeated.

Compared to the draw loom, the Jacquard loom is astonishingly fast. The huge industrial models are capable of 160 weft shots per minute. Furthermore, once the shedding sequence has been determined and the cards arranged in order, operation is completely automatic. The Jacquard loom is used for damasks, brocades, brocatelles, ribbons, and other complex patterns (Fig. 153).

Modern Hand Looms

Several types of looms are in common use among handweavers today. Of these, most are floor looms, equipped with treadles connected to the harnesses. The weaver has foot controls to change the shed, leaving the hands free to throw the shuttle and beat the weft.

Counterbalance Loom   The harnesses in a counterbalance loom (Fig. 154) operate in tandem: as one harness is lowered, the connecting harness is raised. Thus, to create any shed, *all* the warp yarns must depart from the horizontal—some above it and some below. As a rule, counterbalance looms are available with either 2 harnesses or 4, but some have 6 or 8.

Jack Loom   With a jack loom (Fig. 155) each harness works independently. When one set of harnesses is raised, the others remain stationary. Jack looms are made with 4 harnesses or more.

Countermarch Loom   The countermarch loom (Fig. 156) is a rising-shed loom set up like a counterbalance loom, in that all harnesses must be tied to each pedal. The countermarch loom, however, does not depend on paired action. Each harness is operated independently, as on the jack loom. Admirers of this loom like the fact that it not only lifts the harnesses for the particular shed desired but also forces down those harnesses over which the weft is to lie. This makes for a large, clear shed, which is particularly useful when working with a heavy or stubborn warp material. On a jack loom material like this would cause the underlying harnesses to lift a little, making the shed smaller.

The entire tie-up apparatus is more complex with the countermarch loom and requires extra

The French weavers, on the other hand, did not take kindly to the appearance of yet another machine that would eliminate their jobs. Upon his return to Lyons, Jacquard was greeted with such hostility that on three occasions he barely escaped with his life. Jacquard died in poverty in 1834. Inevitably, the advantages of mechanized pattern weaving soon overwhelmed the weavers' objections. The loom ultimately brought great prosperity to the city of Lyons.

The Jacquard loom operates on the same principle as a player piano or a modern computer. Each warp yarn is connected, by means of a cord or *lease*, to a metal needle. A series of cards, one for each weft shot, are punched with holes in a preordained pattern. The cards are then arranged in sequence and laced together to pass through the machine. As each card comes into position, only those needles corresponding to the holes in the cards are released, thus raising the warp yarns attached to those particular needles to create a shed. Any combination of warp yarns can be raised. The weft is shot through, the card moves

below: 154. Leclerc 4-harness counterbalance floor loom. On a counterbalance loom, the harnesses operate in tandem; as one harness is raised, the connecting harness is lowered.

above: 155. Gilmore 4-harness jack floor loom. All the harnesses on a jack loom function independently.

below: 156. In a countermarch loom, all harnesses function independently, but the shed is more like that on a counterbalance loom. For each shed, one or more harnesses are raised, the others depressed.

preparation time whenever the loom is dressed. A countermarch loom has two sets of lamms, one above the other, which permit the combined raising and lowering actions. Countermarch looms come in 4-, 8-, and multiharness versions.

Upright Loom　The upright loom takes many forms (Fig. 299). Some models are equipped with a stationary reed and two heddle frames operated at the base by a pair of treadles. Another type has a simple basic frame that supports the warp beam at the top and cloth beam at the bottom. The latter version has no treadles; warp selection is handled by groups of string heddles operated individually or in groups by the weaver.

Upright looms make excellent frames for tapestry weaves. The lack of shed control becomes less important, since the shot for tapestry is usually very short and changes back and forth often in localized areas. Upright looms are also good for knotted and looped constructions and for hangings. The Navajo weaver operates a loom of this general design.

157. Artcraft 4-harness table loom.

Table Loom On the standard table loom (Fig. 157) all weaving operations must be performed with the hands. In place of treadles the table loom has a set of levers connected to the harnesses, so that in order to change the shed, the weaver must put down the shuttle and manipulate a lever at the side of the loom or on the castle. Table looms usually have 2 or 4 harnesses, but some have as many as 20.

Selecting a Loom

A loom is the most valuable and costly piece of equipment a weaver must purchase. It is a lifetime investment, for a sturdy and well-constructed loom should give efficient service for decades. There are many factors to be weighed in buying a loom. Perhaps the most compelling are the space available, the cost, and—most important—the kind of work the weaver intends to do. The weaver interested primarily in finger weaves might select a tapestry loom (Fig. 299). It is cheaper, requires less floor space, allows the weaver more freedom, and will perform satisfactorily for a number of techniques. However, once this possibility has been eliminated, several variables must be considered in choosing equipment.

Type of Loom The weaver who expects to have only one loom should—if space and money permit—select a floor loom. Table looms are perfectly adequate for weaving samples that are later to be worked up on a floor loom, but the necessity of dropping the shuttle to change the shed makes it difficult to achieve rhythm in weaving. Of course, if space is very limited, or if portability is desirable, the table loom may be the best choice.

There are certain differences in performance with a counterbalance loom, a jack loom, and a countermarch loom. The counterbalance loom is quite efficient when treadling two harnesses against two, but it is less so when only one harness or three are to be raised. In the latter event, the jack loom is easier to operate. Therefore, the weaver may be slightly hampered when attempting a more complicated weave on the counterbalance loom. The countermarch loom might be preferred by the serious weaver. Because it is more complicated mechanically, the weaver should understand the differences between this loom and the jack type and make certain that the chief advantages of the countermarch are worth the added cost and complexity.

Number of Harnesses Most handweavers find that four or eight harnesses are sufficient for the kinds of projects they will undertake. Plain weave requires only a 2-harness loom, but, naturally, the more intricate the weave, the greater the number of harnesses one must have. The weaver interested in experimenting with elaborate patterns would not select a counterbalance loom. Some 4-harness jack looms have space for adding another set of four when money permits. Such a loom is highly practical for the weaver who plans to experiment with pattern weaves.

In addition to pattern complexity, the number of harnesses also affects the density of a potential fabric. For example, if a very dense—that is, a very tightly woven—fabric is to be constructed from relatively fine yarns, a great many warp yarns, and therefore a great many heddles, would be required. A 2-harness loom might not be able to accommodate the necessary number of heddles on only two frames.

Distribution of the warp yarns onto several harnesses also lessens the weight on each treadle. A 4-harness loom should have six treadles, while an 8-harness loom should be equipped with at least twelve.

Weaving Width The size of a loom is designated not by its overall dimensions but by the maximum width of the fabric that can be woven upon it. In other words, a 36-inch loom can produce a web up to 36 inches wide, but the framework of the loom might measure anywhere from 42 inches to 48 inches across. Loom sizes vary from 20 to 60 inches, with a 32-inch maximum for table looms. A web greater than 45 inches in width requires considerable strength on the part of the weaver merely to depress the treadles and throw the shuttle. The small person might not be able to throw and receive the shuttle easily for a loom wider than 36 inches.

Cost　It is always folly to economize on the price of a loom. When buying a loom, particularly a first loom, you should invest in the finest one you can afford. A good machine, made by a nationally or internationally known manufacturer, will almost invariably prove more satisfactory than a bargain, for in the latter case standard parts may be impossible to obtain.

A jack loom is more expensive than a counterbalance loom, which in turn is more expensive than a table loom of the same size. A countermarch loom can be bought for approximately the same price as some jack looms. Few companies in the United States make the countermarch loom, but the loom is quite common in Sweden. Several companies import the loom. The price of all types, as a rule, is directly related to the loom width and the number of harnesses.

Patterns are available from which you can construct your own loom, but this is seldom advisable. Even a fine woodcrafter might have difficulty in achieving the correct balance and proportion of parts that is essential to smooth operation. Furthermore, the cost of labor and materials almost equals that of a readymade commercial loom.

Some of the major loom manufacturers are listed in Appendix C.

Type of Beater　Depending on the way the loom is constructed, the beater may pivot from either the top or the bottom. The overhead type has one disadvantage, in that you must hold it back with one hand while you throw the shuttle with the other. However, very heavy beating, which is necessary for rugs and some other items, is easier with the overhead beater. Weavers disagree about which type is easier to handle, but the balance seems to be slightly in favor of the type that swings from the bottom of the loom. You can develop a comfortable rhythm with either version.

The beater should have a removable reed, so that other dent sizes can be substituted if necessary. Most looms are equipped with a 15-dent reed—fifteen dents to the inch (or six dents per cm). For extremely fine or coarse yarns, a different size may be more convenient. Reed sizes range from four dents per inch to thirty or more, but the average weaver has little occasion to use a reed with a greater concentration than fifteen or twenty per inch (six or eight per cm).

Many looms come with a *shuttle race*, a horizontal extension at the base of the reed along which the shuttle can travel. This accessory is particularly helpful when the warp yarns are widely spaced, for it prevents the shuttle from falling through to the floor.

Type of Frame　A good loom should be constructed from close-grained hardwood with a smooth surface. Folding looms are practical when space is at a premium—many can be collapsed even when threaded—or when portability is desirable, but they are, of course, not as sturdy as rigid looms.

Heddle threading is easier and more comfortable when the breast beam and cloth beam are removable, for the weaver can then sit closer to the harnesses. The distance between the breast beam and the harnesses should be at least 18 inches to ensure a clean shed and even tension.

Some looms have sectional warp beams, with pegs at 2-inch intervals (Fig. 201). This arrangement is more flexible than a plain beam, since the sectional beam can be used for both standard and sectional warping (see pp. 122–123). Warp beams smaller than $\frac{1}{2}$ yard in circumference are impractical. The ratchet wheel releases on the warp and cloth beams should be within easy reach, so that you need not get up to wind the warp forward and retension.

When buying a loom, you should, if possible, check the balance of the shed. In a counterbalance loom the rising and sinking warps should form the same angle with the horizontal. This helps to maintain an even tension in the warp.

Kind of Heddles　Metal heddles are preferable to linen or cotton ones, because they are more durable and they slip more easily along the heddle frame. In order to accommodate various yarn sizes, the heddle eye should be at least $\frac{1}{2}$ inch long. The heddles ought to be detachable from the harness.

Leveling the Loom

It is most important that your loom be absolutely level, for if it is not the shift can affect the fabric you weave. If one side of your weaving pulls down, the fault may lie not with uneven beating or careless weaving practices, but with a slanting floor. Even a fraction of an inch off level can distort the web. To level the loom, use an ordinary carpenter's level, checking first the breast beam and then the back beam. Insert pieces of paper, cardboard, or wood under the corners until the loom is perfectly level in all directions. You should recheck the level occasionally to make sure the balance has not shifted.

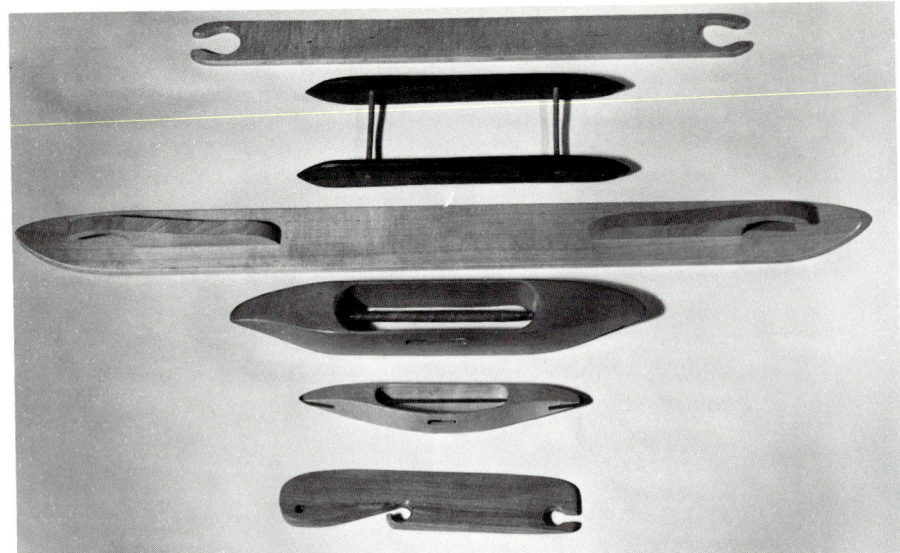

158. Shuttles are available in various designs to accommodate the weft for different kinds of weaving. *Top to bottom:* flat or stick shuttle, rug shuttle, ski shuttle, open boat shuttle, closed boat shuttle, sword beater.

Other Equipment

Loom Accessories

Loom Bench   A loom bench is not essential, but it is usually more comfortable than a stool, because its height is appropriate to that of the loom. Ideally, the stool should be at a height so that your bent elbows, when your upper arms are straight down, will clear the breast beam. This makes the weaving rhythm much easier and helps to prevent fatigue. Many loom benches have slanted tops, which in addition to being comfortable encourage you to lean into your work.

Shuttles   There are many types and sizes of shuttles, each designed to carry the weft yarn for a particular kind of web (Fig. 158). A shuttle containing a *bobbin*, on which the yarn is wound, is more convenient for most textiles, since the yarn unreels smoothly as it is needed. However, in an emergency, a simple flat shuttle can be made from a thin wood strip or tough cardboard.

A *flat* or *stick shuttle* is convenient for bulky yarn or for a narrow web, but it does not release the yarn automatically.

A *rug shuttle* is designed to hold a quantity of rug yarn or other heavy weft material.

The *ski shuttle*, a Scandinavian rug shuttle, is also useful for bulky yarns.

The *boat shuttle*, which contains a bobbin (or, in some cases, two separate bobbins), is most commonly used by handweavers. It is satisfactory for fine weft yarns and adapts well to continuous treadling of the loom, as for yardage, because the yarn is doled out automatically from the bobbin. Bobbins can be made of paper and tape, but pur-

below: **159.** Swedish hand-cranked bobbin winder.

chased bobbins of plastic, metal, wood, or cardboard are more efficient, since they are specially designed to prevent the yarn from falling off.

A *throw shuttle* with a spool is similar in operation to the boat shuttle but will hold a greater quantity of yarn.

Tapestry bobbins, which take the place of a conventional shuttle in finger weaving, are similar to the bobbins used by lacemakers—that is, a shaped dowel form. Flat plastic bobbins for tapestry can also be purchased. If desired, the yarn holders normally used for knitting can serve as tapestry bobbins, or a bobbin can be made from ½-inch dowel cut into 3- or 4-inch lengths and tapered to a blunt point at one end.

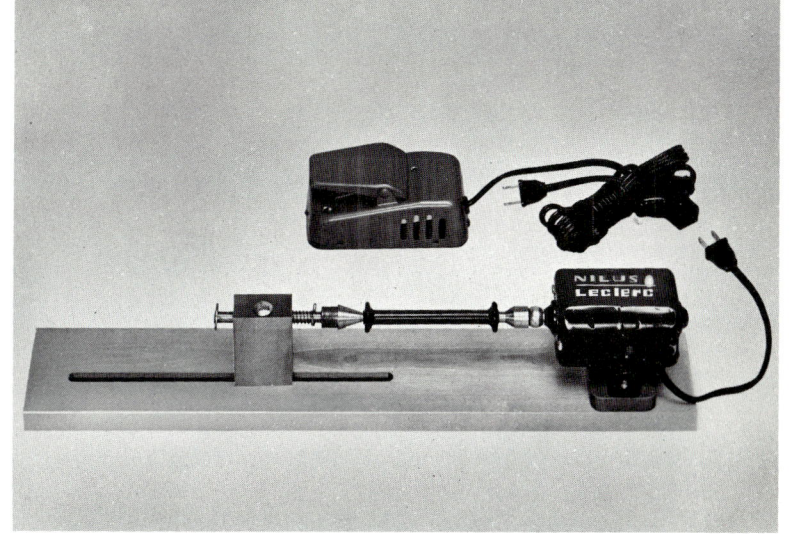

Stretcher The stretcher (Fig. 162), also called a *temple*, is used to maintain a consistent width in the fabric, particularly for yardage or rugs.

Heddle Transfer Aids Thin, pliable steel rods called heddle transfer rods are used for adding and removing heddles from the frames. They also make it possible to store the heddles in an organized manner for easy reuse.

162. Leclerc stretcher, or temple. A stretcher helps to maintain consistent width of a web.

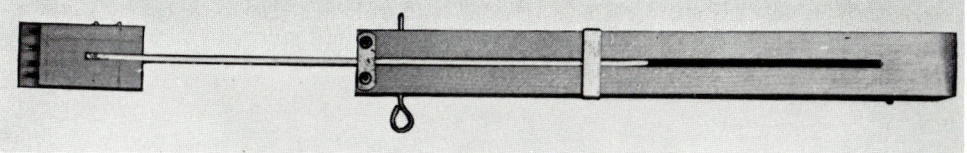

Bobbin Winder Hand-cranked and electric bobbin winders (Figs. 159, 160) are available to fill the bobbins in a boat shuttle. They can also be used to split a spool of warp yarn into several temporary spools. When guiding the yarn onto an electric winder, it is wise to wrap a small piece of cloth around the yarn to avoid friction burns.

Ball Winder A relatively inexpensive and useful accessory, the ball winder is handy for winding yarn from a skein into a ball (Fig. 161). It can also be used to provide multiple sources of yarn for warping with a paddle. This tool makes a flat ball that rests firmly on the floor and pulls from the center, so it does not move around.

Stabilizer A stabilizer is a device that fits over the tops of the harnesses on a loom and prevents them from being raised. It can be locked into place whenever you are not weaving. The stabilizer is particularly useful if your loom stays in a heavily trafficked area, for it will prevent other people from coming along and "improving" your work on the loom or "trying to weave." The weaver who has children will find this a great advantage. You may also want to lock the stabilizer in position when you are threading the heddles, so that you do not accidentally step on a treadle and pull out the yarns you have threaded. The stabilizer is most useful for looms with free-floating harnesses, such as counterbalance looms.

above: **163.** Leclerc warping frame.

right: **164.** Leclerc vertical warping reel.

below right: **165.** Pendleton horizontal warping reel.

Warping Aids

Warping Frame   A *warping frame* or *warping reel* (Figs. 163–165) is required for measuring the warp yarns. Reels are available in both horizontal and vertical models.

Warping Paddle   Warping paddles (Fig. 166) have a series of holes or parallel slots and holes. Experienced weavers use them to warp a number of yarns simultaneously.

Tension Box   A tension box (Fig. 167) is required for sectional warping (see p. 123), in order to give uniform tension to all the yarns as they are wound onto the loom.

Spool Rack   Also called a *warping creel*, the spool rack (Fig. 168) holds the spools or cones of warp yarn during the measuring process. It is essential for sectional warping (see p. 123).

Sleying Hook   A sleying hook or *reed hook* (Fig. 169) is needed to thread the warp yarns through the heddle eyes and the dents of the reed. There are two types available. The common reed hook is a long, flat strip of metal notched at one end. This tool is satisfactory for threading both the heddles and the reed. The Swedish reed hook, on the other hand, is an S-shaped piece of metal or plastic. Too wide to thread the heddles, the latter instrument is more efficient for threading the reed, since it has no sharp hook that might split the yarns. If a Swedish reed hook is used for the dents, a fine crochet hook will serve to thread the heddles.

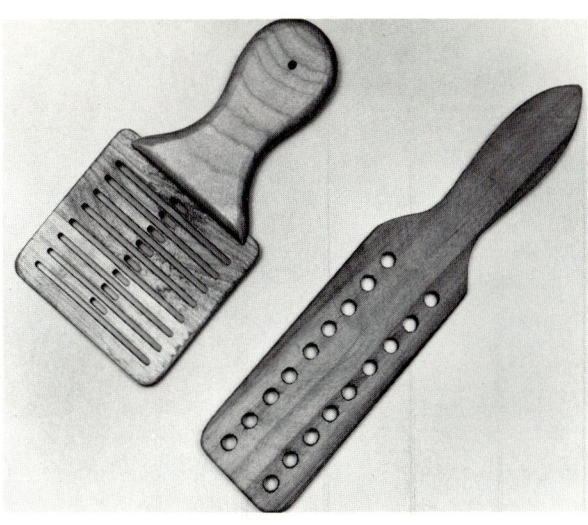

above: 166. Two versions of the warping paddle, used for measuring more than three yarns at once on the warping frame or reel.

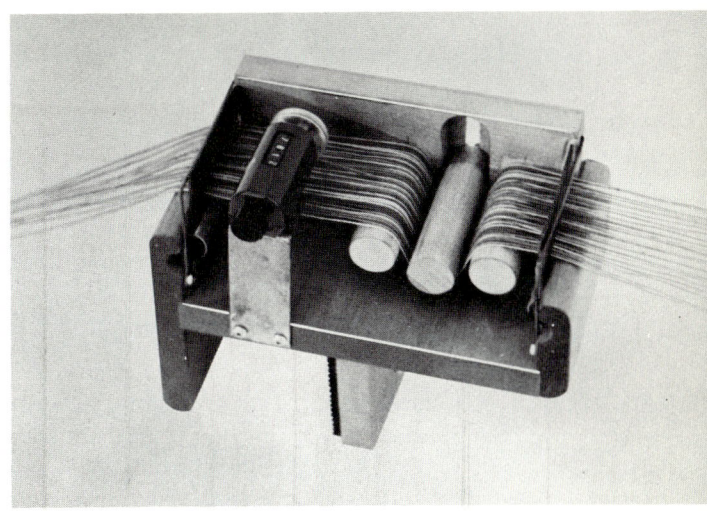

above: 167. Leclerc tension box. A tension box is essential for maintaining uniform tension in sectional warping.

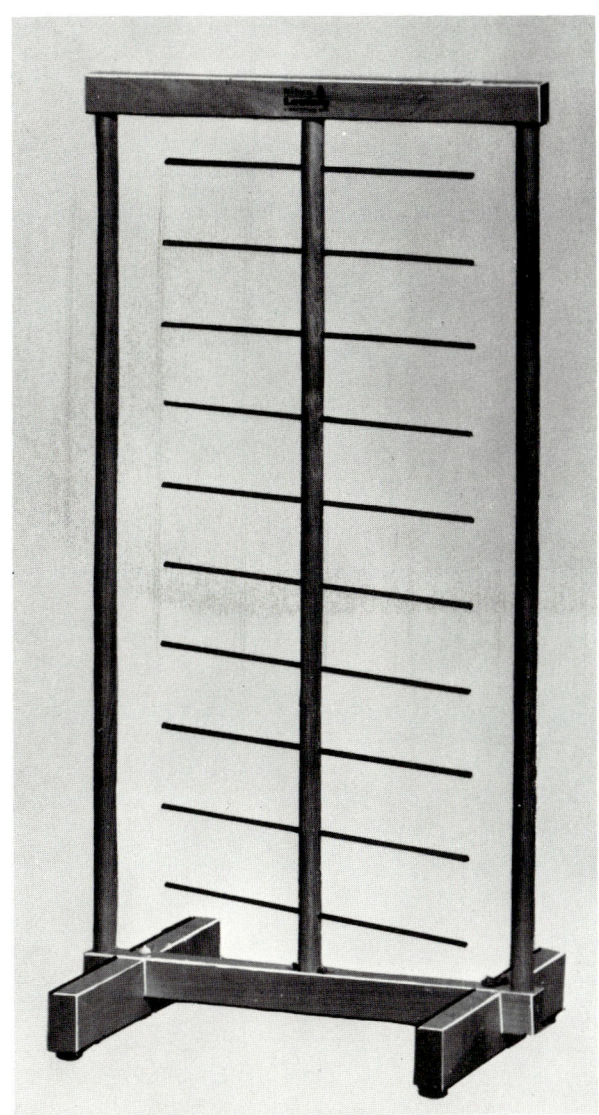

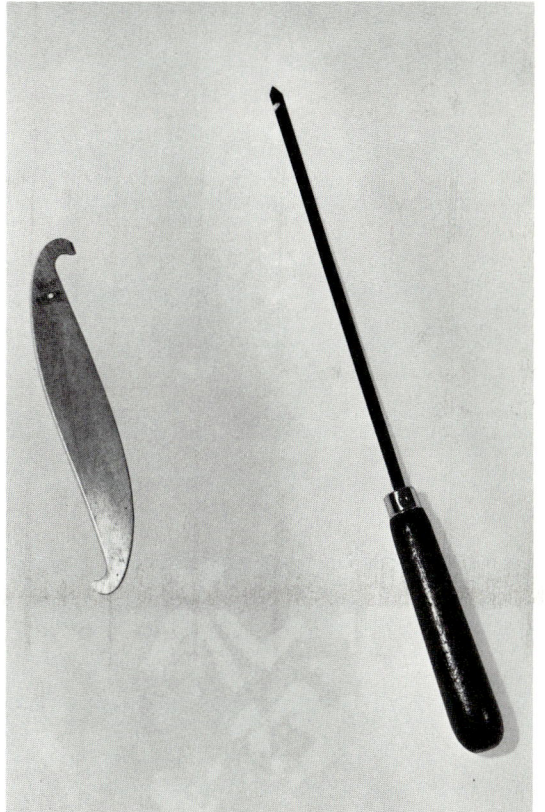

left: 168. Leclerc spool rack or warping creel.

above: 169. A sleying hook or reed hook is needed to draw warp yarns through the heddles and the dents in the reed. The S-shape variety can be used only for the reed.

Swift An *umbrella swift* or a *squirrel cage reel* (Figs. 170, 171) holds a skein of yarn while it is wound onto spools or shuttles. These devices are also practical for winding skeins from balls of yarn in preparation for dyeing.

Lease Sticks A pair of lease sticks (Fig. 172) made of smooth wood or strips of fiberboard, are placed in the warp yarn immediately after it has been wound to maintain the cross (see p. 112).

Spreader You can easily construct a spreader (Fig. 173)—also known as a *warping comb* or *raddle*—from available materials. It functions to spread the warp yarns into 1-inch units all across the loom until the warp has been evenly spaced at its full width. A 1-inch by 2-inch strip of pine slightly longer than the loom is wide can be prepared for this purpose by driving a series of finishing nails into the broader surface of the wood at 1-inch intervals.

Miscellaneous Tools

A variety of small implements, not exclusive to weaving, may prove handy from time to time.

1. A knitting needle is useful with some of the finger weaves.
2. A crochet hook, besides helping to thread the heddles, is essential for some finger weaves. The size of the hook would, in the latter case, be determined by the coarseness of the yarns involved. For heddle threading, of course, the crochet hook must be small enough to pass through the eye.
3. Scissors are indispensible and should be kept at hand always. They must be sharp and *never* used for cutting paper.
4. Straight pins are often required to repair broken warp yarns.
5. A yarn needle with a long eye (½ inch) performs a number of small chores.
6. C-clamps, available at any hardware store, have many uses.
7. Lath sticks are sometimes needed for winding the warp and for spreading the yarns.

Care of Equipment

Properly treated, a loom can last a lifetime—even several lifetimes. As with any piece of fine wood furniture, you should oil or seal the wood to prevent warpage. The loom is delicately balanced, so any warpage of its framework will interfere with proper functioning. Occasionally, parts of the loom may need to be sanded and resealed. The loom should never be stored in a damp place, such as a cellar.

Reeds will rust if they are not lightly oiled when not in use. Some weavers spray them with silicone to prevent this. If a reed has become rusty, you can scrub it with a brush and ground pumice. Metal heddles can also rust, and they will stain the yarns passing through them. Rust is difficult to remove from heddles, so you probably should replace them every few years or whenever you see rust collecting.

Cloth aprons on floor looms and metal warp and cloth sticks should be checked periodically to see that they have not bowed inward from the tension of the yarns.

170. Swedish umbrella swift, for winding skeins.

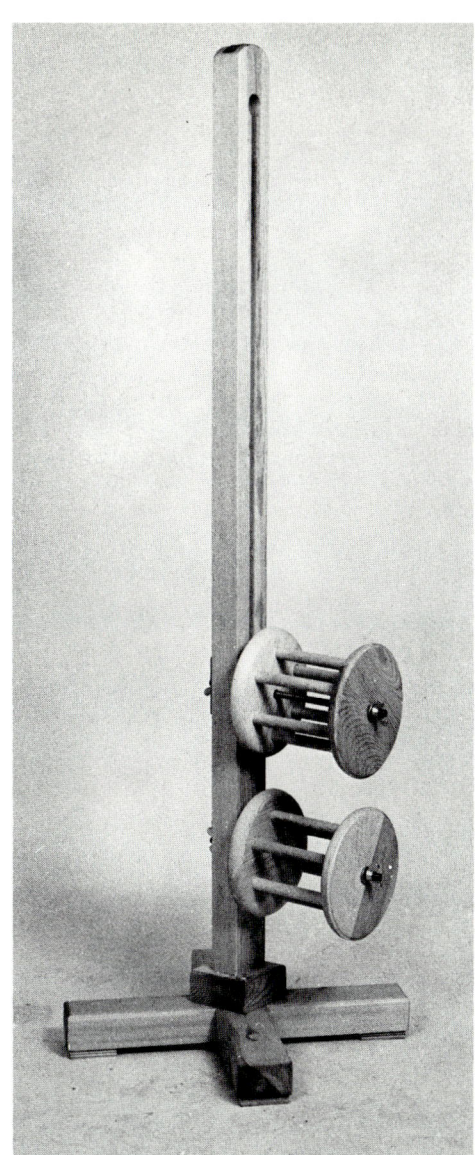

left: 171. Swedish squirrel cage reel, intended for holding skeins of yarn.

above: 172. Lease sticks serve to maintain the cross.

below: 173. A spreader divides the warp into inch units.

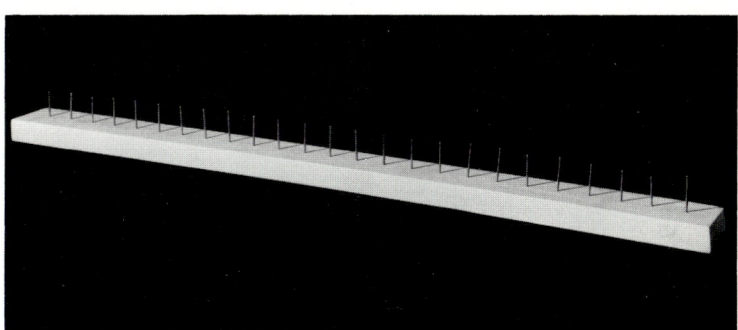

8
Preparation for Weaving

Before weaving can begin, several decisions must be made and a number of preliminary steps carried out. Although there is ample opportunity for variations in pattern once the project is actually on the loom, certain design aspects are necessarily determined in advance and, once established, cannot be changed for that particular web. Such factors include the maximum size of the finished cloth, and therefore the length and width of the warp; the composition of the warp yarns; and the sequence in which the warp yarns are threaded through the heddles and the reed.

When they plan an experimental project, skilled weavers often break some or all of the rules involved in preparing the loom. However, for the average web, using more-or-less conventional yarns, the following steps are taken in sequence:

1. Choose the warp and weft yarns.
2. Calculate the length and width of the warp.
3. Calculate the total quantity of yarn.

4. Wrap the guide string on the warping frame.
5. Warp the required yardage.
6. Secure the cross and choke ties.
7. Chain the warp.
8. Insert the lease sticks in the cross.
9. Spread the warp.
10. Wind the warp.
11. Thread the heddles.
12. Sley the reed.
13. Tie the warp ends at the front of the loom.
14. Check the loom for errors.
15. Prepare the tie-up (floor looms only).
16. Adjust the loom.
17. Fill the shuttle and/or wind the bobbins.
18. Weave the web.

Yarn Calculations

Choosing the Warp and Weft Yarns

The classic web consists of a linen warp and a woolen weft. Through the centuries these two materials have been chosen by weavers all over the world, and the reasons are sound. Linen yarns, which are relatively inelastic, will maintain their proper tension on the loom. Their great strength enables them to withstand the wear and tear of constant beating. Woolen yarns, on the other hand, have neither of these qualities to any real degree, but strength and rigidity are not needed in the weft. Rather, the superior dyeability and filling quality of wool make it ideal for the pattern-carrying element—the weft.

The contemporary handweaver need not be limited by such considerations. Many new yarns, particularly the synthetics, have desirable properties that make them suitable for warp or weft or both. For example, a nylon yarn may be extremely fine yet have more than enough strength for the warp. Furthermore, a variety of finishes—some applied by the manufacturer, some by the weaver—can improve or change the properties of a yarn. An experienced weaver can successfully use yarn that would give a beginner trouble, as many linen yarns do.

A warp yarn must be sturdy enough to withstand the tension of the loom and the repeated movement of the reed. Sturdiness, however, is not the same as bulk. Heavy or bulky yarns usually lack strength, because they are loosely twisted. A warp yarn must be twisted more firmly than a weft, in order to hold its shape when stretched. Ply yarns are most often chosen for the warp, and novelty ply yarns can sometimes be used successfully if they are alternated with more durable fine, smooth yarns. A warp yarn that is very hairy may

create problems, since the loose fibers will cause the mass of warps to mat together, and they will not separate readily to open a shed.

Some fragile yarns can be strengthened by *sizing*, in order to make them suitable for the warp. Sizing also helps to control an extremely hairy yarn.

Sizing

- Boil a solution of linseed gluten to a thick consistency.
- Strain the seeds.
- After the mixture has cooled, dip skeins of yarn that have been tied loosely in several places to prevent tangling.
- Press out the excess sizing.
- Hang the skeins under tension to dry.
- Before the yarn is completely dry, wind it on spools to force the fibers into a compact strand.

There are several different sizing procedures. An alternate method follows.

Alternate Sizing Procedure

This mixture will be sufficient for about 4½ pounds (2 kg) of linen yarn.

6 quarts (5.7 l) water
5¼ ounces (147 g) flour
1¾ ounces (50 g) paraffin

- Boil the flour and water, then remove the mixture from the heat.
- Add the paraffin.
- Beat the mixture until it cools.
- Wind the yarn in skeins and dip it in the mixture, then hang the skeins and weight them for drying. You can also paint the solution directly onto the warp after it is set up on the loom.
- Allow the yarns to dry for 12 hours before weaving.

A weft yarn can be practically any size, either single or ply. It can have any degree of twist. Even uncombed, unspun fibers can be laid into a shed and held in place, as long as the web is not intended for a garment and is not to be laundered often. Also, as Chapter 6 showed, many nonyarn materials can work in a weft. Twisted yarns have a tendency to add firmness to the finished cloth.

Calculating the Length and Width of the Warp

Several factors will contribute to making the finished product smaller in both length and width than the warp as it is set up on the loom. These factors include *loom waste, warp takeup, shrinkage, draw-in,* and *hems.*

Loom Waste   Any web will need additional warp length for tying onto the cloth beam and for extending through the reed and heddles at the end of the web. This extra length is called loom waste. (The portion at the end, after the web is completed, is often referred to as the *thrums.*) The normal allowance for loom waste is about ¾ yard or 27 inches (70 cm). Every loom is different of course. To estimate the loom waste on your loom, tie two pieces of string to the warp stick, bring them through the reed and heddles, and tie to the cloth stick.

Loom waste factor makes it impractical to plan a finished web of less than 1½ yards, since the *percentage* of waste is so high. For example, if you add a ¾-yard waste allowance to a 1½-yard web, the waste is 33⅓ percent. But if the same allowance is added to a 10-yard web, the rate of waste drops to less than 7 percent. Some projects, such as wall hangings, can be designed to use the waste for a finish.

Warp Takeup   The extra amount of warp length necessary to go over and under the weft yarns is known as warp takeup (Fig. 174). An allowance of 10 percent beyond the desired length of the web is usually enough. However, if either the warp or the weft is especially heavy, a greater allowance for takeup may be required.

174. Warp takeup is the extra warp length
consumed as the yarns pass
over and under the weft in weaving.
A similar yarn allowance is required for the weft
as it travels over and under the warp.

Shrinkage   A web nearly always shrinks when the loom tension is released. Shrinkage can also result from finishing procedures—steaming, washing, or whatever. Both types of shrinkage are affected by the composition of the fibers. The only truly reliable way to predict the amount of shrinkage a fabric will undergo is to weave a small sample from the same yarns and then subject the sample to all the usual finishing procedures, taking careful measurements at each stage. But in most

cases an allowance of 10 percent extra warp length should be ample.

Fabric shrinkage can be controlled in a number of ways. A flat, smooth yarn is usually more stable than an irregular or novelty yarn. When yarns of different compositions are combined to make a warp, the rate of shrinkage may be uneven. For example, if rayon and cotton yarns are to be used for a warp, they should be distributed fairly evenly, for a concentration of rayon yarns at one point may cause that area of the web to draw in. Some weavers take advantage of this quality of varying shrinkage to create irregular or crepe effects in parts of the fabric.

Draw-In   As a web is woven, it nearly always draws or pulls in. The finished width of the fabric will therefore be slightly narrower than the sleyed width at the reed. An allowance of 5 to 10 percent is usually adequate. However, if the weft is extremely rigid, no allowance for draw-in will be necessary.

Hems   If the finished web is to be hemmed, this must be taken into account in making the yarn calculations.

The clearest way to demonstrate warp calculations is to give an example. In all the sample calculations that follow, it is assumed that the finished web will be 10 yards (9 m) long and 1 yard (90 cm) wide.

Calculating Length of Warp

- ☐ Determine the desired length of the finished web.
- ☐ Add a 10-percent allowance for warp take-up.
- ☐ Add a 10-percent allowance for shrinkage.
- ☐ Add an allowance of ¾ yard (70 cm) for loom waste.
- ☐ Add the necessary amount for turning hems, if desired.

Example:

length of finished web	10	yards	9 m
allowance for warp take-up (10%)	1	yard	90 cm
allowance for shrinkage (10%)	1	yard	90 cm
allowance for loom waste		¾ yard	70 cm
length of each warp yarn		12¾ yards	11.5 m

If the ends of the web are to be hemmed, an additional length must be allowed for turning. Similar calculations determine the sleyed width of the warp.

<table>
<tr><td colspan="3">Calculating Width of Warp</td></tr>
<tr><td colspan="3">□ Determine width of the finished web.</td></tr>
<tr><td colspan="3">□ Add a 10-percent allowance for draw-in.</td></tr>
<tr><td colspan="3">□ Add a 10-percent allowance for shrinkage.</td></tr>
<tr><td colspan="3">□ Add the necessary amount for turning hems, if desired.</td></tr>
</table>

Example:

width of finished web	36 inches	90 cm
allowance for draw-in (10%)	3.6 inches	9 cm
allowance for shrinkage (10%)	3.6 inches	9 cm
sleyed width of warp yarns	43.2 inches	108 cm

Once the length and width of the warp have been established, you must determine the *number of warp yarns* you will need. This quantity depends on two factors: (1) the size of the yarn; and (2) the *sett* or density of the planned fabric. A tightly woven web composed of fine yarns will, of course, require a great many more warps than an open-work fabric made from heavy yarns.

If you want a reasonably firm web, you can use this simple method for calculating the number of warp yarns.

<table>
<tr><td>Calculating the Number of Warp Yarns: Method 1</td></tr>
<tr><td>□ Wrap the warp yarn around a small object, such as a pencil or ruler (Fig. 175).</td></tr>
<tr><td>□ Lay the yarns as close together as possible without overlapping.</td></tr>
<tr><td>□ Count the number of yarns per inch or centimeter.</td></tr>
<tr><td>□ Divide by two.</td></tr>
<tr><td>□ Multiply that number by the sleyed width of the warp in inches or centimeters.</td></tr>
</table>

Another system for calculating the number of warp yarns is based upon the size of the reed.

<table>
<tr><td colspan="3">Calculating the Number of Warp Yarns: Method 2</td></tr>
<tr><td colspan="3">□ Select a reed.</td></tr>
<tr><td colspan="3">□ Decide how many yarns are to be sleyed in each dent.</td></tr>
<tr><td colspan="3">□ Multiply the reed number by the number of yarns per dent by the width in inches (centimeters) of the warp.</td></tr>
</table>

Example:

reed size	No. 10	4 per cm
yarns per dent	1	1
sleyed width of warp	43 inches	108 cm
number of warp yarns (10 × 1 × 43)	430	432

Calculating the Total Quantity of Warp and Weft

You can now determine the total quantity of warp and weft yarn by simple arithmetic.

<table>
<tr><td colspan="3">Calculating Width of Warp Yarn</td></tr>
<tr><td colspan="3">□ Multiply the number of warp yarns by the length of each yarn.</td></tr>
</table>

Example:

number of warp yarns	430	432
length of each warp	12¾ yards	11.5 m
quantity of warp yarn (430 × 12.75)	5482.5 yards	4968 m

The total quantity of weft yarn must also be calculated in advance to make sure there is a sufficient quantity of the right colors, textures, and weights on hand to complete the project. If the weave is to be *balanced*—that is, the same number of weft yarns as warp yarns per measuring unit—and if the weft and warp yarns are the same size, then the total quantity of weft yarn equals the total quantity of warp yarn.

For an unbalanced weave or one that has yarns of different sizes, you must make a calculation similar to that for the warp. Included in this is an allowance for *weft take-up*—the extra length required for the weft to go over and under the warp.

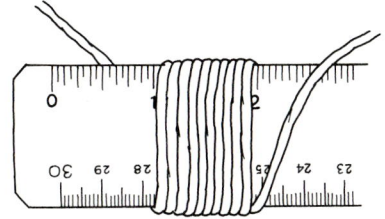

175. One method of calculating the sett, or warp yarns per inch or centimeter on the loom, is to wrap the yarn closely around a ruler or other small object and then divide the number of yarns per segment by two.

Calculating Quantity of Weft Yarn

□ Begin with the width of the fabric as sleyed at the reed.
□ Add a 10-percent allowance for weft take-up.
□ Determine the number of weft shots per inch either by estimation *or* by weaving a small sample and counting the yarns.
□ Multiply the length of each weft yarn by the number of weft yarns.

Example:

width of fabric at the reed	43 inches	108 cm
allowance for weft take-up (10%)	4.3 inches	11 cm
length of each weft yarn (43 + 4.3)	47.3 inches	119 cm
weft shots per inch or centimeter	5	2
length of web (12 yards × 36)	432 inches	1,100 cm
total number of weft shots (5 × 432)	2,160	2,200
quantity of weft yarn (47.3 × 2,160)	102,168 inches	2,618 m
	(2,838 yards)	

The calculation of warp and weft yarns will be simplified for future projects if you keep a precise record, listing all pertinent information, for each web that you weave. With experience, and by evaluating previous webs, you will be able to estimate the yarn requirement with enough accuracy for most projects. A sample Yarn Calculation Form is provided in Appendix B.

Winding the Warp

Warping is a simple enough task, but much of the success of the finished web depends upon the care taken in measuring the warp yarns. The goal is to have every warp end the same length and held at uniform tension. In essence, you need only establish a constant distance—such as the distance between two chairs or around a table top—and wind the yarn around and around until the proper number of warp yarns have been measured. Early weavers wound their yarns around rows of sticks driven into the ground at fixed intervals. Modern warping equipment is not necessarily any more precise, but it eliminates a good deal of walking.

A warping device has two functions: (1) it aids in holding the yarns taut, so that each warp is exactly the same length; and (2) it permits the establishment of the *cross*, the point at which the yarns intersect from opposite directions to maintain their proper sequence throughout the loom-dressing operation. The most common warping aids are the *frame* and the *reel* (Figs. 163–165). The reel is more expensive, but it will measure very long warps—greater than 12 yards, which the frame usually cannot. The warping reel can have either a vertical or a horizontal drum to accept the yarn. Since the reel rotates, the operator stands in one spot to manipulate the drum and the yarns. The warping frame can be either a solid board or a four-sided frame with pegs protruding from it. The pegs must be set into the frame securely enough to prevent their turning inward from the tension of the yarns, for if this occurs, the last warps will be somewhat shorter than the first.

Wrapping the Guide String

The procedures for wrapping the guide string on the reel and on the frame are similar.

Wrapping the Guide String: Warping Reel

□ Select a guide string made from stout cord in a color that contrasts with the warp.
□ Cut the guide string slightly longer than each warp yarn will be to allow for knotting at both ends.
□ Tie the string to the top peg of the reel.
□ Rotate the reel to the left, carrying the string down diagonally to the bottom series of pegs, so that there is just enough string to tie around the last peg at the bottom.
□ If the string is too long or too short, adjust the angle of descent until it fits perfectly.
□ Make sure the distance from the top to the last bottom peg is exactly the length of one warp.
□ Pass the guide string *under* the first peg and *over* the second peg, then tie it to the third (Fig. 176).
□ Push the guide string in close to the reel.

On a warping frame the pegs are a specified distance apart, often 1 yard. Instead of adjusting the angle of descent, as on the reel, you must

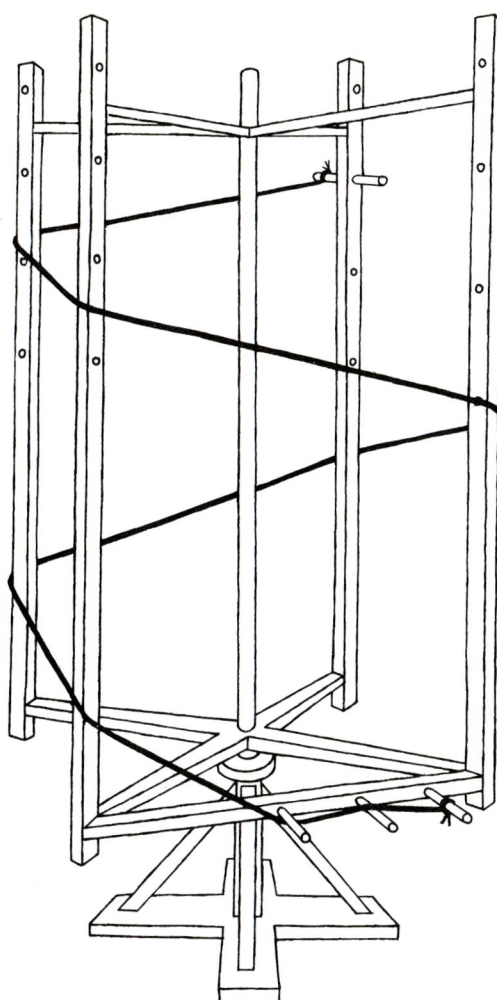

176–177. *The first step in measuring the warp before weaving is to affix a guide string, which establishes a path for the yarn to follow as it is wound on the reel or frame, so that the correct length can be measured.*

left: 176. On the warping reel, the guide string is tied to the uppermost peg and carried down diagonally to the bottom of the reel. The angle of descent is adjusted until the string is exactly the desired length of one warp yarn.

below: 177. On the warping frame, the guide string is initially tied to whichever peg is at a proper distance from the last cross peg to achieve one warp length. The distance between pegs is generally 1 yard.

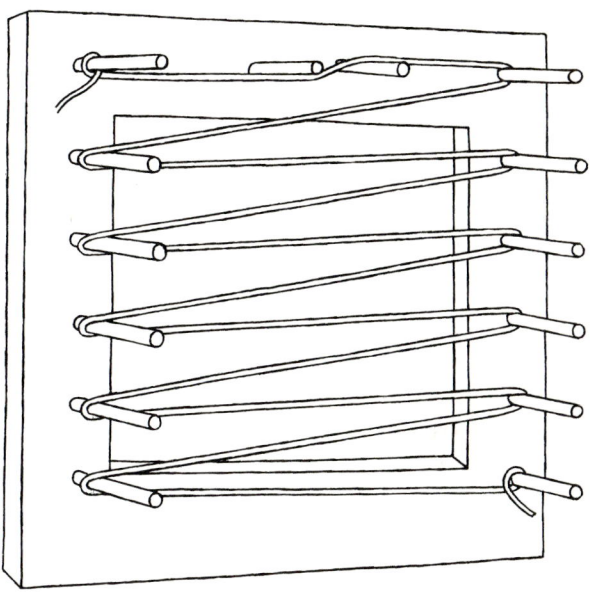

choose the number of pegs that will be involved. For example, the frame in Figure 177 is set up to hold the full 11 yards, which is all this frame can accommodate. If you wanted a warp 10 yards long, you would start at the next peg in sequence, and so on. (A longer warp would need to be measured on a reel.) The cross can be either at the top or at the bottom. Some weavers like to make a cross at *both* ends, to further control the yarns.

Wrapping the Guide String: Warping Frame

☐ Select a guide string made from stout cord in a color that contrasts with the warp.
☐ Cut the guide string slightly longer than each warp yarn will be to allow for knotting at both ends.
☐ Choose the peg at the proper distance from the last cross peg, and tie the cord around it.
☐ Zigzag the guide string back and forth across the frame until you reach the cross.
☐ If the cross is at the top, as in Figure 177, pass the string *over* the first peg, *under* the second, and tie it to the third. Reverse this procedure if the cross is at the bottom.
☐ Push the guide string in close to the frame.

Warping the Yarn

The yarn can now be warped, following the path of the guide string. Never wind the yarns on top of one another, but instead lay them as close together as possible on the pegs. It is most important that you maintain a smooth, even tension throughout the winding, so that all warps will be exactly the same length.

If possible, wind the entire warp on the same day, because atmospheric conditions can affect the tension. For example, rayon yarn stretches on damp days, so yarns warped when the humidity is high will be shorter than those measured on a dry day. Never leave wool yarns stretched on the warping frame or reel any longer than necessary, for continued tension may spoil their elasticity.

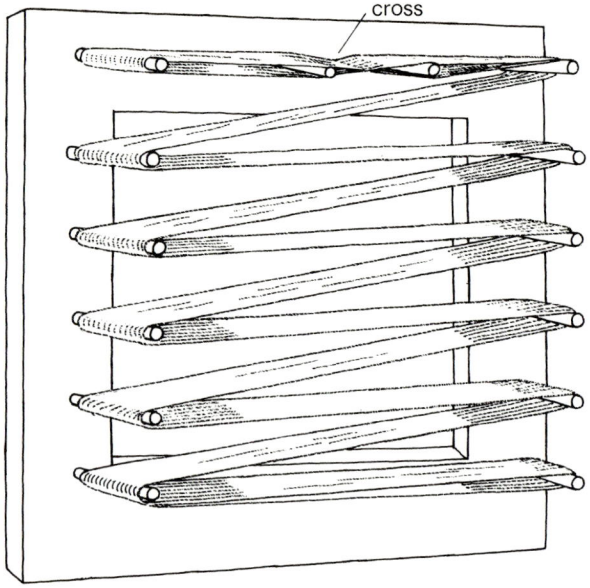

cross

178–179. *The cross is the point*
at which warp yarns intersect
from opposite directions as they are measured.
It maintains the sequence of yarns
throughout the loom-dressing operation.

left: 178. The warp has been properly wound
when every other yarn is crossed
and when each yarn has been placed
next to the previous one, with no overlapping.

below: 179. To establish the cross on the warping frame,
pass the yarn around peg A, over peg B,
under peg C, under and around peg D, over peg C,
under peg B, and over and around peg A.
The directions can be reversed if a cross
is to be made at the bottom of the frame.

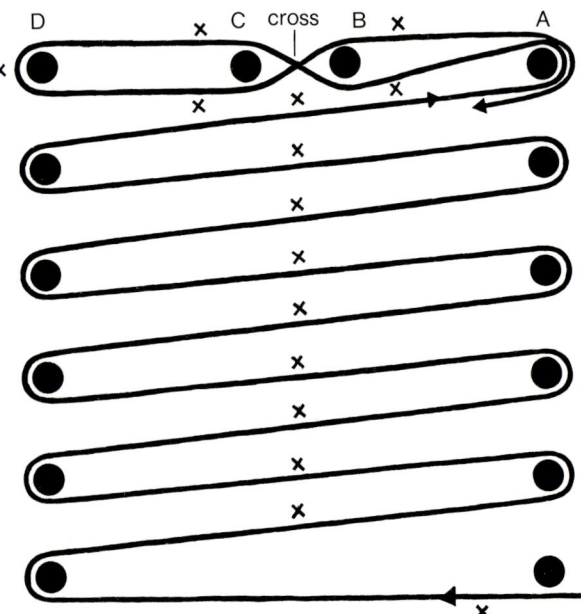

Warping the Yarn: Warping Reel
- Tie the yarn to the top peg on the reel (at the end opposite the cross).
- Following the route of the guide string, bring the yarn down to the bottom pegs (Fig. 176).
- Run the yarn *under* the first peg and *over* the second, then carry it *under* and around the final peg.
- On the return trip, pass the yarn *under* the center and left pegs.
- Continue back to the top of the reel. At this point two complete warp yarns have been measured.

Directions for warping on a frame assume that the cross will be at the top, as in Figure 178. If you prefer to have the cross at the bottom, turn the diagram over and reverse the instructions.

Warping the Yarn: Warping Frame
- Start the yarn at whichever peg is at the proper distance from the last cross peg.
- Following the guide string, zig-zag the yarn across the frame until it reaches the top.
- Following the diagram in Figure 179, pass the yarn around peg A, *over* peg B, *under* peg C, and *under* and around peg D.
- On the return trip, pass the yarn *over* peg C, *under* peg B, and *over* and around peg A.
- Continue back to the starting peg. At this point two complete warp yarns have been measured.

When the warp consists of more than one color or kind of yarn, tie each new yarn at the original starting peg. The yarn can be tied either to the peg itself or to the cut-off original yarn. If you plan to go back to the first yarn later on, you can wrap it around an unused peg to maintain the tension, then unwrap it when you need it. If the warp consists of an *un*even number of yarns, cut the final warp at the cross end of the frame and leave an allowance for tying to the loom.

Dressing the loom is easier when the center of the warp has been marked. Therefore, when half the total number of warp yarns have been wound, tie a cord around all the warps on the reel or frame. This tie is usually made near the cross and left in place when the yarn is taken from the frame.

Some weavers like to divide the warp into inch widths as they measure it. Let us say the sett is to be 10 warp yarns per inch. After you have wound 10 yarns onto the frame or reel (five round trips), drape a contrasting cord about a yard long over

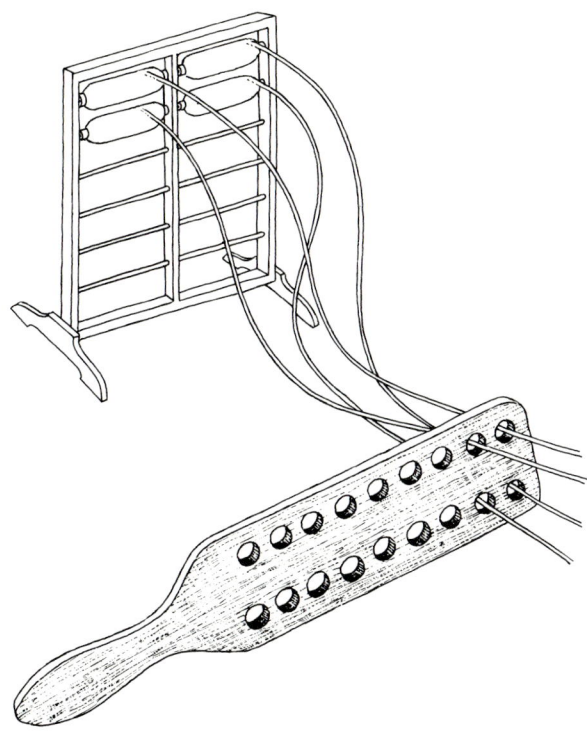

180–185. *Paddle warping is a process by which you can measure up to twenty yarns simultaneously on a warping frame or reel, making full provision for the cross. It is particularly efficient when the warp consists of a sequence of yarns.*

above: 180. To begin paddle warping, arrange the spools of yarn in correct order on the spool rack, then thread them through the paddle in the same sequence.

the yarns at the bottom, and cross the cord underneath. When you have wound another group of 10 yarns, cross the counting cord again, and so on. After all the warp has been measured, tie the counting cord and cut off the excess. (If you do not divide the yarn during warping, you can count it out while dressing the loom.)

In cases where an unusually large number of warp yarns are required, you will have to measure the warp in bouts of about 100 yarns to make handling easier and to prevent the yarns from falling off the pegs. An even number of bouts will automatically indicate the center.

If the warp yarns are consistent in color, texture, and size, an experienced winder can measure from as many as three yarn sources at the same time, thus cutting the warping time to one-third. Feed the yarn from spools in such a way that each strand passes between two fingers. Every point at the cross will then have three yarns over and three under. Groups of four or more yarns require a paddle.

Paddle Warping In some cases it is desirable to measure yarn from a number of sources at once. This is true when the warp is composed of four or more kinds or colors of yarn in consecutive order. Ordinarily, such a pattern would require that each yarn be cut and tied independently. The warping paddle avoids this problem.

The warping paddle is an oblong tool made of wool, metal, or plastic, with a handle and about 20 numbered holes. With the paddle held upright (handle down), the odd-numbered holes are on the left, the even on the right.

Paddle Warping

□ Establish the sequence in which the yarns are to be placed on the loom, in a repeat of up to 20 yarns.

□ Arrange the spools of yarn on a spool rack (Fig. 180), with the odd-numbered yarns on one side, the even-numbered yarns on the other.

□ Thread the yarns through the paddle in order (Fig. 180), with yarn number 1 through hole number 1, and so on.

□ Tie the yarns together, and slip the knot over the starting peg on the frame or reel.

□ Hold the paddle between the thumb and forefinger, allowing the yarn to run between the ring finger and the little finger.

□ Warp as usual until you reach the cross.

□ At the first cross peg, tip the paddle so that the even-numbered yarns go *over* the peg and the odd-numbered yarns run *under* it (Fig. 181).

□ At the second peg, lift the odd-numbered yarns by hand to go over the peg, and let the even yarns run underneath (Fig. 182), thereby establishing the cross.

□ Let all yarns pass over and around the third peg (Fig. 183).

□ On the return trip, turn your wrist to the right, so that the odd-numbered yarns are uppermost.

□ At the middle peg, the number of yarns in the paddle governs the procedure. If you are winding an *even* number of yarns, let the odd-numbered yarns float over the peg and the even-numbered yarns beneath (Fig. 184). If the number of yarns in the paddle is *uneven*, lift the even-numbered yarns over the peg by hand, and let the odd-numbered yarns move below.

□ Reverse this procedure at the third peg (Fig. 185).

□ Continue warping as usual.

Preparation for Weaving **115**

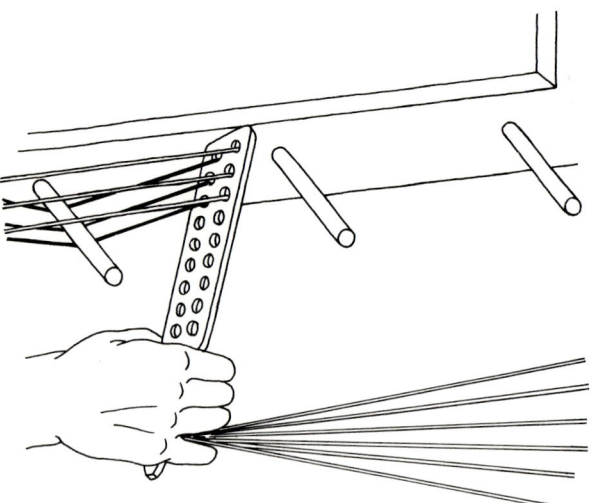

181. At the first cross peg, tip the paddle, so the even-numbered yarns float over, the odd-numbered yarns under.

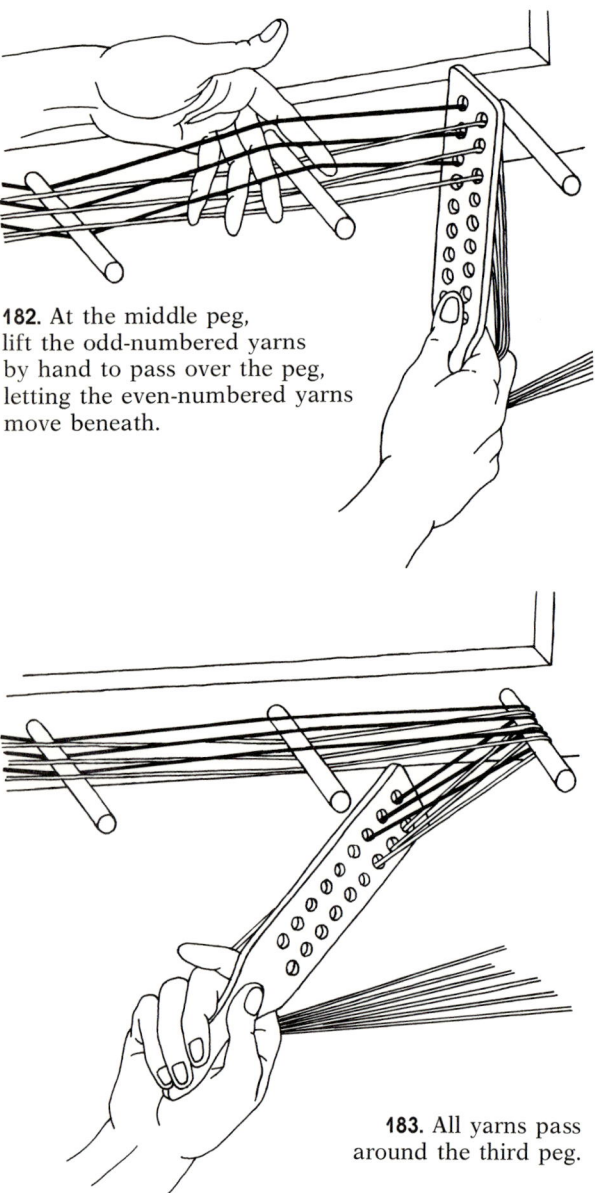

182. At the middle peg, lift the odd-numbered yarns by hand to pass over the peg, letting the even-numbered yarns move beneath.

183. All yarns pass around the third peg.

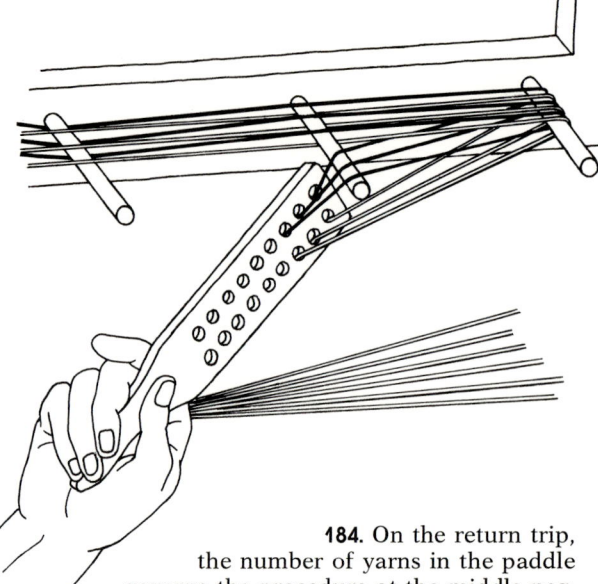

184. On the return trip, the number of yarns in the paddle governs the procedure at the middle peg. If you are winding an *even* number of yarns, let the odd-numbered yarns float over the peg, the even-numbered ones beneath. If the number of yarns is *uneven*, lift the even-numbered yarns over the peg.

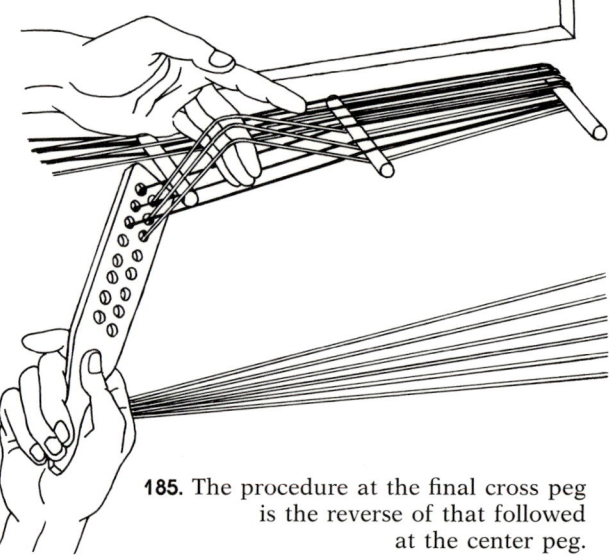

185. The procedure at the final cross peg is the reverse of that followed at the center peg.

If you wish, you can make a second cross at the opposite end of the frame or reel, between the last two pegs. This will let you see at a glance how many units you have wound, and it also helps in dressing the loom. The second cross is made with the entire group of yarns together.

Securing the Ties

When the entire warp—or one complete bout of warp yarns—has been measured, you must fasten a series of ties in order to hold the yarns in proper sequence for removal to the loom (Figs. 186, 187).

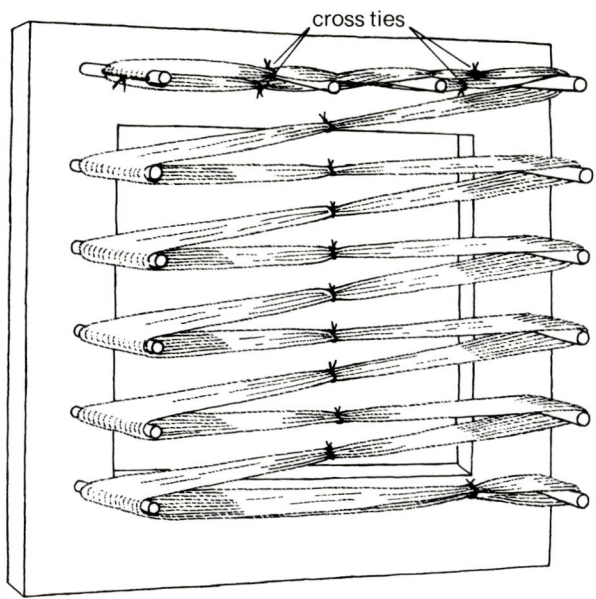

186. The arrangement
of choke ties and cross ties
on a warping frame.

The most important of these are the *lease ties* or
cross ties, which should be made with contrasting
cord so they can be found easily. The cross ties
will maintain the cross until the lease sticks are
inserted (Fig. 189). Therefore, the tie must be secure but need not wrap tightly around the yarns.

In addition to the cross ties, a series of *choke
ties* must be fastened around the yarn to hold the
strands in the same relative positions. These ties
must be wrapped very tightly around the yarn.
Make the first choke tie at the loop on the final
cross peg—the point at which one warp ends and
another begins. Place a second tie about a yard
from the cross, and space the others at intervals of
1 yard. Make the last tie close to the starting peg.

Chaining the Warp

As you remove the yarn from the reel or warping
frame, you must maintain tension to prevent the
strands from tangling. If you are using a reel,
which revolves freely, you should brace it with the
knee or shoulder. Grasp the yarn firmly at the
point of the last choke tie, and remove the peg to
free the yarn. Some weavers cut the yarn at this
point, but if you leave a looped end until the warp
is wound onto the loom, differences in length will
adjust themselves.

Beginning at the starting peg, loop the warp
upon itself as though you were crocheting (Fig.
188) until the entire warp is chained. The warp is
now ready for the loom.

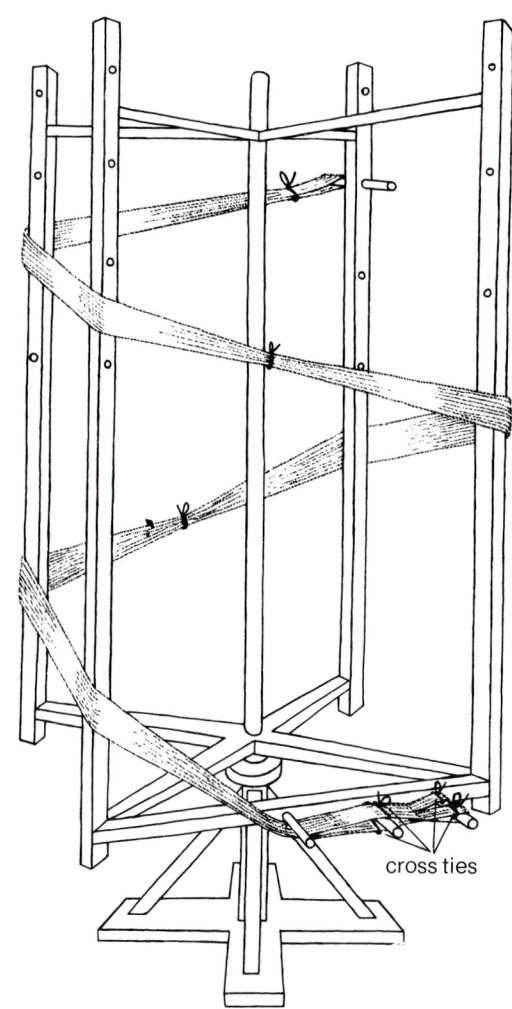

above: 187. The arrangement of choke ties
and cross ties on a warping reel.

below: 188. As you remove the yarn
from the warping frame or reel, loop it
upon itself in the manner of crocheting.
This is called *chaining.*

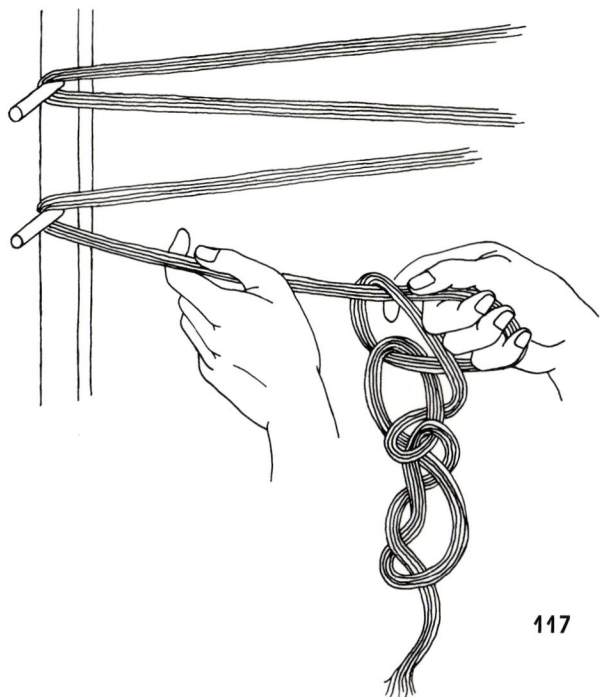

117

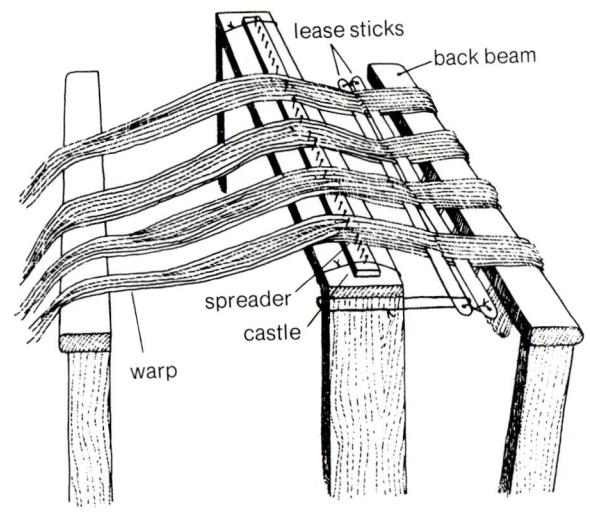

lease sticks

back beam

spreader

castle

warp

189–192. *The term "dressing the loom" is applied to all the preparatory stages involved in setting up the warp for weaving.*

left: 189. Tie the spreader securely to the castle, and insert the lease sticks at either side of the cross. A loose tie connects the two lease sticks, another affixes them to the castle at the back of the loom.

Dressing the Loom

There are almost as many ways of dressing a loom as there are weavers. A procedure that is convenient for one individual may prove awkward for another. The method described on the following pages is certainly not *the* correct way to dress a loom, but if you follow it carefully, you will have a warp that is properly distributed and held under consistent tension. These are always the two most important considerations in dressing the loom. After you have mastered the basic concepts of loom dressing, you may want to experiment with other variations or with methods more convenient for your own loom.

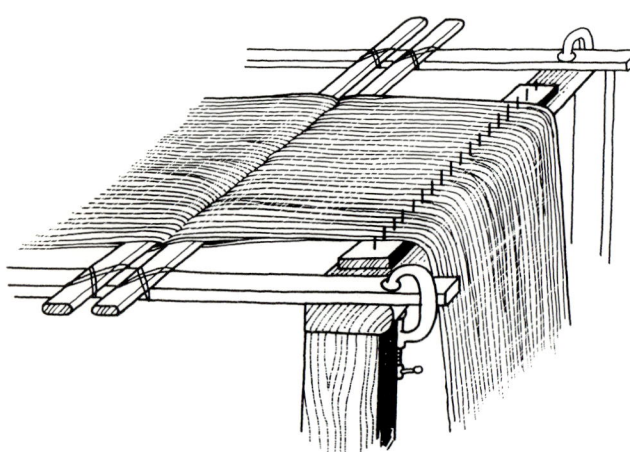

above: 190. On a counterbalance loom, the spreader can be lashed or clamped to the back beam, or to lary sticks lashed between the breast and back beams.

below: 191. A yarn that floats free of both lease sticks can be controlled with a loop of cord.

Placing the Warp Yarns on the Loom
□ If possible, remove the beater frame from the loom, so that it is out of the way temporarily.
□ Place the spreader on the loom, with the nails facing up and the center nail precisely in the middle of the loom (Fig. 189). If the loom has a low castle, the spreader can be fastened there. Otherwise, set lath sticks between the breast and back beams, and clamp the spreader to them (Fig. 190).
□ Drape the chained warp carefully over the spreader, with the looped end near the cross hanging toward the back of the loom and the other ends (cut or uncut) toward the front.
□ If the yarn was wound in bouts, arrange them on the loom in their proper sequence.

Inserting the Lease Sticks

Insert the two lease sticks at either side of the cross, as in Figures 189 and 190. Tie the sticks together, allowing about an inch of space between them. Tie one of the sticks to the back of the loom from the castle. Remove the cross ties.

If you have inserted the lease sticks properly, every warp yarn should be under one stick and

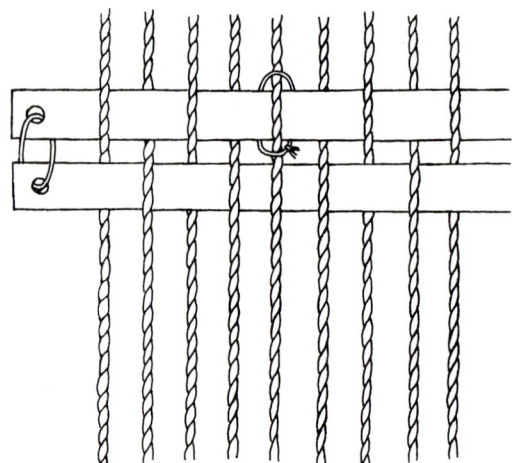

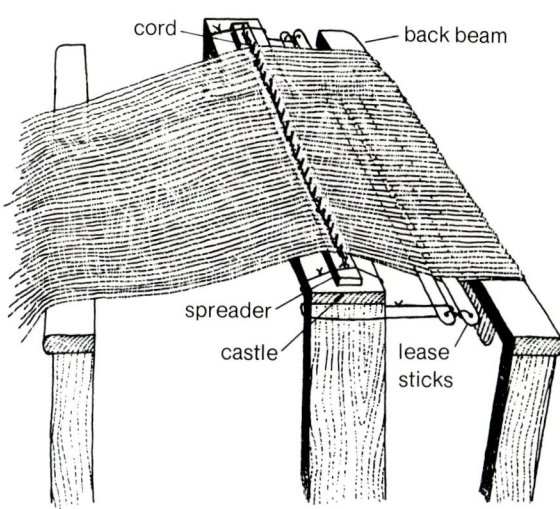

right: 192. The warp yarn is centered on the loom and distributed in inch widths across the spreader.

over the other. However, it is not uncommon, especially with beginning weavers, to find a yarn or two that floats free of the lease sticks—in other words, a yarn that moves under both sticks or over both. This means, of course, that the cross was not made correctly for that particular circuit on the warping frame. When a free yarn is discovered, you should try to locate the position in which it belongs, especially if there is a color or texture sequence in the warp. After you have found the spot, tie a cord loosely around the delinquent yarn and the lease stick (Fig. 191), letting the yarn flow freely but controlling its location in the warp.

Spreading the Warp

The next step is to spread the warp evenly across the loom. Two considerations are important in spreading. First, the warp should be centered exactly on the loom. Second, the number of warp yarns equivalent to an inch of fabric should be placed between each pair of nails (Fig. 192). For example, if the warp is to be sleyed at 10 ends per inch, 10 yarns will be laid in each space. (The equivalent is 4 yarns per centimeter.)

Spreading the Warp

☐ Unchain a sufficient amount of warp to reach over and beyond the spreader.
☐ Find the center nail on the spreader.
☐ Count a number of spaces to one side of the center nail equal to half the inch width of the warp. *Example:* If the warp is to be 36 inches wide, count to the 18th space either left or right of center.
☐ Mark this starting point with a pencil or a piece of tape.
☐ Lay the first inch group of yarns in the starting space. If you used a counting cord, insert the first group separated by the cord. If not, count the yarns individually, choosing first a yarn from one side of the cross, then a yarn from the other side.
☐ Continue across the spreader, laying inch widths in each space, until all the yarn is spread evenly.
☐ Wrap a cord figure-8 fashion around the tops of the nails to prevent the yarns from slipping off and getting out of sequence.

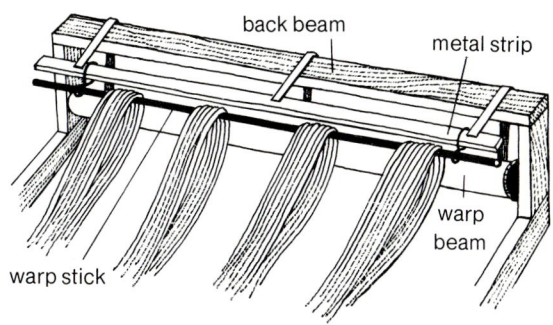

below: 193. Table looms often have a metal strip attached to the warp beam. A rod or stick passed through the loop in the warp yarns can be overcast to this strip.

Attachment to the Warp Beam

The looped end of the yarn must now be attached to the warp beam. The method of attachment depends upon how the loom is equipped. Possibilities include a warp stick and a metal strip (common on table looms); a metal rod and cords; a metal rod and an apron; or simply cords affixed to the warp beam.

Attachment to Warp Beam: Metal Strip

☐ Insert the warp stick or metal rod in the looped end of the yarn (Fig. 193), and tie it temporarily to the back beam.
☐ Distribute the yarns evenly over the stick so they are running in straight parallel lines to the spreader.
☐ Bring the metal strip up over the back beam toward the center of the loom.
☐ Tie the metal strip at both ends to the warp stick (Fig. 193).
☐ Overcast the warp stick to the metal strip with a double length of strong cord, making frequent passes between the warp yarns.

Preparation for Weaving **119**

Attachment to Warp Beam: Metal Rod and Cords

- Insert the warp stick or metal rod in the looped end of the yarn, and tie it temporarily to the back beam.
- Distribute the yarns evenly over the stick so they are running in straight parallel lines to the spreader.
- Find the center of the warp mass, and choose the cord that is attached to the center of the warp beam.
- Pass the center cord over the metal rod between the warp yarns, run it out through the warp loops to the end of the rod, and slip it over the end in a lark's-head knot (Fig. 194). Bring the end of the cord back to its position at the center of the warp.
- Working out from the center to first one side and then the other, insert the remaining cords into the warp at regular intervals in the same manner.

Attachment to Warp Beam: Metal Rods and Apron

- Insert the warp stick or metal rod in the looped end of the yarn, and tie it temporarily to the back beam.
- Distribute the yarns evenly over the stick so they are running in straight parallel lines to the spreader.
- Bring the apron, with a second warp stick running through it, up over the back beam toward the center of the loom.
- Tie the two warp sticks together at each end, and then lace them together along their lengths with heavy cord (Fig. 195).

Attachment to Warp Beam: Cords Only

- Divide the mass of warp yarns into segments according to the spacing of the cords on the warp beam (Fig. 196). *Example:* If the cords appear at intervals of 2 inches, and the warp is set at 10 ends per inch, 20 warps would be tied to each cord.
- Gather each segment of warps in an overhand knot.
- Tie each cord to the warp segment with a lark's-head knot (Fig. 194).

194. The lark's head knot serves many purposes in weaving.

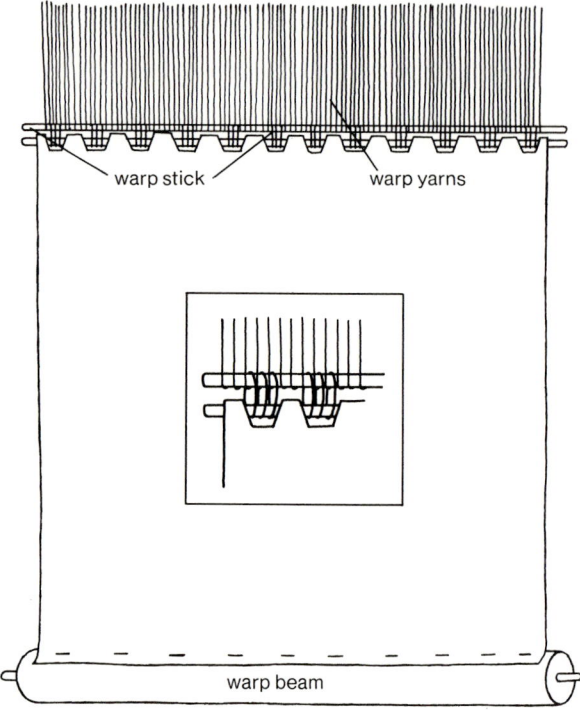

above: **195.** Most floor looms have a metal warp stick joined either by cords or by a canvas apron to the warp beam. Distribute the warp yarns evenly on a separate warp stick, then overcast the two warp sticks together, as the detail shows.

below: **196.** When no warp stick is provided, small bouts of warp yarn can be tied to the beam cords.

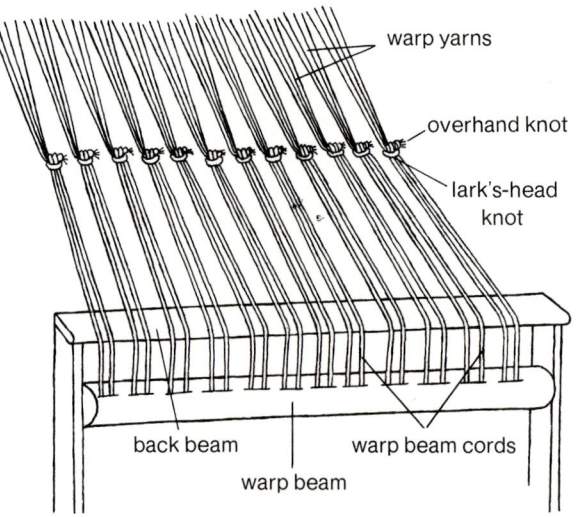

Winding the Warp (Beaming)

Several considerations must be borne in mind as the yarn is wound onto the warp beam, a process often called *beaming*. Excessive handling should be avoided, for it will not only soil the yarns but may tangle them and make them fuzzy. The warp must be wound onto the beam at precisely the width to be sleyed at the reed. Most important, the tension of all the yarns must be consistent, so that none will sag in relation to the others.

A pileup of yarns in certain areas will result in irregular tension as the warp unwinds from the beam. To prevent this, a padding of paper or some other material is usually inserted between layers of yarn on the warp beam. The padding may be pieces of wrapping paper or corrugated paper (Fig. 197). When paper is used, it is cut to the width of the warp beam. A 1-inch fold at each of the outer edges will prevent the yarn from slipping off the paper. Insert the paper at the point where the yarn meets the warp beam. As the yarn is wound

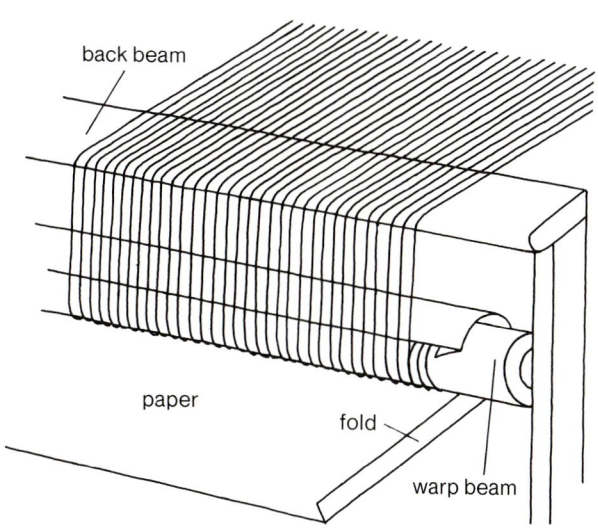

197–199. *Beaming is the process of winding the warp onto the warp beam.*

right: 197. As the warp is beamed, a padding should be inserted between the layers of yarn to prevent bunching and to maintain an even tension.

below: 198. The beaming operation on a floor loom is easier if you have an assistant to hold the yarns and regulate warp tension while you turn the crank.

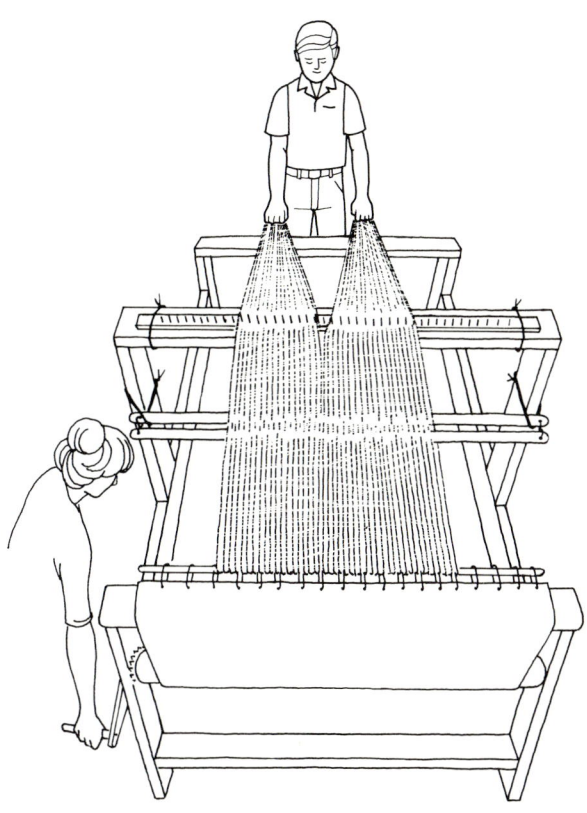

around the beam, it holds the paper in position. Wooden lath sticks (1 by ¼ inch) can be substituted for paper, in which case they are placed against the warp beam and, again, held in place by the yarn. Space the sticks fairly close together for the first revolution of the warp beam, but after that one or two sticks per layer should be sufficient. The sticks should be laid directly on top of one another to avoid creases.

Winding the warp is much easier if you have an assistant to hold the yarns (Fig. 198). This is especially true if the warp is very long or wide, or if it is composed of wool yarns or very fine yarns. The holder should have some knowledge of weaving, in order to understand the importance of maintaining a constant tension. The holder can also deal with any problems that may arise at the front of the loom, while the winder concentrates on the back of the loom.

It is fairly easy for anyone but the novice to wind a table loom without assistance. The winder stands to one side of the loom, holding the yarn in one hand and turning the crank with the other. At any time the unwound yarn can be laid down so that both hands are free to deal with whatever difficulties may present themselves.

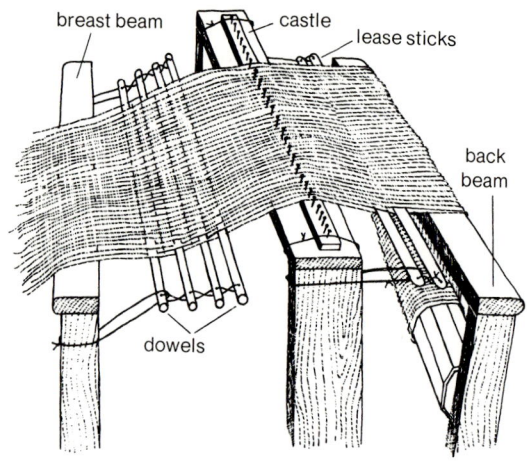

breast beam · castle · lease sticks

back beam

dowels

199. When no holder is available,
you can equalize tension in the warp by inserting
a series of dowels at the front of the loom.

the breast beam. Never attempt to comb through
the yarns with your fingers, for this will spoil the
tension. Instead, separate tangled yarns individually. When 8 to 10 inches of warp hang down over
the castle, winding is complete. The spreader can
now be removed and the yarn dropped down between the castle and the lease sticks.

Sectional Warping

Sectional warping is a process by which the warp
yarns are wound directly from spools onto the
warp beam of the loom. Most of the steps described above—measuring the yarn on a warping
frame or reel, chaining the warp, inserting lease
sticks, spreading the yarn—are bypassed. Special
equipment is required for this method: a pegged
or sectional warp beam, a spool rack, and usually
a tension box. Sectional warping is feasible only
when rather long warps are required.

A sectional warp beam is divided, by means of
pegs, into 2-inch segments. It is generally designed
to hold 1 yard of warp yarn per revolution (although this does not take into consideration the
pileup of yarns on the beam). In order to wind
directly onto the beam you must have on hand a
sufficient number of spools of the warp yarn to fill
one section of the beam. For example, if the warp
is set at 20 ends per inch, a total of 40 spools would
be required.

With a floor loom, the winder may find it impossible to select a convenient position to hold the
warps under tension and at the same time reach
the winding apparatus. Some weavers solve this
problem by inserting a series of smooth, narrow
lath sticks or dowels in the warp at the front of the
loom in positions comparable to those occupied
by the lease sticks (Fig. 199). These rods help to
equalize the tension of the warps as they move
through the loom. They should be sanded and
waxed to make them slide more easily through
the yarn.

As the winding proceeds, remove the choke ties
and unchain the warp at the point where it
reaches the breast beam. The lease sticks serve as
general combs, and the spreader functions as a
distributor, controlling the position of each warp
in relation to the mass of warps. Tangles can be
avoided by shaking the yarn or slapping it against

*200–201. Sectional warping
is a process by which warp yarns
are wound from a spool rack
directly onto the warp beam
of the loom, thus bypassing
the warping frame.
A sectional warp beam
and a tension box are needed
for this operation.*

right: 200. Warp yarns are fed
from a spool rack through
the tension box and attached
to the warp beam
in the order in which
they will appear in the web.
The entire warp length
is wound on one section
of the beam at a time.

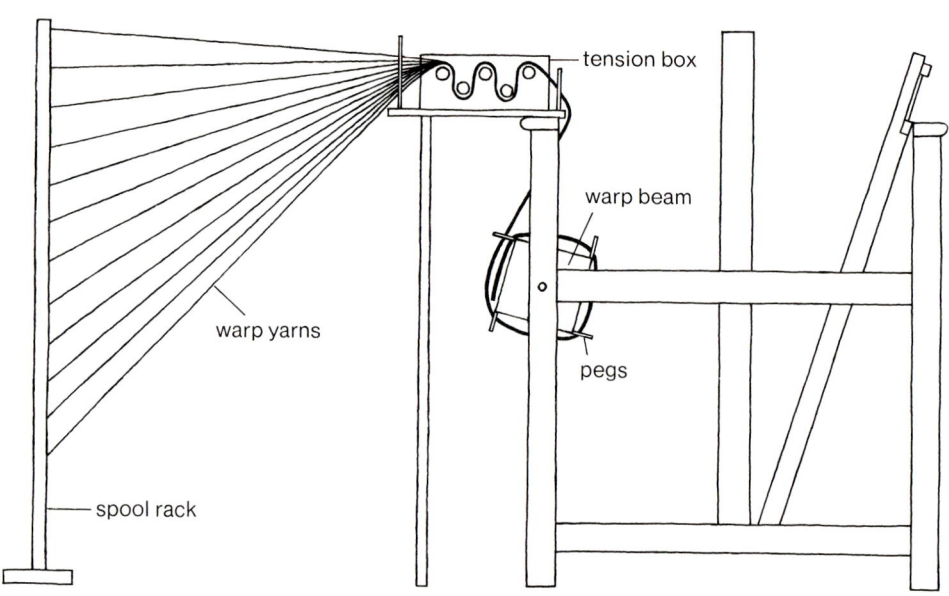

tension box

warp beam

warp yarns

pegs

spool rack

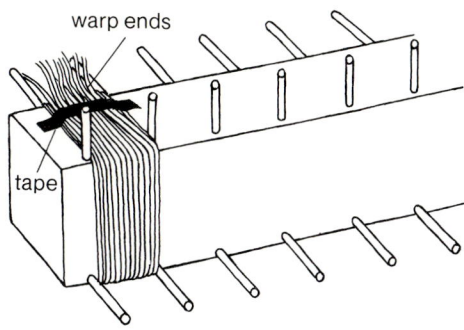

201. After one section has been wound, fix a strip of tape across the yarns, and cut the ends behind the tape. Then proceed to the next section, and so on across the beam.

Sectional Warping

☐ Arrange the spools of yarn on the spool rack in the order in which they will appear in the warp.

☐ Thread the yarns through the tension box in the same order.

☐ Attach the yarns emerging from the tension box to the first section of the warp beam, keeping them in their proper sequence (Fig. 200).

☐ Rotate the beam until the proper length of yarn has been wound.

☐ Fix a strip of masking tape tightly across the yarns, and cut the ends directly behind the tape (Fig. 201).

☐ Proceed across the loom, section by section, being sure to rotate the beam always in the same direction. Count the number of turns carefully, so that all warp yarns are the same length. (Some looms have automatic counters.)

☐ When all sections have been wound, remove the tape and bring the yarns in sequence over the back beam toward the center of the loom.

Threading the Heddles

In preparation for threading the heddles, the breast beam should, if possible, be removed to permit you to sit as close as possible to the harnesses. A low stool can be placed over the treadles so that the heddles are more or less at eye level. The beater frame is still off the loom, and the warp ends are hanging down between the spreader and the harnesses. The lease sticks remain in position,

so that the yarns can be taken in exact sequence. (If the warp ends were measured two at a time on the warping frame, resulting in two yarns over and two yarns under the cross, it does not matter which you take first, as long as you avoid excessive twisting. Of course, if there is a color sequence you must maintain it.

The first step in the threading operation is to make sure there are a sufficient number of heddles on each harness. Although it is not impossible to add a heddle or two at a later point, additions are much easier before threading begins. Metal heddles are correctly positioned if they nest inside each other when pushed together tightly on the frame. Instructions for making a string heddle appear on page 93.

The number of heddles required for a particular web is determined by the sett of the warp and the pattern to be woven. A pattern is normally broken down into units, which are repeated across the loom until all the warps have been accounted for. Figure 202 illustrates one unit of design for the *honeycomb* pattern, a 12-warp unit requiring 3 heddles on each frame of a 4-harness loom. If there were to be 20 units of design across the web (making a total of 240 warp yarns), each harness would require 60 heddles. Similar calculations would be made for different patterns. It is a good idea to record the proper number of heddles for each harness on a piece of masking tape and affix it to the harness for future reference.

Weavers differ on the order in which the heddles should be threaded. Some begin at the left, some at the right, and still others prefer to start at the middle and work to both sides alternately.

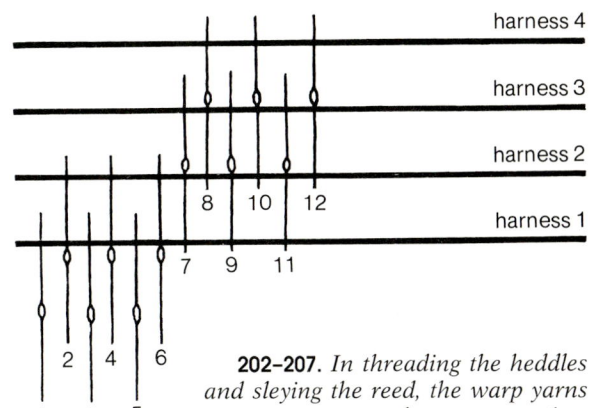

202–207. In threading the heddles and sleying the reed, the warp yarns are taken one at a time in the order in which they occur at the lease sticks.

above: 202. The honeycomb pattern is based on a unit of 12 warp yarns and requires three heddles on each frame of a 4-harness loom.

Beginning at the left is certainly a logical method, since the pattern is then read from left to right. However, any system that you find convenient and that results in the correct threading order will be fine.

The following directions are meant for right-handed people. Left-handed weavers should reverse them.

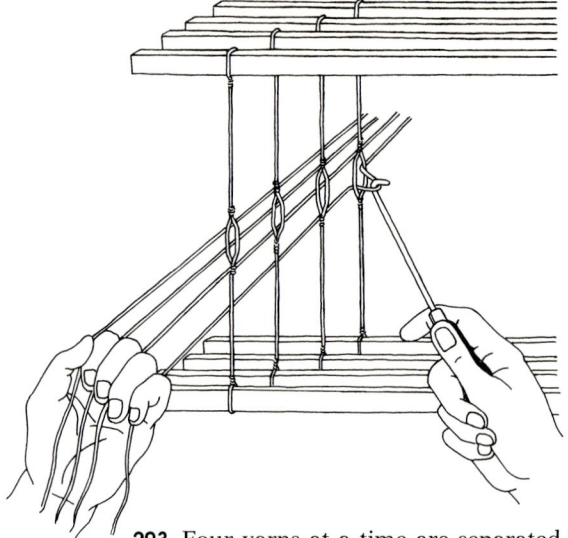

203. Four yarns at a time are separated from the mass of warp to pass through the fingers and be drawn, one by one, through the heddles with a crochet hook or a small sley hook.

Threading the Heddles

☐ If the ends of the warps were not cut upon removal from the warping frame, cut them now.

☐ Push the entire mass of heddles to the extreme right side of the frame.

☐ Separate the number of heddles required for one unit of design. *Example:* The honeycomb pattern shown in Figure 202 requires 12 heddles—3 on each frame.

☐ Select from the lease sticks the first 4 yarns at the left of the warp.

☐ Thread these 4 yarns through the fingers of the left hand (Fig. 203).

☐ With a sley hook or small crochet hook, draw yarn number 4 through heddle number 4, yarn number 3 through heddle number 3, and so forth.

☐ When you have threaded one complete unit of the design—or 8 ends at the most—tie the ends in a *slip knot* (Fig. 204), and let them hang down in front of the heddles.

☐ Repeat for each unit until all the warps have been threaded, checking frequently for errors and correcting them as you go along.

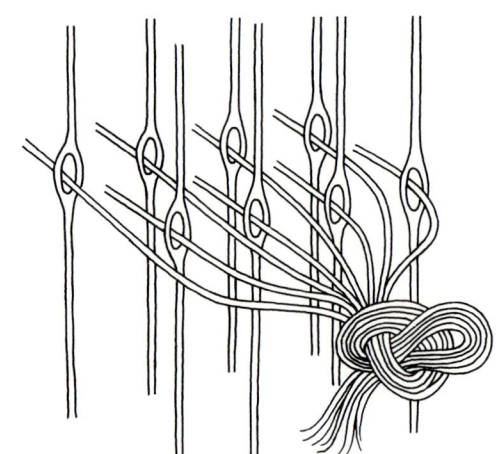

above: 204. After one complete unit of the pattern has been threaded through the appropriate heddles, tie the yarn ends in a slip knot to prevent them from falling out of the heddles and becoming entangled.

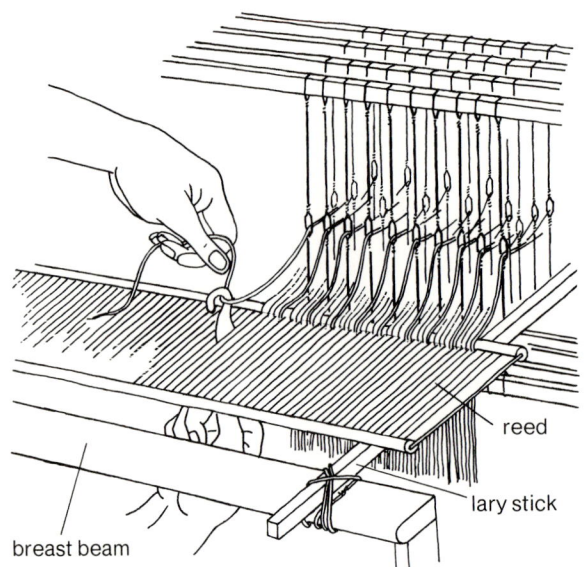

breast beam

reed

lary stick

left: 205. The reed is placed flat on two sticks tied between the breast beam and the back beam. The process of drawing warp yarns through the dents in the reed is called *sleying;* it can also be accomplished with the reed in position in the beater frame.

Sleying the Reed

The reed can be threaded either in position in the beater frame or flat on its side, supported at either end by a lengthwise rod (a *lary stick*) lashed to the back beam and breast beam (Fig. 205). If the first method is used, return the beater to the loom. To sley the reed flat, restore the breast beam.

As with the heddles, the direction of threading is a question of individual preference—right to left, left to right, or center to ends. Right-handed people often find it more comfortable to begin at the right-hand end.

Sleying the Reed

□ Mark the center of the reed so that, when all the yarns are sleyed, the warp will be exactly centered on the loom for balanced beating.

□ Take the yarns in precisely the same sequence as they occur in the heddles to avoid breakage.

□ Draw the yarns through the dents with a sley hook.

□ After each unit is sleyed, tie it with a slip knot to prevent the yarns from falling out of the reed.

The number of warp yarns to be threaded through each dent is determined by several factors: the weight of the warp yarn; the planned density of the fabric to be woven; the material chosen for the weft; the size of the reed; and the design of the fabric. Although it is a common practice to thread 1 or 2 yarns through each dent across the loom, many variations are possible.

The openings in the reed must, of course, be large enough to allow the yarns to flow freely. Therefore, the weight of the warp yarn tends to limit the fineness of the reed. Moreover, it is generally easier to sley 2 or 3 yarns per dent in a relatively coarse reed than to attempt threading a reed finer than 15 dents per inch. On the other hand, grouping yarns in a dent can cause tension problems. For the beginner, one yarn per dent is more comfortable. Sometimes 20- and 30-dent reeds *are* useful, but they require skillful manipulation. (The metric equivalent to a No. 15 reed has 6 dents per centimeter; anything finer than this would be difficult to handle.)

A ridged or shadowed effect can be obtained by grouping warps unevenly in the dents according to a planned sequence (Fig. 206). For example, you might sley 2 or 3 warps per dent for a space of 5 dents, then a single yarn per dent for the next 15 dents, and so on across the loom. Openwork fabrics may call for skipped dents, again in a certain order. When you choose bulky natural materials—such as cattails, branches, or corn husks—for the weft, occasional dents are skipped. By experimenting with different groupings, you can obtain a wide variety of effects.

When the reed has been sleyed, detach the lease sticks from the castle, and tie them loosely to the back beam. They remain in this position throughout the weaving operation. If you sleyed the reed in a horizontal position, resting on lary sticks, return the beater frame to the loom, set the reed into it, and remove the lary sticks. If you sleyed it vertically, in the beater frame, restore the breast beam.

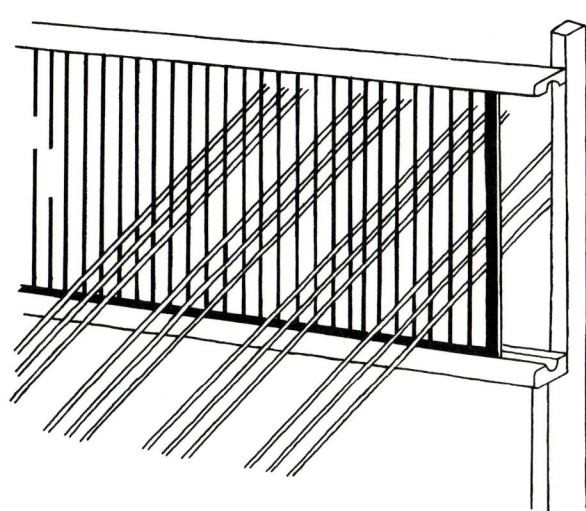

206. A ridged or shadowed web can be produced by grouping warp yarns unevenly in the reed.

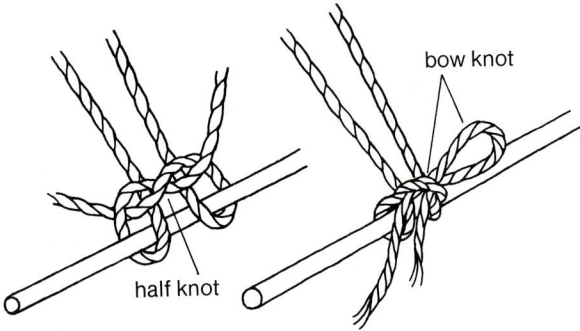

207. The warp yarns are tied to the cloth stick in two steps— first a half knot, then a bow knot.

Tying the Warp Ends at the Front of the Loom

The last step in the loom-dressing operation consists of tying the cut ends of the warp to the cloth beam at the front of the loom.

Tying the Warp Ends

□ Bring the cloth stick (attached by cords or an apron to the cloth beam) up and over the breast beam.

□ Beginning at the center, separate an even number of yarns (usually 6 to 8) and pull them forward.

□ Smooth the yarns, and carry them over and around the cloth stick.

□ Divide the group behind the cloth stick, carry the two sections around, and tie them in a half knot (Fig. 207).

□ Repeat this procedure with a group of yarns at the extreme left edge of the warp and another at the right edge.

□ Continue, alternating groups left and right of center, until all the warp yarns are tied to the cloth stick.

□ Test the warp with the side of your hand to make sure the tension is even throughout.

□ Make any adjustments necessary to equalize the tension.

□ Complete all the ties with a bow knot (Fig. 207).

If the warp yarns are tighter in the center of the loom than at the sides, the resulting web will form an arc, with the high part of the curve at the center. Conversely, if the tension is greater near the selvedges, the fabric will curve upward at the edges. For this reason, it is most important to have equal tension across the warp.

Checking the Loom for Errors

Even the most meticulous weaver will occasionally make a threading error. Common mistakes are:

□ a missed heddle
□ a missed yarn
□ crossed threads
□ too many yarns in one dent
□ a missed dent

If one heddle has been skipped during the threading process, the omission should be corrected before weaving begins. This is relatively easy when the warp is uniform. Set in a new yarn, the entire length of the warp, and thread it through the heddle and the appropriate dent, then tie it in with the proper group of yarns on the cloth stick. Wind the long end around a spool or similar object, and weight it at the back of the loom. A warp composed of different yarns would necessitate rethreading the heddles from the point of the error to the edge or removing one entire unit of the pattern. The latter would narrow the web.

When a yarn has been skipped in threading the heddles, it will not respond to any of the treadles. This situation can sometimes be corrected by removing the yarn altogether. However, if there is a definite threading pattern, a string or corrective heddle (Fig. 140) may have to be inserted.

Yarns that are crossed between the heddles and the reed or between the heddle frames must be rethreaded, for they will prevent a clean opening of the shed and will probably break. Untie the group of yarns containing the errant ones from the cloth stick, rethread the yarns properly, and then attach the entire group once more to the cloth stick in the usual manner.

If, in sleying the reed, you have skipped a dent or drawn too many yarns through a particular dent, you must resley the reed from the point of error to the nearest edge.

An Alternate Method for Dressing the Loom

Some weavers prefer to reverse the process described above and dress the loom from front to back. This method does not require a second person to hold the warp yarns. Instead, a series of dowels or sticks are inserted in the yarn at the front of the loom (Fig. 209), and these dowels comb the yarn and maintain the proper tension during the beaming process. (A second set of dowels can be inserted between the castle and the back beam if desired.) Holes drilled in the ends of the dowels make it easy to lace them together.

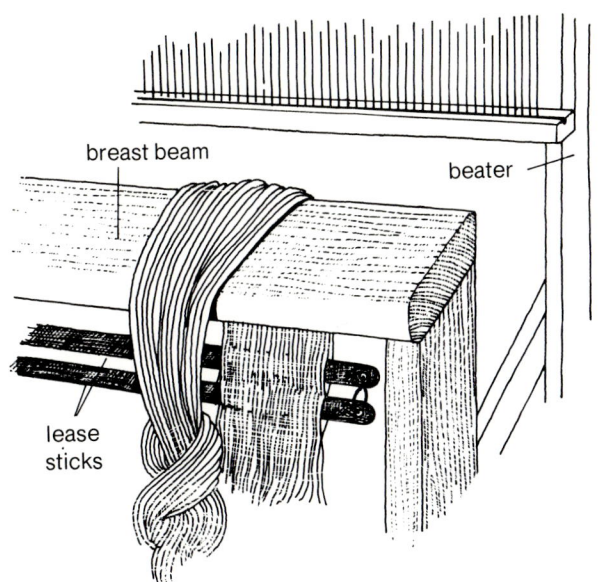

breast beam

beater

lease sticks

208–209. *Some weavers prefer to dress the loom from front to back. In this system, the reed is sleyed first, then the heddles are threaded before the warp is attached to the warp beam.*

left: 208. When the loom is dressed in this manner, the lease sticks are tied between the beater and the breast beam.

below: 209. In order to maintain uniform warp tension during beaming, insert a series of dowels in alternate plain-weave sheds at the front of the loom.

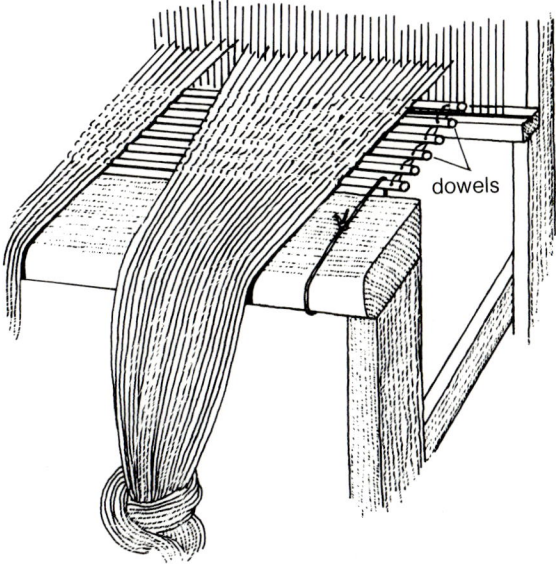

dowels

Alternate Loom-Dressing Method

- ☐ After the yarn has been warped, cut the ends that are near the cross.
- ☐ Insert the lease sticks in the cross, and tie them to the breast beam (Fig. 208), so that all the chained warp hangs down over the breast beam.
- ☐ Spread the yarns on the breast beam.
- ☐ Sley the reed, taking the yarns one at a time in order as they occur at the cross.
- ☐ Thread the heddles from the back of the loom.
- ☐ Attach the ends to the warp beam.
- ☐ If using a floor loom, complete the tie-up (see below).
- ☐ Hand-hold the yarn under sufficient tension to open a shed.
- ☐ Treadle (floor loom) or depress the levers (table loom) to raise harnesses 1 and 3. Insert a dowel in the shed.
- ☐ Treadle or depress the levers to raise harnesses 2 and 4. Insert another dowel in this shed.
- ☐ Continue alternating sheds until there are six or more dowels in position.
- ☐ Lace the dowels together, and tie them between the breast beam and the castle (Fig. 209).
- ☐ Wind the entire warp onto the warp beam.
- ☐ Tie the ends to the cloth stick.

The Tie-Up

The harnesses on a table loom are raised by a series of levers or keys on the right side of the loom or on the castle. Each lever is connected permanently to a single harness, and the weaver can depress one or more levers to create a shed. Once raised, the harnesses remain in position until the shed is changed. Thus, no tie-up is necessary. The instructions given below apply to the floor loom only.

Preparing the Tie-Up

The 4-harness foot-powered loom is equipped with 6 or more treadles connected by lamms to the harnesses. The floor loom differs from the table loom in that the connections are not permanent but can be varied to serve the needs of a particular weaving pattern. Therefore, the treadles must be

Preparation for Weaving **127**

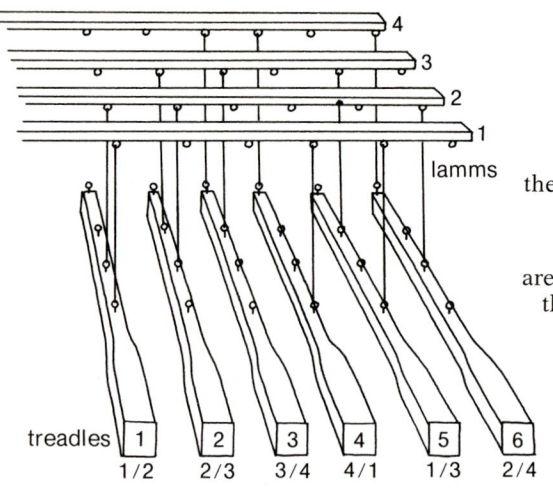

tied to the lamms for each web (Fig. 210). Although this further complicates the loom preparation, it gives the weaver a distinct advantage. Once the tie-up is complete, any desired shed can generally be produced by depressing only one treadle, whereas the same shed might require manipulation of two or three levers on the table loom. With warp yarns that tend to cling, however, it is sometimes useful to tie each treadle to an individual harness so that the harnesses can be treadled separately.

Most weavers establish a permanent numbering system for the harnesses, lamms, and treadles. It does not matter what order is used, as long as you are consistent. On a 4-harness loom it is common to number the harnesses and the lamms 1 through 4 from front to back, and the treadles 1 through 6 from left to right.

On a 4-harness loom it is possible to connect as many as three harnesses to the same treadle (four harnesses attached to the same treadle would raise all the yarns, so there would be no shed). In Figure 210 treadle 1 raises harnesses 1 and 2, treadle 2 raises harnesses 2 and 3, treadle 3 raises harnesses 3 and 4, treadle 4 raises harnesses 4 and 1, treadle 5 raises harnesses 1 and 3, and treadle 6 raises harnesses 2 and 4. This is the *standard tie-up*, which includes twill and plain weave. With it, six different sheds can be created by depressing one treadle at a time. Very complicated weaves sometimes require that two treadles be depressed simultaneously for a particular shed.

The harnesses on a floor loom remain in the raised position only as long as the treadle is depressed. When the foot is removed from the treadle, the harnesses drop and the shed is closed. For this reason, a treadling sequence that alternates

the left and right foot is the most efficient and provides for the steadiest rhythm.

As a rule, the treadles to the left of center (1 through 3) are depressed with the left foot, and those to the right of center (4 through 6) are operated with the right foot. A convenient treadling order might be from the outsides to the center (treadle 1, 6, 2, 5, 3, 4), from the center to the ends (treadle 3, 4, 2, 5, 1, 6), or from left to right (treadle 1, 4, 2, 5, 3, 6). The tie-up should be planned so that the sequence of sheds required by the pattern can be obtained from such a treadling order.

Plain weave or *tabby* (Fig. 234) requires only two treadles; harnesses 1 and 3 are attached to one treadle and 2 and 4 to another. When plain weave forms a significant part of a web, it is normally set up on the innermost treadles or at the right, as in Figure 210.

The method of attaching the lamms to the harnesses and the treadles to the lamms depends upon how the loom is equipped. Some looms have permanent metal connectors that are merely hooked in place. Others have cords with snap-locks on each end. When neither is provided, the cords must be tied individually. Slip one cord through the hole in the lamm and tie it in a half knot (Fig. 211). Double the treadle cord, and tie the cut ends in an overhand knot. Pass the looped end through the hole in the treadle. Fold the looped end over to form a lark's-head knot, and pass the knotted end of the lamm cord through this lark's-head. When the treadle is depressed, the half knot in the lamm cord will be pulled taut against the lark's-head knot in the treadle cord. The height of the lamm can be adjusted by tightening or loosening the half knot where it joins the lark's-head.

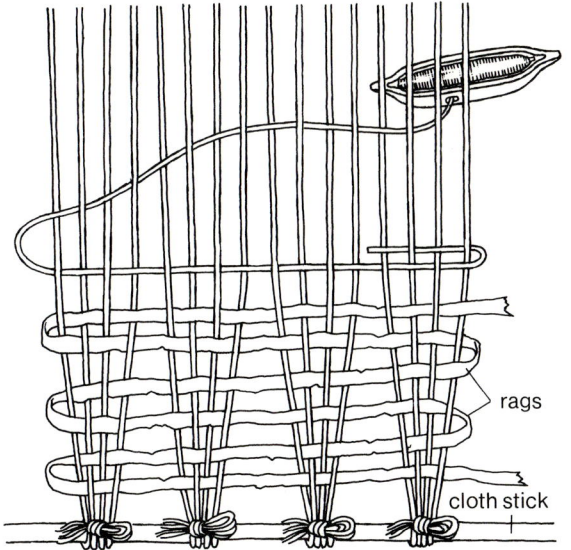

rags

cloth stick

212. Before weaving begins,
the warp yarns should be spread evenly
across the loom by inserting a few shots
of coarse material in alternate sheds.

213. The bobbin is filled with a hand-cranked winder.

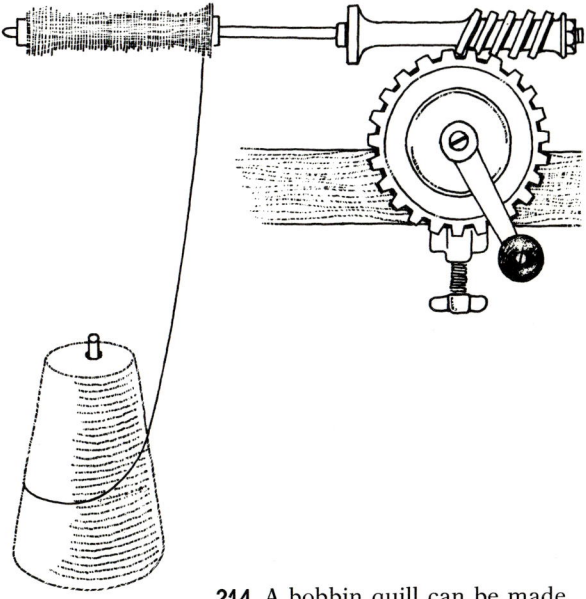

The Weaving Process

Adjusting the Loom

Before weaving can begin, certain minor adjustments must be made to ensure smooth operation of the loom.

Adjusting the Loom

□ Make sure the harnesses all hang at exactly the same height.

□ Adjust the lamms to be roughly parallel to the floor, with the ends connected to the treadles at the same distance from the floor.

□ Adjust the treadles to a height comfortable to you.

□ To spread the warp yarns evenly at the cloth stick, treadle for plain weave (harnesses 1-3 and 2-4 alternately) and insert $\frac{1}{4}$-inch dowels or strips of coarse material into the sheds (Fig. 212).

You can use paper, rags, or heavy carpet warp to spread the yarns. Three or four shots are usually enough to correct the alignment.

Filling the Shuttle

A stick shuttle—used for certain weaves or for unusually heavy weft yarns—must be filled by hand. However, a boat or throw shuttle containing a bobbin is best filled with a hand-powered or electric bobbin winder (Fig. 213). Bobbin quills made of plastic, wood, or cardboard can be purchased, but a homemade quill of sturdy wrapping paper will be satisfactory (Fig. 214). Cut the paper a bit shorter than the bobbin well in the shuttle

214. A bobbin quill can be made by rolling a small piece of paper into a tube and securing it with tape.

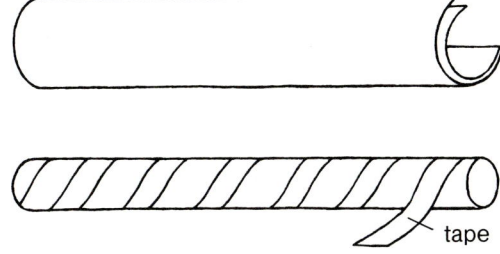

tape

and about 3 inches wide. Wind it into a fine cylinder—just large enough to fit over the bobbin winder—and secure it from top to bottom with transparent tape.

A properly wound bobbin is firm and even. Whether you use an electric or a hand-cranked bobbin winder, one hand must be kept free to guide the yarn onto the quill, thus maintaining a uniform tension. Begin winding by making a small mound of yarn at one end of the quill, then guide

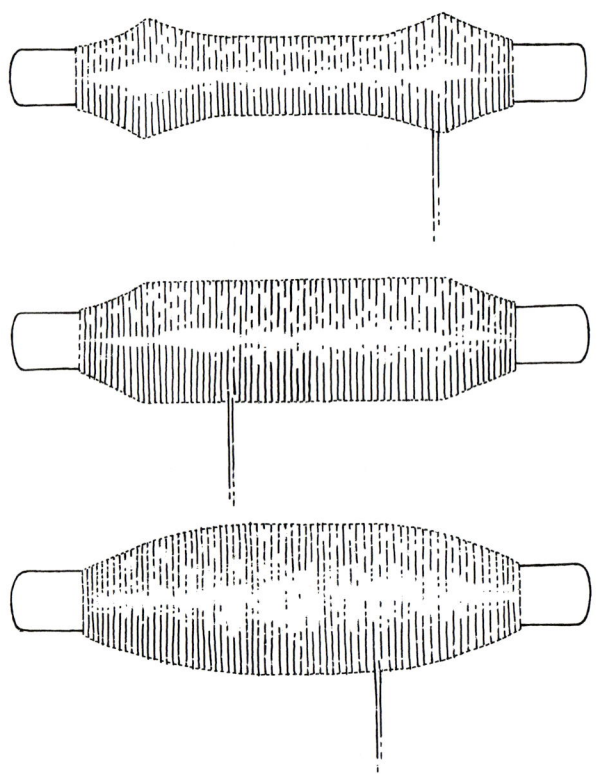

215. The bobbin should be filled first at the two ends and then in the center.

the yarn to the other end to make another small mound. Fill in the middle section of the quill last (Fig. 215).

Weaving the Web

In essence, the weaving operation consists of four steps, the first three done in rhythmic sequence:

1. *Shedding,* the depression of a treadle or lever to open a shed.
2. *Picking,* or throwing the shuttle containing weft yarn through the open shed.
3. *Beating,* or packing the weft yarn against the finished portion of the web.
4. *Taking up and letting off,* the process of winding the warp forward onto the cloth beam as each section of the web is completed.

The Shedding Sequence　　It is customary to record the sequence of sheds (and therefore of treadles or levers) required by a particular web on a piece of tape or paper and to affix it to the loom. For very complicated weaves you may want to assign a code letter to a certain portion of the treadling sequence. For example, "A" might mean "treadle 1-6-3-4." This shorthand method of notation takes the burden off the weaver's memory.

Throwing the Shuttle　　As you throw the shuttle, a sufficient amount of yarn is automatically unwound from the bobbin to make the complete trip across the web. If thrown by the left hand, the shuttle is caught by the right, and the reverse. Pull the weft yarn snugly against the selvedge at the opposite side, but not so tightly that it will cause the web to draw in. Set in the new weft yarn at an angle to the packed filler (Fig. 216) to compensate for the weft takeup that occurs when the yarn is beat in.

Beating　　The appearance of the finished web is greatly affected by the force of the beating and the point at which the beater is pulled forward. Most often, the weft is beat in before the shed is changed or just as the shed is being changed. When the warp yarns tend to cling together (as some woolen yarns do), it may be necessary to change the shed before beating, to encourage the creation of a clean shed for the next shot. Very heavy fabrics, such as rugs, often need a double beating, once before and once after the shed is changed.

The force of beating depends entirely upon the fabric under construction. Heavy fabrics require a firm beating, while delicate or openwork webs are not really "beat" at all. Rather, the new weft yarn is placed gently in position by the beater. With practice, you will acquire a "feel" for the correct amount of force to be applied. Always grasp the beater in the center to ensure even packing. Uniform beating results in weft yarns that are perpendicular to the warp and are evenly distributed throughout the web.

216. Each new weft shot is set at an angle to the finished web to compensate for weft takeup. This prevents excessive draw-in of the fabric.

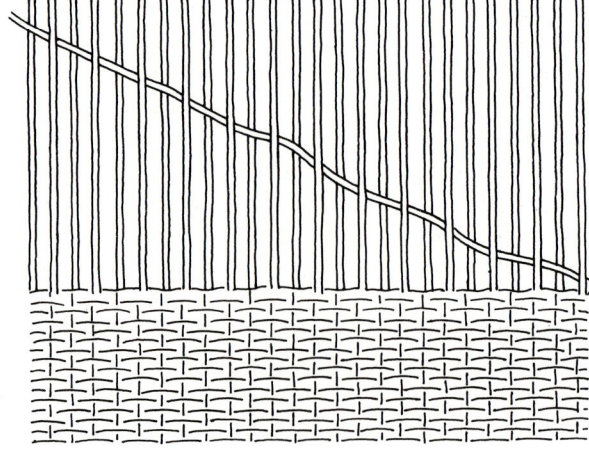

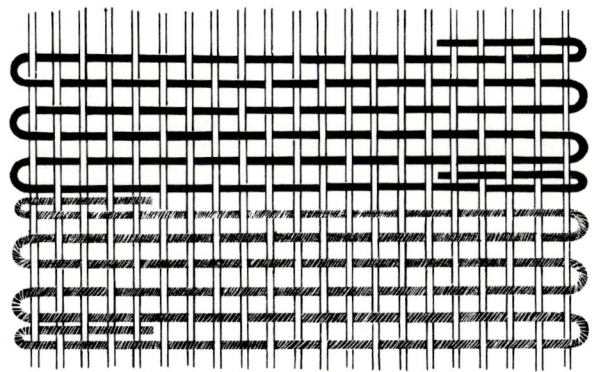

above: 217. When you start a new weft color, leave a tail from the previous color at the selvedge. This tail is wrapped once around the outside warp, then placed back in the same shed before beating.

below: 218. All weft yarns must be interlocked with the outside warp yarns at the selvedge. Sometimes it is easier to do this by weaving alternately with two shuttles.

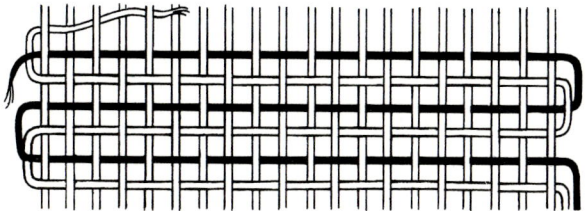

Taking Up and Letting Off   When the shed becomes so small that it is difficult to throw the shuttle easily, you must roll the warp forward onto the cloth beam. The processes of *taking up* finished cloth onto the cloth beam and *letting off* additional warp from the warp beam are done simultaneously. Each time the warp is moved, the overall tension must be adjusted. Only a small amount of warp is rolled forward at any one time, for if the edge of the web is too close to the breast beam or to the reed, the angle of beating will not be uniform all across the fabric.

Changing the Weft Yarns   A new weft yarn is begun when a different color or type of yarn is to be introduced or, in the case of a uniform web, when the supply of yarn on the bobbin has been used up. In either event, the change usually occurs at the selvedge.

When you want to start a new color in the web, leave a short tail of yarn from the first color dangling at the selvedge (Fig. 217). Wrap this tail once around the outside warp, then place it back in the *same* shed before the beater is pulled forward. Carry the tail across the web for a distance of a few warps, and bring it up between the warps. After a few shots of the new color have been inserted and beat in, cut off the protruding tail of

the first yarn cleanly. Follow the same procedure with a tail of the new yarn.

The method for changing shuttles in a uniform weft is similar, except that the tail of yarn remaining from the previous shuttle is inserted in the *next* shed, rather than the same one. Occasionally, when the shuttle empties in the middle of its passage across the web, you can overlap the old and new weft yarns inconspicuously at this point. This procedure is possible only with certain yarns; with others, the overlap would be obvious; the break must come at the selvedge.

Hemming the Start of the Web   In most cases the ends of the web are finished after the entire project has been woven (see Chap. 12). However, it is sometimes desirable to hem the starting edge of the web before it disappears onto the cloth beam, so that it will not unravel when the fabric is removed from the loom. Hemming is easier when the warp is under tension. At the outset of the weaving, let a 3-yard length of weft yarn dangle from the first shed. After you have woven about an inch of the web, thread the extra length of yarn through a needle, and hemstitch the edge of the fabric (Fig. 327).

Maintaining an Even Selvedge   A uniform selvedge forms a straight line parallel to all the warps. It has neither loops of weft yarn nor tightly drawn areas. Only practice will enable you to attain this goal. If the weft yarns are pulled too tightly at the edges, the web will draw in and narrow. This in turn will change the angle of the outside warps at the reed, creating excess friction and possible breakage. Insufficient tension of the warp yarns or inadequate beating may also cause the selvedges to pull inward. When you want an especially firm selvedge, you can thread two or more warp ends through a single dent at the edges of the fabric.

It is important to remember that *all* weft yarns must be interlocked with the warps at the selvedges. When you are weaving alternately with two shuttles, the yarn from one shuttle is always *over* the outside warp, and the yarn from the second shuttle is always *under* the outside warp (Fig. 218). In other words, if shuttle number 1 went *over* the outside warp, the wefts will interlock only if shuttle number 2 is carried *over* the weft of shuttle number 1 before being placed into the shed. Conversely, if shuttle number 1 went *under* the outside warp, shuttle number 2 must be placed *under* the weft of shuttle number 1 before being entered in the shed. All this takes much longer to say than to do, but Figure 218 should make it clear.

Some weaves, particularly certain twills (see p. 141), have a tendency to leave warp yarns floating at the selvedges. Using two shuttles and interlocking them at the edges may solve this problem. Straight twill will leave a skipped or floating warp at both selvedges unless the shuttle is carried from right to left on the 1-2 shed. (This assumes that the threading at the left edge is 1, 2, 3, 4, working from left to right.)

One method of keeping the selvedges even—especially in troublesome weaves—is to add an extra "guide" thread at both edges of the warp. The guide yarns are threaded through the reed but not through the heddles, so they remain in the middle of the shed. Each weft shot enters the shed *over* the guide yarn and emerges *under* the guide yarn at the other side. The guide yarns are therefore woven into the fabric, but they play no role in the pattern.

The Pick Count
The number of weft yarns per inch in a woven fabric is referred to as the *pick count*. In plain weave or one of its derivatives (see p. 139), a *balanced weave* (Fig. 219) has the same number of weft yarns per inch as warp yarns per inch. Two factors create this balance: The warp and weft yarns are of uniform size, and the beating is adjusted to allow for the required number of weft yarns per inch. An *unbalanced weave* (Fig. 220) has an unequal distribution of warp and weft yarns, with one or the other predominating.

A web in which the warp yarns predominate is called a *warp-face* fabric; when the weft yarns dominate the surface of the cloth or completely hide the warp, as in tapestry and some other pattern weaves, the fabric is referred to as *weft-faced*.

Protecting the Fabric on the Loom
When weaving is interrupted, it is a good practice to release the tension on the warp yarns. This is essential with wool or other elastic fibers that might lose their elasticity under prolonged stress. Some materials, including wool and linen, are best woven in a relatively damp room. If the atmosphere is very dry, a pan of water placed under the warp beam or a damp cloth over the beam itself will help to keep the warp moist. You can also spray a section of the warp with a plant mister. No finished yarn should ever be exposed to strong sunlight.

A delicate web may require that paper be wound in on the cloth beam as on the warp beam. If the fabric is very light in color, you can roll sheets of plastic between the layers of the web to help prevent soiling. A knit fabric sewn over the cloth beam like a sleeve will keep the woven fabric from slipping on its first turn.

Measuring the Web
As you weave the fabric, you should keep an accurate measure of its length. One method is to cut a measuring string the exact length of the planned web and place it over the web at the center. Tie the end of the string to the last row of coarse material that you wove in to spread the warp. Then wind the measuring string onto the cloth beam with the fabric. When you reach the end of the string, the web should be the proper length. This system, however, is not advisable when you are weaving many yards of fabric, for the string would create a ridge on the cloth beam. Instead, mark the length by looping a short piece of contrasting yarn over the selvedge warp at the end of each yard. All measurements of the finished web must be taken with the warp tension relaxed, because a measurement made while the yarns are under tension will be inaccurate.

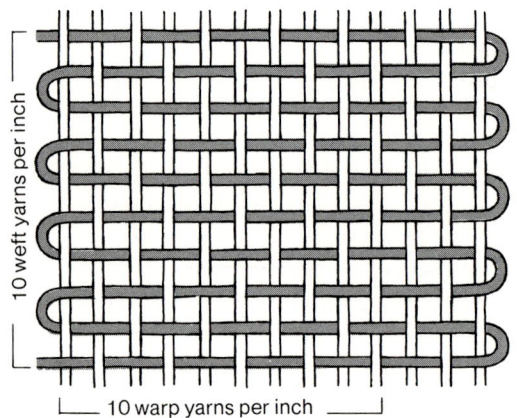

219. A balanced weave has the same number of weft yarns per inch as warp yarns per inch.

10 weft yarns per inch

10 warp yarns per inch

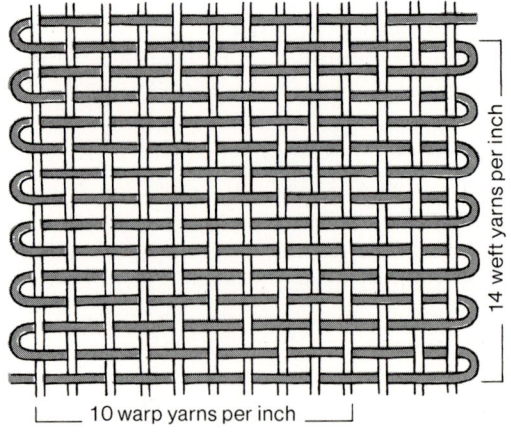

220. An unbalanced weave has an unequal distribution of warp and weft yarns.

14 weft yarns per inch

10 warp yarns per inch

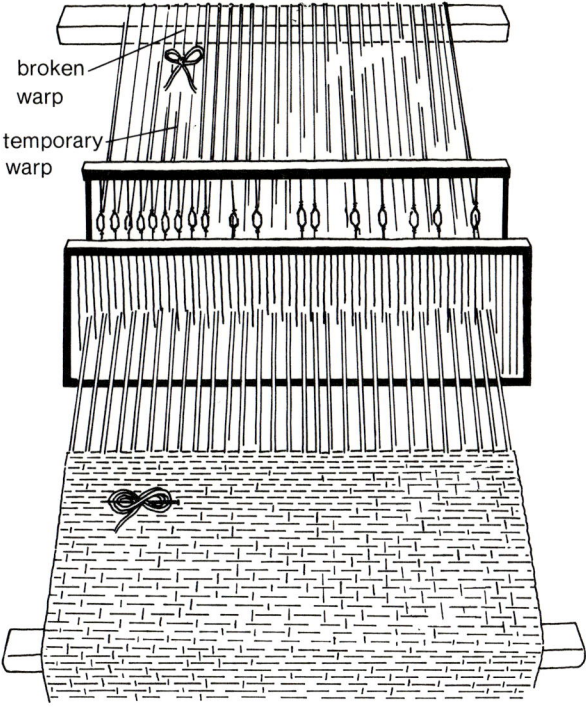

broken warp

temporary warp

221–222. *It is possible to splice a broken warp yarn on the loom by temporarily introducing a length of leftover yarn.*

above: 221. Pull the broken warp yarn out of the reed and heddle, and substitute a new length of yarn. Tie the two ends together at the back of the loom.

below: 222. Continue weaving until the broken end of yarn will reach into the web, then restore it to its position.

Correcting a Broken Warp   If a warp yarn should break during the weaving, or if a knot appears in one of the warps, you can splice the yarn.

Splicing a Warp Yarn

- Cut a piece of leftover warp yarn about 24 inches long.
- Pull the broken yarn out of the reed and the heddle to the back of the loom.
- Substitute the new length of yarn in the appropriate dent and heddle (Fig. 221).
- Tie the broken warp and the new warp together in a bow knot at the back of the loom near the lease sticks.
- Insert a common straight pin about 2 inches into the finished web.
- Pull the new warp to the same tension as the rest of the warp, and wind it figure-8 fashion around the pin.
- Continue weaving until the broken warp end at the back of the loom reaches a point at which it is long enough to extend into the web.
- Insert a second pin in the web, again about 2 inches into the fabric.
- Remove the yarn from the heddle and reed.
- Restore the broken end to its position, and wind it around the second pin (Fig. 222).
- After the fabric is completed, work the loose ends into the web.

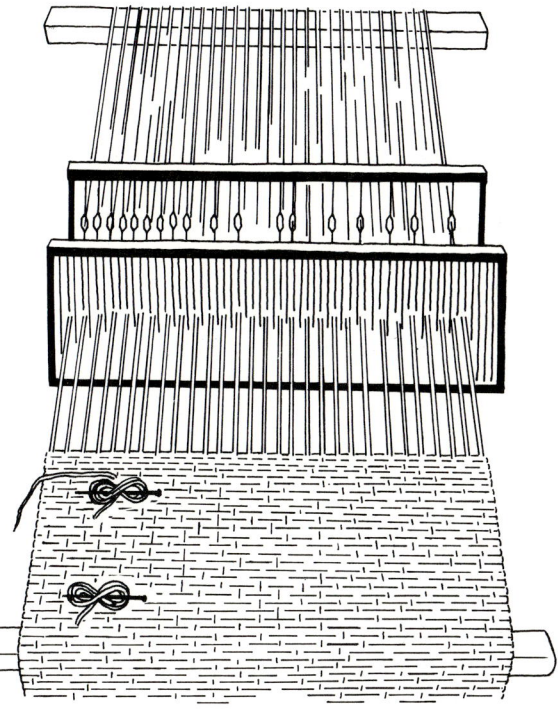

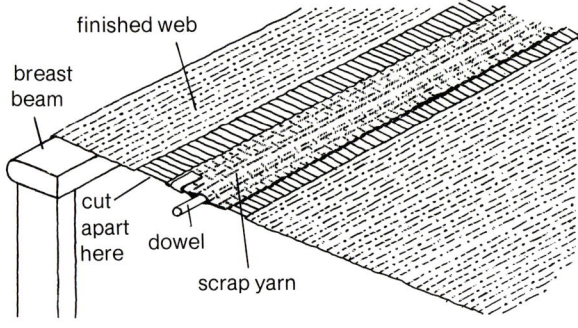

finished web
breast
beam
cut
apart
here
dowel
scrap yarn

above: 223. To remove a portion
of the web from the loom,
weave in a few inches of scrap yarn,
then a dowel, then more scrap yarn.

below: 224. When the dowel reaches the breast beam,
overcast it to the cloth stick.
You can then continue weaving
in the normal manner.

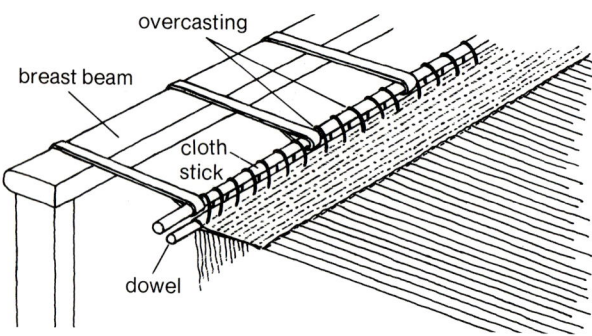

overcasting
breast beam
cloth
stick
dowel

Removing a Portion of the Web   It is possible to remove a portion of the web from the loom without retying the warp ends. A series of woven items, such as a set of place mats, or a great length of yardage may not fit all at once on the cloth beam.

Removing a Portion of the Web
- Complete the first unit or length of material, allowing enough warp at the end to finish the project (a fringe, for example).
- Weave in a weft of scrap yarn for a distance of about 2 inches, and hemstitch or tape it in place (Fig. 223).
- On the next shed, insert a dowel or flat stick wider than the web.
- Follow the dowel with another half inch of scrap yarn.
- Begin the second unit of the web.
- Cut the warps between the finished web and the scrap yarn (Fig. 224).
- Roll back the cloth beam to remove the first unit.
- Bring up the cloth stick, and overcast it firmly to the dowel.
- Adjust the tension, and continue weaving.

Removing the Fabric from the Loom   Weaving is complete when the desired length of fabric has been woven or when the warp can no longer move forward. A sufficient length of warp ends will remain to prevent the fabric from raveling, but if you wish you can hemstitch the web while it is still on the loom (Fig. 327). Cut the warp ends near the heddles, roll back the beam, and remove the fabric.

Drafting is a system of notation used to represent graphically the appearance and mechanics of a weave. A complete draft illustrates the intersections of warp and weft for a particular weave, as well as the threading, tie-up, and treadling sequence necessary to produce the weave.

Drafting has often been compared to musical notation, and in some ways the analogy is accurate. However, unlike the symbols used in music, the shorthand of drafting is not universal. Many different drafting systems are or have been used in different countries and at different times. The method described in this chapter (and in Appendix A) is both simple and quite common, especially in the United States. Once it is understood, you should not find it too difficult to translate other drafting systems that you may encounter.

We occasionally hear of great singers or other musicians who cannot read music. Similarly, many experienced weavers can neither read nor

9

Drafting

write drafts, preferring to design on the loom. It is certainly possible to pursue a career in weaving without ever resorting to paper and pencil. On the other hand, drafting does have several advantages:

1. Drafting is an abbreviated notation. A concise, complete draft will show at a glance what might otherwise require pages and pages of detailed explanation.

2. Drafting can produce an accurate record of all woven projects, giving the weaver an opportunity to build on successful ones and to correct failures.

3. Many variations can be readily visualized on paper. For example, if you have an interesting pattern based on a particular threading order, you may want to see how it will work with a different threading order. By plotting it on paper, you can get a reasonable idea of how the weave will look and also identify problems that may arise. Another possible variation would be a change in color or value in the warp and/or weft. The location and order of different-color yarns will greatly affect the appearance of the fabric. It is much easier to alter the color positions on paper than to wind a series of alternative color sequences and then weave each one of them.

4. Drafting enables you to duplicate another weaver's work for future experimentation. Few serious weavers rely on copying someone else's drafts exactly, but it is often helpful to be able to analyze other weaves in order to find ideas for one's own. In a mutually creative situation, weavers (and, of course, other artists) actively play back and forth against each other, developing and building on each other's ideas.

5. With drafting, it is possible to derive the mechanics of a weave from the appearance of the fabric. This process is often used by people who are interested in historic textiles or those concerned with replicating textiles of the past for restoration.

This chapter introduces the mechanics of the draft and gives only enough information for the reader to understand notations in the following chapters. Full details of the drafting process are provided in Appendix A. Drafts are written on graph paper available from any stationery store.

The Threading Draft

The order in which the warp yarns are threaded through the heddles is referred to as the *draw*. Figure 225 illustrates the draft notation for a *straight draw* on a 4-harness loom, a threading arrangement based on a unit of 4 warp ends repeated across the loom. In this draw, yarn 1 is

225–227. *A threading draft is read from bottom to top as the harnesses occur from front to back.*

225. A straight draw.

threaded through a heddle on harness 1, yarn 2 through a heddle on harness 2, and so forth. After the first four warp ends are threaded, one unit or *repeat* has been completed, and the pattern begins again with harness 1. The threading draft is read from bottom to top as the harnesses occur from front to back on the loom. Therefore, the bottom row of squares represents harness 1, and the top row represents harness 4. An 8-harness loom would, of course, require eight vertical rows of squares. The straight draw is the most common and most universally used, because it forms the basis for all the other drafts. Using the straight draw you can produce all the standard weaves except satin weave (see p. 143).

Another simple threading draft is the *pointed draw*, a version of which is shown in Figure 226. The pointed draw follows the course of the straight draw but interrupts its direction and turns back on itself. The unit can have one or several points. The basic pointed draw, as illustrated in Figure 226, is:

1, 2, 3, 4, 3, 2

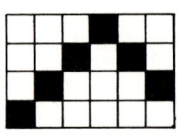

left: 226. A pointed draw.

below: 227. A pointed draw with two points.

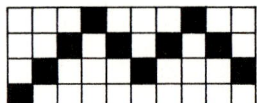

This makes one repeat of the pattern. One variation of the pointed draw (Fig. 227) might be:

1, 2, 3, 4, 3, 2, 3, 4, 3, 2

Appendix A shows a number of other variations and different types of draws.

The Tie-Up Draft

The tie-up draft shows which harnesses are to be lifted simultaneously to create each shed. It is read from left to right for the treadles and from bottom to top for the harnesses. If you are using a 4-harness loom, the tie-up draft might look something like Figure 228, with each vertical row of squares

228. A tie-up draft is read from left to right for treadles, from bottom to top for harnesses. This is the "standard" tie-up.

representing the four harnesses and each horizontal row indicating the six treadles. In Figure 228 the tie-up has the following order:

harnesses 1 and 2 on treadle 1
harnesses 2 and 3 on treadle 2
harnesses 3 and 4 on treadle 3
harnesses 1 and 4 on treadle 4
harnesses 1 and 3 on treadle 5
harnesses 2 and 4 on treadle 6

This is the so-called *standard* tie-up, with the first four treadles arranged for twill, the remaining two for plain weave.

If you are using a table loom, the tie-up draft is not necessary, but you must take into account the harnesses that are to be raised for a particular shed. For example, if the first shed in a pattern calls for treadle 1 to be depressed, then you would manipulate the levers to raise harnesses 1 and 2.

The Treadling Draft

The treadling draft indicates the sequence of sheds that are created for a pattern. Usually, it is read from top to bottom. In Figure 229 the order of treadles for the first repeat of the pattern is:

1, 2, 3, 4, 3, 2, 1, 5, 6

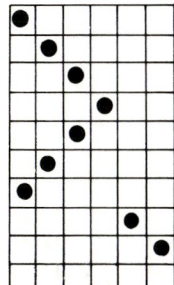

229. The treadling draft is read from top to bottom. When more than one symbol appears in the draft, two or more kinds of weft yarn are indicated.

The use of a table loom requires some interpretation. Going back to the tie-up draft, we can see that the corresponding manipulation of levers would be:

1-2, 2-3, 3-4, 1-4, 3-4, 2-3, 1-2, 1-3, 2-4

Sometimes the instructions for a weave will specify the treadling order merely by a list of numbers, rather than a graphic representation. A series of numbers separated by *commas* generally means *treadles*, while a series separated by *hyphens* stands for either the *levers* on a table loom or the *harnesses* to be raised.

Often one sees another symbol, such as an **X** or a circle in the treadling draft. This is meant to give the weaver special information for a particular web, such as a change in yarn size or color. More information about this, and about drafts in general, is given in Appendix A.

The Cloth Draft

The cloth draft, also known as the *weave draft* or *draw-down*, is a paper diagram of the weave itself. It shows in graphic form what the weave will look like.

Two conventions are followed in preparing the cloth draft. First, the *vertical* rows of squares represent *warp* ends, and the *horizontal* rows signify *weft* yarns. Second, the *dark* squares indicate a point of intersection at which the *warp* yarn is above the weft yarn. The *unshaded* squares are areas in which the *weft* yarn is above the warp yarn.

Usually, the cloth draft is read from top to bottom, actually the reverse of the way the fabric appears on the loom. It is advisable to make at least two repeats of the pattern in order to form an overall impression of the weave and to make sure the joining between units is successful. However, if a very complicated weave is involved, one and one-half repeats across the warp may be sufficient to establish the pattern. Figure 230 illustrates the weave that would result from the threading, tie-up, and treadling drafts in Figures 227 to 229.

above: 230. In the cloth draft, vertical rows of squares represent warp yarns, and horizontal rows weft yarns.

below: 231. A comprehensive draft includes threading, tie-up, treadling, and cloth drafts for a weave.

The Comprehensive Draft

By pulling together all the foregoing elements, one creates a comprehensive draft. Therefore, Figure 231 is the comprehensive draft of the weave represented in Figure 230 and achieved by following Figures 227 to 229. On just a few square inches of paper the weaver notes the appearance of the weave and all the mechanics that produce it.

Deriving the Cloth Draft

In experimenting with a new weave, it is often desirable to draft the pattern on paper before attempting it on the loom, especially when great quantities of yarn are involved. Once a threading draft, a tie-up, and a treadling sequence have been established, you can easily sketch the cloth draft. This method of designing on paper is also useful when you intend to change or vary the pattern. By holding two elements constant (for example, the threading and the tie-up) and varying the third (the treadling sequence), you can see immediately how the pattern will be affected by such changes.

Figure 232 illustrates one and one-half repeats of a pattern weave called *honeysuckle*. It is a good exercise to plot the draw-down or cloth draft for such a complex weave, working from the threading, tie-up, and treadling drafts. Once you have seen how the pattern emerges, the entire concept of drafting should become much clearer.

Using graph paper, begin making marks lightly with pencil, in case you make a mistake. With a regular pattern weave such as honeysuckle, any errors will soon become apparent. Later, the boxes can be darkened with a felt-tipped pen.

First draw the threading, tie-up, and treadling drafts on graph paper. The first shed in the honey-suckle weave is created by treadle 1, which raises harnesses 1 and 2. Starting on the first line of the proposed draw-down, black in a square at each point where either harness 1 or harness 2 is raised. The threading draft shows that warp end 1 is threaded in harness 1 and warp end 2 is threaded in harness 2. Since the shed requires these two harnesses to be raised—thus placing the warp yarn over the weft—the first two squares on line 1 of the draw-down are darkened. Warp end 3 is on harness 3, which is not affected by the first shed, so the third square on the top line is left unshaded. Continue this procedure across the line until one and one-half repeats have been sketched in.

The second shed is plotted in a similar manner on line 2 of the draw-down. This shed calls for treadle 2 to be depressed, which raises harnesses 2 and 3. Therefore, on line 2 of the draw-down each point where either harness 2 or harness 3 is raised will be blacked in. When a sufficient number of sheds have been plotted—in this case 24—the pattern should become clear.

In the following chapters some of the more common weaves are discussed and illustrated by written drafts, occasionally supplemented by photographs of sample webs. However, it is important to remember that drafts, because they are diagrammatic, present an idealized picture of a weave. The choice of yarns and colors has a considerable effect on the fabric's appearance.

Weavers who are interested in pursuing the subject of drafts should refer to Appendix A.

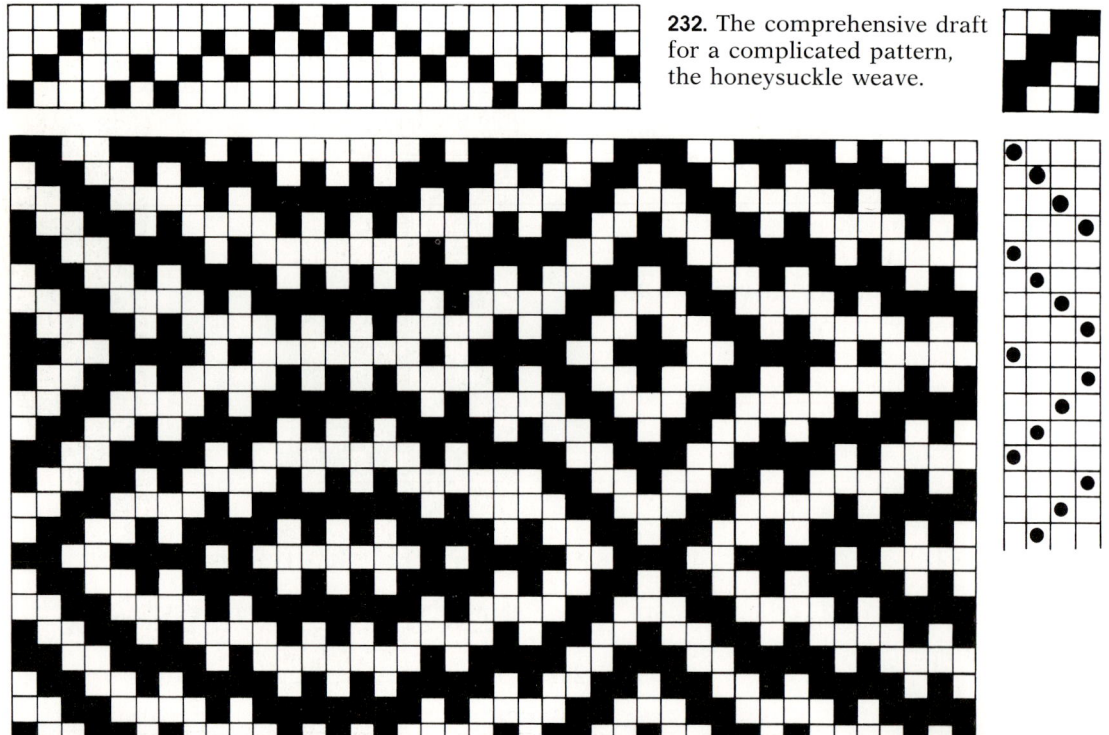

232. The comprehensive draft for a complicated pattern, the honeysuckle weave.

Loom-controlled weaves are those created by the interaction of the harnesses. Pattern variations are produced by altering the threading, tie-up, and treadling sequences, and the weft yarn is usually carried from selvedge to selvedge. There are three basic weave categories: plain weave or tabby, twill weave, and satin weave. Modifications of these three fundamental structures are often called *derivative weaves.*

The Basic Weaves

Plain Weave (*Tabby*)

Plain weave is characterized by a regular interlacing of warp and weft yarns in a 1/1 order (Fig. 233). That is, each weft yarn moves alternately over and under adjacent warp ends, and the sequence is reversed for the alternate weft shots. When the warp is all one color and the weft all another, a checkerboard effect results.

10
Loom-Controlled Weaves

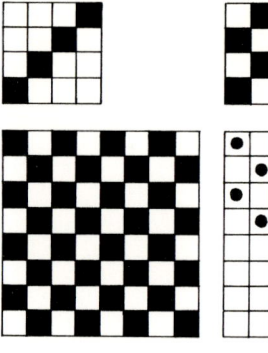

left: 233. Ed Rossbach.
Napkin. 1976.
Cotton welt cord,
24 × 26″ (60 × 65 cm).
Courtesy the artist.

above: 234. Draft for plain weave (tabby).

below: 235. Draft for a 2/2 basket weave.

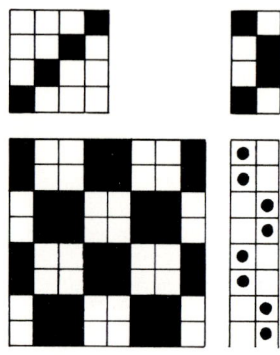

Two harnesses are sufficient to create plain weave, but it is often set up on four to provide a more even distribution of yarns. It is a reversible weave, for the two faces of the fabric are identical. Basic plain weave produces the maximum number of *binding points*—areas in which a single weft yarn is interlaced with a single warp end. Therefore, it is the firmest, most durable weave. The comprehensive draft for basic plain weave is illustrated in Figure 234.

Plain weave was undoubtedly the first construction mastered by prehistoric weavers. Throughout history most fabrics have been woven in plain weave, with color or textural variations providing the major interest. Even today, despite the multiplicity of weaves that are possible on the modern loom, plain weave comprises a very large portion of all woven fabrics.

The two major derivatives of plain weave are *basket weave* and *rep* or *rib weaves.*

Basket Weave A basket weave consists of two or more warp yarns interlaced with two or more weft yarns. For example, a 2/2 basket weave has two warp yarns interlaced as a unit with a unit of two weft yarns. In the warp this effect is produced either by raising two adjacent harnesses simultaneously or by threading two warp yarns through each heddle. The double weft can be created in

several ways. Two shuttles can be passed through the same shed, with a beat after each shot; a shuttle containing two bobbins can be thrown through the open shed; a bobbin wound from two spools simultaneously can be used; a single shuttle can be passed twice through the same shed, with the weft yarn wrapped around the outermost warp yarn before the return trip. The comprehensive draft for a simple 2/2 basket weave is shown in Figure 235.

Rep and Rib Weaves Rep and rib weaves are similar to plain weave except for the yarn concentration (Fig. 236). They are always unbalanced weaves. Usually, *rep* refers to a *warp-face* textile, in which warp yarns are more prominent on the surface of the fabric and may actually cover the weft altogether. A *rib* weave describes a *weft-face* textile in which the weft yarns are more obvious.

236. Warp-face rep and weft-face rib weaves.

warp-face rep   weft-face rib

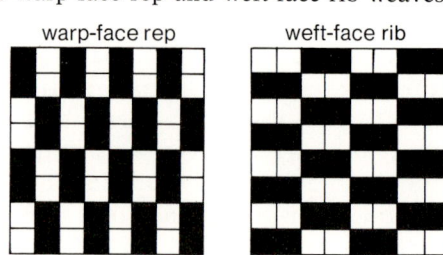

237. Jane Busse.
Loom-shaped jacket.
Tubular twill weave
in linen/rayon
and flax/rayon
with handspun wool
for the pattern.
Courtesy the artist.

The threading and treadling sequences for these weaves are identical to those for plain weave. It is the sett of the warp yarn in the reed that makes the difference. If the warp yarn is set unusually close, it may cover the weft yarn entirely. Conversely, a wide spacing of warp yarns at the reed allows the weft to pack up against itself and cover the warp. For example, suppose with a particular yarn a balanced weave would result from sleying 15 yarns per inch in the reed. If the same yarn were sleyed at 30 ends per inch, a warp-face rep would result; if at 6 or 8 ends per inch, a weft-face rib would be created.

Both rep and rib variations are compact and therefore have more body than the usual balanced plain weave.

Twill Weaves

In twill weaves the binding points of the fabric occur in a diagonal progression across the web, moving systematically to left or right perhaps across one warp yarn with each successive weft shot (Fig. 237). Floats appear in both the warp and the weft. Since the binding points occur less frequently than in plain weave, the fabric is usually more flexible. You can produce a twill with only three harnesses, but twills are usually set up on four or more.

238. A 2/2 straight twill.

Twills are described as *balanced* when the same number of warp yarns always intersect with the same number of weft yarns. For example, a 2/2 twill always has two warp yarns intersecting with two weft yarns (Fig. 238). A balanced twill uses half the treadles each time for developing the sequence. To produce this twill on a 4-harness loom, you would usually treadle

1-2, 2-3, 3-4, 4-1,

while on a 6-harness loom the same result could be produced by treadling

1-2-3, 2-3-4, 3-4-5, 4-5-6, 5-6-1, 6-1-2.

The symbol 3/1 or 1/3 indicates an *unbalanced* twill, which has a higher proportion of floats to

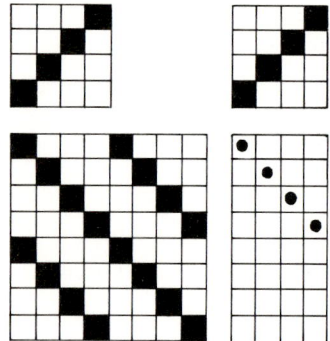

239. A 1/3 straight twill.

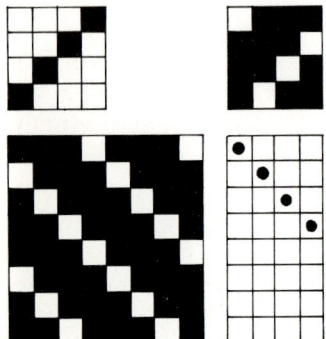

240. A 3/1 straight twill.

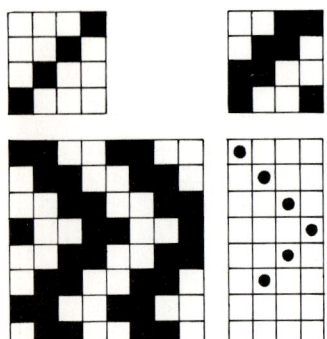

241. A 2/2 reverse twill.

by using different weights of warp yarns or by staggering the sett at the reed (piling up some yarns in a single dent and/or skipping dents in a sequence). The more compact the warp yarns, the steeper the angle of the twill will be. Conversely, a fabric that has low density in the warp will have a flatter diagonal. Another way to produce a flat diagonal is to select a weft yarn that is much heavier than the warp.

By careful planning and combination of the above variables, you can even create an undulating diagonal. One way to do this is to stagger the warp yarns in the reed according to an organized sequence, for example, to gradually progress from a dense sett to a single sley and skipped dent, and then back again. This will cause the angle to shift gradually from steep to flat. The curved angle will also result if the warp consists of groups of yarns varying in size and dented so that the finer yarns are made compact and the heavier yarns spread in the reed. The weft yarn is of uniform size.

Straight Twill   A straight twill has an unbroken diagonal line (Figs. 238–240). When the diagonal rises from left to right, it is referred to as a *right-hand twill;* a *left-hand twill* rises from right to left. On a 4-harness loom, the most common straight twills are the 2/2, the 1/3, and the 3/1.

Reverse Twill   A reverse twill creates a zig-zag effect. To produce it, the treadling sequence is altered, so that the diagonal switches back and forth from left to right (Fig. 241).

Herringbone Twill   A herringbone or chevron twill also shows a zig-zag, but the progression is horizontal rather than vertical. Unlike the straight and reverse twills, the herringbone is threaded on a pointed draw (Fig. 242).

242. A herringbone twill.

binding points. In a 1/3 twill the weft floats over three warp ends and goes under one, while the warp passes under three weft yarns and over one (Fig. 239). This creates a weft-face fabric. The warp-face 3/1 twill has each weft yarn passing over one warp yarn and under three (Fig. 240). Because unbalanced twills require treadling three against one, they are difficult to produce on the counterbalance loom without an attachment.

The diagonal of the twill always reverses in direction on the back of the fabric. Unless the twill is balanced, the two faces will not appear identical.

Considerable variation is possible in the angle of the diagonal. You can alter the diagonal either

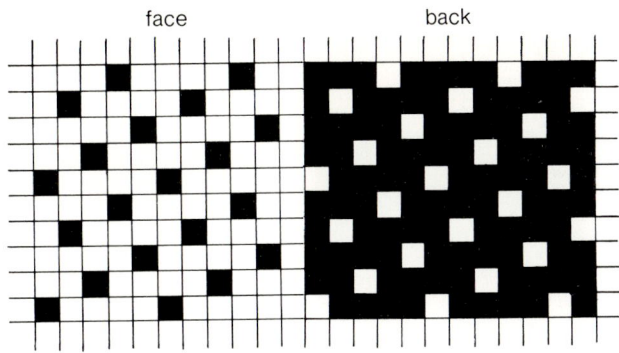

face   back

243. Satin weaves have long floats on the fabric.

Satin Weaves

Satin weaves are characterized by long floats on the surface of the fabric (Fig. 243). Because the binding points are never in contact with one another, the diagonal line typical of twills is fragmented. Satin weave fabric is very smooth and pliable, and the long floats—in either warp or weft—shimmer with reflected light. At least five harnesses, and sometimes ten or fifteen, are required to produce satin weaves.

Loom-Controlled Weaves: A Sampler

The sampler is planned to demonstrate the wide variety of patterns that can be obtained from a single threading of the loom, merely by changing the tie-up and treadling sequences, as well as the color and texture of the weft yarns. Properly labeled, the sampler can serve as an excellent reference for future work.

Samplers may be called *gamps, rags,* or *blankets.* Whatever the name, nearly all weavers use sampling in order to test a new design or to see the effect different textures and colors will have on a standard pattern. Many weavers can design more realistically in fabric than on paper. In fact, special looms capable of producing an 8-inch-wide web are manufactured specifically for testing purposes. As a rule, an 8-inch width is sufficient to produce at least two repeats of a pattern, thereby giving a representative sample of the design.

A great many pattern possibilities and some color effects will appear in the sampler, but this by no means exhausts the potential of the drafts listed. Some of the pattern areas would be suitable for upholstery, others for a coating or suiting yardage, still others for openwork fabrics such as draperies or stoles. The weaver interested in the art fabric will find myriad variations to choose from and develop. In particular, the sampler gives the opportunity to find paired threadings that can be fitted together successfully.

Weaving with eight different threading drafts occasionally results in small areas that are uninteresting. But on the other hand it also provides many surprises in sections where the treadling was planned especially for one draft yet makes equally attractive patterns in others. These bonus results can be very exciting and could have been missed in working with only one threading. Sometimes the back of the fabric, as woven, has a more interesting appearance than the front. You should check both to find the most appealing patterns.

The sampler described on the following pages is planned for a 4-harness loom with—in the case of a floor loom—six treadles. Although the threading pattern is not uniform all across the warp, even a beginner should have no difficulty following the directions. At various points in the course of the sampler you will have to change the tie-up.

Two colors are included in the warp, and fine or textured yarns are occasionally introduced in the weft to demonstrate the interaction of color, weight, texture, and pattern. The choice of colors is left to you. Contrasting colors will show the development of the pattern most clearly and will reveal certain changes of effect caused by color. For example, in some cases the pattern emerging from a dark warp and a light weft would look completely different with a light warp and a dark weft. Until you have more experience, you should avoid black for the warp, since the yarns are difficult to see when threading the heddles.

Specifications for the Sampler

Length of finished web:	8 yards	7.3 m
Length of each warp yarn:	10 yards	9 m
Number of warp yarns:	color A: 130	
	color B: 124	
	total 254	

Amount of warp yarn:	color A:	1300 yards	1188 m
	color B:	1240 yards	1133 m
	total	2540 yards	2321 m

Weft yarn:	8/4 carpet warp in two colors
	soft rug yarn in one color
	fine yarn in one color

Amount of weft yarn:	color A:	3 spools
	color B:	3 spools
	rug yarn:	1 spool
	fine yarn:	1 spool
	total	8 spools

Number of heddles required:	harness 1: 66
	harness 2: 61
	harness 3: 61
	harness 4: 66

Width of finished sampler:	about 15 inches	38 cm
		42 cm
		6 per cm

Width at reed: 17 inches

Size of reed: No. 15

Warping Instructions

The yarns should be warped in the following sequence on the warping frame or reel:

    32 yarns color A
    28 yarns color B
    36 yarns color A
    32 yarns alternating colors A and B
    30 yarns color B
    28 yarns color A
    36 yarns alternating colors A and B
    32 yarns color B
  254

Threading Instructions

Seven different threading patterns are used across the warp: twill (straight draw), goose eye (pointed draw), rosepath III, cord velveret, broken twill, bird's eye, and wheat. The complete threading draft is given in Figure 244. Each draw is to be repeated the specified number of times before proceeding to the next one. Note that the entire warp contains eight pattern *blocks*, and except for the first two, which are threaded in a straight draw, the threading pattern changes each time the color changes.

Sleying Instructions

A single yarn is to be drawn through each dent in a number 15 reed. Therefore, the warp will be 17 inches wide at the reed, with the last inch short one yarn (15 × 17 = 255). In order to center the warp in the loom, divide the excess length of the reed by two. For example, if the reed is 20 inches wide, sleying would begin 1½ inches from the right edge of the reed.

If you are using a metric reed, choose a reed with 6 dents per centimeter. The warp will be 42 centimeters wide at the reed, plus two extra yarns (6 × 42 = 252). Measure to find the center of the reed, and then measure 21 centimeters to either left or right. Sleying is to begin one space beyond that point.

Tie-Up Instructions

Most of the sampler can be woven with the so-called *standard tie-up* (Fig. 245): the first four treadles are tied for twill (1-2, 2-3, 3-4, 4-1) and the remaining two for plain weave (1-3, 2-4). It will become obvious that this is an extremely flexible arrangement. Further instructions for changing the tie-up are given in the section of the sampler devoted to variations. Of course, no tie-up will be needed for a table loom.

below: 244. The threading draft for the sampler is divided into eight pattern blocks. Repeat each draw the specified number of times before proceeding to the next.

right: 245. In the standard tie-up, four treadles are tied for twill, two for tabby.

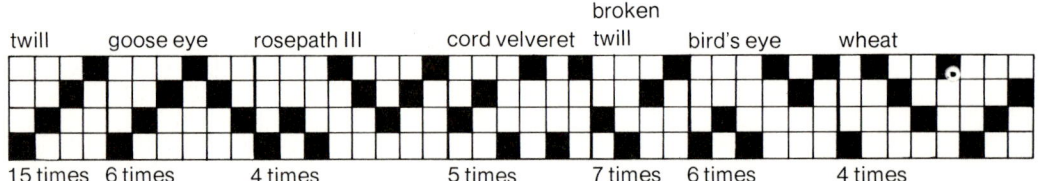

twill   goose eye   rosepath III   cord velveret   broken twill   bird's eye   wheat

15 times 6 times   4 times   5 times   7 times 6 times   4 times

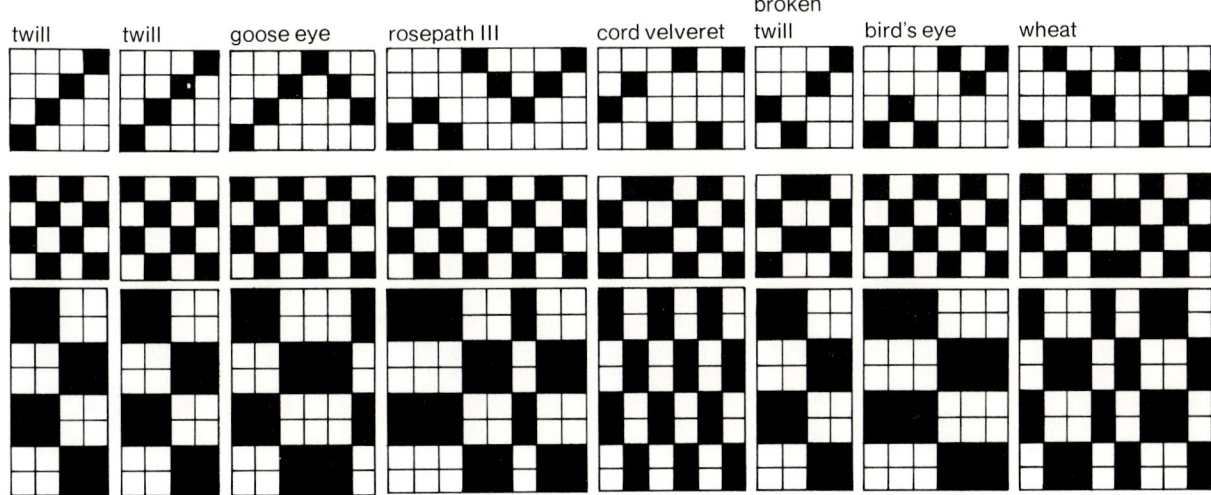

twill	twill	goose eye	rosepath III	cord velveret	broken twill	bird's eye	wheat

above: 246. Draft for the plain-weave and basket-weave portions of the sampler.

right: 247. The plain-weave and basket-weave portions of the sampler, as they appear in fabric.

Weaving Instructions

The directions given in each of the numbered paragraphs below should be followed for a weaving distance of approximately 2 inches (5 cm) to allow for development of the pattern. It is very important to realize that the weave described may appear *only* in the pattern blocks where *both* threading and treadling conform to the needs of that particular weave. For example, even though a tie-up and treadling sequence may specify straight twill, the twill weave will show only in the portions of the sampler that are threaded for straight twill—the first two blocks.

Plain weave (Fig. 246):
1. Treadle 1-3, 2-4; weft yarn in color A. The weave appears in all parts of the sampler except blocks 5, 6, and 8.
2. Treadle 1-3, 2-4; weft yarn in color B.
3. Treadle 1-3, 2-4; weft yarn alternates colors A and B (two shuttles).
4. Treadle 1-3, 2-4; fine weft yarn.
5. Treadle 1-3, 2-4; textured rug yarn in weft.

Basket weave (Fig. 246):
6. Treadle 1-2, 1-2, 3-4, 3-4; weft yarn in color B. The 2/2 basket weave appears only in blocks 1, 2, and 6; block 5, which is threaded for cord velveret, develops a warp-face rep. Figure 247 illustrates part of this section of the sampler.

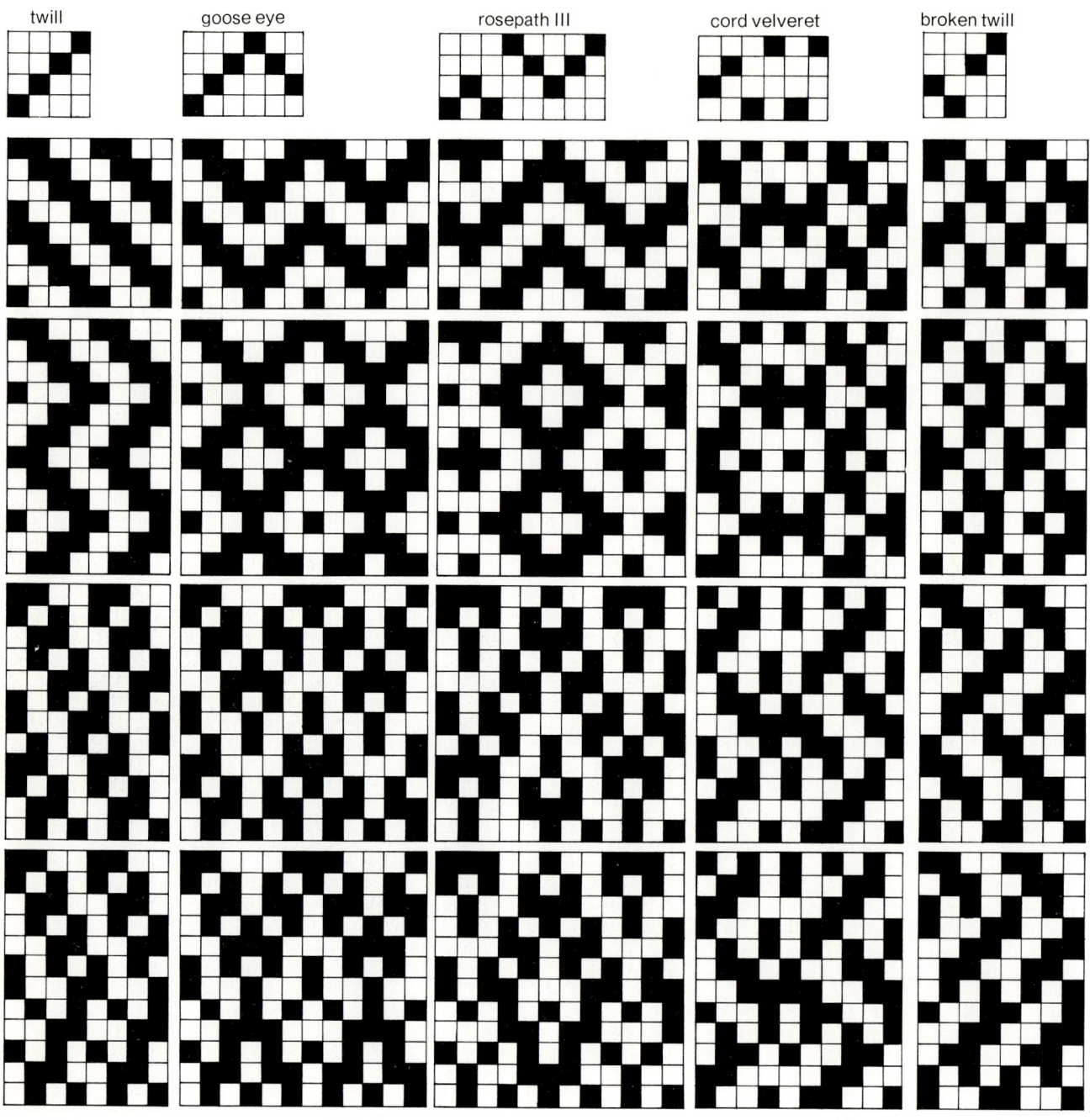

twill   goose eye   rosepath III   cord velveret   broken twill

248. Draft of the twill portion of the sampler.

Twills (Figs. 248, 249):

7. Straight twill—treadle 1-2, 2-3, 3-4, 4-1; weft yarn in color A. The straight twill weave develops only in blocks 1 and 2. Blocks 3, 4, and 7 show the herringbone or chevron twill.

8. Straight twill—treadle 1-2, 2-3, 3-4, 4-1; weft yarn in color B. Since the warp and weft are each a single color in block 1, the fabric is striped diagonally.

9. Straight twill—treadle 1-2, 2-3, 3-4, 4-1; weft yarn alternates colors A and B (two shuttles).

10. Reverse twill—treadle 1-2, 2-3, 3-4, 4-1, 3-4, 2-3; weft yarn in color A. The reverse twill appears only in blocks 1 and 2; a symmetrical diamond pattern is created in blocks 3, 4, and 7.

11. Reverse twill—treadle 1-2, 2-3, 3-4, 4-1, 3-4, 2-3; weft yarn in color B.

12. Reverse twill—treadle 1-2, 2-3, 3-4, 4-1, 3-4, 2-3; weft yarn alternates colors A and B.

Twill alternated with plain weave:

13. Straight twill and plain weave—treadle 1-2, 1-3,

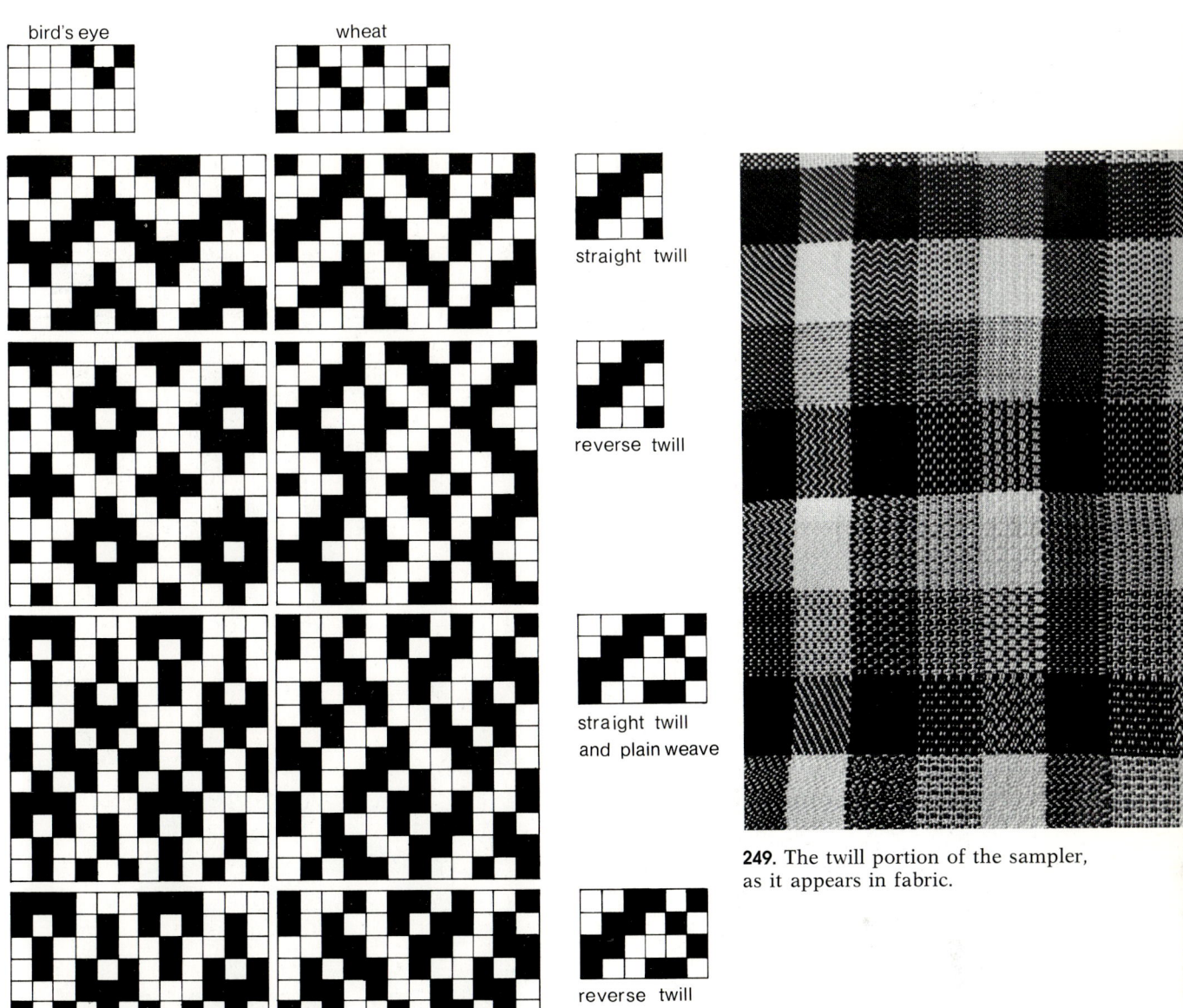

bird's eye

wheat

straight twill

reverse twill

straight twill and plain weave

reverse twill and plain weave

249. The twill portion of the sampler, as it appears in fabric.

2-3, 2-4, 3-4, 1-3, 4-1, 2-4; weft yarn in color A. The pattern is seen only in blocks 1 and 2.

14. Reverse twill and plain weave—treadle 1-2, 1-3, 2-3, 2-4, 3-4, 1-3, 4-1, 2-4, 3-4, 1-3, 2-3, 2-4; weft yarn in color B. The pattern develops only in blocks 1 and 2. Figure 249 illustrates the twill portion of the sampler in fabric.

The weaves in the central portion of the sampler are *tromp as writ,* or treadled in the order in which they are threaded. The term derives from a Colonial expression meaning "tramp as written." Several of the threading patterns have already been treadled. A straight twill treadling (1-2, 2-3, 3-4, 4-1) is the tromp as writ for the twill threading 1-2-3-4. In each case the harness that is threaded plus the adjacent harness that is next in order must be raised to create a balanced weave. For example, when the harnesses are threaded 1, 2, 1, 4, 3, 4 (bird's eye), the treadling sequence is 1-2, 2-3, 1-2, 4-1, 3-4, 4-1.

Tromp as writ (Fig. 250):

15. Rosepath III—treadle 1-2, 2-3, 1-2, 1-4, 3-4, 2-3, 3-4, 1-4; weft yarn in color A. The resultant pattern is similar to that produced when the same threading is treadled for reverse twill (see Fig. 248).
16. Rosepath III—treadle 1-2, 2-3, 1-2, 1-4, 3-4, 2-3, 3-4, 1-4; weft yarn in color B.
17. Cord velveret—treadle 2-3, 3-4, 1-2, 1-4, 1-2, 1-4; weft yarn in color A.
18. Cord velveret—treadle 2-3, 3-4, 1-2, 1-4, 1-2, 1-4; weft yarn in color B.
19. Broken twill—treadle 2-3, 1-2, 3-4, 4-1; weft yarn in color A.
20. Broken twill—treadle 2-3, 1-2, 3-4, 4-1; weft yarn in color B.
21. Bird's eye—treadle 1-2, 2-3, 1-2, 1-4, 3-4, 1-4; weft yarn in color A.
22. Bird's eye—treadle 1-2, 2-3, 1-2, 1-4, 3-4, 1-4; weft yarn in color B.

23. Wheat—treadle 1-2, 1-4, 3-4, 2-3, 1-4, 1-2, 2-3, 3-4; weft yarn in color A.
24. Wheat—treadle 1-2, 1-4, 3-4, 2-3, 1-4, 1-2, 2-3, 3-4; weft yarn in color B. The photograph reproduced in Figure 251 is an example in fabric of the various tromp as writ sections.

broken twill

250. Drafts for rosepath III, cord velveret, broken twill, bird's eye, and wheat tromp-as-writ.

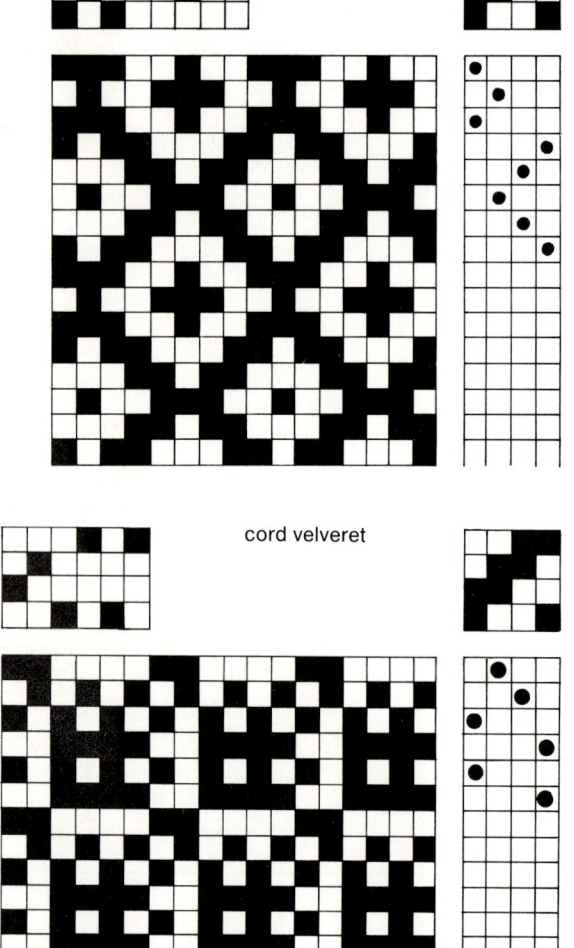
rosepath III

cord velveret

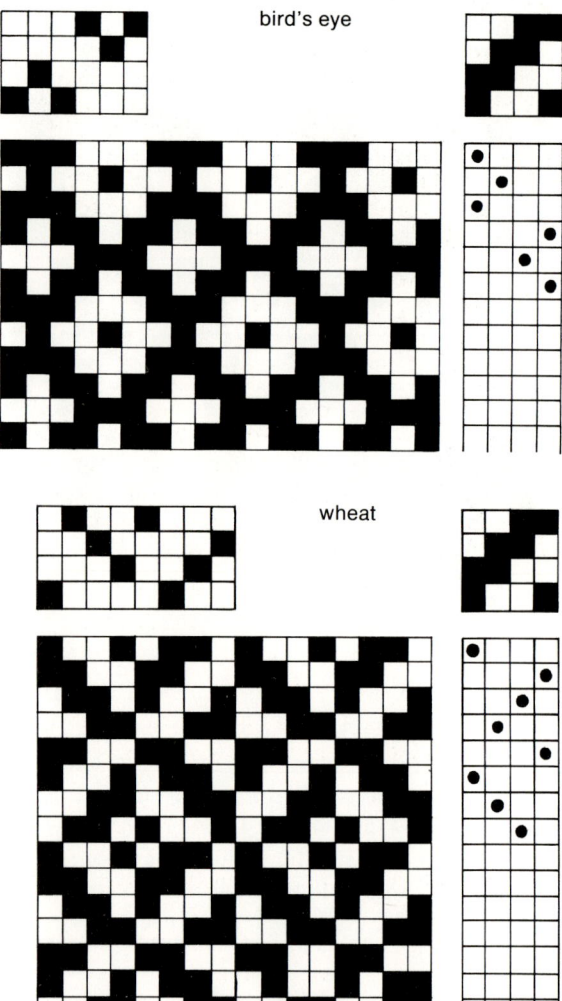
bird's eye

wheat

251. The tromp-as-writ section of the sampler, as it appears in fabric.

27. Tie-up: 1, 2, 3, 4, 1-3, 2-4
    Treadle: 2-4, 1-3, 1, 2, 3, 4
    Weft yarn: color B
28. Tie-up: 1, 2, 3, 4, 1-3, 2-4
    Treadle: 1, 4, 3, 2, 1-3, 2-4
    Weft yarn: color A
29. Tie-up: 1, 2, 3, 4, 1-3, 2-4 (depress two treadles where necessary)
    Treadle: 1-2-3, 2, 2-3-4, 3, 1-3-4, 4, 1-2-4, 1
    Weft yarn: color B
30. Tie-up: 1-2, 2-3, 3-4, 4-1, 1-3, 2-4 (standard)
    Treadle: 1-2, 1-3, 1-4, 2-3, 2-4, 1-2, 3-4, 1-3, 2-3, 1-4, 2-4, 3-4
    Weft yarn: color A
31. Tie-up: 1-2, 2-3, 3-4, 4-1, 1-3, 2-4 (standard)
    Treadle: 2-3, 1-2, 2-3, 3-4, 4-1, 3-4
    Weft yarn: color B

252. Draft of the sampler variations, steps 25 through 40.

25
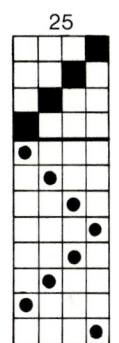

26
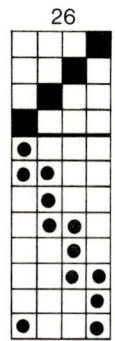

The remaining portion of the sampler is devoted to a series of treadling variations that produce a wide range of patterns. New tie-up instructions are given where necessary, and all the tie-up and treadling drafts are illustrated in Figure 252. Where color variation is important to the development of a weave, this is indicated in the treadling draft by an X for a shot of color A and a • for a shot of color B. In cases where part of a treadling sequence is repeated, it is customary to abbreviate the series as (1, 2, 3, 4)₃ rather than listing each combination individually as 1, 2, 3, 4, 1, 2, 3, 4, 1, 2, 3, 4.

27
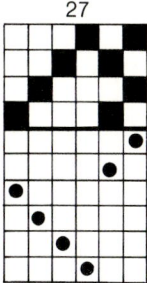

28
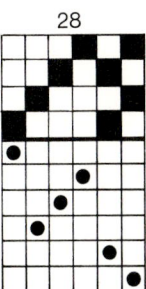

25. Tie-up: 1, 2, 3, 4
    Treadle: (1, 2, 3, 4)₃ (3, 2, 1, 4)₃
    Weft yarn: color A
26. Tie-up   1, 2, 3, 4 (depress two treadles where necessary)
    Treadle: 1, 1-2, 2, 2-3, 3, 3-4, 4, 4-1
    Weft yarn: color B

29
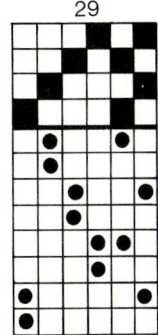

30

31

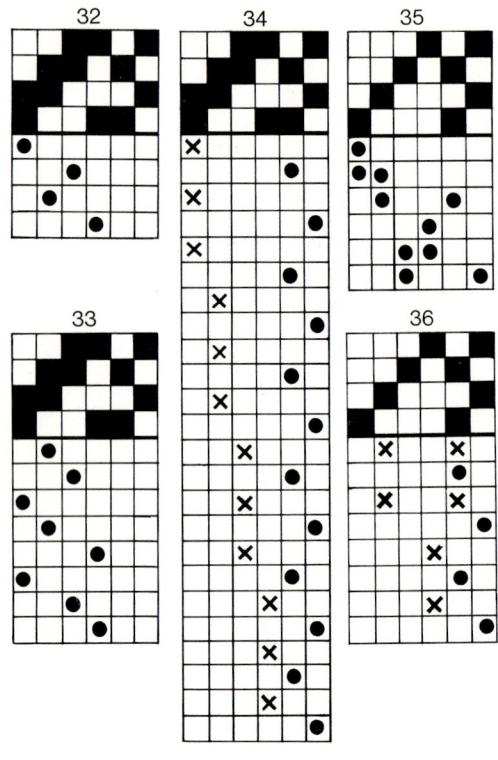

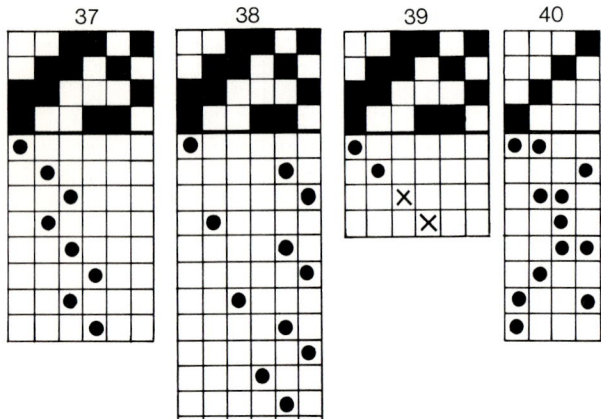

35. Tie-up: 1, 2, 3, 4, 1-3, 2-4 (depress two treadles where necessary)
    Treadle: 1, 1-2, 1-2-3, 4, 3-4, 2-3-4
    Weft yarn: color B
36. Tie-up: 1, 2, 3, 4, 1-3, 2-4 (depress two treadles where necessary)
    Treadle: 1-2-3, 1-3, 1-2-3, 2-4, 4, 1-3, 4, 2-4
    Weft yarn: alternates colors A and B as indicated
37. Tie-up: 1-2, 2-3, 3-4, 4-1, 1-3, 2-4 (standard)
    Treadle: 1-2, 2-3, 3-4, 2-3, 3-4, 4-1, 3-4, 4-1
    Weft yarn: color B
38. Tie-up: 1-2, 2-3, 3-4, 4-1, 1-3, 2-4 (standard)
    Treadle: 1-2, 1-3, 2-4, 2-3, 1-3, 2-4, 3-4, 1-3, 2-4, 4-1, 1-3, 2-4
    Weft yarn: color A
39. Tie-up: 1-2, 2-3, 3-4, 4-1, 1-3, 2-4 (standard)
    Treadle: 1-2, 2-3, 3-4, 4-1
    Weft yarn: colors A and B
40. Tie-up: 1, 2, 3, 4
    Treadle: 1-2, 4, 2-3, 3, 3-4, 2, 1-4, 1
    Weft yarn: color B

Finishing Instructions

If any usable warp remains on the loom after all forty strips have been completed, you can introduce treadling combinations of your own. The sampler can be finished with a few shots of plain weave, as illustrated in Figure 253, and then hemstitched (Fig. 327) to prevent raveling. You may also want to try another of the finishing techniques in Chapter 12. After you cut the sampler from the loom, you should label it to indicate each threading and treadling combination that was used. Labels should be applied in each block along the bottom of the sampler to show the threading arrangement and in each block along one selvedge to indicate the treadling sequence. Iron-on tape is a convenient method for attaching the labels. You will thus have a record of 320 different designs.

The variety in pattern that can be produced merely through the interaction of the harnesses is infinite. After completing the sampler described above, you may wish to experiment with other basic combinations. For example, color can be introduced into both warp and weft in any pattern desired (including random ones) to produce stripes, plaids, and multicolor effects. Textured yarns can influence the development of a weave, as can variations in the sett at the reed. There are hundreds of standard threading arrangements,

32. Tie-up: 1-2, 2-3, 3-4, 4-1, 1-3, 2-4 (standard)
    Treadle: 1-2, 3-4, 2-3, 4-1
    Weft yarn: color A
33. Tie-up: 1-2, 2-3, 3-4, 4-1, 1-3, 2-4 (standard)
    Treadle: 2-3, 3-4, 1-2, 2-3, 4-1, 1-2, 3-4, 4-1
    Weft yarn: color B
34. Tie-up: 1-2, 2-3, 3-4, 4-1, 1-3, 2-4 (standard)
    Treadle: 1-2, 1-3, 1-2, 2-4, 1-2, 1-3, 2-3, 2-4, 2-3, 1-3, 2-3, 2-4, 3-4, 1-3, 3-4, 2-4, 3-4, 1-3, 1-4, 2-4, 1-4, 1-3, 1-4, 2-4
    Weft yarn: alternates colors A and B as indicated

253. The sampler variations, as they appear in fabric. This completes the sampler.

and you might attempt another sampler substituting eight different drafts for those used previously. Several of the more common drafts are illustrated in Appendix A. However, when combining drafts it is important to consider the effect produced at the juncture of two threadings. In some cases modifications must be made to create a smooth transition. Finally, several different treadling sequences can be applied to the drafts in the sampler and those illustrated in Appendix A. No weaver could ever exhaust the possibilities in simple loom-controlled weaves.

Double Weaves

Double weave is a technique in which two sets of warp yarns are interlaced with two sets of weft yarns to create two distinct layers of cloth simultaneously. It is therefore a *four*-element construction. The two layers of fabric are physically attached at one point or at several points. At least four harnesses are required for double cloth, and an 8-harness loom is capable of producing four separate layers of cloth.

The loom is generally threaded on a straight draw for double cloth. Harnesses 1 and 2 weave the upper layer of cloth, while harnesses 3 and 4 weave the lower layer (or the reverse). However, because the top web must be held out of the way while the bottom web is being woven, the treadling sequence might be 1, 2, 1-2-3, 1-2-4 (Fig. 254).

254. Side view, cross section, and draft for double-width cloth, which is joined at one selvedge.

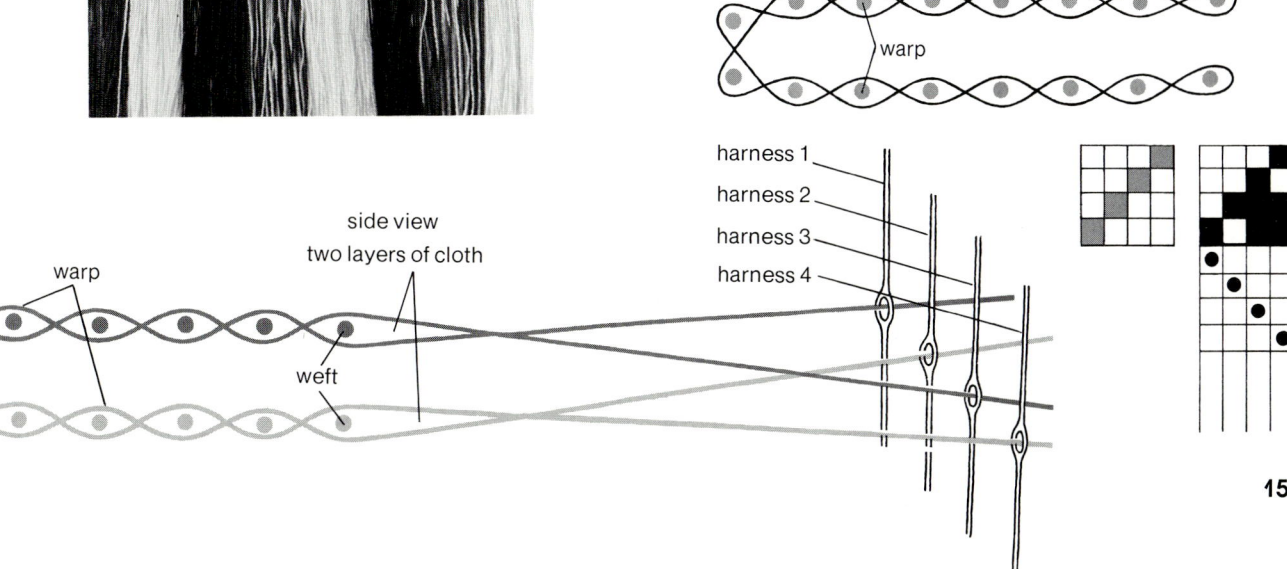

255. When double-width cloth is opened out, it is twice as wide as the fabric width of the loom.

In other words, when the third treadle is depressed (or when levers 1, 2, and 3 are manipulated), the fabric woven on harnesses 1 and 2 is lifted out of the way while at the same time a shed is created between harnesses 3 and 4. Because double cloth requires much treadling of one harness against three, it is difficult to weave on a counterbalance loom.

There are a number of ways to avoid the problem of unbalanced treadling on a counterbalance loom. Some loom manufacturers now offer a special attachment that makes it easier to open a clean shed in treadling three against one.

The sett for double weaves must be rather dense, in order to provide two relatively firm fabrics. Twice as many yarns must be sleyed through each dent as would be needed for a comparable single fabric, since you are weaving two layers of cloth at once.

Double-Width Cloth

By using the double-weave system you can produce a web twice as wide as the loom would normally accommodate. The fabric is woven in such a way that the two layers are joined at one edge and open at the other, so that when it is cut from the loom and opened out, it is twice the weaving width of the loom (Fig. 255). The warp consists of an uneven number of yarns, in order to prevent two warp ends at the joined edge from being woven alike. The joined side must have the last three yarns dented singly. The threading, tie-up, and

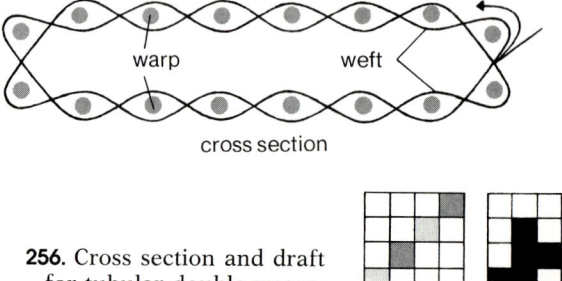

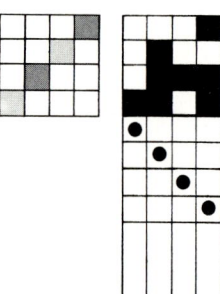

256. Cross section and draft for tubular double weave.

treadling sequences for double-width cloth are those provided in the draft portion of Figure 254.

Tubular Double Weave

Tubular double weave produces a fabric that is joined at *both* edges to create a cylinder of cloth (Fig. 256). It differs from the double-width cloth only in the treadling sequence. The treadling for double-width cloth allows first two weft shots for the top layer, then two weft shots for the bottom; in tubular double weave the weft shots alternate between top and bottom.

The fabric illustrated in Figure 257 was created by reversing the treadling sequence for tubular double weave at planned intervals and by stuffing a padding material between the layers of cloth.

257. In a stuffed tubular weave a padding material is inserted between the layers of fabric during the weaving process. Often, the treadling sequence is reversed from time to time to create sections or pockets of fabric, which are stuffed individually.

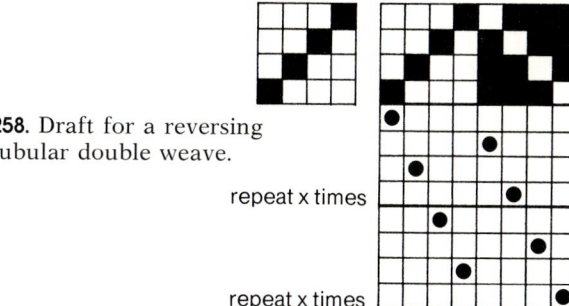

258. Draft for a reversing tubular double weave.

repeat x times

repeat x times

The treadling sequence for the top and bottom sections of the fabric is 1, 1-2-3, 2, 1-2-4; the center section is treadled 3, 1-3-4, 4, 2-3-4 (Fig. 258). This reversal of treadling causes the two layers of fabric to come together and then separate again. Stuffed tubular weaves offer great potential for the artist-weaver (Pl. 9, p. 72; Fig. 259).

Reversed Double Weave

Figure 260 shows a double fabric that is not joined at either edge but that is joined across the warp on the horizontal plane. Two colors have been used in the weft, and the treadling order has been switched at the point of juncture to create a double cloth that reverses upon itself. The draft for this type of web is illustrated in Figure 261. An X represents a weft shot of light-colored yarn, a • a shot of dark-colored yarn. As Plate 10 (p. 72) shows, this construction has far-reaching possibilities in design and scale.

above: 259. Joan Russell.
Full Circle. 1976.
Tubular weave of linen and wool, made in two sections and stuffed on the loom; 6′ (1.8 m) square. Courtesy the artist.

left: 260. A double weave can be reversed, so that the two layers of fabric interpenetrate and exchange positions.

below: 261. Draft for reversed double weave.

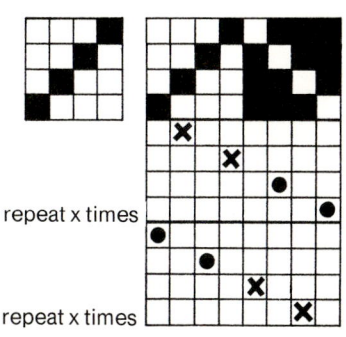

repeat x times

repeat x times

Double Weave Variations

Endless variations are possible with double weaves by changing the points of opening, the interpenetrations, and of course the colors and textures of the yarn. Some effects require the manual intervention of the weaver; these are pattern weaves and are discussed in Chapter 11. An enormous range of effects, however, can be achieved from the action of the harnesses.

In planning the double-weave fabric, a cross-section diagram is useful for organizing the threading. First, the harnesses for each layer must be assigned. Whenever there are crosses or penetrations between layers, these relationships may change.

The treadling sequence can also be planned from the cross-section diagram. It helps to mark arrows on the diagram (see Fig. 262) to keep the development of the fabric in proper order. For example, in weaving a tube you must treadle the top layer immediately after the bottom layer, so that the edges will be closed or the piece continuous. When layers interchange within a particular piece, the treadling pattern must also change.

Some double-weave variations require two or more shuttles, while others are produced by inserting the shuttle at a point other than the selvedge. One of the greatest difficulties in mastering complex double weaves is in keeping track of the yarns that belong to the respective layers and the point of entry for the shuttle, especially when there are frequent crosses and penetrations. Color changes in the warp make convenient breaking points. You can also tie a string through the reed to mark critical points.

Figure 262 shows the diagrams for six different tubular weave variations, and Figure 263 gives the threading, tie-up, and treadling drafts for each, planned for a loom having 8 treadles. The treadling instructions can be adapted easily to the levers on a table loom. For a floor loom with only 6 treadles, you can duplicate this arrangement by tying the first four treadles individually to one harness each and setting up the other two for plain weave (1-3, 2-4). When the treadling sequence calls for 3 harnesses to be raised, you will have to depress two treadles at once.

above: 262. Cross-section of six variations on the tubular double weave.

below: 263. Drafts for six variations on the tubular double weave.

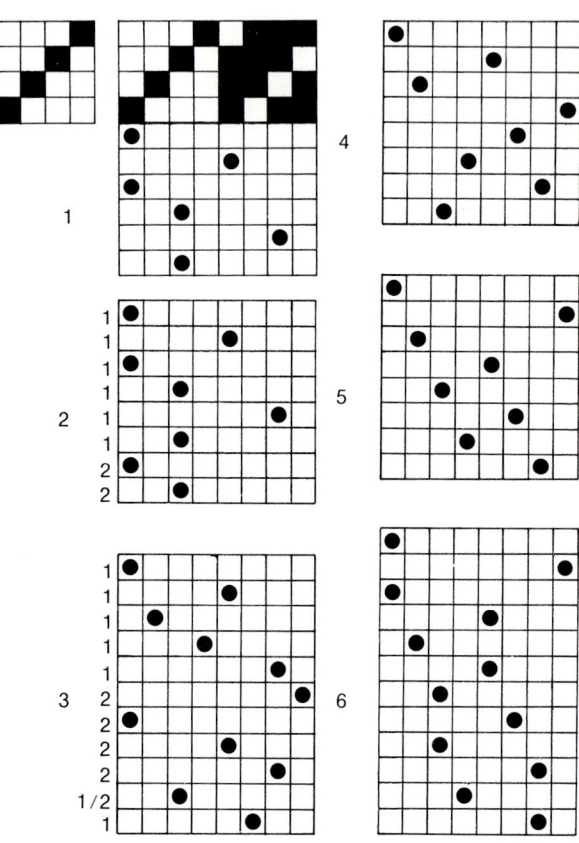

As with other double weaves, these are difficult to do on a counterbalance loom, since the shed does not open cleanly.

1. Center opening—This variation is much like double-width cloth, except that the opening comes in the top surface rather than at the selvedge.

Tie-up: 1, 3, 1-2-3, 1-3-4
Treadle: 1 from opening to right side
           1-2-3 from right edge to left edge
           1 from left edge to center
           3 from center to left edge
           1-3-4 from left edge to right edge
           3 from right edge to center

2. Panel break on the top surface—This construction has a panel in the top surface that is entirely separate from the rest of the textile. You must determine the width and placement of the panel before you begin to weave. Two shuttles are used. The treadling is similar to that for No. 1, except in the panel area. Use the second shuttle for weaving the panel, treadling alternately 1, then 3. Use the first shuttle for the rest of the textile, as described below.

Tie-up: 1, 3, 1-2-3, 1-3-4
Treadle: 1 from opening to right edge
1-2-3 from right edge to left edge
1 from left edge to center
3 from center to left edge
1-3-4 from left edge to right edge
3 from right edge to center

3. Two overlapping sections—This complex structure has four separate openings, two on each surface, none of which go all through the fabric. It requires two shuttles. All break positions must be planned before the weaving starts.

Tie-up: 1, 2, 3, 4, 1-2-3, 2-3-4, 1-3-4, 1-2-4
Treadle: Starting with shuttle #1 on the top surface at the left break point, treadle 1 and weave from left to edge. Treadle 1-2-3, and weave from edge to the same break point, and bring the shuttle out.
Treadle 2 from left break to right break.
Treadle 4, weaving from right break back to left break.
Treadle 1-3-4 to move the weft at the left break from right to left edge of the fabric.
With shuttle #2 treadle 1-2-4, insert the shuttle at left break point, and weave to right break point.
Treadle 1, and continue weaving to right edge.
Treadle 1-2-3, and weave from right to opening at right break.
Treadle 1-3-4, and return the shuttle to right edge.
Treadle 3, and insert shuttle #2 from right edge, weaving to right break point.
In the same shed, insert shuttle #1 to finish its sequence by passing it from the left edge to the left break point.
Treadle 2-3-4, and complete the sequence for shuttle #2, weaving

from right to left ending where the left break opening appears on the back.

4. Middle split on reverse sides—The cross-sectional diagram shows this structural double weave as having a slit at the same point on opposite faces. Actually, the fabric is connected by the continuous piece that makes the lower fabric on one half and the upper fabric on the other. At a chosen point, the upper and lower warp yarns exchange positions. Unless there is a change in the weft color, this variation is woven with one shuttle.

Tie-up: 1, 2, 3, 4, 1-2-3, 2-3-4, 1-3-4, 1-2-4
Treadle: 1 from center to left edge
1-2-3 from left to center
2 from center to right edge
1-2-4 from right edge to center
2-3-4 from center to right
4 from right to center
1-3-4 from center to left edge
3 from left edge to center

5. Figure-8 tube—The figure-8 tube is actually a pair of tubes joined at midpoint vertically. As in No. 4, the warp yarns exchange positions from top to bottom. Only one shuttle is necessary for a uniform weft.

Tie-up: 1, 2, 3, 4, 1-2-3, 2-3-4, 1-3-4, 1-2-4
Treadle: 1 from left to center
1-2-4 from center to right
2 from right to center
1-2-3 from center to left
3 from left to center
2-3-4 from center to right
4 from right to center
1-3-4 from center to left

6. Triple twisted tube—This structure has three tubes connected to one another. It is more complex in appearance than No. 5 but not difficult to weave. One shuttle is sufficient.

Tie-up: 1, 2, 3, 4, 1-2-3, 2-3-4, 1-3-4, 1-2-4
Treadle: Assume the tubes are A, B, C from left to right.
1 from left edge to right side of tube A
1-2-4 from left side of tube B to right side of tube B
1 from left side of tube C to right edge
1-2-3 from right edge to left side of tube C

2 from right side of tube B to left side of tube B

1-2-3 from right side of tube A to left edge

3 from left edge to right side of tube A

2-3-4 from left side of tube B to right side of tube B

3 from left side of tube C to right edge

1-3-4 from right edge to left side of tube C

4 from right side of tube B to left side of tube B

1-3-4 from right side of tube A to left edge

Loom-Controlled Lace Weave

True lace is not made on a loom but with quite different equipment. Some openwork loom-constructed finger weaves resemble lace and are therefore described as lace weaves. These are discussed in Chapter 11. However, there are loom-controlled weaves that also produce a lacy effect—that is, an openwork appearance but still a fairly stable structure (Fig. 264). The most typical weave is often referred to as *Swedish lace*, although this does not indicate a specific threading draft but rather a general method.

Figure 265 shows the threading, tie-up, and treadling drafts for a loom-controlled lace weave. The threading draft is a two-block pattern much like huckaback (Appendix A). This arrangement allows for a looseness in the weave but at the same time a supporting plain-weave structure. The number of repeats in each block can be varied. Each block has five warp yarns tied down by a sixth. Block A is threaded 1, 2, 1, 2, 1, 4; block B is threaded 4, 3, 4, 3, 4, 1. When the two blocks are joined, the repeated 1 or 4 threading is eliminated, so that at points of juncture the blocks share a common yarn. Often, the warp yarns are irregularly dented, with an overall open sett.

The treadling sequence is also two-part. The first section is treadled 1-3, 4, 1-3, 4, 1-3, 2-4; the second 2-4, 1, 2-4, 1, 2-4, 1-3. As with the threading, the repeated treadling is omitted when the sequence changes from one to the other. The beating should be gentle but regular, on a taut warp.

This Swedish lace weave is reversible. Each section of the fabric is warp-faced on one side and weft-faced on the other, and the areas switch positions on the two faces of the textile.

above: **264.** A mock lace weave can be created on the loom through the interaction of the heddle frames, with no finger weaving necessary.

right: **265.** Draft for loom-controlled lace weave.

Weaver-controlled weaves are created through the direct intervention of the weaver. They are often called finger weaves, because at various times the shed or a portion of the shed is opened with the fingers or with some implement—a needle, crochet hook, or *pickup stick*. Weaver-controlled weaves differ from those constructed entirely through the interaction of the harnesses in several respects: either the warp or the weft or both may depart from their strict vertical and horizontal alignments; the weft yarn may appear only in certain portions of the web, rather than being carried from selvedge to selvedge; packing with a beater is often unnecessary or undesirable.

Most finger weaves are based on plain weave. They frequently require short amounts of weft yarn, so a *butterfly shuttle* is more practical than the cumbersome boat shuttle. A butterfly shuttle can be made by wrapping the yarn figure-8 fashion around the fingers (Fig. 266). A loop made from the starting end of the yarn and wrapped snugly around the cross serves to hold the shape.

Weaver-Controlled Weaves

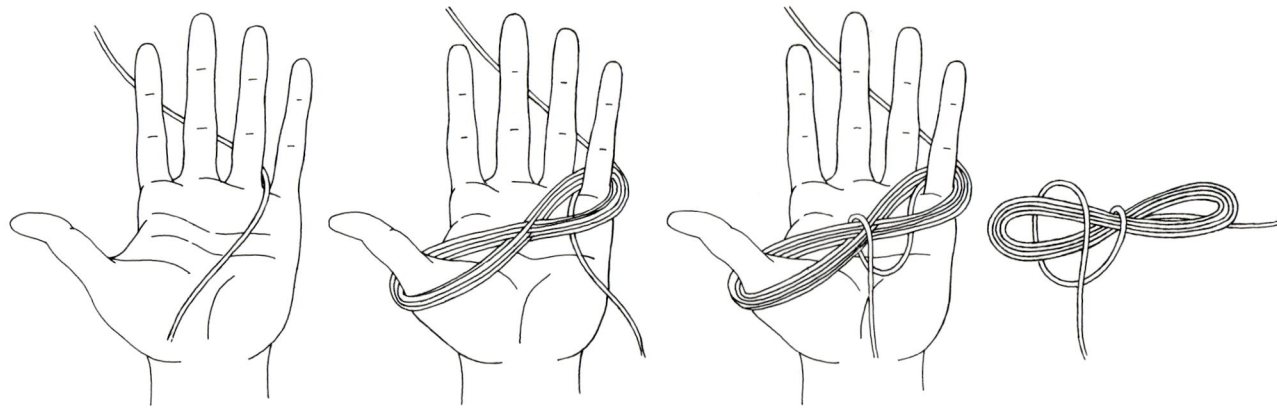

266. A butterfly shuttle can be made by wrapping weft yarn in figure-8 fashion around the fingers. This arrangement is practical for many finger weaves.

Lace Weaves

Lace weaves comprise one of the largest groups of weaver-controlled weaves. They have an open, "lacy" effect and a distortion from the parallel of warp or weft yarns. The most common forms of lace weave are leno, Mexican lace, Spanish lace, Brook's Bouquet, and Danish medallion.

Leno

Leno is a form of *gauze weave*—that is, a weave in which the warp yarns are made to cross each other at certain points. In preparation for leno, the loom is threaded for plain weave on two or four harnesses. A pickup stick that is longer than the web is wide will facilitate crossing the yarns. The stick should also be wider than it is thick, so that when it is placed on end a shed is opened (Fig. 267).

The simplest form of leno is the 1/1 or *single cross*, in which two adjacent warp yarns are crossed upon each other. The yarns must exchange positions in two ways: from top to bottom of the shed and horizontally (or sideways) in the threading order.

There are many variations of leno. Sometimes the leno pattern moves entirely across the web; at

other times it will appear in small sections only. Yarns can be crossed either right to left or left to right. Crossed yarns can alternate with uncrossed ones in a preselected system. The simplest way to explain the mechanics of leno is to give one possible pattern. The directions in the box are for right-handed people. Left-handed weavers should reverse them.

A Basic 1/1 Leno

- Weave a few rows of plain weave to form a base, ending with the shuttle at the right selvedge.
- Open a shed so that the outermost warp yarn at right is down.
- Place the pickup stick, lying flat, on top of yarn 2 (which is up). Reach through the warp with your left hand, grasp yarn 1, cross it behind yarn 2, and place it on the stick to the left of yarn 2.
- Proceed to the left, placing the stick on yarn 4, and crossing yarn 3 behind it to lie on top of the stick.
- Continue across the row in this fashion.
- When all the crossed yarns are on the pickup stick, turn the stick on end, and pass the weft yarn through the resultant shed (Fig. 268).
- Remove the stick carefully, and change the shed.
- On the return trip of the weft, do not cross any yarns. A crossing effect will develop as the yarns untwist themselves.

Some weavers like to work by manipulating the stick alone, without using the left hand. Others find it more convenient to push aside the top yarns with the back of the hand. You can begin the crossing rows from either side of the web and make as many plain-weave shots as you wish between leno rows. However, the leno rows should always begin from the same side and be made on the same shed.

267. Finger weaves often are produced by interlacing a pickup stick through the warp yarns and then turning the stick on end to create a shed.

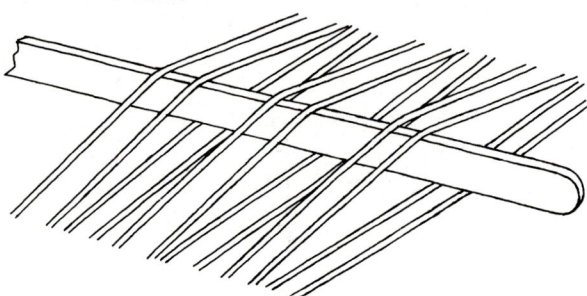

268. Leno is a lace weave in which the warp yarns are crossed at certain points. This is a 1/1 leno, the simplest form.

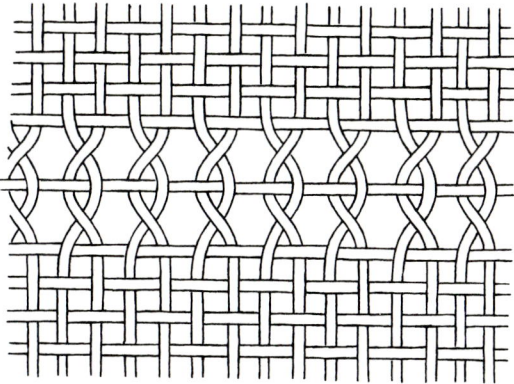

A double or 2/2 leno (Fig. 269) works on the same principle. Following the system used for the above example, start at right and place the stick over warp yarns 2 and 4 (which are up). Cross yarns 1 and 3 behind, and place them on the stick to the left of yarns 2 and 4.

Various other arrangements are possible: three bottom yarns crossed on three top yarns, one top yarn crossed on two bottom yarns, and so forth. Several leno combinations are explored in the sampler (pp. 162–164). Anni Albers' weaving in Figure 270 is an excellent example of leno.

269. A 2/2 leno weave.

270. Anni Albers. *Tikal.* 1958. Pictorial weaving of cotton in leno and plain weave, 35½ × 29½" (89 × 74 cm). From *Objects: USA,* Johnson Wax Collection of Contemporary Crafts, Racine, Wis.

271. In Mexican lace the warp yarns are crossed three times, with the weft inserted in the middle cross.

Mexican Lace

In the Mexican lace variation of leno, the warp yarns are crossed three times, with the weft inserted in the middle cross (Fig. 271). It is usually more open than leno. The major difference between leno and Mexican lace is that in Mexican lace the yarns to be crossed are not adjacent to each other but are farther apart. For example, if you were doing a 2/2 Mexican lace, you would skip one unit of two yarns and cross units 1 and 3.

Mexican lace is just as easy to do as leno, but it requires a special beginning and ending at the selvedges to get the yarns in proper phase. As with leno, it is done on an open shed. If you begin at the right selvedge, with the outermost yarn up, push yarn 1 to the left and under the pickup stick as you draw yarns 2 and 4 (which are down) onto the stick. Repeat this process once, again pushing down one yarn and drawing up two. Then continue with the normal crossing—skipping one unit each time—for Mexican lace. When you reach the left selvedge, you must reverse the beginning arrangement: pushing down two yarns and raising one for a distance of two units.

Because the warp yarns are being drawn farther in a horizontal direction, there is a greater problem of draw-in with Mexican lace than with leno. The fabric tends to become narrow, and the selvedge yarns may break. You can counteract this to some extent by keeping the warp tension slightly looser than normal. As with leno, Mexican lace can be used for a variety of design patterns.

Spanish Lace

Spanish lace is woven by dividing the warp into units and interlacing each unit individually, moving from right to left or left to right across the warp. For purposes of demonstration, the warp yarns in Figure 272 have been divided into groups of three, but in practice, on the loom, you would probably want to group the yarns into larger units—perhaps six to ten yarns.

Spanish Lace

- With the 1-3 shed open, insert the weft at the right selvedge and carry it across one unit of yarns.
- Change the shed to 2-4, and return the weft to the selvedge.
- Change the shed again to 1-3, and carry the weft across the same unit of yarns. Leave the shed open.
- With the 1-3 shed still open, carry the weft yarn down diagonally to the level of the first weft shot but on the second unit of yarns. Make the same S-curve on the second unit.

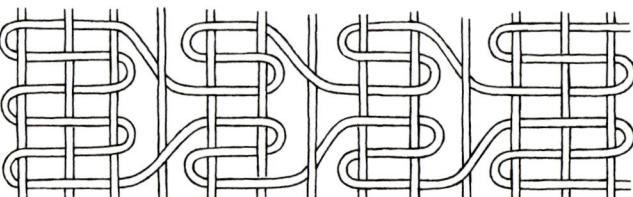

272. To make Spanish lace, divide the warp into sections, and weave each unit individually with a butterfly shuttle. An attractive pattern results when the units are drawn together with spaces in between.

You must ease the weft into position with your fingers or the edge of the shuttle. The beater is never used with Spanish lace. When the weft yarn reaches the left selvedge, a total of three new weft shots—in sections—have been added to the web.

Spanish lace is most effective when the grouped units of warp yarn are drawn together slightly to leave an open slit between them. It is particularly attractive when the weft yarn is heavier than the warp or when it is of a contrasting color. Variety of pattern is achieved by altering the size of the warp units, by staggering the number of weft shots in each unit, or by interspersing areas of Spanish lace with solid plain weave. An adjacent section of plain weave may require extra weft shots to keep the rows even.

Danish Medallion

The Danish medallion is an unusual weave in that the weft yarn departs from its horizontal orientation to make a vertical or diagonal loop on the surface of the fabric (Fig. 273). This loop of yarn is the medallion. It is usually woven with a yarn that contrasts in weight, color, texture, or a combination of these with the warp yarn and ground weft, although a purely textured effect can be produced with identical yarn.

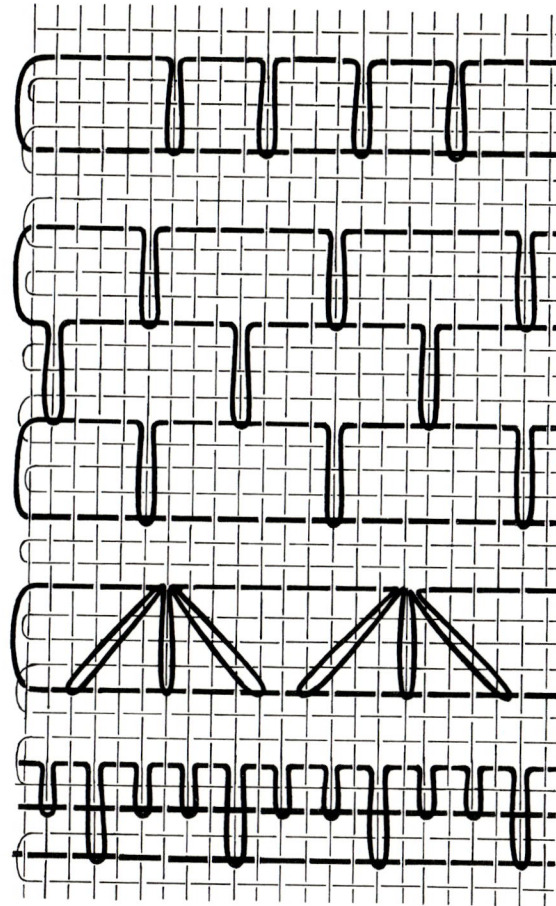

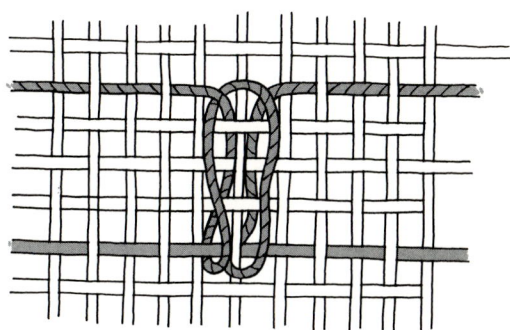

left: 273. Variations of Danish medallion are produced by altering the length, direction, or spacing of the medallion loops.

below: 274. In Danish medallion, the weft yarn departs from its horizontal orientation to make a vertical or diagonal loop on the fabric surface.

275. Brook's Bouquet is a form of warp wrapping in which the weft yarn passes completely around several warp yarns to draw them together.

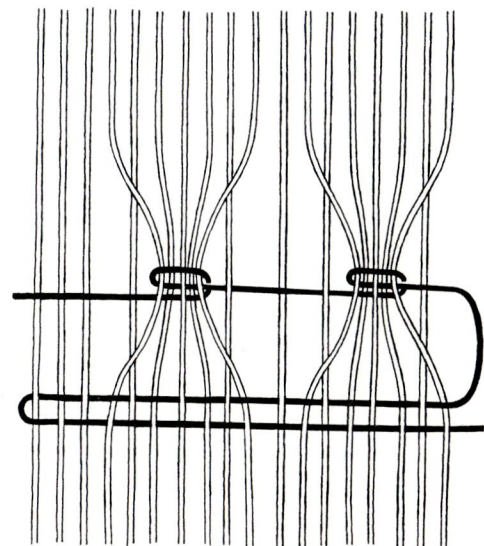

Danish Medallion

□ Pass the medallion yarn through the normal plain-weave shed.

□ Follow this shot with several shots of ground weft (Fig. 274).

□ Enter the medallion yarn in the next shed, passing it through a predetermined number of warp yarns before bringing it to the surface of the fabric.

□ With a crochet hook, catch a loop of the yarn just below the previous medallion weft yarn and at the same horizontal point where the shuttle emerged from the shed.

□ Enlarge the loop to permit the shuttle to pass through it.

□ To finish the medallion, replace the shuttle in the shed at the same spot, and continue across until you want another medallion.

By altering the vertical distance between rows of medallion yarn and the horizontal distance between medallions, you can create a wide range of patterns. You can also produce flowerets, radiating lines, and other designs by catching several loops at the same spot and reentering the yarn at different points in the shed.

Brook's Bouquet

Brook's Bouquet, sometimes called *back stitch*, is a form of warp wrapping made on an open shed. As indicated in Figure 275, the weft yarn passes under a group of warps, wraps around them completely, and then proceeds to the next group. The warp yarn between groups, because it is at the bottom of the shed, is not affected and appears as a single vertical line between the units of Brook's Bouquet. As the weft is twisted around the warps, it should be held tightly enough to draw the warp yarns together, but not so tightly that the weft cannot be beat into position or that two units of warp pull together. Variation in pattern is created by staggering the units of warp to be enclosed or by alternating with sections of plain weave.

Lace Weaves: A Sampler

The sampler cannot possibly explore all the myriad combinations of the various lace weaves. However, the several examples of each will provide you with a key to developing patterns of your own design. The sampler was planned for four harnesses, but since all the lace weaves described are based on plain weave, it could easily be duplicated on two harnesses.

Specifications for the Sampler

Length of finished sampler:	3 yards (2.7 m)
Length of each warp yarn:	3¾ yards (3.4 m)
Warp yarn:	8/4 cotton (carpet warp)
Number of warp yarns:	152 (80 dark, 72 light)
Amount of warp yarn:	570 yards (521 m) (one 4-ounce spool of each color)
Weft yarn:	8/4 cotton (dark, one ¼-pound spool) 8/4 cotton (light, one ¼-pound spool) firm wool (1 ounce) cotton rug yarn (1 skein)
Number of heddles required:	38 on each of four harnesses
Width of finished sampler:	about 9 inches (22.5 cm)
Width at reed:	10 inches (25 cm)
Size of reed:	No. 15 (6 per cm)

Threading, Sleying, and Tie-Up Instructions

Thread the warp in a straight draw (1, 2, 3, 4) throughout. Warp all the dark yarns on one side and the light yarns on the other, so you can see color contrasts develop. Sley one yarn through each dent in the reed. The tie-up is 1-3, 2-4 for the entire sampler.

276. Sections 1 (*above*) and 2 (*below*) of the sampler, showing variations of leno weave.

Weaving Instructions

Weave a dividing band of plain weave at least half an inch wide after each of the pattern areas described below. The sampler has 30 sections in all. The 8/4 cotton is used as weft for the first 22 sections.

1. Four rows of 2/2 leno alternated with three rows of plain weave. The leno twists occur across the entire warp (Fig. 276).
2. Four rows of 3/3 leno alternated with seven rows of plain weave (Fig. 276). There is a 1-inch border of plain weave at each selvedge. Extra weft shots are required in this area.
3. Six rows of 1/1 leno all across the warp, with a single shot of plain weave separating the rows.
4. A 2/2 leno pattern, with eight pairs of twisted yarns followed by eight pairs left untwisted. The pattern is staggered in alternating rows, with three weft shots between rows.
5. Overall pattern of alternating 3/3 leno and plain weave. Six yarns are left untwisted after each leno twist, and there are five shots of plain weave after each leno row.
6. Blocks of 2/2 leno separated by plain weave. There are three shots of plain weave after each twisted row.

277. Section 9 of the sampler, in which 1/2 leno and 2/1 leno are alternated.

7. Staggered pattern of 2/2 leno to create a diagonal line. Only one unit of four yarns is twisted in each row, and every row has a twist. With each weft shot, the yarns to be twisted are those next to the ones twisted in the previous row, moving always in one direction across the web.

8. A broader staggered pattern of 2/2 leno, with four units twisted in each row. As in No. 7, the twists progress to one side of the fabric. In the first row, twist only units 1, 2, 3, and 4. In the second row, twist units 2, 3, 4, and 5. Continue to the center of the fabric, and then reverse.

9. An alternated pattern of 1/2 leno and 2/1 leno all across the fabric. There are three plain weave shots between leno rows (Fig. 277).

10. A pattern of 1/1 leno in which the fourth lower warp yarn is twisted with the first upper warp yarn. Five shots of plain weave separate the pattern rows.

11. Blocks of 3/3 leno surrounded by areas of plain weave. Three weft shots are entered in each twist.

12. A vertical striped pattern created by alternating lenos. Each row has a block of twelve 1/1 lenos followed by a block of three 2/2 lenos. The blocks are kept the same for all the rows.

13. An alternated pattern of lenos. The first row has twelve 1/1 lenos followed by six 2/2 lenos across the web. This is followed by three shots of plain weave. The second twist row is the reverse of the previous one, with six 2/2 lenos followed by twelve 1/1 lenos, and so on.

14. A progression of 1/1, 2/2, and 3/3 leno across the row. The second twist row has consecutive units of 2/2, 3/3, 1/1, and so forth. Five plain-weave shots separate the twist rows.

15. An alternation of 2/2 leno twisted to the left with 2/2 leno twisted to the right, all across the row. One warp yarn must be skipped between twists. Three plain-weave shots separate the twist rows.

16. Leno produced on a closed shed. To make the twists, cross yarns 1 and 2 with yarns 5 and 6, and bring yarns 3 and 4 up through the center of the cross. Yarns 3 and 4 will be above the weft yarn, the others below (Fig. 278). There are five plain-weave shots between the rows.

17. An allover pattern of 2/2 Mexican lace (Fig. 278).

18. Brook's Bouquet twisted around four upper warp yarns all across the row (Fig. 278). Three shots of plain weave separate the pattern rows.

278. Three sections of the sampler: *top:* 16, a leno variation; *middle:* 17, allover 2/2 Mexican lace; *bottom:* 18, Brook's Bouquet.

279. Section 26 of the sampler, illustrating an allover pattern of Danish medallion.

19. A staggered pattern of Brook's Bouquet wrapped around four warp yarns on an open shed, followed by three plain-weave shots. The wrapped warps are alternated in each succeeding row by taking two warp yarns each from adjacent units in the previous row.

20. Brook's Bouquet involving three upper warp yarns, followed by six skipped upper warp yarns. After three pattern rows have been made in this manner, stagger the twists to occur in the middle of the previously skipped section. All rows are separated by three shots of plain weave.

21. An allover pattern of Brook's Bouquet wrapping two warp yarns, followed by five untwisted warp yarns. The twists are in the same position for each row, so that vertical columns develop. One plain weave shot separates rows.

22. Danish medallions at regularly spaced intervals, each spanning four weft shots. The pattern weft yarn is cotton rug yarn.

23. A staggered pattern of Danish medallion. Use one of the two carpet warp colors for this pattern and the other for the ground weft.

24. Danish medallions spaced evenly across the rows and lined up evenly in the various rows, so that they create a vertical column in the fabric.

25. A staggered pattern of Danish medallion with two colors of carpet warp alternated as well as alternated colors in the ground weave.

26. An allover pattern of Danish medallion with three loops in each unit to make a fan or flower effect (Fig. 279).

27. Danish medallion with variation in the size of the units and the length of the loops.

28. Spanish lace with two sizes of weaving units alternated (Fig. 280). The weft yarn is firmly twisted wool.

29. Spanish lace with small and large units alternated both vertically and horizontally (Fig. 280). The weft yarn is again the firm wool.

30. Spanish lace in which the warp yarns have been drawn tightly together to create shaped openings between them (Fig. 281). The weft is beaten tightly to create a warp-face textile. The weft is carpet warp. This method is almost identical to slit tapestry (Fig. 312).

280. Sections 28 (*above*) and 29 (*below*) of the sampler, two variations of Spanish lace.

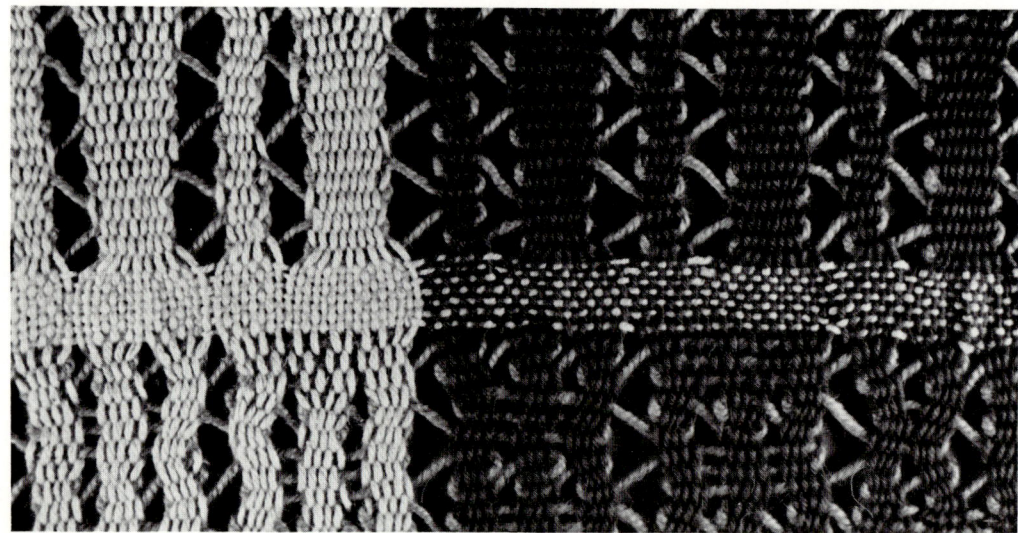

Warp Wrapping

Warp wrapping is, in a sense, an extension of the lace weaves. The weft yarn wraps around several warp yarns to draw them together, thus producing an open, lacy effect. In ancient Peru warp wrapping was done on the backstrap loom, using a needle or a small shuttle to constrict the warp yarns or occasionally the weft. The result was rather like embroidery.

Several techniques can be used for wrapping and gathering the warp, including the simple wrapping discussed in Chapter 15 (Figs. 423, 424). Another common method is the Greek soumak (Fig. 357), which, when pulled taut, produces a diagonal pattern on the surface of the fabric. Figure 282 shows a third technique, the *lockstitch*, which resembles Danish medallion. A small shuttle or butterfly shuttle carrying the pattern weft forms a loop around a selected number of warp yarns and then is passed through that loop to hold the stitch. Other warp-wrapping patterns include the spiral, the figure-8, and the vertical twining technique (Fig. 283).

Pattern Double Weave

Pattern double weaves differ from the loom-controlled variety described in Chapter 10 (pp. 151–156) in that the two layers of fabric interpenetrate and exchange positions at certain points. The pattern is created either by carrying the weft yarn across only part of the web at a time or by lifting certain warp yarns by hand.

281. Section 30 of the sampler, in which Spanish lace is drawn tightly together to create openings.

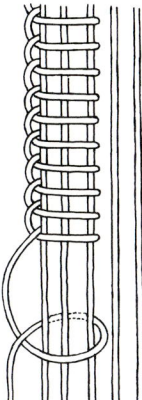

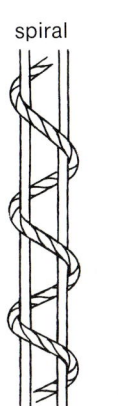   

spiral   figure-8   vertical twining   two yarns

left: 282. Lockstitch can be used for warp wrapping.

right: 283. Four different methods of warp wrapping. *Left to right:* spiral, figure-8, vertical twining, vertical twining with two yarns.

284. Two shuttles—one for each side of the web—are used to create a double cloth in which the two layers exchange positions vertically at the center of the fabric.

A very simple form of pattern double weave is shown in Figure 284. Each layer of fabric has an identical warp and weft, but the two layers cross and exchange positions in the center of the warp. This can be done in several ways.

One method is to carry the shuttle from the center of the web to one selvedge and then back again to the center. An alternate shuttle weaves from the center to the opposite selvedge and back. The heddles are threaded in a straight draw with the warp yarns alternating between the two colors.

Another possible method of creating the vertically exchanging double weave allows the weft yarn to go completely across the web but makes use of a knitting needle or other pickup stick to hold some of the yarns out of the way. The mechanics of this technique are illustrated in Figure 285. Again, the heddles are threaded in a straight draw with the warp yarns alternating colors.

285. Draft for the fabric illustrated in Figure 284.

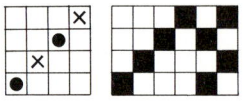

pick up raised yarns on left side
weave across the web with dark weft yarn
weave across the web with dark weft yarn
pick up raised yarns on right side
weave across the web with light weft yarn
weave across the web with light weft yarn

Vertically Exchanging Double Weave

☐ Treadle 2-4, and insert the pickup stick under all the raised warp yarns on the left side of the loom.

☐ Treadle 1, and weave across the web from left to right with the dark weft.

☐ Treadle 3, and weave back across the web to the left edge using the dark weft.

☐ Remove the pickup stick, and beat the fabric firmly.

☐ Treadle 1-3 and insert the pickup stick under all the raised warp yarns on the *right* side of the loom.

☐ Treadle 2, and weave across the web from left to right with the light weft.

☐ Treadle 4, and weave back across the web to the left edge using the dark weft.

☐ Remove the pickup stick, and beat.

The stylized pattern in Figures 286 and 287 was created in much the same manner, with a pickup stick to force pattern warp yarns from the lower layer of fabric into the top layer and the reverse. The only difference from the previous example is that yarns are lifted selectively, not by halves of the warp. This double fabric is reversible: the design appears in light yarn against a dark ground on one side, in dark yarn against light on the other.

As the weave draft shows (Fig. 288), there are six steps involved. First, treadle 2-4 and, with the shed open, place the pickup stick under all the

right: 286. Kyung Rhee.
A Couple. 1976.
Pattern double weave,
29 × 43″ (74 × 109 cm).
Courtesy the artist.

below: 287. Detail of the pattern
double weave in Figure 286.

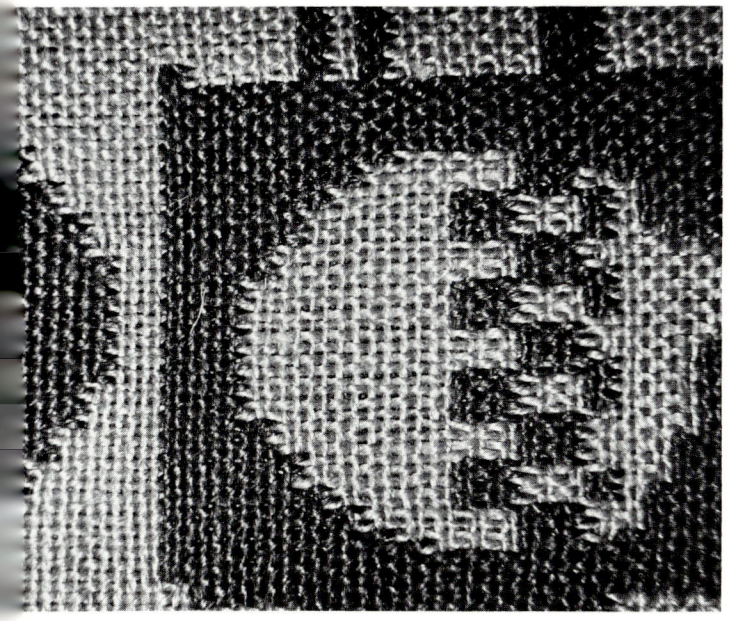

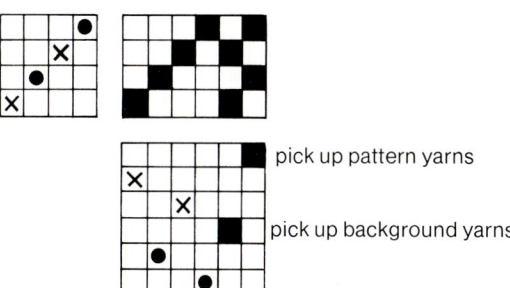

pick up pattern yarns

pick up background yarns

above: 288. Draft for the pattern double weave
in Figures 286 and 287.

below: 289. The pickup stick is threaded
under all the yarns
that are to carry the pattern.

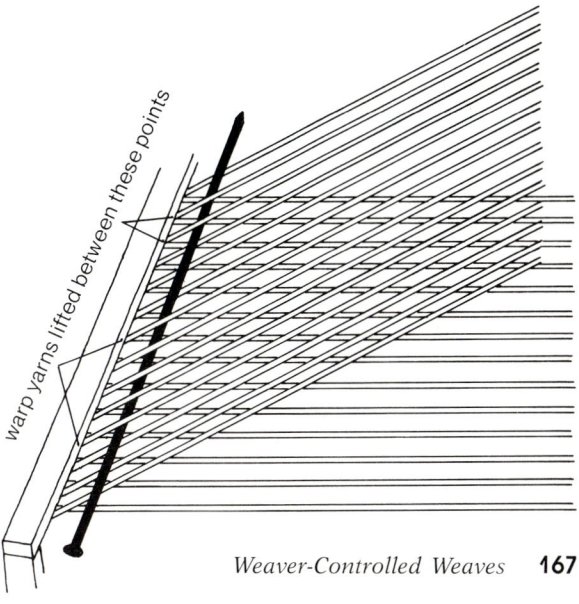

warp yarns lifted between these points

warp yarns that are to carry the pattern (Fig. 289).
Then, with the pickup stick in position, change the
shed. Treadle first 1 and then 3, making each time
a weft shot with the same color yarn as is threaded
in harness 1. Treadle 1-3, and lift all the background yarns onto the pickup stick—that is, all the
yarns not picked up for step 1. Finally, treadle 2
and 4 in turn, and insert the other weft yarn, color
B. When the pattern area increases or decreases—
for example, to create a diagonal line—the change
should affect two adjacent warp yarns in each
row, in order to permit a smooth transition.

Weaver-Controlled Weaves **167**

above: 290. A double cloth can be reversed
in two directions: from front to back
and from top to bottom. This fabric
was woven by combining the techniques
in Figures 261 and 288.

Figure 290 illustrates a slightly more complicated version of the reversible pattern weave. In
this case, the pattern reverses itself both from
front to back and from top to bottom, because the
weave draft has been altered halfway through the
web. At the point of juncture, the treadling is
adjusted as for reversed double weave (Fig. 261).
There are literally infinite variations possible with
pattern double weave.

Brocade

Brocade is a *three*-element construction: in addition to the usual warp and weft, there is a third or
decorative element in the web (Fig. 291). Brocade
can be introduced in the warp or the weft or both.
It can be either *continuous*—running from selvedge to selvedge or from one end of the warp to
the other—or *discontinuous*. A discontinuous brocade, also known as a *laid-in*, *inlay*, or *inlaid*
weave, means that the effect yarns are placed only
in certain areas.

Brocades are most often added to a plain-
weave ground. The plain weave exists independently of the decorative element (Fig. 292), so that if
all the brocading yarns were to be pulled out, the
plain-weave structure would remain intact. Traditionally, the ground is uniform and rather neutral
in color, while the brocade yarn is more intensely

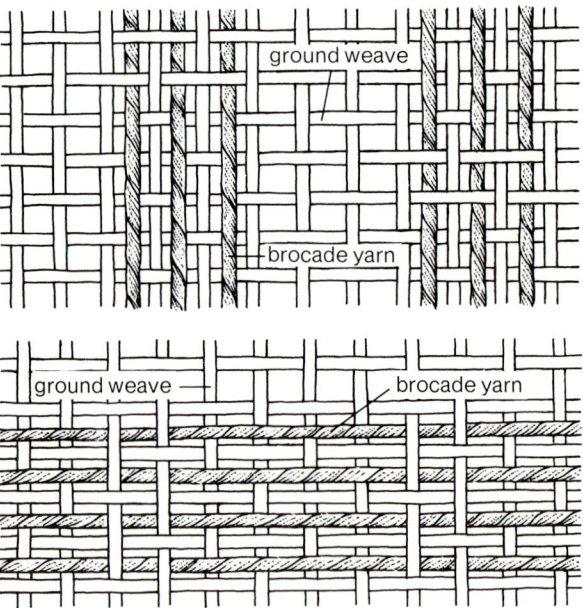

left: 291. Ed Rossbach. *Log Cabin Sham*, detail.
Brocaded overshot in cotton and linen.

above: 292. In brocade, the ground weave exists
independently of the brocading element.
The brocade yarn can be introduced
in either the warp or the weft, or both.

above: Plate 11. Anni Albers.
La Luz I. 1945.
Linen and metal
gimp satine weave
with discontinuous brocade,
$18\frac{3}{4} \times 31\frac{1}{4}''$ (47 × 78 cm).
Collection Richard Lippold,
Locust Valley, N.Y.

left: Plate 12.
Navajo "chief" blanket,
of the Transition Period.
1880–90. Handspun wool with
commercial aniline dyes,
5'3" × 4'2" (1.6 × 1.25 m).
Heard Museum, Phoenix.

above: Plate 13. Grau-Garriga. *Primavera.* Tapestry in cotton, wool, and synthetic fibers; 3′9″ × 2′9″ (1.1 × .8 m). Courtesy Arras Gallery, N.Y.

below: Plate 14. Hermann Scholten. *Boog.* 1973. Wool, 9′9″ × 21′9″ (2.9 × 6.5 m). Provincial Government Building, Zwolle, Holland.

293. A continuous warp brocade, face (*left*) and back (*right*).

colored, heavier, softer, and more elaborate. The fabric is usually woven face down so that, especially with a discontinuous brocade, the weaver can dispose of the effect yarns easily by tying them off or carrying them as floats.

Continuous Warp Brocade

A warp brocade can be woven on only three harnesses. Harnesses 1 and 2 would be threaded for plain weave across the loom, while harness 3 would carry the brocade yarn at each point where it is needed. If desired, a second brocading element could be added on the fourth harness. However, every brocade yarn must have a base yarn on both sides of it to maintain the plain-weave structure. Figure 293 illustrates a simple warp brocade fabric. A basic draft for warp brocade is given in Figure 294.

Continuous Weft Brocade

To create a weft brocade, the heddles are threaded for plain weave, always alternating between an odd-numbered harness and an even-numbered harness. The base weft yarns are shot through alternating sheds, and the brocade yarn, carried on a separate shuttle, is introduced wherever desired but independent of the plain-weave ground. There must be a plain-weave yarn on both sides of every brocade yarn.

Discontinuous Warp Brocade

It is a bit more difficult to introduce a warp brocade yarn for a small area, but some pattern effects may require it. There are several methods for doing this. First, you can splice the brocade yarn onto one of the warp yarns already on the loom in the same manner as you would repair a broken yarn (Figs. 221, 222). You can also tie supplementary rods to the back beam and breast beam to

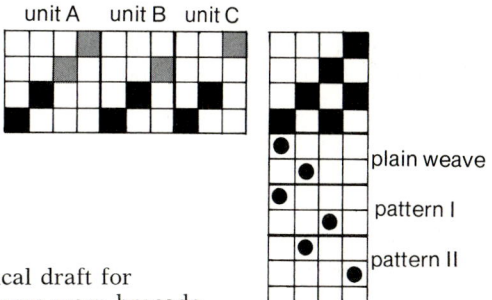

294. Typical draft for a continuous warp brocade.

carry the brocade yarns. When only a few yarns are to be added, they need not be threaded through the heddles; you can simply raise them by hand when necessary. If you do wish to thread the brocade yarns through the heddles, you can either leave extra heddles on the frame when you thread the loom or add string heddles when the brocade yarns are brought in.

Discontinuous Weft Brocade

The simplest method of laying in a weft brocade is to add it to the plain-weave shed (Fig. 295). The loom is threaded in a straight draw and tied up for a 1-3 and 2-4 treadling. Each time the brocade yarn is required, it is placed in the plain-weave shed alongside the regular weft yarn. When the pattern area is completed, the brocade yarn can be

295. A discontinuous weft brocade yarn is usually placed in the plain-weave shed beside the ground-weave yarn.

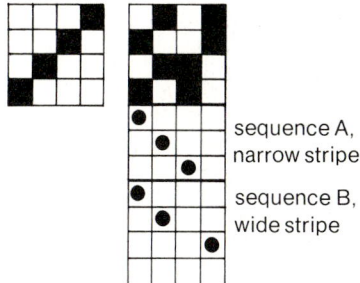

296. Wall hanging in dukagång, from Skåne, Sweden. 1806. Linen and wool, height 27" (68 cm). Nordiska Museet, Stockholm.

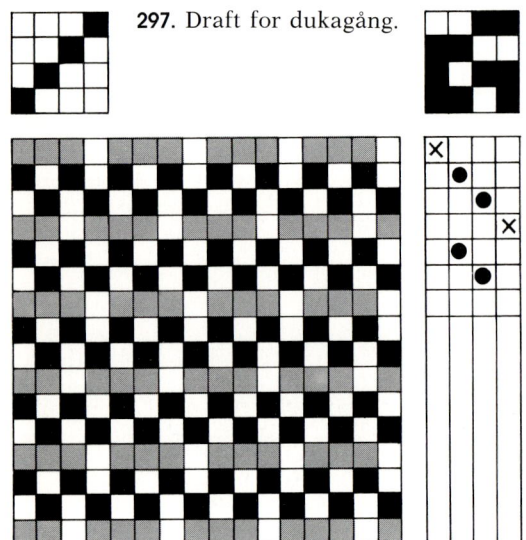

297. Draft for dukagång.

tied off and cut or, if it is to appear again, carried across the back of the fabric (which is up) to the next pattern area.

Of course, it is not essential for the brocaded fabric to be based on plain weave. Twills and other weaves can form the background of a brocade, with the additional yarn laid into some or all of the sheds. In any event, the brocade yarn is generally softer and more decorative than the ground-weave yarns. Following the tradition of opulent Renaissance and Baroque brocades, the pattern yarn is often a metallic (Pl. 11, p. 169).

Dukagång

One variation of the laid-in brocade is Swedish dukagång, in which the decorative yarn floats over three consecutive warp yarns and is tied down by the fourth (Fig. 296). This technique permits greater visibility of the brocade yarn on the surface and produces the "straight little paths in the cloth" from which dukagång takes its name.

As the sample draft (Fig. 297) illustrates, the decorative yarn is not placed in the same shed as the tabby weft. Rather, a separate shed is created for the pattern yarn, followed by one or two shots of plain weave. The fabric is always woven face down. There can be as many as four different dukagång sheds (1-2-3, 2-3-4, 1-3-4, and 1-2-4) or only one. In the sample draft there are two pattern sheds. If the decorative yarn is much heavier than the plain-weave yarn, extra weft shots may be necessary from time to time to fill in the background areas of the fabric and keep the rows even. Sometimes the decorative yarn floats on the back of the fabric to make pattern areas on the face.

Tapestry

A tapestry is a weft-face plain-weave fabric in which pattern areas are built up by free-weaving techniques. The design is often, though by no means always, pictorial. There are many traditional styles of tapestry weaving, each deriving its name from the region or group in which it originated. In some cases the names imply a characteristic pattern or design, in others a particular weaving technique. Often, both elements combine to form an identifiable style. Modern tapestry weavers borrow methods and ideas from many sources, both contemporary and historical, in order to achieve their expressive purposes. With the possible exception of the long-established tapestry

298. Evelyn Anselevicius at work on one of her monumental tapestries. The tapestry being woven is similar to the one shown in Figure 321.

manufactures and some tradition-bound folk artisans, few weavers would insist today that a tapestry must rigidly follow prescribed rules to be "correct." Indeed, the 20th-century weaver is blessed with an enormous wealth of precedent from which to draw inspiration.

Materials

Two considerations are paramount in choosing materials for a tapestry. First, the warp must be strong, smooth, and elastic enough to resist break-

299. A tapestry loom is a vertical frame with only two harnesses. Tapestries woven on such a loom are called *haute lisse*. *Basse-lisse* tapestries are made on a horizontal loom.

age under tension, to stand considerable handling during the weaving process, and to lend body to the tapestry. For this reason, cotton seine cord and cable twine have sometimes been used. In the Scandinavian countries linen has traditionally been the preferred material for tapestry warp. American Indian and Mexican tapestry weavers have favored a tightly spun wool, as did the early European weavers. Tapestries woven in China and Japan utilized silk for both warp and weft.

The second variable is the sett, the density of the fabric. Since it is nearly always desirable for the weft to completely cover the warp, the warp must be sufficiently open to allow the weft to pack around it. Carpet warp can be set at 8 ends-per-inch; a heavier yarn might be set even more openly, but the result will be a coarse tapestry. The closer the sett, the finer the detail can be.

Singles wool yarns have been used traditionally for weft, since they are soft enough to pack readily around the warp. Cotton and silk are often added for accents or textural variation.

Equipment

Tapestries generally are divided into two groups, depending upon the type of equipment on which they are woven. *Basse-lisse* or low-warp tapestries are woven on a standard horizontal loom with two or four harnesses—the same type of loom used for other kinds of flat weaving (Fig. 298). *Haute-lisse* or high-warp tapestries are woven on the vertical two-harness tapestry loom (Fig. 299) or on an upright frame loom (Fig. 401). Because the structure is always plain weave, only two harnesses or shedding devices are required. For very small or simple projects, you could even dispense with harnesses and heddles altogether and interlace with your

300. A tapestry fork serves as beater and reed.

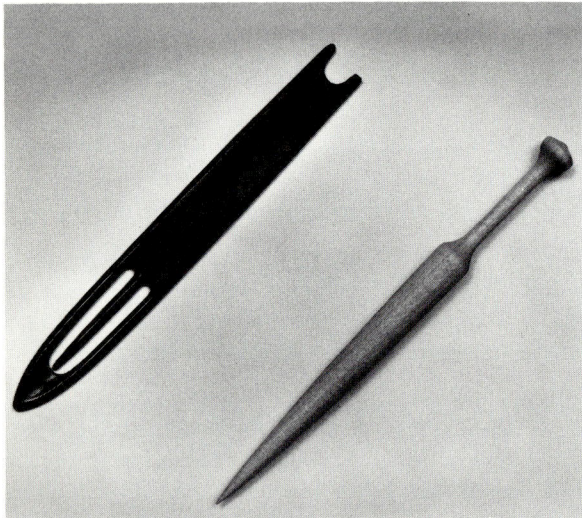

301. Tapestry bobbins, used to hold
the various weft colors for tapestry weaving.

fingers. The weaving proceeds a bit faster on the horizontal loom, but, since tapestries are invariably woven with the face or "right" side *away* from the weaver, you can check your progress only by slipping a mirror under the web. With a vertical loom, you merely walk around to the other side.

An ordinary beater cannot be used for most tapestries. Instead, the weft yarns are laid into place with the fingers, a comb, or a tapestry fork (Fig. 300), a heavy tool that eliminates the need for vigorous packing.

The weft yarns can be wound in small butterfly shuttles or on pointed tapestry bobbins (Fig. 301). A 4-inch length of ¼-inch dowel, tapered to a long, dull point at one end, makes an excellent bobbin.

The Cartoon

The tapestry cartoon is the preliminary drawing used as a guide by the weaver. Many great masters have prepared the designs for tapestry, and their

sketches survive today as oil paintings (Fig. 94). However, the more usual medium is watercolor. Most often the cartoon is drawn to the actual size of the proposed tapestry, but in some styles it is drawn to scale for enlargement on the loom. Either way, the drawing is done in *reverse*, a mirror image of the tapestry to be woven. The cartoon is placed under the warp on a horizontal loom or behind it on a vertical loom. The weaver also works in reverse, from the wrong side of the fabric. Major outlines and pattern areas can be transferred directly to the warp yarns by marking them with a felt-tipped pen (Fig. 302). The ink will not rub off during the weaving, and it will be obscured by the weft in the finished tapestry.

With the advent of Photorealism a number of tapestry weavers have become interested in naturalistic imagery. Many use photographic blow-ups as cartoons, duplicating the original photograph in yarn. This is the technique followed by Helena Hernmarck (Pl. 35, p. 340). Weaving from a photograph should not be thought of as copying or reproduction. Rather, it is the creation of a completely new work of art derived from some other source in a new medium.

302. Detail of Grau-Garriga's *Ecuménisme* in progress, showing the cartoon marks on the warp yarns.

303. Eccentric weft is a tapestry technique in which the weft yarns depart from the horizontal and move at angles to the warp.

Weaving Techniques

In tapestry weaving a single weft yarn seldom, if ever, travels the entire distance from selvedge to selvedge. Rather the weft yarns are built up in pattern areas, with each color moving back and forth in its designated segment of the warp. For very intricate designs a single color of weft yarn might cover only one warp yarn, before disappearing on the back of the tapestry. There are two basic methods of accomplishing this buildup of pattern. You can work in regular horizontal rows, changing colors whenever the design requires it, or you can weave a whole pattern area in one color, working vertically, and then go back to fill in adjacent areas. However, an overhanging shape cannot be woven until the background area has been completed.

304. Diagram of an eccentric weft pattern.

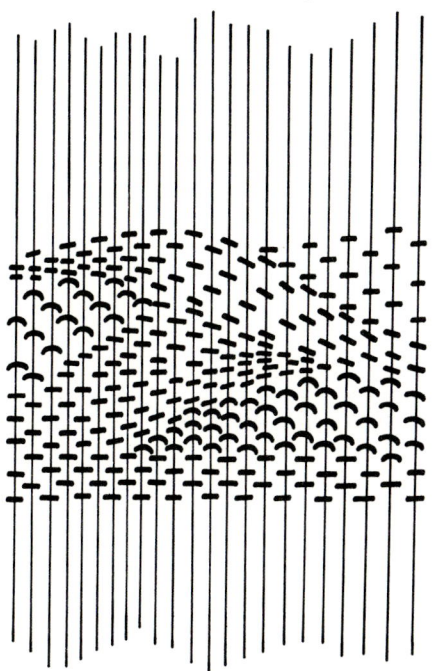

The warp yarns should be held under firm tension and the weft inserted slackly to prevent the web from buckling or drawing in at the edges. Some practice is necessary to acquire the knack of entering the weft yarn. The yarn should be bubbled, so that it will pack around the warp neatly, but there should be no obvious loops, either in the web or at the selvedges. The weft should not be woven for more than about 3 inches before being positioned with the fork, for otherwise you may not be able to correctly gauge the weft length needed for a particular area. If the amount of weft is excessive, bubbles or puckers will appear in the horizontal direction.

A heading of plain weave, twining, or chaining (Figs. 350, 352), woven before the tapestry itself is begun, will help to maintain the horizontal dimension of the fabric. The heading can be removed after the tapestry is cut from the loom. While the weaving is in progress, you can loop short lengths of cord or twine through the tapestry and tie them to the loom (Fig. 401). This system, too, will help prevent the edges from curling and drawing in. The cords should be set about 2 to 4 inches apart.

Some forms of tapestry weaving follow a technique called *eccentric weft,* in which the weft yarns depart from the true horizontal and move in arcs or at acute angles to the warp (Figs. 303, 304). This method is helpful in fitting wedges or lozenges of color into a background area.

A distinguishing feature of tapestries is the presence or absence of *slits,* vertical openings in the web that are created at the point of juncture between two pattern segments. Because the weft yarns move independently within specified areas, vertical lines in the design will always cause slits, unless measures are taken to avoid them. The simplest way to prevent slits in a design composed of many verticals is to turn the entire tapestry on its side and weave horizontally. Thus, the verticals become horizontals, interlocked with the warp,

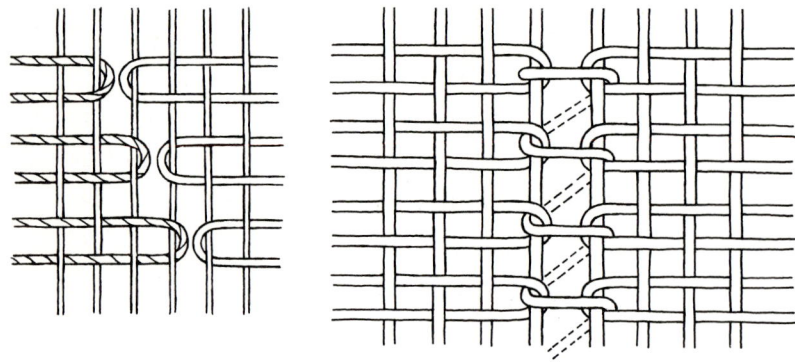

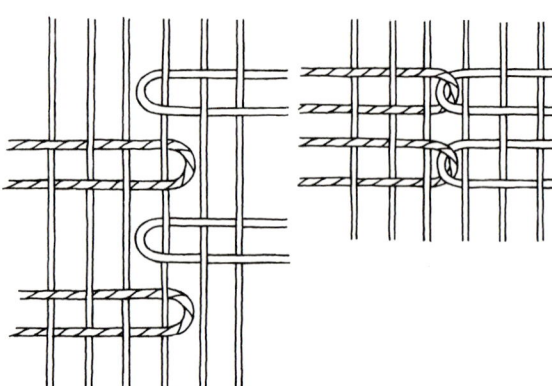

below: 307. Weft yarns can be wrapped
around a common warp yarn
or around each other
to avoid slits.
These two methods
are called dovetailing (*left*)
and interlocking (*right*).

above left: 305. Slits may occur in a tapestry
where two pattern areas meet.
If vertical lines in the pattern are adjusted
so that the weft yarn advances to right or left
one warp yarn at a time, slits will not develop.

above right: 306. Gobelin overcasting is a method for closing slits
by means of a stitch that runs parallel to the weft.

308. A variety of other possible joinings for tapestries.

slit   diagonal interlock   outlining   limning

diagonal dovetail   three warp   diagonal   double vertical interlock

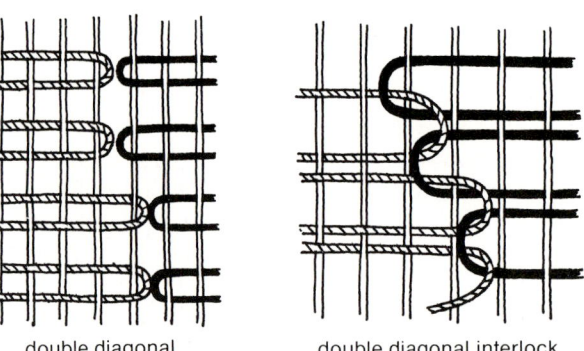

double diagonal   double diagonal interlock

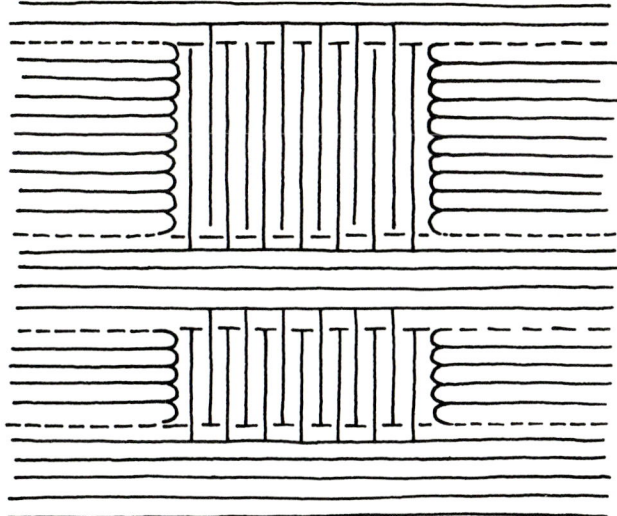

left: **309.** One design possibility for tapestry is to leave sections of exposed warp between woven areas.

above: **310.** Sample fabric based on the exposed-warp pattern in Figure 309.

and no slits occur. If the vertical lines are adjusted so that the weft yarn advances either to the right or to the left one warp yarn at a time (Fig. 305), slits will not develop.

Historically, there have been three basic methods of dealing with slits. Some medieval tapestries exploited them to create a shadowed effect in the fabric. In this event, the slits were simply left open, and their scale was adjusted to the size of the tapestry. The Polish *kilim* also incorporates unsewn slits. In other tapestry styles the slits are sewn closed after the tapestry is finished. A buttonhole stitch worked on the reverse side of the fabric will not be conspicuous if the two sides of the opening are butted together properly, with no overlapping. In French Gobelin tapestries the slits are sewn on the face in an overcast stitch parallel to the weft (Fig. 306). No attempt is made to conceal the stitch. The third method dispenses with the slits altogether. The weft yarns are wrapped around a common warp yarn—a system called *dovetailing*—or around each other (Fig. 307). The latter method of weft interlocking is employed in Scandinavian *rölakan* weaving. Figure 308 shows a number of other arrangements for joining, interlocking, and outlining.

Some tapestries, such as Navajo rugs (Pl. 12, p. 169), are reversible, with the two sides equally finished in appearance. This is done by wrapping the weft ends around a warp yarn at the perimeter of the design area and passing the weft back into the shed. More commonly, the ends of the weft yarn are simply tied off and allowed to hang free on the reverse of the tapestry, so there is only one presentable surface.

The range of tapestry techniques is so broad that this brief discussion can only begin to touch upon the possibilities. Figures 309 and 310 show

one variation, a tapestry with portions of exposed warp yarns. To get a good starting edge after the area of exposed warp, insert a piece of stiff paper or cardboard in the open section. This cardboard can be inserted in the last shed woven, after which the shed is changed for the first row after the exposed warp. You may need to sew the edges around the openings with thread of the same color as the weft to prevent yarns from migrating into the space.

Control of adjacent color areas is of great concern in tapestry weaving. Figure 311 shows how one arrangement was handled. In this instance, the pattern calls for solid color areas abutting striped areas. The weft yarns are interlocked with each other and with a common warp yarn before turning back for the next shed.

311. This sample tapestry fabric shows one method of dealing with adjacent color areas.

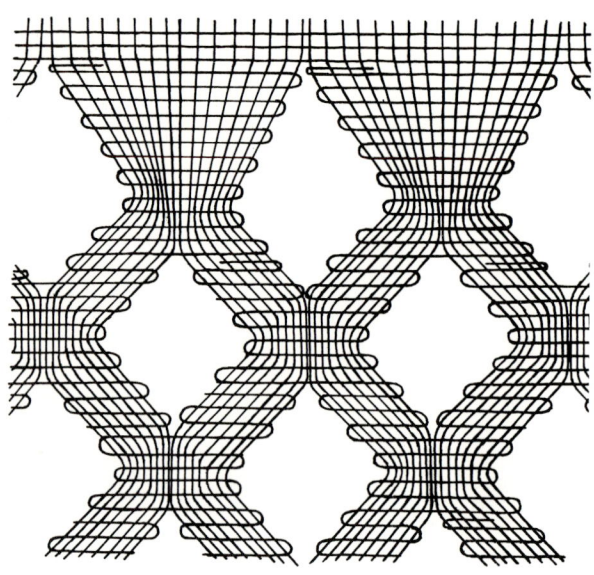

above: **312.** Sometimes the slits that result
from tapestry techniques
are exploited to create openwork fabrics.
This form of openwork was common
in pre-Columbian Peru.

right: **313.** Panel from a garment,
Central Coast of Peru.
A.D. 900–1476.
Slit tapestry with cotton warp
and alpaca weft, height 40″ (100 cm).
Textile Museum, Washington, D.C.

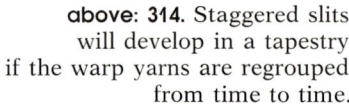

above: **314.** Staggered slits
will develop in a tapestry
if the warp yarns are regrouped
from time to time.

right: **315.** Lenore Tawney.
The Waters Above the Firmament.
1974. Slit tapestry,
12′ (3.6 m) square.
Courtesy Willard Gallery,
New York.

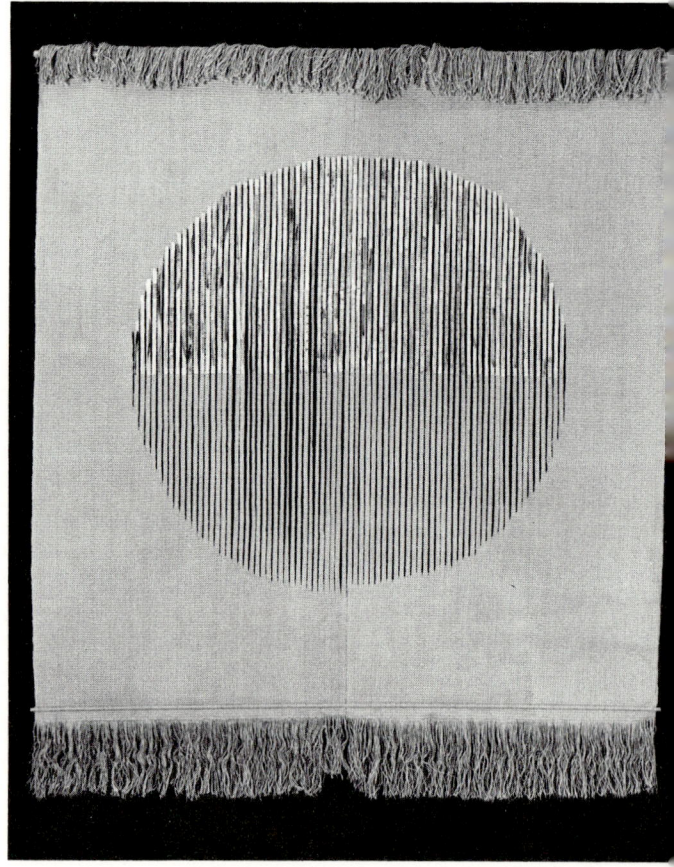

right: 316.
Maria van Blaaderen.
White Knot. 1975.
Woven and plaited,
8′4″ × 7′2″ × 1′6″
(2.5 × 2.15 × .45 m).
Courtesy International
Biennial of Tapestries,
Lausanne, 1975.

below: 317.
Maria van Blaaderen's
White Knot (Fig. 316)
in progress.

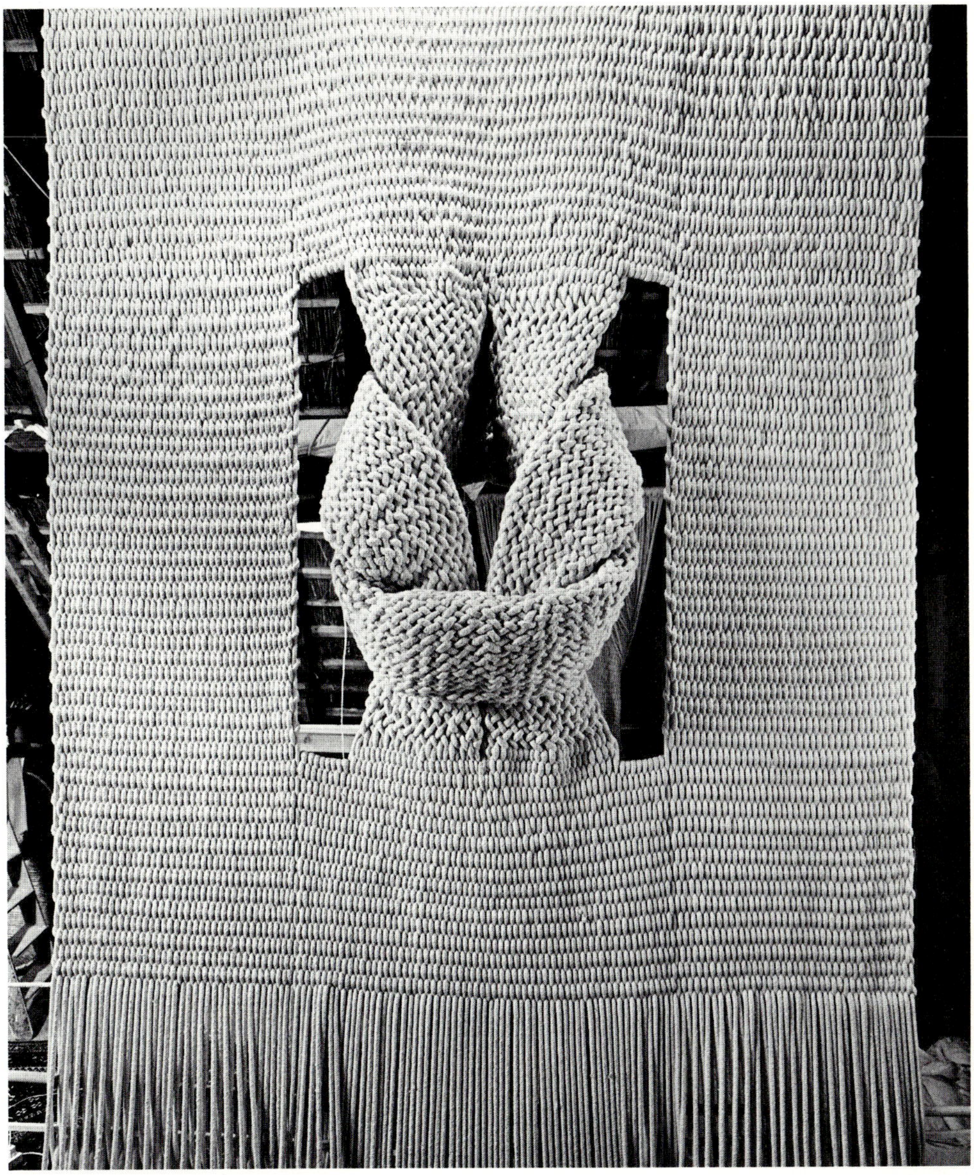

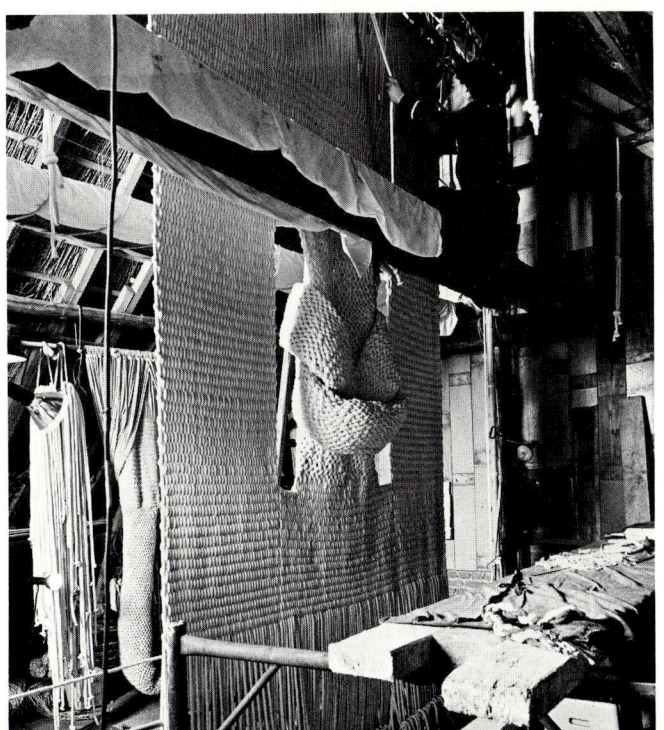

Slit Tapestry

Slit tapestry, more accurately called *woven slit openwork,* is really not a tapestry technique at all, but rather a method in which the warp is divided into sections, each of which is handled independently. The warp yarns are drawn together to produce definite slits in the web (Fig. 312). This method was common in pre-Columbian weaving, such as the Peruvian textile shown in Figure 313. Different effects can be created by regrouping the warp yarns from time to time, so that the staggered slits develop (Fig. 314). Long, narrow slits can create a delicate linear effect, as in Lenore Tawney's *The Waters Above the Firmament* (Fig. 315). Maria van Blaaderen has capitalized on the slit technique by making a huge knot in the center of the tapestry (Figs. 316, 317).

Contemporary Tapestry Weaving

During the past few decades a number of serious artists have attempted to translate the tradition-steeped principles of tapestry weaving into an idiom relevant to the 20th century (Fig. 318). As a result, the art of tapestry has enjoyed an exciting renaissance. Much of this new popularity is traceable to the work of Jean Lurçat, a painter and designer who is credited with reviving the old Aubusson manufactory. The titles of Lurçat's major tapestries—*Liberty, Man, Truth*—evoke the grandeur of their 17th- and 18th-century ancestors, but the forms are bold, fresh, and inventive (Fig. 319). Most of Lurçat's tapestries are conceived on an architectural scale.

All three of the great 17th-century French tapestry works are still in operation. It is interesting to compare an early tapestry woven at Gobelins (Fig. 103) with one created at Aubusson three hundred years later (Fig. 320). The extreme simplification of form and abandonment of naturalistic imagery in the recent work echo the trends of Minimal Art, just as *The Life of the King* mirrored the Baroque style of 17th-century France.

Tapestry has always served to embellish church architecture and public buildings. This use of the textile for large spaces naturally leads to grand scale, with all its special design challenges (Fig. 321). Yet there is long precedent, too, for miniature tapestries, which are meant to be examined in detail at close range (Fig. 322).

left: 318. Stuart Davis design, woven by V'Soske. *Flying Carpet.* 1942. Wool rug, 7'1" × 10' (2.1 × 3 m). Museum of Modern Art, New York (Edgar Kaufmann, Jr., Fund).

below: 319. Jean Lurçat. *Truth.* 1943. Tapestry, 9'8" × 21'8" (2.9 × 6.5 m). Courtesy Galerie la Demeure, Paris.

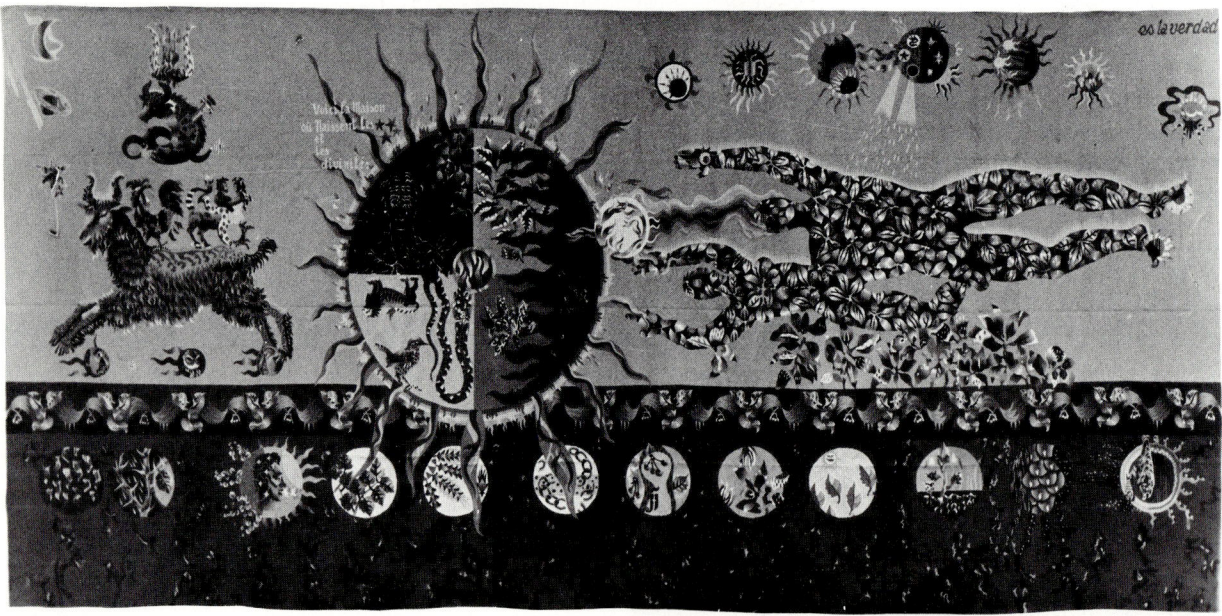

above: 322. Shelley Krapes.
Golden Tears. 1977.
Straw fibers, silk, and linen;
$6 \times 7 \times 2\frac{1}{2}''$ ($15 \times 17.5 \times 6$ cm).
Courtesy the artist.

above: 320. Frank Stella design, woven by Gloria F. Ross.
Tapestry after *Flin Flon XIII.* 1970. Aubusson-style tapestry,
8'10" (2.65 m) square. Courtesy Pace Editions, New York.

below: 321. Evelyn Anselevicius. *Crystallization.* 1974.
Wool, henekin, jute, and goat hair, with weights of quartz,
pyrite, and stalactites.
Colorado School of Mines, Boulder, Colo. (See also Fig. 343.)

The interplay of texture and the projection of three-dimensional form have been among the main preoccupations of the modern weaver. The texture may derive from manipulation of flat-woven forms, as in Adela Akers' *Summer and Winter* (Fig. 323). But the very nature of yarns and other materials used for weaving leads many artists to emphasize lush textural compositions that are a most appropriate celebration of weaving as an art form. This has been a primary characteristic of works by Grau-Garriga (Pl. 13, p. 170; Fig. 324).

With unlimited potential for color control, tapestry weaving offers the possibility of dipping into colors as freely as a painter does into a palette. A more subtle approach is taken by Herman Scholten, whose major interest in recent work has been with progressions of color and value (Pl. 14, p. 170). These tapestries are fascinating because of their very simplicity, as they lead the eye constantly back and forth.

The modern tapestry weaver has by no means disavowed pictorial representation, but merely restated it in terms of a developing culture. Dorian Zachai was trained in classical tapestry methods,

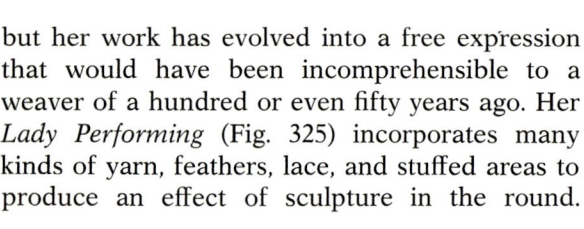

but her work has evolved into a free expression that would have been incomprehensible to a weaver of a hundred or even fifty years ago. Her *Lady Performing* (Fig. 325) incorporates many kinds of yarn, feathers, lace, and stuffed areas to produce an effect of sculpture in the round.

The weaver's task is not quite complete when the woven fabric is cut from the loom. In almost all cases a variety of finishing procedures must be applied to the web, and these can be divided into two general categories. *Edge finishes* prevent the fabric from raveling and sometimes provide a decorative border. *Functional finishes* affect the web itself: they clean it, shrink it, protect it, and change or enhance the appearance of the fibers. A woven project may need either or both.

Edge Finishes

The type of finish that will be applied to the edges of a fabric depends on the nature of the woven article. Each piece is an individual problem. Whatever the finish may be, it should enhance the overall design and not detract from it. Some finishes are virtually invisible, serving only to hold the yarns in place. Others may act as an important part of the design (Fig. 326).

12
Finishing Procedures

326. Hans Widmann.
Compliment to Nature, detail.
1974–75. Woven, knotted,
and braided, with flowers;
width 5′4″ (1.6 m).
Courtesy International
Biennial of Tapestries,
Lausanne, 1975.

The weaver should analyze each web according to the purpose for which it will be used. Yardage, which is to be cut for dressmaking, needs no edge finishing whatever unless the weave is very loose; you may want to run a row of machine zigzag stitching across the fabric to hold the yarns in place. A knotted fringe may or may not be effective on a wall hanging.

To some extent the type of edge finish selected will depend upon the composition of the web. For example, if the warp and the weft are in contrasting colors, a fringe left on the ends would be entirely in the warp color, which may not be desirable. If the warp alone makes a jarring contrast with the web, it may be better to disguise it, by turning back the ends. A fringe of warp yarns can also be wrapped to change both the color and the character of the fringe.

Stitching

Hemstitching, overcasting, cross-stitching, and blanket stitching are all devices to prevent the ends of a woven fabric from raveling. Hemstitch-

ing is easier to do while the fabric is still on the loom and under tension. If necessary, you can hemstitch both ends of the web—the first end after you have woven a few inches but before you roll the fabric forward onto the cloth beam, the other end when you finish the project.

Hemstitching is done on a closed shed. The following directions are intended for right-handed people. Reverse them if you are left-handed.

Hemstitching

- □ Cut a length of weft yarn about three times the width of the web, and thread it through a needle.
- □ Pass the needle up through the fabric at the edge, 2 warp ends in from the selvedge.
- □ Carry the yarn around the outermost 2 warp yarns and behind the fabric, bringing it up through the fabric at a point 2 warp ends from the selvedge and 2 weft shots from the edge (Fig. 327).
- □ Continue this procedure across the web until all the yarns are caught.

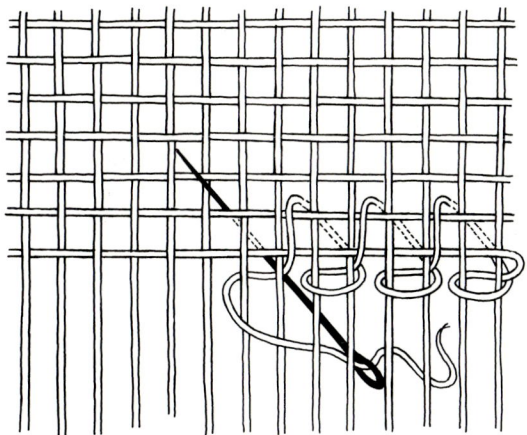

327. Hemstitching.

328. Overcasting.

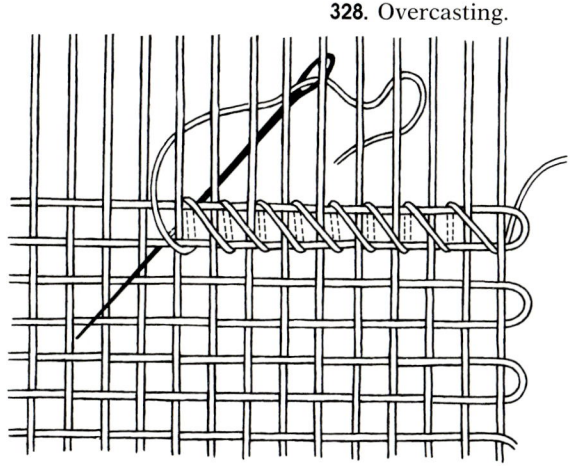

Overcasting, cross-stitching, and blanket stitching can be done either on or off the loom. The overcast stitch is shown in Figure 328. Cross-stitching (Fig. 329) requires a second trip across the web after the overcast is complete. The blanket stitch (Fig. 330) gives a more finished appearance to the fabric.

In addition to these sewing stitches, a number of the finger weaves can be used to finish the edge of a fabric. These include Spanish lace, Brook's

Bouquet, and Danish medallion (Figs. 272, 275, 274). If done in fine yarn or sewing thread, with a color that blends into the web, the stitches will be inconspicuous.

Any of the stitches mentioned can also be used to hold back woven areas when portions of the warp yarn are meant to be left bare. Most of the time it will be better to finish these integral edges while the fabric is still on the loom, so as not to distort the parallel lines of warp yarns.

329. Cross-stitching.

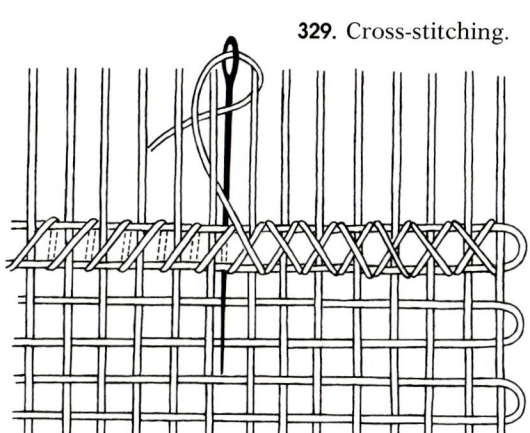

330. Blanket stitching.

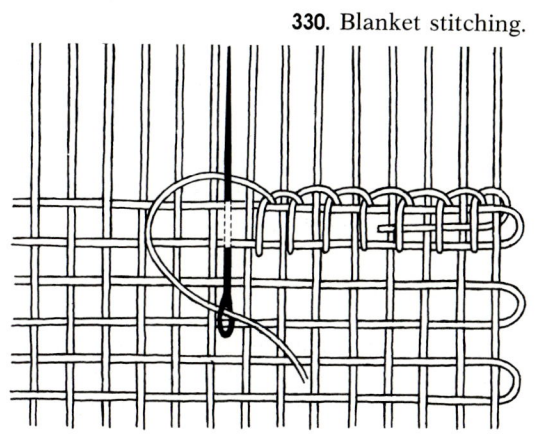

Hemming

A hem is often the best edge finish for a place mat or similar project. When the fabric is very delicate, the hem can be rolled and held in place with tiny stitches (Fig. 331). Otherwise, an ordinary skirt hem about 1 inch wide, plus ¼ inch for turning, is usually sufficient (Fig. 332). In either case, the hemming should be done by hand, so that the stitches are inconspicuous. If warp yarn is used, they will be invisible.

Binding

A fabric that is to be seen from one side only—such as a tapestry or wall hanging—can be finished with seam binding on the reverse side. When you cut the web from the loom, leave an excess warp length of 4 or 5 inches on both ends. Knot the warp ends together at intervals across the fabric to hold the weft in place. Then, turn back the warps and stitch them in position on the reverse side of the fabric. Cover the raw edge with bias tape binding (Fig. 333) or with a facing (Fig. 334). In some cases you may want to cover the entire back with a lining.

Knotted and Braided Fringe

An easy way to make a stable, thick fringe is to twist long warp ends as tightly as possible and then double them back upon themselves (Fig. 335). The double strand will automatically twist into a compact, straight spiral.

A plain knotted fringe is one of the simplest edge finishes to make. As illustrated in Figure 336, the warp ends are grouped and tied in a half knot. Be careful that the fringe is straight and that the ends are parallel to one another. The warp yarn for such a fringe must have a rather tight twist, or the ends will become frayed. Single-ply yarns are not sufficiently durable for a fringe, particularly when the woven article is to be subjected to wear or handling.

above: 333. Binding the raw edge of a fabric.
below: 334. Facing the reverse side of a fabric.

above: 331. A rolled hem.
below: 332. A skirt hem.

335. A simple twisted fringe.

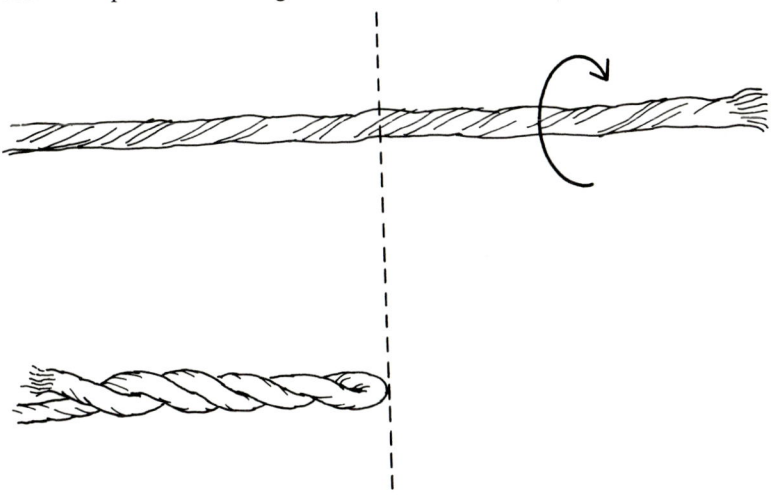

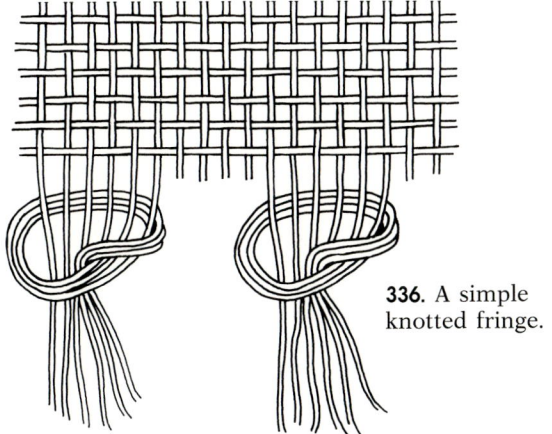

336. A simple knotted fringe.

336–340. *A knotted fringe is a suitable edge finish for many woven projects.*

Figures 337 through 340 illustrate several more complicated knotting techniques often used to finish rugs, shawls, and similar items. The *Philippine edge* (Fig. 337) is both practical and decorative, for it holds the weft yarns in position and at the same time creates an attractive border. The warp ends must be at least 7 or 8 inches long, and even longer if you plan to work a wide border. The Philippine edge is knotted from left to right; if you wish, you can turn the fabric and work the edge in the opposite direction, continuing back and forth for several rows. The *double knot* and the *neolithic knot* (Figs. 338, 339) both provide a firmer edge than the half knot. A system of *locked loops* (Fig. 340), worked from right to left across the edge, provides a decorative transition between the fabric and the fringe.

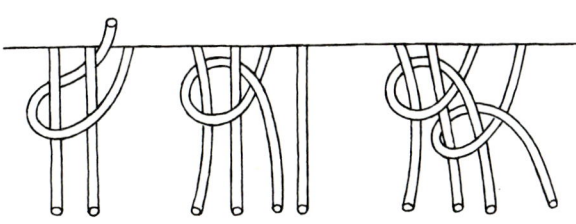

337. Philippine edge.

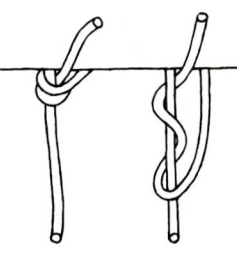

338. Double knot.

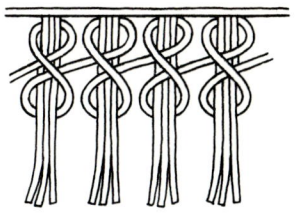

339. Neolithic knot.

340. Locked loops.

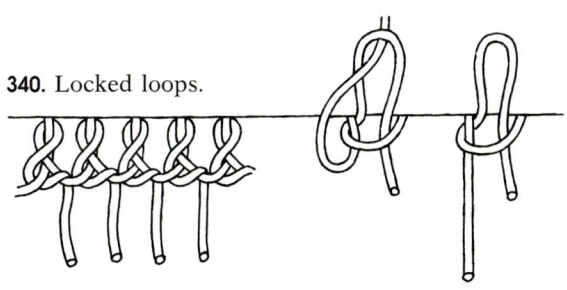

341. Rows of horizontal clove hitches
—a macramé knot—can serve to finish
the raw edge of a woven fabric.

Macramé was originally developed as an edging technique, and it is often used today to finish woven projects. In Figure 341 the warp ends have been knotted in rows of clove hitches (Fig. 412), with and without a fringe. When you do not want a fringe, work the warp ends back into the fabric with a crochet hook and cut them short on the reverse side. The wide border in Figure 342 was also made with clove hitches, in this case diagonal rows that create a diamond pattern.

A heavy braided fringe, interwoven with flowers and other decorative items, serves as a major design element for the wall hanging in Figure 326. Braided fringes can also be effective on garments, since they are much more durable than simple knotted fringes.

For very large projects the weaver may want to weight the bottom of the fringes. In the work shown in Figure 343 (see also Fig. 321), Evelyn Anselevicius neatly accomplished three purposes by knotting uncut chunks of quartz, pyorite, and

stalactites at the bottom of a heavy knotted fringe. The stones provide a stabilizing weight, add a decorative accent, and refer symbolically to the Colorado School of Mines, which commissioned the wall hanging and where it now hangs.

Woven Fringe

A fringe can be woven on one or both ends of a fabric while it is on the loom (Figs. 344, 345). Divide the warp into groups of yarns, and weave each group as a unit with a butterfly shuttle (Fig. 266). After you cut the web from the loom, knot or finish the warp ends in some other way to prevent raveling.

It is also possible to weave a decorative fringe along the *selvedge* of a fabric. The weaving space on the loom must be wide enough to accommodate the web itself, plus the proposed fringe length on both sides. Either a cut or an uncut (looped) fringe can be woven, but in both cases a group of temporary warps must be set into the loom at the outer edge of the fringe.

Weaving a Selvedge Fringe

☐ Tie 3 or 4 warp yarns between the breast beam and the back beam at the point where the fringe will end, passing these yarns through one dent in the reed.

☐ As you weave, carry the weft yarn to the edge of the fringe on some shots but only to the selvedge of the fabric on others (Fig. 346).

☐ Continue weaving in this manner until it is time to roll the fabric forward onto the cloth beam.

☐ Cut the fringe at the ends, and allow it to hang free.

☐ Roll the fabric forward, rolling the fringe onto the cloth beam.

---

342. Shawl with a decorative border of clove hitches.

left: 343. Evelyn Anselevicius.
Crystallization, detail. 1974.
Wool, henekin, jute, and goat's hair,
with weights of quartz, pyorite, stalactites.
Colorado School of Mines, Boulder, Colo.
(See also Fig. 321).

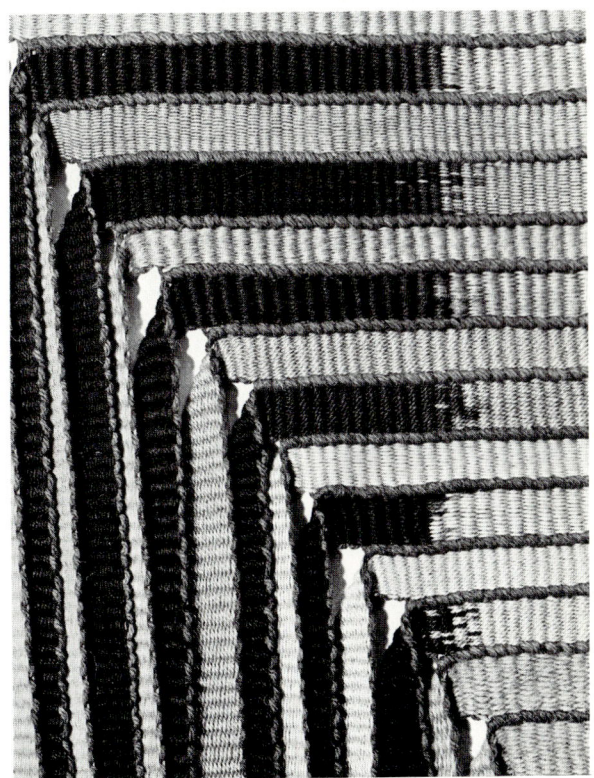

above: 345. Detail of *Confluence*, Figure 344.

below: 346. A woven fringe can be added
to the selvedge of a fabric
by carrying some weft shots
to the extent of the fringe
—marked by a temporary warp yarn—
and the remainder only to the edge
of the fabric.

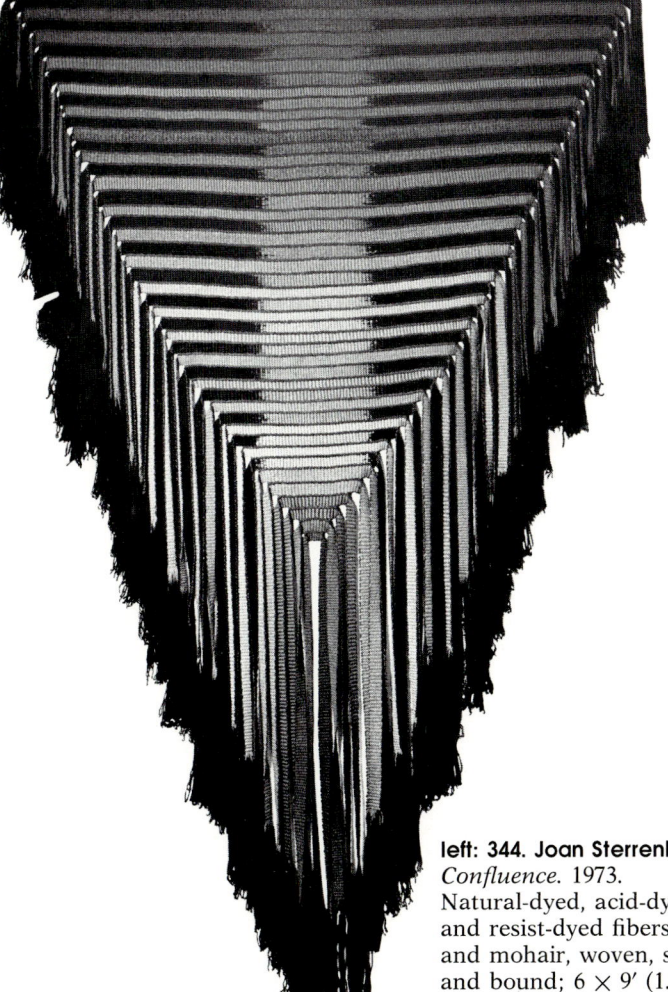

left: 344. Joan Sterrenburg.
Confluence. 1973.
Natural-dyed, acid-dyed,
and resist-dyed fibers of wool
and mohair, woven, stitched,
and bound; 6 × 9′ (1.8 × 2.7 m).
Courtesy the artist.

selvedge

fringe

temporary warp yarns

Finishing Procedures **189**

347. Fabrics are blocked
to make them conform to a desired shape.
Tack the cloth all around to a flat surface,
moisten it, and allow it to dry.

Throughout this process the temporary warps remain stationary. The procedure for making a
looped fringe is similar, except that the temporary
warp yarns are continuous, moving from warp
beam to cloth beam with the rest of the warp. The
temporary warps are threaded through a dent in
the reed but not through the heddles. They are
removed after the fabric is cut from the loom.

Functional Finishes

Cleaning

Most fabrics must be either washed or dry cleaned
after they are taken from the loom, the choice
depending upon the fiber composition of the yarns
involved. The cleaning method should be the same
one to be followed for care of the fabric in use.
Cleaning not only removes any soil that may have
accumulated during the weaving process, but it
also binds the yarns together, improves the *hand*
or feel of the fibers, and preshrinks the fabric.

Special consideration must be given to woolen
fabrics that have been spun and woven *in the
grease*—that is, without prior scouring to remove
surface oil from the sheep's wool. (Weaving in the
grease is common with certain tweed yarns.) Soak
the fabric for about an hour in lukewarm water to

which a few drops of ammonia have been added.
Next, wash the fabric in warm water with a thick
solution of one part detergent to two parts soap,
and then rinse it thoroughly. The washing and
rinsing may have to be repeated two or three times
to remove all the oil. Finally, squeeze the fabric
gently, blot it with a towel, and roll it on a large
blanket-covered tube for drying. It should be left
for at least 24 hours, then rerolled from the opposite direction on another tube. Repeat this procedure until the fabric is completely dry. A gentle
brushing or *napping* will expose the fibers, soften
the fabric, and increase the warmth of a woolen
garment or floor covering.

Blocking

Certain items, such as tapestries or wall hangings,
require blocking to make them conform to the
proper shape. Tack the fabric all around at short
intervals to a solid flat surface (Fig. 347). Then,
moisten it with warm water and allow it to dry
slowly away from sunlight and excess heat.

Starching

Delicate fabrics to be used for wall hangings often
have their shape and body improved by starching.
This is particularly true of fine linens and knitted
fabrics. Dip the entire piece in a starch solution,
and allow it to dry naturally away from the heat.
Afterwards, block the fabric if necessary.

Fireproofing

A textile woven as a commission, especially for a
public place, often must be fireproofed in order to
conform to local laws. Commercial fireproofing
solutions are available, and these should be used
according to the manufacturer's directions.

Spraying

Many weavers like to spray certain types of textiles
to seal the surface, make the fibers permanent and
immune to destruction, give more body to the
piece, and sometimes provide a sheen. Silicone
spray is a common substance used for this purpose. A new technique, spray metalizing, is described in Chapter 21.

Backing

Rugs that are meant to be placed on the floor
should be backed with a coating of latex to prevent slippage.

Other
Construction
Methods

Pile weaves are those that display a raised surface, pushing the normally flat, planar weave into a third dimension. There are two forms of pile weaves, comparable to the low relief and high relief of sculpture. *Low-pile weaves*, such as those produced by chaining, twining, or soumak, have only a slightly elevated surface. Many people do not consider them to be pile weaves at all, but merely a thick, closely woven fabric. Most low-pile weaves are two-element constructions: the weft yarn serves for both the ground and the pile effect.

By contrast, *high-pile weaves* are generally composed of three elements—a warp and weft ground, plus an extra series of yarns running weftwise to form the pile. The pile may vary from a fraction of an inch to several inches or even feet in length. High-pile weaves can be made from a continuous yarn, leaving loops on the surface of the fabric (*uncut pile*), or from short lengths of yarn knotted individually on the stretched warp (*cut*

13
Pile Weaves

348. Sheila Hicks. *Portail de Notre-Dame.*
1973. Natural linen with long wrapped pile,
6'6" × 6' (1.95 × 1.80 m).
Office of the Comptroller
of the Currency, Washington, D.C.

pile). Looped piles can also be severed to produce a cut pile. Long cut piles are often referred to as *shag* weaves.

The common trait of the techniques described in this chapter is that they were originally, or are most frequently, applied to the manufacture of rugs. However, the pile weaves have broken free of any such restraint and are today included in a wide variety of forms—sculpture, wall hangings, upholstery fabric, garments, and other kinds of textiles (Pl. 15, p. 203; Fig. 348).

Only in the 20th century have rugs become a luxury. Before central heating, rugs were stark necessity, providing both warmth and insulation. They served on floors and in doorways, on beds, as sleigh and carriage blankets—anywhere the heavy furlike structure was needed to keep out the cold and give a measure of comfort.

349. *The Ardebil Carpet,* medallion Tabriz rug from the shrine of Sheik Safī at Ardebil, Iran. 1539–40.
Wool pile and silk, 17'6" × 34'6" (5.25 × 10.35 m). Victoria & Albert Museum, London (Crown Copyright).

As noted in Chapter 1, the earliest surviving rug was found in a Scythian grave in Siberia (Fig. 10). With that sole exception, only fragmentary carpets predating the 13th century still exist, although pile weaves were used in many other types of fabrics (Fig. 55). Most of the techniques used for creating rugs originated and reached their highest level of development in the East. We easily free-associate the terms "Oriental" and "Persian" when carpets are brought to mind. Indeed, Persian carpets are among the finest ever produced anywhere in the world (Fig. 349).

Fabric knotting in the rya technique has been an important folk craft in Scandinavia since the 13th century. Only in recent decades, when large quantities of rya-knotted fabrics began to be exported, has the process been applied to rugs. The weaver who had spent weeks or months painstakingly tying thousands and thousands of knots would not have dreamed of putting the result on the floor to be trampled upon. Instead, rya fabrics assumed a place of honor in Scandinavian households and comprised part of a bride's dowry.

Most of the techniques explained in this chapter can be carried out on a simple frame loom, such as any of those illustrated in Chapter 14. It is possible to make a large rya rug in sections on a small frame loom, later sewing the pieces together. But the work moves faster and larger fabrics can be produced on a conventional 4-harness loom.

Low Pile Weaves

Chaining

Chaining is a two-element construction based on plain weave, in which the weft yarn is looped around groups of warp yarns to form a surface pile.

above: **350.** In chaining, the weft yarn is looped around groups of warp yarns to form a low surface pile.

351. A pattern of overall chaining.

Chaining
□ Open a shed, and insert the weft yarn.
□ At the spot where you want the chaining to begin, pull a weft loop to the surface between two raised warp yarns. Draw this loop across for a distance of 2 or 3 warp yarns, and then draw up a second weft loop through the first one (Fig. 350).
□ Carry the second loop over for a distance of 2 or 3 yarns, and pull a third weft loop through the second.
□ Continue this procedure to the point where you want the chaining to stop.
□ Draw the shuttle through the last loop to prevent the chain from unraveling.

The pattern of chaining can follow any direction required by a particular project. The chain can move from left to right or right to left; it can be carried from selvedge to selvedge or appear only in certain portions of the web, in which case it functions as a laid-in design (see p. 168). Two yarns of different colors are sometimes placed in the same shed and chained back and forth alternately, so that adjacent loops vary in color. Whatever the design, each row of chaining should be surrounded by a row or two of plain weave on each side to provide a firm ground for the fabric. Chaining tends to cover neighboring rows of flat weave, and even three consecutive rows of plain weave will usually be hidden by the pile. The sample fabric reproduced in Figure 351 was woven in two colors with a chaining design that is almost entirely laid-in. Chaining is often used as a spacing device on simple looms, replacing the reed that normally maintains the horizontal dimension.

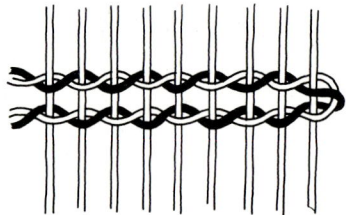

352. Two-strand twining, with a turn to the next row.

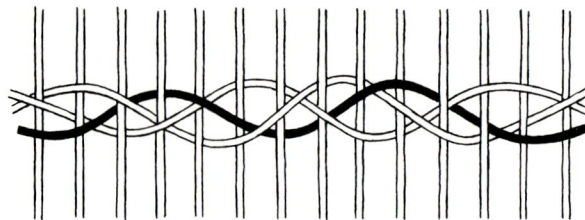

353. Three-strand twining.

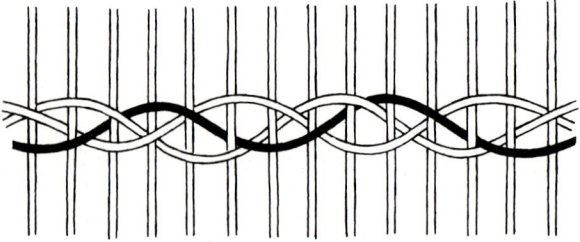

354. Braided-weft twining.

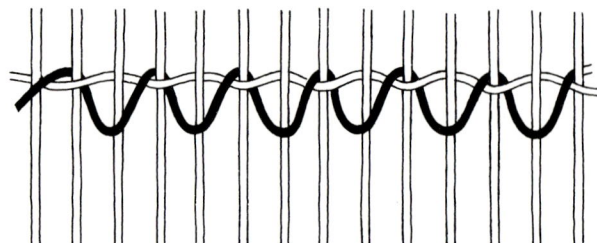

355. Looped twining.

Twining

Twining is a two-element construction in which two or more weft yarns are twisted around one another as they move across the warp. Solid rows of twining nearly always produce a weft-face fabric, for the weft completely obscures the warp.

The simplest form of twining is done with two strands (Fig. 352), often one continuous weft yarn doubled over the outermost warp yarn at one selvedge. The entire weft yarn should be about eight times as long as the distance to be covered. With the center of the yarn carried behind the first warp yarn, draw the ends to the face of the fabric between the first and second warp yarns, twist them around one another (in either a half twist or a full twist), then pass them around the second warp yarn. If you wish, you can cross two or more

356. Jon B. Wahling. *Environment I.*
1972. Jute and metal using warp twining, braiding, and knotting;
8′ × 7′6″ × 1′4″ (2.4 × 2.25 × .4 m).
Courtesy the artist.

warp yarns before twisting. The twists should always be made in the same direction for a single row. When alternate rows are twisted in opposite directions, a chevron pattern develops. Regrouping the warp yarns for subsequent rows will produce a lattice effect. Staggered rows give a twill.

Three-strand twining is a bit more complicated. As illustrated in Figure 353, each of the three weft yarns moves over and under two warp yarns, but the weft yarns are staggered so that they interlock. A variation of this technique consists of braiding three weft strands over the warp, just as one would braid hair (Fig. 354). The Chilkat Indians used three-strand twining for their famous blankets (Pl. 3, p. 37).

Occasionally, twining is adapted to produce a higher pile, by leaving loops on the surface of the fabric (Fig. 355). This is done with the aid of a gauge of some sort, a wooden dowel or knitting needle, for example. Each time one of the weft yarns appears on the face, it is slipped on the gauge before being twisted.

Twining is often done on the vertical warp-weighted loom (Fig. 144) or its cousin, the Ojibway Indian loom (Fig. 405). It is not necessary that the warp be held under tension.

The contemporary handweaver has adapted twining to a variety of purposes. It is used as a trim, to outline pattern areas, to hold back flat

358. A pattern of overall soumak.

weaving around sections of exposed warp, and even for large-scale sculptural constructions (Fig. 356). The solidly twined fabric is thick and quite durable, so it has an obvious application for rugs and mats. Like chaining, a row or two of twining can serve as a spacing element for simple looms.

Soumak

Soumak is the technique that was originally used for making rugs in Caucasia. It is done by wrapping the weft yarn around a warp end or a group of warp ends according to any of several patterns (Fig. 357). The most ornate is the *Greek soumak*, in which the weft yarn is wrapped three or more times around a single warp yarn before proceeding to the next warp yarn. It is also possible to wrap two or more warp yarns at a time, alternating the groups for each row of soumak. For example, if in the first row you wrapped ends:

1-2, 3-4, 5-6, 7-8 . . .

then in the following row wrap ends:

1, 2-3, 4-5, 6-7, 8-9 . . .

The resulting web will be interlocked because of the staggered groups of the wrapped yarns. Closely packed rows of soumak, therefore, conceal the warp altogether to produce a weft-face fabric (Pl. 16, p. 203).

The weft yarn is easiest to work with if it is wound in a butterfly shuttle (Fig. 266). Soumak can be worked on either an open or a closed shed. If the shed is open, only the top layer of warp yarns is wrapped. When rows of soumak are alternated with plain weave, a ribbed effect develops.

The soumak fabric illustrated in Figure 358 was woven by passing the weft yarn over four warp

357. Soumak is a low-pile weave done by wrapping weft yarn around a warp or group of warps. The Greek soumak (*top*) is the most elaborate of the patterns.

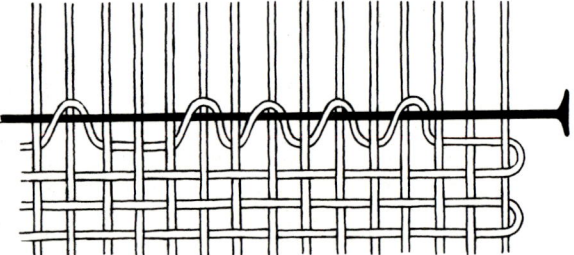

359. Looping is a three-element construction in which a weftwise yarn passes over a gauge to form a surface pile.

ends and back under two. Any other combination of warp yarns could be substituted, depending upon the weight of the yarn and the desired effect. When the soumak is worked alternately from left to right and right to left, a herringbone pattern is created; when all the rows are wrapped in the same direction, a twill results. To change colors, simply carry the first yarn to the underside of the fabric and draw the new color through in the same place. The two ends can be worked into the web vertically in such a way that they are invisible.

Generally, you must take care with soumak to avoid distorting the vertical alignment of the warp, especially with long overshots of 5 or 6 warp yarns. However, you can also take advantage of this tendency for the warp to bunch together and create an openwork fabric. A lattice effect is produced by staggering the warp yarns to be wrapped in various rows.

High-Pile Weaves

Looping

Looping is a three-element construction. The warp and weft ground exists independently of the pile yarn, which can be inserted wherever it is needed. Usually, though not always, the pile yarn is heavier than the plain-weave yarns. Looping is begun in the same manner as chaining.

Looping

□ Open a shed, and insert the pile yarn.
□ Draw loops to the surface between each pair of warp yarns. (When the warp is very dense, draw through every second or third space.)
□ Slip the loops over a gauge—a knitting needle, wooden dowel, or similar object—to maintain a consistent size (Fig. 359). The diameter of the gauge determines the height of the loops.
□ After you have completed one row, beat the pile yarn into place.
□ Follow with a shot or two of plain weave using the regular binder weft.

Maria Chojnacka's tapestry hanging reproduced in Figure 360 exhibits a loop pile only in selected areas (Fig. 361). The result is a sensitive interplay of texture and tonal value. Loops can also be used to emphasize figural or pattern areas, a fact well known and delightfully exploited by the Copts (Fig. 55).

360. Maria Chojnacka. *The Surface.* 1976.
Sisal, mixed technique; 8′ × 13′4″ (2.4 × 4 m). Courtesy the artist.

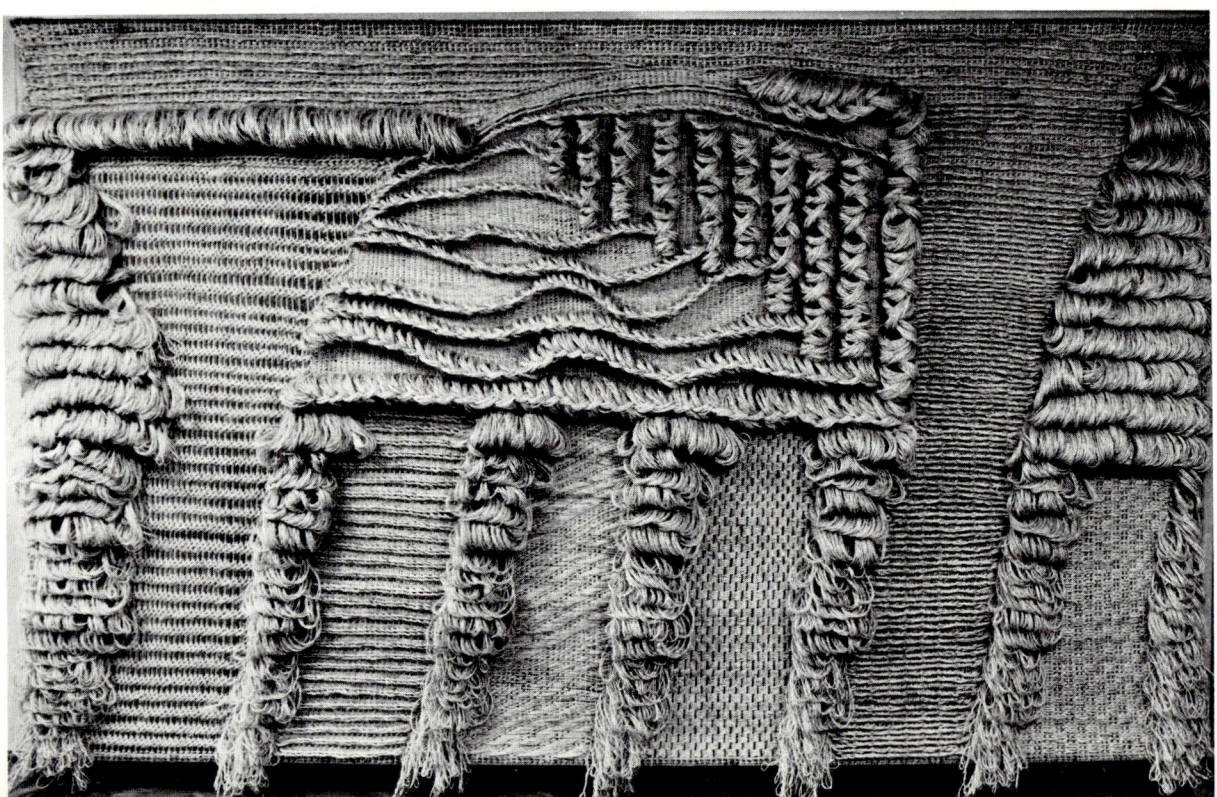

361. Detail of Figure 360, *The Surface.*

below: 362. An overall looped fabric. The checkerboard effect is produced by inserting two pile yarns into each shed and drawing loops only from the color that is needed for that part of the pattern.

The fabric illustrated in Figure 362 is looped over its entire surface in two colors. The checkerboard effect is produced by inserting two pile yarns—one in each color—into the shed simultaneously and drawing loops only from the color that is needed on the surface. The other yarn is absorbed into the plain-weave ground and covered by the looped pile.

Rug Knots

Three distinct knots have been identified in classical rug weaving. The *Ghiordes knot* or *Turkish knot* formed the basis of Turkish rugs and is identical to the Scandinavian rya or flossa knot. Similarly, the *Sehna* or *Persian knot* was employed for making rugs in Persia. The *Spanish knot* is quite rare compared to the other two. While all three knots are still used widely in rug weaving, they have been adopted by contemporary weavers for purposes far removed from floor coverings.

Each of the knots can be made with a continuous weft yarn wound in a butterfly shuttle. The pile is formed by the loops of yarn between each pair of knots, and the loops can be cut or left as they are. It is a more common practice to tie short lengths of yarn individually around the stretched warp ends. The height of the pile thus measures half the length of each yarn, minus the small amount needed for wrapping around the warp.

The weaver has more design freedom in rug knotting than in any other fiber-construction process. The act of tying individual strands of fiber is comparable only to painting, and one's palette consists of all the colors and textures of yarn available. Since the warp and ground weft are invisible and the pile weft is discontinuous, any color can be placed at any point.

Ghiordes Knot

□ Set the warp no denser than 8 to 10 ends per inch to allow room for knotting.

□ Work on a closed shed.

□ Place a length of yarn over two warp yarns and wrap it around them, drawing the ends through the center space (Fig. 363).

□ Pull the knot taut against the previous weft shot.

□ When the row is complete, beat the pile yarns into place.

□ Follow with a few shots of binder weft.

---

363. Individual Ghiordes knots.

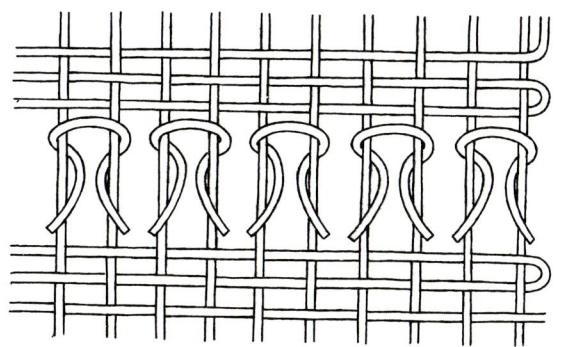

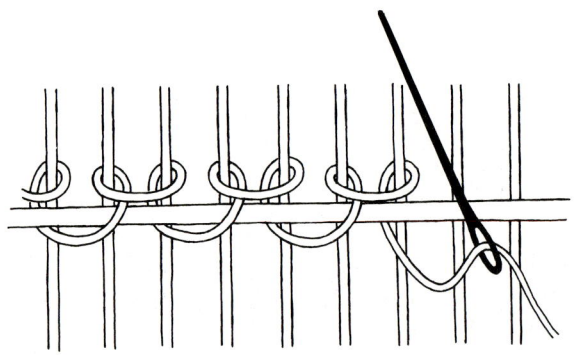

364. Continuous Ghiordes knots.

You can obtain different effects by varying the length of the knotting yarns and the width of the flat-weave strips between the knotted rows. If the pile yarns are relatively short and the knotted rows are close together, the pile will stand straight, whereas rows of long pile yarns set farther apart will cause the pile to sprawl. In classical rug weaving all the pile ends were trimmed evenly to achieve a flat surface. As many as two hundred knots were tied per square inch. Many contempo-

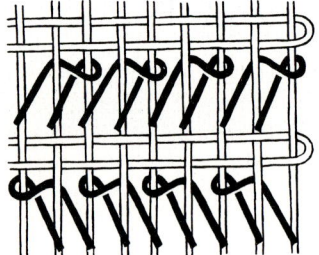

365. Sehna knot.

366. A pile fabric made with Sehna knots. Although several shots of plain weave are inserted after each row of pile knots, the ground weave is completely obscured unless the pile is spread.

rary weavers prefer the informal appearance of random-length pile yarns, which produce an undulating face on the knotted fabric.

The continuous Ghiordes knot is made with a gauge much like that used for looping. The pile weft yarn can be threaded through a needle (Fig. 364) or wound in a butterfly shuttle (Fig. 266). If you want a cut pile, slash the loops between each pair of knots with a knife or razor blade before you remove the gauge. Special Swedish gauges with a cutting groove along one edge facilitate the slashing (Fig. 371).

The Sehna knot is also tied over two adjacent warp yarns. In this case, the pile weft yarn passes under one warp yarn and over and around the other, so that a pile end emerges between each pair of warp yarns (Fig. 365). The knots can be tied so that the pile slants either to the right or to the left, which is a definite design advantage. By tying each knot with two or more yarns simultaneously, you can introduce a variety of colors to build a pattern. Sehna knots can also be made with a continuous yarn looped over a gauge.

Figure 366 shows a sample fabric knotted entirely with Sehna knots, each knot made with two individual yarns. The pile rows have been spread to demonstrate the half inch or so of flat weaving between them. Ordinarily, the pile covers the plain-weave ground completely, and the latter is never visible.

The Spanish knot (Fig. 367) is actually a simple twisting of the pile weft around a single warp yarn. Generally, the knot is made around every second warp end, working alternately in rows. Spanish knots have a greater tendency than the other two to slip out before they can be locked into place with a few ground weft shots, so the knot is usually easier to make with a single continuous yarn worked over a gauge.

We typically think of pile in terms of rugs, with a soft raised surface perhaps an inch or two high. But today's artist-weaver interprets the form much more freely. An area of pile can be introduced in

367. Spanish knots.

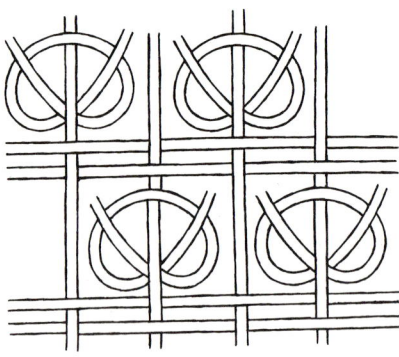

368. Grau-Garriga. *No Domestic.* 1972.
Mixed technique in cotton,
wool, and synthetics.
Courtesy Arras Gallery, Ltd., New York.

any fiber structure for the design content it provides. Since fiber is by nature linear, the linear accent of long pile is particularly expressive of the medium (Fig. 368). We can readily see the endless possibilities for pile knotting, once the stereotype has been abandoned.

Rya and Flossa

The rya or flossa knot is identical to the Ghiordes knot used in Turkish rug weaving (Fig. 363). The only difference is that rya knots generally are made with coarser yarn, and from 2 to 6 strands are handled as one in making a single knot, whereas in Turkish rugs each pile yarn is knotted individually. Rya, which in Finland is called *ryijy*, is for all practical purposes the same as flossa. However, when a distinction is made, the rya fabric is considered to have a longer pile (greater than $1\frac{1}{8}$ inch) and more widely spaced knots. In this

book the two terms are used interchangeably; rya is the term heard most often.

Much tradition governs the rya technique in Scandinavia, particularly in Finland, where any variation on the centuries-old methods and materials is considered by some second only to desecration of the national flag. Wool or goat-hair yarns must be used for the ground, and only wool for the pile. The pile ends are all trimmed to exactly the same height. Formerly, the yarns were colored with natural dyestuffs—leaves, spruce cones, wild rosemary, and various tree barks. The older patterns are generally pictorial, often containing religious symbols. In recent years many rya weavers, even in Scandinavia, have begun to challenge such arbitrary restrictions and experiment with variations in pattern, pile length, and materials. Among the more common designs in modern Scandinavian rya are subtle gradations or explosions of color.

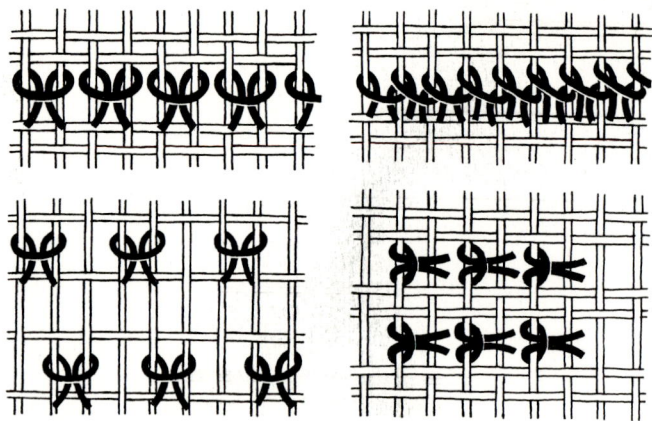

369. Rya is a Scandinavian pile-weaving technique based upon versions of the Ghiordes knot. In recent years it has become associated with rugs. The yarn involved is most often wool, knotted in several strands at a time over warps stretched on the loom. Several versions of the Ghiordes knot used in rya weaving are illustrated here, of which the first (*top left*) is the most common.

Figure 369 illustrates several versions of the rya knot, the first of which is most common. The best materials for conventional rug weaving are an 8/3 or 8/5 linen rug warp and wool rug yarn or wool and goat or cow hair for the ground weft. Swedish long-staple wool rya yarns can be used for the knotting pile. It is rather difficult to estimate the amount of yarn you will need, because the length of the pile, the number of yarns knotted together, the weight of the yarn, and the distance between knotted rows all influence the quantity. Perhaps the easiest method of calculating the total yarn requirement for a given project is to knot a small sample in the same yarns, keeping track of the amount of each color consumed, and multiply that quantity by the number of times the finished rug size will exceed the sample.

The alternative to making a sample involves a fair amount of mathematics. For the following example, it is assumed that the finished rug will be 3 by 5 feet (.9 × 1.5 m); that there will be 308 warp yarns; and that there will be 150 knots in each row, with 4 unknotted warp yarns at each selvedge. The knot in question is the first one in Figure 369.

knots per row	150	
yarns per knot	3	
total pile yarns	450	
(150 × 3)		
pile rows for 5-foot	80	
(1.5 m) length		
number of pile yarns	36,000	
(450 × 80)		
length of each pile yarn	4 in	(10 cm)
total amount of pile yarn	4,000 yds	(3600 m)
weight per skein of yarn	3½–4 oz	(100 g)
length per skein	126 yds	(115 m)
number of skeins	32	
(4,000 ÷ 126)		

The warp and weft ground are calculated in the same manner as for flat weaving (see Chap. 8).

Most rya weavers work from full-scale cartoons prepared in advance and tacked in sections to the loom under the warp. The cartoon need not be in color; tonal gradations can be used to indicate the different shades of yarn. A less cumbersome—but also less accurate—method involves drawing a small cartoon scaled down for enlargement on the loom.

The loom is threaded as for conventional weaving (Fig. 370) using any of the standard drafts—twill, rosepath, bird's-eye, and so forth (see Appendix A). The tie-up should be planned to produce the most compact and simplest ground, perhaps 1-2 and 3-4. In order to prevent excessive narrowing of the web, you can leave a stretcher on the loom during the entire weaving process, moving it to follow the progress of the weaving.

370. The rya knots are made in rows, each row followed by several shots of ground weave.

left: Plate 15. Karen White Boyd.
Shadows of Entropy. 1976.
Shaped tapestry with inlay in polyester,
Christmas tinsel, synthetics, and linen;
3' (.9 m) square.
Courtesy the artist.

below: Plate 16. Adela Akers.
Ceremonial Wall. 1972.
Tapestry with slits and soumak in wool,
goat hair, horsehair, and linen;
8'6" × 6' (2.55 × 1.8 m).
Courtesy the artist.

left: Plate 17. Anne Hornby.
Wall hanging. 1975.
Flossa weave superimposed on cloth
painted with textile dyes,
45 × 26″ (112 × 65 cm).
Courtesy the artist.

below: Plate 18. Jane Busse.
Double corduroy shag rug, detail.
Courtesy the artist.

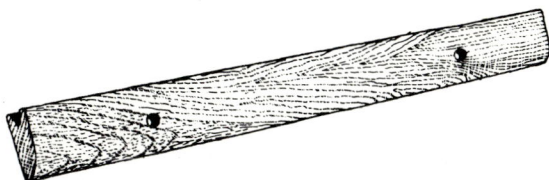

371. Continuous Ghiordes knots can be looped around a Swedish rya stick,
which provides a slot for cutting the loops after each row is finished.

As a rule, no knots are tied on the outside four yarns at each selvedge. Extra filler yarns will occasionally have to be inserted in these narrow bands to take up the space not occupied by the pile yarn and keep the rows consistent. The beating should be quite firm, for a loosely woven rya rug will not wear well.

If a single continuous pile yarn is to be knotted, you can wind the pile loops around a Swedish rya stick (Fig. 371), which provides a slot for cutting the loops before the gauge is removed. However, if a perfectly even pile length is not desirable, the loops can easily be measured around the fingers.

Another method for making a rya rug calls for a two-stage process: First the backing is woven, and later the pile yarns are inserted. To make a separate backing, you must weave an open fabric with space between the filler weft shots to later accept the pile yarns.

Making a Rya Backing

□ Treadle 1-2, and insert a shot of wool filler weft.
□ Treadle 3-4, and insert another shot of wool filler weft.
□ Continue alternating sheds to fill the distance you want between rows of pile knots.
□ Treadle 2-4 and insert a shot of linen warp yarn.
□ Treadle 1-3 and insert another shot of linen warp yarn.
□ Continue, if necessary, to fill a space that will later accept the pile knots.
□ Remove the temporary linen warp yarn.

Linen warp yarn is the best choice for the temporary shots, because it is firm and will be readily visible for removal.

The rug in Plate 17 (p. 204) is an excellent example of freely conceived design in rya. The rather long pile tends to blur outlines and causes pattern areas to flow into one another. Rya is also increasingly used as a design accent, as in the tubular weave "lounge pad" shown in Figure 372.

372. Joan Russell. *The Pad.* 1974.
Handspun wool and linen, tubular weave stuffed on the loom, with rya;
6′ × 3′4″ (1.8 × 1 m).
Courtesy the artist.

Corduroy

In terms of handweaving, corduroy is not a ribbed cotton material but a relatively fast method of creating a shag fabric. The corduroy rug was invented by the English weaver Alastair Morton, and Peter Collingwood has improved upon Morton's idea. A number of contemporary weavers are now working in techniques developed by Collingwood (Pl. 18, p. 204). In essence, the corduroy method is a flat weave with long weft floats on the surface of the fabric, and the floats are cut to form the pile. The pile is, therefore, half the length of the weft float, provided the float is cut precisely in the center of the float.

373. Clara Creager. *Lawn Mower 1974.* 1974. Double corduroy wool rug with lawn mower, rug size 45″ (1.13 m) square. Courtesy the artist.

A corduroy rug (Fig. 373) requires more yarn than a rya rug of comparable size, for the pile yarn is also absorbed into the ground fabric. Furthermore, the design possibilities are as limited as those in any flat-weave textile. You cannot "paint" with fiber. However, the execution of the textile is four times faster than rya knotting. There are two basic drafts for a rug of this type, the *single corduroy* and the *double corduroy*. The latter produces a denser pile and is usually preferred. Like all the other pile techniques described in this chapter, the corduroy weave need not be confined to rugs but can be applied to a wide variety of shag fabrics, including articles of clothing.

The draft for a single corduroy rug appears in Figure 374. In order that the two edges of the fabric will be symmetrical—with either floats or ground weave—the warp should be planned for a half repeat of the threading unit at the right selvedge. The warp is sleyed at about 5 ends per inch, and it is wise to double sley the warp yarns at the two points in the draft where the transition is from 1 to 4 and from 3 to 2 (Fig. 374). The X on the treadling draft indicates a shot of ground weft, the ● a shot of pile weft. At least 4 and sometimes 6 or more pile yarns are set into the same shed simultaneously, so the pile yarn can be finer than the ground yarn.

374. Draft for single corduroy.

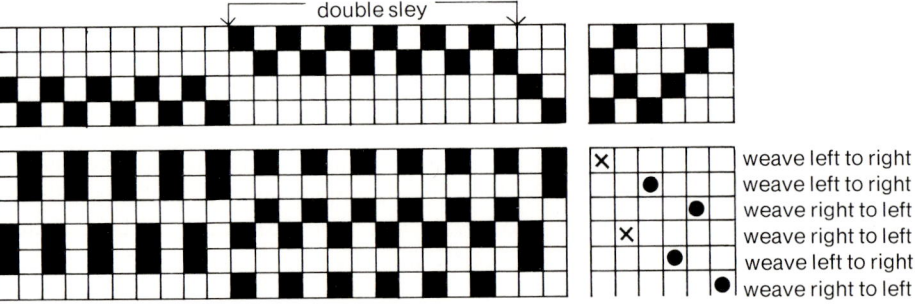

double sley

	weave left to right
X	weave left to right
●	weave right to left
	weave right to left
X	weave left to right
●	weave right to left

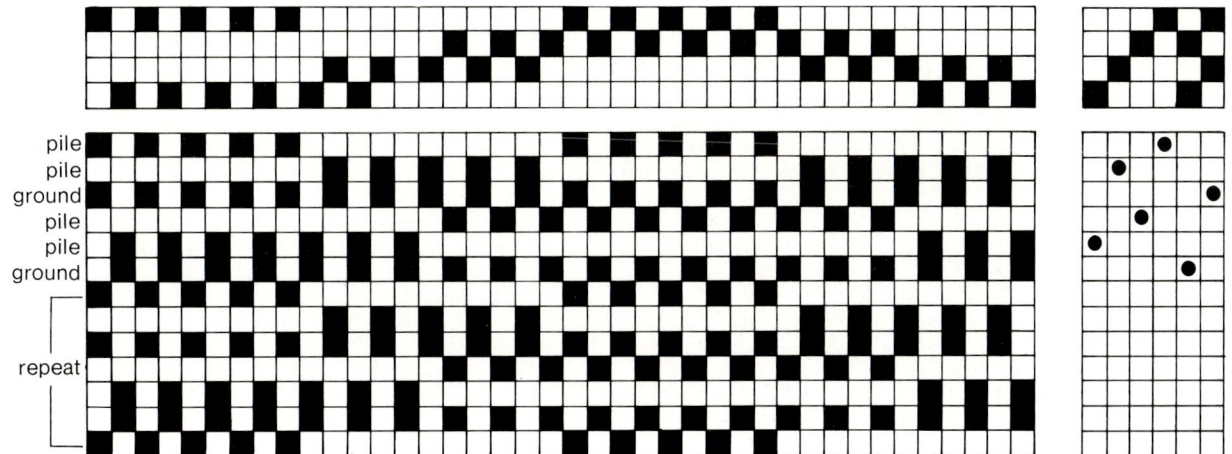

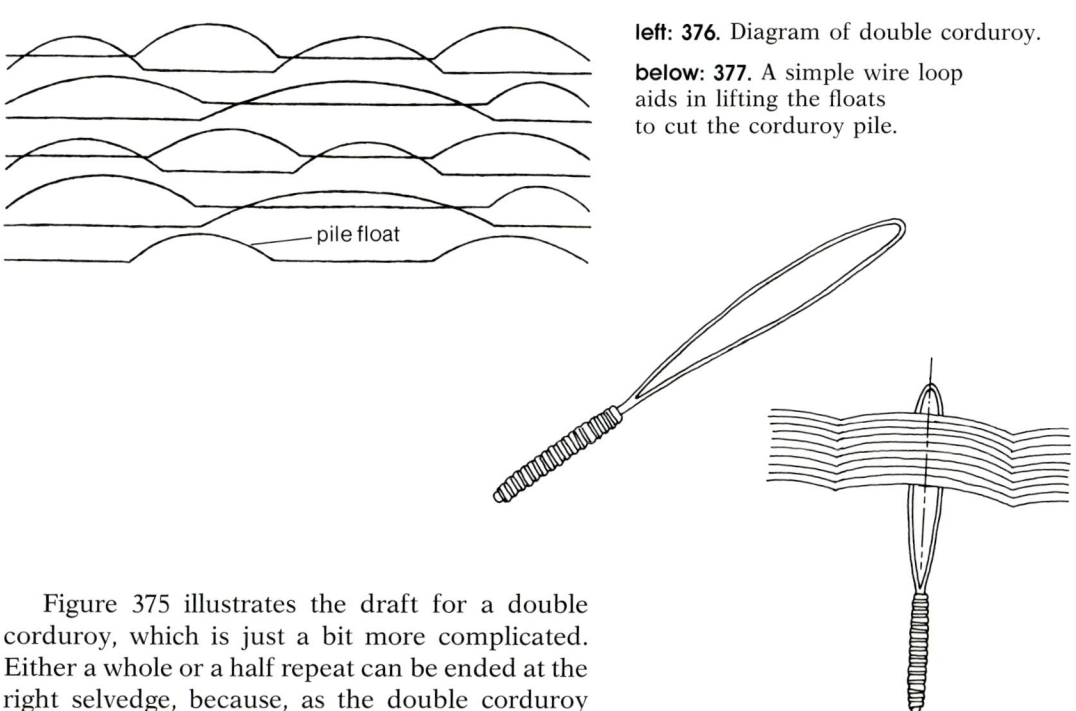

Figure labels: pile, pile, ground, pile, pile, ground, repeat

375. Draft for double corduroy.

pile float

left: 376. Diagram of double corduroy.

below: 377. A simple wire loop
aids in lifting the floats
to cut the corduroy pile.

Figure 375 illustrates the draft for a double corduroy, which is just a bit more complicated. Either a whole or a half repeat can be ended at the right selvedge, because, as the double corduroy diagram in Figure 376 shows, there are nearly always two floats per shot in each repeat of the threading draft.

After 4 or 5 inches of web have been woven and a ground-weave shot inserted to bind the pile, the weft floats in that portion should be cut with a knife or a razor blade. A doubled loop of wire (Fig. 377) will help to lift the pile floats for cutting and prevent accidental slashing of the ground weave. When it is necessary to start a new pile yarn in the center of the web, the ends can be planned to fall in the middle of a float, so they become a precut segment of the pile. The sett at the reed and the density of the weft regulate the closeness of the resulting pile. For example, if the warp is set at 6 ends per inch and 6 individual yarns are inserted

in each pile shed, a fairly heavy shag will result. Of course, the weight of the yarns effects this also.

Hooking

In the strictest sense, hooking is not a weave at all. The process, which in industry is called *tufting*, consists of forcing loops of yarn with a needle through a previously woven backing. The backing material may be burlap, 2-ply monk's cloth, Dura-back, or Warpcloth. But hooking was originally done on fabrics handwoven in the home, and many contemporary weavers use hooking to embellish their woven forms.

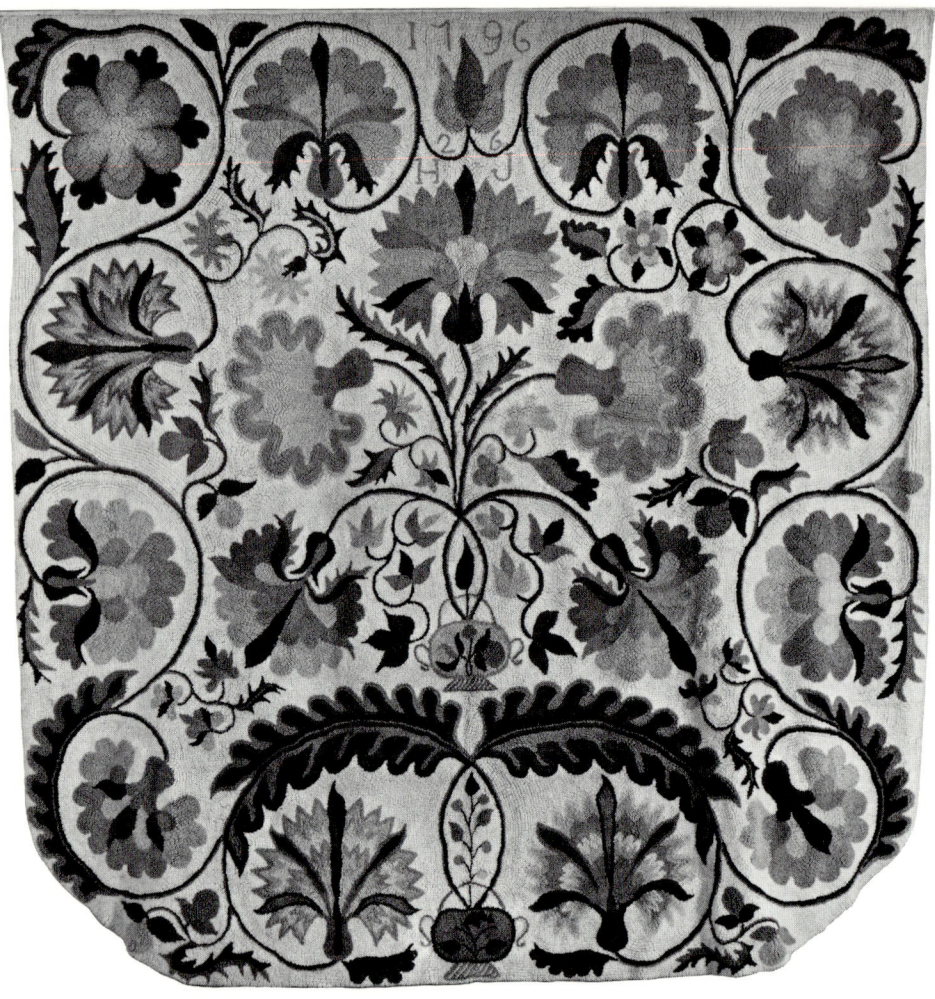

Hooking developed as a handcraft in the United States during the 18th century. A "bedd rugg" hand-hooked by Hannah Johnson in 1796 (Fig. 378) is astonishing in the intricacy and counterpoint of its stylized floral forms. It is interesting to contrast Hannah's rug with one hooked in the United States more than a century and a half later. Bruce Duderstadt's rug (Fig. 379) features rows of circular forms moving in a diagonal procession that seems to suggest the wheels in an enormous machine passing against one another—a phenomenon quite unknown in the pastoral era when Hannah Johnson sat at her hooking frame. The result has a dynamic quality that pushes outside the contours of the rug.

A frame of some kind is essential for hooking, in order to hold the backing material rigid while the loops are hooked through. Figure 380 illustrates a square frame that can be constructed easily from four pieces of high-grade pine attached at the corners in a half-lap joint and secured with glue and wood screws. The frame need not be as large as the project to be hooked, for a portion of the backing can be tacked to the frame at one time, then adjusted as the hooking in each section is completed. The backing material for a given project should be 6 inches longer in each dimension than the planned size of the hooked fabric, to allow a margin for attachment to the frame and for hems. The backing is stapled to the frame or tacked firmly all around with carpet tacks. Alternatively, you can attach a triple thickness of firm fabric permanently to the frame and then overcast the backing material to this fabric.

The design for the hooked project is drawn in reverse on the wrong side of the backing before it is mounted on the frame. All hooking is done from the wrong side, following the sketched outlines.

Wool rug yarn is the best material for a hooked pile. Although cotton yarn can be hooked, it is not nearly as durable as wool, so it is hardly worth the expenditure of time and energy required for hooking a rug. About half a pound of yarn should be adequate for each square foot of fabric.

The only tool needed for hooking is, in fact, a hook. A short-handled crochet hook will work, but

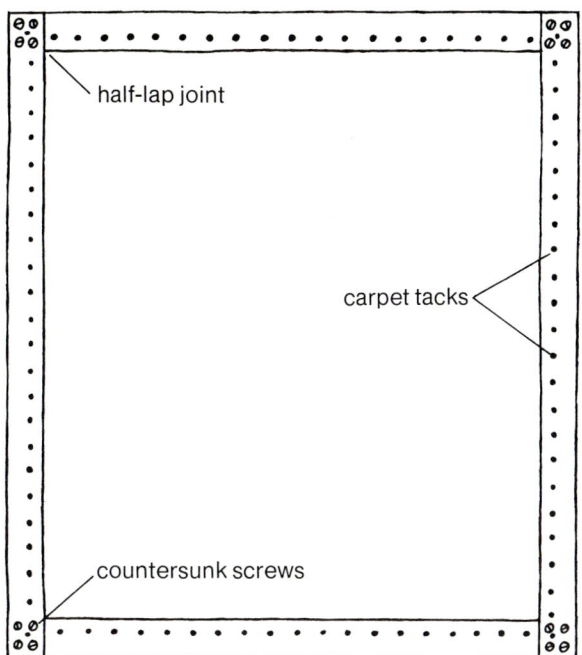

379. Bruce Duderstadt.
Hooked rug. 1972.
Wool on cotton backing,
4′ (1.2 m) square.
Courtesy the artist.

380. A hooking frame is a vertical wooden support to which the backing material is tacked.

half-lap joint

carpet tacks

countersunk screws

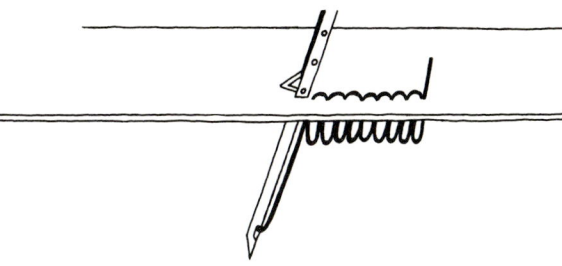

above: 381. The standard hooking tool provides a gauge to control the length of the loops.

below: 382. The pattern to be hooked is drawn in reverse on the wrong side of the backing. The hook is pushed through, and, as it is withdrawn, a loop forms on the face of the fabric.

the standard hooking tool (Fig. 381) is much more efficient, since it provides a gauge to control the length of the loops. The yarn is threaded through the hook, which is then pushed into the backing material from the reverse side to the limit set by the gauge (Fig. 382). As the hook is withdrawn, a

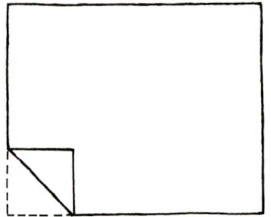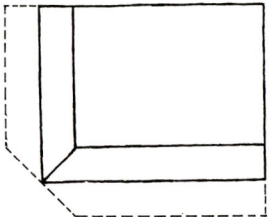

above: 383. After the hooking is completed,
the corners of the fabric are mitered
and the back painted with latex.

right: 384. Sheila Hicks. *Prayer Rug.* 1965.
Wool, hooked with electric pistol,
with braided and wrapped pile;
12′6″ × 3′4″ (3.75 × 1 m).
Museum of Modern Art, New York
(gift of Dr. Mittelsten Scheid).

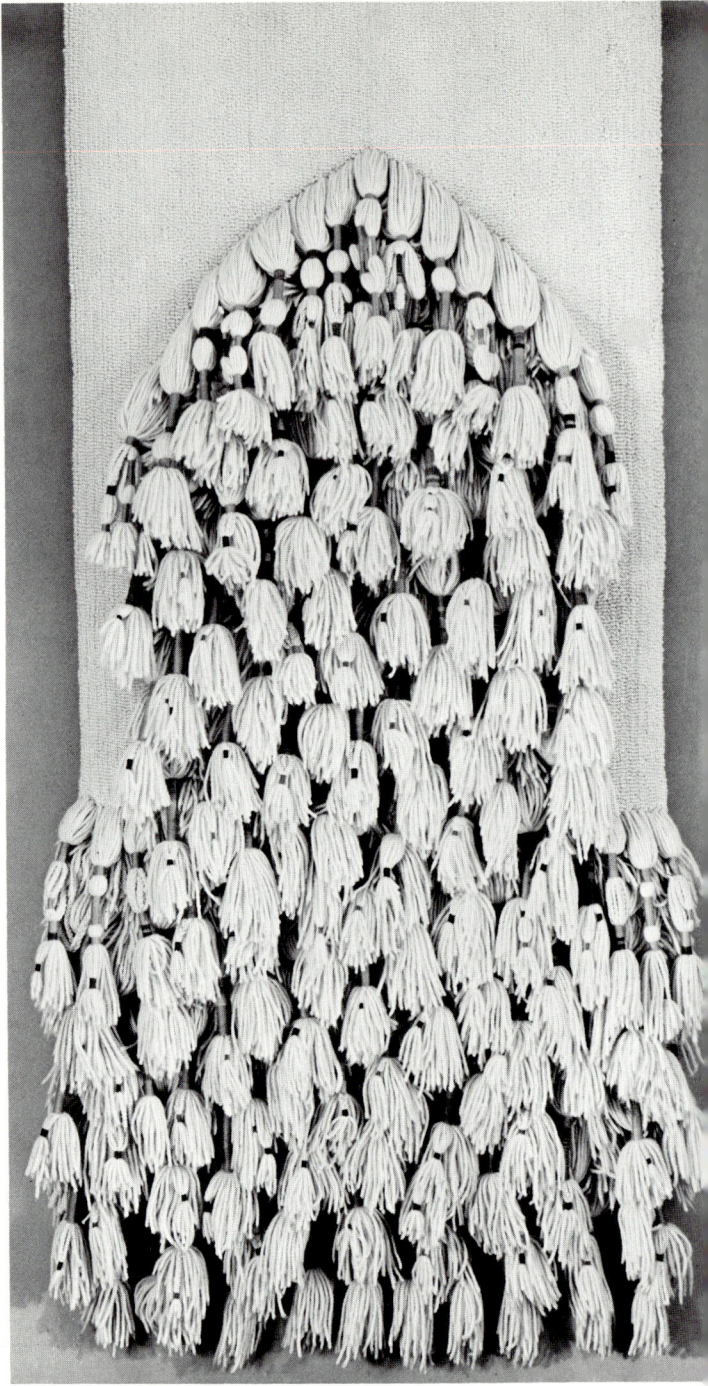

loop forms on the face of the fabric. One normally
works in rows, covering the portion of the design
that requires a particular color.

After the hooking has been completed, the
back of the rug must be painted with latex—available from rug suppliers or mail-order houses—to
prevent the loops from pulling out. First, paint a
narrow strip all around the rug in the area that will
be covered by the hem. Next, miter the corners of
the rug (Fig. 383), and hem the rug all around with
strong carpet thread. Then, paint the entire back
of the rug. About a quart of latex will cover 12
square feet of rug.

Many craftsmen and even manufacturers have
recently begun to experiment with techniques related to hooking. A wall hanging by Sheila Hicks,
though composed of classic yarns, is innovative in
its utilization of an industrial-age method. *Prayer
Rug* (Fig. 384) is a voluptuous cascade of yarns
literally shot through the backing with a mechanical
pistol, a technique Hicks inaugurated in 1963 at the
Arterior Company workshop in Germany. Hicks'
work typifies a willingness among contemporary
fiber artists to avail themselves of all the resources
at hand, no matter how unconventional, in order to
achieve the effect they seek.

Many professional handweavers use simple looms to supplement or even replace the conventional loom. The overriding advantage is cost, for a simple loom can be constructed for a tiny fraction of the amount required to buy a commercial 4-harness loom. If you are a purist, you can even assemble a backstrap loom from sticks and twigs, just as primitive tribes have done for centuries. Only the shed sword and beater need be shaped and refined to any extent; the other components can simply be cut to the proper length.

In addition to the financial aspect, simple looms offer further advantages, both practical and aesthetic. Frame and backstrap looms are lightweight and highly portable; they can be stored in a very small space. Most attractive to some contemporary weavers is the fact that simple looms permit a much more intimate contact between the weaver and the materials. For this reason many beginners prefer to learn the process of interweaving warp and weft on a simple loom, before

Simple Looms

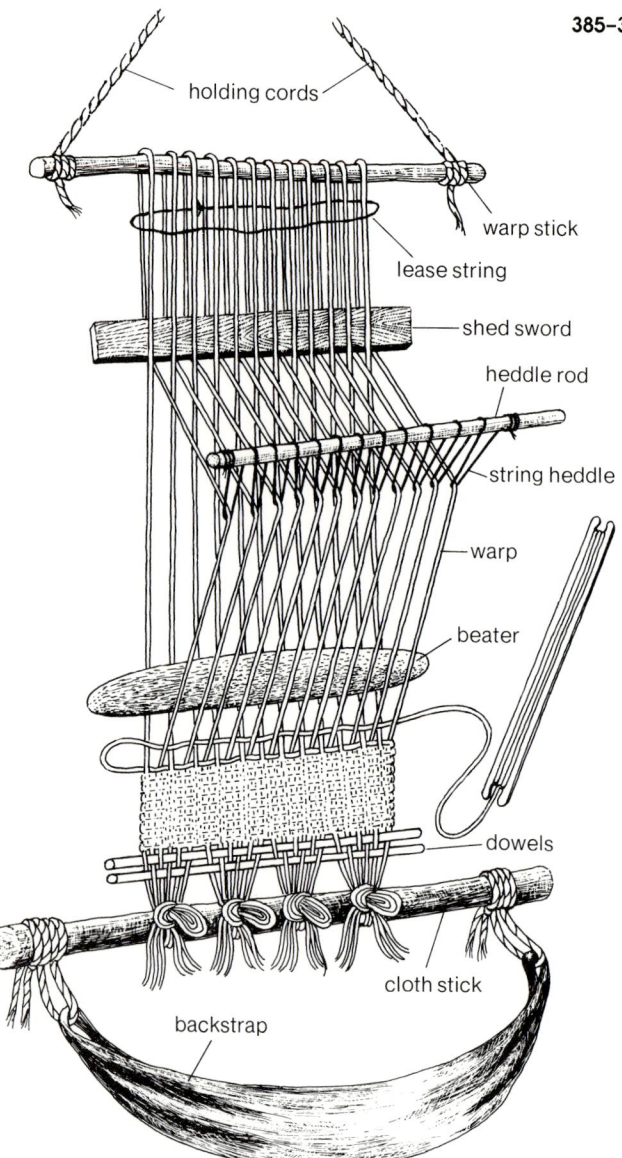

holding cords

warp stick

lease string

shed sword

heddle rod

string heddle

warp

beater

dowels

cloth stick

backstrap

having to master the mechanics of a complex table or floor loom.

Weaving progresses at a rather slow rate on simple looms. However, the range of fabrics that can be constructed is really limited only by the ingenuity and patience of the weaver. A great many of the textiles illustrated in Chapters 3 and 4, notably those from pre-Columbian America, were created on simple looms, and their quality has seldom been equaled in any other time or part of the world.

The Backstrap Loom

A simple backstrap loom has almost all the functioning parts of a modern commercially produced loom, although in crude form. The framework consists of a warp stick and a cloth stick, the former attached to a tree or some other stationary object, the latter joined to a backstrap passed around the weaver's waist (Fig. 385). Often, there is also a cloth roll, next to the cloth stick, around which the finished web is wrapped.

The shedding device may take any of several forms. Figure 386 illustrates a wooden slot-and-eye heddle, used by the Indians in the Great Lakes region of North America. With this ingenious tool, half the warp yarns are passed through the slots, and the other half—the alternate warp yarns—are threaded through the eyes (Fig. 387). When the heddle is lifted, all the warp ends in the eyes are raised to create a shed. When it is pushed down, the alternate ends move to the top of each slot to produce the opposite shed for plain weave. A complicated weave would require that the warp yarns be lifted individually.

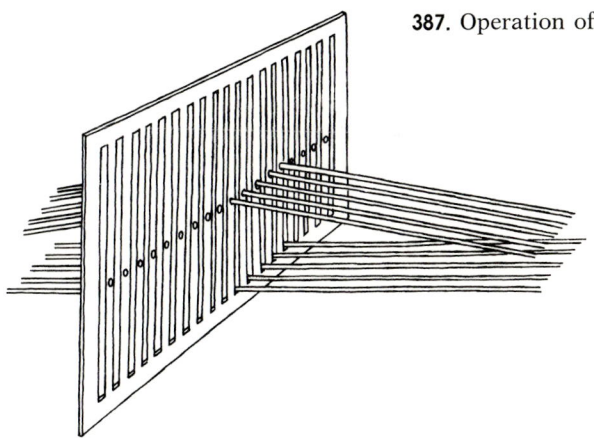

A more common shedding system relies upon a shed roll or *sword* and a heddle rod (Fig. 388). The sword is threaded alternately over and under the warp yarns; when turned on end, it produces the first shed for plain weave. All the yarns that lie under the sword are attached by string heddles (or by one continuous string heddle) to the heddle rod, which when lifted raises the alternate yarns.

The beating mechanism is equally simple. On the Indian version of the backstrap loom the slot-and-eye heddle also serves as a beater. If the sword and heddle rod system is used, an extra stick is inserted in the warp for beating.

Construction of a Backstrap Loom

The backstrap loom can be as wide or as narrow as you can handle with ease. For the beginner, a width greater than about 22 inches (55 cm) is awkward, so all the components of the loom described below have been adjusted to that size. The materials for the backstrap loom include:

> four 22-inch lengths of 1-inch dowel (55-cm lengths of 2.5-cm dowel)
> one 22-inch length of ¾-inch dowel (55-cm length of 1.9 cm dowel)
> two wooden slats, each 22 inches long and 1½ inches wide (55 cm × 3.75 cm)
> one wooden slat, 22 inches (55 cm) long, rounded at both ends and tapered to a knife-like edge along one side for the beater
> one ball of stout twine
> one ball of linen or cotton cord
> one length of cord or tape about 4 feet (1.2 m) long for the backstrap

If you want, you can construct a rigid slot-and-eye heddle similar to that illustrated in Figure 386. This would eliminate the necessity for the linen cord, the ¾-inch dowel, and one of the wooden slats.

For the most part, the backstrap loom is constructed as the loom is dressed. It cannot be fully assembled until the warp is in position.

Preparation for Weaving

The warp yarns can be measured on a warping frame or reel as for conventional weaving. If neither is available, the warp can be wound around the backs of two chairs held at a fixed distance apart, or around two stakes driven into the ground. In any event, some provision should be allowed for making the cross (see pp. 112–114). If you use two chairs or stakes for warping, you can make the cross by winding in a figure-8 manner around the two supports. The cross will lie between the stakes and should be tied with a cord temporarily to hold the yarns in position. For the first project—until you are accustomed to the mechanics of the loom—the warp should be no longer than about 1½ to 2 yards (1.5 m).

388. The shed sword and heddle rod.

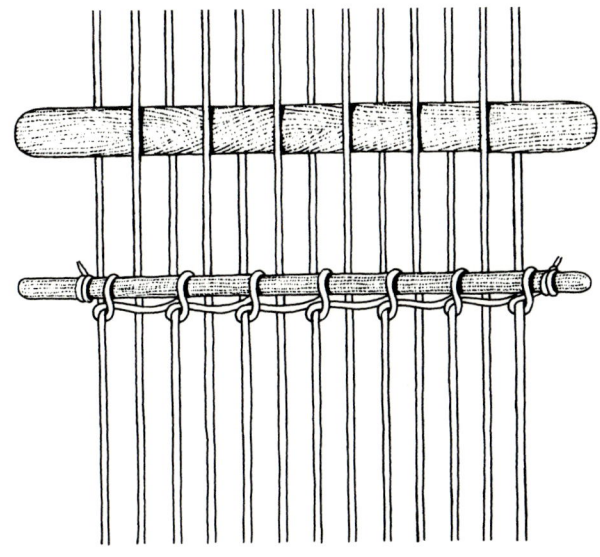

Setting Up the Backstrap Loom

- ☐ Measure the warp yarns, and tie the cross.
- ☐ Cut the warp from the warping device at the end opposite the cross.
- ☐ Slip the looped end near the cross over one of the 1-inch dowels (the warp stick).
- ☐ Attach a length of twine securely to each end of the warp stick, and tie it to your support—a tree, doorknob, or whatever you wish.
- ☐ Cut another length of twine slightly longer than double the width of the warp, and insert it in the cross (to act as lease sticks).
- ☐ Remove the cross ties.
- ☐ Spread the warp on the warp stick.

- ☐ If you are using a slot-and-eye heddle, establish the sheds now. (For a sword and heddle rod, skip this step.) Divide the total number of warp yarns by two, and find the center of the heddle. Count from the center to left the number of slots plus eyes to equal one half of the warp. Mark this point on the heddle. Clasp the heddle between your knees, or prop it between two heavy objects. Working from left to right, draw the warp yarns alternately through a slot and an eye, taking the yarns first from one side of the cross and then from the other. Tie the yarns in a slip knot so they will not fall out of the heddle.

- ☐ Tie the backstrap to one end of another 1-inch dowel (the cloth stick).
- ☐ Pass the strap around your waist in such a way that the cloth stick will be held at a comfortable distance from your body. Fasten the backstrap to the other end of the stick.
- ☐ Attach the cut ends of the warp to the cloth stick with a half knot and bow knot (Fig. 207).

- ☐ With the slot-and-eye heddle, omit the following steps and proceed to weave.

- ☐ If you are using a sword and heddle rod, establish the sheds now.
- ☐ Hold the warp under tension by pressing back slightly on the backstrap.
- ☐ Make the first shed either by lifting gently on the lease cord and passing the shed sword through the opening, or by threading the sword alternately over and under the warp yarns. (If you wish, you can tie a length of cord to each end of the sword to hold it in position.)
- ☐ Turn the sword on end to open a shed.
- ☐ Place the ball of linen or cotton cord in a container (such as a heavy bowl or cooking pot) to the right of the warp.
- ☐ Thread the linen cord across the warp in such a way that it is passed *under* all the warp yarns that are below the sword and *over* all the yarns that are on the sword.
- ☐ Tie the cord to one end of the 3/4-inch dowel—the heddle rod.
- ☐ Starting from the left side, reach through the warp and grasp the cord to the right of the first warp yarn that is *under* the sword (Fig. 389). Pull the cord through the warp, and twist it clockwise in one complete turn to form a loop.
- ☐ Repeat the looping process to the right of each warp yarn that is under the sword.
- ☐ When all the alternate warp yarns have been affixed to the heddle rod, cut the cord, and tie it to the other end of the rod.
- ☐ Pull up on the heddle rod firmly a few times to equalize the loops.
- ☐ Proceed with the weaving.

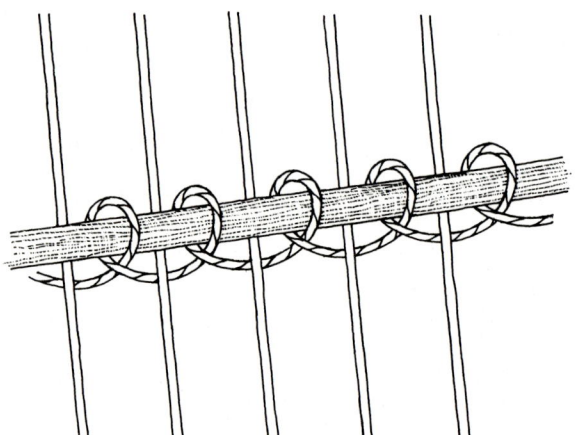

389. A length of cord is looped over the heddle rod, catching all the yarns not engaged by the shed sword. When pulled taut, the heddle rod opens a plain-weave shed.

A boat or throw shuttle is usually too heavy for weaving on a backstrap loom, but a flat stick shuttle will work very well. As an alternate, you can simply wind the weft yarn around a stick bobbin or around a 5-inch length of 1/4-inch dowel that has been pointed at one or both ends. You can point the dowel with a pencil sharpener. For free weaving, you can make a series of butterfly shuttles (Fig. 266)—one for each type of weft yarn.

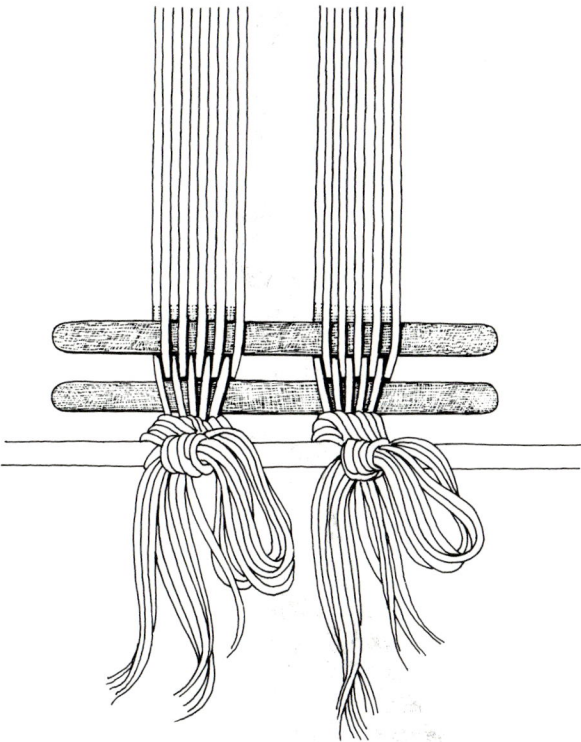

above: 390. To begin weaving on the backstrap loom, insert two dowels in alternate plain-weave sheds near the cloth stick. These dowels help to spread the warp yarns and also serve as a cloth roll as weaving progresses.

below: 391. When a length of fabric has been woven, remove the backstrap from your waist, roll the dowels forward, and secure them by lashing a slat beneath them. Then replace the strap, and resume weaving.

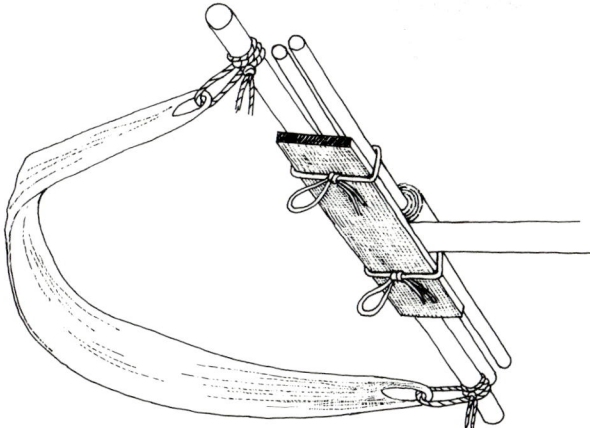

The Weaving Process

To begin weaving, open the first shed and insert one of the remaining 1-inch dowels in the shed. Place the other dowel in the opposite shed (Fig. 390). Besides helping to spread the warp yarns on the cloth stick, these two dowels will serve as a cloth roll. Once the dowels are in position, you can begin weaving. Each weft shot should be beat into

position with either the slot-and-eye heddle or the beater stick. A certain amount of practice is required to master the rhythm of backstrap weaving. Minute shifts of body weight will affect the tension of the warp, so you must make an effort to keep the tension consistent.

When you have woven to the point at which it is no longer comfortable to reach forward and throw the weft, you must roll the web onto the cloth stick. Remove the backstrap from your waist, and roll the three wooden dowels forward. Secure the dowels by lashing the remaining wooden slat to the underside (Fig. 391). Then, restore the backstrap to its position, and proceed with the weaving.

Nearly any weave can be constructed on a backstrap loom, although anything more complicated than plain weave would, of course, mean lifting the warp yarns by hand. The textile can be warp-faced, weft-faced, or balanced, just as on the conventional 4-harness loom. You can also produce a fabric with a selvedge on all four sides, which is impossible on the conventional loom. To make a selvedge on the warp ends, leave the warp loops uncut, and pass a temporary holding cord through each end. Lash these holding cords to the warp stick and cloth stick, and bring the weft directly up against them at both ends.

The Indians of Latin America have developed astonishing dexterity with the backstrap loom (Fig. 392), creating intricately patterned cloth several yards long and often a yard wide.

392. Backstrap weaving of belts and bands, Tetelcingo, Morelos, Mexico.

left: 393. Maria Chojnacka.
Mobile Spatial Composition. 1974.
Sisal, mixed technique
on permanent frames; each segment
40 × 20 × 20″ (100 × 50 × 50 cm).
Courtesy the artist.

below: 394. Joan Michaels Paque.
Mechanistic Movement. 1977.
Synthetic fiber tied and wrapped
on a permanent frame,
6′ × 3′4″ × 6″ (1.8 × 1 × .15 m).
Courtesy the artist.

Permanent Frame Looms

A frame loom is permanent when it becomes an integral part of the woven article created upon it. In this sense, the frame used for sprang (Fig. 425) could be considered a permanent loom, since it cannot be removed without collapsing the sprang-work. Many weavers have experimented with self-contained looms to achieve three-dimensional effects (Figs. 393–395).

Obviously, the permanent loom should reflect the character of the proposed weaving. Four sticks lashed together might be the basis of a rough-textured wall hanging woven from heavy natural yarns. On the other hand, a more "formal" work could be woven on a frame of beautifully grained wood or polished metal. The frame can be of any size or shape required by the particular project.

If the frame loom is made of wood, two principles govern the size of individual members. The frame must be strong enough to support the yarns, and it should relate in terms of scale to the yarn you intend to use. The wooden structure should not overpower the woven fabric, unless, of course, the weaving is intended to remain subsidiary to the framework.

A simple frame loom can be constructed from four lengths of 1-by-2-inch (2.5 × 5 cm) lath attached in a half-lap joint at the corners and secured with glue and countersunk wood screws (Fig. 396). Before the frame is assembled, a hole must be drilled near each end of the uprights to accept a half-inch dowel. Set the dowels at a sufficient distance from the horizontal bars to allow for manipulating the yarns during warping.

Wrap a continuous warp yarn around and around the dowels in figure-8 fashion to within

395. Aurelia Muñoz.
Cometa Anclado. 1974.
White nylon
knotted and wrapped
on a permanent frame,
9'4" × 30' × 30'
(2.8 × 9 × 9 m).
Courtesy the artist.

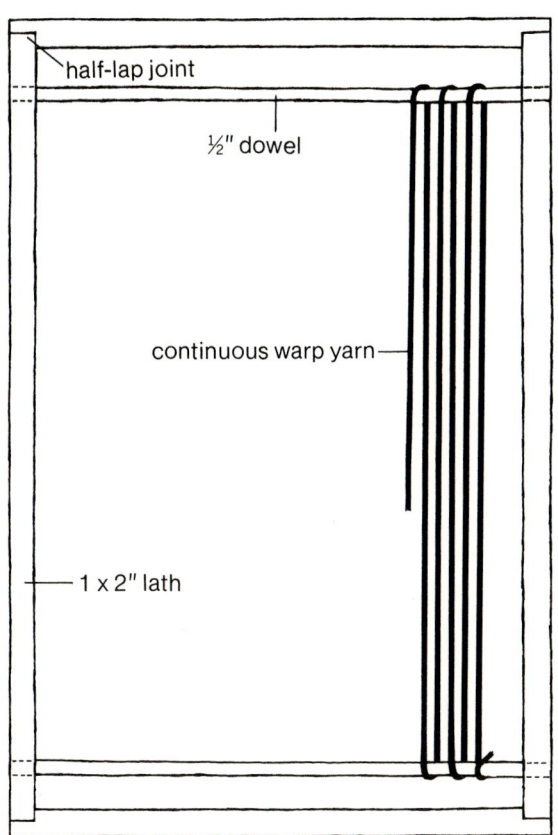

396. A simple frame loom.

half-lap joint

½" dowel

continuous warp yarn

1 x 2" lath

Because frame looms seldom provide for a shedding device, they lend themselves particularly well to finger weaves. The major problem lies in the fact that there is no way to adjust the warp tension. Therefore, a closely woven web is difficult to achieve, for the warp takeup will gradually tighten the yarns until it is almost impossible to open a shed. In extreme cases, the dowels will bow in from the tension in the warp. For this reason, projects woven on frame looms tend to be linear in character, with spaced pattern areas and sections of exposed warp or openwork (Fig. 397). In

397. Frances Schroeder. *Mandala.*
Weaving on permanent metal hoop loom.
The warp for this project
was threaded through yarn covering the ring.
From *Needleweaving: Easy as Embroidery,*
by Esther Warner Dendel.
Philadelphia: Countryside Press, 1972.

about 2 inches (5 cm) of the uprights (Fig. 396). If the warp were carried too close to the uprights, it would be difficult to insert the weft yarn. A few rows of chaining or twining (see pp. 197–199) at the upper and lower ends of the web will help to stabilize the horizontal dimension of the fabric. Any lightweight shuttle or even a tapestry bobbin or needle can be used to hold the weft yarn.

some cases you will find it easier to produce a symmetrical textile if you weave from each end toward the middle.

Reusable Frame Looms

As the name implies, many frame looms can be used over and over again, for the fabric is cut from the loom in the normal manner after weaving. Some looms of this type can be purchased either readymade or in kit form from weaving-supply houses, but they are simple enough to construct, and the problems of delicate balance do not arise, as they do with a complex loom.

I-Form Looms

Among the simplest of frame looms is the I-form (Fig. 398). This device is especially good for small tapestries. The materials needed are:

> one pine board, 1 inch by 5 inches by 30 inches (2.5 × 12.5 × 75 cm)
> two pine boards, 1 inch by 3 inches by 16 inches (2.5 × 7.5 × 40 cm)
> four wooden blocks, 1 inch by 3 inches by 5 inches (2.5 × 7.5 × 12.5 cm)
> eight 2½-inch wood screws
> 102 rustless 1-inch finishing nails
> white glue

Assemble the I-form loom as in Figure 398, with the two crossbars centered on the long baseboard and two wood blocks between them at each end. Glue the parts together, and leave the loom in a wood clamp overnight. When the glue is dry, drill four holes (2 inches or 5 cm deep) from the underside into each end of the baseboard, and countersink a wood screw in each hole so that the head of the screw is even with or just below the surface of the wood. Finally, drive 51 finishing nails in two rows into each of the crossbars. The nails are driven at an angle to counteract the tension of the warp yarns. Each nail projects about ½ inch.

The I-form is warped with a continuous yarn that zig-zags back and forth across the loom. For a denser warp the yarn can be returned in a second trip to the starting point. As with the permanent frame loom, there is no provision for adjusting the warp tension to compensate for yarn takeup, so the loom is more adaptable to loose finger weaves. If you wish, you can make a shed sword and heddle rod similar to those used with the backstrap loom (Fig. 388), but for most free weaving it is simple enough to pick up the yarns manually. A few rows of twining or chaining (see pp. 197–199) at each end of the web will help to spread the warp yarns evenly across the loom. The flat stick shuttle or a series of butterfly shuttles (Fig. 266) are best for holding the various colors of weft yarn. Pointed dowels or large-eyed yarn needles can be used to carry the wool or other kinds of yarn for a tapestry project.

The Indians of ancient Peru undoubtedly utilized a principle similar to that of the I-form loom in constructing shaped garments with a selvedge all around (Fig. 399). By driving nails in a flat surface at each point where the fabric changes direction, you can weave a textile in almost any shape and with a finished edge around the entire border. Because the edges are all meant to be finished selvedges, it is necessary to remove the nails at one end when the fabric has been completed in order to free the textile from the loom.

398. The I-form loom.

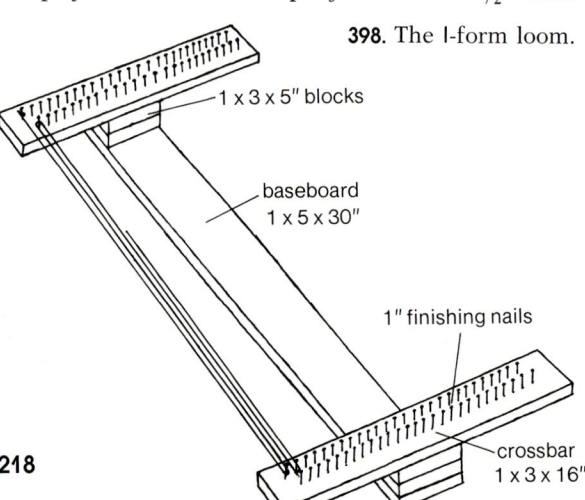

1 x 3 x 5" blocks

baseboard
1 x 5 x 30"

1" finishing nails

crossbar
1 x 3 x 16"

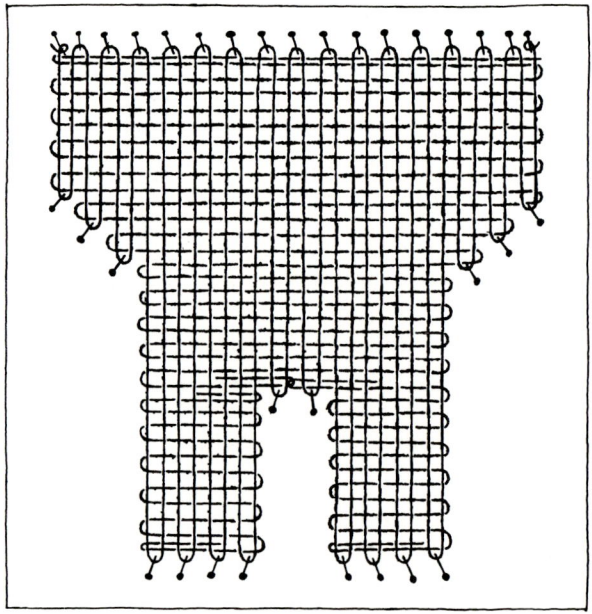

399. The Indians of ancient Peru used a loom based on the I-form principle to construct shaped garments with a finished edge all around.

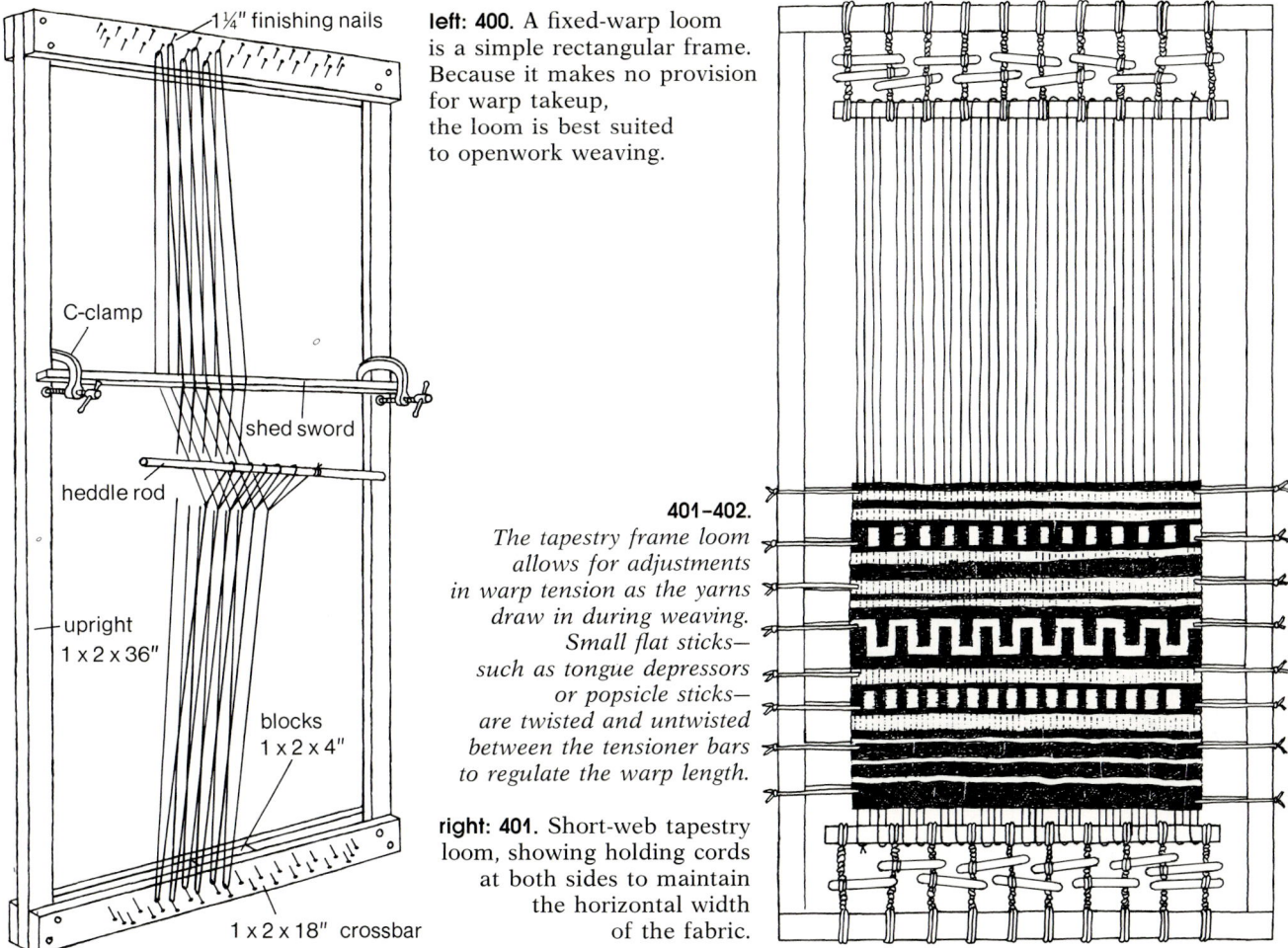

left: 400. A fixed-warp loom is a simple rectangular frame. Because it makes no provision for warp takeup, the loom is best suited to openwork weaving.

1¼" finishing nails

C-clamp

shed sword

heddle rod

upright 1 x 2 x 36"

blocks 1 x 2 x 4"

1 x 2 x 18" crossbar

401–402. *The tapestry frame loom allows for adjustments in warp tension as the yarns draw in during weaving. Small flat sticks— such as tongue depressors or popsicle sticks— are twisted and untwisted between the tensioner bars to regulate the warp length.*

right: 401. Short-web tapestry loom, showing holding cords at both sides to maintain the horizontal width of the fabric.

Square Frame Looms

There are probably thousands of designs for square frame looms, some much more flexible than others. The following section describes four basic designs, of which the first is really a variation on the I-form loom.

Fixed-Warp Loom   The square loom with a fixed warp is quite similar to the permanent frame loom (Fig. 396). It is fashioned from two uprights sandwiched between a pair of horizontal crossbars at each end (Fig. 400). For extra support, a small wood block is nailed between each pair of crossbars at the center. The materials needed are:

> two wooden slats, each 1 inch by 2 inches by 36 inches (2.5 × 5 × 90 cm), for the uprights
> four wooden slats, each 1 inch by 2 inches by 18 inches (2.5 × 5 × 45 cm), for the crossbars
> two wooden blocks, each 1 inch by 2 inches by 4 inches (2.5 × 5 × 10 cm)
> white glue and wood screws or finishing nails
> 64 1¼-inch rustless finishing nails

Assemble the loom as in Figure 400, following the procedure outlined for the I-form loom. Place the finishing nails in two rows—32 nails in each crossbar—and drive them at an angle to support the warp tension. Set them about two per inch except at the edges, where a denser concentration of nails will provide a firm selvedge.

Warping and weaving procedures are the same as those for the I-form loom. The only difference in the square loom is that the selvedges cannot be brought too close to the uprights, or it will be difficult to enter the weft. A shed sword and heddle rod can be constructed and attached to the uprights with C-clamps.

Short-Web Tapestry Loom   The loom described below is most often used for weaving tapestries, but its principles could be applied to almost any small textile. The framework of the loom is identical to that of the fixed-warp loom; however, provision is made for adjusting the warp tension when the yarns draw in during weaving (Fig. 401). The extra materials needed to allow for tension control on the short-web tapestry loom are:

two wooden slats, each 1 inch by 2 inches by 16
   inches (2.5 × 5 × 40 cm)
one ball of linen cord
about twenty small flat sticks—popsicle sticks
   or tongue depressors

The yarn is warped over the two tension slats.
It can be either a continuous warp, wound over
and over the two slats, or individual warp ends,
doubled over one slat and tied to the other. Attach
the tensioners to the uprights with linen cords set
at 2-inch intervals. Insert small twist sticks—such
as popsicle sticks—in the cords and tighten them.
As the weaving progresses and the weft yarns take
up some of the warp length, the twist sticks are
gradually unwound at both ends.

Weaving proceeds in the same manner as on
the fixed-warp loom, with, if desired, a sword and
heddle rod clamped to the uprights. One special
precaution should be taken when creating a tapestry or other closely woven fabric. Short lengths of
linen cord should be looped around the selvedges
and tied—one on each side—to the uprights to
stabilize the horizontal dimension of the fabric.

Long-Web Tapestry Loom   The only advantage of
the long-web loom over the one previously de-

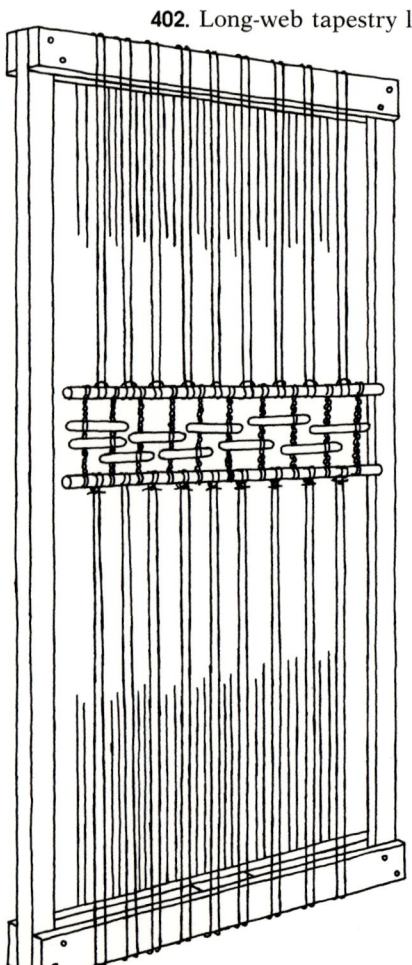

402. Long-web tapestry loom, back view.

scribed is that it can accommodate a web almost
twice as long as the frame. The yarn is warped
over the two tensioner boards in the same manner
as for the short-web loom. However, instead of
attaching the tensioners to the framework of the
loom, join them to each other, by means of cords,
at the back of the loom. The warp yarn thus travels
up and over the top crossbar, down the entire
front of the loom, under the bottom crossbar and
up to the starting point.

You can drive nails into the crossbars, as on the
fixed warp loom, but in this case they serve only as
a general comb and as a spreader for the warp.

As the weaving progresses, you can turn the
web around the loom (Fig. 402), so the working
space is always in the same position. To turn the
yarn and web around, unwind the twist sticks and
slacken the cords holding the tensioners.

Rigid-Heddle Loom   The loom pictured in Figure
403 makes provision for two sheds with a rigid
slot-and-eye heddle, as well as offering the advantage of warp and cloth storage. The heddle frame
rests on a ledge near the center of the loom, in
which position the first shed is open. To change
the shed, you simply press the heddle down. Dowels at either end of the loom serve as the warp
beam and cloth beam. Each has spikes driven into
it, which can be inserted in an eyelet mounted on
the frame. Releasing the spike from the eyelet
allows the roll to turn freely, to let off warp yarn.

The rigid-heddle loom can be constructed with
relatively simple woodworking equipment and
skills. The size can be altered from that specified in
Figure 403. However, if you want a smaller loom
than the one pictured, another of the frame looms
may be more successful. The great advantage of
this model is that it allows for maintaining warp
tension while at the same time permitting enough
slack for warp takeup and for sheds to be opened
easily by the heddle. The distance from cloth beam
to warp beam helps to create this situation. On the
other hand, a rigid-heddle loom much larger than
this would be awkward and cumbersome.

The materials needed are:

two wooden boards each 1 inch by 6 inches by
   30 inches for the horizontal supports
two wooden boards each 1 inch by 4 inches by
   30 inches for the vertical supports
two wooden blocks each $\frac{1}{4}$ inch by $1\frac{1}{2}$ inches
   by 6 inches to form a ledge for the heddle
two 36-inch lengths of 1-inch dowel for the
   warp and cloth rolls
two wooden slats each 1 inch by 30 inches for
   the warp and cloth sticks

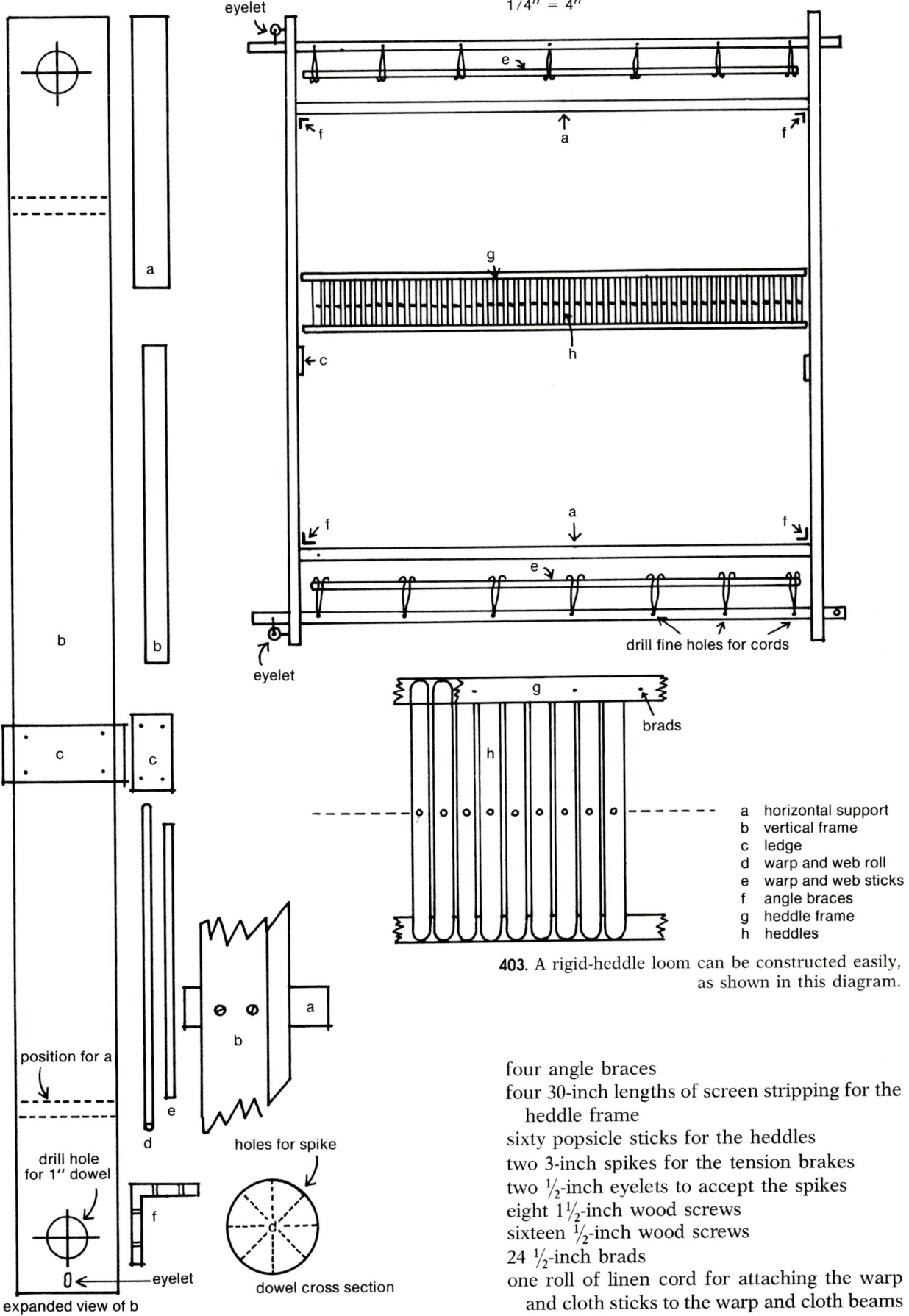

1/4" = 4"

eyelet

e

f — a — f

g

h — c

a

f — f

e

drill fine holes for cords

eyelet

g

brads

h

a   horizontal support
b   vertical frame
c   ledge
d   warp and web roll
e   warp and web sticks
f   angle braces
g   heddle frame
h   heddles

403. A rigid-heddle loom can be constructed easily, as shown in this diagram.

a

b

b

c

c

c

position for a

drill hole
for 1" dowel

expanded view of b

d   e

a

b

holes for spike

f

eyelet

dowel cross section

four angle braces
four 30-inch lengths of screen stripping for the
    heddle frame
sixty popsicle sticks for the heddles
two 3-inch spikes for the tension brakes
two ½-inch eyelets to accept the spikes
eight 1½-inch wood screws
sixteen ½-inch wood screws
24 ½-inch brads
one roll of linen cord for attaching the warp
    and cloth sticks to the warp and cloth beams

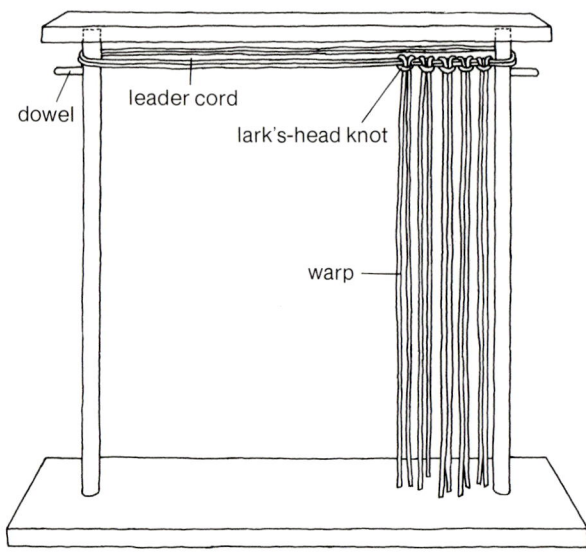

left: 404. Ojibway woven bag, from Bear Island, Leetch Lake, Minnesota. Collected 1903. Basswood fiber. American Museum of Natural History, New York.

below: 405. The Ojibway loom is similar to a warp-weighted loom. It is used primarily for chaining and twining.

The Ojibway Loom

The loom used by the Ojibway Indians is nothing more than a warp-weighted loom without the weights (Fig. 144). The weavers of this tribe, native to the Great Lakes region of North America, employed such a loom for making tightly woven bags of rushes and twine (Fig. 404).

The Ojibway loom consists of two sturdy upright dowels supporting a horizontal crossbar (Fig. 405). A heavy nonelastic cord is wound four or five times around the uprights about half an inch below the crossbar and tied securely. Nails, thumbtacks, or wooden dowels can be added to hold the leader cord in position. All the warp yarns are doubled over the leader cord in a lark's-head knot (Fig. 194) and allowed to hang free. The loom is used primarily for chaining and twining.

Inkle Looms

The inkle loom is the most complex of the frame looms described in this chapter. It can weave a fairly long web, there is a built-in shedding mechanism, and a tension adjustment is provided. However, the *width* of the web is restricted to about 4 inches, and inkle-woven fabrics are usually even narrower. Therefore, the loom is used primarily for weaving decorative bands—belts, headbands, guitar straps, shoulder straps, dog leashes, and trimming bands for garments. Some-

times strips of inkle-woven fabric are sewn together to make a larger, striped textile. In many respects inkle weaving is similar to card weaving (see pp. 244–248), except that on the inkle loom there is a limit to the length of the web, whereas a card-woven fabric could theoretically be infinite in length. Mary Atwater is credited with introducing the inkle loom to the United States. It had long been popular in Scandinavia and in England, where it served for weaving garters and braces.

The loom can be made from high-grade pine, but maple, walnut, or oak will give longer service and provide a more attractive finish. Above all, the framework must be sturdy enough to support yarns under tension. A medium-size inkle loom can be constructed with the following materials:

two wooden boards, each 1 inch by 2 inches by 24 inches (2.5 × 5 × 54 cm)
four wooden boards, each 1 inch by 2 inches by 8 inches (2.5 × 5 × 20 cm)
seven 9-inch (22.5 cm) lengths of $\frac{3}{8}$-inch dowel
two 3-inch (7.5 cm) spikes
eight $\frac{1}{2}$-inch wood screws
white glue
up to sixty 8-inch lengths of linen cord

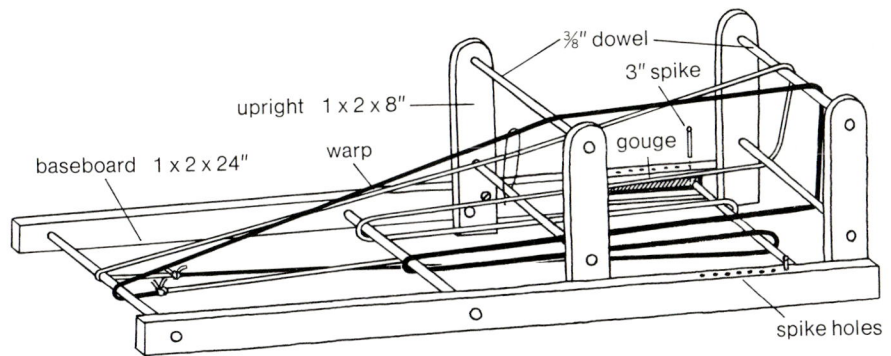

406. The inkle loom is ideal for weaving long, narrow decorative bands. The product of such a loom is generally a warp-face plain-weave fabric.

The fully assembled loom is illustrated in Figure 406. The four 8-inch boards that serve as the uprights are rounded on one end, and two holes are drilled in each to accept the ⅜-inch dowels. The long boards are also drilled with two dowel holes apiece, in the positions indicated in Figure 406. Eight narrow holes—just large enough to accommodate the spikes—are drilled into the 1-inch edge of each baseboard, and the inside face of the wood is gouged out to half the depth of the board in an area ⅜ inch wide and 4½ to 5 inches long around the spike holes. The tensioning dowel that is inserted at this point must be cut slightly shorter than the others, so that it will slide smoothly in the cutout area. The uprights are attached to the baseboards in a half-lap joint, with glue and two wood screws at each juncture.

One continuous yarn is used for the warp, and warping is accomplished directly on the loom. To begin warping, place the spikes in the holes that are closest to the back of the loom. As weaving proceeds and the warp takeup increases tension in the yarns, gradually move the spikes forward. String heddles sufficient to accommodate one-half the warp yarns are tied to the heddle rod dowel. The heddles must be of exactly equal length when tied and must be long enough to catch the yarns coming over the top dowel.

The warping pattern is shown in Figure 406. Each time a yarn passes over the top dowel at the center of the loom, it must be threaded through a heddle. The string heddles, therefore, project through the lower section of the warp. When a new color is introduced into the warp, it should be tied to the end of the preceeding color at the starting point. The final end is tied in an overhand knot to the starting end of the first warp yarn. The tension should be held constant for each circuit of the loom, for it is difficult to adjust after warping.

Inkle looms provide for two sheds. When the yarn is in its normal position, as warped, the first shed is automatically open. To broaden the shed and allow for insertion of the weft, push down the lower layer of yarns by hand. The opposite shed is created by lifting the lower yarns and pushing down those in the heddles.

Whenever the weaving space becomes too small, the entire web can be pulled forward and rolled around the loom. A flat stick shuttle is the best tool for holding the weft yarn, while an ordinary comb can serve as the beater.

Although finger weaving is possible on the inkle loom, the product of the loom is most often a warp-face plain weave (Fig. 407). Because there is no reed, the warp yarns tend to bunch together, all but obscuring the weft yarn. Pattern is achieved by varying the color of the warp. In order for the weft yarn to be as inconspicuous as possible, it should be of the same color as the two edges of the warp.

407. Shirley Marein. Scarf. 1970. Mexican wool, woven on the inkle loom in a traditional American Indian pattern; width 5″ (12.5 cm). Courtesy the artist.

Nonloom Techniques

It is common to classify yarn-interlacement methods according to the number of strands involved and their direction. All fiber construction techniques—except matting and felt-making—can therefore be categorized as either single strand or multiple strand. The major yarn-interlacement systems are grouped as follows:

Multiple strands

knotting
macramé
sprang
plaiting
braiding
bobbin lace
twining
hooking
weaving

The first category is further subdivided into techniques based on one set of yarns oriented in the same direction—such as macramé and sprang—and those having two or more sets of yarns, usually perpendicular to one another—including twining and weaving.

Continuous single strand

crocheting
tatting
netting
knitting
needle lace
coiling

This chapter explores a number of constructions that require no loom, though in a few cases a simple frame or support is necessary. Nonloom techniques are especially appealing to those who cannot or do not wish to invest in a loom, as well as to those who find loom weaving restrictive. Many nonloom constructions can be effectively combined with conventional loom weaving in wall hangings, sculpture, garments, accessories, and similar projects.

Macramé

Macramé is a multiple-strand construction that uses one set of yarns oriented vertically. The technique has long since broken free of its original application to fringes and decorative borders; today it is used for entire garments, wall hangings, sculpture, jewelry, and many other items. Because the knotted structure is extremely strong, it is even suitable for furniture. Two simple knots—the square knot and the clove hitch—are basic to macramé. The great variety of pattern that is possible derives from the endless ways in which the knots can be combined (Pl. 19, p. 237; Fig. 408).

Materials

Any nonelastic cord or yarn that will hold a knot can be used for macramé. Jute, linen, and cotton are the most popular fibers, but many other materials can be adapted for specific projects. Wool yarns—especially knitting yarns—are usually too stretchy for knotting, and excessively hairy yarns will tend to obscure the knots. Nylon cord or twine is usable, but in many cases the ends will have to be melted to prevent the knots from untying. Soft cotton yarns are easier to handle if they are dipped in a starch solution before knotting. The starch can be washed out after the project is completed. Seine cord, packing twine, upholsterer's cord, surveyor's chalk line, and rug yarn are all excellent materials for macramé.

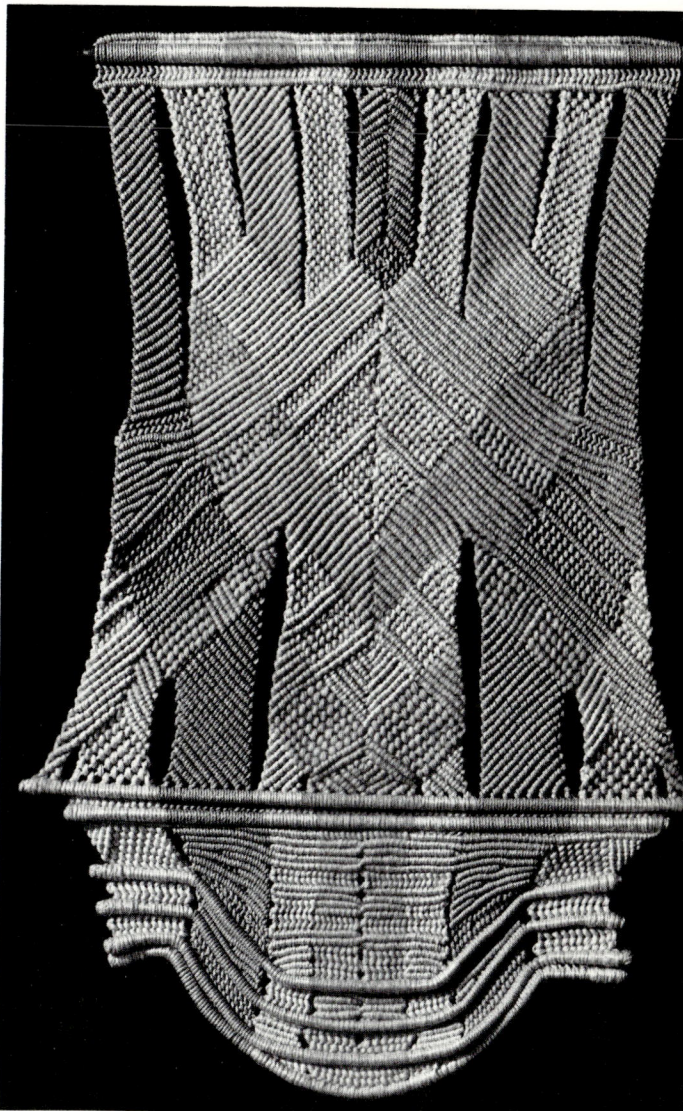

408. Mary Walker Phillips. *White on White.* 1975. Macramé in white wool and white linen, 29½ × 20½″ (74 × 51 cm). Courtesy Hadler Galleries, New York.

Equipment

Sharp scissors and a support of some kind are all the equipment needed for macramé. The support may be removed after knotting is completed or it may be incorporated into the finished article as part of the design. The type of support depends, of course, on the nature of the project to be undertaken. Wall hangings are often knotted on a rigid dowel or metal rod, which becomes a permanent part of the structure. Very large pieces can be knotted on a framework suspended from the ceiling, or on an easel. Tubular knottings originate from any circular support—an embroidery hoop, a lampshade frame, or a length of wire shaped into a circle. Freestanding sculptures may have an armature inside to support the shape.

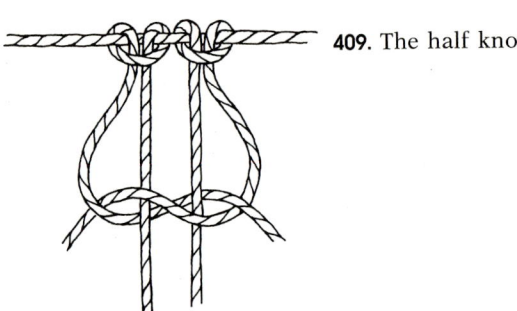

409. The half knot.

410. The square knot.

The Basic Knots

The Half Knot   The half knot or *half square knot* is made on a unit of four cords. The two outside cords make the actual knot, while the inner two are merely foundation cords upon which the knot is built. The foundation cords must be held rigid while the knot is being tied. To make a half knot (Fig. 409) pass cord 4 in front of the foundation cords, then bring cord 1 over cord 4, behind the foundation cords, and through the loop formed by cord 4. If you repeat the half knot over and over on the same four yarns, the result will be a *sinnet* or braidlike band that spirals automatically as the knotting progresses. From time to time the work will have to be turned as cords 1 and 4 automatically exchange positions.

The Square Knot   The square knot is a continuation of the half knot. After a half knot has been tied, pass cord 1, which is now at the right, behind the foundation cords, and carry cord 4 behind cord 1, in front of the foundation cords, and through the loop formed by cord 1 (Fig. 410). Cords 1 and 4 are then back in their original positions. The foundation cords are held rigid throughout. If you tie a series of square knots on the same four cords, the result is a *flat sinnet*. Square knots can also be tied on alternating groups of yarns; if loosely spaced, they produce an allover lacy effect (Fig. 411).

The Clove Hitch   The clove hitch or *double half hitch* is an extremely versatile knot. It can be tied horizontally, vertically, diagonally, or in almost any direction to produce a wide range of effects (Fig. 415).

The *horizontal* clove hitch is illustrated in Figure 412. The first cord at the left becomes the foundation cord; draw it in front of all the other cords, and hold it under tension in a straight horizontal line. (If this tension is relaxed, the knot will not tie properly.) Lift the second cord up and around the foundation cord, then pass it through

the space between the two cords, and pull it taut. Repeat this procedure with cord 2 before continuing to cord 3. Each clove hitch thus consists of *two* loops over the foundation cord with the same knotting cord. When all the cords have been knotted over the foundation cord, you can turn it back and repeat the process from right to left. Cord 1 is thereby returned to its original position.

Rows of horizontal clove hitches are often used to separate pattern areas, because they provide a firm structure to maintain the width of the knotting. They are also excellent for finishing the edges of a handwoven fabric (Fig. 341).

The *diagonal* clove hitch is made in exactly the same manner. The only difference is that the foundation cord is held at an angle, so that the row

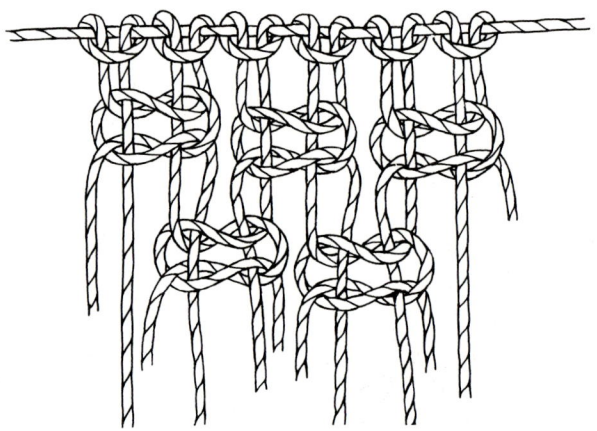

above: **411.** A pattern of square knots on alternating cords.

below: **412.** The horizontal clove hitch.

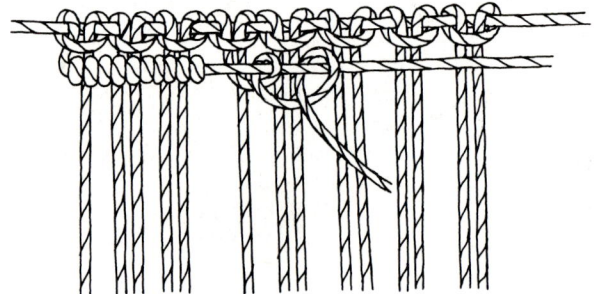

of clove hitches proceeds downward gradually (Fig. 413). An X pattern can be developed by starting a foundation cord from each side of the knotting, with the two cords descending toward the center (Fig. 414). When they meet, the foundation cords are knotted over one another before proceeding toward the opposite edges. Rows of clove hitches tied directly against one another result in an extremely firm structure—strong enough to support a three-dimensional sculpture (Fig. 415).

above: **413.** The diagonal clove hitch is shown proceeding from both sides toward the center.

right: **414.** An X motif in diagonal clove hitches.

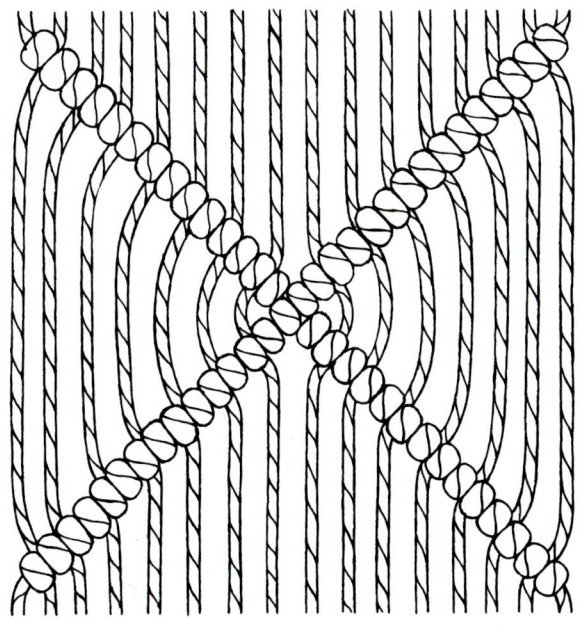

below: **415. Joan Michaels Paque.** *Transcendental Tendencies.* 1977. Self-sustaining construction in knotting and wrapping techniques, synthetic fiber; 3′2″ × 9′3″ × 11″ (.95 × 2.75 × .28 m). Courtesy the artist.

The *vertical* clove hitch (Fig. 416) is made by knotting the cord at far left over each of the remaining cords. Therefore, cord 1 becomes the knotting cord, and all the others serve in turn as foundation cords. When a row of vertical clove hitches is knotted, only the knotting cord appears on the surface. The other cords are completely hidden in the structure.

To make a vertical clove hitch pass cord 1 (at left) behind and around cord 2 so it emerges between the two cords. Repeat this process for the second half of the clove hitch. The knotting cord then moves to cord 3, and so on across the row. If you wish, you can turn back the knotting cord and make a second row from right to left. The vertical clove hitch consumes yarn very rapidly, so the knotting cord must be much longer than the others.

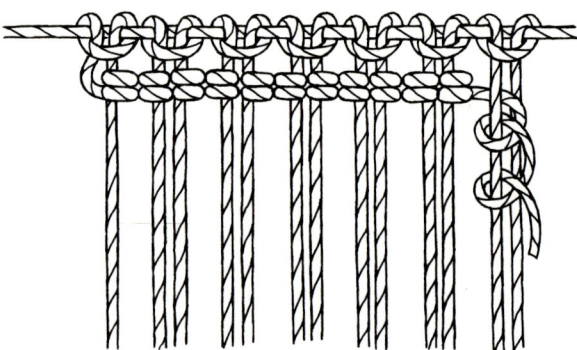

above: 416. The vertical clove hitch.

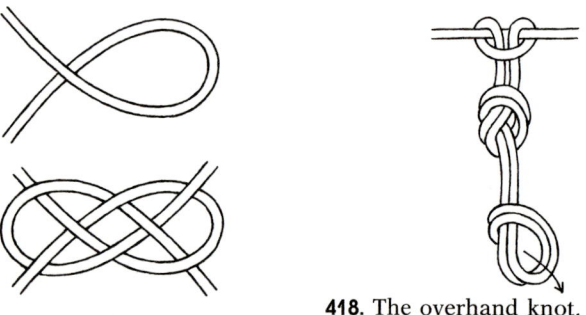

418. The overhand knot.

417. The Josephine knot can be tied with two single yarns or with two groups of yarns handled as a unit.

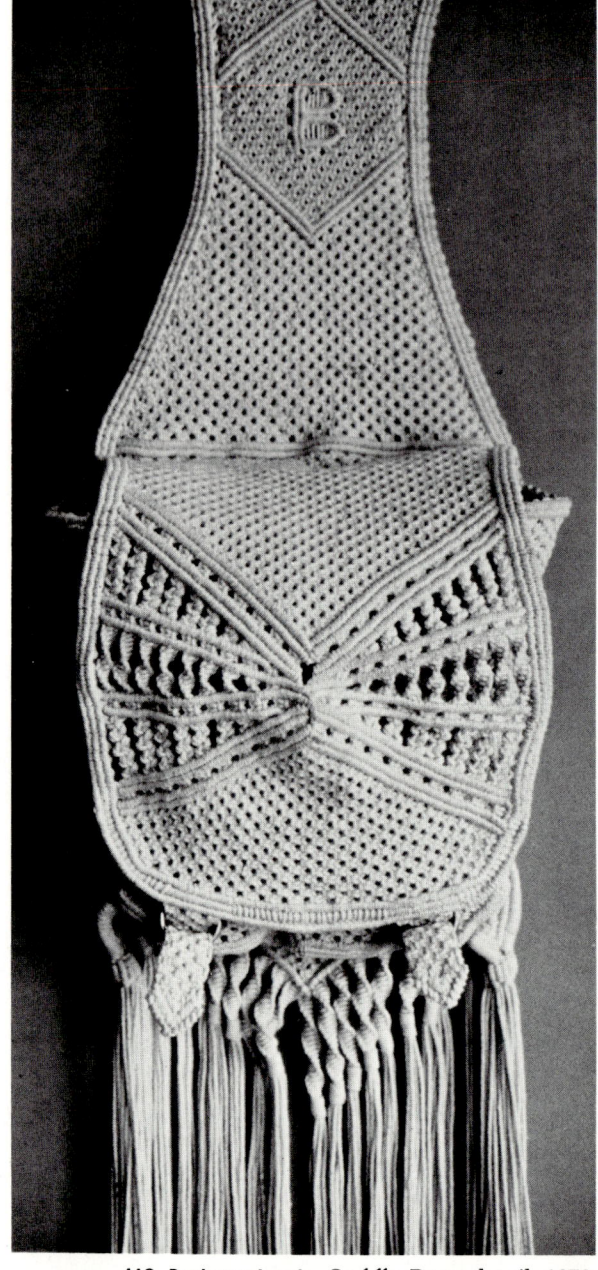

419. Barbara Lewis. *Saddle Bags*, detail. 1972. Macramé in cotton cable cord, 6′6″ × 1′ (2 × .3 m). Collection Bryden Becker, New York.

In addition to the two basic knots, there are special knots that may be encountered from time to time. The *Josephine knot* (Fig. 417) consists of two interlocked loops and resembles a pretzel. It can be tied with two single yarns or with two groups of yarns each considered as a unit. The knot can be pulled taut, but it is usually more attractive if a bit of slack is left in the yarns. The *overhand knot* is a simple loop with the end of the yarn passed through it (Fig. 418). It can be tied with one yarn or with a group of yarns handled as a unit. The *lark's-head knot* (Fig. 194) is frequently used to attach the cords to a support.

Finishing a Macramé Project

Many macramé pieces end in a fringe. When this is not appropriate, the cut ends can be worked back into the fabric with a crochet hook and trimmed cleanly on the reverse side. Cord ends

drawn back onto a fabric of clove hitches are almost invisible. For extra durability you can stitch across the fabric either with a sewing machine or by hand.

The final knots in a macramé project can be secured by painting the reverse side with a transparent glue or clear nail polish. Nylon cords are often subjected to heat so the fibers will melt together and prevent raveling of the knots.

Designing for Macramé

The scope of possibilities for design in macramé—either alone or in combination with other techniques—is very broad. Clothing and accessories, the most popular subjects for knotting in the Victorian era, are still being made today, but with a fresh and inventive approach (Fig. 419). Jewelry is another common application, because of the ease in combining knots with beads, stones, and metals (Fig. 420). The potential for sculpture ranges from rigid, tightly knotted freestanding

left: 420. Chris Yarborough. *Necklace.* Macramé knots in linen with copper wire, copper rods, glass beads, and lead fish weights; 6 × 3″ (15 × 7.5 cm). Collection James A. McCool, Winston-Salem, N.C.

below: 421. Aurelia Muñoz. *Waves of the Sea.* 1976. Knotting in white nylon ropes, 18′9″ (5.4 m) square. Courtesy the artist.

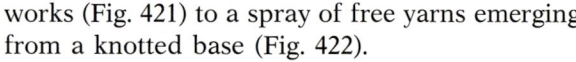

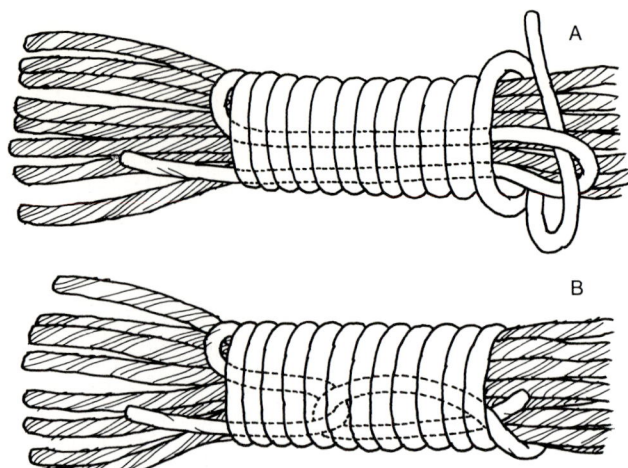

left: 422. Claire Zeisler. *Red Madagascar.* 1971.
Raffia and jute, knotted and wrapped; height 7′8″ (2.25 m).
Courtesy Ruth Kaufmann Gallery, New York.

above: 423. To begin yarn wrapping, make a loop
of the yarn end along the length to be wrapped.
Then, when you have wrapped for a distance,
pull the loop through to conceal the end.

Wrapping

Yarn wrapping is a technique that has attracted
considerable attention in recent years. The process
itself is utterly simple. It involves merely wrapping
the yarns around foundation cords or some other
support and fixing the two ends.

The procedure for attaching the ends will depend upon the length to be wrapped. If you are
wrapping for a short distance, begin by forming a
loop in the wrapping cord along the core to be
wrapped (Fig. 423). Then, while holding the loop
firmly in place, wrap the cord around and around
the length. When you have finished wrapping,
insert the end of the cord in the loop. Pull gently
on the beginning end until the two ends meet
halfway, underneath the wrapping. Clip the rough
ends close to the wrapping.

This system will not work when a very long
section is to be wrapped. In this case, simply wrap
very tightly at the two ends and force the rough
edges under the wrapping with a crochet hook or
other pointed tool.

What makes wrapped works so exciting is the
ingenuity artists have shown in manipulating the
resultant forms. Many of Sheila Hicks' pieces
combine tightly wrapped areas with sections of
free yarn (Pl. 21, p. 237). With their brilliant colors
and rich textural contrasts, these works are among
the purest statements of design in fiber. A different
approach is seen in Olga de Amaral's hangings,
which are cascades of tightly wrapped yarns (Fig.
424). The knotted sculpture in Figure 415 also includes wrapped sections used to create self-supporting three-dimensional form.

works (Fig. 421) to a spray of free yarns emerging
from a knotted base (Fig. 422).

Knotting is often combined with other techniques—weaving, knitting, rya, braiding, and crochet (Pl. 20, p. 237). One of the most obvious combinations is with wrapping.

424. Olga de Amaral. *Una Estera Gris.* 1974.
Horsehair and wool, height 7'3" (2.2 m). Courtesy the artist.

Sprang

Like macramé, sprang is composed of one set of yarns, in this case, parallel warp yarns held under tension at both ends. Nothing need be added to the warp yarns to make the construction. The lacy network is created by twisting adjacent warp yarns and thus interlinking them in a line that moves horizontally across the warp.

The mechanics of sprang are much like those of gauze weave, except that no weft is inserted. Usually, the interlinking is done in the middle of the piece and then pushed to the top and bottom, so that the two halves form a mirror image of one another. When you have twisted the yarns as much as you want (or when they are so tight that it is impossible to continue), the final row of twists must be secured in some fashion. In a wall hanging you may want to insert a rod or stick through

the middle to hold the twists. Otherwise, you can chain across the middle or even add a few rows of weaving or crocheting.

Materials

Sprang can be worked with any relatively elastic yarn or cord—cotton, nylon, or wool rug yarn, for example. As with macramé, an extremely fuzzy yarn will tend to hide the structure, so a clean-surfaced yarn is preferable.

Equipment

A square frame of wood or metal makes a good support for sprang. You can also suspend the sprangwork between two wooden dowels, with vertical rods at either side to maintain the cross-wise stretch. In either case, the horizontal crossbar

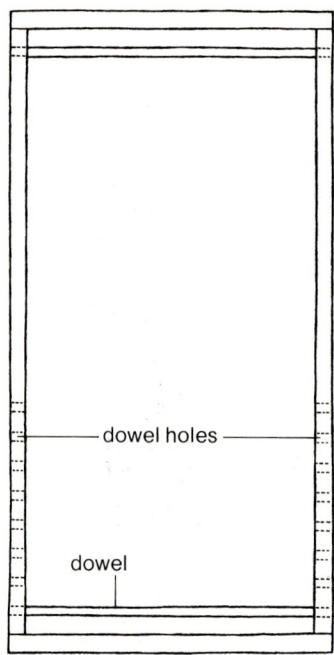

425. A simple rectangular frame for sprang. The lower crossbar is movable so it can be adjusted.

— dowel holes —

dowel

at bottom should be movable, so that it can be raised as the sprang contracts. Figure 425 illustrates a wooden frame that could be constructed easily. The top and vertical portions are fixed, and holes have been drilled at several intervals along the uprights so that the bottom dowel can be raised gradually.

In addition to the frame, you will need a shed stick—either a dowel or a lath stick filed to a blunt point—and several cords to separate the sheds and keep the rows from untwisting. A knitting needle and crochet hook are both helpful.

Mounting the Yarns

To begin the sprang, warp one long continuous yarn onto the frame in figure-8 fashion. Be sure to attach the beginning and end of the yarn at the same end of the frame, either top or bottom (Fig. 426). You will have a series of vertical yarns, the number of which should be divisible by four.

Procedure for Sprang

The first step is to separate the yarns into a shed, with half raised and half lowered. To some extent the warping system will have done this naturally. Run holding cords through the warp to further separate the top and bottom threads. Tie these cords loosely at the top and bottom of the work.

Begin the sprangwork in the center of the warp area. Slip your left hand into the warp between the upper and the lower threads. The first twist is to be

made at the outer right edge of the work. It will involve the first three yarns at right—the first one on top and the first two on the bottom.

The 1/1 Twist for Sprang

□ Working from the right side, bring the first two lower threads to the right of the first upper thread, and pull them to the upper level, pushing the first upper thread to the lower level (Fig. 427).

□ Insert the shed stick to hold this twist.

□ Continue across the row, working to the left, always exchanging one lower yarn for one upper, pulling the lower yarn to the right of the upper. Hold each twist in place with the shed stick.

□ At the end of the first row you should have two upper yarns and one lower one remaining. Pull the lower yarn to the right of *both* remaining upper ones. (This double-yarn selvedge will occur on all odd-numbered rows—that is, on alternating rows.)

□ When you have finished the row, insert a contrasting piece of yarn through the twists. You can tie it loosely to the sides of the frame if you wish. Later, if you make a mistake, you can go back row by row, following the threads, to find the point of the error.

□ The single twists will appear in both the top and the bottom of the work. Using your hands or a stick as beater, push them away from the center.

□ For the second row (and all even-numbered rows), begin at the right side and execute the 1/1 twist by pulling one lower thread to the right of and above one upper thread (Fig. 428).

□ Continue across the row, inserting the shed stick to hold the twists. Insert the contrasting thread, and push the two ends of the sprangwork away from the center.

The sprangwork continues, alternating odd and even rows, until you have no more room to work or are satisfied with the design. If at any point you should be confused about whether you are beginning an odd or an even row, remember that odd rows begin with the first thread at the right in the "up" position.

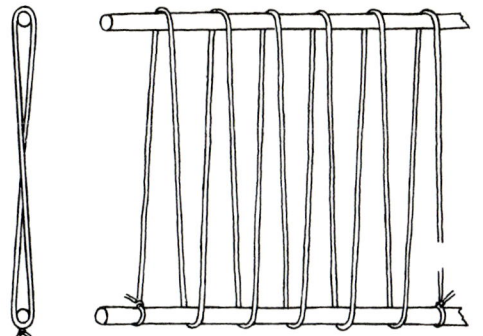

426. To warp for sprang, wrap one continuous yarn around the frame.

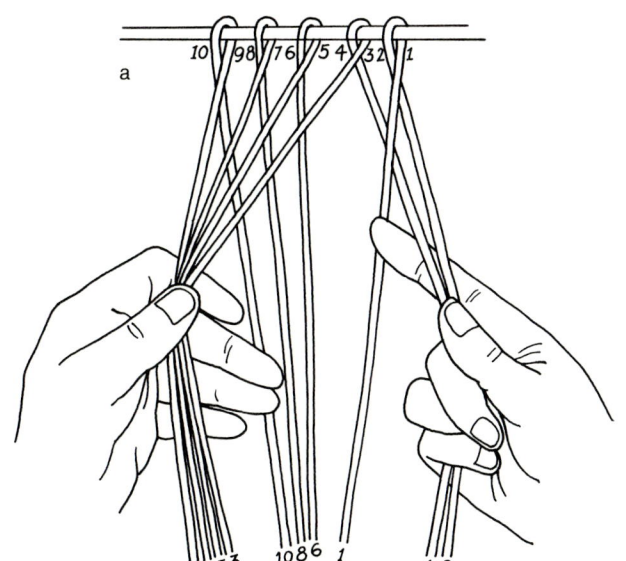

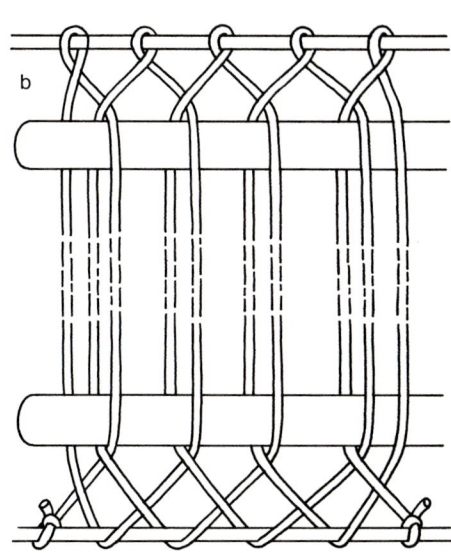

above: **427.** Row one for the 1/1 clockwise mesh. The twists are pushed to the top and bottom of the sprangwork.

below: **428.** Row two for the 1/1 clockwise mesh.

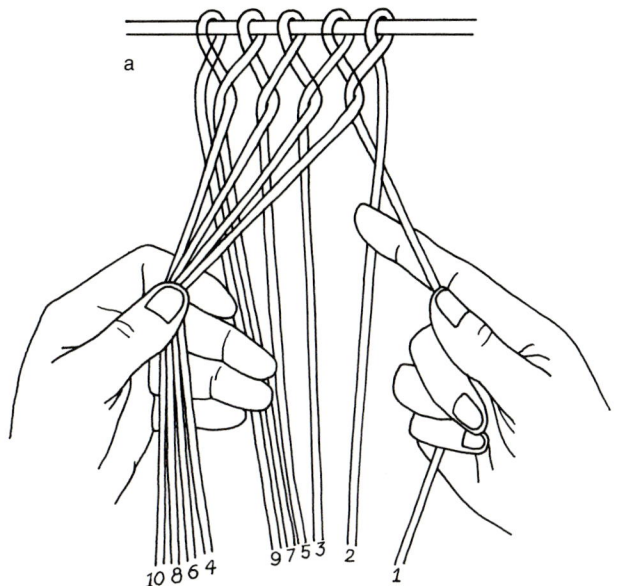

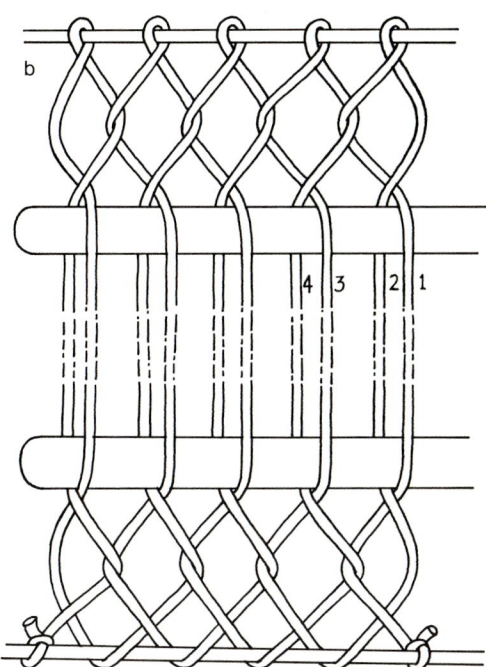

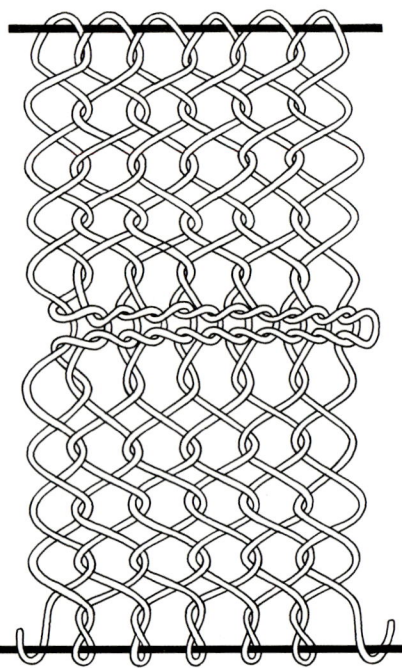

429. When the sprangwork is finished, loop the final twists upon one another to prevent unraveling. You can also leave a dowel or other support in position.

effectively in the wall hanging shown in Figure 430. The yarns in a given area can be left uncrossed for any even number of rows, depending upon the size of the opening you want.

One of the easiest ways to design with sprang is to vary the direction of the diagonal line or wale that develops in the yarns. By alternating the interlinkage of yarns from a clockwise direction (described above) to a counterclockwise, you can stagger the line of the wale.

To make the counterclockwise interlinkage, either turn the frame upside down and work in the manner described in the box, or reverse the manipulation as follows. Place your left hand through the entire shed. Beginning at right, with the first top yarn on the thumb of your left hand, reach to

Once the work has been completed, you will need some finishing device in the center to prevent the twists from coming undone. One method is chaining. As Figure 429 shows, you begin by picking up a loop from the first yarn and proceed by inserting a loop of each subsequent yarn across the row. Finish the chaining by tying off the loop with an appropriate yarn or cord.

Another finishing device, often used in wall hangings, is to insert a permanent dowel through the center to hold the twists. A piece of yarn threaded through with a needlepoint needle can take the place of the dowel.

You can either leave the sprangwork on the frame permanently or remove it. Once off the frame, it can be anchored in various ways, depending upon the effect you want. If you leave the work unanchored, it will twist slightly.

Design in Sprang

Variety of design in sprang can be achieved in several ways. The basic 1/1 mesh can be expanded into a 2/2, a 2/1, a 3/3, or any other combination simply by picking up (or exchanging) different numbers of yarns. Another possibility is the creation of *openings*—points at which the yarns are left uncrossed. This technique has been exploited very

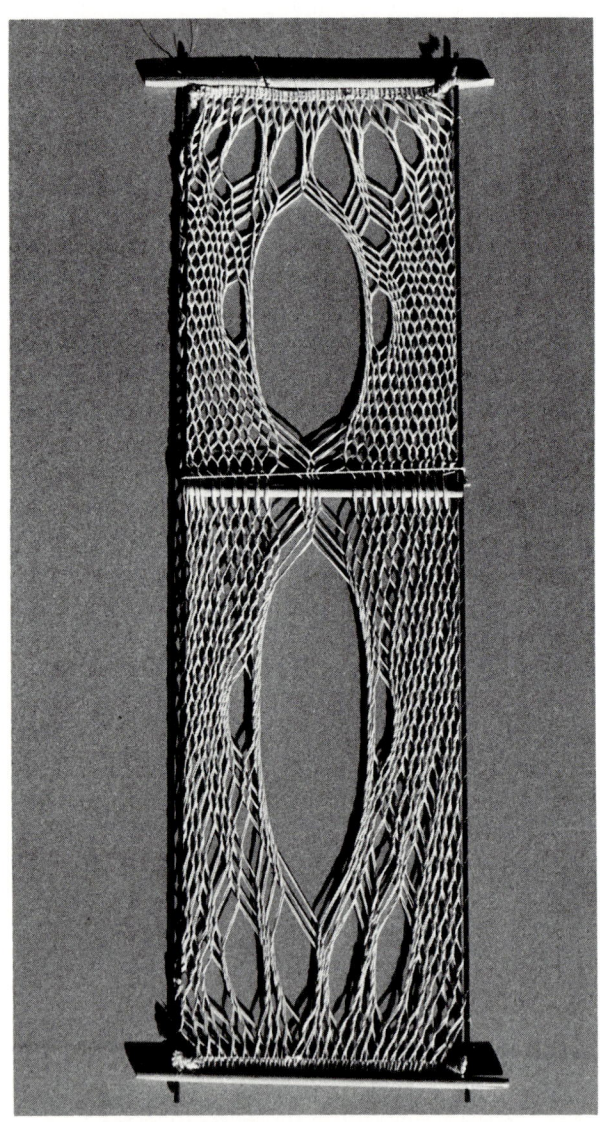

430. Peter Collingwood. Sprang hanging. 1963. White linen, c. 36 × 10″ (80 × 25 cm). Collection Ted Hallman.

the left of the thumb with your right hand, and
pick up the first bottom yarn at the right edge,
then drop the original top yarn. In alternate rows,
you will have to replace two top yarns with one
bottom yarn at the right edge.

Sprangwork is highly elastic in all directions.
Each yarn interacts with every other yarn, so the
overall design cannot be perceived while the work
is incomplete. Until recently sprang was used primarily for wall hangings, but some fiber artists
have begun to apply it to freestanding pieces and
huge environmental works (Figs. 431–433).

Netting

A net is an openwork fabric constructed from a single continuous strand knotted repeatedly over a gauge. In certain variations of the netting technique the twine or yarn is merely looped upon itself, a process known as *knotless netting*. However, the knotted version is more common, and the directions that follow apply to knotted nets.

A wide variety of materials can be used for netting. As with macramé and sprang, relatively nonelastic yarn with a minimum of surface texture will best display the netted structure. Only two pieces of equipment are required: a stick shuttle or netting shuttle and a netting gauge—a dowel or flat strip of wood slightly broader than the filled shuttle (Fig. 434). The width of the gauge determines the size of the open spaces.

The first step in the netting procedure is called *casting on*. Tie a short length of string in a loop, and slip it over a stationary object, such as a doorknob. (Fisherfolk often use their own toes.) Make all the loops for the first row of netting on this holding string.

Oval- or Diamond-Mesh Net

- Grasp the gauge in the left hand, and hold the free end of yarn from the shuttle firmly against the gauge (Fig. 435).
- Move the shuttle up through the holding loop, from back to front, and down again to the gauge, where the yarn is held in position.
- To complete the knot, make a sweeping clockwise curve with the shuttle, and draw it through the curve from back to front and right to left.
- Begin the second knot by passing the yarn around the gauge, then again through the holding loop.
- Once each knot has been tightened, there is no danger of its coming undone.
- After you have made enough knots to cover the width of net you plan, remove the gauge.
- Turn the work, and proceed with the netting again from left to right. This time, the loop of yarn between each pair of knots in the previous row serves as a holding cord (Fig. 436).

434. A netting shuttle and gauge.

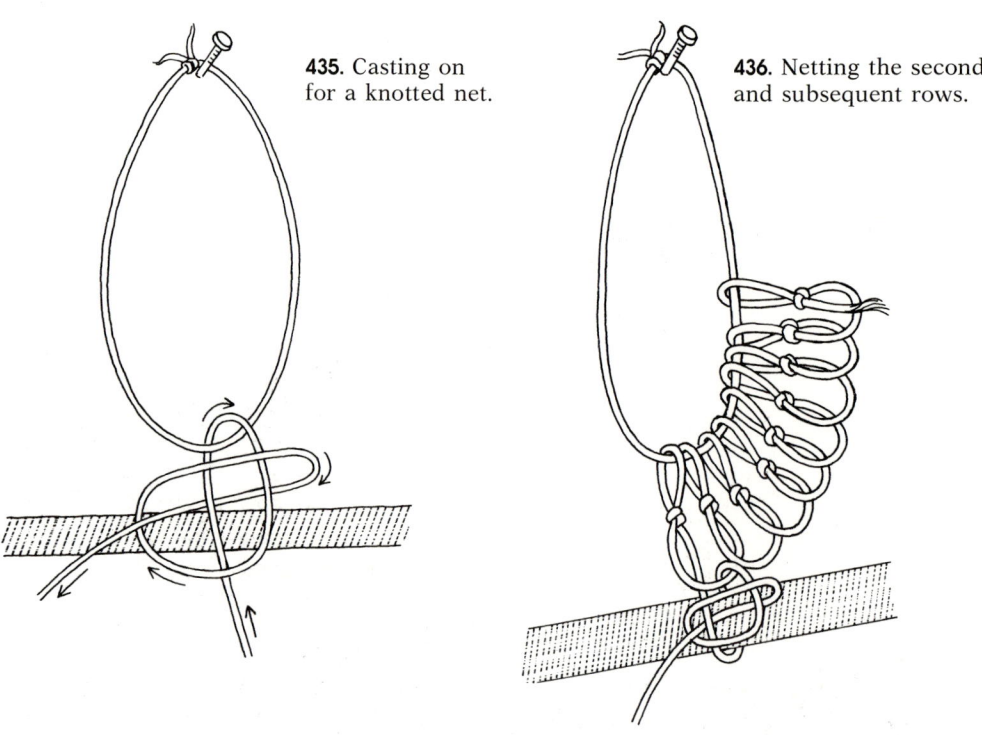

435. Casting on for a knotted net.

436. Netting the second and subsequent rows.

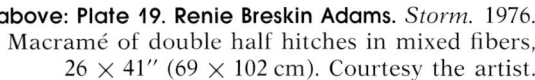

above: Plate 19. Renie Breskin Adams. *Storm.* 1976.
Macramé of double half hitches in mixed fibers,
26 × 41″ (69 × 102 cm). Courtesy the artist.

right: Plate 20. Renie Breskin Adams. *Baby Beak-Nosed Monster.*
1976. Crocheted, with double-half-hitched color wheels,
height 6½″ (16 cm). Courtesy the artist.

below: Plate 21. Sheila Hicks. *Saint-Jean-de-Dieu.* 1973.
Wrapping of linen, cotton, and silk, 5′ × 6′3″ (1.5 × 1.9 m).
Collection Johns-Manville Corp., Littleton, Colo.

above: **Plate 22. Joan Sterrenburg.** *Plaited Ikat III*, detail. 1973. Loom-woven, plaited strips in wool and mohair. Courtesy the artist.

below: **Plate 23. James W. Bassler.** *Soumak.* 1976. Soumak with plaited joinings in silk and wool, 4'3" × 3'11" (1.3 × 1.2 m). Courtesy the artist.

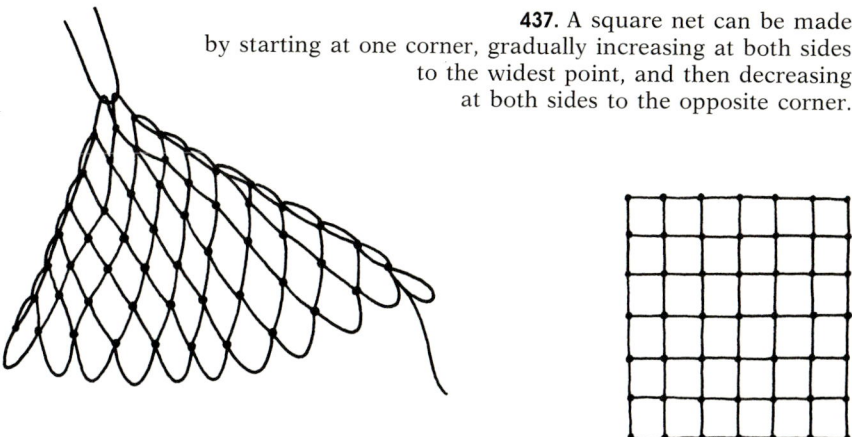

437. A square net can be made by starting at one corner, gradually increasing at both sides to the widest point, and then decreasing at both sides to the opposite corner.

The procedure for making a circular net is only slightly different. The first knot in the second row is hooked onto the first knot in the previous row, and work proceeds in a spiral.

The netting method just described will have mesh openings that are oval or diamond in shape. When you stretch the net lengthwise, the fabric will narrow. This does not happen when the net is made in a square, starting at one corner, increasing to the diagonal of the square, and tapering again to the far corner.

To make a square net, cast on only two loops on the holding cord. With each subsequent row, increase the width of the net by one loop at each side. This is done by making two loops in one, following the procedure outlined above (Fig. 437). When you have reached the desired width, begin decreasing at both sides, by netting the two loops together. You can also make a rectangular net in this fashion. When you have reached the maximum width, begin increasing from one side and decreasing from the other, until you have the proper length. Then, decrease from both sides to the point.

The netting procedure has obvious applications in hammocks, mesh shopping bags, curtains, garments, and similar items. Its lacy structure, alone or in combination with other fiber construction processes, can be adapted to wall hangings and large-scale sculpture (Fig. 438).

438. Loes van der Horst. *Dulobita.* 1972–73. Netting in polypropylene yarn, height 13'2" (4 m). Courtesy the artist.

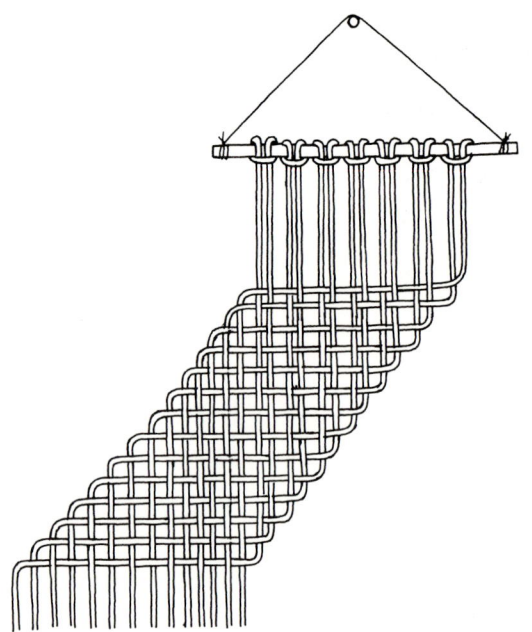

above: 439. Diagonal plaiting.
below: 440. Plaiting in a chevron pattern.

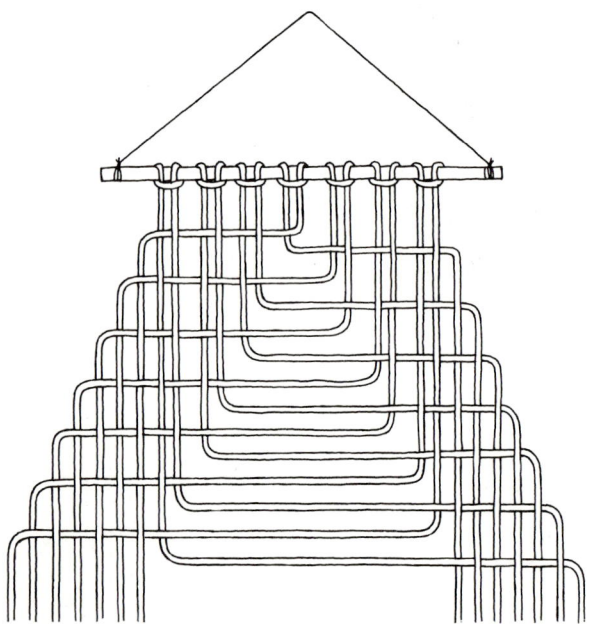

Plaiting and Braiding

Plaiting and braiding are both simple finger-weaving techniques long used by primitive peoples for making belts, straps, bands, animal collars, and other narrow fabrics.

Plaiting is done over a dowel, a stick, or some other holding device. Tie a string at each end of the dowel, so it can be attached to a stationary object. Cut the yarn or twine into lengths at least four times as long as the band is to be, and then double each strand over the supporting rod by means of a lark's-head knot (Fig. 194).

One of the simplest and most common forms of plaiting is the diagonal plait. To begin plaiting, pick up the yarn at far right, and interweave it through the other yarns in turn as for plain weave (Fig. 439). When the yarn reaches the opposite side, drape it over the supporting rod temporarily. Next, weave the second yarn through the fabric in the same manner, interlacing last with yarn 1, which is brought down and allowed to hang free. A diagonal band develops as the process is repeated, working always from right to left. When you finish the plaiting, you can braid or knot the ends together. If you intend the band for a belt, you can tie the initial loops to a buckle.

There are quite a wide variety of possible patterns to be made with the basic plaiting technique. One of these is the *chevron* pattern woven as in Figure 440 by starting at the center and working alternately to the two sides. You can also work from the two edges toward the center. Of course, it is possible to combine several different patterns in the same piece, adding more warp yarns as needed to increase width or change the pattern.

One special variation of plaiting is the Peruvian zigzag, which is constructed around a center yarn that remains stationary. This yarn acts as a stabilizer for the plait. You must have an odd number of warp yarns—that is, an even number plus the central yarn. Interlacing begins at the outside, either the left or the right edge, and works toward the center. Figure 441 shows one possible configuration for the Peruvian zigzag. Plaiting begins with

441. Diagram of the Peruvian zigzag braid. The braiding starts from either side and works toward the opposite side. The center strand (E) is a stabilizer and does not change position.

```
A B C D|E|F G H I
  B C D|E|F G H I A
    C D|E|F G H I A B
      D|E|F G H I A B C
        |E|F G H I A B C D
      D|E|F G H I A B C
    C D|E|F G H I A B
  B C D|E|F G H I A
A B C D|E|F G H I
I A B C D|E|F G H
H I A B C D|E|F G
G H I A B C D|E|F
F G H I A B C D|E|
G H I A B C D|E|F
H I A B C D|E|F G
I A B C D|E|F G H
A B C D|E|F G H
  B C D|E|F G H A
    C D|E|F G H A B
      D|E|F G H A B C
        |E|F G H A B C D
      D|E|F G H A B C
    C D|E|F G H A B
  B C D|E|F G H A
A B C D|E|F G H
```

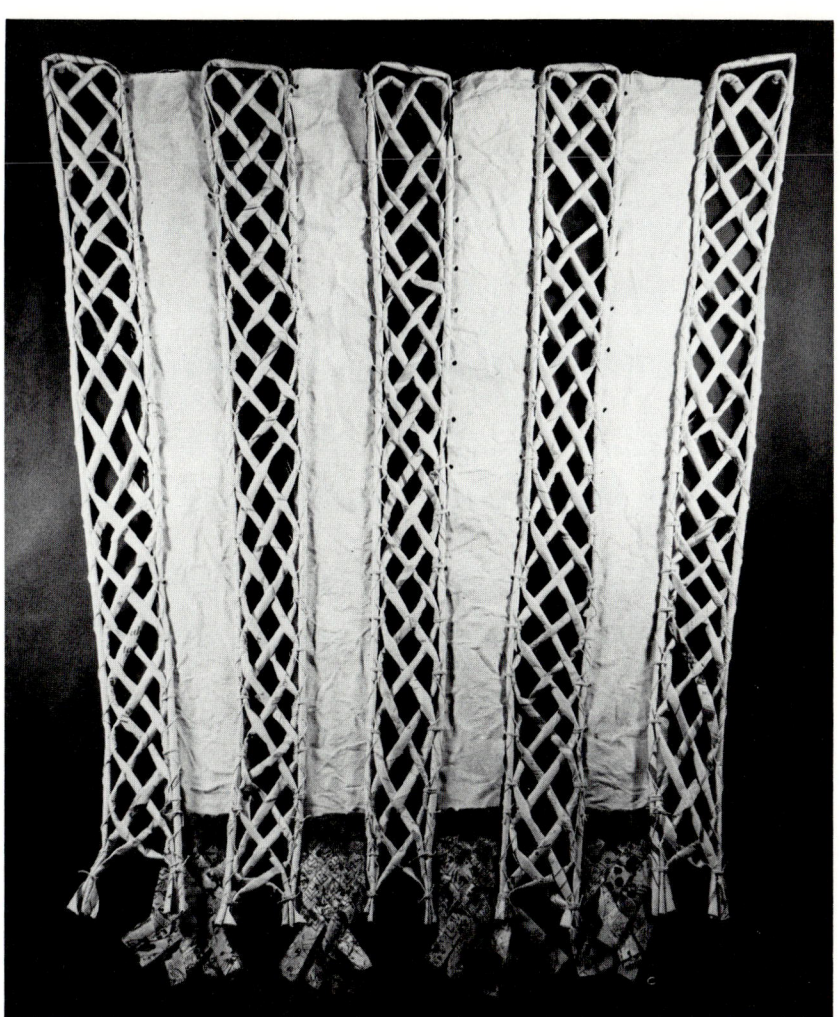

442. Ed Rossbach. *Peruvian Tunic.*
Plaited newspaper, canvas,
and rags; height 4'8" (1.4 m).
Courtesy the artist.

yarn A, which moves under B, over C, under D, over E, under F, over G, under H, and over I. Yarn E, the center strand, does not change position during the entire process.

In its mechanics, plaiting of this type closely resembles conventional weaving. However, it must be remembered that weaving is a two-element construction. With plaiting, the warp yarns serve in turn for the vertical and horizontal members. This identity of vertical, parallel yarns intersecting with one another in pattern is evident in most finished works (Fig. 442, Pl. 22, p. 238).

Three-strand *braiding* is familiar to almost everyone as a method for dressing hair. When the number of strands is increased to four, eight, twelve, or even more, an intricate round braid develops. Four-strand braiding follows the pattern illustrated in Figure 443. Working alternately from left to right, place a strand behind the two adjacent strands, carry it around, and allow it to hang between them. Three-dimensional braids are often woven around a core of yarns (Fig. 444). Any num-

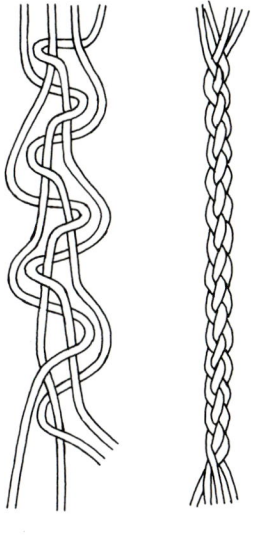

above: 443. Four-strand braiding.

right: 444. Twelve-strand braiding.

ber of strands can be used, but the example demonstrates a twelve-strand braid, actually a braid woven with ten strands around a core of two. When the braid has reached the desired length, the ends can be secured by whipping an extra yarn around them. Braiding often serves as a means for finishing works but can also be the major construction process (Fig. 445).

Spool Knitting

Spool knitting is a process in which a single continuous yarn is looped upon itself, by means of a simple loom, to produce fabric. Spool knitting always results in a tubular cloth.

Spool knitting derives its name from the fact that an ordinary thread spool, or some variation thereof, serves as the loom. The size of the spool regulates the diameter of the fabric produced. To convert the spool to a loom, drive an *un*even number of finishing nails into the top, evenly spaced around the circumference of the spool (Fig. 446). For a larger cylinder of fabric substitute a wooden ring into which dowels have been inserted at regular intervals (Fig. 447). By spacing the nails or dowels close together, you can produce a finer knit.

left: 445. Jon B. Wahling. *Homage to Maija Grotell.* 1974. Braided, knotted, and wrapped sisal, with metal and wood; height 5'8" (1.7 m). Collection Harold Schneider.

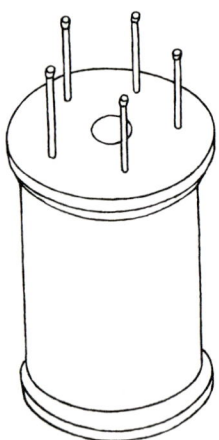

above: 446.
An ordinary thread spool,
with finishing nails
driven into the top,
can be used for spool knitting.

right: 447.
A wooden ring with dowels
inserted at regular intervals
yields a larger tube of fabric.

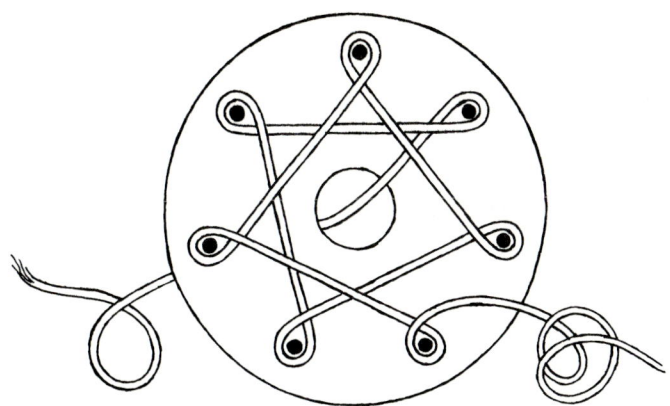

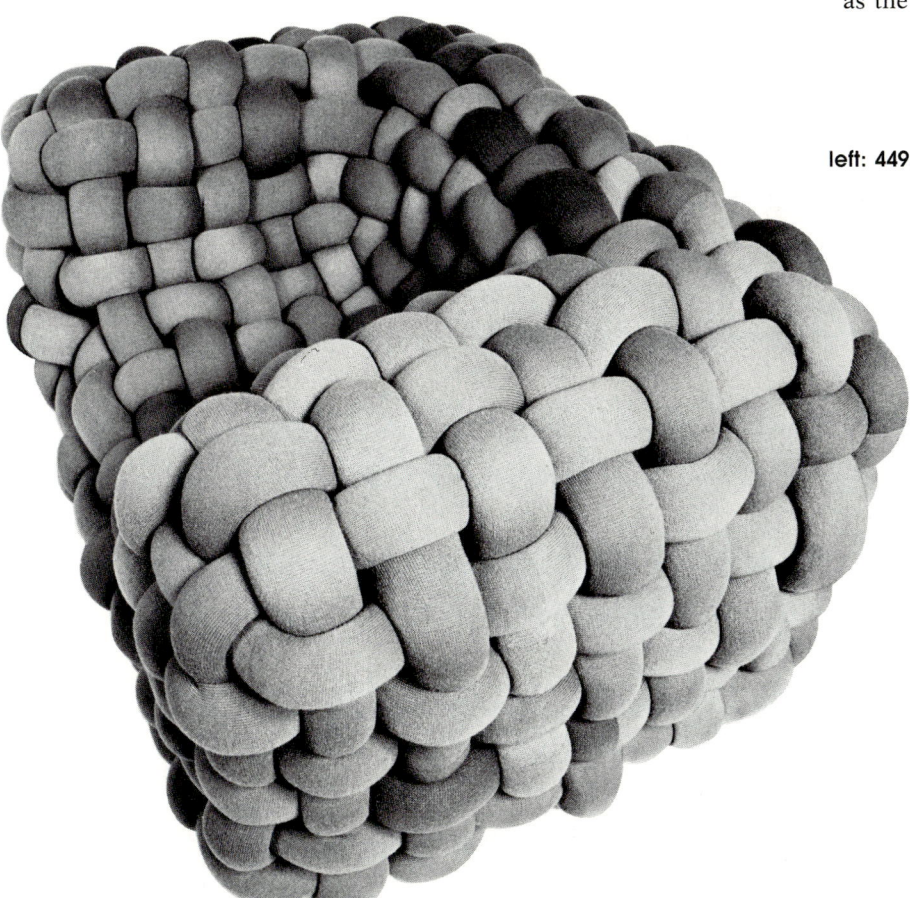

To begin knitting, draw the free end of the yarn through the hole in the center of the spool. Next, wrap the yarn around every other nail on the spool until, after two circuits, each nail has a loop of yarn around it (Fig. 448). Then, rotate the spool to add a second loop around each nail. Lift the first loop on each nail over the second and off the nail with a knitting needle, a crochet hook, or simply with the fingers. Repetition of this process—alternately wrapping the nails and lifting off the lower loop—produces the knit cylinder, which is drawn through the hole in the center of the spool. You can knit by wrapping clockwise, purl by wrapping counterclockwise. The completed fabric will not unravel if each loop is drawn through the adjacent one as for chaining (see p. 197), or if the free end of the yarn is passed through all the loops.

Spool knitting seems the most simple, basic process imaginable. Yet the applications for tubular weaves are almost unlimited, as British artist Ann Sutton has demonstrated. Sutton has created a line of one-of-a-kind chairs, loveseats, and sofas by interlacing tubular-knit structures (Fig. 449). These contemporary seating units have a soft, sculptural quality, with an emphasis on broad, large-scale form and color relationships.

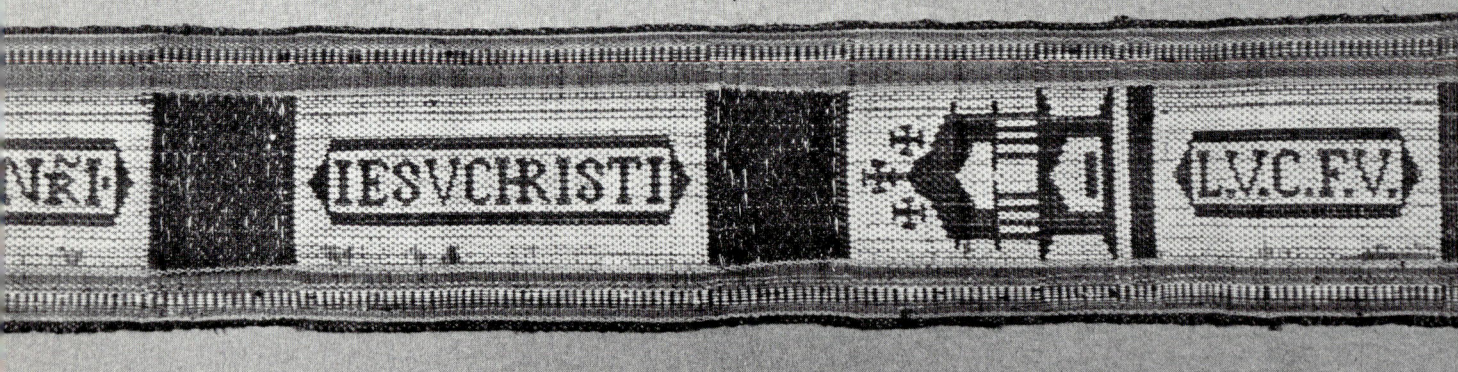

above: **450.** Ecclesiastical stole, detail, from Germany. 16th–17th century. Card-woven silk, linen, and metal. Cooper-Hewitt Museum of Decorative Arts and Design, Smithsonian Institution, New York (gift of J. P. Morgan, 1902-1-404).

451. Weaving tablets, from the Oseberg Burial Ship, Norway. A.D. 830. Wood, 52 tablets in all. University Museum of Antiquities, Oslo.

Card Weaving

Card weaving is a two-element construction with both a warp and a weft. Since ancient times it has been used for making long, narrow bands of fabric (Fig. 450). Square ivory tablets with holes at each of the corners were discovered in Egypt long ago, but at first they were thought to have been part of a game. Later, it was discovered that the cards were used for weaving before the Egyptians developed the warp-weighted loom. Weaving tablets were also found in the Oseberg Burial Ship in Norway (Fig. 451), in this case wooden cards numbering 52 in all. A half-finished band accompanied the tablets.

Card-woven fabric is usually warp-faced. The weft is visible only at the selvedges, and if the weft is the same color as the outside warp ends, it will be barely noticeable. One possible contradiction to the warp-face fabric would be the use of a transparent warp yarn, such as nylon monofilament. In that case, the weft yarns would carry the pattern.

The pattern in card weaving is created in a number of ways. Some are dependent on the colors of the warp and weft, others on size or texture of the yarns. An important variable is the handling of the cards—the ways in which they are turned and the order in which they are taken.

Any smooth, firm yarn can be used for card weaving—linen, cotton carpet warp, crochet cotton, firmly twisted silk or worsted. Soft materials that pull apart easily should be avoided. The only equipment needed is a series of cards with holes punched in the corners. The cards can be triangular, pentagonal, hexagonal, and so forth, but most often they are square, with a hole punched in each of the four corners. Ordinary playing cards, cut square, are excellent for card weaving, or the cards can be made from firm, thin cardboard cut $2\frac{1}{2}$ inches (6.5 cm) square. Holes should be punched at least $\frac{3}{8}$ inch (1 cm) from the edge to prevent them from tearing easily. The number of cards determines the width of the proposed fabric. A novice card weaver should not attempt to handle more than twenty, but with experience you can introduce more cards for greater intricacy.

Preparation for Weaving

In card weaving the cards themselves take the place of harnesses and heddles. Warp yarns are threaded through the holes in the cards according to a planned pattern. Then, the cards are stacked together, and, as they are rotated, the warp yarns twist to open a shed.

The warp can be measured on a conventional warping frame or substitute (such as the backs of two chairs held a fixed distance apart). Warping should follow the color sequence that is planned for a particular project. All the normal warping procedures are adhered to: a cross is made and tied, the warp is chained, and small lease sticks or lease cords are inserted to maintain the cross as an aid in threading the cards (see pp. 112–119).

The pattern for a card-woven band can be drafted on squared graph paper just as for any other kind of weaving, but the method of draft notation is a bit different. In Figure 452 each vertical row of squares represents a single card, and each horizontal row indicates a particular hole in all the cards. It is helpful to number the cards sequentially and to code the holes A, B, C, D, working clockwise. The design in this draft allows for two repeats of a pointed pattern, plus a selvedge border. The drafted squares have been color coded for four different colors of yarn. This system makes it very easy to follow the sequence of colors when threading the cards. Below the draft is a series of slashes, which indicate the *direction* for threading. For example, the first six cards are threaded from the face of the card to the back, the next four are threaded from back to front, and so on. All the holes on a single card must be threaded in the same direction.

To begin threading, stack the cards in order near the lease sticks. Thread each card clockwise according to the draft, and knot the four yarns together on either the face or the back of the card, depending on the direction of threading. A change in the direction of threading is made at each point of emphasis in the pattern. As each card is threaded and the ends knotted, slip the card about 8 inches from the knot. The ends should be kept as even as possible. When all the cards have been threaded, stack them face up, directly on top of one another, with the corresponding holes (A, B, C, D) in the same positions.

Some card weavers use a frame to hold the two ends of the warp. However, if one end is tied to a stationary object—a doorknob or hook on the wall—and the other is tied to the chair in which you sit, the tension can be adjusted easily when necessary just by moving the chair.

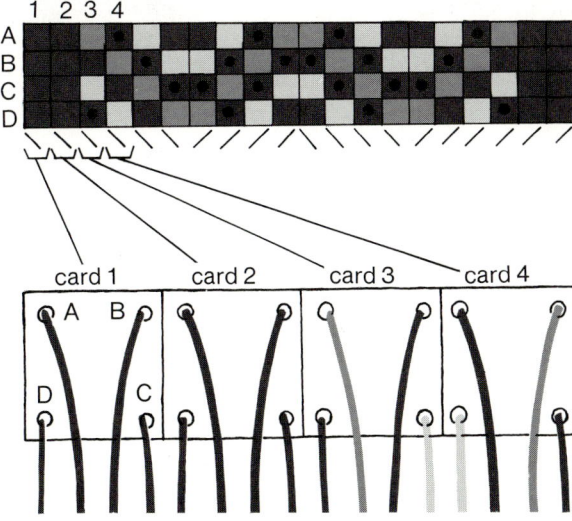

452. A sample draft for card weaving. Each vertical row of squares represents a single card, and each horizontal row indicates a particular hole in all the cards.

453. Candace Crockett demonstrates
the pose for card weaving.
The warp ends are tied
to a fixed object (here a table leg)
and affixed to the weaver's body
as for backstrap weaving.

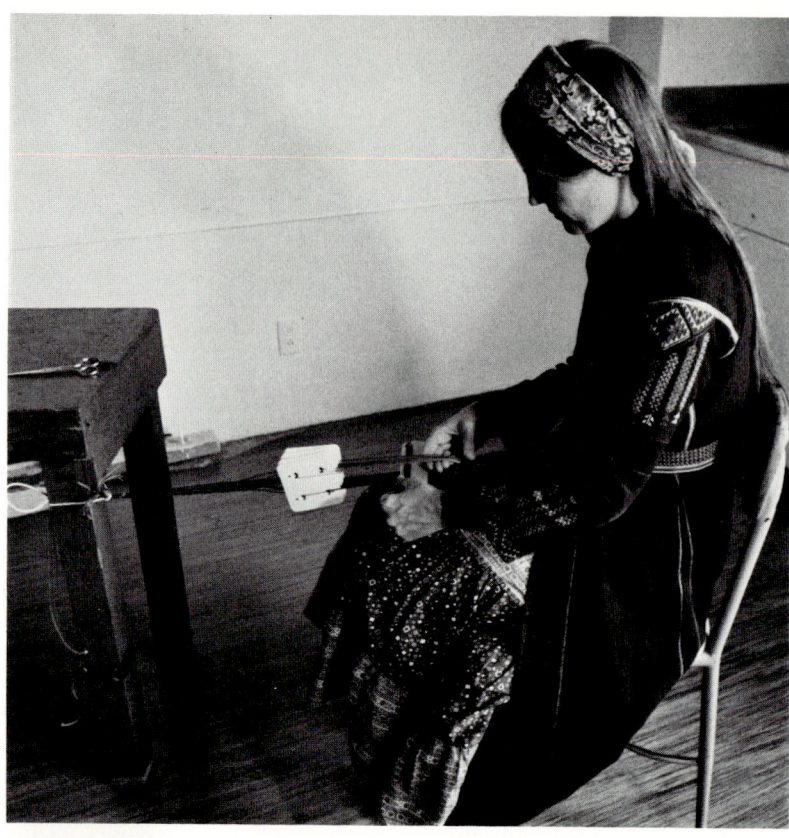

below: 454. A closeup shows the cards
in position to open one shed.

455. Strips of card-woven fabric can be braided
to create a more intricate design. In this illustration,
the band is divided into three strips, each of which
is woven individually. Then, the strips are interchanged
before being rejoined and woven as a unit.

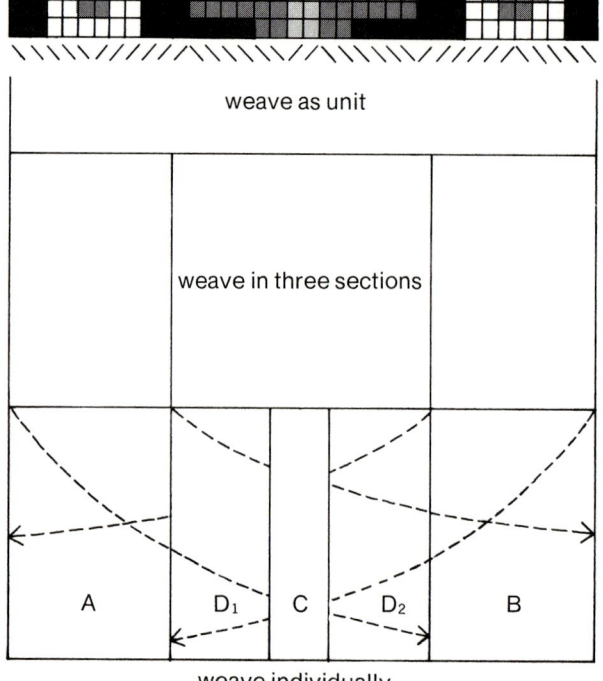

weave as unit

weave in three sections

A   D₁   C   D₂   B

weave individually
place cards for B and A under C but over D₁ and D₂

The Weaving Process

The most efficient posture for card weaving is
shown in Figures 453 and 454. Tie the warp ends to
the back of a chair, and pass them under your
arm. Weaving usually proceeds away from you (as
opposed to the direction on the conventional
loom), but it can move toward you as well.

When the cards are in position, the first shed is
automatically open. Enter a small stick shuttle

246   *Other Construction Methods*

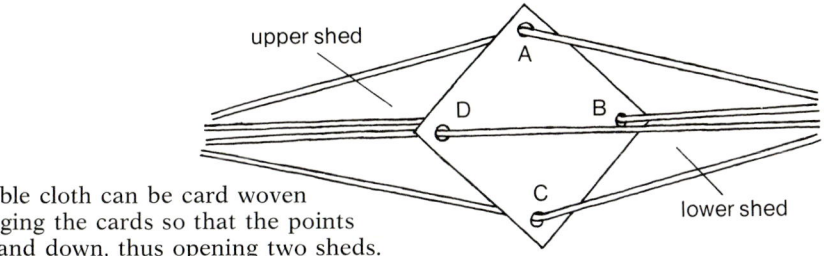

456. Double cloth can be card woven by arranging the cards so that the points face up and down, thus opening two sheds.

containing the weft yarn into the shed. The shed is changed by rotating the cards one quarter turn. Pattern is controlled by the direction in which the cards are turned and the order of the cards. They can be rotated either forward or backward for a set number of times and then back for a certain number of times. When the cards are turned always in the same direction, the warp yarns will gradually become twisted. You can correct this by untying the warp ends and combing out the tangles. You can beat the weft into position with your fingers, a comb, or the shuttle.

A surprising variety of designs can be created with simple card weaving. For example, at any point in the weaving process, you have the option of changing the cards to alter the results without interfering with the threading pattern. One change might be to juggle the order of the cards; another to flip some of the cards but not the others, thus altering the sequence. You can turn some of the cards forward and others backward according to any order you wish.

Figure 455 shows one complicated variation. After a portion of the band has been woven, it is divided into three strips, and each strip is woven as a unit, with the weft yarn carried only to the selvedge of that particular strip. For the third section of the web, the warp yarns are further subdivided, and the center strip is woven in three units. Then, the various strips are braided, with sections *A* and *B* exchanging positions, passing over *D* and under *C*. Finally, the entire band is reunited and woven solidly from selvedge to selvedge.

Both double cloth and tubular weaves are possible in card weaving. To make a double cloth, turn the cards on end, so that the points are facing up and down (Fig. 456), thus opening two sheds. Pass the weft first through one shed and then through the other before turning the cards.

To make a tubular weave, turn the cards in the normal fashion but always introduce the weft yarn into the shed from the same side. The weft will float either over or under the weaving. After ten or more shots, remove the floats by pulling on the floating yarns one by one. This will draw the outer edges of the band together.

Card weaving is generally associated with belts, straps, and other narrow fabrics (Fig. 457). More

457. Card-woven belt with macramé ties.

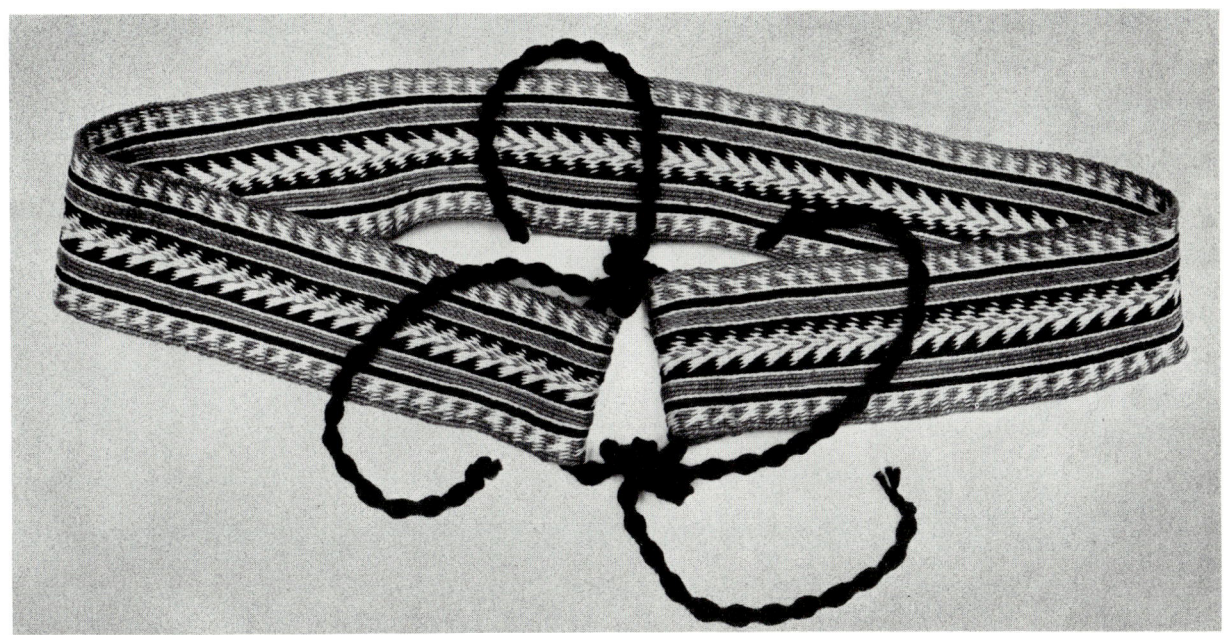

adventurous weavers have experimented with methods of combining the card-woven elements to create hangings and sculptures (Fig. 458). Strips of card-woven cloth can also be sewn together to make striped, patterned fabric or even garments. The simplicity of the technique gives the weaver a freedom of creativeness and manipulation limited only by the imagination.

458. Candace Crockett. *Fragments #9.*
Card-woven strips
of waxed linen in Plexiglas box,
8 × 11 × 1″ (20 × 27.5 × 2.5 cm).
Courtesy the artist.

IV
Spinning
and Coloring

Handspinning of yarns offers several advantages to the designer-weaver, but economy is probably not one of them. The labor involved in fiber preparation as well as in the spinning itself nearly always outweighs whatever saving you may realize by avoiding commercially spun yarns. Still, handspinning currently enjoys a revival similar to that of all the other crafts. By far the strongest argument for handspun yarns is the opportunity to design a yarn ideally suited to a particular end-use. Certain artists have exploited this potential with works in which the yarn construction becomes a major design element (Fig. 459).

The spinning process consists of three basic operations. *Drafting* is the procedure by which prepared fibers are compressed and extended into a continuous strand, or yarn. (Yarn drafting bears no relation whatever to the weave draft discussed in Chapter 9, which is a graphic notation of a

16
Handspinning

459. Berit Hjelholt.
Night. 1975.
Tapestry of handspun
and plant-dyed wool,
linen, and sisal;
8′ × 7′4″ (2.4 × 2.2 m).
Courtesy the artist.

weave pattern.) The *insertion of twist* encourages cohesion of the spun yarn. The *take-up motion* consists of winding the spun yarn onto a spindle or spool for temporary storage.

A History of Spinning

Spinning has been the subject of myth among many ancient peoples and plays a role in a number of fairy tales. *Rumplestiltskin*, one of the fairy tales collected by the Grimm brothers in the 19th century, tells of the gnome who spun flax into gold. In Norse mythology the Norns are characters depicted as spinning the thread of life and purposely tangling it so that it had to be cut short.

Primitive peoples no doubt drew their inspiration for spinning from observing the natural twist of some vegetable fibers. Certain grasses and other cellulosic fibers have a tendency to twist as they dry and are thereby much stronger than in their original state. Increasing skill at the craft of weaving led artisans to seek both longer and more flexible materials. They soon learned to improve

upon this natural twist and to introduce it when it was absent.

In its crudest form, spinning was done with the hands alone. The fibers were drawn out between the fingers of one hand and rolled between the fingers of the other to insert twist. After a length of yarn had been spun, it was wound onto a stick or stone. A variation of this technique consisted of rolling the fibers along the thigh with the palm of one hand while the other hand controlled the drafting.

The most important breakthrough in spinning technology came when it was discovered that the stick used as a base for storing the yarn could be made to rotate by placing a weight at one end, thus inserting twist semiautomatically. This weight, called a *whorl*, became a standard part of the tool. Some authorities believe that primitive spinners got the idea for the whorl when the spindle, which had been stuck in the ground for convenience, came out with clay chunks on it.

Spindle whorls dating from the late Paleolithic Age have been found, so we know that early peo-

left: 460. Double spindle
with yarn in position, Peru.
American Museum of Natural History, New York.

above: 461. Cowichan spindle whorl.
Wood, diameter 7½″ (19 cm).
National Museum of Natural History,
Smithsonian Institution, Washington, D.C.

ples had learned to spin fibers before about 8000 B.C. It is assumed that vegetable fibers were spun before animal fibers, but records show that sheep had been domesticated by about 9000 B.C. The inhabitants of Afghanistan have been credited with establishing the first herds of sheep. The wool from these sheep was long, stiff, and rough. Of the vegetable fibers, flax was first cultivated as a crop at about the same time, so it is clear that there was a demand for fiber by the Neolithic period.

With minor refinements, the stick with a spindle whorl evolved into the *handspindle* (Fig. 460). It is used in almost identical form by many handspinners today. The handspindle resembles a top with an unusually long axis (Fig. 466). It has two parts: the *spindle* portion or shaft, and the *whorl*. In its modern form the spindle is a tapered shaft about 9 inches long with a notch at the top to catch the yarn. The whorl, a disc-shape object mounted on the shaft, provides enough weight to maintain spinning momentum. The use of the handspindle in ancient Egypt and the Swiss Lake region has been well documented. In the cave paintings at Beni Hassan (Fig. 43) the figure at far right is manipulating a handspindle. Prehistoric spindle whorls often were simply a stone or a lump of clay. The American Indians carved their whorls from wood, with intricate stylized designs (Fig. 461).

The spinners of ancient India were particularly renowned for the quality of their yarns. The famed Dacca muslins—transparent, gauzelike cottons—were woven from yarns so fine that a pound equaled 200 *miles* in length. By comparison, the finest yarn in use today would be less than 4 miles long per pound. We can well imagine the skill required for weaving with such a minute yarn. Dacca muslins were woven in 20-yard lengths each

462. Israhel van Meckenem the Elder.
Woman Spinning and Entertaining a Visitor.
c. 1450. Bibliothèque Nationale, Paris.

1 yard wide, a unit that kept two spinners occupied for between ten and thirty days.

Except for minor improvements in the handspindle, the process of spinning underwent little change from earliest times until the Middle Ages (Fig. 462). The spinning wheel was invented in India, although the date is rather uncertain. However, it is much easier to pinpoint the development of the flyer mechanism for spinning. Like almost every other mechanical device, it was first conceived by Leonardo da Vinci in the 15th century.

Leonardo's notebook drawings do not indicate any power source (such as a drive wheel), and it has been suggested that he intended some large external source of power—perhaps a water wheel—to operate the spindle (Fig. 463). Apparently, no model was ever constructed from Leonardo's drawings, but in 1530 Johann Jürgen actually built a flyer spinning wheel based on similar principles. Eventually, a foot treadle was added, thus completing the essentials of the flyer wheel still common today.

463. Leonardo da Vinci. Design for a hand-driven spinning machine with automatic yarn distributor.
c. 1490. From *Codex Atlanticus.* Biblioteca Ambrosiana, Milan.

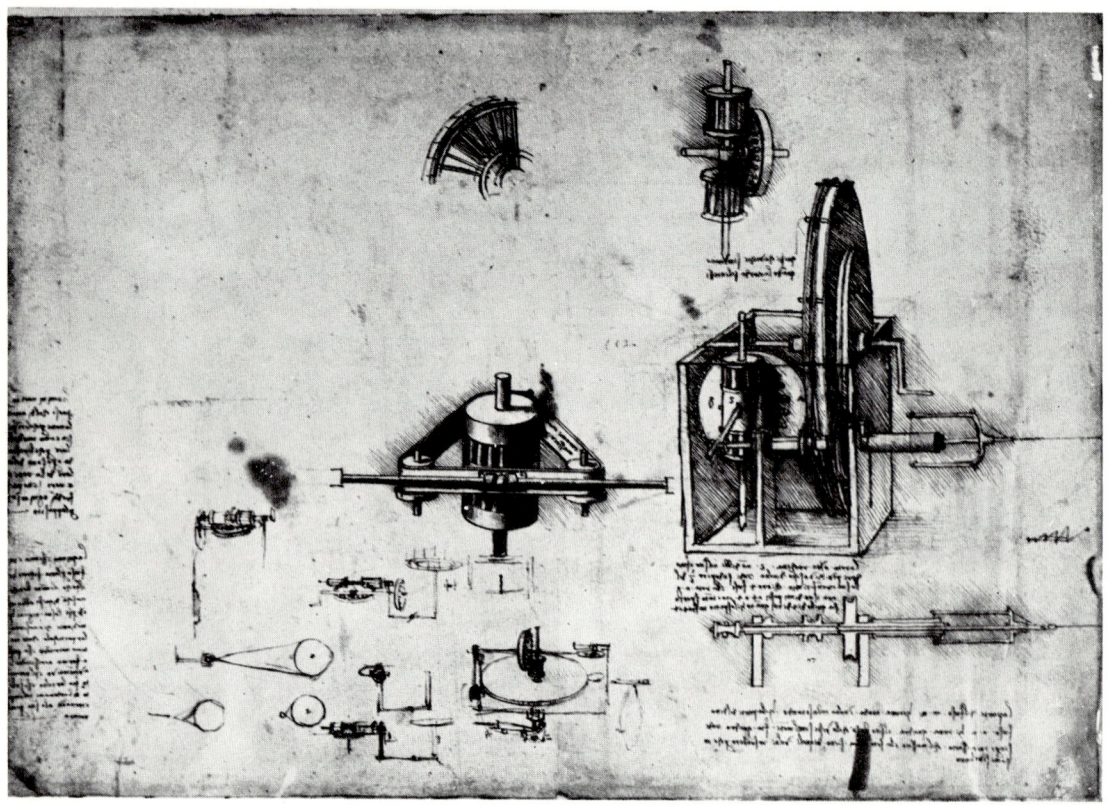

The Industrial Revolution had an equally devastating effect upon the craft of handspinning as it had on handweaving. In the mid-18th century inventions by James Hargreaves, Richard Arkwright (Fig. 464), and Samuel Crompton vastly increased the rate at which yarns could be produced, with the result that handspinning was no longer practical as a profession. However, the craft never completely died out in rural areas or in isolated regions such as the Southern Highlands of the United States. When the interest of 20th-century craftsmen began to grow, there were still spinners to teach the new generation.

Materials for Spinning

Almost any fiber can be spun by the hand processes. Wool and flax are most popular among contemporary spinners, but cotton and hair fibers also used, alone or in blends. In addition, the waste from broken or damaged silk cocoons can be spun into silk yarn, and synthetic fibers—nylon, rayon, acrylic, and so forth—are often cut for spinning. The spinning instructions given here apply primarily to wool.

Natural fibers vary in length, diameter, and inherent *crimp* or waviness, all of which charac-

464. Richard Arkwright. Spinning machine. 1769. Science Museum, London (Crown Copyright).

teristics contribute to their *spinning quality.* Each of the various fibers is sold for spinning in different forms, which require certain preparation.

Flax   Flax fibers are relatively long—from 5 to 20 inches—and have no natural crimp. Flax is often sold to the spinner in a bundle, known as a *strick,* ready to be spun. Usually, the fibers have been *hackled,* a process that is the last stage in the dressing of flax, comparable to the combing of wool yarns.

Silk   Silk to be spun generally is prepared as a combed sliver or *roving*—a thick, ropelike mass of fibers. The typical quantity as purchased is called a *flake* (1 ounce) or a *bell* (16 flakes, or 1 pound).

Cotton   Cotton fibers are much shorter than flax—less than 2 inches long—and evenly convoluted. Occasionally, cotton is offered to the spinner still in the boll, but more often it has been ginned to remove the seeds. Cotton also is available in a battlike form ready to be separated into roving strips for spinning.

Wool   Wool remains unexcelled as a fiber. Its chief characteristics are very high elasticity, a high degree of crimp, good felting quality, low flammability, excellent moisture absorption (making it dye-receptive), and a tendency to give off heat when it absorbs water vapor.

Wool exhibits crimp to a far greater degree than do other fibers, although manufacturers have tried to introduce this quality into synthetic fibers. The greater the number of crimps per inch, the finer the fiber will be. Very fine wool may have as many as 22 to 30 crimps per inch. Spinning is easier when a fiber has high crimp, because the crimp improves the cohesion of untwisted strands. It also gives bulk without weight to the yarn. Crimp remains in the woven cloth, so that the cloth is thicker but has a softer hand, smoother appearance, and better draping quality. Wool lacking in crimp is described as "doggy" wool, a reference to crimp-free dog hair.

The coarser a wool is, the greater will be its strength. Wool can be stretched as much as 30 percent beyond its normal length for short periods of time without harming the fiber. When the fibers are wet, they can be extended as much as 70 percent without breaking, and they have excellent recovery after stretching. Often, the appearance of a particular wool will be described in terms that relate it to luster, silver, silk, or glass. Merino wool is likened to silver, Lincoln and Leicester to silk. The luster in wool brings out the brilliance in dyes.

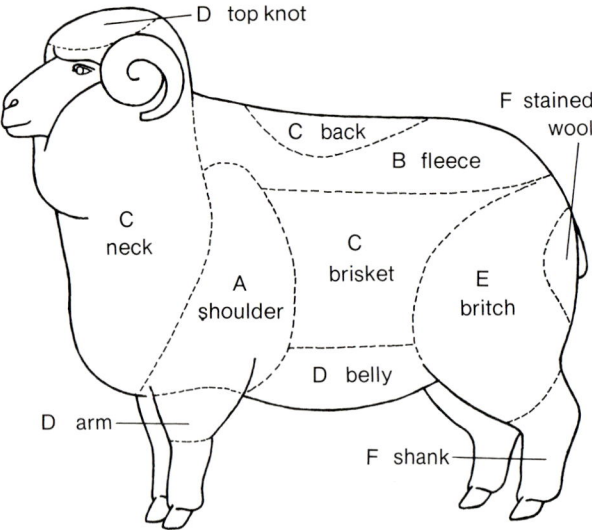

465. Wool fibers can vary in quality even on the same animal. The A indicates the highest grade, the F the lowest.

Wool presents the widest variation in fiber characteristics, depending upon the breed of sheep from which it was taken. Different grades of fiber can be found even in the same breed of sheep or on the same animal (Fig. 465). Wool is finest on the head and shoulders of the animal and coarsest on the hindquarters. The longest fibers grow on the hindquarters, while the head has the shortest wool. The neck and dewlap (the deep folds of skin under the neck of the animal) produce the heaviest yield of fibers. Color can also vary and affect the dyeing properties. Wool is whitest around the head and neck areas, yellow around the tail.

In the centuries since sheep were first domesticated two major changes in wool quality have been effected by cross-breeding. These are the loss of pigment in the wool and the continual growth of the fleece (as opposed to seasonal moulting). Some prehistoric breeds, such as the Soay of Britain, have been preserved for their historical interest but are not used for their wool.

The Merino is among the most ancient breeds of sheep; its wool is still coveted by spinners and weavers, as it has been through the centuries. It is believed that the Merino was introduced into Spain from Africa, perhaps as early as the Roman era. Until 1760 the breed was not found in any other European country, but, after a gift to the French government in that year, the Merino spread to other areas. In the late 18th century Spain exported Merino sheep to her colonies in North America, so that they quickly became established in the new United States.

The Rambouillet, also a superior breed for wool, was developed from the Merino. It has since become one of the foundation breeds for the world, being especially noted for high wool yield. As an experiment, a ram of this breed was permitted to retain his wool for five years, without being shorn. The yield after that period was 100 pounds.

Among the dozen or more breeds of sheep commonly grown in the United States, there is considerable variation in fleece quality. Handspinners can find almost any combination of characteristics they need. The wool differs in staple length, size of crimp, texture, resilience, felting quality, density, color, and dyeability. In choosing a fleece for spinning, you should consider the end-use of the yarn. A yarn to be used for a knit, for example, would need different qualities from that intended for weaving. The table on pages 364–365 summarizes the characteristics of wool found in specific breeds, as well as hair from other kinds of animals.

Wool demands special handling in the preparation stage. It is possible to buy untreated wool fleece from the Wool Cooperatives in the Middle West and at agricultural fairs, as well as from many national and international suppliers (see Appendix C). In buying imported fleeces, the spinner should be alert to the danger of anthrax bacteria possibly contaminating the wool or other animal fibers. Anthrax disease is relatively rare in the United States but is prevalent in some countries of the Middle and Far East. You should avoid buying imported wool or hair fibers that have not been tested and certified free of disease. Contact with infected material can cause illness and even death.

Wool fleeces are available in several states. You can buy whole fleeces directly from a producer after shearing, in which case it will be unscoured and "in the grease." (Never buy the *fell*, which has the sheep's hide as well as the wool.) Sometimes the extremely dirty wool on the outer edges of the shorn fleece will have been removed, leaving a *skirted* wool. If the fleece has been washed to remove part of the lanolin and dirt, it will be described as *scoured*. Some producers offer wool that has been carded but not washed (*greasy carded*) or washed and carded (*scoured carded*). The most expensive form available is called *tops*. This is combed wool ready for spinning without further preparation. Wool *roving* is also sold by the pound. The fibers can be spun in the grease or scoured before spinning (see p. 261).

A higher percentage of foreign material—dirt, grass, twigs, manure—is found in wool than in any other fiber. The spinner should avoid buying wool that is full of burrs or that shows fibers arranged

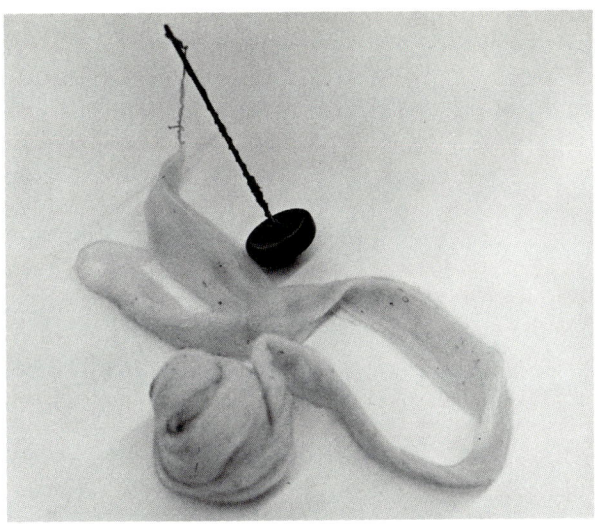

466. A handspindle consists of two parts: the long shaft and the weight, usually mounted near the bottom.

in a disorderly manner throughout the fleece. This indicates that the wool came from a poor-quality animal. *Kemp* is a term that describes the long, coarse, brittle hairs found in some breeds of sheep. These hairs will not accept dye. Occasionally, kemp is included in certain textiles, such as tweeds, to create a surface texture. For the most part, though, a fleece full of kemp will not be suitable for spinning.

Equipment

The equipment needed for handspinning can be divided into three categories: the spinning implements themselves, yarn preparation devices, and skeining tools.

Spinning Equipment

The Handspindle   The basic principle of momentum—that a body set in motion will tend to remain in motion (until some force slows it down)—underlies the functioning of the handspindle (Fig. 466). The body in this case is the whorl, centered at some point (usually near the bottom) on the spindle shaft. When the spindle is twisted, the whorl helps to maintain the momentum of its rotation, which in turn imparts twist to the yarn. The drafting and twisting motions are simultaneous on the handspindle, but the take-up is a separate operation. After a length of yarn has been spun, you must stop, undo the yarn hitches at the top and base of the spindle, and wind the yarn manually. Then, the hitches are restored, and spinning continues. The construction of yarn on a handspindle is therefore much slower than on either type of spinning wheel. On the other hand, the *quality* of yarn spun on a handspindle can be just as high as that produced on a conventional spinning wheel.

There is enormous variation in the style and weight of handspindles. Essentially, however, any spindle that is properly balanced and of a correct weight for the yarn to be spun—that is, heavy enough to establish a twist but not so heavy that it will drag on the yarn—is perfectly acceptable, regardless of the design.

The High Wheel   The high wheel (Fig. 467) is a very simple device. Its framework consists of a *stock*, usually three legs (though sometimes four), a *wheel post*, and a *head post*. The head post supports the *spinning head*, which, as it turns, imparts twist to the spun yarn and builds the yarn on the bobbin spindle. The spinning head is connected by a *drive band* to the large *drive wheel*, which is turned manually to rotate the spinning head. Because the drive wheel is so much larger in diameter than the spinning head, there is a multiplication of motion between the two. For example, if the drive wheel is 40 inches in diameter and the spinning head only $\frac{1}{2}$ inch, one revolution of the drive wheel will cause the spinning head to turn eighty times.

Some high wheels are fitted with a *multiplying head*, which further increases the multiplication of motion. In this case, the large drive wheel is connected by a band to a smaller wheel mounted on the spinning head, which in turn is connected by a second band to the spindle.

467. The high wheel is operated by turning the large drive wheel with one hand, while the other hand draws out the loose fibers to be spun.

468. A treadle powers the flyer wheel, leaving both of the spinner's hands free for drafting the fibers.

The Flyer Wheel   The flyer wheel (Fig. 468) differs from the high wheel in several respects. It is equipped with a foot treadle to turn the drive wheel, leaving both hands free. In place of the spinning head is the *flyer assembly* (Fig. 469), which includes the flyer itself and the yarn bobbin mounted on the spindle shaft. As the flyer rotates, the spun yarn passes through a small opening at the end of the shaft and emerges from an opening at the side. At this point twist is inserted in the yarn. The yarn then moves onto the flyer itself, where it is held in position by hooks for winding onto the bobbin.

Most spinning wheels are planned for right-handed people, and left-handers often find them uncomfortable. In buying a spinning wheel, left-handed people should make sure they can use the wheel easily. Some manufacturers offer left-handed spinning wheels.

The flyer wheel is in many ways the most efficient handspinning device. Its operation is faster than the high wheel and considerably faster than the handspindle. Unlike the high wheel, it leaves both hands free for drafting; unlike the handspindle, its operation is constant.

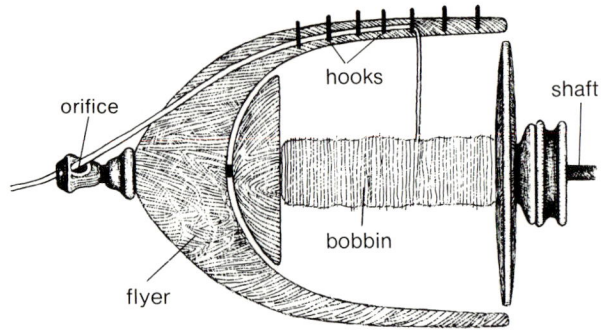

469. The flyer assembly automatically twists the spun yarn. Buildup of the yarn package is controlled by a series of hooks along the top of the flyer.

Fiber Preparation Equipment

Carding Tools   Yarns can be carded either on flat hand cards or on a hand-cranked carding machine. Whichever the case, the actual work is done by the *carding cloth*, comprised of a group of wires or spikes driven through a foundation, usually of leather. The wires are bent at an angle (Fig. 470).

Flat hand cards (Fig. 471) are always used in pairs. The card itself consists of a handle and a

470. The carding cloth wires are bent at an angle to catch the fibers as they are drawn across the card.

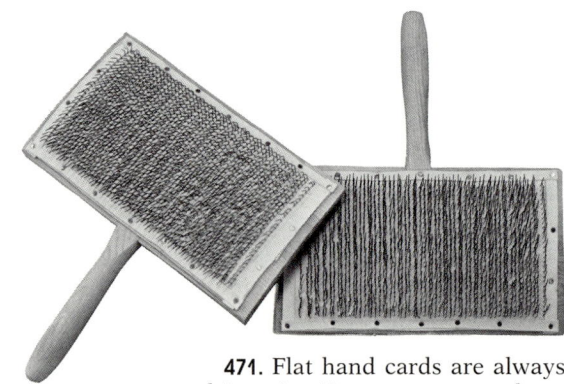

471. Flat hand cards are always used in pairs. You may want to have three sets of cards, with carding cloth in various degrees of coarseness.

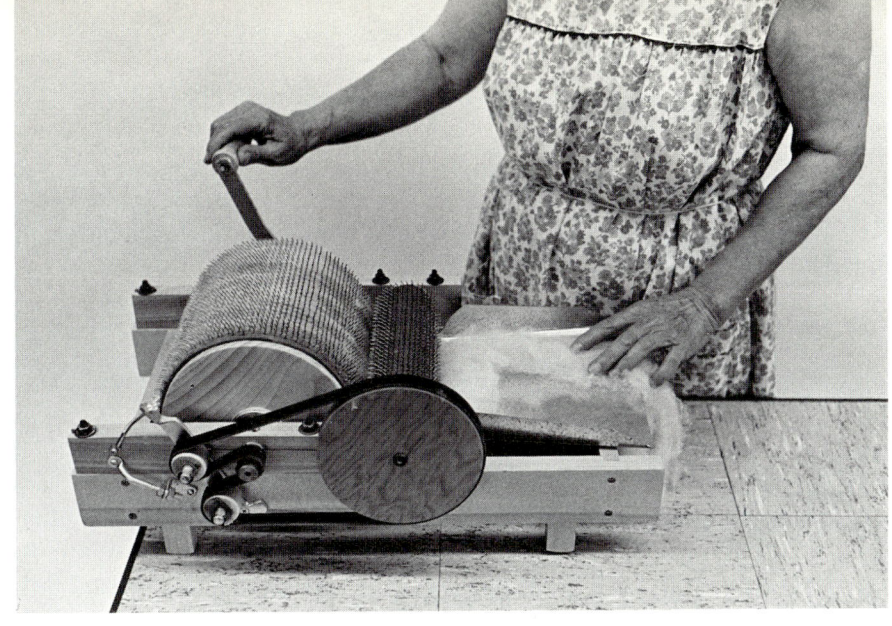

left: 472. The hand-cranked card machine in use.

below: 473. *Wool Comber*, engraving from *The Book of Trades*, 1807. Smithsonian Institution, Washington, D.C.

backing—most often of wood—to which the carding cloth is nailed or attached in some other way. There is a definite top card and bottom card, which should be marked. As the loose fibers are transferred from one card to the other, the very short fibers and any remaining foreign material are carded out, and the fibers are straightened to some degree. You should have several sets of cards with carding cloth in various degrees of coarseness. The condition of particular fibers will dictate the carding cloth to be used. From time to time the wire hooks must be ground to restore their sharpness. Replacement carding cloth is available for when the wires fall out or wear down.

The hand-cranked card machine (Fig. 472) permits somewhat faster carding. The fibers are spread on the *carding pan*, and, as the handle is turned, they are caught by the *small roll* and transferred to the *large drum*. The carding cloth is tacked to both of these rolls.

Combs Many spinners use dog combs or other long-toothed implements for worsted combing, but old-fashioned worsted combs (Fig. 473) are sometimes available. The latter tool consists of a wooden handle from which protrude several rows of very long metal tines. During the combing process each comb in turn is attached by means of a pad to a post or some other fixed object.

Skeining Tools

Once the yarn has been spun and wound into a compact package, it is often desirable to rewind it into skeins, especially for dyeing. Various tools can be used for this, including the umbrella swift shown in Figure 170. A particular favorite with handspinners is the *niddy-noddy* (Fig. 474), which winds a skein 2 yards in circumference. A skein is 40 turns on the niddy-noddy, or 80 yards.

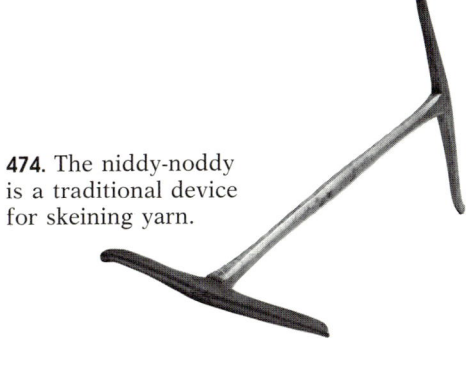

474. The niddy-noddy is a traditional device for skeining yarn.

Planning the Yarn

Ideally, you should consider the end-use to which a yarn will be applied before spinning begins, and even before you begin any fiber preparation. Only in this way can you be sure to spin a sufficient quantity of yarn of uniform size, texture, blend, and quality. Therefore, you should make several decisions even before you buy the fiber.

The choice of a particular fiber or fibers is, of course, the most elementary step in this process. If two or more fibers, colors, or textures are to be blended into the finished yarn, the blending is most often done during fiber preparation.

The second step is to determine the desired weight or count of the finished yarn (see p. 366). It is a good idea to spin a small sample of yarn from the appropriate fiber and to keep the sample at hand during the entire spinning process, especially when large quantities of yarn are to be spun. By referring to the sample from time to time, you can avoid serious deviations from the proper count that might occur when the spinning is done in several sittings. Once the end-use and the yarn count have been determined, you can extrapolate the total quantity of yarn that will be required. If the yarn is to be a ply, with two or more single yarns twisted together (see p. 269), this will also affect the total quantity needed.

The degree of twist to be imparted to the yarn must also be established in advance. This factor is most often expressed in *turns per inch*. Optimum twist is dependent on many variables, including the nature and length of the fibers, the amount of stress the fiber can undergo, and the end-use. Slackly twisted yarns are often suitable for a weft, as well as for knitting and crocheting. In essence, any process that does not subject a specific portion of the yarn to repeated handling can employ a low-twist yarn. On the other hand, a warp yarn—which will be held under tension and subjected to constant beating—should be firmly twisted, as should a yarn to be used for knotting.

Industry considers three degrees of twist for yarns—normal, medium, and hard. *Normal* is 2 twists per inch for weft yarn, $2\frac{1}{2}$ twists per inch for warp; *medium*, 3 twists per inch; and *hard*, $3\frac{1}{2}$ twists per inch. This number is decreased for long wool yarns, because a high degree of twist is not necessary to hold the fibers together. In mohair and alpaca a hard twist would spoil the soft, airy qualities associated with the fibers, so these, too, are twisted more slackly. Crepe yarns require a hard twist to create the proper effect.

Even before preparing the fibers, you should decide whether the yarn is to be spun according to the *woolen system* or the *worsted system*. The terms woolen and worsted do not necessarily mean that the fiber must be wool. Flax and certain synthetic fibers can be spun by either process. Worsted yarns are composed of relatively long fibers arranged in as highly parallel a configuration as possible. The resultant yarns are rather smooth and have few fibers protruding from the yarn surface. To this end, every step in the fiber preparation and spinning processes is aimed at encouraging this parallel arrangement. The fibers are sorted, picked, and carded in such a way that the shorter fibers are winnowed out, and they are subjected to combing as well as carding. Two-handed drafting helps to ensure the parallel orientation of fibers, so worsted spinning on the high wheel is generally not practicable. A yarn spun according to the woolen system is, by contrast, more textured, with many individual fibers protruding from the yarn mass. The yarn includes both short and long fibers that have not been combed, and two-handed drafting is not necessary. Any parallel orientation is accidental.

Fiber Preparation

Of the processes described below, only sorting, teasing, carding, and formation of the rolag or roving are general to all fibers, and even these steps may be omitted occasionally to achieve a particular effect. The remaining processes are required only for a specific fiber (usually wool) or spinning system. The fiber preparation stages have been described in consecutive order; in most cases, several of them can be skipped.

Sorting

Wool fibers purchased in fleece form generally must be sorted for quality, length, and degree of cleanliness before anything else is done. In any fleece there will be portions in which the fibers are longer than in others and sections with finer and coarser fibers. Some parts of the fleece may be so badly stained that they are useless. The type of sorting necessary would depend upon the end-use of the yarn. For example, if the yarn is to be spun according to the worsted system, you would sort for the longer fibers and perhaps save the shorter ones for some other purpose. On the other hand, a high-count yarn to be spun on the woolen system would require sorting for fineness, without much regard to fiber length. Ideally, the sorting should be done on a screen or wire mesh, so that coarse dirt particles and foreign matter can fall through and not recontaminate the wool.

Teasing

Most fibers must be teased, a process by which the tight fiber mass is initially opened up. Teasing also serves to remove dirt particles and to blend the fibers, distributing irregularities evenly throughout the mass.

Natural fibers that contain dirt and foreign material should be teased over a clean surface, such as a large sheet of paper, so that when the particles drop free of the fiber they can be removed easily. An efficient method of working is to place the pile of unteased fibers to one side and, as each batch is teased, transfer it to the other side, with the area directly in front of you kept free for collecting debris.

To begin teasing, separate a handful of fiber from the mass. With a pulling motion, separate the fibers from one another as you gradually transfer them from one hand to the other (Fig. 475). After each handful has been treated, work it gently back into the mass of teased fibers on the other side. The end result of teasing, then, is a blended mass of fibers that are cleaner, fluffier, and more airy than the original mass, not a pile of individual handfuls of fiber.

The degree of force that you apply in teasing depends on the fiber. Firmly packed areas or portions in which dirt has matted the fibers together may need fairly firm pulling, but at no time should your pulling motion be so violent that you damage or break the fibers. Clean fibers may need only one teasing to open up the fiber bundles. However, unusually dirty wool may have to be teased several times, until no more debris falls easily.

Scouring

Wool fibers are often scoured after teasing, though woolens can be carded, combed, spun, and even woven in the grease. Scouring removes the natural oils from the sheep, as well as any dirt that adheres to the fiber after teasing.

It is during the scouring operation that the greatest danger of felting exists, since the conditions for felting—heat, moisture, and pressure—are all present. For this reason it is far better to subject the wool to a series of scourings in warm water and with gentle pressure, rather than trying to speed up the process with too-hot water and excessive agitation.

The vat that you use for scouring should be fitted with a false bottom of screening, so that heavy dirt particles will settle to the bottom and not remain mixed with the fiber. You should use enough water to allow the wool to move freely.

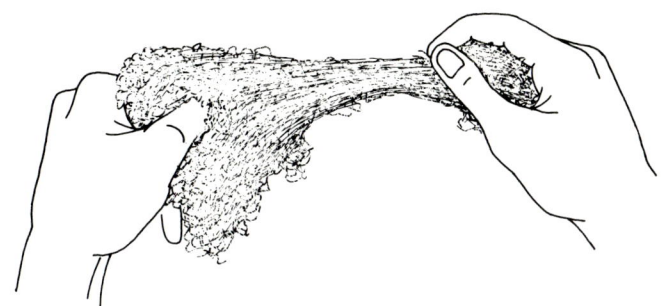

475. Teasing is a process by which the tight fiber mass is first opened and cleaned. It is done with a pulling motion of the hands.

Scouring

□ Fill the scouring vat with warm water, up to 120°F (55°C).

□ Thoroughly dissolve a commercial wool-scouring solution or mild soap in the water. A little vinegar added to a soap solution will cut the suds.

□ Place the wool in the bath in layers.

□ Press the wool gently to circulate it in the scouring solution.

□ From time to time, remove a small sample from the bath and examine it.

□ When all the oil and dirt seem to have been loosened, lift the wool out of the bath.

□ Rinse the wool thoroughly in water of the same temperature, preferably by spraying from above and draining the water from below.

□ Squeeze the fibers very gently to extract excess moisture (or run them through the spin cycle of a washing machine).

□ Dry the fibers in the air or in the cool cycle of an automatic dryer. Very long fibers should be air dried to prevent tangling.

If you scour the fibers before spinning, you must restore some oil afterward to lubricate the fibers and make carding and spinning easier. Special oils are sold for this purpose, but you can also use mineral oil diluted with water. Spray the oil onto the fibers at least 24 hours before you begin the spinning, so that the oil emulsion can penetrate the fiber uniformly.

Carding

Nearly all animal fibers are subjected to at least one carding. To a large extent, the success of the spinning depends on how efficiently the fibers have been carded. Carding opens up the fiber mass to a greater degree than teasing. It also par-

476–483. *Carding is a fiber-preparation step by which the fiber mass is opened to a greater degree than in teasing. Carding also partially aligns the fibers.*

above: 476. Charge the bottom card with fiber.

tially aligns the fibers and helps to remove those that are too short for spinning. This is done by drawing the surface of one carding cloth across the other, either by hand or by machine, in such a way that the fibers are gradually transferred from one to the other.

Hand Carding

The first step in hand carding is to *charge* the first or bottom card with fiber. Hold the card in your left hand, as shown in Figure 476, and draw a small mass of fiber across the carding cloth so that the fibers are caught by the wires. Continue drawing bits of fiber until the card is fully charged. The amount of fiber depends on the type, the degree of entanglement, and several other factors. You will learn by experience how much fiber a card can hold at one time. Too much fiber on the card would prevent thorough carding, while too little would be wasteful of your time.

The actual carding begins when the bottom card has been fully charged. Carding is a continuous operation with two alternating steps—transfer of fibers from one card to the other, and *stripping*. Stripping returns the cards to their condition of one full card and one empty one, without disturbing the fiber arrangement. The amount of carding necessary depends on how thoroughly the fibers were teased, the length of the fibers, and the amount of fiber mixing, if any, to be done.

Hand Carding

☐ Grasp the top card in your right hand, and hold the two cards in the position shown in Figure 477. The handle of the bottom card should point away from you, that of the top card toward you.

☐ Pass the top card lightly but completely over the bottom card, so that some of the fibers transfer to the top card (Fig. 478). Do not let the wires touch, but keep a small distance (the *set*) between them. Use a grazing motion, with the cards moving in parallel lines.

☐ Continue drawing the top card across the bottom one, maintaining the set, until no more fiber will transfer easily.

☐ Strip the top card by reversing it in your hand and drawing it all the way across the bottom card (Fig. 479). For this operation the wires on the carding cloth must actually mesh.

☐ Strip the bottom card as shown in Figure 480.

☐ Return the fibers to the bottom card and continue carding.

☐ When the batch of fiber has been carded, release the fibers from both cards as shown in Figure 481, being careful not to disturb the fiber arrangement.

☐ If the fibers are not to be combed, roll them into a rolag for spinning (Fig. 488).

The angles of the wires on the carding cloth, as they relate to each other, are important to the success of carding. Figure 482 shows the correct relationships for carding and for stripping. In practice, the cards would be held closer together for stripping, so that the wires could interpenetrate to lift the fibers.

477. Stroke the top card across the lower one until no more fiber will transfer easily.

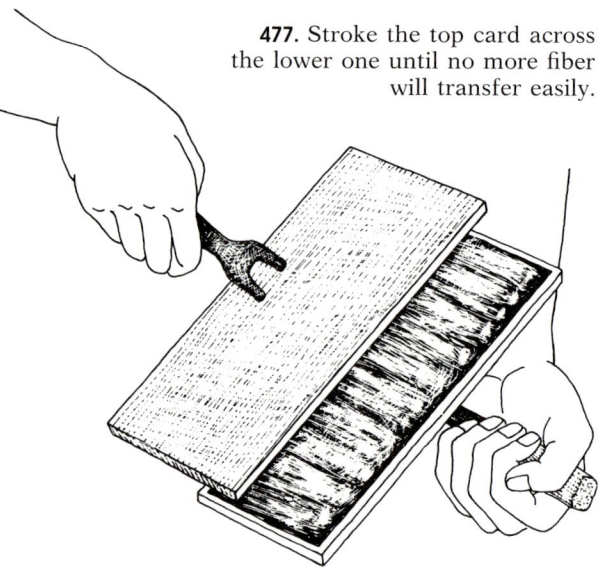

478. Draw the card in a straight line, with no arc.

479. Return all the fibers to the lower card. This is known as stripping.

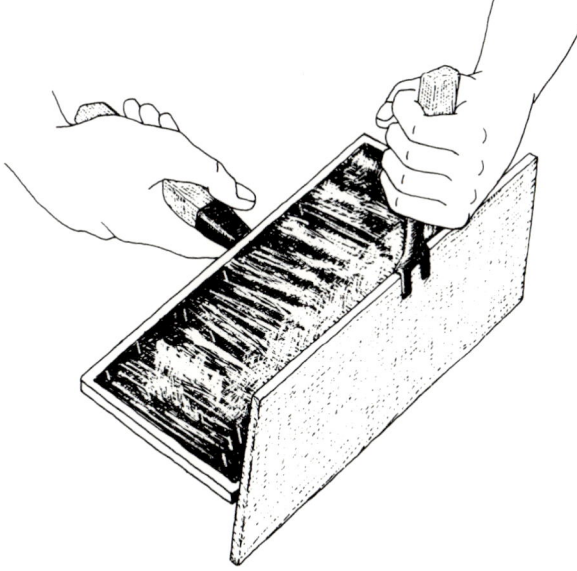

480. Strip the lower card, so that all the fibers are on the top card.

481. Release the fibers from both cards.

A

B

482. This diagram shows the positions of the wires during carding (A) and stripping (B).

Handspinning **263**

Machine Carding The same principles apply to machine carding as to hand carding, except, of course, that the entire operation is faster and more automatic. The machine must first be adjusted to make sure that the two cylinders are exactly parallel to one another and to allow for the correct set between them. The teeth of the two rollers must not be allowed to touch each other but should be $\frac{1}{32}$ of an inch apart. The belt that transfers the movement from the large drum to the small roll must be sufficiently taut to create good traction. The machine needs frequent lubrication; oil holes are provided to lubricate the drum.

To begin carding, spread the fiber evenly across the length and breadth of the carding pan in such a way that it can be caught by the small roll. As you turn the crank, the fibers are picked up by the small roll and gradually transferred to the large drum. A small amount of fiber may remain on the small roll, but this can be left temporarily.

Carding is finished when the fibers have been blended into a soft, evenly distributed layer across the drum. To remove the web, you must pry the wool free across the width of the drum at the bare strip where the two ends of the carding cloth meet. Insert a dowel, knitting needle, or stiff wire in the space under the web to loosen it (Fig. 483). You can tear the web at this point, but do not cut it apart with scissors. When you have loosened one area, rotate the drum backward until the rest of the web is peeled from the teeth.

You should now make the carded web into a long, narrow roving. To do this, divide the web by tearing so that it becomes one long strip, as shown in Figure 484.

Combing

Only fibers to be spun by the worsted system are combed after carding. Combing creates a more

484. The web of fibers that comes from the card machine can be torn into one continuous strip for spinning.

uniformly parallel arrangement of fibers and helps to remove any short fibers that may remain in the rolag after carding.

483. The card machine aligns fibers by gradually transferring them from the small roll to the large drum.

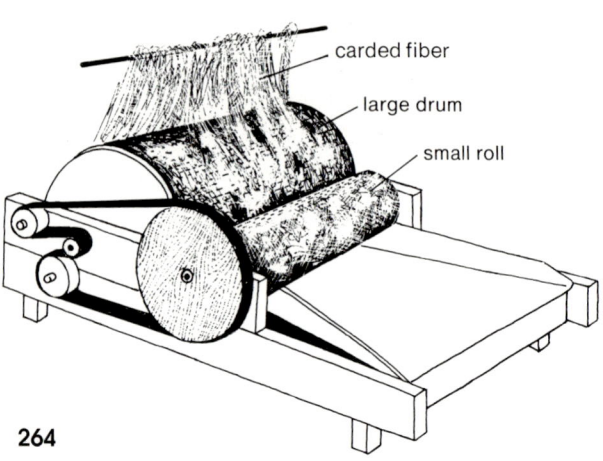

carded fiber

large drum

small roll

Combing

- ☐ Attach one of the two combs very firmly to a fixed support (Fig. 485).
- ☐ Charge the comb by drawing the mass of carded fibers across the tines of the comb so that fibers are gradually caught in the comb.
- ☐ When the first comb is fully charged, draw the second comb repeatedly across the fiber mass, moving ever closer to the first comb and picking up more and more fibers (Fig. 486).
- ☐ Continue combing until the two combs are touching but no more fiber will transfer to the second comb.
- ☐ Remove the fiber remaining on the first comb—the *noilage*—and set it aside.
- ☐ Mount the full comb on the support.
- ☐ Grasp the outermost ends of the fibers in one hand, and draw them out gradually (Fig. 487) in a thick, uniform strand (a *top*).
- ☐ Repeat the combing operation once or twice more if necessary.

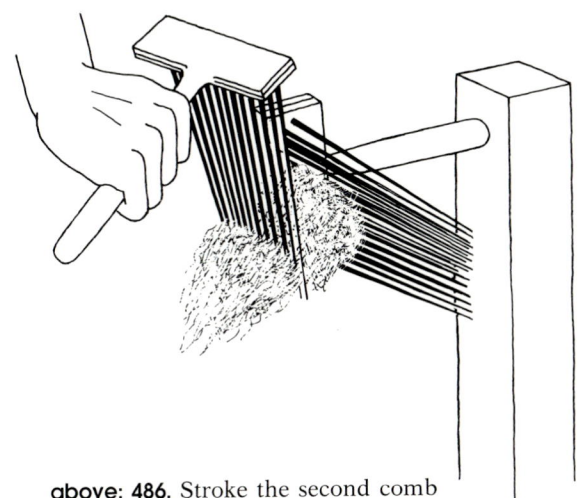

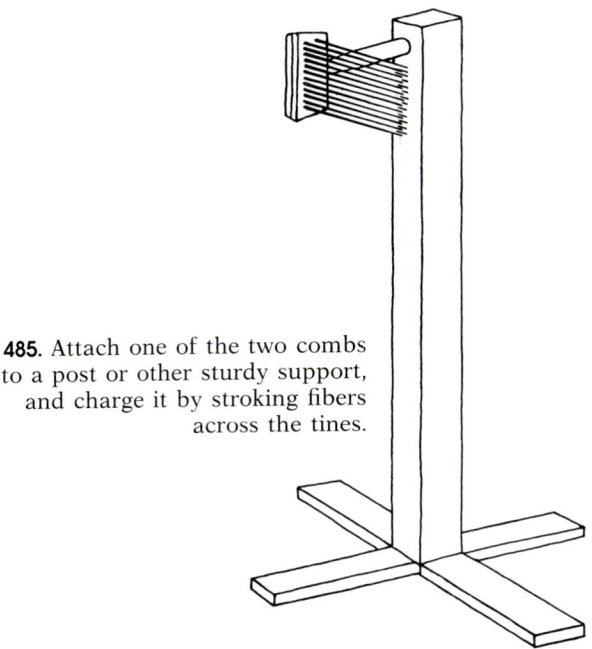

485. Attach one of the two combs to a post or other sturdy support, and charge it by stroking fibers across the tines.

above: 486. Stroke the second comb repeatedly across the first, with the two moving ever closer together, until no more fiber will transfer easily.

below: 487. Draw the fibers from the comb in a thick, uniform strand.

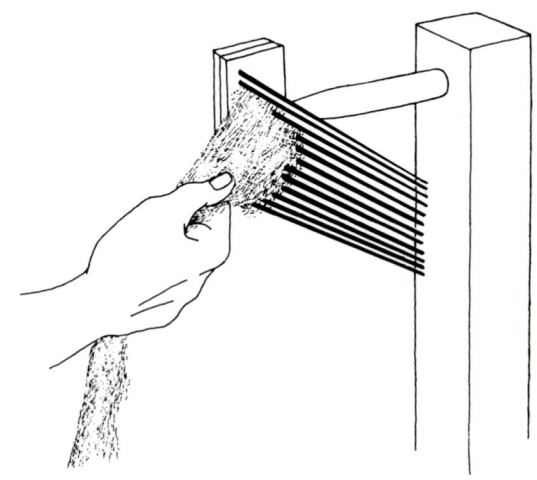

The top drawn from the final combing should be continuous; in other words, as each batch of fiber is combed, you should overlap and piece it with the previous one to form an unbroken top. It should be smooth and uniform, with only long fibers arranged in a parallel configuration.

The noilage left in the first comb will consist of shorter, tangled, or broken fibers that are not appropriate for worsted spinning. However, you should examine this mass of fibers. If too many long fibers are mixed in with the noils, you can recard and recomb the mass to separate the long ones.

Forming the Rolag or Roving

Fibers ready for spinning are in the form of either a *rolag* or a *roving*. Both of these are continuous, compact strands of fibers; they differ only in the way they are formed.

The *rolag* is formed by rolling the mass of fibers that are released from the hand cards. This is done by simply rolling the fibers across a flat surface or the back of one of the cards (Fig. 488).

A *roving* is made by drawing a combed top (or the strip made from fibers that come from the carding machine) through the hands under ten-

488. The formation of the rolag begins as the fibers are removed from the cards.

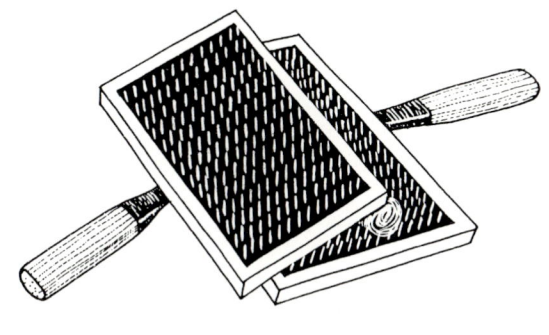

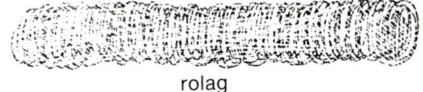

rolag

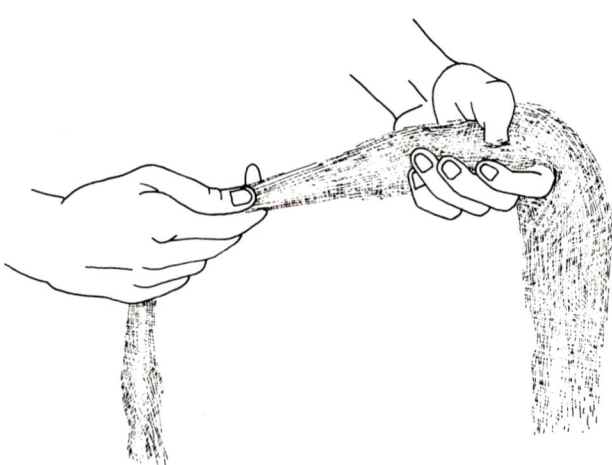

489. The combed fibers are drawn through the hands under tension to form a roving.

sion (Fig. 489). The resultant roving is longer and narrower than the top, but the parallel orientation of the fibers has been maintained or even enhanced. If you plan to spin a fine yarn, you should draw out the top two or three times to create a very narrow roving. The novice spinner will probably have the greatest chance of success with a rolag or roving $\frac{3}{4}$ inch in thickness.

The fiber preparation is now complete, and you can begin spinning.

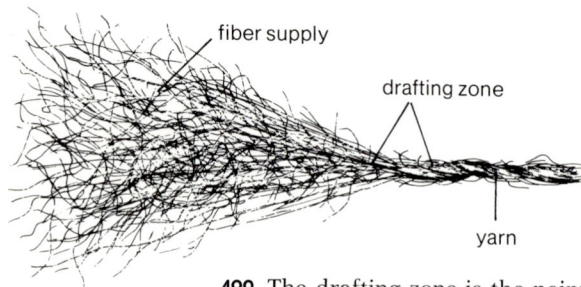

490. The drafting zone is the point at which fibers are drawn out and compressed into yarn. At left is the fiber supply in the form of a roving; at right is the spun yarn.

491. The fibers from two separate rolags or rovings are unraveled slightly so they can be spliced smoothly.

The Spinning Process

Spinning consists of drawing out the roving or rolag into an even finer strand—now a true yarn—giving it a twist, and winding the yarn onto a bobbin or spindle shaft for temporary storage. Figure 490 illustrates graphically the configuration of the fibers at the drafting point. At left is the fiber supply (the rolag or roving) and at right the spun yarn. The center portion of the diagram shows the *drafting zone*, the point at which your fingers regulate the number of fibers allowed to pass through to become yarn. Therefore, the number of fibers in the drafting zone at one time determines the weight of the yarn. Regardless of what spinning tool you use, the twist is actually inserted at a point well beyond the drafting zone, after which it travels back along the yarn toward the fingers.

Spinning always begins by joining, or splicing, a section of the new fiber supply to a length of spun yarn already attached to the spinning mechanism. In order to achieve as smooth a transition as possible, you should unravel the end of the yarn slightly, so that you can join loose fibers to loose fibers. Drafting begins at the point where the yarn is unraveled (Fig. 491). As the fibers move through your hand, there will be increasingly fewer fibers from the old yarn and more fibers from the new source, until the splice is complete.

The Flyer Wheel

The best position for spinning on the flyer wheel is illustrated in Figure 492. The right foot operates the treadle, which turns the drive wheel to rotate the flyer mechanism. Grasp the yarn in both hands, with your left hand controlling the drafting and your right hand the insertion of twist. A steady rate of spinning takes practice to coordinate the treadling, drafting, and twisting motions at the same time.

On the flyer wheel drafting takes place between the left and right hands. Your left hand is held in such a way that only as many fibers are allowed to slip between the thumb and forefinger as are required for the weight of yarn to be spun (Fig. 493). The fingers of your right hand create a tension on the drafted fibers, further attenuating them to the desired yarn thickness. Twisting occurs between the right hand and the flyer mechanism. Twist is inserted at the end of the flyer shaft and travels down the spun yarn toward the hands. Your right hand serves as a brake, preventing the twist from moving into the drafting zone until the proper number of fibers have been drafted. When the draft is correct, the right hand relaxes its grip

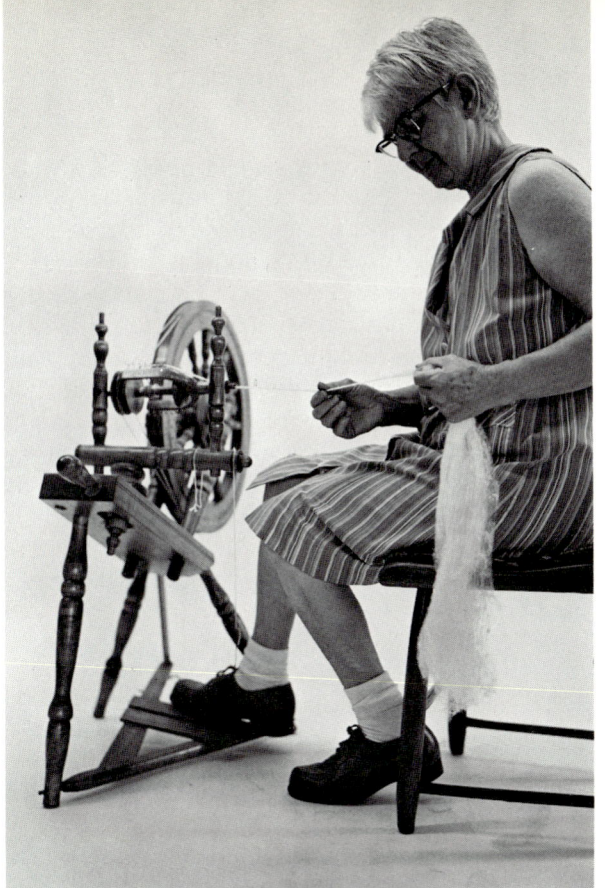

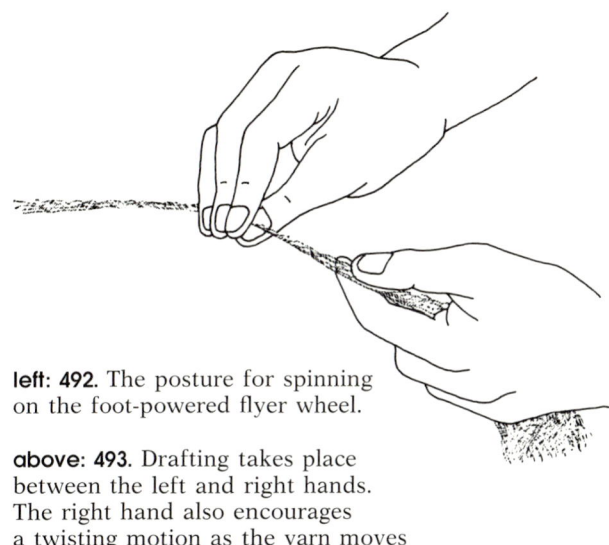

left: 492. The posture for spinning on the foot-powered flyer wheel.

above: 493. Drafting takes place between the left and right hands. The right hand also encourages a twisting motion as the yarn moves toward the flyer assembly.

The High Wheel

Spinning on the high wheel differs in several ways from spinning on the flyer wheel. Only one hand—usually the left—is used for drafting, while the other hand rotates the drive wheel. The drafting hand does not remain stationary, as it does on the flyer wheel, but moves gradually away from the spinning mechanism as a length of yarn is spun. The drafting, twisting, and take-up motions are not simultaneous; rather, spinning must be halted to wind a length of yarn onto the bobbin. In other words, the drafting and twisting are done in one operation and the yarn take-up in another.

The most efficient posture for spinning on the high wheel is illustrated in Figure 494. As your right hand rotates the drive wheel, your left hand

and encourages the twist with a rolling motion of the fingers. After the twist has been inserted, grasp the yarn with the right hand as a brake, and draft new fibers.

The buildup of yarn on the bobbin is regulated by a series of hooks on the arms of the flyer (Fig. 469). In order to permit an even distribution of yarn on the bobbin, you must occasionally stop the wheel and move the yarn from one hook to the next, working back and forth across the bobbin.

494. When spinning on the high wheel, the left hand moves steadily away from the spindle, while the right hand turns the drive wheel.

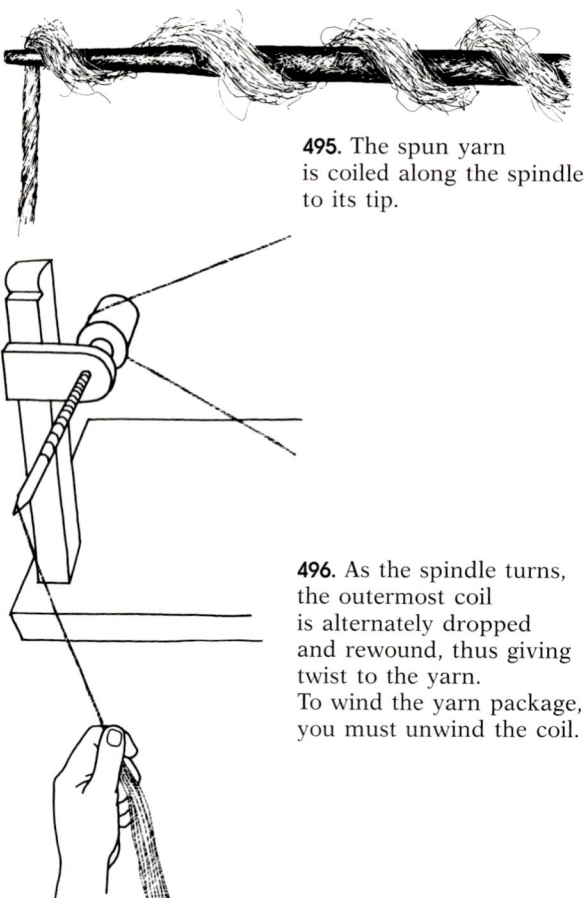

495. The spun yarn
is coiled along the spindle
to its tip.

496. As the spindle turns,
the outermost coil
is alternately dropped
and rewound, thus giving
twist to the yarn.
To wind the yarn package,
you must unwind the coil.

operation of the spindle. The yarn wound around the spindle is hitched at the bottom and top of the shaft (Fig. 498). Before drafting begins, you must flip the spindle to set it in motion. As you draft the yarn through the fingers of both hands, the revolving spindle imparts twist. In this case, it is the spindle that gradually moves away from the hands, rather than the other way around as on the high wheel. Periodically, you must flip the spindle again to renew its turning motion. When you have spun a length of yarn, remove the hitches, wind the yarn around the shaft, restore the hitches, and spin the next bout of yarn. The yarn should be consistent in size, twist, and smoothness, with just enough twist to give it strength.

497. Operation of the handspindle.

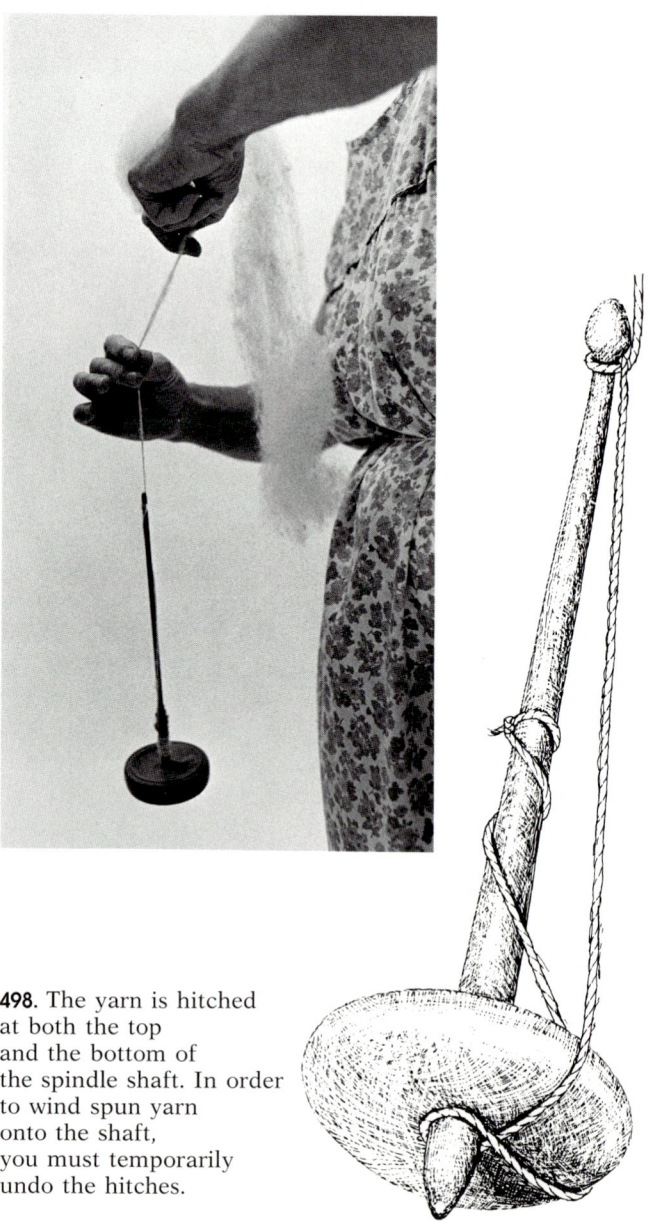

drafts the yarn, moving steadily away from the spindle. As with flyer drafting, only as many fibers as are needed for the correct yarn weight are allowed to slip through the fingers at any given time. The spun yarn is coiled along the spindle to its tip (Fig. 495). When the spindle turns, the outermost coil is alternately dropped and rewound, thus giving twist to the yarn (Fig. 496). In order to maintain an even twist throughout the yarn, the length of yarn spun in each bout and the number of turns of the drive wheel during the spinning of one bout must always be constant. After a length of yarn has been spun, hold the left hand stationary, and turn the drive wheel to give a final twist.

When it is time to wind the yarn, turn the drive wheel in the opposite direction (*backing off*) to remove the coil from the end of the spindle. Then, with the wheel turning in the original direction, wind the yarn onto the inside of the spindle, and build up a new coil to the tip for spinning the next bout of yarn.

The Handspindle

The handspindle offers a great deal of flexibility, because the tool is so simple. Figure 497 shows the

498. The yarn is hitched
at both the top
and the bottom of
the spindle shaft. In order
to wind spun yarn
onto the shaft,
you must temporarily
undo the hitches.

Finishing

After the yarn has been spun, it should be wound into skeins, using either a niddy-noddy or an umbrella swift. If wool yarn was not previously scoured, you will want to scour it now, unless you plan to weave in the grease. Follow the instructions for scouring given on page 261.

If you do not actually scour the yarn, you should at least wash it to remove surface dirt and to "fix" the twist. Dip the skeins of yarn into warm water and mild soap, then hang them to dry with weights on the bottom.

When the yarn has dried completely, the skeins can be rewound into balls if you wish.

Yarn Design

Spinning your own yarn offers a far greater opportunity for achieving special design effects than would be possible in relying strictly on commercial yarns. The design of a finished yarn can be controlled at several stages during the construction process. First of all, certain design decisions are implied in the choice of a fiber or fibers, the selection of a spinning system, and the degree of fiber preparation—all of which are established even before you begin spinning. Further design elements are controlled by the spinning operation itself—the weight of the yarn, the amount of twist, and the presence or absence of slubs or other novelty effects. Finally, the yarn design continues after a single yarn has been spun, for a variety of effects can be achieved by plying two or more yarns together.

The blending of colors, textures, or fibers in a yarn can be done at any point in the construction process. However, the earlier the blending is done, the more thorough a blend will result. For example, when two different colors are to be blended in a yarn—perhaps a dark and a light—the blend might be made when teasing the fibers, so that by the time the yarn has been spun, the two colors will be so completely integrated as to produce a third color. If the blend is made in the carding or combing stage, it will be somewhat less intimate, and so on. The least well integrated blend is produced by twisting together two single yarns of different colors to form a ply. A yarn plied from two colors will have a striped or patterned effect.

The amount of twist to be inserted in a yarn is directly related to its end-use. A warp yarn, for example, needs a tighter twist than a weft yarn. High-twist yarn gives a woven textile strength and smoothness, as well as a firmer hand. The textile woven from a low-twist yarn, conversely, is usually

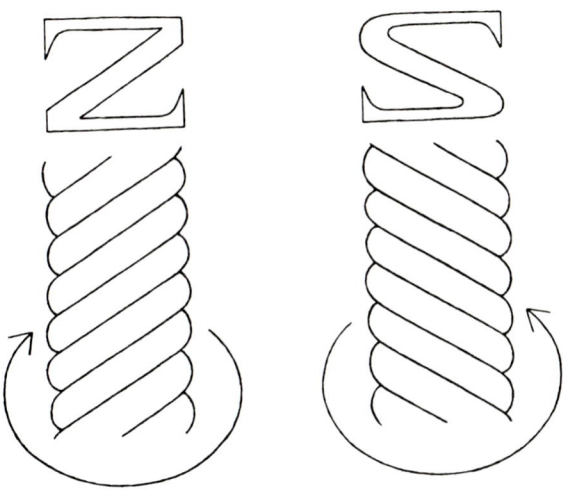

499. Yarns have either a left-hand twist (S twist) or a right-hand twist (Z twist).

softer, fluffier, and more elastic. A low-twist yarn tends to be less durable than a high-twist one, but this factor is also affected by the composition of the fibers. In some cases a very hard twist is desirable. One example of this would be the warp for a Navajo or similar tapestry rug, which is always constructed with excessive twist.

Either a left-hand twist (S twist) or a right-hand twist (Z twist) can be imparted to a yarn during spinning (Fig. 499). In plying two single yarns together, the ply may take the opposite direction from the singles twist or it may be made in the same direction. The latter is sometimes referred to as *cabling*.

To ply two (or more) yarns together, simply attach the yarns to the leader yarn fastened to the bobbin and hold them under tension while you turn the drive wheel in the proper direction, one way for plying, the other for cabling. You can also ply on a handspindle, but the process is much slower, and it is more difficult to control the rate of twist insertion. Interesting effects can be achieved by holding the yarns under different degrees of tension as they are plied. If one yarn is held under greater tension than the other, the taut yarn will form a core with the slack yarn wrapped around it (Fig. 500).

500. A core yarn is made by plying together two yarns held at unequal tension. The taut yarn forms the core, while the other yarn wraps slackly around it.

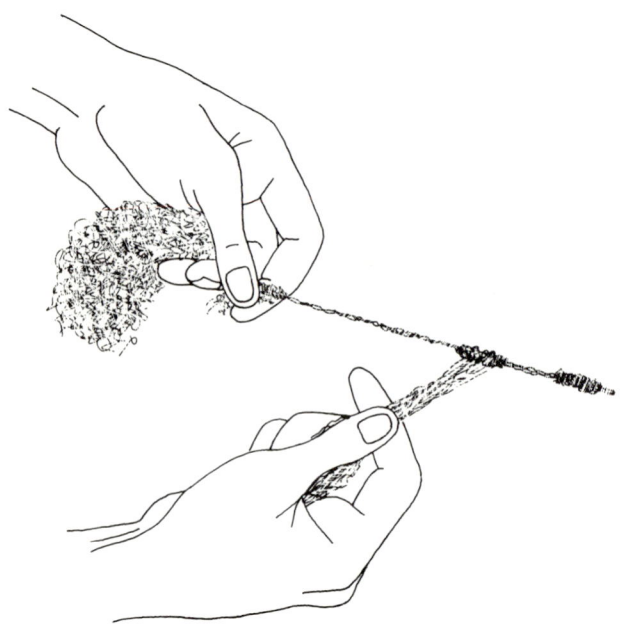

Much of the time your goal in spinning will be to create a yarn that is smooth, even, and regular in diameter. This takes a certain amount of experience, and it is made easier by developing a steady rhythm in spinning. Sometimes, though, you will want to produce an irregular effect. Any of the novelty yarns illustrated in Figure 125 can be created by the hand processes, as well as by machine. Slub and flake yarns are usually constructed during spinning. If, for a short distance, more fibers are drafted at a single time than are required for the normal yarn count, a slub will appear at that point. The slub may be just a tiny bump on the surface of the yarn or a long thickened area. Flakes are produced by introducing a small quantity of unspun fibers into the drafted yarn and allowing the twist to hold them (Fig. 501).

Above all, the great advantage of spinning is that it permits you to make a yarn ideally suited for the end-product (Fig. 502). However, the process can also work in reverse. Experimentation with different design effects may actually suggest a certain end-use and open up new creative possibilities for the fiber artist.

above: 501. Flakes are produced by introducing a small quantity of unspun fibers into the drafted yarn and allowing the twist to hold them in place.

below: 502. Jane Busse. "Bog shirt" with weft effect yarn of handspun brown and white spotted fleece. (See also Fig. 568.)

Many weavers have recently begun to express interest in dyeing their own yarns, particularly with natural dyestuffs. The colors obtained from natural materials (Pl. 24, p. 287) are much more subtle—and infinitely more diverse—than those produced commercially with synthetic dyes. When working with natural dyestuffs there is always an element of chance. Two individuals following exactly the same recipe may obtain quite different results, partly because animal and vegetable substances can vary widely according to climate and geographical location. Furthermore, minute changes in storage and handling procedures will often affect the coloring properties of a dye. However, with experience you can achieve a high degree of predictability.

Color can be introduced at various points in the manufacture of a textile. The fleece from a sheep will occasionally be dyed before spinning, and it is sometimes desirable to dye a fabric after it has been woven. But the most common practice

Yarn
Dyeing

above: 503. **Berit Hjelholt.** *Day.* 1974. Tapestry of handspun, plant-dyed wool, linen, and sisal; 7'10" × 12'6" (2.35 × 3.75 m). Courtesy the artist.

below: 504. Woodcut from *The Plictho: Instructions in the art of the dyers . . . ,* by Gioanventura Rosetti, 1548. Universität Bibliothek, Göttingen, West Germany.

is to add color in the yarn stage (Fig. 503), and that is the procedure emphasized in this chapter.

A History of Dyes

Primitive peoples learned to color their fabrics almost as soon as they learned to make them. Textile remnants discovered in the tombs of Thebes, and dating from about 3500 B.C., show traces of blue indigo dye. It is believed the Egyptians even experimented with dyeing the live sheep. According to Virgil, a sheep that was fed on madder plant would produce red wool!

In the ancient world the Phoenicians were considered masters of the dyeing trade. It was they who developed the rare purple dyes, made from a mollusk found along the coast near Tyre, that were so prized by royalty. Each gram of the dyestuff required twelve thousand of the little animals, and for centuries only monarchs could afford garments colored with Tyrian purple. The Phoenicians were indefatigable traders; their ships sailed the Mediterranean to Gibraltar and beyond, carrying with them a knowledge of dyeing techniques and materials.

A surprising range of colors was available to the early dyers. Safflower yielded reds and yellows, and indigo was used for blue. Madder, an

important red dye, was known to the Egyptians, the Persians, the Indians, the Greeks, and the Romans. In addition to the rich Tyrian purple, there was also a bluer purple called Byzantium. The saffron plant produced yellow, and a tiny insect found on the Kermes oak made a popular red dye. In the Americas, cochineal, obtained from the

505. Walnut hulls, lichens, and oak galls all yield substantive dyes, which do not require the addition of a mordant to make the colors fast.

female of an insect species native to Mexico, provided brilliant red, and logwood bark was used for dark colors. The discovery of mordants—chemical substances that combine with the dyestuffs to make the colors fast—was important to the development of dyeing techniques. Mordants were used in India by 2000 B.C. and perhaps by an even earlier date in the Far East.

In Europe the art of dyeing was a highly secretive one until the 16th century. In 1548 Gioanventura Rosetti of Venice published the first complete printed reference book on dyeing, *The Plictho* (Fig. 504). The product of sixteen years of research, Rosetti's book compiled dye recipes from Venice, Genoa, Florence, and other Italian cities, with special emphasis on the famed reds and blacks of Venice. One can only speculate on what methods Rosetti might have used in persuading dyers to surrender their secret recipes for publication. In 16th-century Italy a black dye was made in the following manner:

> Measure shells of eggs in quantity and make them boil in clear water until it drops by half. Then you remove the shells, and return the water to the fire. Take filings of iron and grindings from the milling of galls so that these things are 2 ounces, roche alum half ounce, gum arabic, very strong lye, and human urine so that the gum and the water be two ounces. Make it boil till it drops to half and this is a good black dye.

The recipe for dyeing "feathers, bones, tables of wood and handles of knives, and all other things" was also rather specific:

> Measure red vinegar very strong as much as you want and put it in a glazed vase and into it much filings of copper and of brass, Roman vitriol, roche alum, verdigris. Put each thing together for several days but first let it boil a little, that is a good boil. You will make a fine tincture of green so strong that never more will it go away.

A green color on skins was produced by combining "apples of the buckthorn of the month of September" with white vinegar or strong wine and roche alum, then allowing this "to boil for the space of saying six paternosters and not more."

The Plictho is subtitled: *Instructions in the art of the dyers which teaches the dyeing of woolen cloths, linens, cottons, and silk by the Great Art as well as by the Common.* This division of dyers into two groups—"those who Dye the greater, and those who Dye the lesser Dyes"—prevailed in Europe well into the 18th century. The great dyes were considered to be Madder-Red, Crimson Violet, Green, Brown Tawney, and Woad and Madder Black, while "blew," red, yellow, and brown were among the lesser colors. In order to qualify as a master dyer of the great dyes one served a four-year apprenticeship, followed by another four years of indenture. It is apparent that air pollution was a problem even in those gentler times, for a text of 1813 cautions: "In the country the scarlet cloth preserves its brightness much longer than in great cities where the urinous and alkaline vapours are more abundant."

Only natural dyes were available until 1856. In that year the English chemist Sir William H. Perkin developed, quite by accident, a synthetic purple dye. Perkin continued his experiments with dyestuffs, and dye chemistry advanced rapidly. By the middle of the 20th century more than fifteen hundred dyes were offered by American manufacturers. However, in spite of the proliferation of chemicals, certain natural materials, such as logwood, are still used in modern dyehouses.

The Dyeing Process

Three major variables affect the ultimate color of a dyed yarn: the nature of the dyestuff, the mordant used, and the fiber content of the yarn itself. Vegetable dyestuffs are capricious. Two batches of goldenrod, for instance, gathered from the identical spot but at different times, might yield different shades of yellow. The same goldenrod, mordanted with copperas instead of with alum, will produce a greenish dye. Woolen and cotton yarns, immersed in the same dye bath, will show different shades of color.

There are two general groups of dye materials. *Substantive dyes* are permanent when heated alone with the fibers. Walnut hulls, lichens, and oak galls are among the few materials in this category (Fig. 505). *Adjective dyes* require the addition of a chemical substance—a mordant—to facilitate absorption of the color and increase its permanence. No dyes are absolutely permanent, except possibly those injected into the solution for a synthetic fiber. However, when properly mordanted, natural dyes can be as long-lasting as their chemical counterparts.

Many yarn distributors offer natural and bleached yarns in wool, cotton, linen, jute, and sisal, as well as in different weights. In general, untreated yarns are stronger than those that have been bleached or stripped of color. A list of the major yarn suppliers appears in Appendix C.

Gathering Natural Materials

There is an optimum time of the year for harvesting most vegetable dyestuffs (Fig. 506). Roots, such as bloodroot, perform best when they are collected in the autumn. Lichens can be gathered all winter, but they are easiest to find in wet weather. Most above-ground plants yield more color if they are harvested in autumn rather than spring, because of the long exposure to sunlight. Day lily leaves, lily of the valley, and rose shoots in particular need much sun. Barks and tree roots should be collected between February and June, when they have the most sap and therefore a more intense color. Berries and fruits—such as ornamental crab apples, grapes, sumac, and pokeberries—must be picked when they are fully ripe; those with the least water content make the best dyes. Leaves, blossoms, twigs, stems, and shoots are generally cut at maturity, although in a few cases the young spring plants are good dye sources. Nuts should be collected after they have fallen to the ground.

A large paper bag or grocery sack is the best container for accumulating vegetable materials, because it is porous and allows the plants to breathe. After harvesting, most dyestuffs can be stored for later processing, although there is sometimes a loss or change of color. Twigs, branches, grasses, and leaves can be tied in bunches and hung from the rafters of a garage or dry basement. Lichens, berries, barks, and roots should be dried slowly in the air and then stored in porous containers until they are needed. Nut hulls and shells must be stored—after drying—in paper bags so they will not oxidize. Some flowers can be dried and preserved, but goldenrod and dandelion must be used fresh.

Materials and Equipment for Dyeing

The following equipment is required at various stages of the dye process (Fig. 507):

glass quart measuring container
stainless steel, Pyrex, or enamel pails and kettles (copper and brass are also usable, but aluminum is too porous, and iron will contaminate the dye bath)
plastic measuring spoons
plastic buckets or dishpans
large glass or plastic funnel
candy thermometer
coffee filter disks
airtight glass jars
glass stirring rod
scale for measuring pounds and ounces (or gram scale)
rubber or plastic gloves

Most of the chemicals listed below can be obtained in drug stores, but they are less expensive if purchased in bulk from a chemical supply house (see Appendix C).

506. With most natural materials, like the birch leaves and goldenrod shown here, there is a best time of the year for harvesting.

507. The equipment needed for dyeing may include: plastic and enamel tubs and kettles, wooden stirring pole, glass jars, scale, plastic funnel, coffee filter disks, plastic measuring bottle, glass stirring rod, measuring spoons, thermometer, rubber gloves.

alum (aluminum potassium sulfate)
chrome (potassium dichromate)
blue vitriol (copper sulfate)
copperas (iron; ferrous sulfate)
tin (stannous chloride)
tannic acid
tartaric acid
Glauber's salts (sodium sulfate)
acetic acid (or vinegar)
sodium benzoate
oxalic and sulphuric acids
ammonia
precipitated chalk
litmus paper

Certain natural materials cannot be grown or harvested in all parts of the United States but can be purchased from commercial suppliers. These include cochineal, indigo, and madder.

Only soft, nonmineralized water should be used for scouring, mordanting, and dyeing yarn. Rain water is the cheapest and most readily available form of soft water, but if it is not feasible to collect large quantities of rain water, distilled water or the moisture from a dehumidifier can be substituted. If necessary, tap water can be temporarily softened by adding one of the following:

1 teaspoon of borax per gallon of water (5 g to 4 l)
2 tablespoons of vinegar per gallon of water (30 ml to 4 l)
a 4-percent solution of acetic acid

A mild soap (not detergent), sal soda, and a water softener are needed for scouring the yarns.

508. In order to extract the dye, you must boil natural materials for several hours, until they release no more color.

Extracting the Dye

The quantities of dyestuff and water needed to make a dye bath depend upon the amount of yarn to be dyed. In general, 1 pound of yarn requires $2\frac{1}{2}$ to 3 gallons of water, plus 1 peck of plant material or 1 pound of nut hulls, wood, or bark. (The approximate metric equivalents are 11 liters of water and 9 liters of plant material or .5 kilogram of bark for .5 kilogram of yarn.) Heavy yarns may require a higher ratio of dye material to water than fine yarns to produce the same color.

Woody materials such as bark, twigs, and roots must be cut into short pieces (1 to 3 inches or 5 cm) or ground with a coarse plate in a food mill. The pieces are soaked for at least 12 and preferably 24 hours, then boiled for 5 or 6 hours. Except for flowers, fruits, and berries, most other natural materials should be soaked for about 12 hours before boiling (Fig. 508). The boiling time varies according to the material, but you can usually see when a dyestuff has yielded all its color. Then, the

509. After all color has been extracted from the materials, strain out the waste matter. The dye bath is then ready for use or storage.

benzoate per quart of liquid and sealing in an airtight container. Dye baths can also be frozen.

Scouring

Before the yarns are processed they should be wound into skeins for easier handling (Fig. 510). Tie the skeins loosely in at least four places, with the beginning and tag end of the yarn tied together. If you intend to dye an unspun wool fleece, it should be placed in a net or cheesecloth bag— large enough to allow adequate movement—to facilitate lifting in and out of the baths. Automatic washers and dryers should not be used for any step in the yarn-dyeing process.

All natural fiber yarns must be scoured to permit even absorption of the dye. Scouring removes the grease and surface soil from woolen yarns and the wax from vegetable fibers.

pulp or waste matter is strained out (Fig. 509), and the dye bath is ready.

In some cases the *pH factor* or acidity-alkalinity ratio of the dye bath can affect the color produced or the quality of the dyed yarn. The addition of either ammonia or oxalic acid to the dye bath—as specified for some dyestuffs in the list on pages 283–290—can increase the acidity or alkalinity of the dye bath and thereby cause varied color results. Litmus paper is used to measure the pH factor of the dye bath.

If the dye bath is not to be used immediately, it can be preserved for several months with no loss of strength by adding 1 teaspoon (4.5 g) of sodium

Wool The scouring solution for wool is based on 2 to 3 gallons of water for each pound of yarn (10 l for each .5 kg). To this is added enough water softener to make the water slippery, 1 to 2 percent sal soda, and a 1 to 3 percent solution of soap. Immerse the yarn, and heat the mixture to a temperature that is comfortable to the hands (110–120°F, 45°C). It should be held at that temperature for 20 minutes to an hour. Then, rinse the yarn thoroughly in at least three changes of warm water, and squeeze out the excess moisture.

510. Yarns are easier to handle throughout the dyeing process if they are tied loosely into skeins. The beginning and tag end of the yarn are tied together.

511. A mordant is a chemical substance that combines with a dyestuff to facilitate its absorption and encourage the development of a permanent color. Here the mordanting chemicals are measured precisely on a gram scale.

Cotton and Linen   Vegetable fibers can stand much higher temperatures than wool. The solution for scouring 1 pound (.5 kg) of cotton or linen consists of 5 parts sal soda, 2 parts soap, and 93 parts water—plus enough water softener to make the water slippery—for a total of 2 to 3 gallons (10 l) of liquid. Boil the yarn in this mixture for 1 to 2 hours, then rinse thoroughly and squeeze to remove excess moisture.

Mordanting

Yarn can be mordanted at various stages of the dyeing process. Sometimes the mordant is added to the dye bath itself, or the yarn is mordanted both before and after dyeing. The most common procedure is to mordant *before* dyeing (*bottom mordanting*), which allows yarns prepared with different mordants to be placed in the same dye bath. One exception to this practice is the copperas (iron) mordant, which is usually added to the dye bath. (By using an iron kettle for the dye bath, you can eliminate the iron mordant. Yarns dyed in this fashion will be darker.)

The mordants most often used with natural dyestuffs are: *alum*, a universal mordant compatible with nearly all dyestuffs and fibers; *tin*, which produces the brightest colors; *chrome*, which tends to brown colors; and *copperas* (iron), a darkening mordant. An excess of alum will make yarns sticky and gummy, while a too-strong concentra-

Mordants for Wool

Mordant	Yarn Quantity	Amount of Mordant	Tartaric Acid	Water	Other Ingredients
alum	1 lb	4 oz	1 oz	3–4 gal	
	4 oz	1¾ tsp	½ tsp	1 gal	
	1 oz	¾ tsp	¼ tsp	1 qt	
	500 g	113 g	28 g	11–15 l	
	100 g	17 g	5 g	4 l	
	30 g	7 g	2.5 g	1 l	
					oxalic acid
tin	1 lb	½ oz	1 oz	3–4 gal	1 Tb
(stannous	4 oz	1 tsp	1½ tsp	1 gal	1 tsp
chloride)	1 oz	¼ tsp	½ tsp	1 qt	¼ tsp
	500 g	14 g	28 g	11–15 l	14 g
	100 g	9 g	7 g	4 l	9 g
	30 g	2 g	5 g	1 l	2.5 g
chrome	1 lb	½ oz	1 oz	3–4 gal	
(potassium	4 oz	½ tsp	1½ tsp	1 gal	
dichromate)	1 oz	¹⁄₁₆ tsp	¼ tsp	1 qt	
	500 g	14 g	28 g	11–15 l	
	100 g	5 g	7 g	4 l	
	30 g	.63 g	2.5 g	1 l	

512. The yarn is removed
from the dye bath after
all the color from the solution
has been extracted.
If left in the dye bath
for cooling, the yarn
will be darker in color.

tion of tin will cause brittleness in woolen yarns. Chrome must be stored in a covered container, for it is very sensitive to light.

Wool　The recipes given in the table (p. 277) can be used to mordant wool yarn with alum, tin, or chrome. Iron mordanting is discussed as part of the dye bath (p. 279). The tartaric acid has no mordanting value but helps to brighten colors.

After the chemicals (Fig. 511) are completely dissolved in the water, add the wet scoured yarn, and heat the solution slowly—over a period of 45 minutes—to the simmering point (200–211°F, 95–99°C). Fine wool yarns are simmered for 20 to 25 minutes; heavy rug yarns are held at the simmering temperature for about 45 minutes. Then, allow the mixture to cool naturally, remove the yarn, rinse, and squeeze out the excess moisture.

The dye bath will produce the best results if the mordant is allowed to age for a short time and if the mordanted yarn is added to the dye bath while still wet. Therefore, when the yarn is removed from the mordant solution, wrap it in a bath towel and allow it to stand for at least 24 hours. However, if the yarn must be held for more than two or three days before dyeing, it can be dried and then resoaked in plain water for half an hour to prepare it for the dye bath. Yarn mordanted with chrome must be kept covered before dyeing, for if light penetrates the fibers, they will turn a grayed blue-green, and this will influence the ultimate color.

Too much tin causes the yarn to become brittle. To lessen the chances of having disastrous results, wash the yarn in soapy water after mordanting.

Cotton and Linen　Vegetable yarns are not susceptible to high temperatures, so they can be boiled safely in mordanting. The following recipes are intended for 1 pound (450 g) of yarn.

alum:	4 ounces (115 g) alum ¼ cup (60 ml) sal soda 3 gallons (11 l) warm water
tin:	2 teaspoons (8.5 g) tin 3 gallons (11 l) warm water
chrome:	1 tablespoon (14 g) chrome (2 Tb or 28 g for darker colors) 3 gallons (11 l) water
tannic acid:	8 tablespoons (113 g) tannic acid 3 gallons (11 l) water

Dissolve the chemicals in the water, then add the yarn and bring the solution to a boil (212°F, 100°C). Fine yarns should be boiled for 1 hour, heavier yarns for 2. Allow the yarn to remain in the bath for 24 hours, then rinse. It should be dyed while still wet or remoistened if allowed to dry.

Because vegetable fibers are not as easy to dye as wool, some people prefer a more complicated three-stage mordanting process, which predisposes the yarn to better dye absorption.

1. Into 3 or 4 gallons of water, dissolve 4 ounces of alum and 1 ounce of washing soda (11–15 l water, 115 g alum, 28 g washing soda). Add the yarn, and boil the mixture for 1 hour. Leave the yarn completely covered by the solution for 24 hours, and then rinse.
2. Make a mixture of 1 ounce of tannic acid and 3 to 4 gallons of water (28 g tannic acid, 11–15 l water). Immerse the yarn, and simmer in solution for 1 hour. Allow this second solution to stand for 24 hours, and rinse the yarn again.
3. Reimmerse the yarn in the first bath, and leave it for 12 hours before rinsing. It should be dyed while still wet.

The Dye Bath

The same instructions apply for dyeing both wool and vegetable fibers. In fact, yarns of different fiber content can be put into the same dye bath simultaneously.

The dye bath should be lukewarm when the wet yarn is immersed. If the yarn is to be mordanted with copperas (iron), 1 ounce of copperas and 1 ounce of tartaric acid (28 g each) are dissolved in the dye solution before the yarn is added. The bath is then heated to the simmering point (200–211°F, 95–99°C) and maintained at that temperature for 10 minutes. Take care to ensure that the yarn remains completely covered by the dye bath. After the solution has simmered for 10 minutes, remove the yarn and dissolve 1 tablespoon (14 g) of Glauber's salts in the dye bath. The Glauber's salts exhaust the color from the dye bath and encourage more uniform dyeing results.

Then, return the yarn to the bath, and simmer it for approximately 30 minutes, or until the desired color is reached. Colors appear darker when the fibers are wet, so make an allowance for lightening as the yarn dries. The yarn can be removed immediately from the hot dye solution (Fig. 512) or permitted to cool naturally in the dye bath, but the latter procedure will tend to darken the colors. If it is necessary to remove the yarn from the dye bath before 30 minutes has elapsed, transfer it to clear water of the same temperature containing 2 tablespoons (28 g) of Glauber's salts, and leave it in that solution for the remainder of the half hour. After removal, rinse the yarn three times, the first rinse at the dye bath temperature, the second somewhat cooler, and the third lukewarm. Then, dry the yarn slowly away from strong light or heat, preferably hung or stretched so it will not tangle.

In spite of all precautions, the final color of the yarn after drying is sometimes uneven. This can be corrected by reimmersing the yarn in the dye bath, to which Glauber's salts have been added in an amount equal to 40 percent of the dry weight of the yarn. The new solution is reheated for an additional 30 minutes. This treatment should level the color throughout the yarn.

It is possible to mordant in the dye bath in a one-step process. The following mordant chemicals, added to the dye bath, will be adequate for $\frac{1}{4}$ pound (110 g) of wool:

alum:	$\frac{3}{4}$ teaspoon (21 g) alum $1\frac{1}{2}$ teaspoons (7 g) cream of tartar
chrome:	scant $\frac{1}{2}$ teaspoon (2.5 g) potassium dichromate
tin:	scant teaspoon (5.5 g) stannous chloride $1\frac{1}{2}$ teaspoons (7 g) cream of tartar
copper:	2 teaspoons (9 g) copper sulfate

Occasionally it is necessary or desirable to subject a yarn to two subsequent dye baths of different colors, a procedure known as *top dyeing*. For example, greens—which are difficult to obtain from a single dyestuff—are often produced by top dyeing blue on yellow. Top dyeing is also useful when the first dye bath is quite unsuccessful. Only mordanted yarns should be top dyed, for otherwise the first color is likely to bleed. It is preferable that the yarn be dry before a second dye bath is attempted, so that the color can be evaluated accurately. Commercially dyed yarns can be top dyed with natural dyes.

To ensure the best possible color fastness, a yarn can be *top mordanted*—that is, mordanted once again after dyeing. However, unless the same mordant is used both before and after dyeing, the color of the yarn will be affected. Some interesting (though rather unpredictable) results can be obtained by bottom mordanting the yarn with one chemical and top mordanting with another.

Special Dye Procedures

Certain dyestuffs require unusual handling in the dye bath. These include madder and indigo.

Madder An eccentric property of madder is that it performs better in tap water than in rain or distilled water. Cut a half pound of madder roots into short pieces ($\frac{1}{4}$ to $\frac{1}{2}$ inch or 1 cm), and cover them with 2 gallons (8 l) of water. Raise the temperature of the water *very slowly*—over a period of an hour—until it is just below the simmering point. Madder roots contain both red and brown dye substances, and if the water becomes hot too quickly, brown will be released. Hold the water at the warm temperature until all the dye has been extracted, then strain out the waste material. Then, add a third gallon (4 l) of water, and immerse the yarn. Hold the dye bath at the simmering point for 15 to 20 minutes or until the proper color is attained. (If the dye bath is permitted to boil, it will turn brown.)

Indigo   The best natural source of blue dye is indigo, which is available commercially in powdered form. Powdered indigo is not soluble in water; it must be dissolved—and the dye extracted—with concentrated sulphuric acid. The recipe for preparing indigo extract consists of:

> 5 ounces (148 ml) 99-percent strength sulphuric acid
> 2½ tablespoons (35 g) indigo powder
> 2½ teaspoons (25 g) precipitated chalk

Sulphuric acid is an extremely dangerous chemical. Serious (or even lethal) burns may result if the fumes are inhaled or if the acid comes in contact with your skin. Therefore, the mixture

513. Indigo dye requires special handling, for it can be dissolved only in concentrated sulphuric acid.

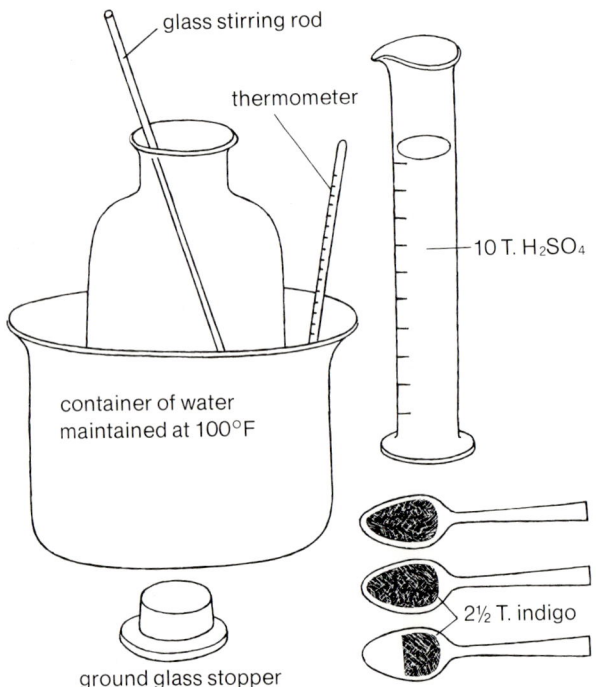

glass stirring rod

thermometer

10 T. H₂SO₄

container of water maintained at 100°F

2½ T. indigo

ground glass stopper

should be prepared outdoors or in a well-ventilated room, and the utmost precaution should be observed in measuring. Only glass implements—containers, measuring beakers, stirring rods—can be used with sulphuric acid, for the acid would literally consume wood or metal objects.

Pour the required amount of acid slowly into a small glass container (Fig. 513). (Pouring against a glass rod set in the middle of the container will help to prevent spills.) Next, add the indigo powder a little at a time, and stir very gently with a glass rod. This will cause the acid to become hot. When all the indigo has been added, the temperature should be between 75° and 100°F (24–38°C), and it is held at this point, with occasional stirring, until the acid and indigo are completely combined (about two hours). Then, seal the container with a tight-fitting glass stopper, and set it in a safe place until the mixture has turned blue, which may take up to two weeks. Finally, add the precipitating chalk a little at a time, and allow the mixture to stand for about three days with occasional stirring. When the chalk is completely dissolved, the indigo extract is ready to use.

Indigo dye is potent and is absorbed very quickly into the yarn. A solution of 1 teaspoon of extract in 2½ to 3 gallons of water will dye 1 pound of yarn to a medium blue. (The metric equivalents are 5 ml extract and 9–11 l water for 500 g yarn.)

The traditional method for working with indigo is to use human urine, which acts as both a dye solvent and a mordant. You can try this old-fashioned system if you wish, but you must be prepared for a very strong, offensive odor. Allow 1 pint (or 480 ml) of urine to ferment for ten days. Then, slowly add 8 tablespoons (113 g) of indigo powder to the urine. Ferment the mixture for another week to ten days, shaking or stirring it once a day. About 1 cup (or 225 g) of the resultant extract will color 1 pound or 500 grams of yarn.

Documenting the Results

When using natural dyes it is most important to keep accurate records so that successful results can be replicated (and unsuccessful ones avoided in the future). A small swatch of yarn from each dye lot should be set aside and labeled with the following information:

> dyestuff employed
> time and place of collection
> mordant and time of mordanting (before or
>   after dyeing or both)
> fiber content of yarn
> date of dyeing

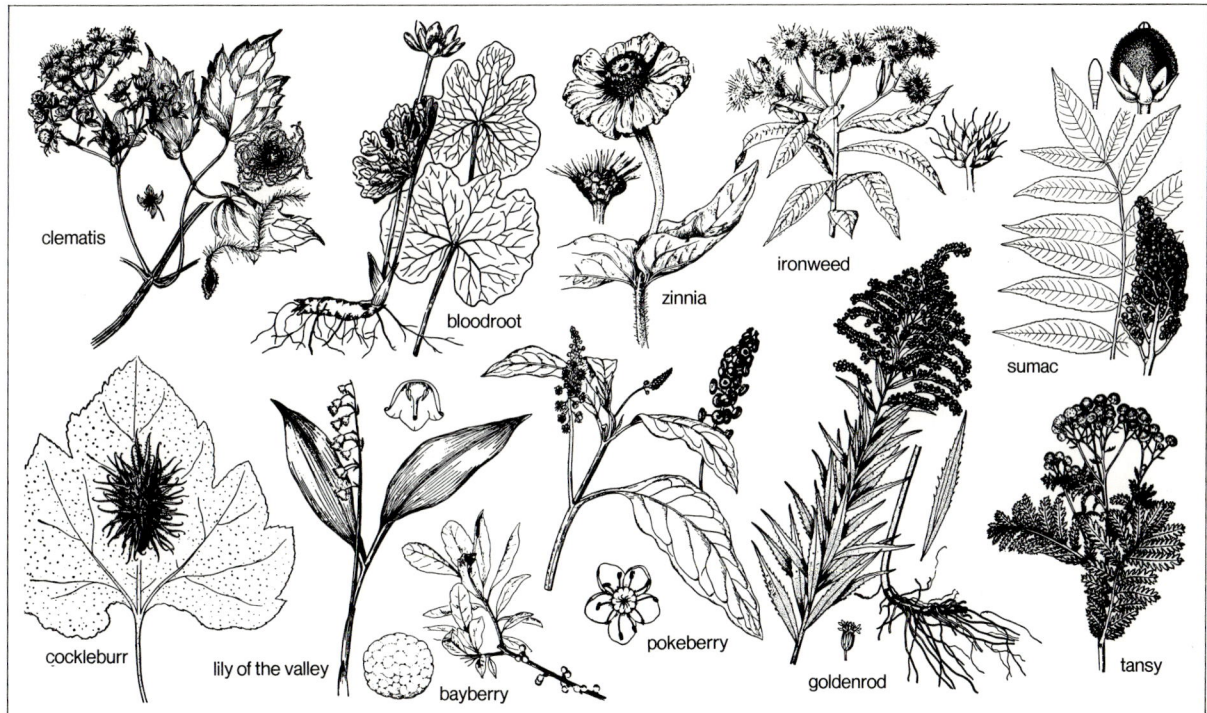

514. These are a few of the many natural materials that can be used for making dyes.

Natural Dyestuffs

Not all natural materials are suitable for making dyes. Some vivid plants and flowers do not release their color and are useless as dye sources. The list on pages 283 to 290 describes natural dyestuffs that are known to be successful (Fig. 514). However, the list is by no means exhaustive. With experimentation you may discover local materials that will produce wonderful dyes.

Synthetic Dyes

The natural dyestuffs discussed above produce highly satisfactory results with wool, but are less successful for cellulosic fibers, including cotton and linen. In working with the latter fibers, either to color them completely or to use one of the patterning techniques discussed in the following chapter, you may want to investigate synthetic dyes. Two general types are of interest to fiber artists—the older vat or oxidation dyes and the relatively new fiber-reactive dyes.

Vat and Oxidation Dyes

Indigo Vat Dye   An indigo vat dye is prepared by mixing the following materials in the order listed. It is imperative to remember that the caustic soda must always be *added to the liquid* and never the

other way around. Adding water to the caustic soda can cause an eruption. The ingredients are:

8 ounces (225 g) plain, uniodized salt
3 ounces (85 g) caustic soda (lye) dissolved in 1 cup (237 ml) water
4 ounces (113 g) sodium hydrosulphite
$\frac{1}{2}$ pound (225 g) indigo grains or powder
2 pints (946 ml) warm water

Be sure to mix the chemicals in a glass or enamel container. This stock solution will be sufficient for a dye bath of about $4\frac{1}{2}$ gallons (17 l) of warm water. Before adding the yarn, sprinkle 1 ounce (28 g) of sodium hydrosulphite on the surface of the water, and stir it gently. This helps to remove air from the dye bath, so that oxidation will take place only after the fabric or yarn has been removed.

Iron-Rust Oxidation Dye   The iron-rust dye calls for a two-step process—first exposing the fibers to the dye, then fixing the dye. The following recipe assumes a fiber quantity of 1 pound (500 g):

1 to 2 cups (2800–5600 g) ferrous sulfate crystals
2 gallons (7 l) water

Wet the fiber thoroughly in plain water, and then place it in the solution, taking care that none of the fiber protrudes from the liquid. (It is advisable to wear rubber or plastic gloves.) Leave the fiber immersed for 5 to 20 minutes, depending upon how deep you wish the orange-rust color to be. You must make tests with a small quantity of fiber before dyeing the whole lot, since the orange color does not appear in the first solution and cannot be gauged. Meanwhile, prepare the fixing solution from the following ingredients:

> 2 ounces (56 g) caustic soda (lye)
> 1 gallon (4 l) water

Again, always *add the lye to the water* and not the reverse. This solution must be handled with extreme caution to prevent burns.

After the fiber has been immersed in the dye bath for the proper time, remove it and immediately place it in the fixing solution. Leave it in the fixer for about 2 minutes, then remove the fiber and rinse it thoroughly. Allow the fiber to remain in the rinse water for about 10 minutes in order to stop the action of the alkali.

Fiber-Reactive Dyes

Fiber-reactive dyes were developed during the 1950s. They are far superior to the older synthetic dyes, because the dyestuff makes a permanent, direct chemical bond with the fibers, thus ensuring colorfastness. Two common trade names are Procion and Cibacron. The Procions are particularly interesting to fiber artists because they react on cellulosic fibers without heat.

Two common household items, salt and soda, are used with the fiber-reactive dyes. The salt can be plain table salt (sodium chloride with iodine), sodium sulfate (Glauber's salts), or rock salt. For the soda, either sal soda (washing soda) or baking soda (sodium bicarbonate) will do, but the latter is more expensive. Depending upon the color desired, the amount of salt can vary widely—from 1 tablespoon (14 g) to 4 cups (1.3 kg). The acceptable range for soda is equally broad. It is advisable to follow the manufacturer's directions and to make several test batches.

With most colors a 4 percent ratio of dye substance to fiber weight will produce a good color. Less than 4 percent will yield a light tint of the color, while more than 10 percent would simply be wasted. The average quantity of dyestuff for 1 pound (500 g) of fiber or fabric is 1 ounce (28 g), but again, this can vary depending upon the color intensity you want. You must remember also that the specific colors differ in densities, so that the constant 1 ounce or 28 grams will require varying teaspoon measures depending on color.

Fiber-reactive dyes are not poisonous, but you should wear rubber gloves to protect your hands from direct contact with the dye bath. Plastic containers are ideal for mixing and dyeing, since there is no heat involved, but you can also use the metal or glass ones suitable for natural dyes. It is essential that the container for the dye bath be large enough to allow adequate circulation of the fibers.

The fiber, yarn, or fabric to be dyed must be thoroughly clean, and fabrics must be free of any commercial finish added during manufacture. Synthrapol is a scouring agent especially formulated for use with textiles. It helps to remove sizing and starch from new fabrics and can also be used to wash out surplus dye. In batik work Synthrapol loosens the wax after dyeing has been completed. The suggested concentration for removing sizing is 1 teaspoon (9 g) per 2 gallons (7 l) of hot water. To rid fabric of excess dye, boil it for 3 to 4 minutes in a solution of $\frac{1}{2}$ teaspoon Synthrapol and 2 gallons of water.

Several alternate procedures are possible for dyeing with Procion dyes, of which this is one:

Dyeing with Procion Dyes

- Dissolve the dye powder in a small amount of lukewarm water (105°F, 40°C).
- Add the salt to the remaining lukewarm water, a small quantity at a time, and dissolve it thoroughly. If the salt does not dissolve completely, there is probably too much for the quantity of water. Add more water.
- Add the dissolved dyestuff to the salt water, and stir slowly but continuously for 10 minutes. Stir twice more, at 10-minute intervals.
- Dissolve the soda in a small amount of lukewarm water, and add it to the dye bath. Make sure it is thoroughly dissolved.
- Wet the fiber, yarn, or fabric in clear water, and transfer it to the dye bath. Stir continuously for 10 minutes.
- Leave the fiber in the dye bath for 1 hour, stirring at 5-minute intervals.
- After 1 hour, remove the fiber, and rinse thoroughly in cold water. Rinse again in hot water with soap (not detergent) added, until no more color flows from the fiber.

The dye reaction lasts for about $1\frac{1}{2}$ hours after the soda has been added. After that, the dye bath is no longer usable.

Fiber-reactive dyes are best and most permanent on cellulosic fibers—cotton, linen, and rayon—but they can also be used on wool and silk, with a slightly different procedure. Follow the manufacturer's directions for the specific fiber.

Material	Mordant(s)	Colors produced
acorn nuts and cups	alum	tan
	alum with oxalic acid	yellow-tan
	tin with oxalic acid	yellow-tan
ageratum	alum	light yellow
	tin	bright yellow
alfalfa	tin and copper	green-gold
	alum	cream
	tin	pale yellow
alder bark	alum	soft brown
apple bark	alum	lemon yellow
	tin	bright yellow
	chrome	brass
	alum and copper with oxalic acid	dark brown
	alum with ammonia	yellow
	alum or tin with copper sulfate	old gold
asparagus plant (fall)	tin	yellow
aster, wild (white)	alum	yellow
	chrome	gold
aster, cultivated (purple)	tin	soft yellow
barberries	alum	yellow-gold to coral
	tin with copper sulfate	light khaki
barberry stem or root	alum	yellow
	tin	deep yellow
bayberry leaves or berries	alum	gray-green to light yellow
	tin	light yellow
	copper	dark brown
beets (entire plant)	alum	tan to red-orange
	tin	gold to yellow-orange
	alum with oxalic acid	light red-orange
	tin with copper sulfate	dark yellow-green
birch leaves	alum	green-yellow to tan
	tin	yellow
	rinsed in weak birch ash lye	red-orange
bittersweet berries	alum	light tan
	tin	bright orange-yellow
	tin with oxalic acid	pink-tan
blackberries	alum with salt	blue-gray
	tin in acid	purple
	alum	brown-purple
blackberry shoots	copper	black
black-eyed susan (blossom)	alum	grayed yellow
	tin	bright yellow
	tin with oxalic acid	light rose
black-eyed susan (cont'd.)	tin and copper with oxalic acid	medium brown
bloodroot	no mordant	orange
	alum	orange and rust
	tin	red and pink
broom, Scotch	alum	yellow
	chrome	gold
broomsedge	alum	green-yellow
	chrome	brass
buck brush berries	tin	light yellow
	alum with ammonia	soft yellow
	tin with ammonia	yellow
buckthorn bark	alum	golden yellow
buckthorn berries	alum	lime green
	tin	orange-brown
	alum with ammonia	gold
	tin with ammonia	bright gold
	alum with oxalic acid	deep rose-tan
	tin with oxalic acid	dark brown
buttercups	alum	yellow
butternut hulls	alum	dull red-orange
	tin	dull yellow-orange
	alum with ammonia	pink-beige
	tin with ammonia	gray-brown
	alum or tin with oxalic acid	bright orange-brown
	copper and alum	medium brown
	chrome	
calliopsis	alum	brick red
camomile blossoms (golden marguerites)	chrome	buff
	alum	gold
canna leaves and stems (fall)	tin	yellow-tan
	alum or tin with ammonia	gray-yellow
	alum or tin with oxalic acid	yellow
	alum	grayed red-orange
carrion plant (berries and leaves, fall)	tin	yellow-tan
	alum with oxalic acid	light yellow
	alum	light yellow-orange
carrot tops		light green-yellow
	tin	bright yellow
	alum or tin with ammonia	bright yellow
	alum or tin with ammonia (fermented)	blue
catnip (fall)	alum	light yellow
	tin	gray-yellow
	tin with oxalic acid	gray-gold
cedar roots	alum	purple
cherry bark	alum	pale rose
	tin	peach

Material	Mordant(s)	Colors produced	Material	Mordant(s)	Colors produced
cherry bark (cont'd.)	alum with oxalic acid	light red-orange	coleus (green and pink)	alum and tin	yellow-tan
	alum with copper sulfate	olive green		alum with oxalic acid	grayed red-orange
cherry wood	alum	tan		tin with oxalic acid	medium brown
	tin	bright gold	coreopsis (blossoms and leaves)	tin	bright yellow
	copper and alum with oxalic acid	dark brown		chrome	burnt orange
	alum or tin with oxalic acid	light grayed red-orange	coreopsis (stalks)	alum	yellow
	tin or alum with ammonia	light red-orange	crabapple, yellow, ornamental	alum	light yellow
				tin	bright gold
	alum with copper sulfate	olive green		alum with ammonia	dark yellow
	alum or tin with copper sulfate and oxalic acid	red-gold	cranberry	alum	pink
				tin	red-gold
				alum with oxalic acid	pink
chestnut, horse (bark)	alum	brown		tin with oxalic acid	light red-violet
	copper	warm gray			
chestnut, horse (leaves and hulls)	chrome	gold		alum with ammonia	grayed pink
				tin with ammonia	dull gold
choke cherry (root and bark)	no mordant	purple-brown	curry powder	alum	bright gold
				tin	bright-orange
choke cherry (fruit)	alum	red	dahlia (blossoms)	alum	yellow
chrysanthemum (blossoms, yellow)	tin	yellow		chrome	orange
			dahlia (leaves, fall)	tin	grayed gold
chrysanthemum (blossoms, red)	alum	medium gray		alum with oxalic acid	dark tan
	tin	bronze			
	alum with ammonia	light yellow		copper and alum with ammonia	warm gray
	tin with ammonia	lime green			
	alum with oxalic acid	red-violet		copper and tin with ammonia	yellow-brown
	tin with oxalic acid	deep red-violet	dandelion root (U.S.)	alum	yellow-brown
clematis (leaves and branches)	alum	yellow	dandelion root (Scotland)	alum	magenta
				copper	dark khaki
cochineal	acids	orange	dandelion (blossoms)	alum or tin	light yellow
	alkalies	crimson violet	dock, broad leaved (leaves)	alum	yellow
	alum	red	dock, broad leaved (root)	alum	dull yellow
	tin	orange-red		chrome	light brown
	copper	deep red-violet		copper sulfate	rich brown
	copper sulfate	red-violet	fennel plant	alum	bright yellow
	chrome with acetic acid	purple		chrome	gold
	oxalic acid	geranium red	fern, bracken (buds, spring)	alum	lime green
	no mordant	rose-pink		chrome	olive green
cocklebur	alum	gold	fern, bracken (shoots)	alum	creamy yellow
	tin with ammonia	yellow		copper	dull green
	chrome	brown	fern, bracken (roots)	alum	dark yellow
	tin with oxalic acid	gold	fern, sweet (summer)	alum	pale yellow
				tin	golden yellow
	copper	dark green		alum or tin with oxalic acid	light red-orange
coleus (purple)	alum	gray-brown	geranium (blossoms, scarlet)	tin	pink
	tin	green-brown			
	alum with ammonia	olive green	gloxinia (blossoms, red)	alum or tin with oxalic acid	deep pink
	alum with oxalic acid	rose		alum	pale pink
				tin	grayed yellow
	tin with oxalic acid	medium gray-brown	goldenrod (blossoms)	alum	yellow

Material	Mordant(s)	Colors produced	Material	Mordant(s)	Colors produced
grapes, Concord	alum	lavender and purple	lichens (cont'd.)	alum or tin with oxalic acid	deep grayed red-orange
grapes, wild	alum	lavender to violet		copper and tin with ammonia	medium brown
hawthorn apples	alum	deep fawn	lichens (Parmelia molluscula)	alum	red-tan to light orange
hickory nut hulls	alum	deep red-orange	lichens (Peltigera)	alum	yellow-tan
	tin	orange		chrome	dark rose-tan
	alum or tin with oxalic acid	deep red-orange	lichens (Umbilicaria pustilata—soaked in ammonia)	alum	deep red-violet
	alum with ammonia	deep brown		tin	red-violet
	tin with ammonia	orange brown		no mordant	deep red-violet
hollyhock (mixed)	chrome	orange and rust	lichens (Usnea)	alum	buff to green-yellow
hollyhock (red)	alum	pink	lilac (branches and leaves)	alum	medium yellow
	tin	deep red		tin	medium yellow
hop, wild (leaves and flowers)	alum	yellow		chrome	warm gray
hop, wild (stalks)	alum	brown-red		oxalic acid and alum or tin	buff
hornbean (inner bark)	no mordant	yellow		oxalic acid, copper sulfate, and alum	green gold
horsebrier fruit	alum	violet		oxalic acid, copper sulfate, and tin	gold
	table salt	blue		copper sulfate and alum or tin	olive green
horsetail stalks	alum	grayed yellow	lily of the valley (fall)	alum	peach
huckleberries, garden	alum	violet		tin	red-orange
	tin	blue		alum with oxalic acid	grayed brown
	alum with ammonia	light blue-green	lily of the valley (spring)	alum	yellow-green
	tin with ammonia	deep green		alum with lime	yellowish green
	alum with oxalic acid	violet		alum with ammonia	greenish yellow
	tin with oxalic acid	deep blue	liver plant (foliage, fall)	alum or tin	clear lemon yellow
	copper and tin with ammonia	dark green	locust seed pods (dark brown)	alum	tan
indigo (roots or powder)	alum	blue		tin	bright orange
	chrome	green		alum with ammonia	grayed yellow-orange
indigo, false	alum	blue		copper and alum with ammonia	dark gray
iris (blossoms)	alum or tin	yellows greens, blues		copper and tin with ammonia	deep bronze
	chrome	green		copper and alum with oxalic acid	warm light gray
ironweed	alum	tan		copper and tin with oxalic acid	gold
joe-pye weed	alum or chrome	yellow			
juniper berries	alum	yellow	locust seed pods (rust)	alum	pale peach
	copper sulfate and ammonia	olive brown		tin	clear yellow
	copper	brown		alum with ammonia	grayed yellow
knotweed	alum	pale yellow		tin with ammonia	yellow-orange
	tin	yellow		alum with oxalic acid	pale peach
	alum with oxalic acid	pink		tin with oxalic acid	light red-orange
	tin with oxalic acid	peach			
lamb's quarter	no mordant or alum	red			
larch needles (newly fallen)	alum	brown			
larkspur (petals)	alum	blue			
larkspur (plant, fall)	alum or tin	grayed tan			
	alum or tin with oxalic acid	medium brown			
lichens (Evernia prunastri)	no mordant	plum			
lichens (green tree)	alum or tin	grayed red-orange			

Material	Mordant(s)	Colors produced	Material	Mordant(s)	Colors produced
locust (yellow)	alum	yellow	onion skins (cont'd.)	tin or alum with oxalic acid	red-orange
lupines (entire plant)	alum	green-yellow		alum with ammonia	gold
madder roots	chrome	red-brown		tin with ammonia	green-gold
	alum	bright red-orange		copper sulfate	yellow-green
	tin	bright orange	Oregon grape (roots, leaves, and stems)	alum	dull green-yellow
	alum with ammonia	light yellow	osage orange (bark or wood chips)	alum	strong yellow-green
	tin with ammonia	clear yellow		tin	yellow
	alum with oxalic acid	bright rust		chrome	gold
	tin with oxalic acid	medium orange	oxalis (foliage, fall)	alum	light peach
maple bark	alum	pink-tan		tin	grayed red-orange
	copper	purple		alum with ammonia	light yellow
marigold, burr (sticktights or pitchfork, fall)	alum	yellow		tin with ammonia	clear yellow
marigold, French (plant and blossoms)	alum	lemon yellow		alum and copper with ammonia	olive green
	tin	bright orange		tin and copper with ammonia	gold
	alum with ammonia	yellow	paprika	alum	tan
	tin with ammonia	yellow-orange	parsley, wild (plant minus roots)	alum	gold or green-yellow
	alum with oxalic acid	tan	pear (sawdust and chips)	alum	peach
	tin with oxalic acid	yellow		tin	rose
	alum and copper	grayed olive		alum with ammonia	red-orange
	copper and tin	orange-brown		tin with ammonia	dusty rose
marigold, American (plant and blossoms)	alum	yellow		alum or tin with oxalic acid	red-orange
	tin	yellow-green		copper and alum with ammonia	warm gray
	chrome	orange		copper and tin with ammonia	cool gray
marigold, marsh (blossoms)	alum	yellow		alum with copper sulfate and ammonia	grayed green
meadow rue (roots)	alum	yellow	peony (blossoms, red and pink)	alum	yellow
mulberry	alum	purple		alum with oxalic acid	red and pink
	oxalic acid	pink	pine cones (long boiling)	alum	dull brown-yellow
	ammonia	blue		alum with oxalic acid	rose-tan
nectarine (leaves, fall)	alum	lemon yellow	plantain (leaves and roots)	alum	green
	tin	bright yellow-orange	plum, Damson (fruit)	alum	strong grayed purple
	alum with ammonia	light yellow	plum, wild (roots)	alum	red-purple
	copper and alum with ammonia	bronze	plum, wild (bark)	alum	red
	copper and tin with ammonia	orange-brown	pokeberry	alum	red and pink
nettle (flowers)	alum	dull gold		chrome	rust
nettle (entire plant)	alum	yellow		tin	bright red
nightshade (berries)	alum	purple	Polyporus lucidus (red shelf fungi or lichens)	alum	pale orange
	tin	blue		tin	pale red-orange
oak, black (bark)	tin	orange on silk		alum or tin with oxalic acid	stronger orange
	alum	yellow			
	chrome	gold			
oak, black (galls or gallnuts)	no mordant	brown			
onion skins (red or yellow)	alum	orange			
	chrome	red to brass			
	tin	yellow-orange			

Walnut staminate flowers; tin mordant

Dandelion plant + ammonia; tin mordant

Cochineal; tin mordant

Cochineal + oxalic acid; tin mordant

Cochineal + copper sulfate; alum mordant

Cochineal + ammonia; alum mordant

Peony flowers + oxalic acid; chrome mordant

Peony flowers + ammonia; chrome mordant

Red chrysanthemum + oxalic acid; tin mordant

Pear sawdust and chips; alum mordant

Pear sawdust and chips + copper sulfate + ferrous sulfate + ammonia; tin mordant

Curry powder; alum mordant

Curry powder; tin mordant

Rock lichen soaked in ammonia and water one week; no mordant

Beet; alum mordant

Beet + chrome; alum mordant

Beet + copper sulfate; tin mordant

Sumac leaves; alum mordant

Sumac leaves + oxalic acid + copper sulfate + ferric sulfate; tin mordant

Cockleburr + ammonia; tin mordant

Hickory nut hulls and young nut; tin mordant

Hickory nut hulls and young nut + ammonia; tin mordant

Garden huckleberries (fermented); tin mordant

Garden huckleberries (fermented) + ammonia; tin mordant

Garden huckleberries (fermented) + oxalic acid; tin mordant

Garden huckleberries (fermented) + ammonia; copperas + tin mordants

Flea bane (or white daisy), entire plant; tin mordant

Flea bane (or white daisy), entire plant; chrome mordant

Flea bane (or white daisy), entire plant + oxalic acid + copper sulfate; alum mordant

Black walnuts + oxalic acid; alum mordant

Fruitwood, ironwood, and wild privet; copperas and tin mordant

Madder (red and brown); alum mordant

Madder (red and brown) + ammonia; tin mordant

Madder (red and brown) + oxalic acid; alum mordant

Madder (red and brown) + copper sulfate, added late; alum mordant

Curly dock; alum mordant

Curly dock + oxalic acid; chrome mordant

Curly dock + ammonia + copper sulfate; alum mordant

Marigold flowers and plants; tin mordant

Buckthorn berries + oxalic acid; tin mordant

Plate 24. Samples of the colors produced by hand-dyeing yarn with natural dyestuffs.

above: **Plate 25. Joan Sterrenberg.**
Gradational Ikat. 1976.
Resist-dyed, loom-woven strips,
stitched and bound, wool and mohair yarns,
acid-dyed; 9 × 8′ (2.7 × 2.4 m).
Collection Monsanto Corporation, St. Louis.

right: **Plate 26. Marian Claydon.** *5 Pieces.* 1976.
Clamp resist in silk, 8′ (2.4 m) square.
Courtesy the artist.

Material	Mordant(s)	Colors produced	Material	Mordant(s)	Colors produced
Polyporus lucidus (cont'd.)	copper and alum with oxalic acid	deep brown	salvia (cont'd.)	copper and alum with ammonia	cool gray
Polyporus versi-color (wavy semicircular grown on trees—soaked in ammonia one month)	alum	pale orange		copper and tin with ammonia	grayed gold
	tin	grayed orange		copper and alum with oxalic acid	grayed dark green
	alum with oxalic acid	grayed orange		copper and tin with oxalic acid	grayed gold
pomegranate skins	alum	yellow	scabiosa (blossoms)	alum	bright green-yellow
	copper with ash lye	violet-blue		tin	yellow-green
poplar (leaves)	alum	lime yellow		alum with ammonia	clear yellow
poplar (bark)	alum	rich yellow		tin with ammonia	green-yellow
	chrome	golden brown		alum with oxalic acid	dusty rose
poplar, Lombardy (leaves)	alum	yellow-brown		tin with oxalic acid	grayed rose
	chrome	brass		copper and alum	dark yellow-green
poplar, Lombardy (catkins)	alum with ammonia	yellow-green		copper and tin	grayed gold
poppy, oriental (petals)	alum with oxalic acid	salmon pink	scabiosa (entire plant)	tin	clear yellow
poppy, oriental (stamens only)	alum with oxalic acid	violet		alum with ammonia	grayed yellow
privet (berries)	alum with salt	blue		tin with ammonia	golden yellow
privet (clippings)	alum	tan		copper and alum with ammonia	grayed olive green
	tin	deep gold			
	copper sulfate	green		copper and tin with ammonia	yellow-brown
	copper and tin with ammonia	golden brown			
	chrome	tan to gold	sedge grass	alum	yellow-green to tan
privet, wild (or ironwood—berries)	alum	tan		chrome	gold
	tin	dark brown		copper	gray-green
	alum with ammonia	grayed gold	seaweed or dulse (spring)	alum with ammonia	yellow-fawn
	tin with ammonia	brass		tin with ammonia	red-brown
	alum with oxalic acid	dusty rose	sheep's sorrel	alum	soft pink
	tin with oxalic acid	dark grayed brown		chrome	mushroom pink
	copper and alum	dark grayed green	smartweed	alum	yellow-green
	copper and tin	dark grayed brown	solomon seal (leaves)	alum	green
purslane, garden	alum	beige	spiderwort (blossoms)	alum	blue
Queen Anne's lace (wild carrot)	alum	pale yellow	sumac (leaves and berries)	alum	tan
	chrome	tan		copper sulfate	green
ragweed (young)	alum	green		copper	gray or gray-brown
	copper and alum	dark green	sycamore (fruit)	alum	gray-yellow
rose bush cuttings	alum	tan	tansy (flower heads)	alum	green-yellow
	copper	green to brown-black		tin	brown
rose bush (wild, fall)	alum	gray to brown	thistle, Russian (entire young plant)	no mordant, but yarn and plant soak together one week while plant ferments	dull olive green
rose hips	alum	grayed rose			
	tin	gold			
rudbeckia (flower heads)	alum	green			
	chrome	green-gold			
saffron (flowers or powder)	alum	yellow	thyme foliage (fall)	alum	grayed gold
salvia (plant with blossoms, fall)	alum or tin	pale yellow		tin	yellow
	tin with ammonia	grayed gold		alum with ammonia	brass
	alum or tin with oxalic acid	peach		tin with ammonia	gold

Material	Mordant(s)	Colors produced	Material	Mordant(s)	Colors produced
thyme foliage (cont'd.)	alum with oxalic acid	grayed red-orange	wahoo (cont'd.)	tin	deep yellow-orange
	tin with oxalic acid	yellow-brown		alum with ammonia	golden yellow
	copper and alum	bronze		tin with ammonia	deep yellow-orange
	copper and tin	grayed red-orange		copper and alum with ammonia	brass
tomato plant (before frost)	tin	clear yellow		copper and tin with ammonia	golden brown
	alum with ammonia	grayed yellow			
	tin with ammonia	grayed golden yellow	walnut, black (hulls)	alum	brown and tan
	copper and alum	cool gray		no mordant	brown
				copper	black and gray
	copper and tin	deep yellow		alum with oxalic acid	red-brown
tulip (petals)	alum	beige and yellow	willow (leaves)	alum	yellow
	oxalic acid	red	willow (bark)	alum or chrome	gold to orange-red and brown
tulip tree (leaves)	chrome	gold			
turmeric	alum	yellow	yarrow	copper	green
wahoo (berries, fall)	alum	pale yellow-orange			

Patterning or printing is a method of selectively introducing color or some other effect into fiber products. By adding color only in certain predetermined areas, one creates a design. It is possible to print yarns—warp or weft or both—before interlacing them, or to print constructed fabrics, whether hand or machine woven.

There are three broad categories of printing: *resist printing*, in which color is applied to all areas except those that have been treated to prevent absorption; *direct printing*, in which color is applied directly in the specific areas desired; and *screen printing* (sometimes called silkscreen), a variation of the stencil process.

Resist printing usually involves dipping the fabric or mass of yarns in color. The dye absorption is thorough, so the two sides will be almost identical. With direct and stencil printing, however, color is usually applied to one side, and this side will have more intense hues and sharper edges on the pattern areas.

18
Yarn and Fabric Patterning

The Spaniards apparently learned ikat from the Moors during the period of the Islamic Empire. A special type of ikat, called *tela de lengua* (cloth of tongue), is associated with Spain. The name derives from the long "tongues" of color that appear on the finished cloth. This effect was produced by dip-dyeing portions of the white linen warp in indigo and interlacing a weft dyed entirely blue. The result was a random streaking of blue and white.

Examples of ikat-patterned cloth have been found in the Americas, but it is not known whether the technique was carried by the *conquistadores* or had been developed previously by the Indians. The Peruvian fabric in Figure 517 is dated roughly to the time of Pizarro's arrival.

Japanese kasuri or kashiri is usually a double ikat, and the patterns are produced in a variety of ways. One ingenious method for controlling the color of the weft involved weaving a fabric with a very coarse warp. The weft yarns were then dyed, the cloth was unraveled, and the colored weft was used to weave another fabric of the same dimen-

above: 515. Lia Cook. *Interweave II,* detail. 1975. Space-dyed photographic weaving, 8 × 4′ (2.4 × 1.2 m). Courtesy the artist.

right: 516. Lia Cook. *Space-Dyed Photographic Weaving,* detail. 1975. Space-dyed cotton yarns woven and stuffed with polyurethane foam. Courtesy the artist.

Resist Patterning of Yarns: Ikat

Ikat is a very old technique that probably originated in Southeast Asia or in India. The process involves resist dyeing portions of the warp or weft yarns after they have been measured but before they are set up on the loom (Figs. 515, 516). When both the warp and weft are patterned, the result is called *double ikat.*

sion. Sometimes the yarns were pressed between boards that had been carved with relief designs, so that when the yarn was immersed in the dye bath, only the background received color. The most meticulous control was exercised by hand rubbing color into selected portions of the yarn. Kasuri is still a highly regarded decorative art among Japanese artisans.

In 20th-century Indonesia ikat is associated with a sacred ritual (Fig. 518), so it is difficult for an outsider to learn the methods practiced in that region. Native Indonesians have been known to err deliberately, rather than disclose a dyeing or weaving secret. Only by trial-and-error experimentation, combined with bits of information gleaned from observation and from the literature, have Westerners been able to duplicate the results.

There is no single procedure for developing an ikat. You must discover the methods that work best for you. The techniques described on the following pages have been proved successful and can be adapted, when necessary, to the needs of a particular project.

above: 517. Warp-ikat fabric, Peru. 13th–16th century. Cotton. American Museum of Natural History, New York.

right: 518. Double-ikat-printed shroud, Dutch East Indies. Late 19th century. Metropolitan Museum of Art, New York (Rogers Fund, 1930).

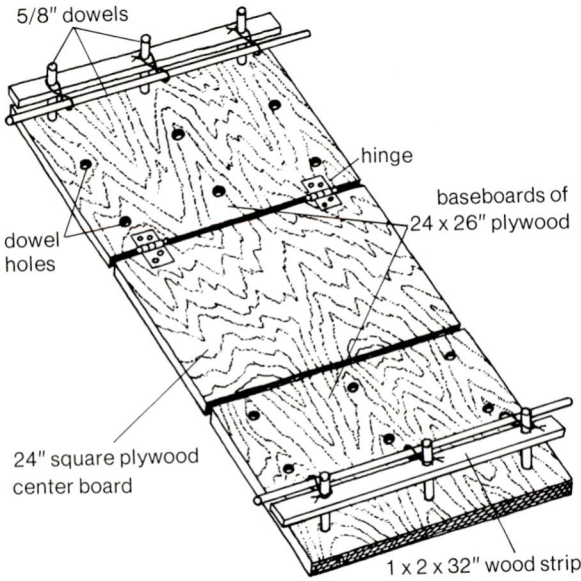

5/8" dowels

hinge

baseboards of
24 x 26" plywood

dowel
holes

24" square plywood
center board

1 x 2 x 32" wood strip

Warp Ikat

The yarns for a warp ikat must be strong, dye receptive, and dimensionally stable. Both natural and synthetic fiber yarns are acceptable, but natural-fiber yarns must be scoured to remove any trace of grease or soil.

You must take extreme care in preparing the warp yarns to make sure they will remain in the same relative positions when threaded on the loom. It is best to warp with one yarn at a time and to make small bouts of 25 to 50 ends each. The length of each warp yarn must, of course, allow for loom waste beyond the pattern area (see p. 110). The cross ties should be loose, so they will not interfere with dye absorption, but a very tight choke tie should be made at each end. These knots will help prevent the yarns from shifting during the dyeing, drying, and loom-dressing.

For your first ikat project a warp length of about 1 to 1½ yards (or roughly 1 meter) will be convenient to handle yet give adequate space in which to design. The longer the warp, the more difficult it is to keep the yarns in their proper order. When the warp is fairly long and/or wide, a series of string guides threaded across will help to control the positions of individual yarns. A loose twining from edge to edge works well, and you can make rows of twining at intervals in the length of the warp. The guide strings should be white or natural in color so as not to stain the warp yarns.

The Frame A stretch frame of some sort is recommended for keeping the yarns aligned before and after dyeing. One design for such a frame requires the following materials:

two pieces of ½-inch plywood, each 24 by 26 inches (60 × 65 cm)

left: 519. The yarn for warp ikat is easier to handle before and after dyeing if it is stretched on a frame.

below: 520. Resists of nonabsorbent material cover sections of the yarn that are not to receive a particular color. Here different-colored balloons serve as a code to indicate which resists should be removed for each dye bath.

one piece of ½-inch plywood, 24 inches (60 cm) square

four metal hinges, with screws

two wooden lath strips, each 1 inch by 2 inches by 32 inches (2.5 × 5 × 80 cm)

six 6-inch lengths of ⅝-inch dowel (15-cm lengths of 1.5-cm dowel)

two 36-inch lengths of ⅝-inch dowel (90-cm length of 1.5-cm dowel)

To construct the frame, drill nine $5/8$-inch (or 1.5 cm) holes in each of the two larger sections of plywood, as in Figure 519. Then, hinge the three sections together, allowing a maximum warp length of 76 inches (1.9 m). Drill each of the two wood laths with three holes to correspond to a row of holes in the plywood.

When you remove the warp from the warping frame, do not make any cut, so that you have a loop at each end. Slip one of the longer dowels through each loop, and lash the dowel to a wooden lath strip. Fit the lath over three of the small dowels set in the row of holes appropriate for the warp length.

The Resists   Warp patterning may require several stages, depending upon how many colors you want. Only one color can be added at a time. The dyeing can proceed either from dark to light or from light to dark, and usually the choice will be governed by the type of resist you plan to use. Since ikat is a resist technique, certain areas of the yarns are prevented from absorbing color, while only the untreated portions are exposed to the dye. Two popular devices are nonporous materials tied to the yarns and a nonabsorbent substance painted on the yarns.

A time-honored method for stopping out the absorption of color in selected areas is to tie non-porous materials—rubber ballons, rubber bands, plastic strips, pieces of inner tube, and so forth—around the sections that are not to receive a particular color (Fig. 520). Strips of plastic from dry-cleaner bags or grocery produce bags work well. Dyeing usually proceeds from the darkest to the lightest color.

For the first dye bath all areas of the warp except those meant to receive the darkest color are covered with the resists. The areas planned for the next-darkest color are uncovered before the second dye bath, and so on until all the colors have been added and all the resists removed. It is wise to code the resists associated with each dye bath, so that only the correct ones are eliminated at each stage.

When a portion of the yarn is top dyed—that is, when a previously dyed section of the warp is exposed to a second or third dye bath—the results are occasionally unpredictable. For example, when the first dye bath is dark blue and a subsequent bath is yellow, the dark blue area of the yarn may assume a greenish cast. It is a good idea to test a small sample of yarn in each dye bath before immersing the entire warp, so that any problems can be corrected. In some cases you may need to reapply a resist to the portions of the warp that have already been dyed with darker colors, so that later dye baths will not contaminate them.

The other major way of creating resists is to paint or stamp a substance onto the yarns. A commercial material called Remyzist, a mixture of organic materials, is often used for this purpose. Remyzist is soluble in cold water but becomes insoluble when the water temperature exceeds 135°F (57°C). Thus, it works well for heated dyes.

When you are working with Remyzist or a similar substance, the dyeing generally progresses from light to dark. This method involves much more color mixing, because it is cumulative: all but the first color is a buildup from those that have been applied before. For the first (lightest) dye bath, no resists are put on the yarns. When that color has dried, the stop-out is painted only on the areas that are to show that first color, and the second dye bath colors all the remaining portions. This procedure continues, with stop-out covering increasingly greater sections of the yarn, until the last color is reached. Each dye bath should be at least 150°F (65°C) when the yarns are entered.

Procedure for Warp Ikat   The first step in ikat dyeing is to plan the pattern of the resists. This is best carried out on the stretcher frame. Sometimes a cut paper cartoon is used to transfer a design to the yarns. Sheets of paper from which the pattern for each color has been cut out are placed in turn on the stretched yarns, and the design is traced in pencil as a guide for applying the resists. If you are working from dark to light, you must apply all the resists before the first dye bath. After dyeing, rinse the yarn thoroughly and stretch it on the frame—which is protected with plastic—to dry. Then, either remove or apply resists for the next dye bath.

With the plastic-ties method, all the resists will be off after the last dye bath. If you are using Remyzist, most of the warp will be covered with resist. You can remove it by rinsing the yarns in cold water, rubbing lightly if necessary.

With any dyeing procedure, prevention of errors is much easier than correction. However, if you should make a mistake—or if the resists should slip causing colors to bleed—you can remove the color by soaking the affected portion of the yarn in a commercial color stripper.

Ikat warps are more efficiently beamed from the front to the back of the loom (see pp. 126–127), so that any yarn slippage that may occur can be rectified. First attach the warp yarns to the cloth beam, then cut and thread them through the reed and heddles. Before you tie the warp to the warp beam, check to make sure the design has not shifted. Then, carefully roll back the entire warp.

You will probably want to choose a weaving pattern that is warp faced, in order to best exploit the design of the warp ikat (Figs. 521, 522; Pl. 22, p. 238; Pl. 25, p. 288). Warp ikat designs are often so striking that they can stand alone, with very little weft interlacement. The coloration itself, rather than any weaving pattern, is the major design interest.

Weft Ikat

The dyeing process for a weft ikat is much the same as that for a warp. However, before stretching the yarns on a frame to tie the resists, you must calculate the length of each weft yarn. You can either estimate this length roughly, allowing a percentage for weft take-up (see p. 111), or, for greater accuracy, weave a small sample to the same width as the projected fabric and then unravel it slightly to measure the length of each weft shot. Once you know the distance, the weft yarns can be measured on a warping frame and then placed on the stretcher.

You should make a cross in this weft during winding, just as you would for a warp (see p. 112) in order to maintain the correct orientation of yarns. Tie a loose cord at either side of the cross.

The weft yarn for a narrow fabric can be wrapped around a small sheet of Plexiglas and then painted with Remyzist for the resist. If you use this system, you can dye the yarn without removing it from the Plexiglas. However, the fact that adjacent wefts are on opposite sides of the Plexiglas makes patterning difficult. Such a procedure might be practical for a double weave.

The weaving process for a weft ikat requires very careful attention, to ensure that the patterned area of the weft falls exactly where you want it.

above: 521. Joan Sterrenburg.
Plaited Ikat VI. 1975.
Resist-dyed wool
and mohair yarns,
woven into strips
and then plaited;
9 × 4' (2.7 × 1.2 m).
Courtesy the artist.

right: 522. James W. Bassler.
*Ikat—Blue, Black,
Orange, and White,* detail. 1976.
Silk and wool warp ikat,
8' × 7'6'' (2.4 × 2.3 m) overall.
Courtesy the artist.

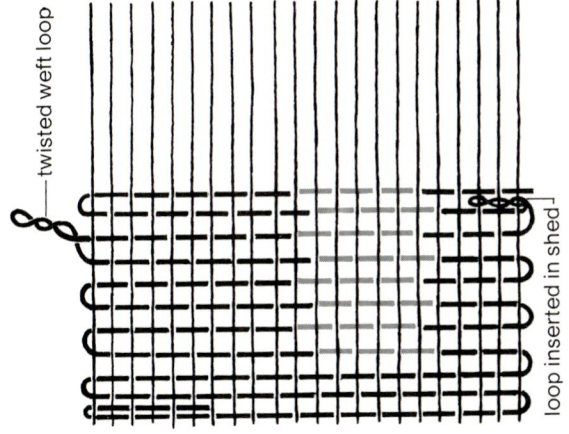

twisted weft loop

loop inserted in shed

You must usually sacrifice perfect selvedges in order to arrive at the desired effect. If a very long loop projects beyond the selvedge once the weft is positioned, the loop can be twisted and inserted back into the shed before beating (Fig. 523). This procedure was followed by the Indians and the peoples of Southeast Asia even in their finest ikats. The weave pattern for a weft ikat is, of course, weft faced (Fig. 524).

While most ikats are planned for a definite pattern, in some cases the ikat process is used to produce a random textured effect (Fig. 525). This device is equally successful when the printing is in the warp.

above: 523.
To control the pattern in a weft ikat, loops of yarn are often twisted and inserted back into the fabric.

right: 524.
Huipile with weft ikat, detail, from Guatemala. Weft-face twill. Textiles and Clothing Department Collection, Iowa State University, Ames.

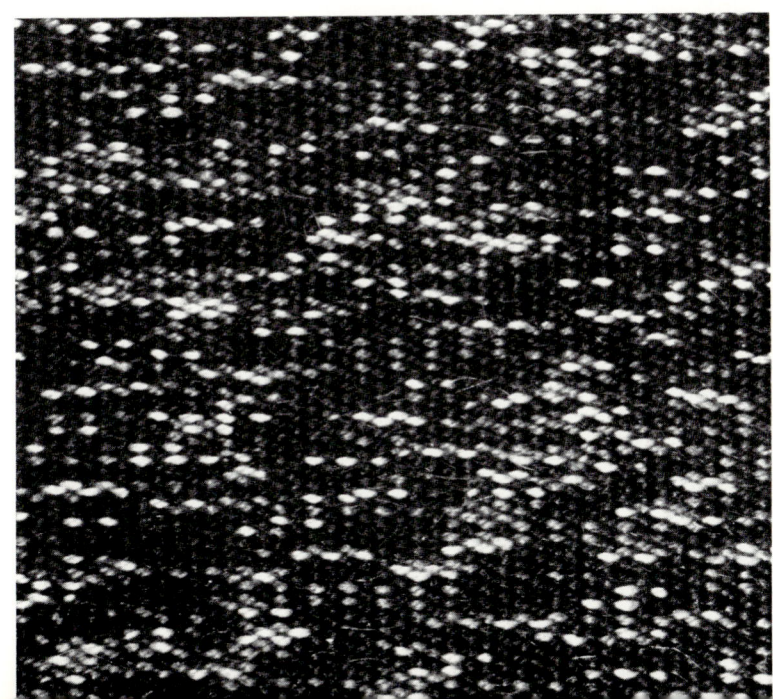

525. Weft ikat printing can be used to produce a random textured surface.

526. Mary Ehlers Mathews.
Double ikat hanging, detail. 1970.
Plain weave in linen.
Courtesy the artist.

Double Ikat

The double ikat combines the two techniques described above to produce a pattern in both the warp and the weft (Fig. 526). To make this method work, you must take the utmost care so that the design coincides in both sets of yarns.

Ikat with Dyed Yarns

Traditionally, ikat has been used on natural or bleached yarns. All color is introduced through the ikat process. However, interesting effects can also be obtained by ikat-patterning previously dyed yarns. For example, you could overdye yarns that are all of one hue but several different values (see Chap. 19) to produce a shaded pattern. In this method you must take special care in selecting the dye or dyes for the ikat, in order to predict how the various colors and the two types of dye will interact. Often, only one dye bath is sufficient to give the yarns a striking pattern.

Bleached Ikat

Previously dyed yarns can also be ikat-patterned by bleaching. Resists are applied to the areas of the yarn where you do not want color *removed*. Either the plastic ties or the Remyzist method will work, but with Remyzist the bleach solution must be heated to 150°F (65°C).

Before attempting a bleached ikat, you must test the yarns to determine the length of time and the strength of the bleach solution required to get the desired result. Some colors go to white, some become grayer as well as lighter, while others change to new related hues. Orange, when bleached, sometimes becomes yellow. Blues are the most perishable (that is, the most readily bleached) and the yellows most stable of the colors. Different yarns bleach at different rates, depending upon their fiber structure and the dyes used. This is important to remember when combining two or more yarns—for example, a nylon and a wool—for bleaching.

You should make tests with several different concentrations of bleach. Full strength is the 5- to 6-percent sodium hypochlorite found in the typical chlorine bleach sold for household use. Some yarns lose their color too quickly at this strength to be of use to the artist, so you will probably want to cut the bleach with one or more parts of plain water. The time needed to get the bleach effect can vary from less than a minute to an hour or more.

After bleaching, rinse the yarns thoroughly. If you follow the Remyzist method, rinse in hot water first to stop the bleach action before attempting to remove the resist in cold water. A small amount of vinegar in one of the later rinse waters will help to counteract the bleach.

Bleached ikat is often a one-step process, but you can also redye parts of the yarn after they have been bleached. Be sure that all the bleach has been neutralized before adding more dye.

Resist Dye Process: Tie-Dye

The tie-dyeing of fabrics works on the same principle as ikat-patterning of yarns. Portions of the fabric are tied to create a resist, and then the entire piece of fabric (or a portion) is dip-dyed.

To create the pattern areas, sections of the fabric are gathered, folded, pleated, or bunched together and then tied tightly with rubber bands (Fig. 527). You can also use waxed string, but the rubber bands are somewhat easier to put on and remove. Often, small items, such as marbles, pebbles, or beads, are tied in with the fabric. After dyeing, there will be an effect of concentric circles or rings (Fig. 528). The tiny circle-and-dot pattern seen in some forms of tie-dye is called *plangi*. In India entire fabrics of plangi have been made by picking up and tying the tiniest bits of fabric in an allover pattern.

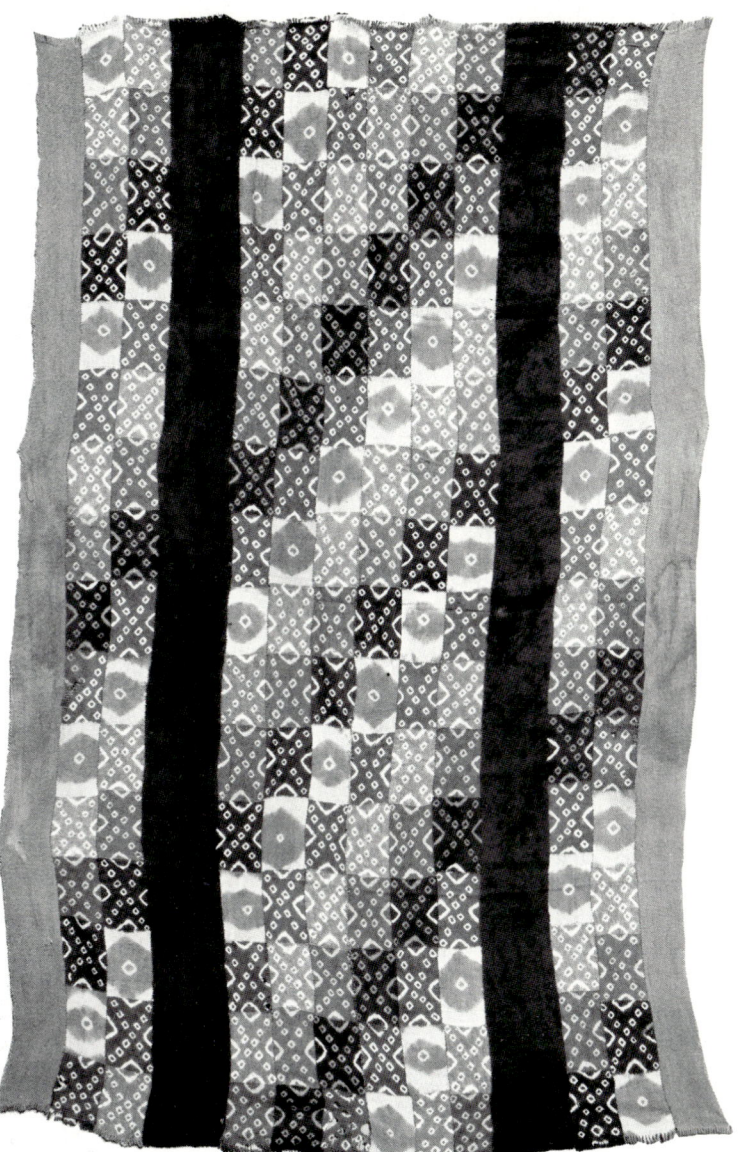

above: 527. For tie-dyeing, the fabric is gathered and tied very tightly in the areas that are to resist color.

right: 528. Mantle, Peru, Middle Horizon (A.D. c. 50–900). Strips of alpaca plain weave, with tie-dyed rectangles. Textile Museum, Washington, D.C.

Tritik is a special kind of tie-dye resist technique done by stitching. Design lines are drawn on the fabric, and then stitched over with long stitches by hand or machine. Then, the stitches are drawn up to create a compact mass of fabric, and dye absorption is prevented in the immediate area of the stitching (Fig. 529).

Another variation of the resist dye method is *clamp resist*, which uses clamps to draw the fabric together to prevent dye absorption (Pl. 26, p. 288).

Resist Dye Process: Batik

Batik is a patterning method that employs wax or a similar nonporous material for the resist. Liquid wax is painted or brushed onto the fabric according to a planned design, then allowed to harden, after which the fabric is immersed in dye. When there are several colors involved, more wax can be added after each dye bath. After the dyeing process is finished, the wax is removed by boiling the fabric in water. Some people use other substances for batik work, such as a starch-paste material, but wax is most common.

The fabric for batik must be chosen with consideration for both the original color and the fiber content. The fabric need not be white, but it must be light enough in value to accept overdyeing. Most synthetic-fiber fabrics, with the exception of rayon, do not dye easily. Silk is perhaps most often used for batik work, but cotton and linen can also be batik-patterned successfully. The fabric should be washed thoroughly to remove any starch or sizing applied by the manufacturer.

Applying the Wax Resist The wax for batik work is sold in commercial preparations. Normally, it is a mixture of 1 part beeswax to 2 or 3 parts paraffin. Before application, it must be heated to about 250°F (120°C). It is not advisable to heat the wax to temperatures higher than 280°F (140°C), because the wax penetration will be too rapid to allow control. You must take great precautions in heating the wax to avoid burns. The pan should be heavy and have a broad, thick base and no long handles that could cause tipping. Keep a pan lid nearby, so that if the wax should become too hot and ignite you can quickly smother the flames. Wax that is too hot will smoke, froth, and sizzle when the brush is inserted.

Brushes in various sizes make good applicators for the wax. Also available are special batik tools that hold a small reservoir of wax and are capable of drawing fine lines and making small dots.

Some artists work from cartoons and transfer the design to the fabric in pencil before beginning to apply the wax. However, many people today prefer to design directly on the cloth, which allows for great freedom in expression.

In preparation for applying the resist you can either lay the fabric on a flat surface or hold it taut by tacking to a simple wooden frame. Often both sides of the fabric are coated to ensure complete stopping out.

The Dye Procedure Batik presents a special problem in dye selection, because the dyes must be used cold to prevent melting the wax. Most supply houses offer dyes formulated for batik work. The fiber-reactive dyes described in Chapter 17 work especially well on cellulosic fibers (cotton, rayon, and linen) but are difficult to use on

529. In the tritik method, the fabric is stitched and drawn together to create a resist. Courtesy James W. Bassler.

530. Catherine E. Milovich. *Untitled.*
Batik on handwoven Indian silk,
using fiber-reactive dyes;
9′ × 3′9″ (2.7 × 1.1 m).
Courtesy the artist.

silk. As with other patterning processes, you should make a series of test samples before committing the entire fabric. Properly documented, these samples can serve as useful guides for future work in batik.

For a multicolor work, the dye baths usually progress from lightest color to darkest. The first color is applied to all or nearly all of the fabric, and then wax is painted on the areas that are not to receive the second color. Increasing amounts of resist are added before each dye bath, until the cloth is nearly covered. This process involves considerable color mixing.

If you want to reverse the order of dyeing and work from dark to light (or to dye each color individually with no mixing), you must remove the wax after each bath and reapply it in other areas.

Removing the Wax   Thick layers of wax can be removed by scraping. You can also place the fabric between layers of newspaper and iron it. To remove any wax residue from the fabric, boil it in water. You can recover the wax for future use by skimming it off the top when the water has cooled. Some artists like to leave a thin film of wax in textiles meant for hanging, because the wax makes colors more luminous as light passes through them. A bit of wax also gives body to the cloth.

Design Variations in Batik

Considerable variation is possible in batik designs (Fig. 530). For instance, if you crumple or fold the fabric before immersing it in the dye bath, the wax will crack, allowing dye to penetrate in thin lines.

This technique can be used to create a crackle effect. Another possible variation involves dipping the entire fabric in wax, allowing it to dry, and then scratching through it with a fine, blunt-ended instrument to allow dye penetration in those areas. A textured background can be achieved by splattering the wax onto the cloth.

Direct Printing on Fabric or Yarns

Direct printing is, in fact, the most "direct" method of applying color to fiber. It involves simply stamping or rolling color onto the yarns or fabrics in selected areas. Usually, direct-printed designs are repeat designs, with the size of the repeat governed by the size of the applicator. However, there is nothing to prevent you from simply painting dye onto the fabric in any free-form design you choose.

The most common hand process for direct printing is *block printing*, in which the design is stamped onto the fabric from a block of wood, linoleum, or some other material into which the design has been carved in relief. Wood blocks, linoleum blocks, and carving tools are readily available from craft-supply outlets. Wood provides the most durable surface, capable of standing up and holding detail for a great many impressions. However, if your carving skill is limited, you may prefer to work with the softer linoleum.

Designs for block printing are usually fairly simple (Fig. 531), because the carving process makes fine detail difficult for all but the most experienced carvers. The designs take much of their interest from the repeat pattern.

A simple block print can be made in the following manner. Draw the design directly on the block, bearing in mind that it will print in *reverse*. Carve away from the block all the portions that you do not want to print. The design will then stand out in relief. Roll viscous dye onto the block, and then press it directly onto the fabric or yarns.

Screen Printing on Fabric or Yarns

Screen printing is a very straightforward method of transferring designs to a surface. Recent developments in the technique have greatly expanded its sophistication, both in terms of the kind of imagery it can produce and the method of applying images to the screen. If you expect to become deeply involved in screen printing work, you should consult a text devoted to the method. However, you can experiment with a few simple materials and procedures.

Screen printing is a development from *stencil printing*, in which a precut pattern is placed upon the surface to be printed; one traces around or inside the pattern to transfer the design. For screen printing, a fabric mesh—traditionally of silk

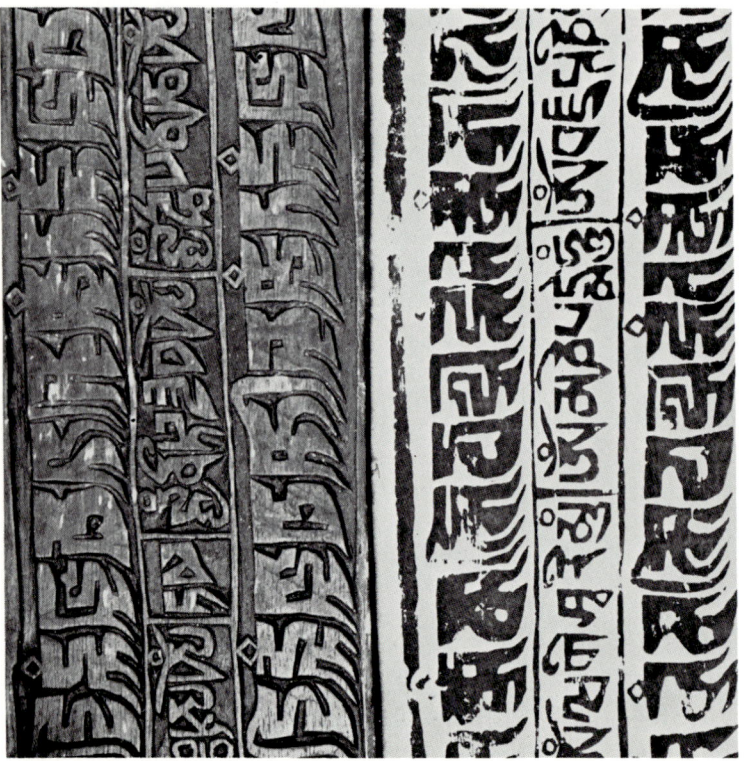

531. A wood block (*left*) and the fabric printed from it (*right*).

but now more commonly of nylon or polyester—is stretched tightly in a frame, and all the areas that are *not* to print are stopped out with a substance that closes the pores in the mesh. Next, the frame is placed over the printing surface, and a thick, viscous dye or textile paint is forced through the screen. The dye penetrates the screen only in the portions that have not been coated, and thus a design is transferred to the fabric.

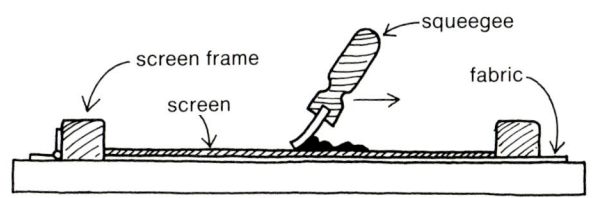

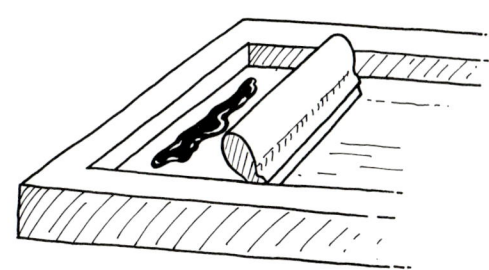

532. In screen printing, a squeegee drawn across the screen forces dye through the pores in the screen mesh to the fabric beneath.

The Screen   Most people who do a lot of screen printing work make their own screen frames, but ready-made screens can be purchased in a variety of sizes and with screen meshes of varying densities. If you plan to make a multicolor design, it is more efficient to have one screen for each of the colors to be used.

Preparing the Screen   There are numerous methods for fixing the image to be printed on the screen mesh. One of the simplest calls for the following materials:

glue (such as Lepages Original Glue, Franklin Hide Glue, or similar products)
shellac
poster or watercolor paint
alcohol or acetone
brush
cardboard

Preparing the Screen

□ Place the drawing of the design you wish to reproduce under the screen.

□ Mix a little poster paint with the glue to make it visible.

□ With a brush dipped in glue, coat the screen in all the *positive* printing areas from the drawing.

□ When the glue has dried, coat the entire screen with shellac, using a small piece of cardboard to spread it.

□ Once the shellac has dried, wash out the glue with a spray of cold water. The shellac also will lift in the areas that were covered by the glue, so that you will have a screen with the image areas open and the background areas stopped out with shellac.

□ Hold the screen up to the light, and make sure that all the nonprinting areas are completely blocked. If there are pinholes, touch them up with a brush dipped in shellac. (The alcohol or acetone is used to remove the shellac from the screen once the printing is completed.)

The Dye   Commercially sold textile paint is excellent for making the print. You can also use one of the fiber-reactive dyes described in Chapter 17, provided you add a thickening agent. A simple gum tragacanth thickener can be made from:

7 parts gum tragacanth
100 parts water

Sprinkle the powdered tragacanth over the water, and leave it for 2 or 3 days to absorb the moisture. Then, heat the mixture in a double boiler for 8 hours at a temperature of 150°F (66°C). This thickener can be mixed with the fiber-reactive dyes and will not affect the colors.

Printing on Fabric   To print through the screen onto fabric, you need only stretch the fabric taut on a flat, waterproof table and place the screen on top in the area where you want the image. With a *squeegee*—a tool that has a sharp rubber blade attached to a handle—spread the dye over the entire area of the screen (Fig. 532). The dye will penetrate to the fabric only in the areas left open on the screen.

Printing on Warp Yarns   A warp is best printed after it has been installed on the loom.

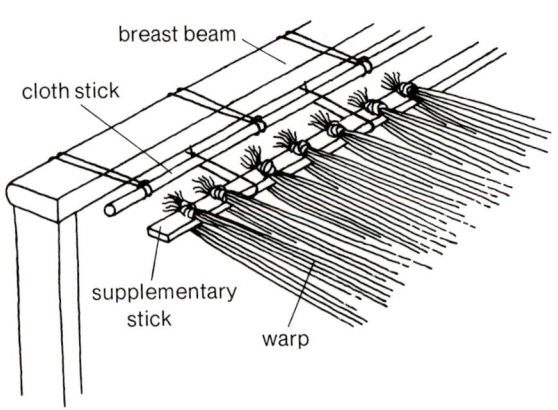

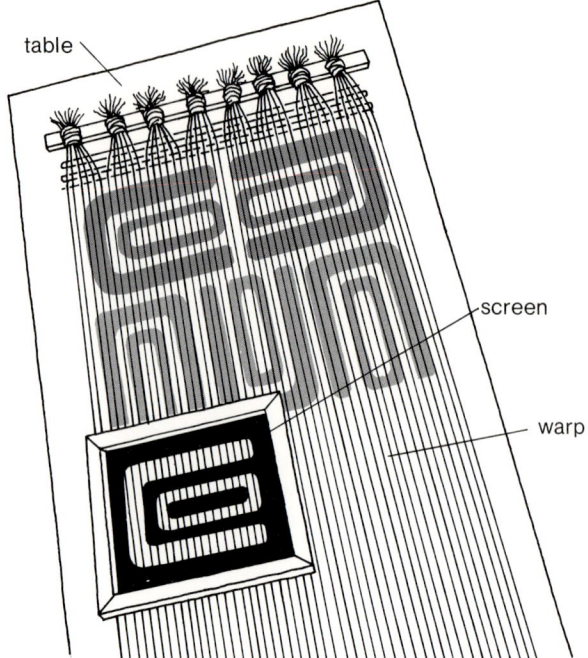

above: **533.** A warp that is to be screen printed should be attached to a supplementary cloth stick, which is in turn tied to the cloth stick of the loom. This system permits easy removal and reattachment of the warp yarns.

right: **534.** The screen is placed on the warp, and paint or dye is forced through it.

Arranging the Warp for Printing

☐ Attach the warp yarns to the warp stick individually with lark's-head knots (Fig. 194) to inhibit the slippage of the yarns.

☐ Beam, thread, and sley the warp yarns in the usual manner (see Chap. 8).

☐ Instead of attaching the cut ends directly to the cloth stick, tie them to a supplementary metal or wooden rod, and then tie this rod to the cloth stick (Fig. 533). This permits easy removal and reattachment of the warp yarns.

☐ After you have dressed the loom and adjusted the warp tension at the cloth stick, remove the cords joining the supplemental rod to the cloth stick.

☐ Unwind the yarn from the warp beam, and extend it to its full length on a waterproof table in front of the loom.

☐ Arrange the yarns carefully, so that the horizontal spacing is, as nearly as possible, equal to the sleyed width at the reed.

☐ Place the screen on the warp, and force the dye through with a squeegee (Fig. 534).

When more than one color is to be printed, the several screens must be *registered* or aligned, so that all the colors printed in a given portion of the warp fall in the proper relation to one another. A simple method of registering the screens is to affix small pieces of tape to the table under the warp and line up each screen with the tape marks. Take care to avoid moving the warp when you position or lift the screens.

After the warp has been printed, allow the paint or dye to dry completely. Then, roll the warp carefully back onto the warp beam, and reattach the supplementary rod to the cloth stick.

There is almost always a certain amount of yarn slippage during the beaming and weaving processes, which causes the sharp outlines to become blurred. For this reason, large, simple designs are often the most successful. You will probably want to select a warp-face weaving pattern to allow the design to show to best advantage. Because the yarns invariably rotate to some extent during weaving, the pattern is nearly as complete on the reverse side as on the face. You can take advantage of this effect in a room divider or other freestanding project.

V

Design
in the
Fiber Arts

Throughout this text the word *design* has been used rather freely, often as a synonym for pattern or motif. No attempt has been made to establish a definition for the concept. In fact, it is in some ways more difficult to *explain* design than it is to *do* it. However, before attempting to catalogue the components of design and the principles that govern its implementation, we must clarify our terminology. Therefore, for purposes of this discussion, design is defined as *the ordered arrangement of parts to make a whole.* The *parts*, in this case, are the raw materials of weaving—the fibers, yarns, and miscellaneous objects weavers have at their disposal. The *whole* is, of course, the finished product—the wall hanging, sculpture, garment, yardage, or whatever. Order*ed* does not necessarily mean order*ly*, for a tangled mass of yarns may in fact be planned and therefore designed (Fig. 540).

It is impossible to make anything without designing it, either consciously or unconsciously, for design implies a series of choices: the choice of one yarn over another, the choice of one color

19
Elements
and Principles
of Design

535. **Joan Michaels Paque.** *Intersections.* 1977.
Wall relief structure in synthetic fibers.
Courtesy the artist.

instead of a second, the choice of a particular size or shape. The weaver's concern is not with designing *per se*, but with creating an *effective* design—one that fulfills the requirements of the item to be woven and that at the same time satisfies the artist's aesthetic goals.

Design is sometimes divided into two categories—*structural* and *decorative*. The first refers to the inner skeleton, the "body" of an object, the second to its surface treatment or embellishment, which can be varied without modifying the structure itself. Yet structural and decorative design are inseparable; neither can exist without the other. One cannot embellish the surface of nothing, nor can one create a structure with no surface, and that surface must have some degree of decorative design, however simple. Weaving exemplifies this bond especially well, for both structural and decorative design are carried by the yarns. If the two kinds of design are to be divided at all, it is only to illustrate their very intimate connection, for effective design results only when decoration expresses structure and structure supports decoration.

A concept related to design is that of *form*, which at one time was considered to be synonymous with shape. However, the form of an object encompasses not only its external shape but its inner structure, the mode of expression, the interrelationship of parts.

We often hear the expression "form follows function." This means that a work of art or industry is not successful if it does not fulfill the purpose for which it is intended. Thus, for example,

an umbrella that is physically beautiful but does not keep out the rain is not effectively designed; a chair that is so overdecorated that it discourages sitting fails in its function and therefore in its form. In weaving this notion is best understood in terms of functional objects—place mats, bedspreads, garments, and the like. A furry, high-pile place mat might be interesting and amusing and even attractive, but it would certainly cause the dishes to wobble about. Moreover, such considerations are equally relevant to nonutilitarian items. A wall hanging planned for a particular spot is not effective if its design is so striking that it dominates the whole room, unless, of course, the sole purpose of the room is to display that particular wall hanging.

In creating a woven object—or indeed, anything at all—the individual must work with certain visual elements: shape, line, space, texture, light, and color. Actually, such "elements" can be isolated only in theory; in practice they are inextricably bound together. Shape cannot exist without establishing a line, and color is meaningless in the absence of light. Space is delineated by the presence of shapes and lines. Nevertheless, one must identify these elements in order to see their relationships in a work of art.

Design Elements

Shape

The shape of any object is fairly self-evident. Terms such as round, square, oval, or cubic are generally understood (Fig. 535). Certain of the items a weaver will undertake to produce have their shapes predetermined: a place mat is usually rectangular within a limited range of size; a tablecloth must cover the table; a garment conforms generally to the outlines of the body. But what of a sculpture or wall hanging? Will it be two- or three-dimensional, rigidly geometric or free form? In planning—that is, in designing—the shape of an object the weaver must take into account the limitations of equipment and materials.

A loom-constructed web will have its size and shape restricted to some extent by the size and complexity of the loom. A very fine yarn may be unable to support a large sculptural construction. When a weaving contains pictorial elements, its shape can either control or be controlled by those

536. Arleen Schloss.
Ceiba in Fawn I. 1973.
Ramie and latex,
10′ × 8′2″ (3 × 2.5 m).
Courtesy the artist.

elements. For instance, the narrative scenes of 17th-century tapestries are contained by the traditional square or oblong shape of the fabric (Fig. 100). All action exists within those perimeters. On the other hand, the figure in a tapestry may actually control the outline of the weaving (Fig. 325). In the end, the shape of a woven object is successful if it fulfills the purpose—functional, aesthetic, or both—that object is to serve.

Line

Line is closely related to shape, for the external contours of an object create a line. In basic math-

ematical terms, a line is an extension of a point. It can move in any direction, be straight, curved, or convoluted. A woven object displays many kinds of lines. When the warp and weft yarns are heavy, contrasting in color, or loosely woven, they can produce a distinct line (Fig. 536). By comparison, the warp and weft in the tapestry shown as Figure 537 are so tightly meshed as to be imperceptible except at very close range. This is essential to the amusing trompe l'œil subject.

We often speak of the *quality* of a line, the characteristics implied by such adjectives as broad, narrow, bold, sketchy, crisp, delicate, smooth, and so forth. When the warp and weft

537. Archie Brennan.
Kitchen Range. 1974.
Tapestry weave
in cotton and wool,
40 × 52″ (100 × 130 cm).
Collection Michael Laird,
Edinburgh.

above: **538. Marguerite Carau.** *Yellow with White Band and Opening.* 1974.
Sisal, 6′ × 6′1″ (1.79 × 1.83 m). Courtesy the artist.

below: **539. Marguerite Carau.** *Ivory with Yellow Angle.* 1976.
Sisal, 6′ × 6′1″ (1.79 × 1.83 m). Courtesy the artist.

above: 540. *Entanglements*, a participatory event of the *Fiber as Medium* symposium, 1971, cosponsored by the University of California, Los Angeles, and the Pasadena Art Museum.

below: 541. **Maria Chojnacka.** *Diminuendo*, detail. 1975. Sisal. Courtesy the artist. (See also Fig. 598.)

yarns describe a line, the yarns themselves establish its quality. A fine carpet warp is very different in appearance from a slub, chenille, or bouclé yarn, yet each produces a single continuous line. Similarly, the lines created by color, texture, or pattern areas can exhibit many different qualities. Another variable of lines is their *direction*—vertical, horizontal, diagonal. In general, horizontal lines are associated with calmness and repose, vertical lines with force and stability, and diagonal lines with action, interrupted motion, or anxiety. A diagonal line seems to possess more energy than a horizontal line, whereas a line that is slightly off "true" can be disturbing (Figs. 538, 539; Pl. 27, p. 321). Of course, such interpretations are by no means absolute, for the impact of a work is influenced by other factors—color, texture, shape. Line is a very powerful tool, which designers must learn to control for their own purposes.

Space

Space is the three-dimensional volume in which form occurs. It is also the distance between forms, a condition that changes constantly when form is set in motion. Space is often described as *positive* or *negative*, the positive referring to form and the negative to the void between forms. On a flat surface considerations of space involve the relationship of forms to one another and in some cases the impression of three-dimensional space created by

means of perspective and other optical devices (Fig. 537). In a free-form sculpture the problem of space becomes somewhat more complex, for the object's space includes not only the relationship of forms and the area between them but the whole environment of the sculpture. When we approach a large sculptured hanging and move around or inside it, we become part of its space and interact with it in ever-changing ways (Fig. 540).

Texture

Texture refers to the surface quality of an object (Fig. 541). The most obvious form of texture is

542. Barbara Shawcroft.
Group of interchangeable forms.
Crocheted mohair, cotton roving,
wool, and horsehair;
height of tallest form 8″ (20 cm).
Courtesy the artist.

left: **543. Arlene Stimmel.**
Snake Coat. 1974. Crochet,
wool and metallic fibers.
Courtesy the artist.

below: **544. Nathan Shapira**
and **Larsen Design Studio.**
Galaxy. 1969. Hand print on satin.
Jack Lenor Larsen, Inc., New York.

tactile, the feeling of smooth, rough, grainy, hairy, rippled, or whatever that we experience when we run our hands over a surface. If we were to touch one of Barbara Shawcroft's "interchangeable forms" (Fig. 542), our fingers would transmit the sensation of "fuzzy" or "hairy" that the artist has contrived with her use of horsehair, mohair, and rough wool yarns. Yet, in a sense, this texture is *visual,* for we know just by looking at a photograph of Shawcroft's forms more or less what they would feel like. An elaborate learning process begun at birth has trained us to recognize by sight alone textures that are essentially tactile (Fig. 543). Much of the charm of rya rugs, for example, derives from the impression of warmth and luxuriousness that is created when we see them, even before we touch or walk upon them (Pl. 17, p. 204).

There is another class of textures that are predominantly or entirely visual, exemplified by the

Larsen Design Studio's *Galaxy* (Fig. 544). This fabric presents a grainy, pebbled appearance, yet the surface is absolutely smooth to the touch. A more sophisticated interpretation of known facts enables us to translate the sensation of touching a handful of grain or pebbles into a purely visual experience. Texture of this sort is usually created through the use of color or pattern. For example, an all-black or all-white surface provides little visual texture, but by placing black on white or white on black in selected areas or in prearranged patterns, one can simulate a wide variety of textures.

Texture is of great importance in weaving, particularly with utilitarian objects (Fig. 545). A garment or upholstery fabric that is to come in contact with the body must be pleasing to the touch as well as to the eye, or its function is violated. Psychological response to texture is almost as powerful as to color. Certain textures repel us, others make us long to stroke them; furry piles create an impression of warmth, crisp linens and silks a sense of coolness. The designer must be aware of subtle reactions to texture—both visual and tactile—and the way in which it can enhance a work.

Color and Light

Color is by far the most complex of the visual elements. Many scientists have taken as their life's-work the investigation of color phenomena. While the modern textile designer has little need for an in-depth study of color theory, some knowledge of the characteristics of colors, and how they interact, will be useful.

In its purest sense, color is the prismatic breakdown of white light into separate hues—red, orange, yellow, green, blue, and violet (Fig. 546). Black is the absence of light and therefore of color. Strictly speaking, black and white are not colors at all, but since they are used as such in everyday life, they can be considered along with the "real" colors.

Color is implicit in everything, for the eye cannot separate an object from its background unless there is some color contrast. This contrast may be of *hue*, of *value*, or of *intensity*, the three color dimensions that are generally identified.

Hue The pure state of any color is referred to as its *hue*. For example, *red* is the name of a hue, and when we speak of red as a hue we mean a pure red, unmodified and unmixed. A hue is considered *primary* when it cannot be mixed from other colors. Generations of color theorists have disagreed about what the primary hues actually are, although there always seem to be three. To a physi-

above: 545. Dorothy Liebes.
Drapery fabric, detail. c. 1946.
Cotton, wool, chenille,
silk, and metal.

below: 546. Color is
the prismatic breakdown
of white light
into separate hues.

cist red, green, and blue are the basic colors, while in pigments the primaries are magenta, yellow, and turquoise—the bases for mixing all other colors. Despite these differences of opinion, color theory can be understood equally well in any of the various systems.

The traditional color wheel (Pl. 28, p. 321) takes as its primary colors red, yellow, and blue. The combination of two primary colors in the proper amounts will create a *secondary* color, such as orange—the product of red and yellow. *Tertiary* or *intermediate* colors derive from the combination of adjacent primary and secondary colors. Red-orange, yellow-green, and blue-violet are examples of tertiary colors. An infinite range of colors can be produced by combining the primary hues in different proportions—1:1, 1:2, 1:3, 1:4, and so on, until the variations are not discernible even to the eye of a trained colorist.

Value Value is the lightness or darkness of a color. The *normal value* of any hue is the state in which it appears in the prismatic spectrum produced by white light. According to this criterion, yellow is a light color and blue is a dark color. However, any color can exhibit a range of values that deviate from the normal value of the hue. Colors that are lighter than the norm are referred to as *tints*; those that are darker are called *shades*. Pink is a tint—a deviation toward the light end of the spectrum—of red.

Albert Munsell has devised a scale of values that helps to standardize the range of colors and to measure value. On this vertical scale, white is at the top and black at the base. Between the two extremes are seven distinct gradations (Pl. 28, p. 321), referred to as high light, light, low light, middle value, high dark, dark, and low dark. It is possible to establish the normal value of any color in its appropriate position on the value scale. Thus, pure green is the equivalent of low light, while tints or shades of green fall at other points on the scale. Similarly, pure yellow is equal to high light, yellow-green to light, orange to low light, red-orange and blue-green to middle value, red and blue to high dark, red-violet and blue-violet to dark, and violet to low dark. Any variation from these positions constitutes a change of value.

Intensity The third dimension of color is called *intensity, chroma,* or *saturation*. It refers to the relative purity or grayness of a color. A hue can be bright or dull by degrees, depending upon the amount of contamination by a dissimilar color. For example, yellow would contaminate violet, since there is no yellow in pure violet; therefore, a violet with much yellow mixed in would exhibit a *low degree of saturation* (or intensity or chroma). Pure yellow, by contrast, has high intensity. By combining equal parts of the three primary colors, one produces a *neutral*—theoretically gray, but in practice often a muddy brown.

Color in Weaving The textile arts are unique in their use of many fine strands of color. Two or more colors woven intimately into a web tend to merge and blend at a distance. The equal distribution of two yarns that are pure but contrasting in color can result in a neutral color effect. For instance, if a warp is all of orange and a weft entirely blue, the completed fabric may give the impression of a neutral when viewed straight on, but turning the fabric slightly on the bias will cause either blue or orange to emerge as the dominant color. When the hues of warp and weft are vividly contrasting, the mixed color may sparkle.

To the viewer with a trained eye, color can be observed in all but pure black and white. Dull colors or grays nearly always reflect some hue. We speak of "warm" grays that perhaps contain some yellow, or "cool" grays that show traces of green or blue. Neutrals are very important to the contemporary handweaver, but they are seldom mere grays and browns (Pl. 32, p. 339). Like the bark of a weathered tree, the soft neutrals, under close scrutiny, reveal the mellow tones of many colors.

Colors are almost magical in use. If we stare at something red for a few minutes and then look away toward a white surface, we see an afterimage that is green. This effect is produced because the eye becomes color fatigued. For much the same reason, yellow placed against green will not look the same as yellow placed against red.

When two closely related hues are laid side by side, the intensity of each is reduced by means of *simultaneous contrast* (Pl. 29, p. 322). Each original hue becomes cloaked in a veil of its complement and thereby is grayed to a certain extent. On the other hand, when *contrasting* hues are adjacent to one another, each becomes more brilliant, because it has acquired a small portion of the other hue's complement (Pl. 30, p. 322). In general, black tends to make all hues appear more intense. Often, the use of several closely related hues can produce greater sparkle than a single color.

Everyone has intuitive and psychological reactions to color, and the designer can exploit these reactions in choosing the yarns for a particular project. Reds and yellows seem to suggest "warm" (Pl. 31, p. 322), while blues and greens give one an impression of "cool." Light values appear cooler than dark values. In general, warm colors seem more aggressive and advancing; cool colors tend to recede. Dark values are "heavier" than light values. Bright colors have a greater impact on the viewer than dull colors, so a relatively small proportion of bright color can be incorporated into a weaving, and the result will still be stimulating. The association of hues that are all of the same intensity creates the greatest possible force.

There are several ways that colors can be varied without actually changing their hue components. Chief among them is the alteration of surface texture to produce lights and shadows that subtly affect the color. A shiny surface reflects light, while a soft or pile fabric tends to absorb light, thus darkening the color.

The designer will find unlimited inspiration by observing the ways in which color and texture combine in nature. Perhaps the most important thing to know about color is that *any* hue can be employed successfully in a woven object and any two or more colors can be combined, provided their values, intensities, and proportional relationships are handled with sensitivity.

Design Principles

The principles of design are guidelines to be considered in developing a design. They are not rules, for there can be no rules governing imagination and ingenuity. In fact, the skilled designer may deliberately contradict some or all of these principles to create a particular effect. More often, the principles of design will be applied to a work by some critic or viewer *after* the work has been completed, for they are so much a part of the artist's training and background that he or she has unconsciously observed them in tracing the idea. The experienced artist does not mutter, "Now I'm doing proportion," or "It's time to put in some balance." We are much more likely to hear the artist say, "Yes, that works," or "That doesn't work." Whether a design "works" is a highly subjective judgment based partly on such nebulous concepts as taste and aesthetic sensibility, as well as long observation of designs that *do* work.

It would certainly be possible to formulate a design that embodies to perfection all the textbook principles, and yet produce an object that nobody would bother to look at. Nevertheless, virtually every work of art makes at least a token reference to the principles of design in either a positive or a negative manner. Works that attempt to shock, puzzle, astonish, or even repel the viewer in order to convey an idea do so because they violate conventions of "good" design. In fact, terms like "good" and "bad" are seldom used in relation to design, because they imply a universal standard that simply does not exist. Rather, we speak of a design as being *effective* or *successful*, and any design is so when it satisfies the artist's aesthetic impulse and reaches the desired audience.

There is little agreement about just how many design principles there are. Some writers put the number at five, others at three or six. Actually, these differences are just a problem in semantics, for one authority will divide into two sections a concept that is lumped together by someone else. For purposes of this discussion, four seems an adequate and understandable number, those four being *proportion, balance, emphasis,* and *rhythm.*

Proportion

Proportion refers to the relationships of size or other measurable quantity among the elements in a design or between an object and its environ-

right: 547. If a small circle is placed in a large square, it seems out of proportion to the field of the design.

below: 548. When the circle is enlarged or repeated many times, the proportion becomes more harmonious.

 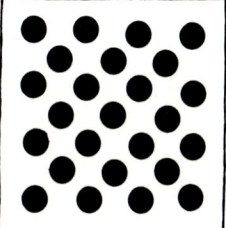

ment. For example, if you plan to design an area rug, you must consider the proportion of the pattern or color areas to the overall size of the rug and—if its destination is known—the proportion of the whole rug to the part of the floor it will occupy.

A related term, which is generally used to indicate specific dimensions or a mathematical ratio, is *scale*. Almost everyone is familiar with the devices of *scale models* and *scale drawings*, which imply that regardless of the size of the finished product, the relationships of the individual members will remain the same. A tapestry cartoon that is scaled 1:2 could be woven 1 foot by 2 feet, 2 feet by 4 feet, and so on. If the cartoon contains a figure that occupies half the space of the design, the same figure will always occupy half the space, even if the tapestry measures 50 by 100 feet.

The scale of any woven form must always be considered in relation to something else, for scale is a relative concept. For example, if one were to stand in front of Clair Zeisler's *Red Forest* (Fig. 587), the work would seem very large in scale compared to the human body. Yet if the same construction were hung inside a much larger enclosure, such as an airline terminal, it would be smaller in scale relative to its environment. Similarly, each individual yarn is small in scale compared to the knotting as a whole.

The term *out of proportion* has become part of our everyday vocabulary. When someone belabors a point that seems trivial, people speak of this as being "out of proportion" to the significance of the subject. The same principle can be applied to a design. For example, if a small circle is placed in a very large square (Fig. 547), it seems out of proportion to the overall field of the design. However, if the little circle is repeated many times or is enlarged considerably, the proportion becomes

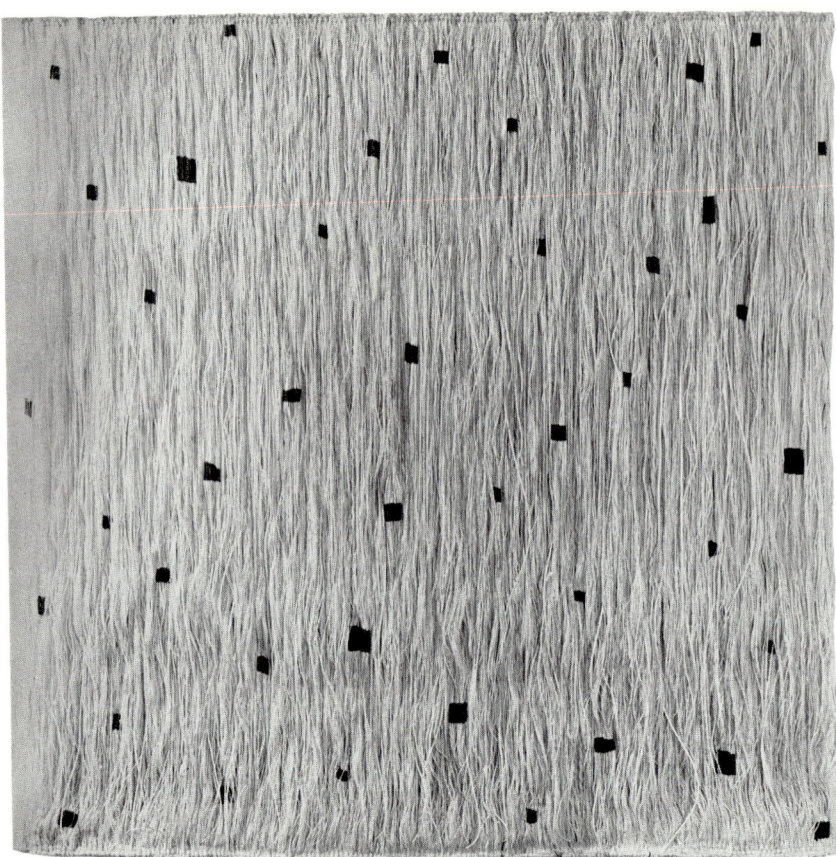

549. Désirée Scholten.
Red Dots. 1976.
Linen, plastic, cotton, wool,
and rayon; 4′4″ (1.3 m) square.
Courtesy the artist.

more harmonious (Fig. 548). The forms in Figure 554 are very large, but their proportion to the overall size of the tapestry is elegant and satisfying. By contrast, a wall hanging by Désirée Scholten (Fig. 549), which is similar in actual size, contains tiny squares and rectangles, but the repetition of the forms creates a sense of proportion.

These two examples are fairly extreme. In most cases, the proportional relationships in a woven object are more subtle and complex: the proportion of one yarn to another; that of one color to a second, a third, a fourth, or more; the relationship between open areas and sections of solid weaving; the width of stripes or the scale of a plaid; the proportion of figures or patterns to each other and to the web as a whole—all these are important design considerations. Often, a slightly altered proportion can change the whole appearance of a design. A "sense of proportion" is largely intuitive and is frequently arrived at by trial and error. This is one instance in which predesigning on paper can be a real advantage to the weaver.

Balance

Balance is the condition that exists when all forces present are in a state of equilibrium. In a woven form, or in any work of art, balance is achieved when the *visual weight* of one sector of the composition equals the visual weight of the other side. This concept of visual weight includes many factors: the colors (hues, values, and intensities), textures, sizes, shapes, and lines present in the various pattern areas. A large light area might be effectively balanced by two smaller darker areas, because the visual weights are equal.

A total absence of balance is comparable to the experience of singing "do-re-mi-fa-sol-la-ti . . ." Most people feel a sense of incompleteness, even anxiety, and are literally forced to add the final "do." Some woven constructions take advantage of this phenomenon, deliberately leaving the viewer vaguely uneasy. But it is human nature to seek balance, and most weavers try to achieve it in their work.

Balance is often divided into two categories: symmetrical and asymmetrical. *Symmetrical* balance, occasionally called formal balance, refers to a composition in which the two sides (or four quadrants or whatever) form a mirror image of one another (Fig. 550, Pl. 32, p. 339). There is a tendency for symmetrically balanced designs to give the impression of calm, repose, even dignity, but of course this is not always the case. When a weaving contains energetic curves and lines or bold, vibrant colors, it will not be really restful no matter how perfect its symmetry.

A composition that exhibits *asymmetrical* or informal balance requires a bit more sophistication on the part of both designer and viewer. The two halves of the work are not identical, yet their visual weights are sufficiently alike to balance the composition (Fig. 551). The effect is one of movement and spontaneity. This is not to say that asymmetrical balance is in any way "better" or more interesting, for extremely sensitive and challenging designs can be set within the limits of absolute symmetry. However, asymmetrical balance does present the designer with yet another problem to solve. The visual weights carried by the two sides of a design can be equalized by any number of devices—by adjusting color, texture, size, shape, or the placement of forms.

Without implying any criterion of effective design, it is safe to say that symmetrical balance is easier to do. One simply repeats in the second half

right: **550. Jon B. Wahling.** *Environment I,* detail. 1972. Twining, braiding, and knotting in jute and metal. Courtesy the artist.

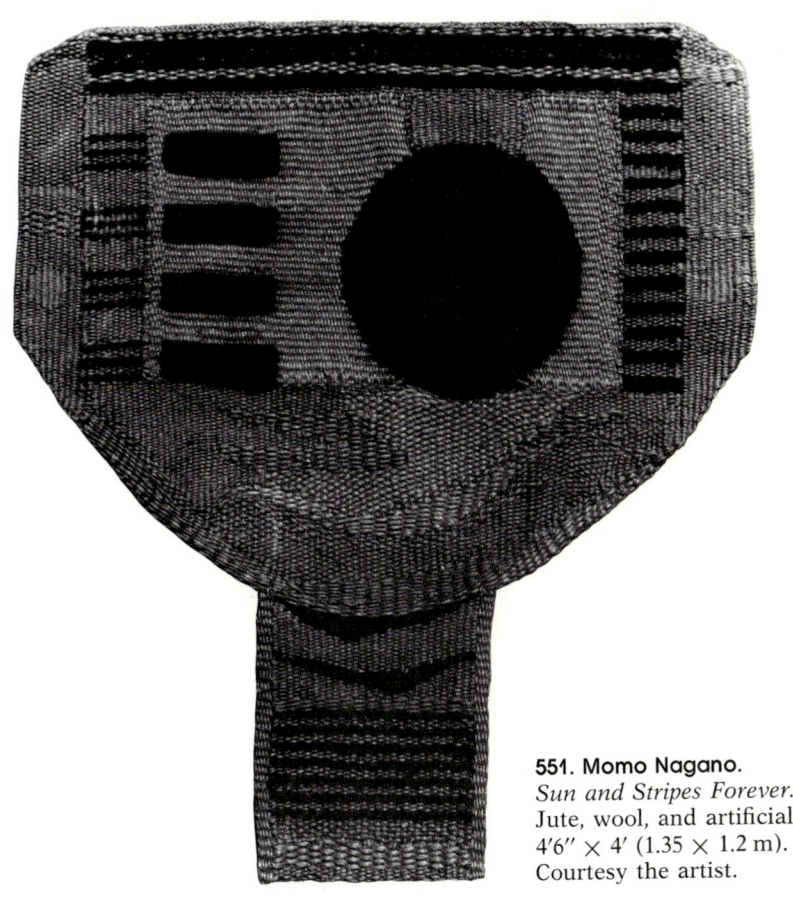

551. Momo Nagano.
Sun and Stripes Forever. 1975.
Jute, wool, and artificial silk,
4'6" × 4' (1.35 × 1.2 m).
Courtesy the artist.

Elements and Principles of Design **317**

of the design what one has done in the first. Like proportion, asymmetrical balance is largely a matter of intuition and judgment. The artist is not dealing with measurable quantities, such as "two small dark circles equal $27\frac{1}{2}$ and one large red triangle equals 8 visual weights." After much experimentation the designer learns to sense when a composition is balanced, and in this case, too, designing on paper is very helpful.

Emphasis

Emphasis suggests that one particular part of a design catches and holds the viewer's eye more than any other (Fig. 552). Our attention is directed—either gradually or immediately—to some focal point or points and is held there.

A *repeat design* such as is found in most yardage, wallpaper, and upholstery fabric, has no real point of emphasis, except to a limited degree within each unit of the motif (Fig. 553). The size of the repeat can vary from a fraction of an inch to several square feet, but the principle remains the

left: 552. Marguerite Carau.
Ivory with Cutout. 1971. Sisal,
$5'9\frac{1}{2}'' \times 6'1\frac{1}{2}''$ (1.74 × 1.81 m).
Courtesy the artist.

above: 553. Larsen Design Studio.
Carrickmacross. Double weave of wool in patterned Bawneen (Irish tweed), a traditional wool cloth of Ireland. Jack Lenor Larsen, Inc., New York.

same—identical forms repeated over and over in a theoretically infinite space. Interest is created by the flow of rhythm from one motif to the next, so an exaggerated point of emphasis in each pattern area is unnecessary or undesirable. When a small-scale repeat design is viewed from a distance, it often gives the impression of overall texture, rather than discrete pattern.

A *unit design,* on the other hand, generally has some focal point and often subsidiary focal points. Most of the individual projects a weaver will undertake—wall hangings, sculptures, tapestries, place mats, pillow covers, rugs, even some garments—are based on the unit or self-contained design. The point of emphasis can be created by several means, including a dominant color, a change of texture, the convergence of sight lines, a contrasting shape or size, or an unexpected detail. The center of interest in Figure 554 is fairly obvious even to the casual observer; it is all but in the very center of the composition. Moreover, this focal placement is reinforced by the fact that the circle is the only classic form in the whole design.

The opposing shapes embrace and direct attention to it. By comparison, the focal point in Marguerite Carau's tapestry is much more subtle—it is the little notch to one side (Fig. 552). Because it is unexpected, it becomes all the more riveting.

The point of emphasis in a design allows the viewer's eye to rest momentarily and enriches by contrast the less demanding areas of the composition. In general, its strength is in proportion to the subtlety or impact of the design as a whole. Lacking a focal point, the unit design runs the risk of becoming mere background for something else that is more compelling.

Rhythm

Rhythm is a sense of continuity or recurrence, a succession of spaced intervals. In a visual design rhythm causes the eye to travel from one part of the composition to another until the entire work has been perceived.

In weaving rhythm can take a variety of forms, just as in music we recognize several kinds of

554. Luis Feito, design, woven at the Atelier de Saint-Cyr. *Guadarrama.* 1971.
Tapestry, 6'3" × 8'5" (1.86 × 2.55 m). Collection La Demeure, Paris,
courtesy International Biennial of Tapestries, Lausanne, 1971.

rhythm—waltz, march, syncopated, and so on. The smooth flow of gently curved lines provides quite a different rhythm from the staccato of sharply angled turns or spaced individual forms (Fig. 555). Rhythm helps to create the particular atmosphere or expression of any design.

Aside from these four principles, we could cite other factors that contribute to effective design, such as honesty of materials or relevance to one's time. For a weaver to copy any of the designs in Part I of this text would be no more appropriate than an Athenian temple constructed at the corner of Broadway and 42nd Street, or a rock group playing madrigals. Designs that are relevant to some period in history are useful for study or even experimentation, but they do not express the unique character, feeling, and experience of the 20th century.

In terms of weaving, honesty of materials suggests that a yarn is chosen for its own innate qualities, because it can best fulfill the requirements of a certain project. It does not make sense to use nylon yarns when wool would do a better job, simply because synthetic yarns are "modern." Plastic that is made to look like wood remains imitation wood, but plastic used as plastic can be exciting and contemporary. The weaver should be acquainted with all the available materials, in order to choose the one best suited to any situation. Each provides its own kind of comfort, durability, and aesthetic potential.

All these guidelines and principles are worthless when one element is missing: the inspiration and imagination of the designer. That is one quality we cannot categorize under neat headings and subheadings, yet somehow we always know when it is there—or not there.

555. Sheila Hicks. *Macro-Tissage.* 1974.
White linen, 9′ (2.7 m) square.
Courtesy Modern Master Tapestries, Inc., New York.

Plate 27.
Marguerite Carau.
Beige with Yellow Diagonal.
1974. Hemp and sisal,
4' (1.2 m) square.
Courtesy the artist.

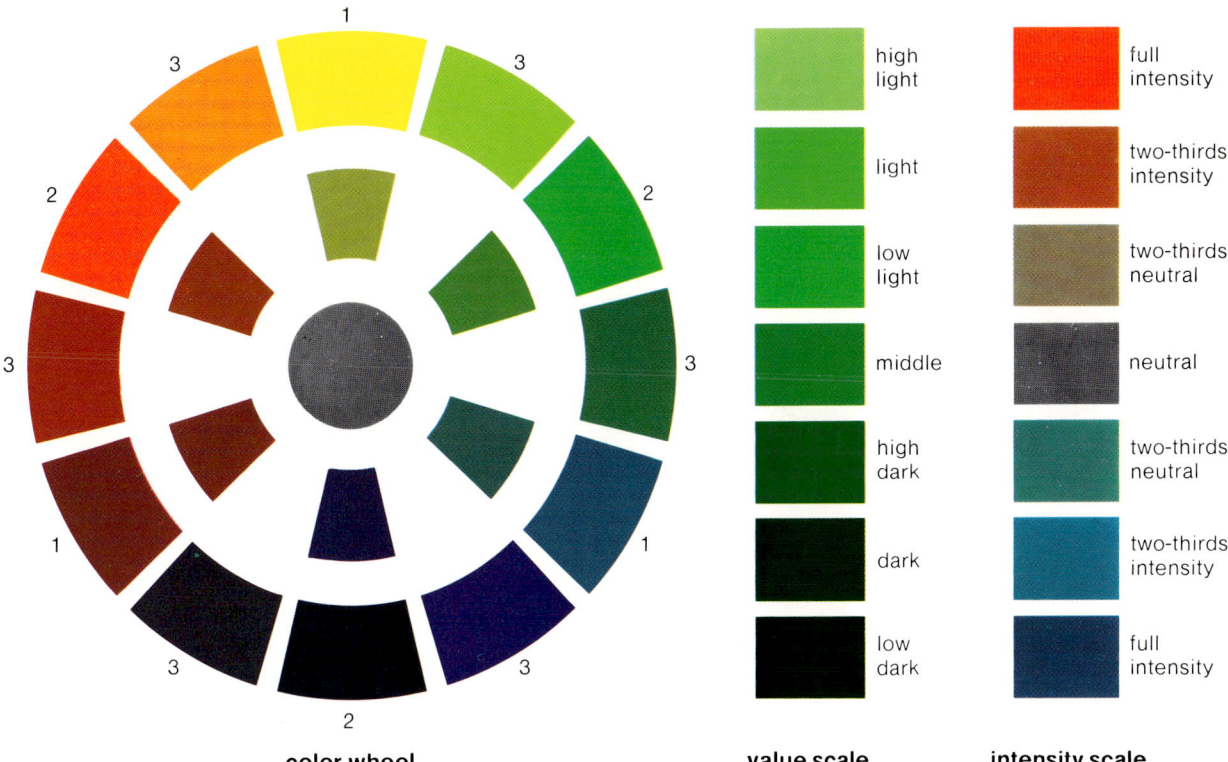

color wheel   value scale   intensity scale

Plate 28. The traditional color wheel takes as its primary colors red, yellow, and blue.
In this representation, the numeral 1 indicates a primary color, 2 a secondary color, 3 a tertiary color.
The value scale shows seven different values for the hue green; the intensity scale demonstrates
levels of saturation for orange and blue, approaching neutral gray.

321

The preceding chapter explored design in terms of selected elements and principles. However, designing for the loom—as for any other medium—can also be considered as a series of *decisions:* decisions about the nature of the product to be woven, the fiber, color, and texture of the yarns; the form or pattern of the weaving (or both); the mechanics of the loom setup; and the final assembly of the woven fabric. Each of these decisions serves to limit the range of choices for those that follow. For example, the type of fabric to be woven determines, to some extent, the selection of a yarn; the characteristics of the yarn limit the form of the weaving or the other way around; the yarn and the pattern prescribe the loom setup; and all of the foregoing control the finished appearance of the web. From this point of view, design can be seen as an infinite range of choices, gradually narrowing until each element has been harmoniously incorporated into an end-product.

Designing for the Loom

Design Decisions

Choosing the Project

When a weaver is filling a commission, the nature of the product is determined. Often, the client will also have specific ideas about color, materials, size, shape, and other variables. However, the student or independent weaver, working to achieve his or her own expression, has no such guidelines. Obviously, the first group of projects to be eliminated from consideration are those that are beyond the weaver's level of experience or the complexity of the available loom. This still leaves a huge body of potential projects, some of which are described in the second section of this chapter. The weaver's own taste and preferences are perhaps the most compelling factors in this choice, but these should be tempered by practicality.

The product of the loom is often divided into two categories: the functional fabric, which serves some utilitarian purpose; and the art fabric, which is solely the aesthetic expression of the weaver. This division, however, is by no means rigid. Many functional items, if they are sensitively designed, will evoke an aesthetic response, and often the art fabric can have an indirect function, such as the decoration of a particular space.

In some ways the design of functional objects is easier. This is true because one's expectations are guided by other examples. For instance, in weaving a pillow, one can look at other hand-woven pillows, assess their strengths and weaknesses, and then seek new solutions.

Designing an art fabric, by contrast, means giving concrete form to one's own ideas, and there is nothing available for comparison. The gifted designer does not copy another's work. The art object is always unique.

A question many weavers never grapple with is: What is the point of weaving this product by hand? The mere fact of being able to say "this is handwoven" seems hardly adequate when one realizes the great expenditure of labor involved in any handwoven object. There are, in fact, many items that *can* be more efficiently produced by machine, and the simple duplication of power-loomed fabrics is not a worthy investment of the weaver's time. The handmade product must exhibit some extra quality, some feature of design or execution that would be impossible to achieve on an industrial level.

Selecting the Materials

Once the nature of the project has been established, the next step may be either selection of appropriate materials or the creation of an idea. One or the other can come first, or the two elements may be conceived simultaneously in the weaver's mind.

When a utilitarian product is to be woven, the choice of yarns or other materials is often the first consideration, for questions of *suitability*—which seldom arise in sculpture or wall hangings—must be dealt with. A coarse, hairy yarn would not be suitable for a scarf or some other garment that will touch the wearer's skin, nor would a very fine, gossamer yarn be appropriate for a cloak that is meant to provide warmth. A tablecloth, place mat, or set of napkins must be constructed from yarns that are easily cleaned; a drapery or upholstery fabric woven from flammable yarns would clearly be unsuitable.

After the specific requirements of the proposed fabric have been satisfied, one basic rule governs the selection of the materials: Buy the best-quality yarn you can afford. Labor is the most expensive ingredient in any handcrafted item, and your production time is the same regardless of whether you use cheap materials or good ones. No matter how much skill and imagination you contribute, the finished product will always reflect the quality of its raw materials.

Permanence is another important consideration in the choice of materials. Unfortunately, it is not unknown for weavers to deliberately build obsolescence into their products by using materials that will deteriorate in a relatively short time, such as jute or foam rubber. This is a contradiction to the craft aesthetic. But the weaver who inadvertently employs a short-lived material is almost as guilty for not having become informed about its properties.

Developing the Idea

The equivalent in weaving of an artist's sketchbook is the set of woven samples, carefully marked for loom setup and yarn types (Fig. 556). A generous book of samples will provide endless inspiration, because in many cases a slight change of color, texture, or pattern will transform an insignificant design into something truly exciting. Perhaps a tiny corner of a sample could be expanded into a full-scale design. Besides the woven samples, many designers keep an "idea book," with notes, sketches, and perhaps paper cutouts or patterns in three dimensions.

A systematic program of thinking and planning is essential to predictable results. Experimentation with materials and techniques, to learn their potentials and limitations, will augment sketches.

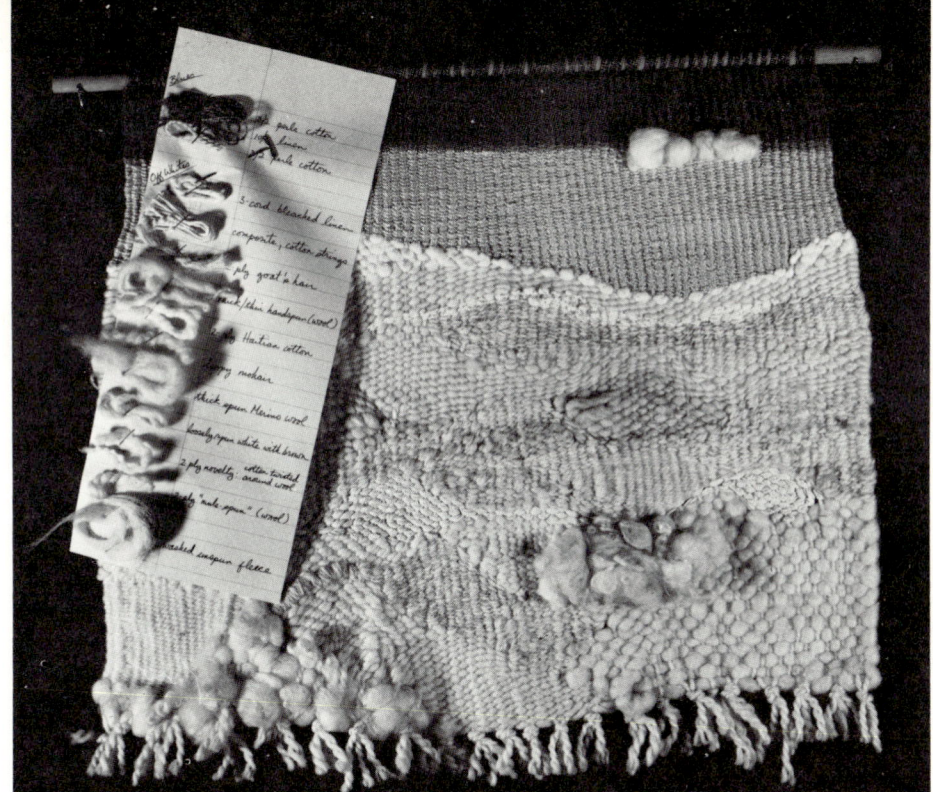

556. Weaver's sample, including swatches of yarns used
and a test fabric. A detail of the tapestry
made from this sample appears in Plate 7 (p. 71).

Evaluation at various stages can be extremely helpful, whether by oneself or one's friends and fellow weavers. Above all, the weaver must be in control of materials and processes in order to achieve the desired results. The design phase can be agonizing, but it is the most truly creative part of weaving.

So many options present themselves! Will the fabric be stiff or soft and pliable, solid or openwork, textured or smooth, shaped or rectangular, subtle in color or polychrome, two-dimensional or three, boldly patterned or simple? By weaving a sample or a series of samples with the projected end-product in mind, you will soon begin to narrow your range of choices. In the case of a large free-form structure, you may even wish to build a scale model and weave the piece in small scale before actually committing great quantities of yarn to the project.

It is rare for the inventive weaver to sit down at the loom without some idea of what he or she intends to do. Simply by designing and weaving one fabric, you will probably think of two or five or a dozen other designs to try. Part of the challenge and fascination of weaving is that your hands can seldom keep up with your head.

Choosing the Technique

The development of an idea limits but does not always dictate the loom mechanics that will be used to produce it. Often, the same result can be achieved in a variety of ways, and you must decide upon the most appropriate as well as the most economical method. For example, when the design calls for great color variation in one set of yarns, that variation can more easily be introduced in the warp, so that after the loom has been dressed, weaving can proceed with a minimum of shuttle changes and references to the design plan. It is not uncommon for a weaver to spend more time in *planning* the loom setup than in actually weaving the web. (Sometimes, too, a great portion of the time is spent in finishing the piece after it comes off the loom.)

The amount of time and energy that will be expended in weaving the fabric is closely related to the complexity of the treadling. Numerous harnesses and shuttles slow the weaving process and also increase the chances of making a mistake. Of course, there are situations in which a very involved treadling pattern is required, but sometimes the desired effect can be produced more easily in some other way. A thorough knowledge of the loom and what it can do may save a great deal of time.

The manner in which the warp yarns are set up on the loom is so crucial to the appearance of the fabric that it deserves special mention. By spacing the warp yarns irregularly—that is, by uneven grouping in the reed—you can create a striped or ridged pattern that is particularly effective in fabrics that are exposed to light, such as room dividers, casements, and lamp shades. Sometimes very fine yarns can be made more versatile by an unusually close sett or even by threading two or three yarns through a single heddle. When highly elastic warp yarns are interspersed with dimensionally stable ones, the warp tension can be controlled fairly well.

In the following section considerations of loom setup and materials are discussed in relation to certain kinds of projects.

Planning Specific Items

Almost anything that is typically made of fiber—and a few things that are not—can be handwoven on the loom. The list that follows presents only the broadest suggestion of potential projects for the handweaver and is in no way exhaustive of the possibilities for works in fiber.

Wall Hangings and Sculpture

It sometimes, though rarely, happens that the design for a wall hanging or sculpture will spring, fully conceptualized, into the weaver's mind. It is all there—idea, materials, techniques, colors, scale, and perhaps the yarn or yarns. All that is necessary is to fit the weave mechanics to this mental picture. On the other hand, the weaver may occasionally enter the studio with the intention of creating a wall hanging but not the slightest clue about how to begin.

In most cases, however, the situation falls somewhere between these two extremes. You have a germ of an idea that must be expanded and developed into a full-scale plan for a wall hanging. Perhaps you have come upon a new yarn that intrigued you, or been struck by a special combination of colors. Perhaps you have been inspired by the work of another weaver, either contemporary or historical. Or, you may simply have noticed a pattern—in another art medium, in some object, in nature, in the immediate environment—that suggested the design for a wall hanging. Whatever the stimulus, this fragmentary idea must somehow be translated into warp and weft, into a satisfying combination of design *elements* that embodies, insofar as appropriate, the design *principles* outlined in the previous chapter.

The approximate size and shape of a wall hanging or sculpture are often among the first variables to be decided. It is difficult to visualize a design without forming some notion of its desirable proportions—a small oblong, a long narrow strip, a massive mural-size tapestry. The oblong shape—a rectangle that is longer in one dimension, hung either vertically or horizontally—has long been popular for wall hangings. Yet virtually any size or shape can be worked into an effective design if the various elements are handled sensitively. Most weavers would faint at the suggestion that they create a wall hanging nearly a football field long and less than 2 feet high, yet that is precisely what the designers of the *Bayeux Tapestry* (Fig. 67) accomplished nearly a thousand years ago. A three-dimensional sculpture presents the weaver with yet more decisions, for the size and shape must relate not only to a wall but to a whole environment.

The visual organization of a wall hanging is another major design question. It may range anywhere from a simply woven rectangle in which the major interest lies in color and shape relationships through an elaborate pictorial tapestry. If you intend to develop a wall hanging whose idea can be conveyed most effectively using abstract or geometric shapes, you may decide first to sketch the plan on paper or even cut out the shapes and rearrange them until you arrive at the most effective combination. A pictorial design may be subjected to a long series of sketches before you achieve precisely the effect you are seeking. The idea is determined first, and the weave mechanics must be adjusted to correspond. When a specific yarn, color, or color relationship has been the initial stimulus, you must determine above all how best you can exploit it.

A wall hanging or sculpture should be an intensely personal expression on the part of the weaver. A glance at the illustrations in this book, as well as exposure to craft exhibitions and publications, will give the student weaver an idea of how other designer-artists have interpreted fiber as an art medium.

There is considerable interest today in the three-dimensional art fabric. Most webs produced on conventional looms are flat, rectangular planes, but there is no reason they need remain that way. A number of simple devices will enable you to introduce structure, shape, and three-dimensionality into the products of an ordinary loom.

Some forms develop because of slits or openings in the fabric (see Chap. 11). These openings make it possible to manipulate portions of the web or to intersect two or more webs to create structure (Fig. 557).

Three-dimensionality is a natural by-product of double-weave or multilayer fabrics. Tubes, cylinders, and similar constructions, stuffed or padded and joined in different ways, can be handled with great freedom in creating sculptures (Fig. 558).

left: 557. Jacques Douchez.
Maroon and Orange Interlacings 74. 1974.
Mixed technique, slit tapestry;
10' × 6'2" × 2' (3 × 1.85 × .6 m).
Courtesy the artist.

below: 558. Jean Stamsta.
Tarzan's Rope. 1977.
Tubular weave in wool and synthetics,
39'4" × 10" (11.8 m × 25 cm).
Courtesy the artist.

Often, in creating sculpture or other art fabrics it is desirable to have a certain rigidity either in the whole web or in portions of it. This can be produced in several ways. The mechanics of the weave itself will have some effect upon rigidity. For example, a plain-weave fabric is more inflexible than a twill weave of comparable yarns and sett. On the other hand, plain-weave surfaces usually lie flat, while twills have a tendency to curl. This curl can be emphasized, if desired, by experimenting to find just the right combination of warp and weft yarns.

Some fibers are innately more rigid than others—jute, sisal, and linen, to name a few. High twist and plying add stiffness to a yarn, and cord tends to be more inflexible than simple yarn. This stiffness can be enhanced by an unusually dense sett in the warp yarns. An extremely firm web will result when truly rigid materials such as wire are introduced.

Creases or folds reinforce stiffness, and pronounced folds can be achieved in several ways.

Interlocking of weft yarns between warp ends as in the tapestry technique (Fig. 307) causes a natural fold to develop along the line of interlocking. Another method of making a crease is to leave a few warp yarns unwoven for a distance and then wrap the skipped yarns tightly. (See Chap. 15 for wrapping procedures.)

559. In planning shaped items, you can weave darts by using tapestry techniques, then pull the fabric together after it is off the loom. These drawings show one system for making vertical darts (*above*) or horizontal darts (*below*).

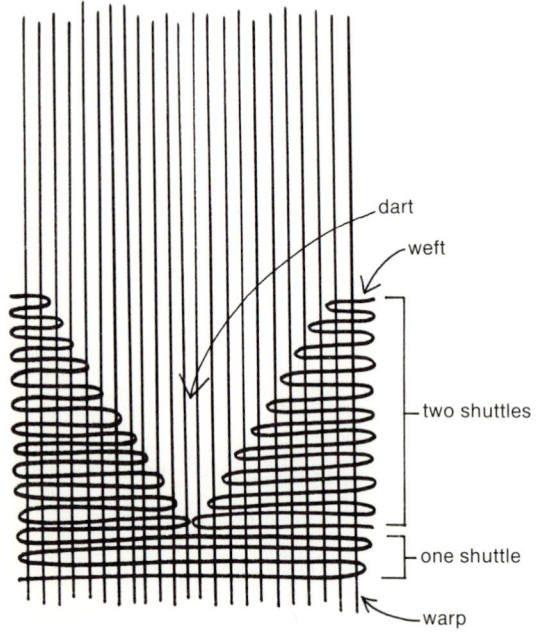

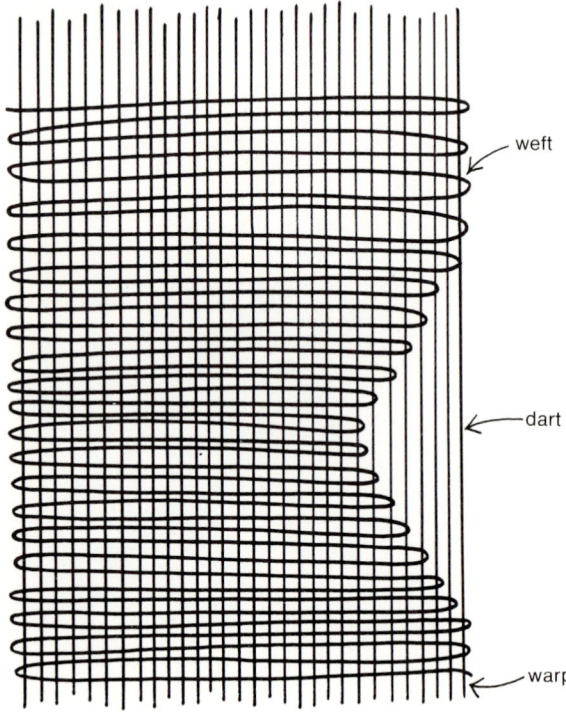

Solid flat fabrics can take on a third dimension if they are gathered in some way, for example, if the corners are brought together. Gathering can be done in several ways. If the web is fairly open (that is, not tightly packed) and not overly long in relation to the weight of the warp yarn, certain key warp yarns can be pulled from one end or from both to compact the fabric. When the warp is set up for double weave, you can leave certain portions of the lower layer unwoven and use the open yarns as gathering strings. A warp that is not strong enough for pulling can have sturdy yarns inserted at strategic places for later gathering.

Weftwise gathering is also possible with either the normal weft yarns or special gathering yarns inserted where necessary. If you plan to gather while the fabric is still on the loom, you will have draw-in problems unless you remove the reed. Horizontal gathering is easier on simple looms, such as the backstrap.

The darts and tucks used in the construction of garments can also help to shape nonfunctional fabrics. If you want to make a dart without the extra bulkiness of fabric, you can actually construct the dart on the loom with tapestry techniques (Fig. 559), then pull the two sides together later on.

A wide range of shaped, geometric pieces can be woven directly on the loom for later assembly. Figure 560 shows only a few of the possibilities. The method combines tapestry techniques with portions of unwoven warp. Experimentation with the box or cube form will demonstrate the many possibilities for this kind of shaping.

As you can see from Figure 560, there are several different approaches to making the box shape, with or without a lid. Choice of one pattern over the other would be governed by the placement of color or pattern areas. If you wish, you can reinforce the fold lines to give extra crispness. If the crease runs weftwise on the loom, simply make several weft shots in the same shed. A warpwise crease can be made firmer by having two or more adjacent yarns lifted together at the crease lines. When you are using tapestry techniques, as several of the patterns in Figure 560 require, interlocking of the weft yarns will automatically create a natural fold.

Garments and Accessories

Throughout history many cultures, including the Indians of Peru, have shaped garments on the loom, with a minimum of post-weaving construction—that is, cutting and sewing. The sari of India is an example of such a garment. Today, this prac-

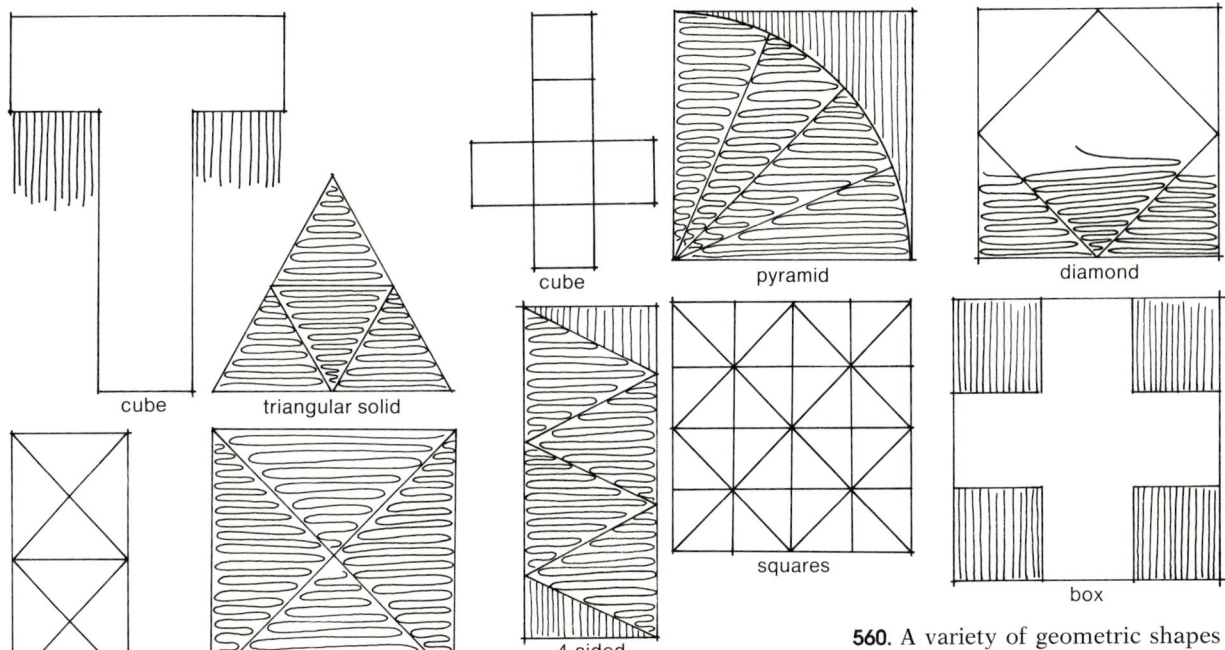

cube

cube

triangular solid

squares

square

4-sided
solid pyramid

pyramid

diamond

squares

box

560. A variety of geometric shapes
that can be woven flat on the loom.
Many assemble into three-dimensional forms.
Some portions of the warp are left unwoven.

tice is gaining new popularity with handweavers (Pl. 33, p. 339). Among the garments that can be fabricated in this manner are ponchos, shirts, skirts, dresses, vests, coats, jackets, and trousers. Frequently, a seam or two is all that is needed before the article is ready to wear.

Figure 561 illustrates one method of constructing a poncho—a simple, blanketlike outer garment (Fig. 562). The plan calls for two lengths of fabric each about 15 inches wide and 30 inches long (finished dimensions). Only two seams are required to assemble the poncho, but a dart at the shoulder enhances the fit. Some forethought is necessary to ensure that the design meshes properly when joined length to width. A plaid will be easier to match if it is square, and small patterns join more readily than large ones.

561. Plan for a loom-constructed poncho,
based on two lengths of fabric
each about 30 × 15″ (75 × 37.5 cm).

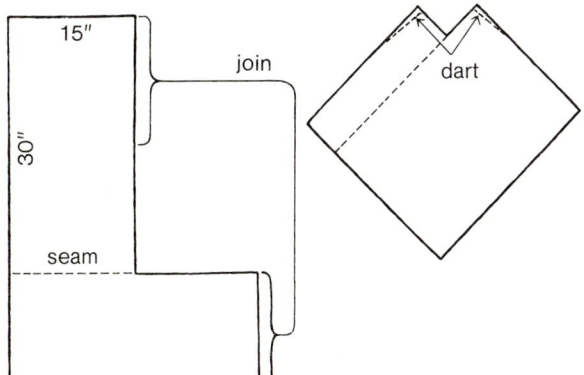

15″

join

dart

30″

seam

562. Loom-constructed poncho
with fringe, woven in two sections
and seamed at the shoulders.

Designing for the Loom   **329**

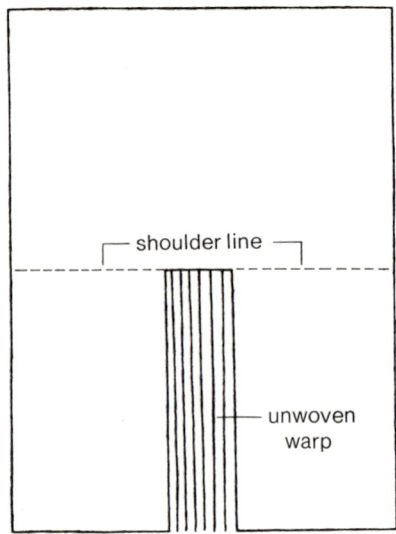

shoulder line

unwoven warp

above: **563.** A one-piece poncho can be constructed on the loom by leaving the warp yarns unwoven in one section for the neck opening.

right: **564. Ulla Nass.** Hooded poncho. "Harness lace" (the artist's own technique combining plain weave and leno). Courtesy the artist.

below: **565.** Pisac-type poncho, Chahuaytiri, Peru. 1967. Wool, 4'6⅝" × 4'1½" (1.4 × 1.25 m). American Museum of Natural History, New York (on loan from Grace Goodell). This poncho was made in two pieces and seamed down the center.

left: 566. Loom-constructed wool jacket
with card-woven trim at neckline, front, and armholes.

A wider loom permits construction of a one-piece poncho (Fig. 563), with the warp yarns left unwoven in one section to allow for a neck opening. Button or tie closures at the neckline and under the arms complete the garment. The standard measurements can be adjusted to fit the intended wearer and could even be scaled down to make a baby's sweater. With further trimming and shaping you can turn the poncho into a vest or sleeveless jacket. Wool and mohair yarns will produce a very warm covering (Figs. 564, 565), while cotton or linen could be used for a lightweight summer wrap. By choosing the yarns and the weave draft with care, you can build a draping quality into the fabric, thus compensating for the loose fit.

A basic shirt or jacket can also be woven in one piece, but this construction requires a bit of cutting and sewing (Fig. 566). The pattern in Figure 567 allows for a decorative band—perhaps card or inkle woven—around the bottom of the shirt, which improves the fit at the hipline. A T-shape slit is cut in the center for the neck opening. Figure 568 shows a somewhat simpler design, the plan for the bog shirt illustrated in Figure 502.

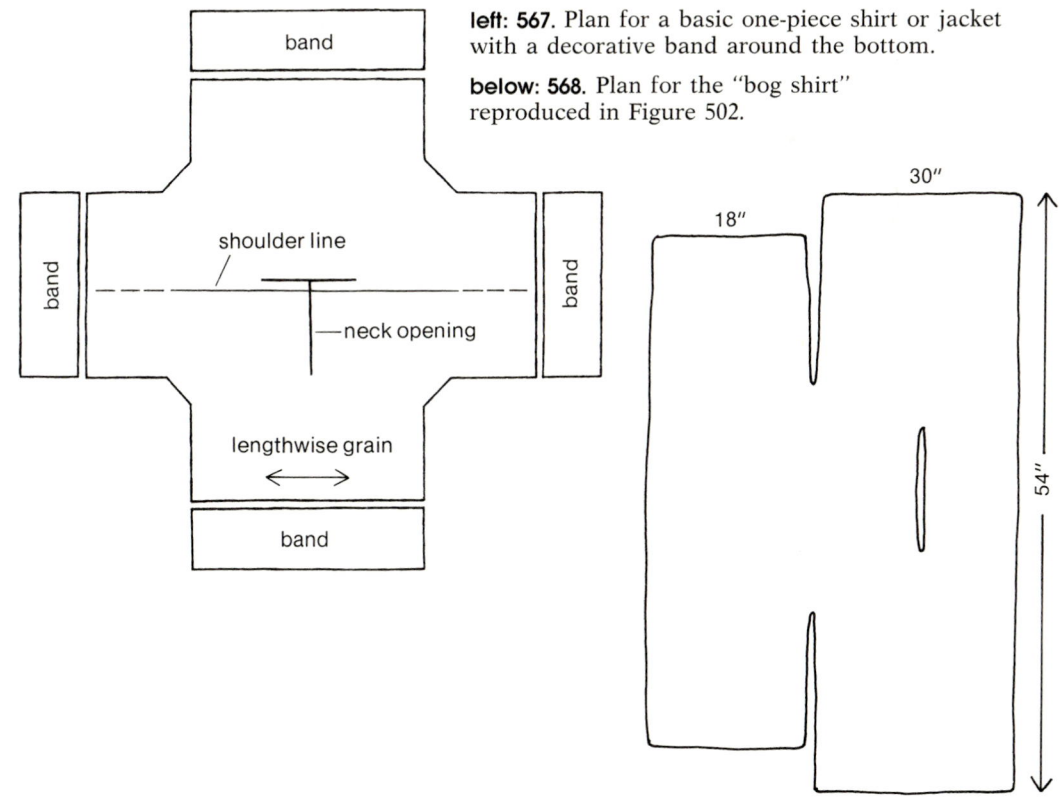

left: 567. Plan for a basic one-piece shirt or jacket with a decorative band around the bottom.

below: 568. Plan for the "bog shirt" reproduced in Figure 502.

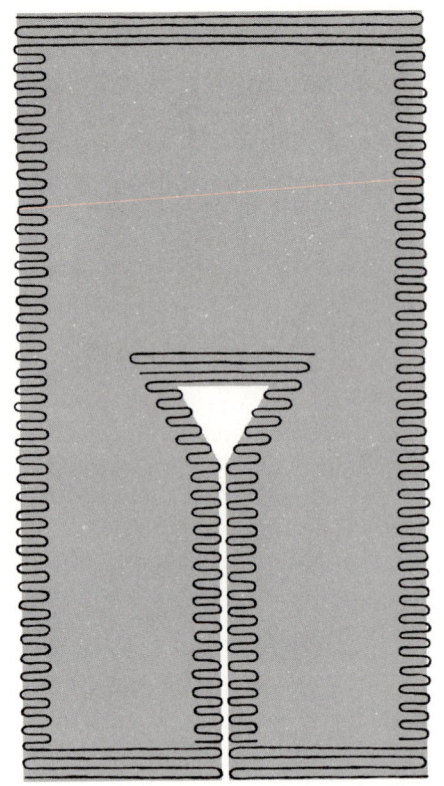

full width in a curve 2 inches high. For the sleeves, the full width was woven in two layers over a distance of 7 inches. Finally, an inch was woven at each side for the shoulders, leaving a 7½-inch opening for the neck. The bottom of the dress was hemmed, and the shoulders were sewn together by hand. The unwoven warp ends were pulled to the inside of the dress, tied, and sewn to the inside.

Pile weaves seem particularly appropriate for winter accessories such as hoods, mittens, and muffs, since they provide both actual and psychological warmth. A simple hood can be contructed from a rectangular length of fabric stitched in half at one selvedge to form the back seam. The chin ties are added separately.

above: 569. Plan for a straight vest with a laid-in trim around all edges.

right: 570. Jane Busse. Tubular weave loom-constructed dress in cotton and rayon. Courtesy the artist.

One of the easiest garments to make is a straight vest (Fig. 569), which is woven in one piece and reinforced around the edges with a laid-in or free-weaving technique. The portion of the web that is intended for the neck opening is left unwoven, and the free warps are cut away after the weaving is completed. The sides can be laced or otherwise joined under the arms.

A loom-shaped dress is a more complicated structure, but it can be exciting and challenging to plan. Figure 570 shows a dress designed by weaver Jane Busse, and Figure 571 gives the draft. It was woven from cotton and rayon yarns, which provide enough bulk to hold the circular shape, with silk for the dark pattern bands. The dress is a tubular weave, begun at the bottom. Shaping was done by tapering inward to the waistline and then out again for the sleeves. After the first light pattern band at the bottom, 4 warp ends (in one dent) were dropped at each edge for every ⅞ inch of weaving until the dress was 19 inches wide at the waist. Next, the weaving continued straight upward for a distance of 4½ inches. Then the outer warp ends were gradually picked up again to the

571. Draft for
the loom-constructed dress
shown in Figure 570.

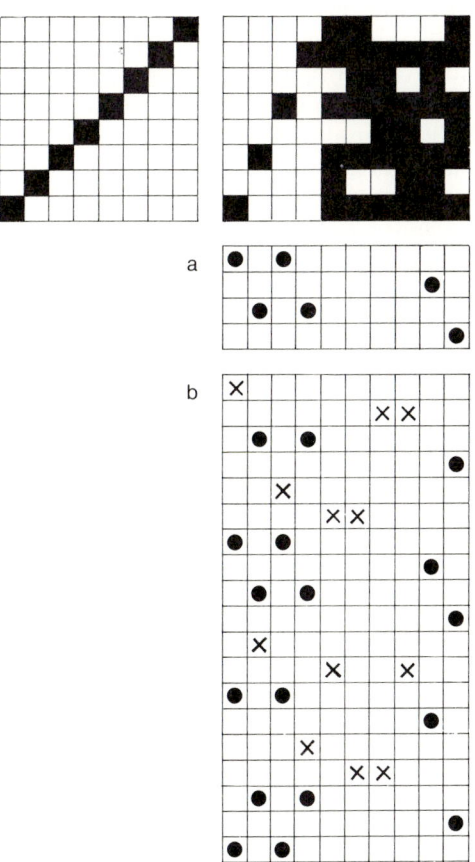

above: 572. Shoulder bag with card-woven strap.
Plain weave, looping, chaining, and overlaid techniques;
linen warp, wool weft.

below: 573. Place mats are among
the easiest items to weave on the loom.
Any of the finishing techniques described in Chapter 12
can be used to bind the raw edges.

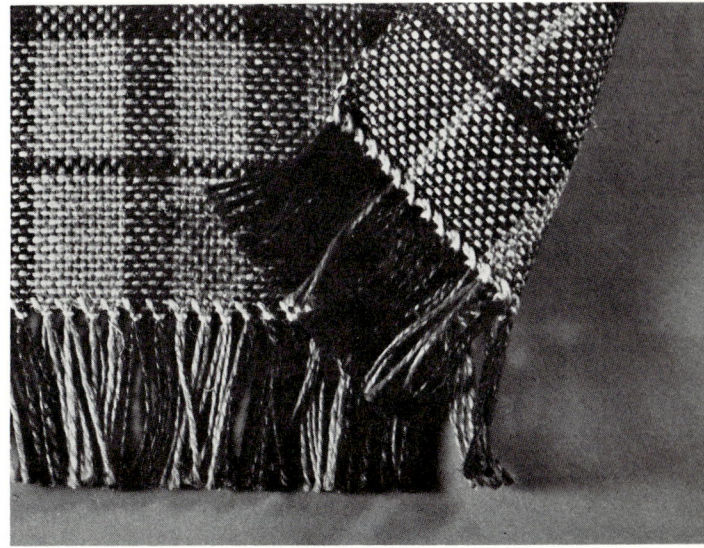

Scarves, which are often left fringed at the ends, should be woven in such a way that they drape attractively. A tightly packed plain weave would probably result in a too-stiff fabric, unless the yarns are very fine. Mohair yarns are soft and pleasant to the touch, so they are very popular in scarves. However, since they are hairy and tend to stick together, they are easier to handle in the weft, with a more dimensionally stable yarn for the warp. If you use mohair yarns in the warp, you should keep the sett quite open to prevent the yarns from binding together. An open warp will also show the character of the yarn to better advantage. The standard sizes for scarves include 15 by 48 inches (40 × 120 cm), 8 by 36 inches (20 × 90 cm), and 10 by 15 inches (25 × 40 cm), not counting the fringe, if any.

Shoulder or hand bags in a wide variety of shapes and sizes can be woven in one piece, with handles added separately (Fig. 572). The bag can be a simple envelope or can be shaped with stiffeners and, if desired, lined on the inside. Tubular weave (see pp. 152–153) provides a very simple construction that is finished on three sides even

before the fabric is removed from the loom. An allowance of 2 to 3 inches is left at the top for hemming. The straps could be braided, knotted, card woven, or inkle woven.

Table Linens

The term *linen* is a convention used to describe domestic textiles. Actually, tablecloths, napkins, and place mats can be woven from any flat, smooth fiber (Fig. 573). For a greater textural interest, you might choose raffia, grasses, or corn husks (Fig. 574), provided the surface is level. The only requirements are that the fabrics be rather firm and easy to clean. The standard sizes for table linens are:

tablecloth:	52 inches square
	52 by 70, rectangular or oval
	60 by 84, rectangular or oval
	60 inches round
	132 cm square
	63 by 175 cm
	56 by 75 cm
place mats:	13 by 19 inches
	32–35 cm by 43–55 cm
napkins:	dinner, 18 inches square
	(41 cm square)
	luncheon, 14 inches square
	(36 cm square)
	tea, 12 inches square
	cocktail, 5 by 8 inches

Of course, these sizes can be adjusted to fit an unconventional table or preference. In all cases an allowance must be made for hems or—on the place mats—a fringe, if desired. Sets of napkins or place mats can be woven on a single continuous warp and cut apart after weaving. However, each should be a unit design, so that they do not look like yardage cut into pieces.

Place mats need not be identical in design to comprise a set; often they are woven from the same yarns but with a slightly different pattern. Clearly, a striking unit design would be wasted when the mat is covered by china, so the pattern is generally rather subdued.

Yardage

Handwoven dress goods are no longer the major output of the loom, as was the case until the early part of this century, but many weavers still specialize in custom yardage. The fabric for men's garments is generally woven to between 27 and 30 inches (about 70 cm) in width (plus allowances for shrinkage and draw-in), while women's yardage is woven to 36 or 42 inches (90 or 105 cm). It is a bit difficult to weave wool or other bulky yardage on a table loom, because the cloth beam will not accommodate great quantities of woven fabric. However, if you plan a garment requiring many yards of wool material, you can overcome this difficulty by laying out the pattern in advance and calculating manageable segments of fabric that correspond to the cutting arrangement. Each portion is then woven individually.

Drapery and Upholstery Fabric

Drapery fabric presents a unique challenge to the weaver: The material must be just as attractive when it is hung in multiple folds as when it is flat. In addition to being relatively nonflammable and easy to clean, the casement or drapery fabric should offer special light-transmitting or light-blocking qualities, depending upon the use for which it is intended. Some drapery materials are designed to block out light altogether, while others merely screen the light and are either transparent or translucent. In the latter event, a subdued line or pattern can add visual interest while still maintaining the fabric's role as background for the more striking elements in the room. The drapery fabric should be sleyed as wide as possible on the

below: 574. Detail of table mat with widely spaced wool warp and corn husk weft.

right: 575. Plan for a pillow cover seamed down the center of the back.

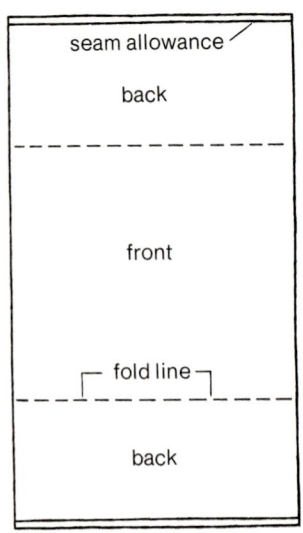

576. Ulla Nass. *Peru,* bedspread-blanket. 1976. "Harness lace" (the artist's own technique combining plain weave and leno) in cotton and wool, 5′6″ × 6′10″ (1.65 × 2.05 m). Courtesy the artist.

loom, and particular attention must be paid to making the selvedges even and smooth.

The finished width of upholstery fabric should be at least 32 inches (80 cm), which is the standard size for cushions, including a seam allowance. Therefore, the web would be sleyed to about 36 inches (90 cm) to account for shrinkage and draw-in. A firm, compact, and abrasion-resistant fabric, with no long floats on the surface, will give the longest wear. Cotton is the most common warp material, but linen or certain synthetic fibers might also be used successfully. Considerations of scale are important in designing fabric for a specific piece of furniture, because a large, bold pattern could easily overwhelm a delicate chair.

Home Furnishing Accessories

The handweaver will find ample opportunity in the area of home furnishing accessories. Pillow covers, flat cushions, screens, dividers, throws, and rugs are only a few of the possibilities.

A pillow cover makes a good beginning project, but its design can be sophisticated enough to challenge even the most experienced weaver. Pillows can be woven flat and sewn to shape after weaving. In order to hide the seam on the reverse side,

the weaving begins with a portion of the back, then proceeds through the front of the pillow cover to the remainder of the back (Fig. 575). Alternatively, a tubular weave can be used, with ample seam allowances at either end for turning in. Rug knots, lace weaves, or any other decorative device can be used with the greatest freedom. Since a pillow is by nature an accent, the design can be as bold, as amusing, even as eccentric as your taste allows.

Bed covers or spreads offer another area in which design can be as individual as the weaver (Fig. 576). Spreads are seldom used for warmth nowadays but serve a purely decorative function. Just as the traditional coverlet was woven in two or three panels to cover the bed, the contemporary bedspread must generally be planned in units to be stitched together after weaving. These units need not be parallel to the length of the bed. Among the many techniques that have potential for bed covers are double weaves, brocades, lace weaves, ikat, and silkscreen.

Still another area open to exploration is that of wall coverings. A handwoven wall covering should be more than just a variation on commercial wallpapers. It can be considered as a wall hanging that happens to be attached to the wall. Interesting or novelty yarns and natural plant materials such as grasses would be among the possible materials, but they must be small enough in scale to keep the thickness as flat as possible. Most materials require a special coating (such as silicone spray) to make the surface shed dust, to give durability, and to protect from insects.

Weave Analysis

Many designers are interested in historical weaves and like to copy all or a portion of an old pattern for adaptation in their own work. In addition, weavers are occasionally commissioned to replicate fabrics of the past for reconstruction of historical landmarks. It is necessary to have a sample of the original fabric that is large enough to provide at least three repeats of the pattern in both directions and that can be picked apart for analysis. Any pile or nap on the surface of the material should be removed by burning to reveal the underlying structure.

The first step in weave analysis is to ravel a fringe for about ¼ to ½ inch on two adjacent edges of the fabric. A strong yarn needle is the best tool for this purpose. Next, establish the direction of warp and weft. The warp yarn can usually be recognized, because it is the stronger, less elastic yarn, it is parallel to the selvedge, and it is more regular in placement.

Patterns are most often based on repetition of individual design units. With a pin, mark on the fabric the end points of two units of design in each direction. Then, plot a corresponding area on graph paper in the following manner. Lift the first weft yarn to determine its horizontal arrangement across the warp within the two pattern units. Each time the warp appears *over* the weft, make a mark on the paper. Repeat the same process with all the other weft yarns until the pattern area is complete.

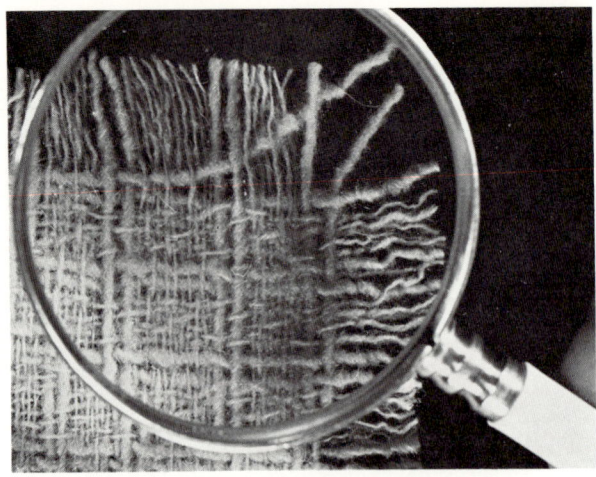

577. To analyze a weave from a sample, unravel a fringe on two adjacent edges of the fabric, and then plot on graph paper the pattern of interlacement for one unit of the weave. A magnifying glass helps to sort out fine yarns.

When very fine yarns are involved, a magnifying glass will help (Fig. 577). It is wise to indicate the color, weight, and texture of the warp and weft yarns as the work progresses. For future reference a sample of each yarn can be cut and placed beside the graph. After the plotting is complete, the weave draft should resemble the pattern of the actual fabric. From this, a threading and treadling order can be derived.

Design for the loom can be as simple or as complex as you wish to make it. Some weavers work almost exclusively in plain weave, preferring to create a visual effect with color or texture. Others employ a limited range of yarns but seek ever more intricate patterning. Through constant experimentation with different ideas, you will eventually find your own direction.

The term *handweaving* or even *weaving* limits, to some extent, our comprehension of the work that is being done today in yarn interlacements and fabric construction. Perhaps it is more appropriate to describe individuals engaged in such enterprise as *fiber artists*, a broad designation that embraces not only the handweaver who works with a conventional loom, but also the designer-consultant to industry, the artisan whose medium is technically a nonwoven form, and the artist whose aesthetic works are based for the most part on fiber or yarn.

There is little agreement about what exactly constitutes a craft, as opposed to an art. Traditionally, media such as weaving, ceramics, glassblowing, metalwork, and so forth have been considered "minor arts," distinguishable from the "major arts" of painting and sculpture. However, many of the works reproduced in this book, though undeniably weaving, are closer to painting and sculpture than to the average person's notion of a handcrafted object. Similar difficulties arise in the other fields as well. If the construction of a stoneware pot is to be considered a craft, is the design

The Contemporary Fiber Artist

578. Daniel Graffin. *Indigo Quadrangulaire.* 1975. Knotted, stuffed, and woven; 17'10½" × 18'2⅜" (5.4 × 5.5 m). Courtesy International Biennial of Tapestries, Lausanne, 1975.

techniques, while the potential of older, traditional materials and methods has been pushed to limits undreamed of a century ago. Weaving as a profession, as a life's-work, has been reestablished in a manner quite different from the guild weaving of three or four hundred years ago. Finally, the subject matter of weaving or of fiber construction in general has undergone a drastic reinterpretation (Fig. 578). Indeed, the manipulation of fibers, yarns, and fabrics has undoubtedly changed more in the last two or three decades than it did in the previous two or three millennia.

Innovations in Fiber Craft

New Materials

Fifty years ago the materials of weaving were essentially those that had been in use for fifty centuries: wool, linen, cotton, and silk. Since the 1920s a tremendous variety of new fibers and yarns have been developed, and the end is not in sight. In many cases the technology needed to produce miracle fibers has been a side effect of space research. Even now, fabrics capable of conducting electricity are being woven from carbon/graphite yarns. The cloth has the hand and drape of fiberglass, but electrical power is distributed throughout by means of metallic conductors. The potential end-uses include bedding, heated clothing, and upholstery material for automobiles. In the Soviet Union electrically heated suits are manufactured for outdoor work in temperatures to −75°F. At the other extreme, garments fabricated from heat- or fire-resistant fibers are also a by-product of space exploration. A fabric made from graphite yarns, trademarked Thornel, is stronger than steel yet 40 percent lighter than the aluminum in jet airplanes. Thornel yarns are not practical for apparel, since they break when bent over a small radius, but they have many other potential applications.

One of the most interesting of the new materials available to the fiber artist is metal—not in the form of metal objects added to a weaving, but molten metal actually sprayed onto the fibers. This technique has been explored by Jeffrey J. Bayer, of the University of Alabama, in collaboration with several weavers.

The metallizing process, done in much the same way as paint is sprayed, provides a weatherproof, durable, metallic surface. It can add body to an otherwise limp form and make it freestanding. Either ferrous (iron-based) or nonferrous metals—including stainless steel, aluminum, brass, copper, nickel, and zinc—are capable of being sprayed. The coating can be sprayed over the en-

of a large-scale architectural ceramic mural also a craft? If not, where precisely is the dividing line between art and craft? Questions of this nature have been raised time and again, but never answered in a manner that is generally satisfying. Many of the individuals whose work is illustrated in these pages would prefer to be called artists. In the end, we have used the term "craft" in the same way that painting or sculpture is described as a craft—a serious endeavor that implies the highest standards of design, materials, ingenuity, and workmanship.

Fiber construction in the latter part of the 20th century is an enormous field. The designer-artist has available a wealth of new materials and new

left: **Plate 32. Karen White Boyd.**
Actinomorphic Monument. 1975.
Tapestry of wool and linen,
4′ × 1′10″ × 1′10″ (1.2 × .55 × .55 m).
Courtesy the artist.

below: **Plate 33. Ann-Mari Kornerup.**
Tapestry-woven dress. Flax and wool.
Courtesy Den Permanente, Copenhagen.

Plate 34. Renie Breskin Adams.
Breakfast with a Blueberry Muffin.
1973. Crocheted cotton,
8½″ (21 cm) diameter.
Courtesy the artist.

right: Plate 35.
Helena Hernmarck design,
executed at Alice Lund's Textile
Workshop, Borlange, Sweden,
under the artist's direction.
Cloudscape. 1975.
Tapestry of linen rug warp;
wool, linen, and nylon weft;
25′ (7.5 m) square.
Collection United States
Automobile Association,
San Antonio, Tex.

below: Plate 36. Arlene Stimmel.
Blue Stripe Kimono. 1976.
Machine knit and
hand crochet in wool.
Courtesy the artist.

Stitch-Knit   Stitch-knit is based on an industrial technique known as *Mali*. The concept of the *Malimo* machine, one version of the process, is essentially quite simple. Two sets of yarns—a warp and a weft—are laid perpendicular to one another. However, rather than interlacing the two elements, the machine actually stitches them into position in the manner of sewing. Other Mali machines create pile fabrics, web textiles, and yarn.

The possibilities for adapting Mali principles to hand fiber craft were explored in a special tapestry exhibition held in Prague in the mid-1960s. All the tapestries in the show were created by laying yarns or fabric remnants on a heavy nonwoven backing and then stitching the various elements together (Fig. 580). The major advantage of this technique is that it permits a wide range of textural combinations. Furthermore, it overcomes many of the limitations encountered in conventional loom weaving; one can reproduce almost any pattern or effect one wishes. Both the design problems and the results are much like those of collage.

left: 579. Marilyn Meltzer. *J. B.'s Phoenix*, detail. 1975. Sisal and jute sprayed with zinc and bronze. Courtesy the artist.

below: 580. Antonin Kybal. *Brown Cathedral.* c. 1966. *Art protis* tapestry. Courtesy Art Centrum, Prague.

tire work or limited to specific areas (Fig. 579). Sometimes the original fiber texture is allowed to show through, while at other times the coating may completely cover the fiber. In the latter case, the fibers serve as a form—a kind of armature—for the metal structure. The fiber choices are somewhat limited, because molten metal can be sprayed only on fibers that will withstand the heat of the metallic spray.

The metallizing process would have limited interest for most weavers, because the cost of the equipment is prohibitive. However, it could offer exciting possibilities for the weaver who works with large fiber sculptures, particularly in commission work for public buildings.

Experimental Techniques

The search for new methods to fulfill the increasing needs of new forms has encouraged the contemporary designer-artist to tap many sources, both old and new. In some cases handweavers have borrowed techniques originally developed for industry. In others they have reexamined traditional hand processes in light of their potential for 20th-century expression.

above: **581. Gayle Luchessa.** *Red Felt.* 1976.
Felt of wool and dog hair with brass foil, 44 × 20 × 6″
(110 × 50 × 21 cm). Copyright © Gayle Luchessa.

below: **582. Arleen Schloss.** *Homage to Brenda Grant.* 1973.
Ramie and flax with rhoplex, 7′6″ × 10′ (2.25 × 3 m).
Collection Area Arts Foundation, Amarillo, Tex.

Felting and Related Techniques   As noted in Chapter 2, felting is an ancient process that predated weaving in many parts of the world. Many of today's fiber artists have rediscovered felting, since its simple heat-and-pressure principles allow great freedom in manipulating forms. Gayle Luchessa's *Red Felt* (Fig. 581) combines wool, dog hair, and brass foil to create exciting contrasts of color, texture, and material.

The techniques for making paper resemble felting in many ways. Arleen Schloss has experimented with these methods to make a series of works, such as the one illustrated in Figure 582. The fibers are first soaked, either with a garden hose or in the rain, which causes the fibers to shift and intermesh into one thick layer. Then, the pieces are dried and pressed. The resultant forms have the effect of the "controlled accident."

Basketry   Another ancient medium that has enjoyed a renaissance is basketry. Although the basic interlacement methods have remained much the same, weavers are investigating new materials and creating forms totally different from the seed carriers of long ago (Fig. 583). Many "baskets" today function less or not at all as containers but exist as striking forms in themselves.

Knitting and Crocheting   Both single-strand interlacements, knitting and crocheting have long been considered appropriate for the construction of utilitarian items, generally articles of clothing. Only recently has their great potential for nonfunctional works of art—sculpture, wall hangings, and tapestry—begun to be realized.

Mary Walker Phillips has utilized her training as a weaver in designing large-scale knit wall hangings and upholstery fabric (Fig. 584). She often works in linen or unconventional materials and blocks her finished work, thereby sacrificing the elastic quality normally characteristic of knit fabrics to emphasize the overall design.

above: **583. Gary Trentham.** Basket. 1977. Waxed linen. Courtesy Hadler Galleries, New York.

below: **584. Mary Walker Phillips.** *Bell Frilling Knitting.* 1976. Red armature wire with white and red glass beads and gold bells, 24 × 16″ (60 × 40 cm). Courtesy the artist. (See also Fig. 135.)

The Contemporary Fiber Artist   **343**

585. Olga de Amaral.
Wrapped Blue Net. 1973.
Horsehair and wool,
9'2" × 5'10" (2.8 × 1.8 m).
Courtesy the artist.

below: **586. Lia Cook.** *Space-Dyed Photographic Weaving.* 1975.
Space-dyed cotton with polyurethane foam shaping and photographic-contact printing,
7' × 10'6" × 1' (2.1 × 3.15 × .3 m). Courtesy the artist.

587. Claire Zeisler. *Red Forest.* 1968. Square-knotted forms in dyed jute, height 8′ (2.4 m). Collection First National Bank of Chicago.

Renie Breskin Adams has used the basic crochet method, sometimes combined with other techniques, to create witty, freestanding forms (Pl. 34, p. 340). Her work demonstrates the potential for sculptural construction in all fiber interlacings, not just in crochet.

Wrapping Yarn wrapping (see Chap. 15) is often considered purely as a means to embellish or complete works in other techniques. For instance, the ends of a woven piece are sometimes wrapped to make a fringe. However, entire works can be created from wrapped yarns (Fig. 585). The wrapped element can be almost as rigid as wire, so that one has the ability to construct self-supporting works—to draw lines in space.

Photographic Techniques Techniques derived from photography have found their way into many art forms—painting, sculpture, printmaking, ceramics—and weaving is no exception. Various methods can be used to transfer a photographic image onto yarns or woven fabrics. The *Photographic Weaving* by Lia Cook in Figure 586 was made by first space-dyeing the yarn in skeins (see Chap. 18), then weaving with shaped foam rubber to make the undulating wefts. The panels were then coated with a light-sensitive substance and exposed to contact-size photographic negatives.

The Professional Weaver

The individual who earns a livelihood from weaving or some other fiber craft generally falls into one of three categories: the teacher; the workshop weaver, with or without apprentices or assistants; and the design consultant to industry. Some professional weavers actually fill all three roles, in addition to lecturing and giving demonstrations. The possibilities of a career in weaving are much greater now than they were a decade ago, but, as one might expect, the competition is also much greater. Each of the career choices makes certain demands and offers its special rewards.

The Workshop Weaver

The monumental yarn constructions of Claire Zeisler (Fig. 587) require a considerable amount of hand knotting and wrapping. In order to keep pace with the demand for her work, as well as with her own creative urge, Zeisler employs several assistants, who do most of the actual tying. The artist herself—thoroughly acquainted with the mechanics of yarn—designs the sculptures, supervises their execution, and makes whatever modifications are needed before each piece is finished. This workshop approach has provided Zeisler with a stimulating challenge.

588. Magdalena Abakanowicz. Environmental wall. 1971. Sisal, wool, and flax, especially spun for the project; 24'9" × 81'3" (7.4 × 24.4 m). S'Hertogenbosch, Holland.

A similar approach has been taken by Magdalena Abakanowicz (Fig. 588), whose massive environmental tapestries could not possibly be woven by a single person. The viewing public is occasionally shocked to learn that a work of art was actually executed by someone other than the artist whose name it bears, sometimes even without his or her direct involvement. Yet such a workshop situation has a very long precedent; great masters like Raphael and Rubens had assistants, and in some works only the principal figures were executed by the artist himself. Abakanowicz' medium—yarn and specifically sisal—and her forms are very much her own, and they express the artist's hand as personally as though she had thrown each weft shot herself.

Sheila Hicks has established a number of workshops in the last several years, but their purpose and outlook are rather different from the shops of Zeisler and Abakanowicz. At the forefront of a trend that is becoming more and more

common among prominent designer-weavers, Hicks has collaborated with native artisans in Chile, India, and Morocco to revitalize the local weaving industries. The result is a superb blend of traditional cultural elements and the unerring design sense of the artist (Fig. 589). Not until she had thoroughly studied the country and its ancient weaving techniques did Hicks attempt to influence the Moroccan weavers. This symbiotic relationship between a 20th-century artist and a centuries-old craft tradition has benefited both, for the Moroccan weavers have been exposed to a fresh new outlook, while Hicks has absorbed ideas that will remain forever a part of her total design concept.

There is some evidence that the medieval guild system of apprenticeship is gaining new popularity as a method for learning or perfecting the craft of weaving. In an apprentice situation the advanced student not only benefits from the direct one-to-one supervision of a master weaver but also gains practical experience by taking part in the execu-

589. Sheila Hicks. Wall rugs from the *Sejjada* series shown at the Galerie Bob Rouah, Rabat, Morocco, 1971. Height of each rug 7'7" (2.3 m). Courtesy the artist.

tion of commissioned works. Furthermore, the student has the unique opportunity, unknown in the classroom, of observing the business end of a weaving shop—pricing, billing, packing, shipping, and so forth. There are obvious advantages to both master and apprentice.

Design for Industry

The textile industry is one of the largest in the world. In addition to clothing and home furnishings, textile manufacturers supply fabric for upholstery in cars, trains, planes, buses, and ships; for theaters and other public buildings; for industrial purposes; even for sports equipment.

In the first flush of the Industrial Revolution there were no real designers in the great weaving mills. Rather, the emphasis was on imitating designs from other sources, and as the machines became more sophisticated, there was a tendency to reproduce the most elaborate, fussy patterns, simply to demonstrate the marvels of the power loom. Even today, some textile mills do not employ staff designers. However, many hire as consultants skilled handweavers to supply designs.

The major problem confronting the industrial designer is machine-controlled efficiency. The power-loom operation is not financially successful unless the machine can be set to produce a large quantity of fabric with a minimum of human intervention. The manipulation of multiple harnesses and shuttles is time-consuming for the machine, just as it is for the hand loom; consequently, the power loom works best when the complexity of the design is warp-oriented. Industrial looms are becoming ever more automatic, and attempts are being made to utilize the computer in designing for the loom, as well as in controlling the weave mechanics.

Dorothy Liebes achieved her first success as a studio weaver (see Chap. 5), filling commissions for architects, decorators, and wealthy clients across the United States. Her involvement with industry began when she accepted a position with Goodall Fabrics in Maine. As stylist for home furnishings, Liebes strove to maintain a hand-loomed quality in the mass-produced fabrics (Fig. 590).

590. Dorothy Liebes for Goodall Fabrics, Inc. Drapery fabric, detail. 1946. Power loomed in an overshot technique with cut fringe; wool, cotton, and metallic fiber.

591. **Jack Lenor Larsen, Inc.** *Pavilion Cloth,*
from the *Pleasure Dome of Kublai Khan* collection.
Knitted casement fabric in cotton.
Courtesy Jack Lenor Larsen, Inc.

Later, E. I. du Pont de Nemours & Co. assigned her the enviable task of experimenting with their new synthetic fibers. Until her death she served as design consultant for Bigelow-Sanford and Sears, Roebuck & Company. The experience of Dorothy Liebes proves that excellence of design is not incompatible with large-scale production.

Jack Lenor Larsen operates his own fabric house in New York, from which he distributes power-loomed fabrics on a limited-production basis. By keeping his output relatively small, he has been able to create an incredibly diversified line and at the same time maintain a high level of quality in design (Fig. 591). Larsen's particular genius has been in adapting the power loom to a surprisingly wide range of design effects. Rather than forcing the design to conform to the needs of the machine, he has let the design come first.

In addition to the New York operation, Larsen maintains handweaving shops in nine countries, including Haiti, Colombia, and Mexico, all staffed with native weavers. Through these foreign branches he is able to renew his touch with the authentic character of the hand-loomed fabric.

Boris Kroll also directs his own textile firm, working primarily with Jacquard-loomed fabrics (Fig. 592). Kroll supervises every stage of the manufacturing process, from the spinning and blending of fibers into yarn, through the dyeing, to the actual fabric design. It is his conviction that the creation of a textile requires total design involvement, that the character of the yarn is just as important as the weaving pattern.

The cooperation of art and industry in the creation of fabric has proved so successful that we can expect to see more of it in the years to come. The industrial age can best fulfill its potential when machines provide the muscle and human beings supply the heart and soul.

Weaving: Art and Craft

Regardless of whether weavers consider themselves artists or artisans, their work art or craft, many of the same standards apply: honesty of

592. **Boris Kroll Fabrics.** *Himalaya, Everest, Monolith, Pinnacle,* and *Calcutta,* from the *Naturals* collection. Jacquard weave in natural, undyed wool and nylon. Courtesy Boris Kroll Fabrics, Inc.

593. Archie Brennan. *Muhammad Ali/TV.* 1973.
Tapestry in cotton and wool with foam rubber filling,
3'8" × 5'2" × 8" (1.1 × 1.55 × .2 m).
Courtesy Edinburgh Tapestry Company Ltd.

materials, effectiveness of design, care of execution, and fidelity to function, be it utilitarian or aesthetic. Weaving is such an enormous field that there is room for all sorts of products.

Weaving as an Art Form

The outstanding weavers in the United States today are choosing the same paths as their counterparts in painting and sculpture. Neither size nor dimension is an obstacle in the creation of a form, and sedate rectangles are no longer compulsory.

To a certain extent weaving of the past two decades has tended to reflect contemporary trends in painting and sculpture. In the work of many prominent artist-weavers can be found elements of Pop Art (Fig. 593), a style that derives its forms and spirit from aspects of the mass culture; of Op (or optical) Art (Fig. 594), a form concerned with

594. Carol Kurtz. *Untitled.* 1974. Wool and cotton, monk's-belt weave;
5' × 4'2" (1.5 × 1.25 m). Courtesy the artist.

left: 595. Herman Scholten.
Square Purple Yellow. 1976.
Rib weave and plain weave
in wool, linen, and sisal;
8'4" (2.5 m) square.
Museum Boymans-van Beuningen,
Rotterdam.

below: 596. Magdalena Abakanowicz.
Human Structure Images,
from the cycle *Alteration.* 1974–75.
Linen, thread, and glue;
approximately life size.
Courtesy the artist.

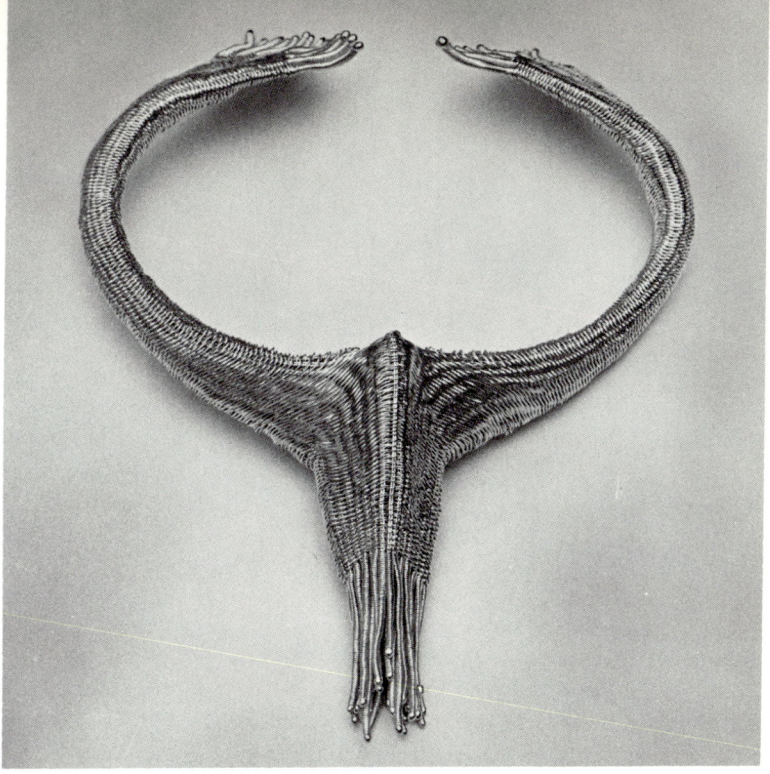

597. Mary Lee Hu. *Neckpiece #5.* 1969. Wrapped and woven fine and sterling silver. Courtesy the artist.

the response of the eye to visual stimuli often of an illusory nature; and of Minimal Art (Fig. 595), which attempts to limit art to the most basic elements of color, plane, and form. The 1970s have brought to weaving, as to the other arts, an interest in Photorealism—or ultranaturalistic representation based on the aesthetic of photographic imagery (Pl. 35, p. 340).

Some critics would argue that the fiber arts have taken the lead, that fiber construction has begun to establish styles for the other media to imitate. A suggestion of this identity is evident in the molded fiber structures of Magdalena Abakanowicz (Fig. 596), as well as in her monumental tapestry works (Fig. 588). We see this trend to create new idioms of form and design also in the wrapped works by Sheila Hicks (Pl. 21, p. 237) and the huge environmental works by Loes van der Horst (Fig. 599). Once we put aside the conventional ways of thinking about fiber as a medium, we realize how very little its potential has been exploited.

Weaving as a Humanizer

Our surroundings today are highly standardized. Our homes, schools, offices, machines, tools, furnishings, cars, and other paraphernalia are mass-produced according to certain limited design standards. One of the few areas left in which it is relatively easy and inexpensive to create individuality—and therefore a touch of humanity—is in fabrics, in clothing and home furnishings made of fiber. If we are to seek personal identity in the fabrics of everyday living, these items must be in some way unique, in some way more beautifully crafted or individually expressive than the mass-produced garments and furnishings of industry.

It is entirely possible for an article of clothing to be more-or-less conventional in design, yet display an artistry of fabric that sets it apart from the standardized product of the industrial mills (Pl. 36, p. 340). The handweaver has great freedom to exercise ingenuity in the creation of loom-constructed garments (see pp. 328–333) and yardage for clothing. Subtle decorative effects that would be impossible or prohibitively expensive on power equipment can imbue the hand-loomed fabric with rich, personal qualities.

Even greater impact is achieved by the garment that steps outside convention to create new lines and forms. Such innovative designs make us question the standards and rules of dress that are normally adhered to. There is no reason why a garment must conform to a particular shape; as long as it performs its function—contributing to modesty, warmth, ease of movement, or whatever—it can be considered an effective design.

Jewelry is an area in which people always have expressed their individuality, but only recently have fiber and the fiber techniques been involved. This interest began with macramé, which, when knotted on delicate yarns, has an obvious application for jewelry (Fig. 420). But jewelers also have begun to explore the possibilities of precious metals—gold and silver—interlaced in fiber techniques (Fig. 597). Fine gold and silver wires, used in basketry or weaving processes, combine the delicate tracery of the technique with the intrinsic value of the material.

above: **598. Maria Chojnacka.** *Diminuendo.* 1975. Mixed technique in sisal, 7′ × 12′4″ (2.1 × 3.7 m). Courtesy the artist. (See also Fig. 541.)

below: **599. Loes van der Horst** design, executed by Mick Eckhout. *Bijlmermeer.* 1974–76. Net construction over water, polypropylene cable on steel tube poles; greatest height 52′6″ (16 m). Commissioned by the city of Amsterdam.

The same humanizing principles can be applied to interior design—upholstery fabric, room dividers, casement and drapery materials, accessories, and the like. There is ample opportunity for the handweaver to express individuality in the embellishment of the home. In Colonial times nearly all furnishings were homemade, and many families still treasure heirlooms meticulously crafted by great-grandparents. No machine can ever hope to duplicate the qualities of warmth and humanity—perhaps even of durability—inherent in an object patiently created by human hands.

Weaving as Environment

A fiber structure qualifies as "environment" either when it actually encloses us or when it so imprints itself upon a space that we must interact with it and respond to it (Fig. 598). The experience of standing, sitting, walking, *being* inside a woven environment is completely different from that of viewing a form hung on the wall (Fig. 599). At any museum exhibition the largest crowd collects around the work of art that can be touched, crawled through, sat upon, and generally brought into direct contact with the viewer (Fig. 600). One is instinctively drawn to an object that can be made a part of oneself and that one can be a part of. Many contemporary artists in various fields have been attracted by the concept of environment, for anything less than total immersion in the artist's form forces one's perception to be affected, often subliminally, by adjacent objects. The artist who creates an environment controls as fully as possible the viewer's aesthetic experience. And, in essence, any woven form, however small, however utilitarian, provides the observer with an aesthetic experience.

600. **Wilhelm and Eva Heer.** *Spielwildnis*, detail. 1973.
Knotted rope, 13'1" × 13'1" × 9'10" (3.9 × 3.9 × 2.9 m) overall.
Courtesy International Biennial
of Tapestries, Lausanne, 1973.

Appendices

Appendix A
Drafts and Drafting

Chapter 9 introduced the basics of drafting and gave enough information for the reader to follow explanations in the text. Weavers who are interested in the concept of drafting or who enjoy planning on paper may wish to pursue the subject further. This appendix gives more detailed information about the threading draft and draw-down, or cloth draft. On the following page are pictured some of the more common drafts used on the 4-harness loom. The profile draft, a shorthand method of draft notation, is also explained in this appendix.

In Chapter 9 two of the most-used types of draw were presented: the *straight draw* (1, 2, 3, 4) and the *pointed draw* (for example, 1, 2, 3, 4, 3, 2). The weaver involved in pattern weaves should also be familiar with two other categories of threading draft: the *broken draw* and the *intermittent draw*.

The broken draw has a sequence that begins as a straight draw but breaks, then starts again in the opposite direction. One example would be:

1, 2, 4, 3

A more complex broken draw might be:

1, 2, 3, 4, 2, 1, 4, 3, 2, 1, 3, 4

The intermittent draw breaks from the straight sequence and skips one or more harnesses before beginning again. This form with skipped intervals enlarges, to an extent, the resulting pattern. Usually, the break occurs between the first and last yarns in a line sequence. One example of an intermittent draw would be:

1, 2, 3, 2, 3, 4, 3, 4, 1, 4, 1, 2

There are, of course, many more complicated threading drafts, but most are intended for looms with more than four harnesses and are thus beyond the scope of this book.

The weave draft or draw-down can be especially useful in planning color relationships on paper. Drafting with several colors in either the warp or the weft or both can be somewhat complex. However, it does show how even the most basic weave can provide unusual effects of patterning with careful planning and distribution of colors. You can use either different symbols or even the actual colors in felt-tip pen to indicate the yarn colors in the draw-down.

The easiest way to begin color drafting is with two colors in the warp. The color unit may not always coincide with the threading unit. It may extend over several repeats of the threading. It is usually easier to start plotting the treadling pattern row by row with a pencil dot. When the overall pattern has been determined, you can go back with colored felt-tip pens to fill in the squares for color change. One point may seem obvious but can be overlooked: Remember that the warp will have the same color consistently in a vertical line and will be colored the same every time that warp yarn shows on the surface.

After the warp color positions have been established, the weft yarns are those remaining blank on the draw-down. The weft color, naturally, will be the same all across each horizontal row.

A good exercise—in both drafting and design in general—is to take a simple plain-weave or twill pattern and do a number of draw-downs with color variation, increasing the complexity as you go along. You might

357

Common Drafts for the
4-Harness Loom

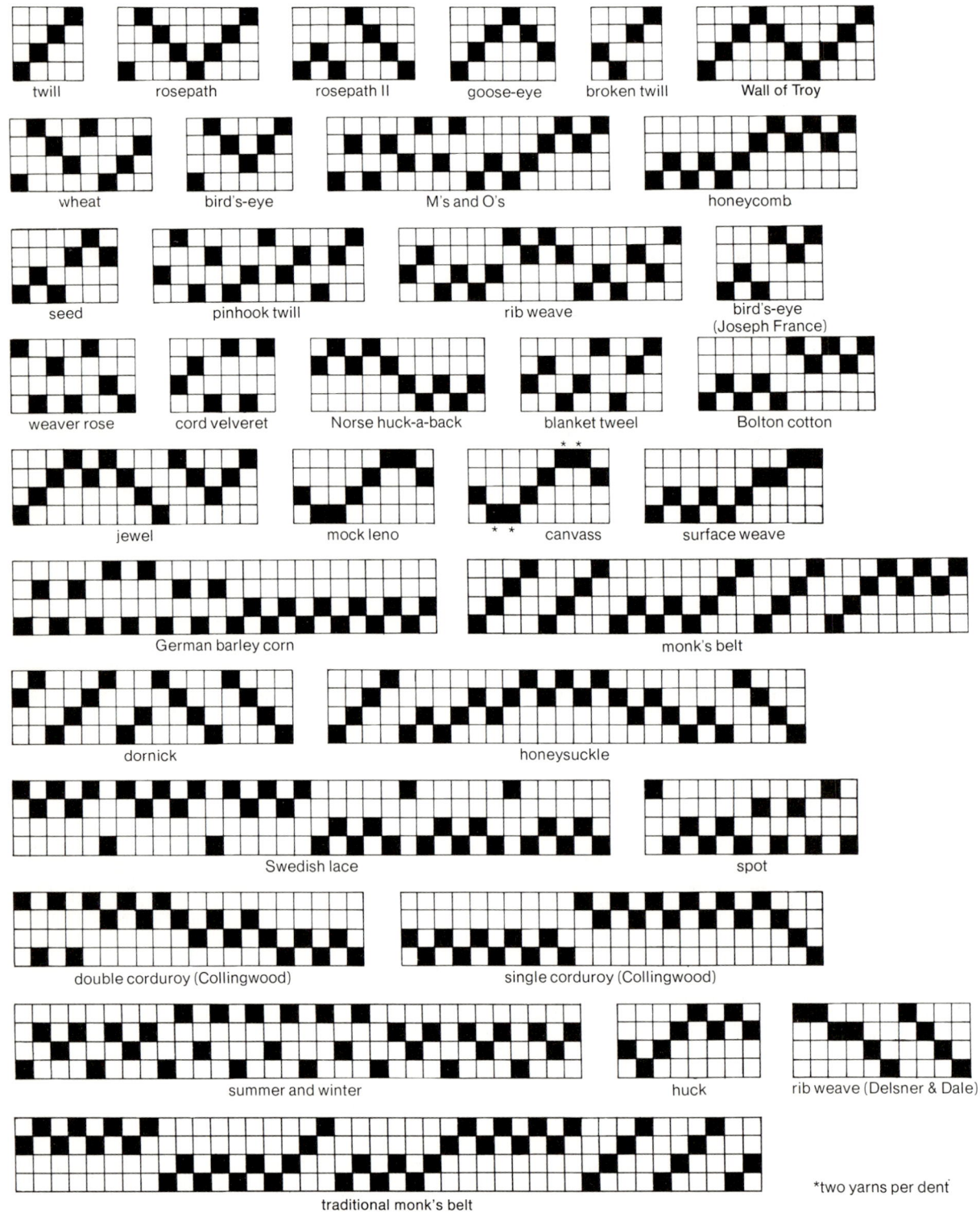

twill   rosepath   rosepath II   goose-eye   broken twill   Wall of Troy

wheat   bird's-eye   M's and O's   honeycomb

seed   pinhook twill   rib weave   bird's-eye (Joseph France)

weaver rose   cord velveret   Norse huck-a-back   blanket tweel   Bolton cotton

jewel   mock leno   * *   canvass   surface weave
* *

German barley corn   monk's belt

dornick   honeysuckle

Swedish lace   spot

double corduroy (Collingwood)   single corduroy (Collingwood)

summer and winter   huck   rib weave (Delsner & Dale)

traditional monk's belt   *two yarns per dent

begin with two colors in the warp, then add a third, then perhaps vary the weft color. Of course, the symbols or colors that you choose to mark the weave draft need not represent actual color change but can also stand for differences in weight or texture of the yarns. The draft shows *relationships*, rather than the real appearance of the fabric.

The Profile Draft

A profile draft is a short method of notation for unit pattern weaves. It is used often by designers to enlarge, scale down, or vary a pattern weave and is most helpful in creating original drafts.

Drafts for combination weaves (block designs) are developed from composites of several individual units indicating the threading sequences. The basic unit for a 4-harness loom may consist of a sequence of as few as two yarns. This individual unit, when several unlike units are arranged in a composite draft, is referred to as a *block*. The units chosen for compound drafts might be identical to one of the common twill threading drafts repeated all across a warp.

Designing with a compound threading draft is a matter of distributing the two or more units of design in order to achieve the desired results. The profile draft simplifies the process by reducing the long series of squares that would be found on a full threading draft to just a few squares. This simplified type of notation is used when the threading draft consists of two or more basic blocks. In the

profile draft, the square no longer represents a single yarn. Rather, each square on the draft denotes one *unit*, which often is composed of four warp yarns.

There is no standard interpretation of the profile that applies to every situation, except in relation to a specific weave. The individual unit threading information must be provided at some point for each profile draft. The key for interpreting the shortened draft version is essential.

When you work with a profile draft, you are starting with preconceived units of threading. The design therefore refers to an arrangement of the *units* for the designed fabric, rather than an arrangement of individual yarns. The weaver can more readily give attention to proportions and to the overall design, instead of concentrating on the yarn-by-yarn threading order. A profile draft also makes it easier to thread the heddles, because you are repeating whole blocks from the profile draft.

Summer-and-winter is a typical unit weave for which you may wish to set up a profile draft. This pattern weave produces at least two units of a twill, has only small weft overshots, and has a draft that will make plain weave. Two harnesses are devoted to making the plain weave to give the background structure to the fabric. Therefore, if you are threading a 4-harness loom, there are only two harnesses left for carrying the pattern yarn. Since only one harness is needed to make a single pattern block, there are two pattern blocks possible on the 4-harness

601. Threading drafts for three versions of the summer-and-winter weave. In each case, the full draft is at left, the profile at right.

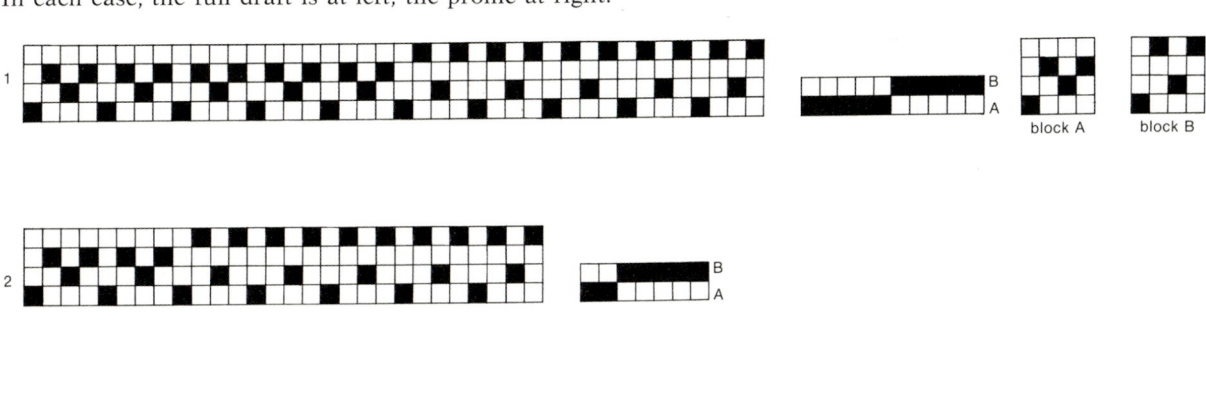

loom. Looms with more harnesses allow you one extra pattern block for each additional harness. The yarns making the background are threaded alternately with the pattern warp yarns.

The figure on page 359 shows three possible drafts for the summer-and-winter weave. In each case, the full threading draft is at the left, the profile draft at the right. In version No. 1, the two blocks of the pattern have been isolated to make the relationships clearer.

As you can see from draft No. 1, there are two different threading blocks:

1, 3, 2, 3

and

1, 4, 2, 4

In the full draft at left, block A is repeated five times, and then block B is repeated five times. The profile draft at right reduces this notation to just ten squares, instead of the forty squares needed for the full draft. Once the blocks have been identified (at far right),

602. Profile draw-down and full draw-down for three versions of the summer-and-winter weave.

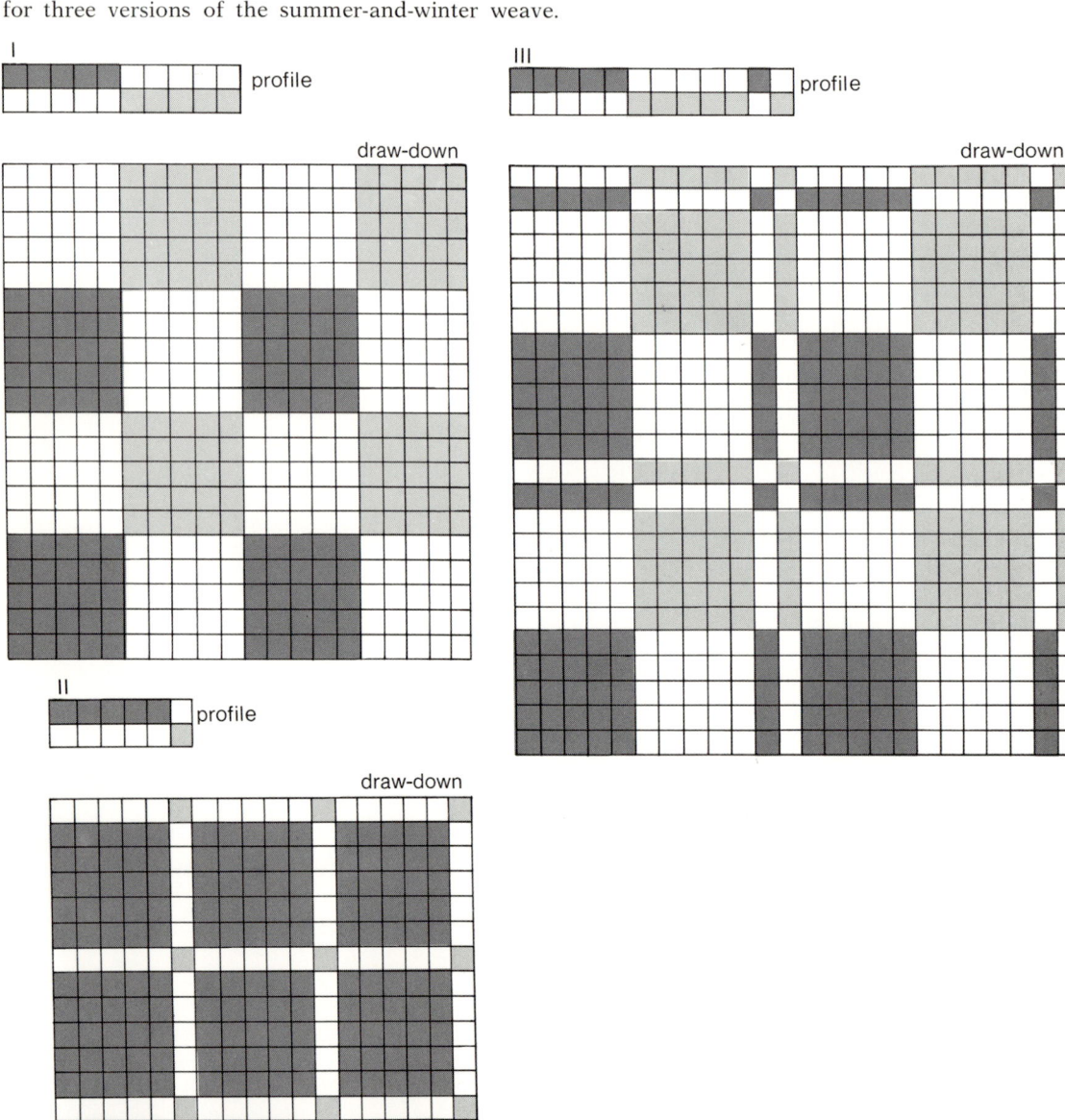

there is no need to show every single yarn in the threading pattern.

The weave draft or draw-down can also be reduced to a profile, which serves as a guide for the pattern arrangement without indicating either the placement or the precise number of individual yarns. The figure that follows shows both the profile draft and the long weave draft for three different threading arrangements of summer-and-winter. In each case the profile draft indicates a *relationship*, and the long draft presents a *scale* based on that relationship.

Many pattern books, particularly those dealing with Early American designs, employ the profile system exclusively. If you are interested in more intricate patterning, you should cultivate a facility for profiles.

Appendix B
Records

Sample Yarn-Calculation Form

---

title/description of project _____

finished length _____

allowance for warp take-up (10%) _____

allowance for shrinkage (10%) _____

allowance for loom waste _____ ¾ yard _____

allowance for hems _____

total warp length _____

finished width _____

allowance for draw-in (10%) _____

allowance for shrinkage (10%) _____

allowance for hems _____

width at reed _____

sett: _____ × _____ = _____
     ends per inch   width at reed   total warp yarns

warp quantity: _____ × _____ = _____
                   warp yarns   length of warp   yards

_____ ÷ _____ = _____
warp quantity   am't per spool/pound   No. of spools/pounds

weft quantity: _____ + _____ = _____
                   width at reed   10% take-up   length of one weft

_____ × _____ = _____
weft yarns per inch   length of warp   No. weft shots

_____ × _____ = _____
length of one weft   No. weft shots   weft quantity

_____ ÷ _____ = _____
weft quantity   am't per spool/pound   No. of spools/pounds

Sample Weaving Record

title/description of project _____

woven by _____ date _____

	warp	*weft*

yarn type _____   _____

size   _____   _____

color   _____   _____

warp: No. warp yarns _____

      order of warp _____

      total yardage _____

      total weight _____

      finished length _____

weft: total yardage _____

      total weight _____

      finished width _____

loom _____ reed _____ e.p.i. _____

draft name _____

No. harnesses _____ No. treadles _____

No. heddles: _____ _____ _____ _____ _____ _____ _____ _____

     frame 1   frame 2   frame 3   frame 4   frame 5   frame 6   frame 7   frame 8

cost of project: _____ selling cost: _____ _____

                                                            wholesale   retail

comments _____

Appendix C
Sources of Materials and Equipment

Looms and Weaving Equipment—Manufacturers and Distributors

Albion Hills School of Spinning, Dyeing, and Weaving, R.R. 3, Caledon East, Albion Hills, Ontario, Canada

Gunnar Andersons, Vä vakedsverkstad, 792 00 Mora, Sweden

Beka, Inc., 1648 Grand Ave., St. Paul, Minn. 55105

Bexell & Son, 2470 Dixie Highway, Pontiac, Mich. 48055 (*Cranbrook looms*)

Dick Blick, P. O. Box 1267, Galesburg, Ill. 61401 (*table looms, floor looms*)

Gina Brown Fibrecrafts, 2207 Fourth St. S.W., Calgary, Alberta, Canada T2S 1X1

Gallagher Tools, 318 Pacheco, Santa Cruz, Calif. 95062

E. E. Gilmore, 1032 N. Broadway, Stockton, Calif. 95205

The Good Wool Shop, 1119 Corydon Ave., Winipeg, Manitoba, Canada R3M 0X4

Greentree Ranch, 163 N. Carter Lake Rd., Loveland, Colo. 80537

J. L. Hammett Co., 10 Hammett Place, Braintree, Mass. 02184

Harrisville Designs, Harrisville, N.H. 03450 (*loom rentals available*)

Herald Looms, 118 Lee St., Lodi, Ohio 44254

Kessenich Looms, 7463 Harwood Ave., Wauwatosa, Wis. 53213 (*looms for the handicapped available*)

Walter Kircher, 355 Marburg/Lohn, Postfach 1408, Germany (distributed by Greentree Ranch)

Lillstina, Inc., 66 Hawley St., Binghamton, N.Y. 13901

Lillstina of Canada, 4A John St., Weston, Ontario, Canada M9N 1J3

Loomcraft, P. O. Box 65, Littleton, Colo. 80120

Looms 'n Yarns, Box 4605, Berea, Ohio 44017 (*countermarch looms, Glimåkra looms*)

Macomber Looms, Beech Ridge Rd., York, Maine 03909

Maplewood Enterprises, Chatham, Mich. 49816 (*backstrap loom*)

Newcomb Loom Co., Davenport, Iowa 52808

Nilus Leclerc, Inc., L'Isletville 6, Quebec, Canada (East Coast distributor: P. O. Box 491, Plattsburg, N.Y. 12901; West Coast distributor: 2799A Del Monte St., West Sacramento, Calif. 95691)

Northwest Looms, Box 4872, Bainbridge Island, Wash. 98110 (*Pioneer looms*)

The Norwood Loom Company, Box 272, Baldwin, Mich. 49304

Pendleton Shop, Sedonia, Ariz. 86336

Ries Knotique, 13042 82 St., Edmonton, Alberta, Canada T5E 2T5

Schacht Spindle Co., 1708 Walnut St., Boulder, Colo. 80302

School Products Co., Inc., 1201 Broadway, New York, N.Y. 10001

Structo Division, King-Seeley Thermos Co., Freeport, Ill. 61032

Toika Finnish Loom Corp., P. O. Box 2, Millwood, N.Y. 10546

Tools of the Trade, R.F.D., Fairhaven, Vt. 05743

Ulltex Inc., P. O. Box 918, Demond Ave., North Adams, Mass. 01247 (*countermarch looms*)

The Village Weavers Ltd., 551 Church St., Toronto, Ontario, Canada M4Y 2E2

Weaver's Loft, 1021 Government St., Victoria, B.C., Canada

Dyes

Accolite Pigments, American Crayon Co., Sandusky, Ohio 44870 (*Helizarin dyes*)

Allied Chemical Corp., 1411 Broadway, New York, N.Y. 10036, Att. Mrs. K. H. Jones, 6th Floor (*acid dyes for wool and silk; bulk quantities only*)

Bachmeier and Co., Inc., 154 Chambers St., New York, N.Y. 10007 (*acid, direct, aniline, benazel, chlorantine, and basic dyes*)

Cerulean Blue, P. O. Box 5126, Seattle, Wash. 98105

Ciba Chemical and Dye Co., 7535 Lincoln Ave., Skokie, Ill. 60076

Comak Chemicals Ltd., Swinton Works, Moon St., London, N1, England (*natural dyes*)

Craftsman's Dyes, George Wells, 565 Cedar Swamp Rd., Glen Head, N.Y. 11545

W. Cushing and Co., Perfection Dyes, Kennebunkport, Maine 04046

Fab Dec, Box 3062, Lubbock, Tex. 79410

Fecel Gifts, Inc., 7147 S.W. 8 St., Miami, Fla. 33144

C. D. Fitz Harding-Bailey, St. Auryn, 15 Dutton St., Bankstown, N.S.W. 2200, Australia (*natural dyes*)

Glen Black Handwoven Textiles, 1414 Grant Ave., San Francisco, Calif. 91433 (*Procion dyes*)

Handcraft Wools, Box 378, Streetsville, Ontario, Canada (*Ciba dyes*)

I. C. I. America, Inc., Box 1274, 151 South St., Stamford, Conn. 06904

The Mannings, R.D. 2, East Berlin, Pa. 17316

Nature's Herb Co., 281 Ellis St., San Francisco, Calif. 94102

Naz-Dar Co., 1087 N. Branch St., Chicago, Ill. 60622

New England Earth Crafts, 149 Putnam Ave., Cambridge, Mass. 02139

Old Fashioned Herb Co., 581 N. Lake Ave., Pasadena, Calif. 91101 (*lump and powdered indigo root*)

Pioneer Handspinning, 89 E. Second North, Hyde Park, Utah 84318 (*seeds for growing dye plants*)

Putnam Fadeless Dyes, Monroe Chemical Co., 301 Oak St., Quincy, Ill. 62302

Pylam Products Co., Inc., 95-11 218 St., Queens Village, N.Y. 11429 (*Procion dyes*)

Harry E. Saier, Dimondale, Mich. 48821 (*seeds for growing dye plants*)

Shag Rag Weavers, Route 1, P. O. Box 55B, Green Mountain, N.C. 29740 (*lichens*)

Straw Into Gold, P. O. Box 2904, Oakland, Calif. 94618

Village Weaving Center, 434 Sixth Ave., New York, N.Y. 10011 (*natural dyes and mordants*)

World on a String, P. O. Box 405, June Lake, Calif. 93529

World-Wide Herbs, 11 Saint Catherine St. W., Montreal 18, Quebec, Canada

Batik and Screen Printing Supplies

Advance Process Supply Co., 400 N. Noble St., Chicago, Ill. 60622

Arthur Brown and Bro., Inc., 2 West 46 St., New York, N.Y. 10036

Batik Craft Supplies, 1 Industrial Rd., Woodbridge, N.J. 07075

Batik International, 15455 Milldale Dr., Los Angeles, Calif. 90024

Dharma Trading Co., Box 1288, 1952 University Ave., Berkeley, Calif. 94701

Fezandie and Sperrie, Inc., 103 Lafayette St., New York, N.Y. 10013

Gager's Handicraft, 3516 Beltline Blvd., St. Louis Park, Minn. 55416

MacMillan Arts and Crafts, Inc., 9520 Baltimore Ave., College Park, Md. 20740

Resin Coatings Corp., 5900 Miami Lakes Dr. E., Miami Lakes, Fla. 33014 (*Remyzist*)

Saks Art and Crafts, 1103 N. Third St., Milwaukee, Wis. 53203

Screen Process Supplies Mfg. Co., 1199 E. 12 St., Oakland, Calif. 94606

Yarns

A. A. A. Cordage Co., Inc., 3730 W. Montrose, Chicago, Ill. 60618

Gina Brown Fibrecrafts, 2207 Fourth St. S.W., Calgary, Alberta, Canada T2S 1X1

J. Hyslop Bathgate and Co., Galashiels, Scotland (*wool yarn and oddments*)

Belding Lily Co., P. O. Box 88, Shelby, N.C. 28150 (formerly Lily Mills)

Stanley Berroco, Inc., 140 Mendon St., Uxbridge, Mass. 01569

Briggs and Little, York Mills, Harvey Station P. O., York County, New Brunswick, Canada

William Condon and Sons, 65 Queen St., P. O. Box 129, Charlottetown, P.E.I., Canada

Contessa Yarns, P. O. Box 37, Lebanon, Conn. 06249

Coulter Studios, 118 E. 59 St., New York, N.Y. 10022

Creative Handweavers, P. O. Box 26480, Los Angeles, Calif. 90026

Dharma Trading Co., Box 1288, 1952 University Ave., Berkeley, Calif. 94701

Frederick J. Fawcett, Inc., 129 South St., Boston, Mass. 02111

The Fiber Studio, Foster Hill Rd., Henniker, N.H. 03242

Filature Lemieux, Inc., St. Ephrem, Beauce, Quebec, Canada

Folklorico, 522 Ramona St., P. O. Box 625, Palo Alto, Calif. 94302

Fort Crailo Yarns Co., 2 Green St., Dept. 3, Rensselaer, N.Y. 12144

The Good Wool Shop, 119 Corydon Ave., Winnipeg, Manitoba, Canada R3M 0X4

Greentree Ranch, 163 N. Carter Lake Rd., Loveland, Colo. 80537

Handcraft Wools, Box 378, Streetsville, Ontario, Canada

The Handweaver, P. O. Box 1271, Sonoma, Calif. 95476

Harrisville Designs, Harrisville, N.H. 03450

Henry's Attic, 5 Mercury Ave., Monroe, N.Y. 10950

House of Kleen, P. O. Box 224, North Stonington, Conn. 06359

Ironstone Yarns Warehouse, P. O. Box 196, Uxbridge, Mass. 01560

Lundgren, Inc., 540 W. Main St., Northboro, Mass. 01532 (*rya and other Swedish yarns, cow's hair, rya backing*)

The Mannings, R.D. 2, East Berlin, Pa. 17316

Mexiskeins, P. O. Box 1629, Missoula, Mont. 59801

Nature's Fibres, Box 172, Newbury, Vt. 05051 (*silk*)

Newfoundland Weavery Ltd., 99 Yorkville Ave., Toronto, Ontario, Canada *and* 170 Duckworth St., St. John's, Newfoundland, Canada

Oregon Worsted Co., P. O. Box 02098, Portland, Ore. 97202

Paternayan Brothers, Inc., 312 E. 95 St., New York, N.Y. 10028 (*wholesale*)

Rammagerdin, Hafnar Straeti 5 & 17, Reykjavik, Iceland (*natural undyed wools*)

Robin and Russ, 533 N. Adams St., McMinnville, Ore. 97128

Shelburne Spinners, 2 Howard St., Burlington, Vt. 05401

The Silver Shuttle, 1301 35 St., N.W., Washington, D.C. 20007

Paula Simmons, P.O. Box 12, Suquamish, Wash. 98392 (*handspun yarn*)

Tinkler and Co., Inc., Box 17, Norristown, Pa. 19494

The Village Weavers, Ltd., 551 Church St., Toronto, Ontario, Canada M4Y 2E2

Village Weaving Center, 434 Sixth Ave., New York, N.Y. 10011

Weaver's Loft, 1021 Government St., Victoria, B.C., Canada

The Weaver's Loft, Ltd., Anchorage House, Historic Properties, Halifax, Nova Scotia, Canada

The Weaver's Place, 109 Osborne St., Winnipeg, Manitoba, Canada R3L 1Y4

George Wells, The Ruggery, 565 Cedar Swamp Rd., Glen Head, N.Y. 11545

Wettehoffin Katilollisuusopettajaopisto, Hämeenlinna, Finland

Wilde Yarns, John Wilde & Bro., Inc., 3705 Main St., Philadelphia, Pa. 19127

Clinton L. Wilkinson, 64 Virginia Ave., Charlotte, N.C.

The Yarn Barn, Hobbycraft Center, 1249 Fourth Ave., Prince George, B.C., Canada

The Yarn Depot, Inc., 545 Sutter St., San Francisco, Calif. 94102

Spinning Wheels and Equipment

Albion Hills School of Spinning, Dyeing, and Weaving, R.R. 3, Caledon East, Albion Hills, Ontario, Canada (*wheels*)

Anchor Chest Co., Box 107, Salem, Ohio 44460

Ashford Handicrafts Ltd., P. O. Box 121, Rakaia, New Zealand (*wheels*)

Clemes & Clemes, 650 San Pablo Ave., Pinole, Calif. 94564

C. D. Fitz Harding-Bailey, St. Auryn, 15 Dutton St., Bankstown, N.S.W. 2200, Australia (*wheels*)

E. B. Frye and Sons., Inc., Wilton, N.H. 03086

Greentree Ranch, 163 N. Carter Lake Rd., Loveland, Colo. 80537

Handcraft Wools, Box 378, Streetsville, Ontario, Canada

M. W. Klein, 1053 Blue Heron Dr., Sanibel, Fla. 33957

The Mannings, R.D. 2, East Berlin, Pa. 17316

The Merri Weaver, 1112 Rowand Ct., Voorhees, N.J. 08043

Pirtle Spinner, 21501 St. John Lane, Huntington Beach, Calif. 92646

Lucien Quellet, Manufacturers des Rouets, Village des Aulnais, Cité L'Islet, Quebec, Canada

Romni Wools, 3779 W. Tenth, Vancouver, B.C., Canada V6R 2G5 and 319 King St. W., Toronto, Ontario, Canada M5V 1J5

School Products Co., Inc., 1201 Broadway, New York, N.Y. 10001 (*wheels, cards, fleece, spindles, spinning oil*)

Paula Simmons, P. O. Box 12, Suquamish, Wash. 98392 (*carding and spinning oil*)

Obadia Tharp Co., 8406 S.W. Eighth Ave., Portland, Ore. 96219 (large wheels)

The Village Weavers, Ltd., 551 Church St., Toronto, Ontario, Canada M4Y 2E2

Weaver's Loft, 1021 Government St., Victoria, B.C., Canada

Whitehorse Mountain Woodworks, P. O. Box 23, Green Spring, W. Va. 26722

Spinning Materials

Cambridge Wools, Ltd., P. O. Box 2572, Auckland, New Zealand (*scoured natural wools*)

Freed Co., P. O. Box 394, 415 Central Ave., N.W., Albuquerque, N.M. 87103 (fleece)

Greentree Ranch, 163 N. Carter Lake Rd., Loveland, Colo. 80537 (*wool and flax*)

Indiana Botanic Gardens, Inc., P. O. Box 5, 626 177th St., Hammond, Ind. 46325 (*flax seed*)

Jones Sheep Farm, Peabody, Kan. 66866 (*fleece*)

Alistair Mathieson, P. O. Box 431, Waterloo, Ontario, Canada N2J 4A9 (*New Zealand fleece*)

Newfoundland Weavery, Ltd., 99 Yorkville Ave., Toronto, Ontario, Canada *and* 170 Duckworth St., St. John's, Newfoundland, Canada

The River Farm, Route 1, P. O. Box 169A, Timberville, Va. 22853

Robin Hill Farm, R.R. 4, Box 721, Newburgh, Ind. 47630

Romni Wools, 3779 W. Tenth, Vancouver, B.C., Canada V6R 2G5 *and* 319 King St. W., Toronto, Ontario, Canada M5V 1J5 (*unspun silk, flax, fleece, angora*)

Straw Into Gold, P. O. Box 2904, Oakland, Calif. 94618 (*cotton*)

Wilson's Holiday Farm, Route 2, Waupun, Wis. 53963

Chemicals

The following chemicals firms will send information about local distributors.

FMC Corporation, Inorganic Chemicals Division, 633 Third Ave., New York, N.Y. 10017

Merck and Co., Inc., General Offices and Laboratories, Rahway, N.J.

Spectro Chem Inc., 1354 Ellison Ave., Louisville, Ky. 40204

Rug Hooking Supplies

Norden Products, P. O. Box 1, 222 Waukegan Rd., Glenview, Ill. 60025

Rittermere Craft Studios Ltd., P. O. Box 240, Vineland, Ontario, Canada

Beads

Earthy Endeavors, 12130 E. Philadelphia, P. O. Box 817, Whittier, Calif. 90601

Sondra Lund, 2641 Crestview, Newport Beach, Calif. 92660

Mumby's Beads, 2931 E. Grace Lane, Costa Mesa, Calif. 92625

Reeves Knotique, P. O. Box 5011, Riverside, Calif. 92507

Yone, Inc., 478 Union St., San Francisco, Calif. 94133

Feathers, Shells, Reed, and Cane

Fiberfold Ltd., 49 Edward St., Buffalo, N.Y. 14202

Gettinger Feather Co., 200 Fifth Ave., New York, N.Y. 10018

Straw Into Gold, P. O. Box 2904, Oakland, Calif. 94618

Naturalcraft, Inc., 2199 Bancroft Way, Berkeley, Calif. 94704

Appendix D

Characteristics of Common Sheep Breeds and Other Animal Fibers

Breed or animal	Where raised	Colors	Texture	Fleece weight	Staple length	Crimp number per inch	British spinning quality count	Felting and other special qualities
Cheviot	England Norway Australia	white-faced	very soft	5–7 lb 2.25–3.18 kg	2–6 in 5–15.2 cm	8–9	50–56	easy to spin, dyes easily, dense
Columbia	U.S.A.	white		11–13 lb 5–6.9 kg	3½–5 in 8.8–12.7 cm		56–60	dyes easily
Corriedale	New Zealand Australia U.S.A.	white	fairly soft, silky	10–15 lb 4.5–6.8 kg	4–6 in 10–15 cm	small 14–16	56–60	dyes readily
Cotswold	England U.S.A.	white	luster, curly locks	9 lb 4.17 kg	10–14 in 25–35.5 cm	wide; wool hangs in ringlets 14–18	44–46	tends to mat
Dorset horn	England Australia	black-faced	crisp, springy, has kemp	5–9 lb 2.2–4.17 kg	3½–5½ in 8.8–13 cm		50–56	
East Friesian (Westphalian rattail)	Germany	white-faced		9 lb 4.17 kg			48–56	felts easily
Finnish Landrace	Finland U.S.A.			5–7 lb 2.2–3.18 kg			50–60	
Hampshire	England U.S.A.	black-faced	luster, coarse	7–11 lb 3.18–6.9 kg	2¾ in 7 cm	small, springy	50–58	
Herdwick	England Norway	white, black, graded	springy, harsh, has kemp	3–4 lb 1.36–1.81 kg	6–8 in 15–20 cm		28–40	
Karakul	S. Africa U.S.A.	black, gray	coarse, wiry	8 lb 3.63 kg	8–10 in 20–25 cm		40–46	
Kivircik	Turkey	white-faced	fine				44–56	
Leicester	U.S.A. England Australia	white	luster, fine, silky	7–11 lb 3.18–5 kg	14 in 35.5 cm	wide, 3–4	40–46	

Breed or animal	Where raised	Colors	Texture	Fleece weight	Staple length	Crimp number per inch	British spinning quality count	Felting and other special qualities
Lincoln	U.S.A. Canada England	black-trimmed	coarse, luster	12–20 lb 5.44–9 kg	10–16 in 25–40.6 cm	wide 1–2	30–44	
Merino	Spain Australia U.S.A. England	white	fine, soft, silky	7–10 lb 3.18–4.5 kg	1½–3 in 3.7–7.6 cm	26–28	56–80	
Montedale	U.S.A.			8–20 lb 3.63–9 kg	3–6 in 7.6–15 cm		56–58	
Oxford Down	England U.S.A.	black-faced, brown, black	coarse, springy	10–12 lb 4.5–5.44 kg	3–6 in 7.6–15 cm		46–50	hard to dye an even color
Rambouillet	France U.S.A.	white	fine	10–18 lb 4.5–8.17 kg	2–3 in 5–7.6 cm		62–70	easy to spin
Romney	England U.S.A. Australia	white	luster, semi-coarse	10–12 lb 4.5–5.44 kg	7–8 in 17.7–20 cm	wide	46–50	easy to felt
Scottish Black-face	England	black-trimmed	coarse	4–5 lb 1.81–2.2 kg	8–15 in 20–38 cm		28–40	
Shetland	England	white-faced	soft	3½ lb 1.6 kg	3½ in 8.8 cm		46–58	easy to felt, tend to moult
Shropshire	U.S.A.	black-faced, white	fine	8–10 lb 3.6–4.5 kg	4 in 10 cm	small, springy	50–58	
South Down	England	white, black-faced	fine, fairly uniform	5–7 lb 2.2–3.18 kg	3 in 7.6 cm	fine 14–18	56–60	felts easily, hard to spin
Spaelsau	Norway							
Suffolk	England	black-faced		6–7 lb 2.72–3.18 kg	2–5 in 5–12.7 cm		56–58	easy to spin
Targhee	U.S.A.			11–20 lb 6.9–9 kg	2½–4½ in 6.4–11.4 cm		58–64	

Breed or animal	Where raised	Colors	Texture	Fleece weight	Staple length	Crimp number per inch	British spinning quality count	Felting and other special qualities
Tunis	Tunisia		coarse, silky		2–4 in 5–10 cm			easy to spin
Vlachia	Greece	Brown, black	fine, hairy	2–5 lb .9–2.2 kg	7–10 in 17–25 cm		28–40	easy to spin
Angora rabbit clipped or plucked every 3 months	France England Netherlands U.S.A.	white	silky, soft, springy, fluffy	7–14 oz 225–390 g	3–8 in 7.6–20 cm	slight		felts easily; dyes lighter than wool; used with other fibers
Angora goat 2 clips a year	Turkey Texas S. Africa	white	fine, soft, silky	3–6 lb 1.36–2.72 kg	10 in 25 cm	tight lock		does not felt
camels' hair	Mongolia China N. Africa	tan, fawn	fine, springy		15 in 38 cm			poor felting; hair is shed
cashmere goat	China Russia Iran Afghanistan	gray, brown, white	down, silky texture of kitten's fur	8 oz 23 g	1½–3½ in 3.7–8.8 cm	uniform crimp all along fiber	40–80	
mohair goat	Turkey S. Africa U.S.A.		hard, stiff, high gloss	5–6 lb 2.25–2.27 kg	8–12 in 20–30.4 cm	none		
musk ox (qiviut)	Alaska Greenland	Gray	warm, fine, silky, light weight	6 lb 2.72 kg	2–5 in 5–12.7 cm		20–40	will not shrink when boiled; dyes easily
alpaca vicuna llama	Peru Boliva Chile	black, gray, fawn, brown	fine, coarse hairs, kemp	4–7 lb 1.81–3.18 kg	8–12 in 20–30.4 cm 16 in, 40.6 cm	llamas and alpacas have crimp 4–8	50–70	felts easily
cow's hair	Canada Japan India Iran S. America	variety of browns, grays	very coarse	½–2 lb 23–90 g				
horsehair	S. America Canada	white and other colors	coarse		15–40 cm longer from mane & tail			

Appendix E
Selected Yarn Designations

Common Yarn Count for Natural-Fiber Yarns

cotton		worsted		wool or linen	
size	*yards per pound*	*size*	*yards per pound*	*size*	*yards per pound*
1	840	1	560	1	300
3/2	1260	6/1	3360	1½ lea	450
4/4	840	9/1	5040	5/1 (Scottish)	1500
4/12	280	10	5600	5½/1	1650
5/2	2100	10/2	2800	6/3	600
8/2	3360	10/4	1400	6/4 (Swiss)	450
8/4	1680	12/2	3360	7/2	1050
8/6	1120	12/3	2240	8/1 (dry spun)	2400
10	8400	15/2	4200	8/5 (Swedish)	450
10/2	4200	16/2	4480	9/3	800
10/3	2800	18/2	4800	10	3000
12/4	2520	20/2	5000	10/1 (dry spun)	2700
16/2	6720	22/2	6160	10/2 (wet spun)	1500
16/4	3280	26/2	7260	10/2 (dry spun)	1350
16/6	2240	32/2	8960	10/5	540
20/2	8400			12	3600
20/3	5600			14	4200
20/6 (floss)	2800			14/2	2100
24/2	10000			15/2	2250
24/3	6720			16	4800
30/2	12600			16/2	2400
34/2	14000			18/2	2700
50/3	14000			18/6	900
				18/8	675
				20	6000
				20/2	3000
				30	9000
				30/2	4500
				40/2	6000
				40/3	4000
				50/2	7500
				50/3	5000
				60/3	6000
				70/2	10500
				140/2	21000

Miscellaneous and Novelty Yarns

name	description	approximate yards per pound
macramé yarns		
English seating cord		250
8-cord cable twist		920
jute cord	small	250
	medium	166
	large	100
	2-ply	300
jute-tone		420–440
navy cord	18/3	2200
nylon stitching twine	small	425
seine cord, cotton	large	207
	#18	358
nylon	small	233
sisal	large	100
	lace yarn	1900
cotton	3-cut cotton chenille	225–230
	6-cut chenille	425–450
	12-cut chenille	1200–1500
rayon flake		2500
linen	12-fold (parallel)	1450
silk		
douppioni (Scottish)	7/2	2100
	12/1	10000
	14/1	11760
silk tweed	60/2	12800
spun silk		
wool		480
eiderdown		1850
English Donegal tweed	singles	1000
loop or brushed mohair	large loop	400–500
rug yarn, U.S.		600
Scandinavian	fine	320
	heavy	680
cowhair		560
acrylic, rug yarn	3-ply	440
	4-ply	

Common Knitting Yarns

general name	yards per pound	fiber content
fingering	2720–2800	Orlon and/or wool
pompadour	2160	wool
baby yarn	2240	wool
sport yarn	1600–2200	wool and/or nylon, acrylic
bulky	400–600	wool

Appendix F
Metric Conversion Tables

When dealing with foreign suppliers or consulting references printed abroad, the weaver should be able to convert readily from the American system of weights and measures to the metric system, employed by virtually every country outside the United States. The following tables provide multipliers for converting from metric to U.S. and the reverse; the multipliers have been rounded to the third decimal place and thus yield an approximate equivalent.

Metric to U.S.

to convert from:	to:	multiply the metric unit by:
length		
meters	yards	1.093
meters	feet	3.280
meters	inches	39.370
centimeters	inches	.394
millimeters	inches	.039
area and volume:		
square meters	square yards	1.196
square meters	square feet	10.764
square centimeters	square inches	.155
cubic centimeters	cubic inches	.061
liquid measure:		
liters	cubic inches	61.020
liters	cubic feet	.035
liters	*U.S. gallons	.264
liters	*U.S. quarts	1.057
weight and mass:		
kilograms	pounds	2.205
grams	ounces	.035
grams	grains	15.430
grams per meter	ounces per yard	.032
grams per square meter	ounces per square yard	.030

U.S. to Metric

to convert from:	to:	multiply the U.S. unit by:
yards	meters	.914
feet	meters	.305
inches	meters	.025
inches	centimeters	2.540
inches	millimeters	25.400
square yards	square meters	.836
square feet	square meters	.093
square inches	square centimeters	6.451
cubic inches	cubic centimeters	16.387
cubic inches	liters	.016
cubic feet	liters	28.339
*U.S. gallons	liters	3.785
*U.S. quarts	liters	.946
pounds	kilograms	.453
ounces	grams	28.349
grains	grams	.065
ounces per yard	grams per meter	31.250
ounces per square yard	grams per square meter	33.333

*The British imperial gallon equals approximately 1.2 U.S. gallons or 4.54 liters. Similarly, the British imperial quart equals 1.2 U.S. quarts, and so on.

Bibliography

Part I: The History of Fiber Arts

Ackerman, Phyllis. *Tapestry—The Mirror of Civilization.* New York: Oxford University Press, 1933.

Amsden, Charles Avery. *Navaho Weaving.* Albuquerque: University of New Mexico Press, 1949.

Atwater, Mary M. *The Shuttlecraft Book of American Handweaving.* New York: The Macmillan Company, 1956.

Bird, Junius B. *Paracus Fabrics and Nazca Needlework.* Washington, D.C.: National Publishing Co., 1954.

Birrell, Verla. *The Textile Arts.* New York: Harper & Row, 1959.

Bennett, Wendell C., and Junius B. Bird. *Andean Culture History.* New York: American Museum of Natural History; Handbook Series No. 15, 1949.

———. *Ancient Art of the Andes.* 2d ed. New York: Museum of Modern Art, 1966.

Broholm, Hans C., and M. Hald. *Bronze Age Fashion.* Copenhagen: Nyt Nordisk Farlag, 1948.

Burnham, Dorothy. *Cut My Cote.* Toronto: The Royal Ontario Museum, 1973.

Burnham, Harold B., and Dorothy K. Burnham. *Keep Me Warm One Night.* Toronto: University of Toronto Press, 1972.

Daumas, Maurice. *A History of Technology and Invention.* Vol. 1. New York: Crown Publishers, Inc., 1969.

Davidson, Mildred, and Christa C. Mayer-Thurman. *Coverlets.* Chicago: Chicago Art Institute, 1973.

D'Harcourt, Raoul. *Textiles of Ancient Peru and Their Techniques.* Seattle: University of Washington Press, 1974. Paperback reissue of 1962 reprint of 1934 classic.

Forbes, Robert J. *Studies in Ancient Technology.* Vol. 4, "Textiles." New York: W. S. Heinman, 1964.

Goodrich, F. L. *Mountain Homespun.* New Haven, Conn.: Yale University Press, 1931.

Hall, Eliza. *A Book of Handwoven Coverlets.* Boston: Little, Brown & Company, 1914.

Hoffman, Marta. *The Warp Weighted Loom.* Oslo: Oslo University Press, 1964.

King, Mary Elizabeth. *Ancient Peruvian Textiles.* Greenwich, Conn.: New York Graphic Society, 1965.

Murray, Margaret. *Tomb of Two Brothers.* Manchester: Sherratt and Hughes, 1910.

Naylor, Gillian. *The Bauhaus.* London: Studio Vista, 1968.

———. *The Arts and Crafts Movement.* Cambridge, Mass.: M.I.T. Press, 1971.

Neumann, Eckhard. *Bauhaus and Bauhaus People.* New York: Van Nostrand Reinhold, 1970.

Nordland, Odd. *Primitive Scandinavian Textiles in Knotless Netting.* Oslo: Oslo University Press, 1961.

O'Neale, Lila. *Textile Periods in Ancient Peru.* Berkeley, Calif.: University of California Press, 1930.

Roth, Ling H. *Studies in Primitive Looms.* Halifax: Sott Brothers, Ltd., 1950.

Rowe, Anne Pollard. *Warp-Patterned Weaves of the Andes.* Washington, D.C.: The Textile Museum, 1977.

Santangelo, Antonio. *A Treasury of Great Italian Textiles.* New York: Harry Abrams, Inc., 1964.

Threads of History. The American Federation of Arts, 1965.

Tidball, Harriet. *Thomas Jackson, Weaver.* Shuttle Craft Guild Monograph No. 13. Lansing, Mich.: Shuttle Craft Guild, 1964.

Ubbelohde-Doering, Heinrich. *The Art of Ancient Peru.* New York: Frederick Praeger, 1952.

Van Stan, Ina. *Problems in Pre-Columbian Textile Classification.* Tallahassee, Fla.: Florida State University Press, 1958.

Weigert, Roger Armand. *French Tapestry.* Newton Centre, Mass.: Charles T. Branford Company, 1963.

White, Margaret. *The Decorative Arts of New Jersey.* Princeton, N. J.: D. Van Nostrand Company, Inc., 1964.

Part II: Handweaving on the Loom

Flat Weaving

Albers, Anni. *On Weaving.* Middletown, Conn.: Wesleyan University Press, 1965.

Baizerman, Suzanne, and Karen Searle. *Latin American Brocades: Explorations in Supplementary Weft Techniques.* St. Paul, Minn.: Dos Tejedoras, 1976.

Bennett, Noel, and Tiana Bighorse. *Working with the Wool: How to Weave a Navajo Rug.* Flagstaff, Ariz.: Northland Press, 1971.

Black, Mary E. *New Key to Weaving.* Milwaukee, Wis.: Bruce Publishing Company, 1957.

Blumenau, Lili. *The Art and Craft of Handweaving.* New York: Crown Publishers, Inc., 1955.

———. *Creative Design in Wall Hangings.* New York: Crown Publishers, Inc., 1966.

Cyrus, Ulla. *Manual of Swedish Handweaving.* Newton Centre, Mass.: Charles T. Branford Company, 1956.

Davenport, Elsie. *Your Handweaving.* Pacific Grove, Calif.: Craft & Hobby Book Service, 1970.

Davison, Marguerite P. *A Handweaver's Pattern Book.* Swarthmore, Pa.: M. P. Davison, 1963.

Emery, Irene. *Primary Structures of Fabrics.* Washington, D.C.: The Textile Museum, 1966.

Frey, Berta. *Seven Projects in Rosepath.* Berta Frey, 1959.

Gallinger, Osma. *Joy of Weaving.* Scranton Pa.: International Textbook Company, 1950.

Garrett, Gay. *Warping All By Yourself.* Santa Rosa, Calif.: Thresh Publications, 1975.

Hooper, Luther. *Handloom Weaving*. London: Sir Isaac Pitman & Sons, Ltd., 1934.

House, Florence. *Notes on Weaving Techniques*. New York: Elizabeth Salisbury, 1964.

Lewis, Alfred Allan, with Julienne Krasnoff. *Everybody's Weaving Book*. New York: The Macmillan Company, 1976.

Moorman, Theo. *Weaving as an Art Form*. New York: Van Nostrand Reinhold, 1975.

Nye, Thelma M., ed. *Swedish Weaving*. New York: Van Nostrand Reinhold, 1972.

Pyysalo, Helvi. *Handweaving Patterns from Finland*. Newton Centre, Mass.: Charles T. Branford Company, 1958.

Reed, Tim. *Loom Book*. New York: Sunstone Press, 1973.

Regensteiner, Else. *Weaver's Study Course*. New York: Van Nostrand Reinhold, 1975.

Selander, Malin. *Swedish Handweaving*. Göteborg: Wazäta Förlag, 1959.

_____. *Weaving Patterns*. Göteborg: Wazäta Förlag, 1956.

Thorpe, Azalea Stuart, and Jack Lenor Larsen. *Elements of Weaving*. Garden City, N.Y.: Doubleday & Company, 1967.

Thorpe, Heather G. *A Handweaver's Workbook*. New York: The Macmillan Company, 1966. Paperback reissue, 1974.

Tidball, Harriet. *Double Weave: Plain and Patterned*. Shuttle Craft Guild Monograph No. 1. Lansing, Mich.: Shuttle Craft Guild, 1960.

_____. *Two-Harness Textiles: Loom Controlled*. Shuttle Craft Guild Monograph. Lansing, Mich.: Shuttle Craft Guild, 1967.

_____. *The Weaver's Book: Fundamentals of Handweaving*. New York: The Macmillan Company, 1962.

_____. *Woolens and Tweeds*. Shuttle Craft Guild Monograph. Lansing, Mich.: Shuttle Craft Guild, 1961.

Tovey, John. *The Technique of Weaving*. New York: Van Nostrand Reinhold, 1965, reissued, 1975.

Waller, Irene. *Designing with Thread*. New York: The Viking Press, 1973.

Worst, Edward. *Weaving with Foot-Power Looms*. New York: Dover Publications, 1974. Reissue of 1924 classic.

Zielinski, Stanislaw A. *Encyclopedia of Hand-Weaving*. New York: Funk & Wagnalls Company, 1959.

Znamierowski, Nell. *Step-by-Step Weaving*. New York: Golden Press, Inc., 1967.

Tapestry

Beutlich, Tadek. *The Technique of Woven Tapestry*. New York: Watson-Guptill Publications, 1971.

Coffinet, Julien. *Pratique de la Tapisserie*. Geneva; Editions du Tricorne, 1977.

_____, and Maurice Pianzola. *Tapestry: Craft and Art*. New York: Van Nostrand Reinhold, 1974.

Constantine, Mildred, and Jack Lenor Larsen. *Beyond Craft: The Art Fabric*. New York: Van Nostrand Reinhold, 1973.

Jobé, Joseph. *Great Tapestries: The Web of History from 12th to 20th Century*. Lausanne: Edita S.A., 1965.

Kahlenberg, Mary Hunt, and Anthony Berlant. *The Navajo Blanket*. New York: Frederick A. Praeger, Inc., 1972.

Mattera, Joanne. *Navajo Techniques for Today's Weaver*. New York: Watson-Guptill Publications, 1975.

Paque, Joan Michaels. *Design Principles and Fiber Techniques*. Shorewood, Wis.: J. & H. Paque, 1976.

Pendleton, Mary. *Navajo and Hopi Weaving Techniques*. New York: Collier Books, 1974.

Rhodes, Mary. *Small Woven Tapestries*. Newton Centre, Mass.: Charles T. Branford Company, 1973.

Tidball, Harriet. *Contemporary Tapestry*. Shuttle Craft Guild Monograph No. 12. Lansing, Mich.: Shuttle Craft Guild, 1964.

Weigert, Roger-Armand. *French Tapestry*. Newton Centre, Mass.: Charles T. Branford Company, 1963.

Wells, Oliver N. *Salish Weaving—Primitive and Modern*. Chilliwack, B.C., Canada: Salish Weavers, 1973.

Part III: Other Construction Methods

Pile Weaves

Collingwood, Peter. *The Techniques of Rug Weaving*. New York: Watson-Guptill Publications, 1968.

Lewes, Klares, and Helen Hutton. *Rug Weaving*. Newton Centre, Mass.: Charles T. Branford Company, 1962.

Tod, Osma Gallinger, and Josephine Couch Del Deo. *Rug Weaving for Everyone*. New York: Bramhall House, 1957.

Willcox, Donald. *The Technique of Rya Knotting*. New York: Van Nostrand Reinhold, 1971.

Wilson, Jean. *The Pile Weaves: Twenty-Six Techniques and How to Do Them*. New York: Van Nostrand Reinhold, 1974.

Znamierowski, Nell. *Step-by-Step Rugmaking*. New York: Golden Press, Inc., 1972.

Simple Looms and Nonloom Techniques

Atwater, Mary Meigs. *Byways in Handweaving*. New York: The Macmillan Company, 1967.

_____. *Guatemala Visited*. Shuttle Craft Guild Monograph No. 15. Lansing, Mich.: Shuttle Craft Guild, 1965. Reprint of 1946 edition.

Chamberlain, Marcia, and Candace Crockett. *Beyond Weaving*. New York: Watson-Guptill Publications, 1974.

Collingwood, Peter. *The Technique of Sprang*. New York: Watson-Guptill Publications, 1974.

Crockett, Candace. *Card Weaving*. New York: Watson-Guptill Publications, 1973.

Dendel, Esther Warner. *Needleweaving: Easy as Embroidery*. Philadelphia: Countryside Press, 1972.

Depas, Spencer. *Macramé Weaving and Tapestry: Art in Fiber*. New York: The Macmillan Company, 1973.

Fisch, Arline M. *Textile Techniques in Metal*. New York: Van Nostrand Reinhold, 1975.

Graumont, Raoul, and Elmer Wenstrom. *Square Knot Handicraft Guide*. Cambridge, Md.: Cornell Maritime Press, 1949.

Gubser, Elsie H. *Bobbin Lace*. McMinnville, Ore.: Robin and Russ Handweavers.

Harvey, Virginia I. *Color and Design in Macramé*. New York: Van Nostrand Reinhold, 1971.

_____. *Macramé: The Art of Creative Knotting*. New York: Van Nostrand Reinhold, 1967.

_____. *Split-Ply Twining*. Santa Ana, Calif.: HTH Publishers, 1976.

_____, and Harriet Tidball. *Weft Twining*. Shuttle Craft Guild Monograph No. 28. Lansing, Mich.: Shuttle Craft Guild, 1969.

Ikle, Charles, *The Plangi Technique*. New York: Needle and Bobbin Club Bulletin, Vol. 25, No. 2, 1941.

Kliot, Kaethe. *Bobbin Lace: Form by the Twisting of Cords*. New York: Crown Publishers, 1973.

Marein, Shirley. *Off the Loom: Creating with Fibre*. New York: The Viking Press, 1973.

May, Florence Lewis. *Hispanic Lace & Lace Making*. New York: Hispanic Society of America, 1939.

Meilach, Dona Z. *Macramé—Creative Design in Knotting*. New York: Crown Publishers, Inc., 1971.

Naumann, Rose, and Raymond Hull. *The Off-Loom Weaving Book*. New York: Charles Scribner's Sons, 1973.

Nordland, Odd. *Primitive Scandinavian Textiles in Knotless Netting*. Oslo: Oslo University Press, 1961.

Phillips, Mary Walker. *Creative Knitting*. New York: Van Nostrand Reinhold, 1971.

_____. *Step-by-Step Knitting*. New York: Golden Press, Inc., 1967.

_____. *Step-by-Step Macramé*. New York: Golden Press, Inc., 1970.

Redman, Jane. *Frame Loom Weaving*. New York: Van Nostrand Reinhold, 1976.

Skowronski, Hella, and Mary Reddy. *Sprang Thread Twisting: A Creative Textile Technique*. New York: Van Nostrand Reinhold, 1973.

Snow, Marjorie, and William Snow. *Step-by-Step Tablet Weaving*. New York: Golden Press, Inc., 1973.

Swanson, Karen. *Rigid Heddle Weaving—New and Innovative Techniques on an Easy-to-Use Loom*. New York: Watson-Guptill Publications, 1975.

Taber, Barbara, and Marilyn Anderson. *Backstrap Weaving*. New York: Watson-Guptill Publications, 1975.

Part IV: Spinning and Coloring

Spinning

Bowen, Godfrey. *Wool Away/The Art and Technique of Shearing*. New York: Van Nostrand Reinhold, 1974.

Davenport, Elsie. *Your Handspinning*. London: Sylvan Press, 1964.

Fannin, Allen. *Handspinning: Art & Technique*. New York: Van Nostrand Reinhold, 1970.

Hochberg, Bette. *Handspinner's Handbook*. Santa Cruz, Calif.: Bette Hochberg, 1976.

Jenkins, J. Geraint. *The Wool Textile Industry in Great Britain*. London: Routledge and Kegan Paul Ltd., 1972.

Kluger, Marilyn. *The Joy of Spinning*. New York: Simon & Schuster, Inc., 1971.

McKinney, John. *The Sheep Book*. New York: John Wiley and Sons, Inc., 1959.

Ryder, M. L., and S. K. Stephenson. *Wool Growth*. London: Academic Press, 1968.

Simmons, Paula. *Spinning and Weaving with Wool*. Seattle: Pacific Search Press, 1977.

Von Bergen, Werner. *Wool Handbook*. 2 vols. 3d ed. New York: John Wiley and Sons, Inc., 1969.

West, W. C. *Anyone Can Build a Spinning Wheel*. Santa Rosa, Calif., Thresh Publications, 1975.

Yarn Dyeing

Adrosko, Rita J. *Natural Dyes and Home Dyeing*. New York: Dover Publications, Inc., 1971.

Bemis, Elijah. *The Dyer's Companion*. Reprint. New York: Dover Publications, 1973.

Bolton, Eileen. *Lichens for Vegetable Dyeing*. Newton Centre, Mass.: Charles T. Branford Company, 1960.

Brooklyn Botanical Garden. *Dye Plants and Dyeing—A Handbook*. Brooklyn, N.Y.: Brooklyn Botanical Gardens, 1964.

Colton, Mary-Russell Ferrell. *Hopi Dyes*. Flagstaff, Ariz.: Northland Press for Museum of Northern Arizona, 1965.

Dana, Mrs. William Starr. *How to Know the Wild Flowers*. New York: Dover Publications, 1963.

Davenport, Elsie. *Your Yarn Dyeing*. Pacific Grove, Calif.: Craft & Hobby Book Service, 1970.

Davidson, Mary. *The Dye Pot*. Middleboro, Ky.: Mary Davidson.

Kershaw, K. A., and K. L. Alvin. *The Observer's Book of Lichens*. London: Frederick Warne & Co. Ltd., 1966.

Kramer, Jack. *Natural Dyes: Plants and Processes*. New York: Charles Scribner's Sons, 1972.

Larsen, Jack Lenor, Alfred Buhler, Bronwen Solyom, and Garett Solyom. *The Dyer's Art: Ikat, Batik, Plangi*. New York: Van Nostrand Reinhold, 1975.

Leggett, William E. *Ancient and Medieval Dyes*. New York: Chemical Publishing Company, 1944.

Lesch, Alma. *Vegetable Dyeing*. New York: Watson-Guptill Publications, 1970.

Mairet, Ethel. *Vegetable Dyes*. London: Faber and Faber, 1946.

Robertson, Seonaid M. *Dyes from Plants*. New York: Van Nostrand Reinhold, 1973.

Robinson, Stuart. *A History of Dyed Textiles*. Cambridge, Mass.: M.I.T. Press, 1969.

Rosetti, Gioanventura. *The Plictho*. Translated by Sidney M. Edelstein and Hector C. Borghetty. Cambridge, Mass.: M.I.T. Press, 1969.

Thurston, Violetta. *Use of Vegetable Dyes*. Leicester, England: Dryad Press, 1943.

Tidball, Harriet. *Color and Dyeing*. Shuttle Craft Guild Monograph. Lansing, Mich.: Shuttle Craft Guild, 1965.

Weigle, Palmy. *Ancient Dyes for Modern Weavers*. New York: Watson-Guptill Publications, 1974.

Part V: Design in Fabric Construction

Albers, Anni. *On Designing*. Middletown, Conn.: Wesleyan University Press, 1961.

Albers, Josef. *The Interaction of Color*. Rev. ed. New Haven, Conn.: Yale University Press, 1975.

Bevlin, Marjorie E. *Design Through Discovery*. New York: Holt, Rinehart and Winston, 1977.

Biegeleisen, J. I., and J. A. Cohn. *Silk Screen Techniques*. New York: Dover Publications, 1958.

Brodatz, Phil. *Textures: A Photographic Album for Artists and Designers*. New York: Dover Publications, 1966.

Bucher, François. *Josef Albers Despite Straight Lines*. New Haven, Conn.: Yale University Press, 1961.

Byström, Ellen. *Printing on Fabric*. New York: Van Nostrand Reinhold, 1976.

Chevreul, M. E. *The Principles of Harmony and Contrast of Colors and Their Applications to the Arts*. New York: Van Nostrand Reinhold, 1967. Based on the first English edition of the book, 1854.

Frey, Berta. *Designing and Drafting: Basic Principles of Cloth Construction.* New York: The Macmillan Company, 1958.

Hartung, Rolf. *Creative Textile Design: Thread and Fabric.* New York: Van Nostrand Reinhold, 1964.

Itten, Johannes. *The Art of Color.* New York: Van Nostrand Reinhold, 1966.

Johnston, Meda Parker, and Glen Kaufman. *Design on Fabrics.* New York: Van Nostrand Reinhold, 1967.

Lubell, Cecil. *Textile Collections of the World.* New York: Van Nostrand Reinhold, 1975.

Marx, Ellen. *The Contrast of Colors.* New York: Van Nostrand Reinhold, 1973.

Oelsner, G. H. *Handbook of Weaves.* New York: Dover Publications, Inc., 1951.

Posselt, Emanuel A. *Technology of Textile Design.* Philadelphia: Textile Publishing Company.

Robinson, A.T.C., and R. Marks. *Woven Cloth Construction.* London: The Textile Institute, 1967.

Robinson, Stuart. *A History of Printed Textiles.* Cambridge, Mass.: M.I.T. Press, 1969.

Segal, William. *Encyclopedia of Textiles.* 2d. ed. Englewood Cliffs, N.J.: Prentice-Hall, 1972.

Scheidig, Walther. *Crafts of the Bauhaus.* New York: Van Nostrand Reinhold, 1967.

Schwalbach, Matilda, and James Schwalbach. *Screen Process Printing.* New York: Van Nostrand Reinhold, 1970.

Weigle, Palmy. *Color Exercises for the Weaver.* New York: Watson-Guptill Publications, 1976.

Book Suppliers

Book Barn, Farmington Valley Arts Center, Avon Park North, Box 256W, Avon, Conn. 06001

K. R. Drummond, 30 Hart Grove, Ealing Common, London W5, England

Museum Books, Inc., 48 East 43 Street, New York, N.Y. 10017

The Unicorn, 5525 Wilkins Court, Rockville, Md., 20852

Wittenborn and Co., 1018 Madison Avenue, New York, N.Y. 10021

Periodicals

American Fabrics, 24 East 38 Street, New York, New York 10016.

Craft Horizons, published by the American Crafts Council, 16 East 52 Street, New York, New York 10022.

Creative Crafts. This publication is out of print, but back copies are available from libraries.

Form, Swedish Society for Industrial Design, Svenska Slojdföreningen, Box 7047, S-103 82, Stockholm 7, Sweden.

Handicrafter. This publication is out of print, but back copies are available from libraries.

Handweaver & Craftsman, 220 Fifth Avenue, New York, New York 10001.

Quarterly Journal of the Guilds of Weavers, Spinners and Dyers. Subscriptions available through: Mary Barker, 1 Harington Road, Brighton 6, England.

Shuttle, Spindle and Dyepot, Handweavers Guild of America, 339 North Steele Road, West Hartford, Connecticut 06117.

Webe Mit. Subscriptions available through: 705 Baiblingen bei Stuttgart, Postfach 65, Germany.

Copies of *Ciba Review,* a trade journal published in Basle, Switzerland, are available in most large libraries. The following issues may be of special interest:

#1	*Medieval Dyeing*
#2	*India, Its Dyers, and Its Colour Symbolism*
#4	*Purple*
#5	*Tapestry*
#7	*Scarlet*
#8	*The Dressing of Hides in the Stone Age*
#9	*Dyeing and Tanning in Classical Antiquity*
#10	*Trade Routes and Dye Markets in the Middle Ages*
#12	*Weaving and Dyeing in Ancient Egypt and Babylon*
#14	*Clothing Making in Flanders*
#15	*Pile Carpets of the Ancient Orient*
#16	*The Loom*
#18	*Great Masters of Dyeing in 18th Century France*
#20	*The Development of the Textile Crafts in Spain*
#21	*Weaving and Dyeing in North Africa*
#23	*The European Carpet*
#24	*The Basle Ribbon Industry*
#27	*The Textile Trades in Medieval Florence*
#28	*The Spinning Wheel*
#29	*Venetian Silks*
#30	*The Essentials of Handicrafts and the Craft of Weaving among Primitive People*
#33	*Bark Fabrics of the South Seas*
#34	*The Development of Footwear*
#35	*The Hat*
#36	*Indian Costumes*
#37	*Textile Ornament*
#38	*Neckties*
#39	*Madder and Turkey Red*
#40	*Turkestan and Its Textile Crafts*
#44	*Ikats*
#45	*The Crafts of the Puszta Herdsman*
#54	*Basketry and Woven Fabrice of European Stone and Bronze Age*
#58	*Batiks*
#59	*The Reel*
#63	*Basic Textile Techniques*
#68	*Dyeing among Primitive Peoples*
#76	*Early American Textiles*
#84	*Maori Textile Techniques*
#85	*Indigo*
#88	*Swedish Peasant Dress*
#110	*Damask*
#117	*Tablet Weaving*
#133	*Coptic Textiles*
#136	*Peruvian Textile Techniques*
1961/3	*Gold and Textiles*
1963/2	*Early Chinese Silks*
1964/6	*Knitting Techniques*
1965/1	*Nonwovens*
1965/2	*Flax*
1965/3	*Yarn and Thread*
1967/1	*Animal Motifs on Fabrics*
1967/4	*Japanese Resist-dyeing Technique*
1968/2	*Textiles in Biblical Times*
1969/2	*Greek Contemporary Handweaving*
1969/3	*Bamboo*

Glossary

Terms italicized in the definitions are themselves defined within the glossary.

adjective dye   A dye that requires a *mordant* to produce fast color.

apron   A canvas fabric nailed to the *cloth beam* and *warp beam* on some *looms*. The aprons help to maintain the *warp* in its proper position.

back beam   Part of the framework of a *loom;* a rigid beam at the back of the loom that supports the *warp* and maintains its horizontal position.

back stitch   See *Brook's Bouquet.*

backstrap loom   A simple horizontal *loom* on which *warp tension* is maintained between a stationary object and the body of the weaver.

balanced weave   A *weave* in which the number of *warp* yarns per inch is equal to the number of *weft* yarns per inch.

bark cloth   See *tapa cloth.*

basic weave   A specific system of yarn interlacement not derived from any other system. The basic weaves are usually considered to be *plain weave, twill,* and *satin.*

basket weave   A *derivative* of *plain weave* created by consistently interlacing two or more *warp* yarns with two or more *weft* yarns.

basketry   A *weaving* technique that employs semirigid materials to create a self-supporting object.

basse lisse   A *tapestry* woven on a conventional horizontal *loom.*

bast fiber   A woody *fiber* from a plant such as jute, flax, sisal, or hemp.

batten   See *beater.*

beaming   The process of winding the *warp* yarns onto the *warp beam.*

beater   The framework that supports the *reed* on a *loom.* The beater swings freely to pack the *weft* yarn into position.

bight   See *bout.*

blanket   In *weaving,* a trial *web* or sampler.

block   A pattern unit or section of a *weave.*

blocking   A finishing process applied to *fabrics* to make them conform to a desired shape.

bobbin   A spool around which the *weft* yarn is wrapped for *weaving.* Often, the bobbin fits into a larger *shuttle.* Also, a yarn-carrying tool for lace-making, *tapestry,* and several other techniques.

bobbin lace   A form of *lace* worked with several individual threads each wrapped around a spool or bobbin.

bobbin winder   A simple hand-cranked or electric machine for winding *yarn* onto a *bobbin,* spool, or *quill.*

bottom mordanting   The application of a *mordant* to a material before it is dyed.

bouclé yarn   A looped *novelty yarn* similar to a *ratiné.*

bout   In weaving, a group of *warp* yarns treated alike.
1. One complete circuit of yarn on the *warping frame.*
2. One group of yarns tied together at the *cloth stick.*
3. One group of yarns *warped* and *chained* together.

braiding   A simple *finger weave* used to create decorative bands.

breast beam   Part of the framework of a *loom;* a rigid beam at the front of the loom that supports the *warp* and maintains its horizontal position.

brocade   A three-element construction in which a decorative yarn is added to a *plain-weave* or other simple ground. Brocades can be *loom-controlled* or *discontinuous.*

Brook's Bouquet   A *lace weave* in which the *weft* yarn is wrapped around several *warps* to draw them together.

butterfly shuttle   A miniature skein of *weft* yarn wound around the fingers, used for *tapestry* or other *finger weaves.*

cable yarn   A *yarn* composed of two or more *ply yarns* twisted together.

card clothing   A set of wires or spikes protruding from a foundation, used in *carding.*

card sliver   A thick strand of partially aligned *fibers;* the product of the *carding* operation.

card weaving   A simple *weaving* technique in which hole-punched cards or tablets, through which the *warp* yarns are threaded, take the place of a *loom* and *harnesses.* The result is a narrow band of *warp-face fabric.*

carding   The process of separating and partially aligning loose *fibers* in preparation for *spinning.*

cartoon   A preliminary sketch used as a guide for pattern *weaving,* especially for *tapestry* or *rya.*

castle   The uppermost part of the *loom* framework, which supports the *harnesses.*

chaining   A *weaving* technique in which the *weft* yarn is looped around groups of *warp* yarns to form a surface *pile.*

chaining the warp   The process of looping the *warp* upon itself to prevent tangling during the transfer from the *warping frame* to the *loom.*

chiné   See *ikat.*

choke ties   Lengths of cord wrapped tightly around the *warp* yarns to maintain their order during transfer to the *loom.*

chroma   See *intensity.*

cloth beam   A cylindrical member at the front of the *loom* around which the woven *fabric* is wound.

cloth stick   A rod attached to the *cloth beam* upon which *warp* yarns are mounted.

clove hitch   One of the principal knots used in *macramé.*

combing A process by which loose *fibers* are straightened and sorted for length prior to *spinning* according to the *worsted system*.

cord yarn See *cable yarn*.

corduroy In handweaving, a *weave* that provides for long *weft floats* on the surface of the *fabric*, which are cut after weaving to create a *pile*.

corkscrew yarn A *novelty yarn* created by twisting together *yarns* of different diameters, sizes, or *fiber* contents, or by varying the speed or direction of twist.

counterbalance loom A floor *loom* in which the *harnesses* operate in tandem. As one harness is raised, the connecting one is lowered.

crepe yarn A highly twisted *yarn*.

crimp The waviness of a *fiber*.

crochet A single-element construction in which a *yarn* is looped upon itself by means of a notched hook to create *fabric*.

cross The point at which the *warp* yarns are alternated around pegs on the *warping frame* or reel during the *warping* operation. The cross maintains the correct sequence of yarns. Also called the *lease*.

cross ties Preliminary ties made in the *warp* yarn to maintain the *cross* until the *lease sticks* are inserted.

damask A reversible patterned *fabric* created from a combination of *satin* and *sateen* weaves.

Danish medallion A *lace weave* in which the *weft* yarn departs from its horizontal orientation to create a loop on the surface of the *fabric*.

denier The basic unit of size of a *filament yarn*, equal to the weight in grams of 9000 meters of yarn.

dent One space in the *reed* of a *loom*.

derivative weave A modification of a *basic weave*.

design The ordered arrangement of parts to make a whole; loosely, a pattern or motif.

discontinuous weave Any *weave* in which some of the *weft* yarns do not run from *selvedge* to selvedge but appear only in certain portions of the *web*.

double weave A *weave* that produces two distinct layers of cloth simultaneously, often connected or interpenetrating at some point.

double-face fabric Any *fabric* with two structurally identical sides.

draft A graphic representation of the appearance and/or mechanics of a particular *weave*.

drafting In spinning, the process of compressing and extending loose *fibers* into *yarn*.

draw The *draft* of a threading pattern for the *loom*; the order in which the *warp* yarns are threaded through the *heddles*.

draw-down The graphic representation of a *weave* on paper; a weave *draft*.

draw-in The tendency for a *web* to narrow on the *loom* during the *weaving* process; a particular order of threading *warp* yarns through the *heddles*.

dressing The preparation of the *loom* for *weaving*, which includes: *beaming*, threading the *heddles*, sleying the *reed*, and tying on to the *cloth stick*.

dukagång A Scandinavian *laid-in weave* (brocade) in which the decorative yarn *floats* over three consecutive *warp* yarns and is tied down by the fourth.

dyestuff Any material, natural or synthetic, that can be used for imparting color to an absorptive subject, such as a *yarn*.

eccentric weft A *weaving* technique in which the *weft* yarn departs from its horizontal orientation to move in arcs or at acute angles to the *warp*.

embroidery Ornamental stitchery applied with a needle to a *fabric* ground.

ends Individual *warp* yarns.

fabric A construction made from *fibers*; a *textile*.

felt A nonwoven *fabric* constructed by interlocking loose *fibers* through a combination of heat, moisture, and pressure or friction.

fiber A material, either man-made or derived from natural sources, capable of being spun into *yarn* or thread.

filament fiber A *fiber* that can be measured in yards or miles. Silk and all manufactured fibers are filament length. Compare *staple fiber*.

filler See *weft*.

finger weave A *weave* created through the direct intervention of the weaver by manipulation of individual *warp* yarns with the fingers or a *pickup stick*.

flake yarn A *yarn* to which small tufts of *fiber* have been added at irregular intervals.

float Any portion of a *warp* or *weft* yarn that extends without intersection over two or more units of the opposing set of yarns.

flossa See *rya*.

flyer wheel A *spinning* device that *drafts* and twists the *fibers* simultaneously. Power is supplied by a foot treadle.

frame loom Any simple square or rectangular *loom*, usually lacking *harnesses* and a *beater*.

gamp A trial *web* or sampler.

gating The process of adjusting the *loom* after it has been *dressed* but before *weaving* begins.

gauze weave A *lace weave* created by crossing or twisting selected *warp* yarns before inserting the *weft*.

Ghiordes knot A classic knot used to create *pile* rugs and for *rya* weaving.

God's-eye A diamond-shape emblem worked by wrapping *yarn* continually around two crossed sticks; a ritual symbol in Latin America.

guide string A preliminary measuring cord used to establish the correct *warp* length and pattern of winding on the *warping frame* or reel.

guimpe yarn See *ratiné yarn*.

hand The touch or feel of a *fabric*.

handspindle The simplest *spinning* device consisting of a disc-shaped weight centered on a long notched shaft.

hank A unit of measure for cotton, wool, and silk *yarns*. A hank of cotton or silk yarn equals 840 yards; a hank of worsted yarn equals 560 yards; a hank of woolen yarn equals either 300 or 1600 yards.

harness A frame that supports a group of *heddles* on the *loom*.

haute lisse A *tapestry* woven on a vertical *tapestry loom*.

heddle A wire, strip of metal, or cord with an eye in the center. One (or more) *warp* yarns are threaded through each heddle to control the separation of the warp and create a *shed*.

heddle frame See *harness*.

heddle rod A device that performs the function of a *harness* on simple *looms*.

herringbone A *derivative* of the *twill* weave.

high wheel A *spinning* device that drafts and twists the fiber in two operations. Power is supplied by manually turning the large drive wheel.

hooking The process of forcing loops of *yarn* through a previously woven backing to create a *pile* fabric.

hue The pure state of any color.

ikat The process of *resist* dyeing portions of a *warp* or *weft* (or both) before *weaving* to create a pattern.

inkle loom A simple *loom* used for *weaving* narrow bands of *warp-face fabric*.

inlay, inlaid See *laid-in weave*.

intensity The relative purity or grayness of a color.

jack loom A floor *loom* in which each *harness* operates independently.

Jacquard loom A complex power *loom* capable of producing elaborate pattern *weaves*.

jaspé See *ikat*.

kasuri, kashiri See *ikat*.

kilim A classic Polish form of *tapestry*.

knitting A single-element construction in which a *yarn* is continually looped upon itself by means of needles to create *fabric*.

knob yarn See *nub yarn*.

lace A decorative openwork *fabric* created by twisting fine threads together to form a pattern. See also *needle lace, bobbin lace*.

lace weave An openwork *weave* usually characterized by a distortion from the parallel of *warp* or *weft* yarns.

laid-in weave A *finger weave* in which decorative *weft* yarns are added to a *plain-weave* ground in selected portions of the *web*.

lamb's wool Wool clipped from sheep less than eight months old.

lamm, lam A bar that connects the *harnesses* to the *treadles* on a floor *loom*.

lary sticks Temporary supports fastened between the *breast beam* and the *back beam* of a *loom*, used by some weavers during the loom-*dressing* operation.

lea A unit of measure for linen *yarn*, equal to 300 yards.

lease, leish, leash See *cross*.

lease sticks A pair of smooth, flat sticks used to maintain the *cross* in the *warp* yarns before and during *weaving*.

leno A *lace weave* created by crossing selected *warp* yarns in a certain pattern prior to inserting the *weft*.

line Flax (linen) *fibers* longer than 12 inches.

linsey-woolsey A Colonial expression referring to *fabric* woven from a linen *warp* and a wool *weft*.

linters Waste *fibers* that are too short for *spinning*. Linters are used in the manufacture of rayon, a *synthetic fiber*.

lockstitch A *weaving* technique in which the *weft* wraps tightly around several *warp* yarns to draw them together and create an openwork effect.

loom Any device used for *weaving* that performs the minimum function of holding the *warp* yarns taut and in their proper positions.

loom-controlled weave Any *weave* that is created solely through the interaction of the *heddles* and *harnesses* on a *loom*. Compare *finger weave*.

loop yarn A *novelty yarn* in which a curling effect yarn is held in place around a core by a binder yarn.

looping A high-*pile weave* in which loops of *weft* yarn are left on the surface of the *fabric*.

macramé A technique in which a set of parallel yarns are knotted together to create a decorative *fabric*.

Mali An industrial *fabric*-construction process—with applications for handweaving—in which two sets of *yarns* or yarns and pieces of fabric are stitched together in the manner of sewing.

manufactured fiber A *fiber* created in the laboratory that contains no natural ingredients; loosely, any nonnatural fiber. Compare *synthetic fiber*.

matting The process of constructing a nonwoven *fabric* from pounded mulberry bark. See also *tapa cloth*.

mercerization A finish applied to cotton to improve its luster, strength, and dyeability.

merino yarns *Yarns* spun from a mixture of wool and cotton in any proportion.

Mexican lace A variation of *leno*.

mock double cloth A three-element *weave* composed of two sets of *weft* yarn but only one *warp*. The *fabric* resembles both *brocade* and *tapestry*.

monofilament yarn A *yarn* composed of only one *fiber filament*.

mordant A chemical substance that combines with a *dyestuff* to enhance absorption of the color and to make the color fast.

multifilament yarn A *yarn* composed of two or more *fiber filaments*.

multiharness loom Any *loom* with more than four *harnesses*.

natural fiber Any *fiber* derived from plant or animal sources. The four most common natural fibers are cotton, linen, wool, and silk.

needle lace A form of *lace* composed of stitches and knots made with a single continuous thread in a needle.

netting A looping and knotting technique worked on a single continuous strand to produce openwork *fabric*.

novelty yarn A complex *yarn* characterized by irregularities of size, twist, or effect.

nub yarn A *novelty yarn* in which a decorative strand is wrapped repeatedly around a core to form an enlarged segment.

overshot A *weave* characterized by *weft floats* on a *plain-weave* ground.

paddle, warping paddle A flat tool with a handle and two parallel rows of holes or slots, used for measuring several *yarns* at once on the *warping frame* or reel.

paddle warping The process of measuring several *warp* yarns simultaneously with the aid of a paddle.

Persian knot See *Sehna knot*.

pick See *weft*.

pick count The number of *weft* yarns per inch in a woven *fabric*. Compare *sett*.

picking 1. In *weaving*, the act of throwing or passing the *weft* yarn through a *shed* in the *warp*. 2. In *spinning*, a hand operation in which the compact mass of *fibers* is initially opened and blended prior to *carding*.

pickup stick A narrow pointed needle or rod used for manipulating the *warp* yarns for a *finger weave*.

pile weave A *weave* characterized by strands or loops of *weft* yarn protruding from the surface of the *fabric*.

plain weave A *basic weave* created by consistently interlacing one *warp* yarn with one *weft* yarn.

plaiting A simple *finger weave* used primarily to create decorative bands.

ply yarn A *yarn* in which two or more single strands are twisted together.

primary color A color that cannot be mixed from other colors.

profile draft An abbreviated method of graphic notation for unit pattern weaves; a short *draft*.

quill The shaft around which the *weft* yarn is wound in a *bobbin* or *shuttle*.

raddle See *spreader*.

ratchet   A braking device on both the *warp beam* and the *cloth beam* of a *loom*, which prevents them from turning and holds the *warp* under *tension*. The ratchet is released to roll the warp forward.

ratiné yarn   A *novelty yarn* in which a bulky yarn is looped around a core yarn and held in place with a binder.

raw silk   Silk that has not been degummed and still contains the serecin secreted by the silkworm.

reed   A comblike device set into the *beater* on a *loom*. The reed helps to maintain the horizontal position of the *warp* yarns and also beats each new *weft* yarn into position.

reed hook   See *sley hook*.

rep weave   A derivative of *plain weave* in which the pattern of interlacement is extended either vertically or horizontally.

reprocessed wool   Wool that has been reclaimed from *fabric* scraps that were never used.

resist   Any material that is applied to a surface before dyeing or printing to prevent absorption of ink or dye in the area covered.

reused wool   Wool reclaimed from used *fabric*.

rib weave   See *rep weave*.

rölakan   A classic Scandinavian form of *tapestry*.

roving   1. An untwisted *yarn*. 2. A condensed mass of *fibers* ready for *spinning* into yarn.

rya   A Scandinavian *pile weave* based on the *Ghiordes knot*.

ryijy   The Finnish name for *rya*.

sateen   A *weave* similar to *satin* but with *floats* in the *weft* direction.

satin weave   A *basic weave* characterized by long *floats* on the surface of the *fabric*.

saturation   See *intensity*.

scaffold yarns   Extra *yarns* added temporarily to a *warp* or weft on the *loom* to contribute color, density, texture, or some special effect.

scouring   A cleaning bath that removes dirt and natural oils from wool *fibers*, *yarns*, or *fabrics*. Vegetable fibers are also scoured before dyeing.

secondary color   The product of two *primary colors*.

sectional warp beam   A *warp beam* divided into 2-inch segments, essential for *sectional warping*.

sectional warping   A method of measuring the *warp* yarns directly on the *loom*, thus combining the *warping* and *beaming* operations.

seed yarn   Similar to a *nub yarn*, but with smaller segments.

Sehna knot   A classic knot used to create *pile* rugs, especially in Persia.

selvedge, selvage   The lengthwise or *warp*wise edge of a woven *fabric*; the point at which the *weft* yarns bind the warp to form a finished edge.

sericulture   The cultivation of the silkworm for the production of silk.

sett, set   The density of a *fabric*; the number of *warp* yarns per inch, especially as *sleyed* at the *reed*.

shag weave   Any *weave* that incorporates a long, cut *pile*.

shed   The space between separated *warp* yarns through which the *weft* yarn is passed. A shed is created by raising one or more *harnesses* or *heddles*.

shed sword   A flat stick used for creating a *shed* on simple *looms*.

shedding   The process of creating a *shed* in the *warp* by manipulation of *harnesses* or *heddles* on the *loom*.

shoddy   See *reused wool*.

shot   One passage of the *weft* yarn through a *shed*; also, one weft yarn.

shuttle   A tool on which the *weft* yarn is wrapped so it can be passed through a *shed* in the *warp*.

shuttle race   An extension at the base of the *reed* which supports the *shuttle* as it moves across the *warp*.

silk-screen printing   A form of *stencil printing* in which dye is squeezed through a stretched mesh of silk that has been painted with a *resist* in the areas that are not to print.

singles yarn   A *yarn* composed of only one strand.

sizing   A finishing process applied to *yarns* to make them stronger and more compact.

skeleton yarns   See *scaffold yarns*.

sley hook   A tool for threading *warp* yarns through the *dents* in a *reed* prior to *weaving*.

sleying   The process of drawing the *warp* yarns through the *reed* on a *loom*.

slit   A vertical opening in a *web*, especially in *tapestry*, created at the juncture of two pattern areas.

slit tapestry   A form of *tapestry* in which long slits or openings are created in the *fabric* by *weaving* sections of the *warp* independently.

slot knitting   A *knitting* process worked through an opening in a board to create flat *fabric*.

slub yarn   A *novelty yarn* that is left untwisted at intervals to produce bulky areas.

solution dyeing   The process of introducing color into the liquid solution for *synthetic fibers* before they are extruded.

soumak   A low-*pile weave* in which the *weft* yarn is wrapped around a *warp* yarn or a group of warp yarns according to one of several patterns.

Spanish knot   A classic knot used to create *pile* rugs.

Spanish lace   A *lace weave* in which segments of the *warp* are woven individually.

spinning   The process of drawing out and twisting loose *fibers* to form a continuous strand of *yarn*.

spool knitting   A *knitting* process worked on a thread spool or disc to create a cylindrical *fabric*.

spool rack   An upright frame used to hold spools or cones of *yarn* during the measuring or for *sectional warping*.

sprang   A single-element construction in which a set of stretched *warp* yarns are twisted upon one another to form a symmetrical pattern.

spreader   A flat stick with nails or spikes protruding at one-inch intervals; used to distribute the *warp* yarns evenly on the *loom*.

square knot   One of the principal knots used in *macramé*.

square knotting   See *macramé*.

squirrel cage reel   See *swift*.

staple fiber   A short *fiber* that can be measured in inches or fractions of inches. All *natural fibers* except silk are staple length. Compare *filament fiber*.

stencil printing   A method of transferring an image or design to a surface by tracing around a pattern.

stretcher   A device for maintaining consistent width of *fabric* on the *loom*.

string heddle   A *heddle* made of linen cord.

substantive dye   A dye that is permanent when heated alone with the material to be colored; a *dyestuff* that does not require a *mordant*.

swift   A device used to hold a skein of *yarn* while it is wound onto spools or *shuttles,* or to wind a skein from a cone or spool.

synthetic fiber   A *fiber* made by chemical means but composed partly of vegetable materials; loosely, any non-natural fiber. Compare *man-made fiber.*

tabby   See *plain weave.*

tablet weaving   See *card weaving.*

takeup   The extra *yarn* allowance needed for lacing over and under the opposing set of yarns in *weaving.*

tapa cloth   A nonwoven *fabric* once common in Africa, Hawaii, and the South Pacific, made by pounding bark from the paper mulberry tree.

tapestry   A *weft-face plain-weave fabric* in which the *weft* yarns are *discontinuous;* usually decorative or expressive.

tapestry fork   A tool that takes the place of a *beater* and *reed* in *tapestry* weaving.

tapestry loom   A vertical two-*harness loom* used primarily for *finger weaves. Tapestries* woven on such a loom are referred to as *haute lisse.*

tela de lengua   A Spanish form of *ikat* printing, usually in blue dye on white yarns.

temple, template   See *stretcher.*

tension   In *weaving,* the tautness of *warp* yarns during the measuring process and when stretched on the *loom.*

tension box   A machine used to maintain uniform *tension* in the *warp* yarns during *sectional warping.*

tertiary color   A color produced by combining adjacent *primary* and *secondary* colors.

textile   A construction made from *fibers;* often used to refer specifically to woven *fabric.*

thread count   The number of *warp* and *weft* yarns per inch in a woven *fabric.*

thrums   The unweavable portion of the *warp* yarns required for tying on to the *loom.* Also called *loom waste.*

tie-up   The connections between the *harnesses* and the *lamms* and between the lamms and the *treadles* on a floor *loom.* Also, the process of making such connections for a particular *weave.*

top   A thick strand of long, partially aligned *fibers;* the product of the *combing* operation.

top dyeing   The process of dyeing a second color over a previous one.

top mordanting   The application of a *mordant* to a material after it has been dyed.

tow   Flax (linen) *fibers* shorter than 12 inches.

treadle   A foot lever that controls the raising of *harnesses* on a floor *loom.*

tromp as writ   A term signifying that a *weave* is to be *treadled* in the same order as the *harnesses* are threaded.

tubular double weave   A *weave* that produces two distinct layers of *fabric* connected at both *selvedges.*

tufting   An industrial form of *hooking.*

Turkish knot   See *Ghiordes knot.*

Tussah silk   Silk from cocoons of uncultivated silkworms.

twill   A *basic weave* characterized by diagonal lines.

twining   A two-element construction in which two or more *weft* yarns are twisted around one another as they interlace with the *warp.*

ultimates   Short lengths of flax *fiber* ready for *spinning.*

umbrella swift   See *swift.*

unbalanced weave   A *weave* in which either the *warp* yarns or the *weft* yarns are more concentrated. Compare *balanced weave.*

value   The lightness or darkness of a color.

virgin wool   New wool that has never before been made into *yarn.*

warp   A set of yarns that are parallel to one another and to the *selvedge* or longer dimension of a woven *fabric;* the lengthwise element in a woven construction.

warp beam   A cylindrical member at the back of a *loom* around which the unwoven *warp* yarns are wound.

warp stick   A rod attached to the *warp beam* upon which *warp* yarns are mounted.

warp-face   Describes a *fabric* or *weave* in which the *warp* yarns predominate or cover the *weft* completely.

warping   The process of preparing the *warp* yarns for the loom: measuring, establishing the *cross, chaining.*

warping comb   See *spreader.*

warping creel   See *spool rack.*

warping frame, warping reel   Simple devices for measuring the *warp* yarns prior to *weaving.* Both make provision for establishing a *cross* in the yarns.

warp-weighted loom   An upright *loom* used by many ancient cultures, in which the *warp* yarns are suspended from a horizontal bar and weighted at the bottom.

weave   A particular pattern or order of interlacement for *warp* and *weft* yarns.

weaving   The process by which two sets of threads of any substance are interlaced at right angles to form a continuous *web.*

web   The *fabric* created by interlacing *warp* and *weft;* the product of the *loom.*

weft   A set of yarns or other material perpendicular to the *selvedge* or longer dimension of a woven *fabric;* the crosswise element in a woven construction.

weft-face   Describes a *fabric* or *weave* in which the *weft* yarns predominate or cover the *warp* completely.

wild silk   See *Tussah silk.*

woof   See *weft.*

woolen system   A *spinning* process wherein relatively short, un*combed* wool or flax *fibers* are made into *yarn.*

worsted system   A *spinning* process wherein long, *combed* wool or flax *fibers* are made into yarn.

yarn   A continuous strand of material spun from drawnout and twisted *fibers.*

yarn count   The size or relative coarseness or fineness of a *yarn. Filament fiber* yarns are measured in *deniers;* the greater the number, the coarser the yarn. *Staple fiber* yarns are measured in *hanks* (cotton, wool, and silk) or *leas* (linen); the greater the number, the finer the yarn.

Index

Photographic Sources

A.C.L. ©, Brussels (71); Abrams Photo-Graphic, Phoenix, Ariz. (Pl. 12); Alinari–Art Reference Bureau, Ancram, N.Y. (45, 47, 59, 70, 92, 93); American Crafts Council, New York (113); American Museum of Natural History, New York (4, 17, 404); Anderson–Art Reference Bureau, Ancram, N.Y. (98); Archives Photographiques, Paris (67, 68, 91); David Arky, New York (Pl. 9); Alan W. Ashe, Asheville, N.C. (115); Barceló Fotos, Barcelona (130); James W. Bassler, Malibu, Calif. (529); John Charles Bell (21, 581); Bexell & Son, Pontiac, Mich. (156); Donald E. Busse, Cincinnati, Ohio (237, 570, Pl. 18); R. Camprubi, Barcelona (368); Ciba-Geigy Limited, Basel (19, 56); Donald Cordry, Cuernavaca, Mexico (392); John Creel (137); Don Cyr, New Haven, Conn. (466–468, 471, 472, 476, 478, 492, 494, 497, 505–512); Bevan Davies, New York (582); Carolyn Deal (564, 576); Jonas Dovydenas, Chicago (422); E. I. DuPont de Nemours & Company, Wilmington, Del. (117–120); Gay Emlen (Pl. 8); George Gardner, Belle Harbor, N.Y. (347); Martine Gilchrist, New York (562, 566); Giraudon, Paris (2); D. R. Goff, Quicksilver Photography, Columbus, Ohio (356, 445); Peter P. Gray, Blauvelt, N.Y. (37); Richard Gross, Los Angeles (127); Ted Hallman, Willowdale, Ontario (430); © Jane Hamilton-Merritt, Redding Ridge, Conn. (146); Bob Hanson, New York (135, 542, 584); Virginia Harvey, Seattle, and William Eng (341); Hoa-Qui, Paris (1); Marek Holzmann, Warsaw (116); Ruth Kaufmann Gallery, New York (Pl. 14); Bernard Kester, Los Angeles (540); Sam Kimura (325); Jules Kliot, Berkeley, Calif. (39, 431–433); Carol S. Kurtz, Rockville, Md. (594); J. Sergo Kuruliszwili, Warsaw (131, 360–361, 393, 541, 598); Maria Kwong (145, 551); L. Larsen, Copenhagen (9, 66); Eino Makinem, copyright © National Museum of Finland, Helsinki (370); Rush J. McCoy, Golden, Colo. (321, 343); Metropolitan Museum of Art, New York, and Soprintendenza Archeologica della Toscana, Florence (46); Modern Master Tapestries, Inc., New York (Pl. 21); Modern Master Tapestries, Inc., New York, and Al Mozell, New York (348); Al Mozel, New York (320); Ann Münchow, Aachen, West Germany (58); National Gallery of Art, Washington, D.C., Index of American Design (106); Nilus/Leclerc, Inc., L'Isletville, Quebec (299); Jan Nordahl, Sodertalje, Sweden (588); Novosti Press Agency, Moscow (16, 51); Maarten D'Oliveira, Amsterdam (595); Henry Paul Paque, Shorewood, Wisc. (31, 394, 415, 535); Robert Perron, New York (55); William Piltzer, San Anselmo, Calif. (18); Eric Pollitzer, Hempstead, N.Y. (125, 140, 158, 166, 169, 172, 173, 255, 257, 260, 284, 290, 300, 301, 331–334, 342, 351, 358, 362, 366, 457, 572, Pl. 11); Susan Rayfield, New York (Pl. 7); Sam Sawdon, London (449); Claus P. Schmid (550); Charles Seeley (28); Service Photographique, Paris (103); Tim Smith, Winston-Salem, N.C. (24, 134, 420); Smithsonian Institution, Washington, D.C. (473); Soprintendenza alle antichità Egittologia, Turin, and Rampazzi Ferruccio, Turin (44); Soprintendenza alle antichità Egittologia, Turin, and Foto Rosso, Turin (40); Soprintendenza ai Monumenti ed alle Gallerie dell'Umbria, Perugia (85); Alan Sweetman (407); Teigens Fotoatelier, Oslo (73); U.S. Department of the Interior, Washington, D.C., Indian Arts and Crafts Board (3); O. L. Varela, Washington, D.C. (88); © J.-C. Varga, Paris (424); Jan Versnel, Amsterdam (121, 549, 599); David Vine, New York (133, 247, 249, 251, 253, 474); Charles Vorhees (373); William Ward, Cleveland (558); John K. Wilkie, Edinburgh (537, 593); A. J. Wyatt, Philadelphia (52); Yale Studios, New York (161); Zauho Press, Tokyo (89).

Figs. 143 and 148 from "Studies in Primitive Looms" by H. Ling Roth, from *Royal Archaeological Institute Journal*, #47–48, 1917–18. Fig. 151 from *Traditional Crafts of Japan* by Charles Pomeroy (New York and Tokyo: John Weatherhill, Inc., 1967–68). Fig. 152 from *Historic Textile Fabrics* by Richard Glazier (London: B. T. Batsford Ltd., 1923). Fig. 423 redrawn from *Backstrap Weaving* by Barbara Taber and Marilyn Anderson (New York: Watson-Guptill Publications, 1975). Figs. 427, 428 redrawn from *The Techniques of Sprang* by Peter Collingwood (New York: Watson-Guptill Publications, 1974). Fig. 514 from *The New Britton & Brown Illustrated Flora* by Henry A. Gleason (New York: New York Botanical Garden, 1952). Pl. 33 from *New Design in Weaving* by Donald J. Willcox (New York: Van Nostrand Reinhold, 1970).

Work by Lurçat: Permission © A.D.A.G.P., Paris, 1977. Work by Widmann: Permission © S.P.A.D.E.M., Paris, 1977.